PUERTO RICO

SUZANNE VAN ATTEN

Contents

Although every effort was made to make sure the information in this book was accurate when going to press, research was impacted by the COVID-19 pandemic. Some things may have changed during this crisis and the recovery that followed. Be sure to confirm specific details when making your travel plans.

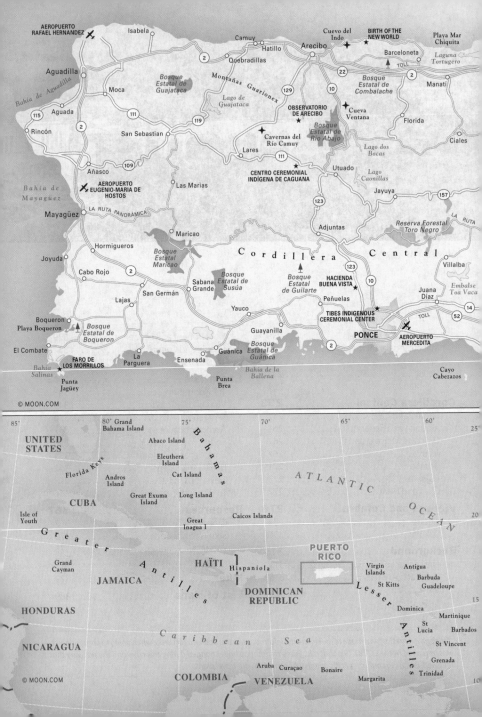

Map 1 (top — Puerto Rico)

Aeropuerto Rafael Hernandez
Isabela
Camuy
Hatillo
Quebradillas
Cuevo del Indo
Arecibo
BIRTH OF THE NEW WORLD
Playa Mar Chiquita
Barceloneta
Laguna Tortugero
TOLL
Aguadilla
Moca
Montañas Guarionex
2
Bosque Estatal de Guajataca
129
Lago de Guajataca
10
Bosque Estatal de Combalache
Manati
22
115
Aguada
111
OBSERVATORIO DE ARECIBO
Cueva Ventana
Bosque Estatal de Río Abajo
Florida
2
Rincón
2
San Sebastian
119
Cavernas del Río Camuy
Lago dos Bocas
Ciales
Lares
111
Añasco
109
Las Marias
CENTRO CEREMONIAL INDÍGENA DE CAGUANA
Utuado
Lago Caonillas
Bahía de Mayagüez
AEROPUERTO EUGENIO-MARIA DE HOSTOS
123
Jayuya
157
LA RUTA PANORÁMICA
Reserva Forestal Toro Negro
LA RUTA
Mayagüez
Maricao
Adjuntas
Hormigueros
Cordillera Central
Villalba
Joyuda
Bosque Estatal Maricao
Bosque Estatal de Guilarte
123
Embalse Toa Vaca
Cabo Rojo
2
Sabana Grande
Bosque Estatal de Susúa
Bosque Estatal Buena Vista
HACIENDA BUENA VISTA
10
Juana Díaz
Lajas
San Germán
Peñuelas
14
Yauco
TIBES INDIGENOUS CEREMONIAL CENTER
52
Boqueron
Playa Boqueron
Bosque Estatal de Boqueron
Guayanilla
PONCE
AEROPUERTO MERCEDITA
El Combate
La Parguera
Ensenada
Guánica
2
TOLL
Faro de los Morrillos
Bahía Salinas
Punta Jagüey
Punta Brea
Guánica
Bosque Estatal de Guánica
Bahía de la Ballena
Cayo Cabezazos

© MOON.COM

Map 2 (bottom — Caribbean)

85°   80°   75°   70°   65°   60°   25°
UNITED STATES
Grand Bahama Island
Abaco Island
Bahamas
Eleuthera Island
Florida Keys
Andros Island
Cat Island
ATLANTIC
CUBA
Great Exuma Island
Long Island
Isle of Youth
Great Inagua I
Caicos Islands
OCEAN
20
Greater Antilles
HAÏTI
Hispaniola
PUERTO RICO
Virgin Islands
Antigua
Grand Cayman
Barbuda
Guadeloupe
JAMAICA
Antilles
DOMINICAN REPUBLIC
St Kitts
Lesser
HONDURAS
Dominica
15
Martinique
Caribbean Sea
St Lucia
Barbados
NICARAGUA
Antilles
St Vincent
Grenada
Aruba
Curaçao
Bonaire
Trinidad
COLOMBIA
VENEZUELA
Margarita
10

© MOON.COM

Puerto Rico

Isla del Encanto, which translates to Island of Enchantment, is Puerto Rico's nickname for good reason. Sandy beaches, palm trees, and tropical breezes make it a favorite getaway for the sun and surf crowd. Rugged mountains and a verdant rainforest attract adventure travelers, and lavish hotels with oceanside golf courses embrace vacationers who crave luxury.

But Puerto Rico is more than a picture postcard. Centuries of indigenous, African, and Spanish influences can still be experienced as part of Puerto Rico's vibrant cultural life today.

The hip, bustling metropolis of San Juan boasts world-class restaurants, and casinos and clubs keep the late-night set up until dawn. Yet, a simple stroll through the cobblestone streets of Viejo San Juan steeps visitors in a concentrated dose of the island's history and cultural life.

Natural beauty abounds in the many protected coves, mangrove lagoons, caves, and mountain streams. They provide the perfect backdrop for an immersion into the sensual pleasures of the tropics. Venture out from San Juan and discover El Yunque National Forest with its semitropical rainforest; the northwestern karst country with its limestone caves; and three bioluminescent bays, where

Clockwise from top left: La Coca Falls in El Yunque National Forest; Cruceta del Vigía in Ponce; antique Puerto Rican pottery; fishing boats on Vieques; the dome of El Capitolio in San Juan; colorful houses on a hillside in San Juan.

kayakers can paddle in water that glows glittery shades of green, blue, or white at night.

Puerto Rico's central mountain region is one of the most dramatically beautiful areas of the island, where high mountain peaks, canyons, lush vegetation, orchids, streams, and cooler temperatures prevail. The indigenous Taíno culture was once a stronghold here, and their ancient ruins and petroglyphs can be found throughout the area.

All that is to say that there is a lot more to Puerto Rico than beaches. But if it is spectacular beaches you want, there are plenty to be found, as well as a bounty of water sports, from surfing and diving to fishing and sailing.

Life is vivid in Puerto Rico. The sun shines brightly, rainbow-hued buildings pop with color, and tropical music fills the air. Prepare to be enchanted.

Clockwise from top left: sentry box overlooking San Juan Bay; roadside fruit vendor in Mayagüez; cobblestone street in Viejo San Juan; Yokahu Tower in El Yunque National Forest.

10 TOP EXPERIENCES

1 **Explore the Rainforest:** Take a scenic driving tour of **El Yunque National Forest,** one of the most easily accessible rainforests in the world—or get out and hike its many trails (page 114).

ᨆ ᨆ ᨆ
ᨆ ᨆ

2 **Party in the Streets:** Celebrate with locals in popular party districts like La Placita in Santurce (page 69), Boca de Cangrejos in Piñones (page 111), and Calle San Sebastián in Viejo San Juan (pictured, page 69).

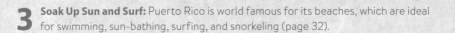

3 **Soak Up Sun and Surf:** Puerto Rico is world famous for its beaches, which are ideal for swimming, sun-bathing, surfing, and snorkeling (page 32).

4 **Feast on Traditional Cuisine:** Travel **La Ruta del Lechón** in the Cordillera Central (page 258) to dine on roast whole pig, or head to Luquillo's famous *kioskos* (page 127), where you can sample an array of traditional fritters.

^
^
^

5 **Unleash Your Adventurous Spirit:** Plunge into a pool at the base of a waterfall. Fly on a zipline. Go white-water rafting. Trek through the jungle. The possibilities are endless (page 31).

6 **Get to Know the Local Culture:** Dance to the rhythms of *bomba* and *plena* music in Viejo San Juan (page 64), join in the revelry of Hatillo's Festival de la Máscaras (page 250), or visit the Museo del Cemí (page 269) in Jayuya to learn more about the island's Taíno culture.

7 **Paddle across a Glowing Bay:** Take a kayak or a boat ride into one of the island's three **bioluminescent bays** and be mesmerized by the underwater light show (page 34).

8 **Savor the Flavor of Coffee:** Visit coffee farms, stay overnight in a historic hacienda, and sip aromatic beverages produced locally—from bean to cup (page 24).

9 **Discover Puerto Rico's Wild Side:** The island has thousands of acres of undeveloped, protected land, including the stunning stretch of wilderness beach in **Piñones** (page 111), the subtropical **Bosque Estatal de Guánica** (page 225), and the secluded beaches and coves of **Vieques National Wildlife Refuge** (page 286). >>>

10 **Wander through Historic Cities:** Stroll the cobblestone streets of **Viejo San Juan** (page 41) and take in the colonial architecture. In **Ponce** (page 149), visit indigenous ceremonial grounds and a 19th-century coffee plantation.

Planning Your Time

Where to Go

San Juan

Situated on the northeast coast, sophisticated, fast-paced San Juan is Puerto Rico's capital and largest city. Its heart is **Viejo San Juan,** the original walled city founded by Spanish settlers in 1521, home to two fortresses: **Castillo San Felipe del Morro** and **Castillo de San Cristóbal.** Other significant neighborhoods include **Isla Verde,** with the city's best beaches and most exclusive hotels, and **Condado,** considered the tourist district, where you'll find high-rise hotels, upscale restaurants, and casinos. In nearby **Santurce** is a burgeoning arts district, home to galleries, studios, and **Museo de Arte de Puerto Rico.**

Because the island is only 111 miles by 36 miles, you can take a **day trip** to anywhere in Puerto Rico from San Juan, although traffic and narrow, windy roads if you venture into the mountains can make your drive take longer than you might expect. Popular day trips include El Yunque National Forest in Río Grande, the beach and *kioskos* in Luquillo, the colonial city of Ponce, and Fajardo, for boating, diving, and fishing excursions.

El Yunque and the East Coast

The east coast contains some of Puerto Rico's most popular tourist sights, starting with **El Yunque National Forest,** a 28,000-acre nature preserve in the Sierra de Luquillo and home to the island's rainforest. Nearby is **Playa Luquillo,** a gorgeous, municipal beach in Luquillo. Just beyond the Luis Muñoz Marín International

Spanish colonial architecture in Viejo San Juan

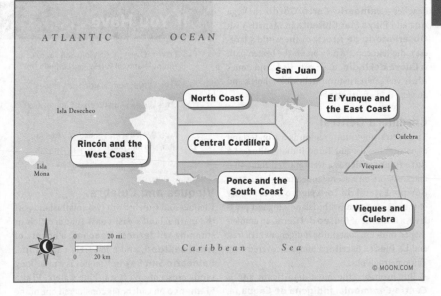

Airport in San Juan is **Bosque Estatal de Piñones,** a beautiful stretch of wilderness beach with a wooden boardwalk for biking and walking.

Fajardo is the boating center of Puerto Rico, where you can go diving, snorkeling, fishing, sailing, and kayaking. It is also home to the bioluminescent **Laguna Grande.** All-inclusive packages are available at resorts in **Río Grande,** home to two world-class golf courses. The southern region of the east coast is the least touristy part of the island and features several narrow beaches and good seafood restaurants.

Ponce and the South Coast

Ponce, the island's second-largest city, boasts scores of beautifully restored neoclassical and Spanish Revival architecture, a large and thriving plaza, and a strong cultural heritage preserved in its many museums. Just north of town is one of the island's two major indigenous cultural sites. **Centro Ceremonial Indígena de Tibes** was once home to two indigenous tribes, the Igneri and the Pre-Taínos. Also north of town is **Hacienda Buena Vista,** a former 19th-century coffee plantation that has been restored. In the

southern foothills of the mountains are the restorative natural hot springs of **Aguas Termales de Coamo.**

Rincón and the West Coast

Within the west coast region are the fun-loving surf towns of **Isabela, Rincón,** and **Aguadilla;** the colonial cities of **Mayagüez** and **San Germán;** the fishing village of **Boquerón;** the bioluminescent bay in **La Parguera;** and the salt flats of **Cabo Rojo.**

In addition to being a major destination for surfing and diving, the west coast has one of the island's loveliest public beaches, **Balneario de Boquerón.** And it is also home to two major forests, **Bosque Estatal de Guajataca,** a 2,357-acre subtropical wet forest in the north, and **Bosque Estatal de Guánica,** a 10,000-acre subtropical dry forest in the south.

North Coast

Much of the north coast is **karst country,** distinguished by limestone hills and caves, which makes for lots of rocky beaches and seaside cliffs. But there are two terrific sandy beaches—**Balneario Cerro Gordo** in Vega Alta and **Playa Mar Chiquita** in Manatí. Visit **Observatorio de Arecibo,** the world's largest radio telescope. And a bit off the beaten path is **Cueva del Indio,** huge petrified sand dunes where you can see natural arches, blow holes, and ancient Taíno petroglyphs.

Cordillera Central

The central mountain region is a wonderland of natural beauty and Taíno Indian culture. **La Ruta Panorámica** is a well-marked route that takes visitors on a scenic tour through the area. **Bosque Estatal de Toro Negro,** in the center of the region, contains the island's highest peak. Jayuya is the site of **Museo del Cemí,** an amulet-shaped museum containing indigenous artifacts, and **La Piedra Escrita,** a boulder covered with Taíno petroglyphs.

But probably the most significant site is **Centro Ceremonial Indígena de Caguana,** a Taíno archaeological site dating to AD 1100 in Utuado. Also in Utuado is **Bosque Estatal de Río Abajo,** a subtropical humid forest, and **Cueva Ventana,** a cave with a window that offers a breathtaking view. The region is also home to **Ruta del Lechón,** a scenic drive through the eastern mountains that passes by many *lechoneras,* traditional Puerto Rican restaurants specializing in whole, fire-roasted pig.

If You Have . . .

- **Three Days:** Visit Viejo San Juan, El Yunque National Forest, and Luquillo.
- **Five Days:** Add Fajardo and Vieques.
- **One Week:** Add Culebra, Caguas, and Cayey.
- **Two Weeks:** Add Ponce, Utuado, Arecibo, and Rincón.

Vieques and Culebra

Vieques and Culebra are two small islands off the main island's east coast that are rich in stunning **wilderness beaches,** a bounty of **fresh seafood,** and a leisurely pace of life. **Balneario Sun Bay** in Vieques is a mile-long sandy crescent on crystal-blue waters. **Playa Flamenco** on Culebra is considered one of the best beaches in the United States. Both islands are renowned for their spectacular diving and snorkeling.

Vieques is also the site of **Mosquito Bay,** Puerto Rico's most outstanding bioluminescent bay, where the water glows an electric blue at night. If you need a history fix, Vieques is home to **El Fortín Conde de Mirasol,** the last fort built by colonial Spain.

When to Go

The climate in Puerto Rico is classified as tropical marine, which means it is sunny, hot, and humid year-round. The average year-round temperature ranges from 80°F on the coast to 68°F in the mountains.

Puerto Rico has two seasons. **Dry season** is January-April. This is when humidity is the lowest, and temperatures hit an average high of 84°F and an average low of 71°F. It should be noted that rain does occur during dry season, but at a much lower rate than in summer and fall. Airline tickets and hotel room rates tend to be higher during dry season. From December through the end of dry season is **high season** for the tourist industry throughout much of the island, including San Juan, Vieques, Rincón, and resort areas, such as Dorado and Río Grande.

Rainy season is May-November, when an average of 4-6 inches of rain falls each month. The island's hottest months are June-September, when temperatures average 89°F, but it can spike as high as 97°F on the coast. The rainy season is

Playa Luquillo

also hurricane season. Airline ticket prices and hotel room rates are often reduced during rainy season.

In some parts of the island, particularly areas such as Cabo Rojo and La Parguera that cater primarily to Puerto Rican tourists, high season coincides with summer, when children are out of school.

Recovering from Hurricane Maria

In September 2017 Hurricane Maria made landfall in Puerto Rico around Patillas on the southeast coast and spent the next 24 hours or so churning over land on a diagonal path before it exited the island around Arecibo on the northwest coast. The category 4 storm brought heavy rains and 100 mph winds. It also decimated the electrical system, which cast the entire island into darkness for months. Some parts of the island were without power for an entire year. Just two weeks earlier, the island had endured Hurricane Irma, which had already crippled the power grid and destroyed homes. The combined impact of those two storms had a devastating effect on Puerto Rico, resulting in some 3,000 deaths.

Many residents of the island are still coping with the loss of homes, health, and income due to the storms. But recognizing the importance of tourism to the island's economy, Puerto Rico's leaders successfully fast-tracked efforts to restore the tourism infrastructure. Efforts also began to construct mini power grids so the electrical power system would be less vulnerable to future storms. Today, tourists may not even notice lingering effects of the storms, but the dollars they spend on the island go a long way in helping residents continue to recover.

To have the greatest positive impact, tourists are encouraged to patronize **small, independent businesses** and **roadside vendors,** preferably with cash. Support the local agriculture industry by buying fresh produce from **farmers markets,** and stock up on bags of **local coffee** for souvenirs. Tip your servers and hotel staff

damaged structures in Rincón after Hurricane Maria

well. Visit smaller towns and communities around **Patillas,** the central part of the Cordillera Central, and **Vieques,** where recovery has been slowest.

Those who want to do more may want to seek out **volunteer opportunities,** which are a great way to meet residents and learn about life on the island. To get started, visit the websites of the nonprofit organizations **All Hands and Hearts** (www.allhandsandhearts.org) and **World Central Kitchen** (www.wck.org).

The Best of Puerto Rico

It would take at least a month to fully explore Puerto Rico, but this one-week whirlwind tour gives visitors a little taste of everything Puerto Rico has to offer: beaches, nature preserves, colonial cities, surf and dive spots, and golf.

Day 1: Viejo San Juan

Arrive the night before and plan to spend your whole first day in **Viejo San Juan,** starting with *café con leche* and a *mallorca* for breakfast at **La Bombonera.** Wander the cobblestone streets and shop for hand-rolled cigars at **El Galpón** and **The Cigar House** or *vejigante* masks at **Puerto Rican Arts and Crafts.**

For lunch, fuel up on baked empanadas at **Maví,** then tour one of the Spanish forts, **Castillo San Felipe del Morro** or **Castillo de San Cristóbal.** In the afternoon, enjoy a rum tasting at **Casa Melaza.**

For dinner, feast on stuffed mofongo on the rooftop bar at **Punto de Vista,** then enjoy an after-dinner cocktail at **La Factoria.** Explore its maze of secret bars, including **Shing-a-Ling,** a late-night salsa bar.

Day 2: El Yunque National Forest

Rent a car and drive to the town of **Palmer.** Dine on bacon waffles at **Lluvia,** then walk across the street to **Portalito Hub,** the visitors center for **El Yunque National Forest.** Pick up a map and drive south to just short of the summit of El Yunque. Along the way, stop at **La Coca Falls** and **Yokahu Tower** to admire the views.

Proceed to the **Palo Colorado Information Center,** and follow the signs on a short, two-minute walk to see **Baño Grande,** a stone pool built in the 1930s. Serious hikers may want to make the strenuous hike to the summit of El Yunque and back.

Drive to the **Luquillo** *kioskos* and lunch on a variety of fritters, then head next door to **Playa**

Playa de Jobos in Isabela

Follow the Coffee Trail

In the 19th century, Puerto Rico was a major exporter of coffee. The industry has waxed and waned in the years since. Notably, it took a big hit from Hurricane Maria in 2017. Entire crops of coffee beans were wiped out, and because it takes three years for a new plant to produce, product was limited for several years. But the industry is slowly building back, and there are still plenty of ways to experience the history and the flavors of Puerto Rico's coffee heritage. The best time to visit coffee farms is during harvest season (Sept.-Dec.).

- **Festival del Café** (page 163): A weeklong celebration (mid-Feb.) of Yauco's main crop, featuring parades, award ceremonies, musical and dance performances, arts and crafts, and food vendors.

- **Café Hacienda San Pedro Tienda y Museo** (page 270): The café is located on a coffee farm in Jayuya, serving coffee drinks and selling bags of freshly ground and whole bean coffee. A museum next door displays coffee-processing equipment dating back to 1931.

- **Hacienda Buena Vista** (page 157): Established in 1833, this former coffee plantation in Ponce has been restored by the Conservation Trust of Puerto Rico. Guided tours are available in Spanish and English.

- **Hacienda Gripiñas** (page 270): Relive the glory days of Puerto Rico's 19th-century coffee trade by spending the night at this former coffee plantation.

Hacienda Buena Vista is a working coffee farm.

- **Hacienda Pomarrosa** (page 269): Take a two-hour tour of this working coffee farm near Jayuya. Enjoy a cup or two of the product, which is grown and processed on-site.

- **La Fiesta del Acabe del Café** (page 277): Celebrate the end of harvest season at a three-day celebration in Maricao (mid-Feb.). Festivities include musical performances, crafts, and food vendors.

Luquillo and spend the afternoon swimming and sunning at one of the island's most beautiful beaches. Drive back to San Juan and freshen up before dining at **Jose Enrique** in **Condado.**

Day 3: Santurce and Loíza, San Juan

Take a taxi or Uber to Calle Serra in **Santurce** and have Spanish tortilla for breakfast at **El Patio de Solé.** Stroll up and down Calle Serra, admiring the incredible **street murals.** Tour **Museo de Arte de Puerto Rico** and view its art collection spanning from the 17th century to the present.

Order lunch at the window of a bright yellow storage container at **Tresbé,** and find a shady table on the deck to dine on *pinchos*, ceviche, and tamarind chicken wings.

Next, explore the **Loíza** neighborhood. Stroll along **Calle Loíza,** shopping at boutiques and thrift stores such as **Len T. Juela** and **Electroshock.** Head to **Lote 23** food truck park for dinner and dine on pork sandwiches and frosty cocktails.

In the evening, join the street party at **La Placita**. Order a drink from a sidewalk bar and wander the streets people-watching and dancing to salsa music.

Day 4: Fajardo

Drive an hour east from San Juan to **Fajardo** and enjoy a brunch of coconut pancakes or eggs Benedict while admiring the views at **Las Vistas Café**. Take a water taxi to one of the small islands in the **Reserva Natural La Cordillera**, and spend the day swimming and sunning on a deserted beach.

In the afternoon, take a **sunset cocktail cruise** on a catamaran with **Salty Dog**. For dinner, dine on smoked meats and grilled seafood at **La Estación**. Stay the night at the **Fajardo Inn**.

Day 5: Vieques

Wake up early and head to the airport in Ceiba. Catch a 10-minute flight to **Vieques**. Grab a cup of coffee and a pastry at **Isla Nena Café** at the airport while you wait for your rental car to be dropped off.

Explore the historic sites of **El Fortín Conde de Mirasol** and **El Faro Punta Mulas**, and visit the **Vieques Conservation and Historical Trust**. Enjoy a Cuban sandwich at **Panadería La Viequense**, then take a horseback ride on the beach with **Esperanza Riding Company**.

Have an early dinner of Caribbean-inspired Mexican cuisine at **Coqui Fire Café**. After dark, take a bio-bay kayak tour of **Mosquito Bay**. Toast your adventure over a craft beer at **Duffy's Esperanza**. Stay the night at **Malecón House**.

Day 6: Culebra

Enjoy a breakfast of avocado toast and fruit smoothie at **Rising Roost Market & Café**, then catch the passenger ferry to **Culebra**. Snorkel with sea turtles on a guided tour with **Culebra Island Adventures**.

Dine on a burrito at **Zaco's Tacos** for lunch, then spend the afternoon swimming and sunning at **Playa Flamenco**. For dinner, chow down on whole fried snapper at the **Krusty Krab** and drink your dessert in the form of a bushwhacker cocktail at **Mamacita's**. Stay the night at **Club Seabourne**.

Day 7: Caguas and Cayey

Catch a 15-minute flight to **Ceiba**, pick up your rental car, and drive to **Caguas** and visit **Jardín Botánico y Cultural de Caguas**. Take a short scenic drive through the mountains along the **Ruta del Lechón** in **Cayey** and stop at **Los Pinos** *lechonera* to feast on roast pork with chicharrón, *pasteles*, rice and beans, and *tostones*.

Go for a swim at **Charco Azul**, a natural freshwater pool, then head back to **San Juan** and say goodbye to the island.

The Best of San Juan, Vieques, and Culebra

San Juan makes a convenient launchpad for getaways to the islands of Vieques and Culebra. Some people go to Vieques or Culebra for the day, just long enough to take in a water sport and have a meal. A few hop back and forth between the two. Vieques is the most diverse in terms of accommodations, restaurants, and water sports. Culebra is the sleepier, less-developed of the two. Both islands are rustic and boast spectacular stretches of pristine coastline and clean, clear waters ideal for diving and snorkeling.

Day 1: San Juan

Time to hit the beach. Rent a car for the day and head for **Ocean Park.** Stop at Walgreens for a Styrofoam cooler and some sunscreen, and then go to **Kasalta Bakery** for a quick breakfast of *quesitos* (cheese pastries) and coffee. While you're there, pick up picnic provisions: cheese, bread, ceviche, beer, water, and a bag of ice.

Head to **El Alambique Beach** in **Isla Verde,** where you can rent lounge chairs and umbrellas and supplement your picnic with *piraguas* (snow cones) and *frituras* (fritters) from beachside vendors. While away the day swimming, riding Jet Skis, parasailing, surfing, or just soaking up the rays.

Return to your hotel to shower off the sand, and then take a taxi to **Miramar** and dine on traditional Puerto Rican cuisine in a romantic atmosphere at **Casita Miramar.** Finish the night on the dancefloor at **Tántalo** in **Santurce.**

Day 2: Vieques

Catch a morning flight to **Vieques** from Isla Grande Airport in San Juan. Pick up a rental car and head straight to **Balneario Sun Bay** to spend the early part of the day swimming and sunbathing. Nosh on pizza and fritters from beachside vendors for lunch.

In the afternoon, check out **La Ceiba de Vieques,** a 275-year-old Ceiba tree, then drive to the site of the historic **Playa Grande Sugar Mill** and wander through the woods exploring the ruins.

In the evening, dine on exceptional seafood and Puerto Rican-inspired dishes at **El Quenepo.** Afterward, sing karaoke and have a nightcap at **Saint Voodoo's Mar Azul.**

Day 3: Vieques

Enjoy a leisurely breakfast at **Carambola** at the Inn at the Blue Horizon. Take a half-day tour fishing for amberjack and tarpon with **Caribbean Fly Fishing** and spend the afternoon exploring the deserted beaches at **Refugio Nacional de Vida Silvestre de Vieques** wildlife refuge. In between, pick up a bag of empanadas from **El Resuelve** for lunch.

In the evening, take a kayak tour of the bioluminescent **Mosquito Bay.** Enjoy a late-night meal of traditional Puerto Rican food at **El Guayacán,** a place so casual you don't even have to return to your guest room first and change.

Day 4: Culebra

Take the ferry to **Culebra.** Hit **Pandeli Bakery** in Dewey for a breakfast sandwich or pastry and stock up on sunscreen before heading to **Playa Flamenco,** where you'll want to rent lounge chairs and umbrellas and spend the day swimming, sunbathing, and walking the mile-long crescent of pristine beach.

When hunger pangs strike, visit one of the beachside kiosks and lunch on pizza, empanadas, *pinchos,* and fried seafood. In the afternoon, go for a challenging hike through a mangrove and boulder forest to **Playa Resaca,** a coral reef beach ill-suited for swimming but an important nesting site for sea turtles.

For dinner, enjoy creative dishes that combine Caribbean and Italian cuisines at **El Eden.** Dance

A Day and a Night in San Juan

Thousands of visitors flock to San Juan every week to start their Caribbean cruise vacations. The savvy ones book a hotel room, come a day early, and spend some time exploring the port of origin. The city is so compact and easy to navigate—it's a breeze to squeeze a lot of fun into 24 hours.

DAY

Catch an early flight and arrive midday in San Juan. Check into **Olive Boutique Hotel** in **Condado** and stroll around the lagoon at **Parque Nacional Laguna del Condado Jaime Benítez.**

Walk over to the gorgeous, mid-century-era resort **Caribe Hilton** and have a piña colada at the bar. Catch a taxi to **Viejo San Juan** and visit the **Cuartel de Ballajá,** an 1854 Spanish barracks, home of the **Museo de las Americas.**

NIGHT

In the evening, dine on upscale, creative interpretations of Puerto Rican cuisine at **Cocina Abierta,** then try your luck at the gaming tables at **Casino del Mar** at **La Concha Resort.**

Take a taxi or Uber to **Calle Loíza** and go salsa dancing at **Pisa Viejo** nightclub. Return to

San Juan Harbor at night

Condado and have a late-snack at **Latin Star Restaurant,** which is open 24 hours.

the night away to live salsa music or DJs at **La Lobina.**

Day 5: Culebra

To fully appreciate all Culebra has to offer, you need to get underwater and explore the rich sea life. Take a one-tank dive with **Culebra Divers** or take a snorkel kayak tour with **Kayaking Puerto Rico.** Afterward, enjoy a late lunch of seafood tacos and fresh fruit margaritas at **Zaco's Tacos.**

In the afternoon, take a drive around the island and visit the **Museo Histórico de Culebra El Polvorin.** For dinner, dine on creative Caribbean cuisine at **Susie's Restaurant** and end the evening with a nightcap at **The Sandbar.**

Day 6: Back to San Juan

Fly back to Isla Grande airport in San Juan. Spend the day wandering around **Viejo San Juan.** Take a guided tour of **La Fortaleza,** a UNESCO World Heritage site and home to the Puerto Rico governor since the 16th century. Enjoy a traditional Puerto Rican lunch at **Cafeteria Mallorca.** Then visit **Cuartel de Ballajá.** Originally barracks for Spanish soldiers, it's now home to **Museo de las Americas,** featuring a large collection of Latin American and Puerto Rican folk art.

Dine in elegance on the chef's six-course tasting menu at **Marmalade.** End the evening with a chocolate-flavored after-dinner cocktail at **Casa Cortés ChocoBar.** Prepare to fly home the following day.

Cordillera Central Road Trip

Gorgeous tropical jungle, hiking trails, natural pools, and indigenous culture are just some of the attractions in the Cordillera Central, the island's interior mountain range. Take four days to fully explore this mountain getaway. You'll need a car and plenty of time for travel; allow a minimum of one hour for every 50 kilometers (31 mi) when traveling mountain roads. Try to stay on main roads whenever possible.

Day 1

Fly into San Juan, rent a car, and drive 32 kilometers (20 mi) south to **Caguas.** Tour the lush grounds and historic ruins at **Jardín Botánico y Cultural de Caguas.** Head 23 kilometers (14 mi) south to **Cayey** and dine on juicy pit-roasted pork and other local delicacies at one of the *lechoneras.*

If there's time, walk it off on a short hike in **Reserva Forestal de Carite,** a subtropical humid forest. Spend the night in luxury with gorgeous mountain views at **El Pretexto** in Cayey.

Day 2

From Cayey, drive 20 kilometers (12 mi) northwest along **La Ruta Panorámica** to **Aibonito,** stopping by **Mirador Piedra Degetau** to take in the amazing view. Continue along La Ruta Panorámica for 16 kilometers (10 mi) to **Barranquitas.** Visit the town square and tour **Museo Luis Muñoz Rivera,** the former home of the poet, journalist, and politician.

Head 32 kilometers (20 mi) north to **Orocovis** and go ziplining, rappelling, and mountain biking at **ToroVerde.** Drive 48 kilometers (30 mi) west to **Jayuya.** Stay the night in **Hacienda Gripiñas,** a former 19th-century coffee plantation.

Day 3

In Jayuya, tour **Museo del Cemí,** a museum featuring excavated artifacts from the island's indigenous Taíno culture. Stop by **Casa Museo Canales** next door to tour a traditional *criolla*-style house.

Vieques

Romantic Escapes

Puerto Rico's beautiful beaches, balmy breezes, and lush tropical foliage provide a perfect backdrop to a romantic getaway.

VIEJO SAN JUAN

Book your stay at **Hotel El Convento,** a former Carmelite convent that dates back to 1651; request the romantic getaway package including a bottle of champagne, rose-petal turndown service, and chocolate-covered strawberries. Spend the day strolling through the historic town's cobblestone streets, playing hide-and-seek in **Castillo San Felipe del Morro,** and sipping café au lait at **Poetic Café.** At night, dine on expertly prepared French cuisine beneath a crystal chandelier at **Trois Cent Onze.**

LA PARGUERA

La Parguera is a romantic spot with an old-fashioned, rustic charm. Stay the night at **Parador Villa Parguera,** an old-fashioned inn with pleasantly landscaped grounds right on the water. The next day go sailing to **Los Cayos,** where you can find your own private beach for swimming, sunning, and snorkeling. Dine at any number of excellent seafood restaurants in town, and take a private nighttime boat tour of glittery **Bahía Fosforescente.**

CULEBRA

Nothing says romance, privacy, and seclusion like Culebra. Hop a flight to this small island off the coast of Fajardo. Stay at **Club Seabourne,**

Hotel El Convento in Viejo San Juan

a small, lovely property on Fulladoza Bay, featuring private villas with luxurious beds and glass showers. Explore the primitive beaches in the **Culebra National Wildlife Refuge,** or go to famous **Playa Flamenco** and walk until you find a secluded spot. At night, dine at **Susie's Restaurant,** specializing in fresh, seasonal seafood and produce. Stop by **Mamacita's** for a Bushwhacker, a sensuous and potent blend of Bailey's, Kahlua, Amaretto, coconut cream, rum, and ice cream.

Next, visit **La Piedra Escrita,** a boulder covered with Taíno petroglyphs, located by a large natural pool where you can take a cool dip. Take a hike to **Torre Observación** in **Bosque Estatal de Toro Negro** and admire the view from one of the highest points on the island. Camp overnight or return to Hacienda Gripiñas.

Day 4

From Jayuya, drive 29 kilometers (18 mi) west to **Utuado** and explore **Centro Ceremonial Indígena de Caguana,** an archaeological site dating back to AD 1100 featuring *bateyes* (ball courts), monoliths, and petroglyphs left behind by the Taíno.

Head 16 kilometers (10 mi) north toward Arecibo and stop for a 15-minute hike to **Cueva Ventana** for breathtaking views of the island's northern karst country. Take the highway 81 kilometers (50 mi) northeast to San Juan.

The Best of the West

Puerto Rico's west coast has a different vibe than San Juan and the east coast. The landscape is much more rugged, encompassing everything from salt flats and a subtropical dry forest to petrified sand dunes and a bioluminescent bay. It is also home to party-hearty surf towns and a colonial city that retains its Old World elegance.

Day 1: Aguadilla

Fly directly into **Aguadilla.** Pick up a rental car and take a driving tour of the town. Visit **Parterre J. de Jesus Esteve,** an elegant, shady park built in 1851, with a natural spring running through it. On a hill behind the park is **Pintalto Casas de Colores,** a brilliantly colored, massive public art project featuring a mural that stretches across more than a dozen contiguous houses.

Park the car and stroll along **Paseo Real Marina,** a promenade that stretches for miles along the waterfront. Dine on fresh seafood, ribs, or curry at the **Aguadilla Food Truck Park,** then drive south to **Rincón** and stay the night.

Day 2: Rincón

Start the day with caramelized banana French toast and fresh-pressed juice at **The English Rose.** Take a surf lesson at **Rincón Surf School.** Enjoy one of the *criolla*-style daily specials at **Café Puya** for lunch.

Take a snorkel cruise with **Katarina Sail Charters,** then watch the sun set over a rum punch during happy hour at **Calypso Café.** Dine on coriander-encrusted pork tenderloin in a tamarind glaze overlooking the water at **La Copa Llena at The Black Eagle.**

Have an after-dinner drink at **Roots.** Night owls will want to stroll around the plaza and hit a couple other bars, including **Rincón Beer Co.** and **Gylro.**

Day 3: Mayagüez

Grab a quick bagel and coffee from **Café 413** and drive south to **Mayagüez.** Take a walking tour of the city's colonial sites, including the large, Spanish-style **Plaza Colón** at the center of town. Facing it is **Catedral Nuestra Señora de la Candelaria,** a cathedral established in 1763. Nearby is **Casa de los Cinco Arcos,** a striking example of *criolla*-style architecture built in 1865.

For a midday snack, stop by **Plaza del Mercado,** a large farmers market filled with vendors selling everything from fresh produce to herbal remedies. Dine on traditional Puerto Rican cuisine in an elegant setting overlooking the plaza at **Cassabe.**

For dessert, try a slice of *brazo gitano,* a traditional Mayagüez pastry, at **Ricomini Bakery.** For late-night fun, try your luck at **Mayagüez Resort & Casino.**

Day 4: Boquerón and Cabo Rojo

Drive 30 minutes south to **Boquerón.** Visit **Refugio de Aves de Boquerón,** a bird sanctuary featuring a boardwalk through a mangrove swamp. For lunch, dine at **Terramar Restaurant** on the house special, pizza topped with churrasco, lobster, and bacon.

Proceed 10 minutes south to the **Cabo Rojo Peninsula,** the most southwestern point of Puerto Rico. Drive to the end of PR 301 and take a 15-minute hike to **Faro Los Morrillos,** the only lighthouse in Puerto Rico the public can enter. Admire the view of waves crashing into red cliffs along the coast.

Visit the **Cabo Rojo salt flats,** then go to **Playa El Combate** and rent Jet Skis from **BAMA Boqueron Aqua Marine Adventures.** Dine alfresco on a seafood feast overlooking the ocean at **Annie's Restaurant.** Stay the night and plan on driving 75 minutes back to Aguadilla for departure the next day.

Seek Thrills

- **Trek in El Yunque National Forest** (page 114): Bypass the paved trails in El Yunque Recreation Center to hike **El Toro Trail,** an arduous 2.2-mile trail that passes through *tabonuco,* sierra palm, and cloud forests and offers spectacular views of the south coast.

- **Go Diving in La Pared** (page 222): This world-class dive site near La Parguera features a wall that drops from 55 feet to more than 1,500 feet in depth, and visibility ranges 60-150 feet. See moray eels, parrotfish, and rare black coral.

- **Camp on Mona Island** (page 194): Pitch a tent on an uninhabited subtropical island with 20 miles of coastline, most of which is vertical cliffs more than 200 feet high. Hike the island's trails and snorkel or dive the crystal-clear waters.

- **Go Kiteboarding in San Juan** (page 60): With **Kite Puerto Rico,** you can learn how to soar on a kiteboard in four lessons.

- **Traverse San Cristóbal Cañon** (page 261): Hike, rappel, and bodysurf your way through one of the biggest canyons in the Caribbean. At 4.5 miles long and 500-800 feet deep, it's a great place to test your mountaineering skills.

- **Surf in Rincón** (page 191): Head to **Surf 787 Resort** for a crash course in surfing with overnight accommodations in Rincón.

- **Zipline through ToroVerde** (page 263):

ancient stone head in El Yunque National Forest

This adventure park in Orocovis boasts a variety of aerial challenges, including The Beast, a 4,745-foot double harness zipline. There are also canopy tours, a hanging bridges tour, rappelling, and a mountain bike course.

- **Jump into a Waterfall Pool** (page 175): Plunge from a rope swing into the pools of not one, but two waterfalls at **Gozalandia Cascadas.**

Sun and Surf

No two beaches are alike in Puerto Rico. *Balnearios* are large, government-maintained beaches with bathroom and shower facilities, picnic tables, and snack bars. Some have lounge-chair rentals, lifeguards, and campsites. Expect to pay $3-5 per vehicle to get in, and be aware that they get crowded on weekends and holidays.

There are also many wilderness beaches, which are typically remote and devoid of development and facilities. Some beaches have big waves best suited to surfing, and others are as calm as bath-water and ideal for swimming. Some, especially along the north coast, are rife with strong currents. They're beautiful to look at, but not safe for swimming. One thing all the beaches have in common is their accessibility to the public. There is no such thing as a private beach in Puerto Rico.

Best *Balnearios*

PLAYA LUQUILLO (PAGE 125)

Playa Luquillo, formally called **Balneario La Monserrate,** is considered one of the island's most beautiful beaches. It features a **wide flat crescent of sand,** a **shady palm grove,** and **calm shallow waters.** A couple of **food vendors** sell fritters and piña coladas, among other refreshments. There are several picnic shelters, as well as toilets and shower facilities. Camping is allowed with a permit.

BALNEARIO SUN BAY (PAGE 289)

Balneario Sun Bay is **Vieques's crowning jewel** of beaches. Pull your car to the edge of a sand dune and mark your spot on the smooth sand. Shade is spotty here, so bring a beach umbrella if you plan to stay for the day. Modest picnic shelters, bathrooms, and shower facilities are available. Camping is allowed with a permit.

PLAYA FLAMENCO (PAGE 304)

Culebra is the lucky site of Playa Flamenco, one of "America's Best Beaches," according to the

Travel Channel. The wide, mile-long, horseshoe-shaped beach boasts **fine white sand** and **calm, aquamarine water.** Unlike Puerto Rico's other publicly maintained beaches, Playa Flamenco is **home to two hotels**—Villa Flamenco Beach and Culebra Beach Villas. An abandoned graffiti-covered tank on the sand is a reminder of the U.S. Navy's presence. Camping is allowed with a permit.

BALNEARIO DE BOQUERÓN (PAGE 214)

The size of the parking at this **long white-sand beach** rimmed by **calm waters** is a testament to the size of the crowds that flock here, especially during Boquerón's high season in the summer. The property is quite **shady,** and in addition to the usual showers, toilets, and picnic tables, there is a huge **events pavilion,** a **baseball field,** and a **cafeteria.**

BALNEARIO CERRO GORDO (PAGE 239)

Balneario Cerro Gordo in Vega Alta on the north coast is a large **protected cove** with **calm waters** and a **pristine sandy beach** surrounded by hills covered in **lush vegetation.** It boasts one of the **best campgrounds** of any of the *balnearios* because of its spacious location atop a hilly peninsula overlooking the ocean. There's also **great surfing** to be had here.

Best Beaches for Surfing

Although surf spots can be found all around Puerto Rico's coastline, the most popular area is the northwest coast in the municipalities of Isabela, Aguadilla, and Rincón.

PLAYA DE JOBOS (PAGE 176)

Playa de Jobos in Isabela is an island favorite among surfers. The break point off Punta Jacinto is renowned for its **right-breaking tube.** The challenge here is parking, only available on narrow strips of sand along the roadside. Within walking distance are a number of casual restaurants and bars.

DOMES (PAGE 192)

Rincón is the surfing capital of Puerto Rico, thanks to literally dozens of popular surf sites. By far the favorite is Domes, located in front of the green domes of an abandoned nuclear power plant known by the acronym BONUS. This **easy-access** spot features **long hollow waves.** Domes is often crowded, especially on weekends.

STEPS BEACH/
TRES PALMAS (PAGE 192)

Located in Rincón, this is a **world-class site for experienced big wave surfers.** The waves here are very long and fast. Waves reportedly reach heights of 40 feet.

WILDERNESS BEACH (PAGE 184)

Aguadilla also boasts several outstanding surf spots. One popular spot is Wilderness Beach, located on the former Ramey Air Force Base. Just drive right through the golf course to get there. **Waves break right and left,** and swells reach up to 16 feet in height. Nearby **El Rincón Surf Shop** is a great source of information on current conditions and hot spots.

Best Beaches for Snorkeling and Diving

Puerto Rico's best snorkeling and diving is done offshore, but there are two beaches where underwater life can be explored.

BALNEARIO EL ESCAMBRÓN (PAGE 57)

The publicly maintained beach in the San Juan neighborhood of Puerta de Tierra features a **small crescent beach** on a **protected cove.** On the ocean floor is a collapsed bridge that provides an excellent site for underwater exploration.

PLAYA CARLOS ROSARIO (PAGE 304)

For easy access to a site rich in marine life, visit Playa Carlos Rosario, a narrow beach flanked by boulders and a protruding **coral reef** in Culebra. The underwater visibility is usually quite good here, and the coral reef, where you can see all kinds of **colorful fish** and **coral formations,** is teeming with marine life.

Best Wilderness Beaches
BOSQUE ESTATAL DE
PIÑONES (PAGE 111)

Bosque Estatal de Piñones offers several miles of **gorgeous, undeveloped** beach just minutes east of San Juan. Drive along PR 187 and look for sandy unmarked roads along the coast where you can pull your car right up to the beach and climb down the sand dunes into the water. For lunch, grab an *empanadilla* and *coco frio* from one of the food kiosks on the way. Plan on leaving by late afternoon because the sand fleas tend to attack when the sun starts to go down.

PLAYA MAR CHIQUITA (PAGE 240)

Playa Mar Chiquita in Manatí is a **tiny protected cove** located at the base of limestone cliffs on the north coast. A **coral reef** nearly encloses the calm, shallow basin of water, which is **ideal for taking small children swimming.** When you need some respite from the sun, explore the **cliffside caves.**

CULEBRITA (PAGE 304)

It requires a boat ride to get there, but Culebrita, a *cayo* off the coast of Culebra, is the place to go if you really want to get away from it all. In addition to multiple beaches perfect for **swimming** or **shore snorkeling,** there are several **tidal pools** and a lovely, abandoned **lighthouse.** To get there, either rent a boat or catch a water taxi at the docks in Dewey.

Explore Bioluminescent Bays

By day, a bioluminescent bay looks like any other body of still water. The only way to see its bioluminescence is by taking a boat ride or paddling a kayak into the lagoon at night. For the best visibility, go when there's a new moon.

MOSQUITO BAY (PAGE 284)

If you see only one bio-bay, make it Mosquito Bay in Vieques. When it's at its best, the water here glows an electric blue.

Mosquito Bay is accessible by kayak or by small electric-powered boat. Tours take about 90 minutes and cost $50-65. No kayaking experience is necessary. **Kayak tour operators** include:

- **Jak Water Sports**

- **Taíno Aqua Adventures**

- **Melaya's Tours**

- **Travesias Isleñas Yaureibo**

El Viequesnse Sea Tours offers **electric boat tours.** Tours are best booked 24 hours in advance to ensure availability.

LAGUNA GRANDE (PAGE 131)

The only way to access this lagoon in Fajardo is by kayak tours, which traverse a mangrove canal. When conditions are optimum, the water glows a glittery green.

Tours last about an hour and cost $45-50. No previous kayaking experience is necessary. Outfitters include:

- **Kayaking Puerto Rico**

- **Eco Adventures**

- **Yokahu Kayaks**

- **Las Tortugas Adventures**

- **Island Kayaking Adventures**

bioluminescent waters

Puerto Rico Access Tours offers bio-bay tours that are wheelchair-accessible and adaptive for guests with special needs. All Fajardo tours are best booked at least 24 hours in advance.

BAHÍA FOSFORESCÉNTE (PAGE 222)

La Parguera, a 2.5-hour drive southwest of San Juan, is home to Puerto Rico's most visited bio-bay. Unfortunately, the tourist town's ambient light means that the bay's glow has been diminished to subtle specks of white.

Thirty-minute gas-powered motorized boat tours cost $8-10. Small boat operators include **Gina at Johnny's Boats** and **Aleli Tours.** The 72-foot *Fondo de Cristal III* is a multi-tiered party boat that blasts loud rock music.

San Juan

San Juan, Puerto Rico, is arguably the most cosmopolitan city in the Caribbean.

The second-oldest European settlement in the Americas, it is a place where world-class restaurants and luxury hotels compete for space alongside glitzy nightclubs and casinos; where Spanish colonial and neoclassical buildings line cobblestone streets; where designer stores and import shops beckon tourists' dollars; where art, music, and dance thrive in its theaters, museums, and festivals; and where you're never very far from wide strips of sand and surf, ideal for sailing, surfing, and swimming.

Established by Spain in 1521 on the northeastern coast of Puerto Rico, San Juan stretches along 25 miles of coastline and 10 miles inland.

Highlights

Look for ★ to find recommended sights, activities, dining, and lodging.

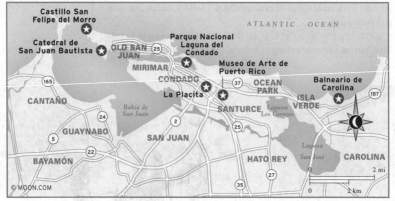

★ **Take in the views at Castillo San Felipe del Morro:** The imposing Spanish colonial fortress known as **El Morro** was designed to spot enemies entering San Juan Bay (page 41).

★ **Catedral de San Juan Bautista:** Established in 1521, this cathedral is the oldest existing church in the western hemisphere (page 49).

★ **Parque Nacional Laguna del Condado:** Fresh water and salt water blend together in the **Condado Lagoon.** A popular recreation area for running, walking, kayaking, and stand-up paddleboarding, it is also home to brown pelicans and manatees (page 52).

★ **Explore the Art Scene:** The impressive **Museo de Arte de Puerto Rico** (page 53) showcases island art from the 17th century to the present. The **street murals in Santurce** (page 56) are even more of-the-moment.

★ **Lounge in the sun at Balneario de Carolina:** This long, wide stretch of white sand beach is far from the high-rises of San Juan and dotted with lots of shady palm trees. It's one of the best beaches in the city (page 58).

★ **Party in La Placita:** By day, this plaza, formally known as **Plaza del Mercado,** hosts a popular farmers market. By night, it's the apex of a roving street party (page 69).

It spans 30,000 acres of coastal plain, encompassing rivers, bays, and lagoons, and is home to 347,000 people.

The heart of the city is historic Viejo San Juan, also known as Old San Juan, a 45-block grid of blue cobblestone streets lined with pastel-colored 16th-, 17th-, and 18th-century buildings trimmed with ornamental ironwork, flanked by two Spanish fortresses and surrounded by a 400-year-old wall. By day its streets crawl with tourists shopping for souvenirs and designer duds. At night it throbs with locals and tourists alike, partaking of some of the city's finest restaurants and bars. Along the bay, cruise ships dock.

Proceeding eastward along the coast from San Juan is Puerta de Tierra, a small neighborhood with a large park, a public beach popular with sunbathers and snorkelers, and the stately capitol building, the seat of the island's government. Next is Condado, the city's glitzy tourist district where high-rise hotels and casinos jockey for position with modern condominium and apartment buildings for the best views of the Atlantic Ocean. The main thoroughfare, Avenida Ashford, is lined with upscale restaurants, shops, and parks. Continuing eastward is Ocean Park, a fine stretch of beach with a stately residential community, a handful of guesthouses, and a growing cluster of restaurants. The final, most eastward community is Isla Verde, the densely developed home to the city's most spectacular beaches and exclusive resorts, as well as the Luis Muñoz Marín International Airport.

But it isn't just about the beaches in San Juan. Many of the city's charms can be found inland. Miramar, a high-rise residential neighborhood, is home to Condado Lagoon, Isla Grande regional airport, and the Puerto Rico Convention Center District, which continues to expand its tourism and entertainment footprint with new hotels, casinos, theaters, and more.

Loíza traditionally was the commercial center for San Juan's urban, working-class community, but it has transformed in recent years into a thriving bohemian arts district accompanied by a profusion of hip new restaurants, bars, boutiques, and hostels surrounded by spectacular street murals. It is a sub-barrio of Santurce, where the modern Museo de Arte de Puerto Rico is located, and Plaza del Mercado, a historic farmers market that doubles as La Placita, the focal point for a nightly street party that spills out into the surrounding streets, which are lined with traditional and trendy restaurants, bars, and clubs.

Travel farther inland for a locals-only experience in Hato Rey, the city's financial center; Río Piedras, home of the main campus for the Universidad de Puerto Rico; and the bedroom communities of Bayamón and Guaynabo.

As in any large city, all is not paradise. San Juan is a densely populated metropolis choking on its automobile traffic. A heavy cruise-ship trade dumps thousands of tourists in Viejo San Juan several days a week. American fast-food restaurants proliferate. The illegal drug trade is a source of violent crime.

But despite its big-city ways, San Juan retains its elegant charm and Spanish, Afro-Caribbean heritage. It is firmly planted in the 21st century, but its rich history endures and its sophisticated culture continues to thrive and evolve.

PLANNING YOUR TIME

It's possible to hit San Juan's highlights in one whirlwind **long weekend,** but it's equally possible to spend a whole month here and not see all the city has to offer.

Several spectacular day trips are less than an hour's drive east of San Juan, the most popular being the rainforest in **El Yunque Caribbean National Forest,** and **Playa Luquillo,** considered one of Puerto Rico's most beautiful beaches. Foodies can get their fill of fritters on a tour of *chinchorros* in Piñones.

Previous: Plazuela de la Rogativa, named after its sculpture by Lindsay Daen; outdoor café in Viejo San Juan; street art in Viejo San Juan.

San Juan

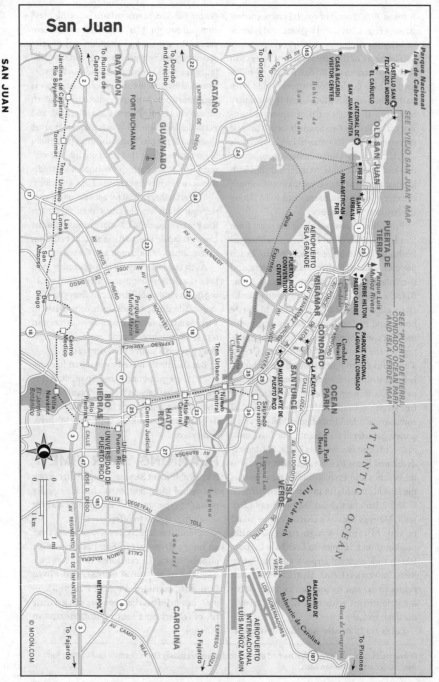

Parque Nacional
Isla de Cabras

CASTILLO SAN
FELIPE DEL MORRO

EL CAÑUELO

CASA BACARDI
VISITOR CENTER

SAN JUAN BAUTISTA

CATEDRAL DE
SAN JUAN BAUTISTA

OLD SAN JUAN

SEE "VIEJO SAN JUAN" MAP

Bahía
de
San Juan

PIER 2

PAN-AMERICAN
PIER

BAHÍA
URBANA

PUERTA DE
TIERRA

Parque Luis
Muñoz Rivera

CARIBE HILTON

PASEO CARIBE

SEE "PUERTA DE TIERRA,
CONDADO, OCEAN PARK,
AND ISLA VERDE" MAP

AEROPUERTO
ISLA GRANDE

PUERTO RICO
CONVENTION
CENTER

Laguna del
Condado

Condado
Beach

PARQUE NACIONAL
LAGUNA DEL CONDADO

MIRAMAR

CONDADO

SANTURCE

LA PLACITA

CALLE LOÍZA

OCEAN
PARK

MUSEO DE ARTE DE
PUERTO RICO

Sagrado
Corazón

Ocean Park
Beach

ATLANTIC

Isla Verde Beach

ISLA
VERDE

Laguna Los
Corozos

OCEAN

Boca de Cangrejos

BALNEARIO DE
CAROLINA

Balneario de
Carolina

AEROPUERTO
INTERNACIONAL
LUIS MUÑOZ MARÍN

To Piñones

CAROLINA

To Fajardo

EXPRESO DE DIEGO

CATAÑO

FORT BUCHANAN

GUAYNABO

BAYAMON

To Ruinas de
Caparra

To Dorado
and Arecibo

To Dorado

To Dorado

Jardines de Caparra/
Río Bayamón

Tren Urbano
Torrimar

Las
Lomas

San
Alfonso

De
Diego

Centro
Médico

RIO
PIEDRAS

Río
Piedras

HATO
REY

UNIVERSIDAD DE
PUERTO RICO

Uni de
Puerto Rico

Centro
Judicial

Villa
Nevárez

El Jardín
Botánico

CALLE

AV JOSE D. DIEGO

CALLE DEGETEAU

CALLE SIMON MADERA

AV REGIMIENTO
65 DE INFANTERIA

METROPOL

To Fajardo

AV CAMPO REAL

EXPRESO DE DIEGO

AV J. F. KENNEDY

Agua Expreso

Marín Peña
Channel

Tren Urbano

Nuevo
Central

Hato
Rey
Central

Laguna
San José

Laguna
de
Guaynabo

AV JESÚS T. PIÑERO

AV F. D. ROOSEVELT

EXPRESO AMERICA

AV BARBOSA

TOLL

AV BALDORIOTY DE CASTRO

AV ISLA
VERDE

AV LOS
GOBERNADORES

EXPRESO
LOÍZA

AV F. JUNCOS
AV PONCE DE LEON
AV MUÑOZ RIVERA
AV ASHFORD
AV FERNÁNDEZ JUNCOS

0

0   1 km
0   1 mi

© MOON.COM

ORIENTATION

Six municipalities make up greater San Juan: San Juan, Cataño, Bayamón, Guaynabo, Trujillo Alto, and Carolina. The eight barrios and sub-barrios that most visitors gravitate to are Viejo San Juan, Puerta de Tierra, Condado, Ocean Park, Isla Verde, Miramar, Loíza, and Santurce. Five of those communities are on the water, and they are all within about 30 minutes of one another by car, taxi, or bus.

Viejo San Juan

Viejo San Juan is the historic center of Puerto Rico. The 500-year-old walled city is filled with beautiful pastel-colored colonial buildings, Spanish forts, art and history museums, plazas, restaurants, bars, shops, and ship docks. Many of the island's must-see sites are located here. They include two Spanish fortresses, **Castillo San Felipe del Morro** and **Castillo de San Cristóbal;** the historic churches **Catedral de San Juan Bautista** and **Capilla del Cristo;** and a couple of terrific museums, including **Museo de las Americas.**

The best way to see Viejo San Juan is **by foot.** The narrow, one-way roads are tricky to drive and often congested, and parking is limited. Sturdy walking shoes are recommended; it's easy to turn an ankle on the cobblestones.

Getting into and out of Viejo San Juan is easy. The main public bus terminal, **Covadonga Bus Terminal,** is at the corner of Calle la Marina and Calle J. A. Corretjer, near the cruise-ship piers. A taxi stand is nearby, just south of Plaza de Colón at Calle Tetuán and Calle Recinto Sur.

Puerta de Tierra

Geographically this small spit of land is part of Viejo San Juan, but it's located outside the walled city and lacks the cobblestone streets and charm. Nevertheless, despite its size (little more than half a square mile), it packs in a diversity of sights.

Puerta de Tierra is the home of many government buildings, including **El Capitolio.** But it's also the site of the classic midcentury modern **Caribe Hilton; Paseo Caribe,** a large multi-use development with a vibrant, high-end shopping district, food hall, and restaurants; **Fuerte San Jeronimo,** a diminutive fort; **Parque Luis Muñoz Rivera,** a lovely park; **Balneario El Escambrón,** the closest public beach to Viejo San Juan; and **Sixto Escobar Stadium.**

Capilla del Santo Cristo de la Salud, on Calle del Cristo

Condado

The strip of beachfront property between Viejo San Juan and Ocean Park has undergone countless facelifts. From its heady, glamorous days in the late 1950s to a period of decline in the 1980s to a new era of prosperity in the 2000s, Condado has seen some ups and downs. It is home to some of San Juan's flashiest resorts—**The Condado Plaza, La Concha Resort,** and **Condado Vanderbilt.** It is also home to high-end restaurants, including **José Enrique, Cocina Abierta, Mario Pagan Restaurant,** and **1919 Restaurant,** as well as a number of casinos.

There's more to Condado than commerce: most notably the long, wide stretch of **beach.** The pedestrian-friendly neighborhood boasts a gorgeous seaside park, **Ventana al Mar** (Windows to the Sea), as well as **Laguna del Condado,** a small, natural lagoon offering watersports and a wide boardwalk.

Ocean Park

Nestled between Condado and Isla Verde, Ocean Park is an upscale residential community featuring shady streets and beautiful old homes, many of them outstanding examples of Caribbean-style midcentury modernist architecture. Visitors are free to come and go on weekends, but after 6pm a guard checks IDs, so expect to wait at a checkpoint to get in. On weekends, car traffic is limited to residents and patrons of the restaurants and guesthouses.

Ocean Park is renowned for its long, wide strip of **beach,** which isn't dominated by high-rise buildings and resort hotels. The beach is popular with kiteboarders. **Playa Último Trolley,** also known as **Ocean Park Beach,** is an easily accessed public beach with free parking. Across the street, **Parque Barbosa** features several sports fields as well as a track for biking, walking, and running.

Commercial development in Ocean Park was once limited to just a handful of businesses, including the outstanding **Kasalta** bakery, but restaurants and guesthouses have cropped up to serve visitors who gravitate to the neighborhood's chill vibe.

Isla Verde

Isla Verde is renowned for its long, wide beaches, luxury resorts, and some spectacular nightclubs and casinos. When you're catching rays on the beach or partying the night away in a glitzy hot spot, Isla Verde can feel as glamorous as South Beach.

The main thoroughfare, the congested Avenida Isla Verde, is lined with a wide variety of fast-food joints, pizzerias, and **souvenir shops.** To see Isla Verde's **gorgeous coast,** you'll need to head to one of the high-rise hotels and condominiums that line every inch of the way. (There are a few other ways to see the coast: an entrance at the end of Calle Tartak, and a few narrow, hard-to-see walkways between buildings.) The best way to enjoy Isla Verde is to ensconce yourself in one of the cushy resorts. The community has the added benefit of being home to the **Luis Muñoz Marín International Airport.**

Loíza

The neighborhood of Loíza (not to be confused with the municipality of the same name on the east coast) is defined by one street, **Calle Loíza,** which stretches 14 kilometers (9 mi) between Calle Wilson and Parque Barbosa. It's only one block away from Calle McLeary, the main artery through Ocean Park's commercial district, but it feels like it's a world away.

Formerly the commercial center of Santurce, it has been transformed into a bohemian **arts district** filled with stunning street murals, creative restaurants and bars, and **hipster boutiques.** At night it turns into a lively **entertainment district** for the young and young at heart. This is one of the hippest places in San Juan.

Santurce

Santurce is a large swath of central San Juan that stretches from Puerta Tierra in the west to Isla Verde in the east, encompassing the sub-barrios of Condado, Miramar, and Loíza, among others. It is home to the modern **Museo de Arte de Puerto Rico** and the **Centro de Bellas Artes Luis A. Ferré performing arts center,** as well as a number of contemporary art galleries, art collectives, and design centers. Eye-popping **street art murals** can be seen along Calle Cerra.

Santurce is also the site of **Plaza del Mercado,** also known as **La Placita,** a thriving farmers market by day and a lively street party scene at night.

Miramar

South of Condado, opposite from Laguna del Condado, Miramar has traditionally been home to the city's upper middle class. The neighborhood's main one-way thoroughfares—Avenida Ponce de León and Avenida Fernández Juncos—run parallel from one tip of the community to the other, and a drive along either one reveals modern highrise apartment buildings, classic **colonial homes,** and **trendy restaurants** that abut boarded-up storefronts and abandoned buildings scrawled with graffiti.

On the western tip of Miramar, along San Juan Bay, is the Puerto Rico Convention Center District. At its center is the modern and massive **Puerto Rico Convention Center.** The Sheraton Puerto Rico Hotel & Casino and several other corporate hotels occupy this area. Construction of a $150 million entertainment complex called El Distrito (The District), featuring a large, modern plaza with an outdoor stage, massive video screens, a multiplex cinema, and space for restaurants and bars, is underway.

Miramar is also home to **Isla Grande Airport,** San Juan's regional airport, which provides air service to the Caribbean.

Greater San Juan

Outside San Juan's popular tourist areas are communities central to the lives of San Juan residents. **Hato Rey** is the city's business and financial district, chock-full of banks and restaurants that cater to office workers. It's connected by the Tren Urbano metro system to **Río Piedras,** home of the Universidad de Puerto Rico, and the residential communities of **Bayamón** and **Guaynabo.** On the western shore of San Juan Bay, across from Viejo San Juan, is **Cataño,** home of Casa Bacardí.

Sights

VIEJO SAN JUAN
Historic Sites
★ CASTILLO SAN FELIPE
   DEL MORRO

Castillo San Felipe del Morro (501 Calle Norzagaray, 787/729-6777, www.nps.gov/saju, daily 9am-6pm, $10 adults, free for children 15 and younger), commonly called **El Morro,** is an impressive sight to behold no matter what direction you come from. From San Juan Bay, which the fort was constructed to protect from attack, it's a daunting display of military defense featuring four levels of cannon-bearing batteries that rise 140 feet from the sea. From Viejo San Juan, the approach is more welcoming, thanks to an

enormous expanse of grassy lawn and breathtaking views of the shore. It's easy to see why this is a popular spot for kite-flyers.

Inside Castillo San Felipe del Morro is a maze of rooms, including gun rooms, soldiers' quarters, a chapel, turreted sentry posts, and a prison connected by tunnels, ramps, and a spiral stairway. The foundations for El Morro were laid in 1539, but it wasn't completed until 1787. It successfully endured many foreign attacks by the English in 1595, 1598, and 1797, and by the Dutch in 1625. During the Spanish-American War, the United States fired on El Morro and destroyed the lighthouse, which was later rebuilt. On Saturdays and Sundays, guided tours are offered in Spanish and

Viejo San Juan

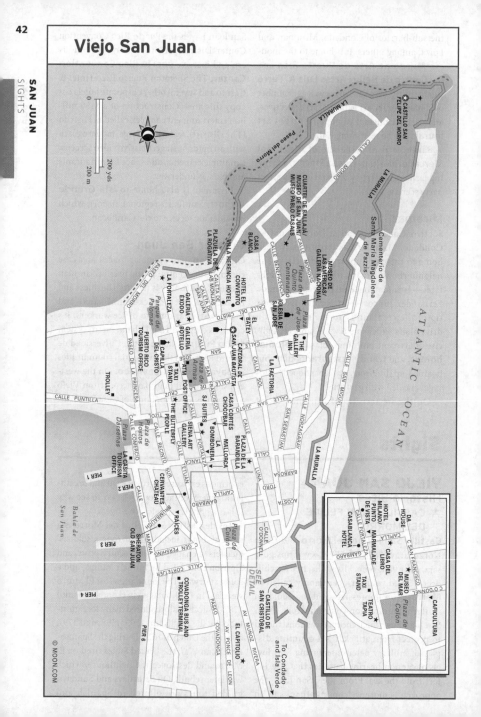

0
0

200 yds
200 m

ATLANTIC OCEAN

Bahia de San Juan

★ CASTILLO SAN FELIPE DEL MORRO

LA MURALLA

Paseo del Morro

CALLE DEL MORRO

LA MURALLA

CUARTEL DE BALLAJA/
MUSEO DE SAN JUAN/
MUSEO PABLO CASALS

CASA BLANCA

Cementerio de Santa María Magdalena de Pazzis

PLAZUELA DE LA ROGATIVA

VILLA HERENCIA HOTEL

HOTEL EL CONVENTO

MUSEO DE LAS AMÉRICAS/
GALERÍA NACIONAL

Plaza del Quinto Centenario

CALLE BENEFICENCIA

CALLE MORROS

PASEO DEL MORRO

CALETA DE LAS MONJAS

LA FORTALEZA

GALERÍA EXODO

GALERÍA BOTELLO

CAPILLA DEL CRISTO

TROLLEY

CALLE PUNTILLA

PUERTO RICO TOURISM OFFICE

PASEO DE LA PRINCESA

Parque de Palomas

CALLE DEL CRISTO

CALLE SAN JOSÉ

CALLE DE LA CRUZ

ATM

TAXI STAND

POST OFFICE

EL BATEY

CATEDRAL DE SAN JUAN BAUTISTA

★ SAN JUAN BAUTISTA

Plaza de Armas

SJ SUITES

THE BUTTERFLY PEOPLE

CALLE SAN FRANCISCO

CASA CORTÉS CHOCOBAR

SIENA ART GALLERY

LA BOMBONERA

MALLORCA

IGLESIA DE SAN JOSÉ

Plaza de José Casals

THE GALLERY INN

LA FACTORIA

CALLE SOL

CALLE LUNA

CALLE SAN SEBASTIÁN

CALLE NORZAGARAY

CALLE SAN JUSTO

CALLE SAN MIGUEL

LA MURALLA

Plaza de Hostos

CALLE COMERCIO

CALLE RECINTO SUR

PLAZA DE LA CATEDRAL

CALLE FORTALEZA

CALLE TETUÁN

CALLE TANCA

CALLE RECINTO SUR

CALLE SAN JUSTO

CALLE O'DONNELL

Plaza de Colón

LA CASITA TOURISM OFFICE

CERVANTES CHATEAU

RAÍCES

SHERATON OLD SAN JUAN

CALLE LA MARINA

CALLE BRUMBAUGH

CALLE GEN PERSHING

CALLE CORTELIER

PIER 1

PIER 2

PIER 3

PIER 4

PIER 6

COVADONGA BUS AND TROLLEY TERMINAL

Plaza Dársenas

CALLE COMERCIO

PASEO COVADONGA

AV COVADONGA

AV PONCE DE LEÓN

AV MUÑOZ RIVERA

EL CAPITOLIO

CASTILLO DE SAN CRISTÓBAL ★

SEE DETAIL

To Condado and Isla Verde

CALLE BARBOSA

CALLE ACOSTA

CALLE TORO

CALLE GAMBARO

CALLE CAPILLA

SEE DETAIL

DA HOUSE

HOTEL MILANO/ PUNTO DE VISTA

MARMALADE

CAPILLA

CASABLANCA HOTEL

CASA DEL LIBRO

C SAN FRANCISCO

CALLE FORTALEZA

GAMBARO

C O'DONNELL

MUSEO DEL MAR

TAXI STAND

TEATRO TAPIA

Plaza de Colón

CAFICULTURA

© MOON.COM

English. The admission fee also includes entry to Castillo de San Cristóbal.

CASTILLO DE SAN CRISTÓBAL

Castillo de San Cristóbal (Calle Norzagaray at the entrance to Viejo San Juan, 787/729-6777, www.nps.gov/saju, daily 9am-6pm, $10, free for children 15 and younger) is the large fortress at the entrance to Viejo San Juan by Plaza de Colón. Before it was built, two significant attacks from land—first by the Earl of Cumberland in 1598, later by the Dutch in 1625—convinced the Spanish that protecting the walled city from attack by sea alone was not adequate.

The fort's construction began in 1634 and was completed in 1783. The fort eventually encompassed 27 acres of land, although some of it was destroyed to accommodate the expanding city. The fort's defense was tested in 1797 by another unsuccessful attack by the British. After the United States won the Spanish-American War, it took control of the fort and used it as a World War II observation post. Today, a section of the fort is open to the public, who can wander freely among its intriguing array of tunnels, ramps, stairways, batteries, magazines, soldiers' quarters, and turreted sentry posts. The admission fee also includes entry to El Morro.

CASA BLANCA

Casa Blanca (1 Calle San Sebastián, 787/725-1454, Wed.-Sun. 9am-noon and 1pm-4pm, gardens open daily 9am-4pm, $5 adults, $3 children, students, and seniors) was the island's first fortress and was originally built as a home for the island's first governor, Juan Ponce de León, although he died on his quest for the Fountain of Youth before he could ever take up residence. Construction began in 1523, and for more than 200 years it served as the residence of Ponce de León's descendants. Today it's a museum of 17th- and 18th-century domestic life featuring lots of impressive Spanish antiques. Don't miss the cool, lush gardens that surround the house and the views of both San Juan Bay and the Atlantic Ocean.

LA FORTALEZA

La Fortaleza (Calle Fortaleza, 787/721-7000, ext. 2211, 2323, and 2358, daily 9am-4pm, free) was the first fort built in Puerto Rico, completed in 1540 to provide refuge for the island's original Spanish settlers. Partially

Castillo San Felipe del Morro

burned by the Dutch in 1625, it was rebuilt in the 1640s and received a new facade in 1846. It has been the official residence of the governor of Puerto Rico since the 16th century, which gives it the distinction of the longest continuous use of an executive mansion in the western hemisphere. It is included on the UNESCO list of World Heritage sites. Guided tours are limited to the gardens and 1st floor.

LA MURALLA
La Muralla (The Wall) is the grand, dramatic, and impenetrable wall that once surrounded Viejo San Juan and still stands strong today along the coast and bay. Nearly 400 years old, the wall took 200 years to complete and stands 40 feet high and 45 feet thick in some places. The wall once had five gates that permitted access into the city, but only one, La Puerta de San Juan, remains today.

LA PUERTA DE SAN JUAN
Built in 1635, the commanding red **La Puerta de San Juan** (end of Calle Caleta de San Juan) is the last remaining gate, of the original five, to provide access through La Muralla into the walled city. Located at the end of Calle Caleta de San Juan, the 16-foot tall, 20-foot thick door was the main gate to the city.

PASEO DEL MORRO
The beautiful **Paseo del Morro** is a broad, 5-kilometer (3-mi) promenade outside La Muralla, tracing San Juan Bay. It spans from Paseo de la Princesa, north past La Puerta de San Juan, around Castillo San Felipe del Morro, back through a gate (open daily 9am-6pm), and across the vast lawn in front of El Morro. Boasting stunning views of the bay and city wall, the promenade has royal palms, public art, and gardens along its length. There is not much shade, so sunscreen and a hat or parasol are recommended.

PASEO DE LA PRINCESA
The **Paseo de la Princesa** is a wide, shady promenade from Plaza de Hostos at Calle Tizol to San Juan Bay at the southern end of Paseo del Morro. Along the way is the Tourism Company of Puerto Rico, the remains of La Princesa prison, and a couple of restaurants. Outdoor musical performances and artisan fairs are often held here, and food vendors frequently sell treats like *piraguas* (snow cones) and *dulces* (candies).

LA PRINCESA
La Princesa (2 Paseo La Princesa, 787/721-2400, www.prtourism.com, Mon.-Fri.

La Fortaleza

8am-4:30pm, free), also known as **El Presidio del San Juan** and **Carcel de San Juan**, was a federal prison built in 1837 that remained active until 1976. More than 600 prisoners were housed here at one time. It is now home to the Tourism Company of Puerto Rico. Pass through the reception room and art gallery into the courtyard, and you can tour three prison cells and the courtyard where executions by hanging were held.

CUARTEL DE BALLAJÁ
Cuartel de Ballajá (Calle Norzagaray beside Plaza del Quinto Centenario near the entrance to Castillo San Felipe del Morro) is a massive structure that once housed 1,000 Spanish soldiers. Built in 1854, the former barracks is three levels high with interior balconies and a dizzying series of arches that overlook an enormous courtyard. It was the last major building constructed by the Spanish in the New World. Today it houses several museums, including the **Museo de las Americas** and a number of restaurants, bars, and cafés.

CEMENTERIO DE SANTA MARÍA MAGDALENA DE PAZZIS
Cementerio de Santa María Magdalena de Pazzis is the city's historic cemetery, outside the city wall just east of Castillo San Felipe del Morro and accessible from Calle Norzagaray in Viejo San Juan. In addition to a neoclassical chapel, there are many significant burial sites of some of the city's early colonists, as well as the tomb of Pedro Albizu Campos, the revered revolutionary who sought independence for the island of Puerto Rico. Avoid going alone or at night. Next door is **La Perla**, an impoverished community notorious for its drug trade; its illicit activities are known to spill over into the cemetery. If you don't want to venture in, you can get a great view of it from Plaza del Quinto Centenario on Calle Norzagaray.

TEATRO TAPIA
Teatro Tapia (Calle Fortaleza at Plaza de Colón, 787/721-0180 or 787/721-0169, www.teatropr.com) is one of the oldest theaters in the western hemisphere. The lovely Romantic-style building was constructed in 1824 and renovated in 1987. Named after Puerto Rican playwright Alejandro Tapia y Rivera, the 642-seat theater still hosts a variety of performing arts events.

The only way to tour the interior is during an event, but this significant architectural landmark is worth viewing from the outside.

Paseo de la Princesa

Saving La Muralla

Viejo San Juan is a walled city overlooking San Juan Bay.

The most enduring symbol of Puerto Rico is La Muralla. Nearly 400 years old, the city wall is composed of rock, rubble, and mortar that wraps around Viejo San Juan from the cruise-ship piers on San Juan Harbor to the capitol on the Atlantic Ocean. Its iconic sentry boxes serve as a symbol of the island's Spanish heritage and resilience in an ever-changing world.

Begun by Spanish colonists in the 1600s, the wall took 200 years to complete and has withstood multiple attacks by the English, the Dutch, and the Americans. But what proved nearly impenetrable to foreign attack has been rendered defenseless by modern life. Automobile traffic, pollution, and misguided attempts to preserve it have endangered the wall.

Forty-five feet wide and 40 feet high in some spots, La Muralla is crumbling in places. In 2004 a 70-foot section below the heavily traveled Calle Norzagaray fell, underscoring the urgency of stepping up preservation efforts. It wasn't the first time the wall's fragility was made apparent. A larger section fell into San Juan Bay in 1938, and in 1999 a Soviet oil tanker ran aground, damaging the wall's northwest corner.

When the U.S. Army seized Puerto Rico in 1898, it took over maintenance of the wall and attempted its first preservation efforts. Concrete was used to patch La Muralla, but that only served to add weight to the wall and trap moisture inside it, which weakened the structure over time.

Now a UNESCO World Heritage site, La Muralla is maintained by the U.S. Park Service, which has been overseeing efforts to repair the wall.

Along with the fortresses of El Morro and San Cristóbal that adjoin it, the wall attracts 1.2 million visitors a year. Chances are, with the help of preservation efforts, it will continue to assert its soaring beauty and cultural significance as the proud protector of Viejo San Juan for years to come.

ANTIGUO CASINO DE PUERTO RICO

One of the most striking sights at the entrance to Viejo San Juan beside Plaza Colón is **Antiguo Casino de Puerto Rico** (1 Ave. Ponce de León, 787/690-5482, www.antiguocasinopr.com), a stunning blue beaux arts-style building appointed with elaborate gardens, balconies, and ornate moldings. Originally a social club established in 1917, the building has served various purposes since that time, including as the officer's club for the U.S. Army during World War II. It's a popular site for weddings, quinceañeras, and corporate events. The building is not open to the general public, but it's worth walking around outside to admire the exterior.

History Museums
MUSEO DE SAN JUAN

Museo de San Juan (150 Calle Norzagaray, 939/454-2594, www.facebook.com/MuseodeSanJuan, Tues.-Sat. 9am-noon and 1pm-4pm, Sun. noon-5pm, free) is in the city's former marketplace, built in 1857. In 1979 it was converted into a city museum. It contains two exhibition spaces, one housing temporary exhibits illuminating various aspects of the city's history, the other a permanent exhibition that gives a comprehensive look at the city's history from its geographical roots to the 21st century. The superb exhibits include reproductions of old photographs, maps, prints, and paintings that tell the city's story. All of the text describing the exhibits is in Spanish.

LA CASA DEL LIBRO

A depository of more than 8,000 books dating back to the late 15th century, including a first edition of *Don Quixote,* **La Casa del Libro** (255 Calle del Cristo, 787/723-0354, www.lacasadellibro.org, Thurs.-Sat. 11am-5pm, $5 adults, $4 children) features rotating exhibits of books from its collection, as well as exhibits devoted to the art of book printing and binding.

MUSEO DEL MAR

Museo del Mar (360 Calle San Francisco, 787/977-4461, www.elmuseodelmar.com, Wed.-Sun. 10am-5pm, $6 adults, $3 children 5-12) boasts a small but impressive collection of nautical items, ranging from letters purportedly written by King Ferdinand V and Queen Isabella I, to dozens of lifesavers from the world's largest collection (as proclaimed by Guinness World Records). The items are all from the private collection of José Octavio Busto, founder and president of Continental Shipping Inc.

Art Museums and Galleries
MUSEO DE LAS AMERICAS

Museo de las Americas (Cuartel de Ballajá, 2nd Fl., on Calle Norzagaray beside Plaza del Quinto Centenario, 787/724-5052, www.museolasamericas.org, Tues.-Fri. 9am-noon and 1pm-4pm, Sat.-Sun. noon-5pm, $6 adults, $4 children, students, and seniors) is located inside **Cuartel de Ballajá,** an enormous structure that once housed 1,000 Spanish soldiers. The museum contains a fantastic collection of Latin American folk art, including masks, musical instruments, clothing, pottery, baskets, and tools. Highlights include altars representing Santería, voodoo, and Mexico's Day of the Dead celebration. Don't miss the collection of vintage santos, Puerto Rican wood carvings of saints. Wall text is in Spanish and English except in the second smaller exhibit dedicated to Puerto Rico's African heritage. The **Tienda de Artesanías** (787/722-6057, Tues.-Fri. 9am-noon and 1pm-4pm, Sat.-Sun. noon-5pm), on the 1st floor, has a small but quality selection of locally made crafts for sale.

GALERÍA BOTELLO

Galería Botello (208 Calle del Cristo, 787/723-9987 or 787/723-2879, www.botello.com, Mon.-Sat. 10am-6pm, free) is a significant art museum dedicated to the work of Angel Botello. Born in Spain, the renowned artist spent most of his life in the Caribbean, eventually settling in Puerto Rico, where he opened this gallery. Although he died in 1986, the artist lives on through his paintings and sculptures on view at the gallery, which also exhibits solo shows by contemporary artists.

SIENA ART GALLERY

Siena Art Gallery (253 Calle San Francisco, 787/724-7223, www.sienaartgallery.com, Mon.-Sat. 11am-6pm, free) is a fine art gallery featuring Puerto Rican and Caribbean artists, including Mikicol and Rafael Colon Morales.

GALERÍA ÉXODO

Located in two galleries a few steps apart, **Galería Éxodo** (200-B Calle del Cristo and 152 Calle del Cristo, 787/725-4252 or 787/671-4159, www.galeriaexodo.com, daily 11am-7pm, free) specializes in Caribbean art and represents 60 contemporary artists.

THE BUTTERFLY PEOPLE

The Butterfly People (257 Calle de la Cruz, 787/723-2432 or 787/723-2201, www.butterflypeople.com, daily 11am-6pm, free) is a unique gallery that sells fantastic colorful pieces composed of real butterflies mounted in Lucite.

Religious Sites
★ CATEDRAL DE SAN JUAN BAUTISTA

Catedral de San Juan Bautista (151-153 Calle del Cristo, 787/722-0861, www.catedralsanjuan.com, Mon.-Thurs. 9am-noon and 1:30pm-4pm, Fri. 9am-noon; Mass: Sat. 9am, 11am, and 7pm, Sun.-Fri. 12:15pm) holds the distinction of being the second-oldest church in the western hemisphere, the first being Catedral Basilica Menor de Santa in the Dominican Republic. The church was first built of wood and straw in 1521 but was destroyed by hurricanes and rebuilt multiple times. In 1917 the cathedral underwent major restoration and expansion. The large sanctuary features a marble altar and rows of arches, with several side chapels appointed with elaborate statuary primarily depicting Mary and Jesus. In stark contrast is a chapel featuring an enormous contemporary oil painting of a man in a business suit. It was erected in honor of Carlos "Charlie" Rodríguez, a Puerto Rican layman who was beatified in 2001 by Pope John Paul II. Catedral de San Juan Bautista is the final resting place of Juan Ponce de León, whose remains are encased in a marble tomb. It also holds a relic of San Pio, a Roman martyr.

CAPILLA DEL SANTO CRISTO DE LA SALUD

Built in 1753, the tiny picturesque **Capilla del Santo Cristo de la Salud** (south end of Calle del Cristo, 787/722-0861), sometimes referred to as **Cristo Chapel,** is one of the most photographed sights in San Juan. Legend has it that horse races were held on Calle del Cristo. One ill-fated rider was speeding down the hill so fast he couldn't stop in time and tumbled over the city wall to his death, and the chapel was thus built to prevent a similar occurrence. An alternative end to the legend is that the rider survived and the church was built to show thanks to God. Either way, the result was the construction of a beloved landmark.

The chapel is rarely open, but it's possible to peer through the windows and see the ornate gilded altarpiece. Beside the building is **Parque de Palomas,** a gated park overlooking San Juan Harbor that is home to more pigeons than you might think imaginable. Birdseed is available for purchase if you want to get up close and personal with your fine feathered friends.

IGLESIA DE SAN JOSÉ

Iglesia de San José (Calle San Sebastián at Plaza de San José, 787/725-7501) is one of the oldest structures in Viejo San Juan. Built in the 1530s, it was originally a chapel for the Dominican monastery, but it was taken over in 1865 by the Jesuits. The main chapel is an excellent example of 16th-century Spanish Gothic architecture. Originally, Iglesia de San José was Juan Ponce de León's final resting place, but his body was later moved to Catedral de San Juan Bautista. Ponce de León himself is said to have donated the wooden 16th-century crucifix. Unfortunately, the church has been closed since 2000 as painstakingly slow efforts to preserve the building have been underway. In 2013 the National Fund of Historic Preservation added it to its list of historic sites in danger of disappearing.

1: Museo de las Americas 2: Catedral de San Juan Bautista 3: Plaza de Armas

PARROQUIA SAN FRANCISCO DE ASIS

Located by Plaza de la Barandilla, adjacent to Plaza Salvador Brau, **Parroquia San Francisco de Asís** (301 Calle San Francisco, 787/724-1131, www.capuchinospr.org; Mass: Sun. 8am, 9:30am, 11am, and 5pm, Tues.-Sat. 12:15 pm) was built in 1876. It has undergone various renovations over the years, but it remains true to the beautiful simplicity of its Gothic design, marked by high archways, a rustic altar, and plain wooden pews. A crypt in the basement contains remains dating back to the early 1800s.

Plazas and Parks

Most every town in Puerto Rico has a main plaza at its center that is flanked by a church and an *alcaldía* (town hall). Bigger towns like San Juan have several. There is no better way to spend the morning than strolling the perimeter of a plaza or sitting on a bench sipping coffee and watching the parade of people pass by. The plazas are also popular sites for arts festivals and evening concerts. Not surprisingly, the largest concentration of historic plazas and parks is in Viejo San Juan.

PLAZA DE ARMAS

Plaza de Armas (Calle San Francisco at Calle de la Cruz and Calle San José) is the main square in Viejo San Juan and a great place to people-watch. Once the site of military drills, it contains a large gazebo and a fountain surrounded by four 100-year-old statues that represent the four seasons. A couple of vendors sell coffee and snacks, and there's a bank of pay phones popular with cruise-ship visitors eager to check in with those back home. Across the street on Calle de la Cruz is a small grocery store. Across Calle Cordero is an ATM.

PLAZA DE COLÓN

Plaza de Colón (between Calle Fortaleza, Calle San Francisco, and Calle O'Donnell) is a large square at the entrance to Viejo San Juan by Castillo de San Cristóbal. In the center is a huge pedestal topped with a statue of Christopher Columbus, whom the plaza is named after. There's a small newsstand on one corner, and several restaurants and shops surround it on two sides. Unfortunately, there's little shade, so it's not that pleasant for lingering when the sun is high.

PLAZA DE LA BARANDILLA

Located by Carlos Albizu University, the large **Plaza de la Barandilla** (Calle Tanca between Calle San Francisco and Calle Luna) was buried beneath asphalt and concrete for 80 years until it was discovered in 2005. It was restored at a cost of more than $3 million. A popular spot for outdoor concerts, it is a welcome respite of open space and sky in the midst of Viejo San Juan's density, and it provides a welcoming access to Calle Luna via a sweeping set of steps.

PLAZA DEL QUINTO CENTENARIO

Plaza del Quinto Centenario (between Calle Norzagaray and Calle Beneficencia near the entrance to Castillo San Felipe del Morro) is Viejo San Juan's newest park. Built in 1992 to commemorate the 500th anniversary of Christopher Columbus's "discovery" of the New World, the plaza features a striking 40-foot sculpture, Tótem Telúrico, created by local artist Jaime Suárez from black granite and ceramics. The plaza provides a great view of the historic cemetery, El Morro, and all the kite-flyers who gather on the fort's long green lawn.

PLAZUELA DE LA ROGATIVA

One of Puerto Rico's most beautiful pieces of public art is in **Plazuela de la Rogativa,** a tiny sliver of a park tucked between the city wall and Calle Clara Lair just west of El Convento in Viejo San Juan. At its center is a spectacular bronze sculpture called *La Rogativa,* designed by New Zealand artist Lindsay Daen in the 1950s.

The piece depicts a procession of three women and a priest bearing crosses and torches. It commemorates one of San Juan's most beloved historic tales. In 1797 a British fleet led by Sir Ralph Abercrombie entered San Juan Bay and prepared to launch an attack in hopes of capturing the city. Because the city's men were away protecting the city's inland fronts, the only people remaining behind were women and clergy. In hopes of staving off an attack, the governor ordered a *rogativa*, a divine entreaty to the saints for help. As the story goes, the town's brave women formed a procession, carrying torches and ringing bells throughout the streets, which duped the British into thinking reinforcements had arrived, prompting them to sail away, leaving the city safe once again.

PLAZA DE JOSÉ

Plaza de José (Calle San Sebastián and Calle del Cristo) is in front of the Iglesia de San José and features a statue of its most celebrated parishioner, Juan Ponce de León. After successfully thwarting another attack by the British in 1797, citizens of San Juan melted the enemy's cannons to make the statue. This is a popular gathering place for young locals, especially at night when the string of nearby bars gets crowded.

PLAZA DE EUGENIO MARÍA HOSTOS

Plaza de Eugenio María Hostos (between Calle San Justo and Calle Tizol) is a bustling shady spot near the cruise-ship piers. On weekends it turns into a craft fair, and there are often food vendors selling fritters and snow cones. Just across the street, at **Plaza de la Dársena,** concerts are often held on the weekends on a covered stage overlooking the harbor.

PARQUE DE PALOMAS

Parque de Palomas (beside Capilla del Santo Cristo de la Salud on the south end of Calle del Cristo) is home to countless pigeons. A vendor sells small bags of birdseed for those who take pleasure in being swarmed by the feathered urban dwellers. Kids love it!

BAHÍA URBANA

Located along Piers, 6, 7, and 8 on San Juan Bay, **Bahía Urbana** (Ave. Fernández Juncos, 787/977-2777) is a pretty, wide open park with a paved promenade and large swaths of green space, gorgeous water views, pleasant seating areas, and public art.

PUERTA DE TIERRA
Fuerte San Jerónimo

Fuerte San Jerónimo (behind the Caribe Hilton in Puerta de Tierra) is the only fort in San Juan that isn't part of the San Juan National Historic Site. Instead, it's overseen by the Institute of Puerto Rican Culture and managed by the Caribe Hilton, on whose property it now sits. Various sources date its origins to the 17th and 18th centuries, but little is known about it. It's rarely open to the public, but it can be seen from Puente Dos Hermanos bridge in Condado and the grounds of Caribe Hilton in Puerta de Tierra.

El Capitolio

El Capitolio de Puerto Rico (Puerto Rico capitol building, Ave. Luis Muñoz Rivera, 787/721-5000, ext. 301/311, www.tucamarapr. org, Mon.-Fri. 8:30am-4:30pm, free) is the seat of government for Puerto Rico, where the legislature and the senate meet, and where political protests are held. It is an imposing building completed in 1929 and constructed in the Neoclassical Revival style of architecture. The marble dome was added in 1961. The interior features stained glass and murals created by some of the island's most revered artists, including Jose Oliver, Rafael Tufino, and Jorge Rechani. Tours (reservations required) are conducted in English and Spanish.

Walter Otero Contemporary Art

Walter Otero Contemporary Art (402 Ave. Juan Ponce de León, 787/998-9622, www.facebook.com/WalterOteroContemporaryArt, Tues.-Fri. 10am-6pm, Sat. 10am-2pm, free) represents more than 20 modern Caribbean artists and hosts rotating exhibits year-round.

Puerta de Tierra, Condado, Ocean Park, and Isla Verde

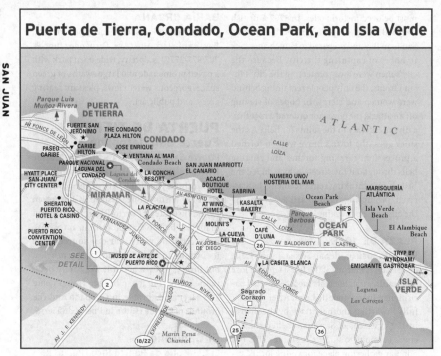

Parque Luis Muñoz Rivera

Once a heavily shaded park filled with massive ceiba trees, Parque Luis Muñoz Rivera (between Ave. Ponce de León and Ave. Muñoz Rivera) took a big hit from Hurricane Maria. The park's old-growth trees were wiped out, making this a much sunnier spot than it used to be. But it's still a lovely green space. Providing a welcome reprieve from the city's urban atmosphere, the park features formal gardens, fountains, walking trails, a children's play area, and a pavilion.

CONDADO
★ Parque Nacional Laguna del Condado

Parque Nacional Laguna del Condado Jaime Benítez (Ave. Baldorioty de Castro between Condado and Miramar, daily 24 hours) is a park that houses the **Condado Lagoon.** The lagoon is bordered by a wide boardwalk, with a public ramp for launching kayaks and canoes. Several natural restoration projects are ongoing at the site, including a sea-grass restoration project in the lagoon and the cultivation of red mangrove trees, ceibas, and other native plants around its shore.

Parque Luchetti

A lovely oasis of quiet and lush green flora just two blocks away from the hubbub of Avenida Ashford, **Parque Luchetti** (between Calle Magdalena and Calle Luchetti at Calle Cervantes) is a hidden gem of a park. Shaded benches, flowering shrubs, palm trees, and bronze sculptures make this the perfect spot to relax or picnic. One of the highlights is a whimsical bronze sculpture called *Juan Bobo and the Basket.* Created in 1991 by New Zealand artist Lindsay Daen, who made the statue *La Rogativa* in Viejo San Juan, it's inspired by a local fable.

Ventana al Mar

A welcome expanse of green space with a stunning view of the Atlantic along Condado's

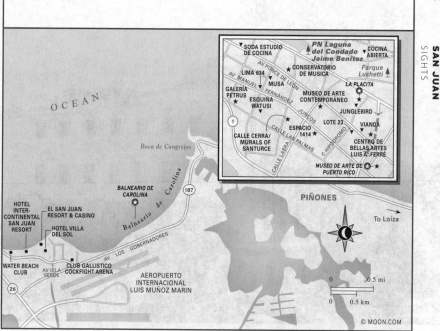

© MOON.COM

high-rise row, **Ventana al Mar** (1054 Ave. Ashford, beside La Concha Resort) provides easy access to the beach, as well as benches and lounges for relaxing. On one side is an attractive strip of restaurants, ranging from casual to upscale, and an outdoor area filled with tables and chairs for dining alfresco.

SANTURCE
Art Museums and Galleries
★ MUSEO DE ARTE DE
  PUERTO RICO

Without a doubt, the crown jewel of San Juan's cultural institutions is **Museo de Arte de Puerto Rico** (299 Ave. José de Diego, 787/977-6277, www.mapr.org, Tues. and Thurs.-Sat. 10am-5pm, Wed. 10am-8pm, Sun. 11am-6pm, $6 adults, $3 children 5-12). Even visitors with only a passing interest in art will be bowled over by the volume and quality of work produced by the many gifted artists who hail from this small island.

The 130,000-square-foot neoclassical structure opened in 2000 and was renovated in 2011. It is devoted to Puerto Rican art from the 17th century to the present. The wall text is in Spanish and English. Exhibition highlights include works by the celebrated Francisco Manuel Oller, a European-trained, 17th-century realist-impressionist, as well as a striking selection of *cartels,* a midcentury poster-art form distinguished by bold graphics and socially conscious themes.

Don't miss the contemporary art section on the 2nd floor. One room is devoted to Rafael Trelles's 1957 installation *Visits to the Wake,* inspired by Oller's famous 19th-century painting of a family attending a child's wake, called *El Veloria.* The piece combines video, sculpture, found objects, and life-size cutouts of the painting's characters to astounding effect. Another remarkable work is Pepón Osorio's installation titled *No Crying Allowed in the Barbershop.* The simulated barbershop explores issues of male vanity, rites of passage, and early lessons in masculinity.

1

2

There are also exhibition spaces for rotating shows, a children's gallery, a modern sculpture garden, and the Raul Julia Theater, featuring a curtain made of *mundillo*, a traditional handmade lace. A gift shop is also on-site.

MUSEO DE ARTE CONTEMPORÁNEO DE PUERTO RICO

In a striking redbrick Georgian structure completed in 1918, **Museo de Arte Contemporáneo de Puerto Rico** (Escuela Rafael M. de Labra, corner of Roberto H. Todd and Ave. Ponce de León, 787/977-4030, 787/977-4031, or 787/977-4032, www.museocontemporaneopr.org, Tues.-Fri. 10am-4pm, Sat. 11am-5pm, $5 adults, $3 children, seniors, and visitors with disabilities) has two small exhibition spaces featuring rotating exhibitions from its permanent collection.

GALERÍA PETRUS

Galería Petrus (726 Calle Hoare, Miramar, 787/289-0505, http://petrusgallery.com, Mon.-Fri. 10am-6pm, Sat. noon-5pm) is a contemporary art gallery that hosts temporary shows featuring contemporary paintings, sculptures, and graphic arts from the 1960s to the present. The gallery specializes in Caribbean artists, including painters Carlos Dávila Rinaldi, Santiago Flores Charneco, and Luis Hernández Cruz, and sculptor Carlos Guzmán.

ESPACIO 1414

Espacio 1414 (1414 Ave. Fernandez Juncos, 787/725-3899, www.espacio1414.org, by appointment only, email info@berezdivincollection.com) was established by art collectors Diana and Moises Berezdivin to house their collection of contemporary conceptual art with an emphasis on emerging artists. The nonprofit gallery is also the site of occasional visiting exhibitions.

1: El Capitolio 2: Fuerte San Jerónimo and Condado Plaza Hilton

Performing Arts

CENTRO DE BELLAS ARTES LUIS A. FERRÉ

Centro de Bellas Artes Luis A. Ferré (Ave. Ponce de León, 787/620-4444 or 787/725-7334, www.cba.gobierno.pr) is a fine arts performance space hosting classical, jazz, and folk concerts, as well as theater and dance productions. This is also the place to see *zarzuela*, a form of Spanish operetta, performed. Home to the Puerto Rico Symphony Orchestra and the annual Casals Festival, it has four halls; the smallest seats up to 200 and the largest seats around 2,000. Ample parking is available on-site.

CONSERVATORIO DE MUSICA DE PUERTO RICO

Renowned cellist Pablo Casals established the **Conservatorio de Música de Puerto Rico** (951 Ave. Ponce de León, Miramar, 787/751-0160, www.cmpr.edu) in 1959, and it underwent extensive renovation in 2011. The music conservatory provides undergraduate, graduate, and community education programs in areas of musical performance, composition, jazz, and education. The conservatory hosts a variety of performances by students, faculty, and guest artists.

MIRAMAR
Puerto Rico Convention Center

The **Puerto Rico Convention Center** (100 Convention Blvd., 800/214-0420, www.prconvention.com) lays claim to being the largest, most technologically advanced convention center in the Caribbean, with 580,000 square feet of meeting space that can accommodate up to 10,000 people. Events include art fairs, Puerto Rico Comic Con, bridal shows, volleyball championships, and shopping expos.

GREATER SAN JUAN

Museo del Niño de Carolina (corner of Avenida Camp Rico and Fidalgo Diaz Carolina, Carolina, 787/257-0261, www.museodelninocarolina.com, Wed.-Fri.

☆ The Murals of Santurce

street art mural on Calle Cerra

Art doesn't just live in galleries and museums in Puerto Rico. It explodes in riotous colors and arresting images from the streets of Santurce. Just stroll along **Calle Cerra,** a formerly derelict part of town, and view one stunning mural after another. The massive pieces are the work of local artists Celso Gonzalez, Vero Rivera, Bob Snow, and Alexis Bousquet, among others. Bousquet helped launched the island's mural movement in 2010 when he founded **Santurce es Ley** (www.facebook.com/santurceesley), a street art festival. In addition to the annual festival, which occurs late in the year and attracts up to 10,000 people, Santurce es Ley hosts pop-up events and epic after-parties featuring the island's hottest DJs.

Once the festival is over, the new additions to this incredible outdoor gallery remain. The quality of the murals is phenomenal, and the subject matter ranges from comical to poignant. Many capture the pride of Puerto Rican heritage; some contain social commentary. As a result of the project's popularity, Santurce has experienced a revival. New restaurants, coffee shops, and bars have opened, making Calle Cerra a destination.

The momentum behind the movement continues to grow. Murals have started popping up in other cities around the island, and a new initiative was launched in 2020 to encourage mural artists from around the world to participate.

There is no better way to spend an afternoon than walking along Calle Cerra, marveling at the artwork and stopping in the neighborhood bistros. Start at **Avenida Juan de Ponce de León** and head southwest to **Avenida Las Palmas,** where the concentration of murals is greatest. Be sure to explore the side roads and empty lots around the area so you don't miss anything.

9am-5pm, Sat.-Sun. 10am-6pm, $10 adults, $6 children 1-14, $5 seniors) is a hands-on, interactive educational center featuring more than 100 exhibits. Kids can put on a play, deliver a weather report on TV, take the controls in the cockpit of an actual airplane, and more. There

is also a playground, go-kart racing ($5), and a petting zoo ($2 adults, $1 children).

El Cañuelo (end of PR 870 on Isla de Cabras, Toa Baja, www.npr.gov/saju, park access daily 8:30am-5:30pm, $2), also known as **Fortín San Juan de la Cruz,** is the ruins of a tiny fortress across the bay from Castillo San Felipe del Morro. Originally constructed of wood in the 1500s, it was destroyed in an attack by the Dutch in 1625. The current stone structure was built in the 1670s. Its purpose was to work in concert with El Morro to create cannon crossfire at the mouth of the bay. The public is not allowed to enter the fort, but surrounding it is a modest park with a small recreation area, picnic tables, and a terrific view of El Morro.

Hato Rey
Parque Luis Muñoz Marín (off PR 18 between Ave. Jesús Piñero and Ave. F. D. Roosevelt, 787/480-7777, Wed.-Sun. 8:30am-5pm) in Hato Rey is a modern 140-acre park with walking and bike trails, a children's play area, golf practice grounds, an amphitheater, pavilions, and more.

Cataño
CASA BACARDÍ VISITOR CENTER
Casa Bacardí (PR 165, km 6.2, 787/788-8400, www.bacardi.com/casa-bacardi, Mon.-Sat. 9am-4:30pm, Sun. 10am-4:30pm, $15) offers an expansive visitors center and premium tours where you can learn all about Bacardí rum. On the rum tasting tour ($50), visitors can taste all the varieties of rum in the Bacardí portfolio. Learn how to make three classic rum drinks on the mixology tour ($60).

Established in Cuba in 1862 by Don Facundo Bacardí Masó, Bacardí is the top-selling rum in the United States and is still owned and operated by its founder's descendants. No rum is made on the site of the visitors center, which features displays and historical objects that tell the history of the business.

To get to Casa Bacardí, it's a 10-minute ride from Viejo San Juan on the **ferry** (daily 6am-9:40pm, $0.50 each way) operated by **AcuaExpreso Cataño** (Calle Marina, Pier 2, Viejo San Juan, 787/729-8714 or 787/788-0940). The ferry runs every 30 minutes except Monday-Friday 6am-10am and 3:45pm-7pm (holidays excluded), when it increases frequency to every 15 minutes.

Guaynabo
RUINAS DE CAPARRA
Ruinas de Caparra (PR 2, km 6.4, 787/781-4795, Mon.-Fri. 8am-noon and 12:30pm-4pm, free) is the site of Juan Ponce de León's first settlement on the island, established in 1508. All that's left are a few crumbling walls and foundations, but there is a small museum containing some historical documents and Taíno artifacts pertaining to the site.

Recreation

Puerto Rico's west coast is better known for diving and surfing, but there are opportunities to do both in San Juan. The most popular water sport these days seems to be stand-up paddleboarding. Riding personal watercraft like Jet Skis is also popular. And good old-fashioned swimming, sailing, and fishing never go out of style.

BEACHES
Balneario El Escambrón
The closest beach to Viejo San Juan is

Balneario El Escambrón (Ave. Muñoz Rivera, Puerta de Tierra, Mon.-Thurs. 8am-5:30pm, Fri.-Sun. 8am-6pm, free, $5 parking). The publicly maintained site offers basic amenities, such as public restrooms, showers, snack bar, lifeguards, and an outfitter renting scuba gear, snorkel gear, and kayaks. The small crescent beach is on a cove protected by a coral reef, so the water is quite calm, and there is excellent snorkeling and diving to be had along a collapsed bridge. Steer clear at night.

Condado Beach

Condado Beach (along Ave. Ashford) is a perfectly fine beach for swimming and sunning, although the terrain is hillier, the sand coarser, and the water less crystalline than San Juan's finer beaches in Isla Verde or Ocean Park. As in Isla Verde, the beach is lined with high-rise buildings, but it is easier for the public to access it thanks to several parks along the way, including **Ventana al Mar, Plaza Ancla,** and **Parque del Indio.** The farther east you go, the wider the beaches get.

Ocean Park Beach

The pretty **Ocean Park Beach** (along Park Blvd.) is called **Playa Último Trolley** by locals. When the island's electric trolley system ceased operation in 1946, a trolley car was converted into a snack bar and placed in Parque Barbosa across the street. (The trolley car is no longer there.) There are no facilities, but the beach is cleaned and raked daily, and a swimming area is protected with nets to keep out sea creatures. On weekends, lounge chairs are available for rent, and street vendors patrol the boardwalk selling snacks and beverages.

Parque Barbosa (end of Calle McLeary) is right across the street from Ocean Park Beach and is the perfect place to park when visiting the beach. It isn't the prettiest or best-maintained park in San Juan, but it does have hiking, jogging, and bike paths. Its proximity to a large public-housing project may deter some visitors.

El Alambique Beach

El Alambique Beach (Calle Tartak, Isla Verde) is a popular destination for sun-worshippers and water sports enthusiasts. Roughly 4 kilometers (2 mi) long, its wide stretches of sand and rolling surf make for great swimming, surfing, and windsurfing.

To access the beach, go to the end of Calle Tartak by the San Juan Water Beach Club Hotel. Parking is limited, but there is a turn-around where you can unload your coolers and beach chairs. Once you find a spot to park

the car, there is a pedestrian pathway from Avenida Isla Verde. On weekends and all summer long, vendors rent out beach chairs and sell *piraguas* (snow cones). This is a popular spot to windsurf, parasail, ride Jet Skis, and take out small sailboats.

★ Balneario de Carolina

Balneario de Carolina (PR 187, Ave. Boca de Cangrejos, 787/757-2626, ext. 4650, 4651, or 4652, May 15-Aug. 15 daily 8am-6pm, Aug. 16-May 14 Tues.-Sun. and holidays 8am-5pm, free, $4 parking) is a gorgeous, 4-kilometer (2-mi) stretch of undeveloped beachfront with lots of shady palm trees, located between Isla Verde and Piñones and maintained by the municipality of Carolina. It's best suited for swimming and sunning. The facility features picnic shelters, bathroom facilities, food vendors, and plenty of parking. Traffic along Avenida Boca de Cangrejos can slow to a crawl on weekends, so get there early and plan to leave late.

DIVING AND SNORKELING

San Juan may be home to some beautiful beaches, but its snorkel and dive spots are virtually nil. Local outfitters typically head east toward Fajardo for underwater exploration tours.

Ocean Sports (3086 Ave. Isla Verde, 787/268-2329, www.osdivers.com, Mon.-Fri. 9am-7pm, Sat. 9am-6pm, $115-175) rents and sells snorkel and scuba equipment and operates shore tours around San Juan. Boat tours can be arranged for groups of three or more and require a one-hour or two-hour drive.

Scuba Dogs (Balneario El Escambrón, Ave. Muñoz Rivera, 787/783-6377 or 787/977-0000, www.scubadogs.net, Mon.-Thurs. 8am-4pm, Fri.-Sun. 8am-5pm) rents scuba and snorkel equipment and offers tours. One-hour snorkel tours range $55-80. Scuba tours start at $75, with three-hour beginner tours ranging $125-150.

1: Condado Beach 2: Ocean Park Beach

Aqua Adventure (Caribe Hilton, 1 Calle Geronimo, Puerta de Tierra, 787/636-8811 or 787/860-3483, http://scubapuertorico.net) offers snorkel and scuba tours, plus SNUBA tours, a combination of snorkeling and scuba diving. The 90-minute snorkel tour is $69; a one-hour scuba or SNUBA tour costs $88 per tank; and a two-hour Discover scuba dive tour for beginners is $159.

SURFING

Puerto Rico's primo surf spots are found on the west coast, but in San Juan, **Isla Verde**'s waves are just big enough to give novice surfers a challenge. Instructors with **Wow Surfing School & Water Sports** (787/955-6059, www.wowsurfingschool.com, daily 9am-5pm) offer two-hour private surf lessons on land and in the water, including board rentals, for $85 at The Ritz Carlton San Juan in Isla Verde. Group rates are available. Equipment rentals include surfboards ($25/hour), paddleboards ($30/hour), kayaks ($25/hour), and snorkel equipment (from $15/hour). Jet Ski rentals and tours are available from San Juan Marina in Miramar and El San Juan Hotel in Isla Verde ($80-150 for 30- to 90-minute tours). Operators must be 21 or older; passengers must be at least 12.

Pine Grove Surf Club (Pine Grove Beach, Isla Verde, 787/361-5531 or 787/403-8803, www.pinegrovesurfclub.com, daily 8:30am-5pm) offers private surf lessons ($75/hour), surfboard rentals ($25 for 2 hours), snorkel tours at Playa El Escambrón ($45/hour), and paddleboard tours in Piñones ($55/hour).

Caribbean Surf School (787/637-8363, www.caribbeansurfpr.com, daily 7am-10pm) also offers lessons, tours, and equipment rentals. Surfboard rentals are $30-40 per day, and a one-hour surfing class is $65 (price includes day-long surfboard rental).

Tres Palmas Surf Shop (1911 Calle McLeary, Ocean Park, 787/728-3377, www.trespalmaspr.com, Mon.-Sat. 10am-7pm, Sun. 10am-6pm) is the source for all your surfing needs, including boards, board shorts, flip-flops, sunglasses, T-shirts, bathing suits, and more. Rentals are $30 for surfboards, $35 for fun boards, $40 for long boards, and $25 for body boards.

STAND-UP PADDLEBOARDING

SUP Action (482 Ave. Manuel Fernández Juncos, 787/637-2338, Mon.-Fri. noon-6pm, Sat.-Sun. 9am-6pm) rents paddleboards ($17/day) and kayaks ($20-30/day) and leads private tours ($70) in Condado Lagoon. The best way to reach this business is via text.

KITEBOARDING

Learn to kiteboard in four lessons at **Kite Puerto Rico** (Numero Uno Beach House, 1 Calle Santa Ana, Ocean Park, 787/726-5010, www.kitepuertorico.com). IKO-certified instructors provide instruction in four three-hour sessions. The only requirement is participants must be good swimmers. Rates are $375 for one session, $1200 for four, including gear. This is also the place to buy and rent kiteboarding gear.

KAYAKING

Take an illuminated nighttime tour of the Condado Lagoon with **Night Kayak** (Serafina Beach Hotel, 1045 Ave. Ashford, 787/248-4569, www.nightkayak.com, from $49). Climb aboard a double kayak tricked out with LED lighting and take a guided tour of the lagoon after dark. If you're lucky, you may see some marine life, including tarpon, sea stars, turtles, lobsters, and stingrays. The tours last one hour and are suitable for all skill levels. One-hour stand-up paddleboard tours (ages 14 and up, from $59) are available for experienced paddleboarders only.

E-Bike & Kayak (San Juan Marriott Resort, 1309 Ave. Ashford, Condado, 340/344-4381, www.ebikeandkayak.com) leads one-hour illuminated kayak tours ($49) nightly at 7pm and 9pm for all ages. (There must be at least one participant age 16 or older in each two-person kayak.) The company also leads bike tours (from $89) on electric bikes.

BOATING
Marinas

There are three marinas in San Juan. All three have fuel and water. The largest is **San Juan Bay Marina** (Ave. Fernandez Juncos, Miramar, 787/721-8062, www.sjbaymarina.com), with a capacity of 191 boats, including 125 wet slips, 60 dry-stack spaces, and six spaces for yachts more than 100 feet long. There's also a restaurant on-site.

Club Náutico de San Juan (482 Ave. Fernández Juncos, Miramar, 787/722-0177, www.nauticodesanjuan.com) is a secure port in San Juan Harbor featuring 117 wet slips that can accommodate vessels 30-250 feet long. Amenities include a clubhouse, a fueling port, and 24-hour guard service. Club Náutico de San Juan also offers sailing lessons (787/667-9936) for children age 6 and older, and it hosts the annual International Regatta (Feb.) and the International Billfish Tournament (Sept.).

Boat Tours and Rentals

Sail the seas on the 83-foot topsail schooner *The Amazing Grace* with **Old San Juan Harbor Tours** (between Piers 3 and 4, Viejo San Juan, 787/860-3434, www.eastislandpr.com). Daily 90-minute tours are $79 for adults and $69 for children 4-11. Daily two-hour sunset tours (Oct.-Apr. 5pm, May-Sept. 5:30pm) are $95 for adults and $85 for children 4-11. Boarding begins 30 minutes prior to departure.

Wow Surfing School & Water Sports (787/955-6059, www.wowsurfingschool.com, daily 9am-5pm) offers Jet Ski rentals and tours ($80-150 for 30- to 90-minute tours) from San Juan Marina in Miramar and El San Juan Hotel in Isla Verde. Operators must be 21 or older, and passengers must be at least 12. Also available are two-hour private surf lessons ($85 including board rental) at The Ritz Carlton San Juan in Isla Verde. Group rates are available.

FISHING

Caribbean Outfitters (Cangrejos Yacht Club, 787/396-8346, www. fishinginpuertorico.com) offers fishing and fly-fishing charters throughout Puerto Rico, Vieques, Culebra, the Dominican Republic, and St. Thomas with Captain Omar. Three-quarter-day kayak fishing trips are $600 for one person, $750 for two, including gear and bait. Light tackle fishing ventures start at $375 for one person for a half-day. Deep-sea fishing starts at $575 for a half day, $850 for three-quarters of a day, and $1,175 for a full day.

Magic Tarpon (Cangrejos Yacht Club, 787/644-1444, www.puertoricomagictarpon.com) offers fly-fishing outings for up to two anglers for $350 for four hours or $460 for eight hours. Reef fishing outings for barracuda, yellow tail, snapper, sharks, and more are $340-475 for 1-4 people.

CLIMBING, CAVING, AND ZIPLINES

Hacienda Campo Rico (Ave. Campo Rico, Carolina, 787/523-2001, www.haciendacamporico.com) is a wonderland for thrill-seekers looking for a new challenge to conquer. Take a half-day **zipline tour** ($95-105) and admire the views of lagoons, ocean, plantain groves, and mountains from five ziplines, one measuring 1,000 feet long. Other options include a three-hour expedition combining **ziplining and cave rappelling** ($129, meal included), **horseback riding** (from $75), and **ATV tours** (from $95). From the San Juan airport, go south on PR 26. Exit on Avenida Campo Rico and head east. Go over the bridge and pass through five traffic lights. The road ends at the entrance to Hacienda Campo Rico. Just past the guard gate, turn right, then turn right again at the intersection. Look for the terra-cotta colored house, which is where you'll park.

Book Hacienda Campo Rico tours through **EcoQuest** (New San Juan Building 6471, Ste. 5A, Isla Verde, 787/616-7543 or 787/529-2496, www.ecoquestpr.com) and get round-trip transportation from San Juan for $20 per person.

GOLF

Río Bayamón Golf Course (PR 171 at Ave. Laurel, Bayamón, 787/740-1419, www.municipiodebayamon.com, Mon.-Sat. 7am-6pm, Sun. 6am-8pm, $65 greens fee) is the only golf course in the metropolitan San Juan area. The public course is 6,870 yards and par 72. Facilities include a driving range, putting green, pro shop, and restaurant.

HORSEBACK RIDING

Hacienda Campo Rico (end of Ave. Robert Sánchez, Carolina, 787/523-2001, www.haciendacamporico.com, daily 9am and 3pm) provides guided horseback tours for $75 per person for two hours. Private tours are also available. Riders must be at least 8 years old and weigh less than 250 pounds. Closed-toe shoes are required. Arrive 45 minutes prior to your tour's start time.

BICYCLING

San Juan Bike Rentals (787/554-2453, www.sanjuanbikerental.com, Mon.-Fri. 7am-6pm, Sat. 9am-6pm, from $22.50 for 4 hours) is a mobile bike rental service that delivers road, mountain, hybrid, and cruiser bikes anywhere in Viejo San Juan, Condado, Ocean Park, Isla Verde, and Miramar.

E-Bike & Kayak (San Juan Marriott Resort, 1309 Ave. Ashford, Condado, 340/344-4381, www.ebikeandkayak.com) leads a 2.5-hour bike tour ($89) from Condado to Viejo San Juan on electric bicycles. The bikes are available in two styles: a cruiser or a tandem. The 14-kilometer (9-mi) ride is for confident, experienced bike riders only, ages 16 or older. Tour times are 10am and 2pm daily. For an added adventure, take the Night E-Bike Tour (daily 6:30pm, $109), illuminated by LED lights. Nighttime kayak tours ($49) are also available.

YOGA

Ashtanga Yoga Puerto Rico (1950 Calle McLeary, Ocean Park, 787/677-7585, www.ashtangayogapuertorico.com, daily, from $16) offers classes and workshops in beginning yoga, rocket yoga, breath and bandha, and alignment. Mats and water are provided. Some classes are taught in Spanish.

SPAS

Dimly lit and decorated in saturated shades of deep blues and magenta, **Cloud Spa** (Gallery Plaza, 103 Ave. De Diego, 5th floor, 939/204-0496, www.cloudspa.cloud, daily 10am-7pm) has an otherworldly feel that provides a soothing backdrop to an array of relaxing, restorative services, including massages ($110-165), reflexology ($55-110), and facials ($125-185). The spa's magnesphere therapy session promises to balance the nervous system using low level magnetic fields.

Eden Spa (331 Recinto Sur, Bldg. Acosta, Viejo San Juan, 787/721-6400, Mon.-Sat. 10am-7pm) offers pure luxury pampering, including caviar facials, four-hands massage, honey-butter body wrap, chakra-balancing treatments, Reiki—you name it, Eden Spa has got it. Packages run $148-198.

Zen Spa (1054 Ave. Ashford, Condado, 787/722-8433, www.zensparetreat.com) provides 85-minute massages ($95-145) and facials ($95-165). There's another location at the Sheraton Puerto Rico Hotel & Casino (200 Convention Blvd., San Juan, 787/522-8433).

Entertainment and Events

NIGHTLIFE

If club- and bar-hopping is your thing, you've come to the right place. San Juan knows how to party. Electronic music is prevalent, as is hip-hop and reggaetón, Puerto Rico's home-grown brand of hip-hop, combined with Jamaican dancehall and Caribbean musical styles. There's renewed interest among young adult locals in the Afro-Caribbean sounds of *bomba* and *plena*, and the sounds of salsa are ubiquitous. The legal drinking age is 18, and there's no official bar-closing time, so many establishments stay open until 6am. Things often don't get started until after midnight, so take a disco nap and put on your dancing shoes. It's sure to be a long, fun-filled night.

Viejo San Juan

There are two sides to Viejo San Juan's night-life. On the southern end near the cruise-ship docks are the more commercial and chain establishments like Señor Frog's. But the farther north you go toward Calle San Sebastián, the more authentic the offerings get. If you need a place to rest your feet and just chill with a cool beverage, there are a wide variety of bars, both casual and upscale, where you can actually have a conversation, at least in the early part of the evening. The later it gets, though, the more crowded and louder it becomes.

★ **La Factoria** (148 Calle San Sebastián, 787/412-4251, www.lafactoriapr.com, daily 6:30pm-4am, $6-16) is a classic drinking spot with exposed beams, black-and-white parquet floor, distressed concrete walls, and a weathered antique bar. The bartenders serve creative cocktails like the signature drink, Hijos de Borinquen, which features Don Q rum, lemon, apricot liqueur, and cinnamon with a floater of Jamaican rum on top. La Factoria serves a small menu of better-than-average bar food, including sliders and bruschetta. There's more to this spot than meets the eye: Wander through the unmarked doors past the

bar and the bathrooms and discover a labyrinth containing even more bars. **Vino** is a wine bar where DJs spin late into the night. **Shing-a-Ling** is a late-night salsa dance club, and **El Final** is the place to go for last call. The newest addition is **La Cubanita** (51 Calle San José, 787/365-9339, www.facebook.com/lacubanitavsj, daily 6pm-4am, $3-12), which also has a separate streetside entrance. It keeps up the vintage cocktail bar vibe in a more intimate space, specializing in expertly mixed, complex cocktails using fresh fruit juices.

La Vergüenza (280 Bulevar del Valle, Calle Tanca at Calle Norzagaray, 787/949-9784 or 787-595-4517, Sun.-Wed. 11am-11pm, Thurs. 11am-midnight, Fri.-Sat. 11am-2am, Sun. 11am-11pm, $5-12) is a tri-level dive bar with two rooftop decks overlooking Viejo San Juan and the Atlantic Ocean. A young crowd comes here for the cheap drinks and Puerto Rican food. A DJ spins Latin music on Friday nights, and on Sunday afternoons from 3pm-8pm, a live salsa band performs outside the bar and a crowded dance party breaks out on the dead-end street.

Primarily a lounge, **Mono Stereo** (150 Calle San Sebastián, 787/910-6111, http://mono-stereo.business.site, drinks $3-9, food $10-14) specializes in classic cocktails. But it also serves an above average food menu featuring tacos al pastor, pork belly bao, chicken pad Thai, and clay pot macaroni and cheese.

Beer aficionados flock to **La Taberna Lúpulo** (151 Calle San Sebastián, 787/721-3772, Mon.-Thurs. 6pm-2am, Sat. 1pm-2am, Sun. noon-2am, $11-30). The corner bar with dramatic archways and shelves lined with beer bottles sets the stage for sampling more than 30 craft beers on tap, as well as a pub menu of quesadillas, empanadas, and the like. There's also a full bar. No table service.

Tres Cuernos (359 Calle San Francisco, 787/724-3840 or 787/723-2733, Mon. 10am-6pm, Tues.-Sun. 10am-2am) is a large,

Dance the Night Away

Bomba and *plena* musicians perform at La Terreza de Bonanza.

When it comes to music, Puerto Rico is world renowned for salsa, a lively fusion of jazz, African polyrhythms, and Caribbean flair, performed by ensembles on drums, keyboards, and horns. Salsa originated with Puerto Ricans living in New York City, but the island quickly claimed it for its own. Among its grand masters are Tito Puente, Celia Cruz, and El Gran Combo de Puerto Rico. Contemporary stars include Marc Anthony, Ile, and Pirulo y la Tribu. Dancing to salsa or watching the experts in action on the dance floor is as fun as listening to the music.

The roots of **salsa music** can be heard in Puerto Rico's earliest known musical styles, *bomba* and *plena,* which are experiencing a renaissance among the island's youth. Originating in African culture, both musical forms are propelled by hand drummers. Fast-paced *bomba* features call-and-response vocals and is accompanied by frenzied dancers who compete to match their steps to every beat of the drum. In *plena,* the emphasis is on the lyrics of the songs, which recount stories about current events or local gossip.

- **Pisa Viejo** (page 65): This popular nightclub on trendy Calle Loíza features salsa bands throughout the week. **Free dance lessons** are offered Thursday nights before 10pm.

- **La Vergüenza** (page 63): The street outside this dive bar on the edge of Viejo San Juan turns into a lively **outdoor dance party** on Sundays from 3pm-8pm when a salsa band performs in a vacant lot across the street.

- **Shing-a-Ling** (page 63): Hidden in a labyrinth of speakeasy-style bars in Viejo San Juan, Shing-a-Ling is a late-night club that's great for **salsa dancing.**

- **La Terreza de Bonanza** (page 67): On Monday nights starting at 7pm, this open-air *chinchorro* in Santurce becomes the hottest place in town to see **live *bomba* and *plena* performances.**

bare-bones dive bar specializing in 31 flavors of $1 *chichaitos*, a traditional anise-flavored shot, and $1.50 Medalla beers. A changing menu of Puerto Rican dishes such as *arroz con pollo* and *carne guisada* is served for lunch (daily 10:30am-3pm, $6 a plate).

Looking for all the world like an old jail cell, ★ **El Batey** (101 Calle del Cristo, 787/725-1787, daily noon-4am, cash only) is a barren dive bar covered top to bottom with scrawled graffiti and illuminated by bare bulbs suspended from the ceiling. There's one pool table and an interesting jukebox with lots of jazz mixed in with classic albums by the likes of Tom Waits, Jimi Hendrix, and Sly Stone. If you order a martini, they'll laugh at you. This is a beer and shots kind of place.

Condado

From the street level, **Di Zucchero Lavazza Restaurant & Lounge** (1210 Ave. Ashford, 787/946-0835, http://dizuccheropr.com, lounge Fri.-Sat. 11pm-4am) is a hip Italian coffee bar and restaurant specializing in pasta, pizza, and panini in a dramatic red-and-black setting appointed with ornate white chandeliers. Venture upstairs and discover a massive two-level nightclub that continues the baroque theme from downstairs but sets it against an industrial-chic backdrop. Five extensively stocked bars serve up to 500 clubgoers who come to dance to techno music, check out experimental film projections on the walls, and canoodle on overstuffed couches in dark corners.

Oasis Bar Tapas & Lounge (6 Ave. Condado, 787/781-5172, www.facebook.com/oasispr, daily 24 hours, $2-8) is a divey gay bar featuring cheap drinks, go-go dancers, indoor and outdoor seating, and a small menu of bar bites like empanadas, hot dogs, and chicken wings.

Isla Verde

One of San Juan's most glamorous bars is **Mist** (2 Calle Tartak, 787/728-3666, www.waterbeachhotel.com, Sun.-Wed. 11am-11pm, Thurs. 11am-midnight, Fri.-Sat. 11am-3am),

atop the San Juan Water Beach Club Hotel. This posh rooftop bar features white leather sofas and beds arranged around tiny tables under a white awning. The minimal lighting is limited to elaborate Indonesian lanterns and candles, which complement the panoramic view of the city lights.

On the 1st floor of the San Juan Water Beach Club Hotel is **Zest** (2 Calle Tartak, 787/728-3666 or 888/265-6699, www.waterbeachhotel.com, 7am-10pm daily), a more intimate restaurant and bar. The attraction here is the interesting wall behind the bar—it's made from corrugated tin over which water pours all night long.

Another popular hotel hot spot is **Club Brava** (El San Juan Resort, 6063 Ave. Isla Verde, 787/791-2761 or 787/791-2781, www.bravapr.com, Thurs. 10pm-5am, Fri.-Sat. 11pm-5am). This popular dance club packs in the upscale, trendy set, who dance to an eclectic mix of dance-club tunes, salsa, and '80s rock. Reservations are required for table service.

Pa' Pical (63 Ave. Isla Verde, 787/448-0526, daily 11am-2am, $4-9) is a hopping little dive bar serving strong drinks and tasty empanadas, tacos, and a $5 lunch special featuring ribs, fried pork chops, and chicken breast in garlic sauce.

Loíza

For some of the hottest salsa dancing in town, go to **Piso Viejo** (1917 Calle Loíza, 787/662-0828, http://pisoviejo.com, Wed.-Sat. 6pm-2am, Sun. 6pm-midnight, $8-12). Enjoy classic cocktails and specialties, and nosh on wings, ceviche, and sliders, because you're going to need your energy to keep up on the dance floor, especially after 10pm when the action heats up. There are free salsa lessons on Thursday nights.

Tántalo (1912 Calle Loíza, 787/249-7988, www.facebook.com/TantaloLoiza, Mon.-Wed. 4pm-midnight, Thurs.-Fri. 4pm-2am, Sat. noon-2am, Sun. 10am-midnight, cocktails $3-35, food $12-22) is a large, colorful, high-energy club where mixologists concoct

a variety of creative cocktails including flaming fishbowl punches perfect for sharing. The menu features small bites. DJs spin music at night.

Barrio Social Bar (1920 Calle Loíza, 787/510-3809, Tues.-Thurs. 5pm-3am, Fri.-Sat. 5pm-5am, Sun. 6pm-2am, $1-5) attracts a young, lively crowd with cheap drink specials, DJs, and live music—mostly reggaetón and techno.

The appeal is straightforward at **El Tap Bar** (1969 Calle Loíza, 787/545-4955, www.facebook.com/eltappr, Sun. and Tues.-Thurs. 3pm-10pm, Fri.-Sat. 3pm-2am, food $8-12, beer $1-9). Sit down at the long stretch of bar and peruse the 46 labeled taps on the wall behind it. Pick your pleasure, ranging from local brews to imports and ciders, in the size of your choosing, from a six-ounce glass to a growler. The menu of hummus, tacos, sliders, tuna tartare, and ceviche is simple and good.

Loíza 2050 Whiskey Bar (2050 Calle Loíza, Santurce, 787/726-7141, Sun. and Thurs. 5pm-10pm, Fri.-Sat. 5pm-midnight) got its start 25 years ago as a pizza joint, but it has become a popular hot spot for the young, hip crowd, attracted by the large selection of craft beers and whiskeys. And you can still get a pizza to soak up the booze.

Santurce

★ **Esquina Watusi** (801 Calle Cerra, 787/388-7434, Mon.-Thurs. 3pm-1am, Fri.-Sat. 3pm-3am, Sun. 3pm-midnight, $1-8) is like no other bar in Puerto Rico. It's on an urban street corner, but it looks like a shack in the Cordillera Central that's been tricked out in bright green and yellow paint. Inside it appears to be a bodega selling sodas, cigarettes, and basic sundries, yet people come from miles around to buy beer or a cheap cocktail and sit in one of the folding chairs scattered around the sidewalks outside. On any given night you can find 40 or 50 young adult artists, musicians, and professionals gathered

around, perfecting the art of hanging out and people watching as classic car owners cruise by, drum circles break out, and who knows what else crops up or passes by. Be sure to check out all the cool street murals on the surrounding buildings.

La Terraza de Bonanza (1751 Ave. Eduardo Conde, 787/508-8877, daily 10am-1am, $2-7) is a classic urban *chinchorro*, a casual, open-air bar where locals gather. The food (tacos, nachos, quesadillas) is cheap, and so are the drinks. Don't order anything fancy: This is a beer and a shot kind of place. The best time to come is Monday nights after 7pm when dozens of *bomba* and *plena* musicians and dancers gather to perform on the streetside stage. Order at the window and try to wrangle a seat at one of a handful of picnic tables if you have to sit. But you'll probably want to dance once the music starts.

Trendy ★ **Junglebird** (254 Calle Canals, no phone, www.colectivoicaro.com/junglebaobao, Thurs.-Sat. 6pm-3am, Sun. 5pm-1am, $9-10) is a cool, dark, tropical tiki bar near La Placita with a copper-top bar and green neon lights that give the place a moody vibe. The menu is segmented into four categories: beer, wine, traditional tiki drinks, and delicately balanced tropical drinks made with fresh fruit juices and given playful names like Bastard Goes Bananas and Adios Pantalones. The ever-changing food menu is small and designed to accompany a beverage, but it's surprisingly good, like the Lenny Crabitz, a perfectly grilled cheese sandwich with five kinds of cheese, fried green tomato, and lump crab meat.

At the nexus of all that is hip in Santurce, which is experiencing an arts renaissance, is **La Respuesta** (1600 Ave. Fernandez Juncos, no phone, www.larespuestasanturce.com, hours vary by event), a graffiti-covered industrial space that hosts DJs, live bands, and art exhibitions that celebrate both emerging young artists and oldsters with an edge. Musical acts run the gamut from hip-hop and R&B to metal and Latin jazz. Wednesday night is *Noche de Cine*, featuring film screenings. By

1: ancient ceiba tree in San Juan **2:** Esquina Watusi in Santurce

The History of Puerto Rican Rum

Sugar production was integral to Puerto Rico's modern history. It was the bounty of sugarcane that first brought an influx of Europeans to the island in the 1800s. Eventually the island was dotted with sugarcane plantations, sugar refineries, rum distilleries, and shipping operations. Around the turn of the 19th century, the sugar industry declined, but that didn't stop the rum-making operations. Today, most of the world's supply of rum is produced in Puerto Rico. **Bacardí** is the top-selling brand, but it's not the only game in town. Serralles Distillery in Ponce produces the well-regarded brand **Don Q.** Most locals recommend **Ron del Barrilito,** made in Bayamón, as the island's most prized brand. In recent years, several small-batch craft rums have come to market, including **Rum Caray,** made in Juncos, and **Trigo,** which is from Bayamón.

Here are some ways to explore the flavors and history of the island's favorite elixir:

- **Casa Bacardí Visitor Center** (page 57) is a popular tourist attraction devoted to the history of the top-selling rum in the United States, which is still owned and operated by descendants of founder Don Facundo Bacardí Masó. No rum is made on-site, but you can see displays of historic objects used to make rum in its early days and advertisements through the years. Special rum tasting and mixology tours are available for an additional fee.

- **Castillo Serrallés** (page 154) is proof of how lucrative rum production was for its makers. Built atop a mountain overlooking Ponce in 1934 for Eugenio Serrallés, founder of Serrallés Rum Distillery, this stunning four-story Spanish Moroccan-style mansion contains many of the Serrallés family's original furnishings. One room in the house has been converted into an exhibition space that explains and illustrates how sugarcane is processed and turned into rum.

- **Casa Melaza** (page 73) is a petite shop in Viejo San Juan that bills itself as a "rum boutique." Owner Antonio Lizardi is a wealth of information about local rums. In addition to all the major brands, he carries an excellent selection of small-batch and aged rums ideal for sipping.

- The **piña colada,** a frozen concoction of rum, coconut cream, and pineapple juice, originated in San Juan. There's no disputing that. But, the question remains: Who invented it? Ramon "Monchito" Marrero, a bartender at **Caribe Hilton** (page 95), claimed to have made the first one in 1954 after three months of experimentation. Rumor has it that Joan Crawford said the drink was "better than slapping Bette Davis in the face." But Spanish-born bartender Ramon Portas Mingot also claims to have made the first one at the restaurant **Barrachina** (page 77) in 1963. The difference between the two versions is Caribe Hilton makes it with ice and Barrachina makes it with water and freezes it before blending it. You can try one at both establishments and decide for yourself which one is best.

- **Chichaito** is a clear, thimble-sized drink often served after a traditional Puerto Rican meal, as well as in most bars. (Its name is slang for "little fornicator.") It is made from equal parts rum and anise-flavored liqueur and is downed in a single gulp that packs a powerful punch. **La Casita Blanca** (page 89) in Santurce sends out a complimentary round after dinner, and the bar **Tres Cuernos** (page 63) in Viejo San Juan serves 31 flavored versions.

- **Taste of Rum** (www.tasteofrums.com) is an annual festival held in March that offers the opportunity to sample an array of Puerto Rican rums. Held at Paseo La Princesa in Viejo San Juan, the one-day event also features educational seminars, competitions, live music, dancing, and food vendors.

day this place looks like an abandoned warehouse, but it smokes at night.

The late-night party crowd goes to **Taberna los Vázquez** (1348 Calle Orbeta, 939/269-1531, http://taberna-los-vazquez. business.site, Wed. 5pm-11pm, Thurs.-Fri.

5pm-2am, Sat. 2pm-2am, Sun. 2pm-midnight, beer $1-3, food $4-10) for karaoke, salsa dancing, and the all-day happy hour. The bar serves a light menu of octopus salad, *tostones*, and *pinchos*.

Santurce has several popular gay bars.

They typically don't get started until 10pm at the earliest, and the later it gets, the livelier they become. Shoot pool, play video games, sing karaoke, check out the drag show, and hit the dance floor at **Circo Café** (650 Calle Condado, 787/725-9676, Mon.-Wed. 9pm-5am, Thurs.-Sun. 9pm-6am, no cover, drinks $3-8). Formerly Junior's Bar, **Toxic Night Club** (613 Calle Condado, 787/478-8602, www.facebook.com/toxicnightclub, Fri. 11pm-6am, Sat. 11pm-10am, $5 cover) is a small dance club with DJs, go-go dancers, and drag shows. For a more chill scene, stop by **Tia Maria's Liquor Store** (326 Ave. de Diego, 787/724-4011, Mon.-Tues. 2pm-1am, Wed.-Thurs. 2pm-2am, Fri.-Sun. 3pm-3am, cash only), a small, low-key bar with two pool tables and a reputation for stiff drinks.

PARTY DISTRICTS

There's no doubt about it: Puerto Ricans love a good party, and it seems as if there's always one going on somewhere. San Juan has a couple of unofficial party districts where the concentration of bars and restaurants creates a street-party atmosphere that attracts young locals and tourists alike to bar-hop and people-watch. Although generally safe and contained, these areas can experience a certain level of rowdiness and petty crime, particularly the later it gets and the more alcohol is consumed. Visitors are encouraged to have a good time, but they should take care to keep their wits about them.

★ La Placita

Santurce's historic marketplace, **La Placita** (Calle Roberts), more formally known as **Plaza del Mercado,** is at the heart of a street party that spills into the surrounding narrow roads lined with bars, restaurants, and lounges. La Placita attracts a mostly local crowd of all ages, including blue collar workers, young professionals, and foodies. Instead of partying down with tourists, beachcombers, and the cruise-ship crowd, you can share a drink with folks who are blowing off steam after a hard day's work.

A high concentration of small bars and restaurants serve cheap drinks and local cuisine, and a bandstand hosts live music. The streets get especially crowded Thursday, Friday, and Saturday nights.

Calle San Sebastián

In Viejo San Juan, party central is along Calle

La Placita

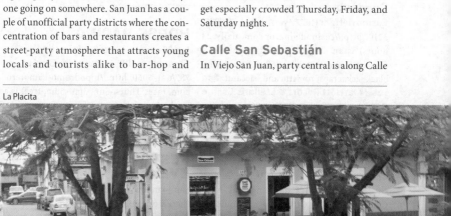

San Sebastián. Restaurants, bars, clubs, and pool halls of every stripe line the street, making it a great place to bar-hop door-to-door. Standard stops include **Nono's** and **Balcones de Nono's** (109 Calle San Sebastián, 787/725-7819, daily noon-3am), **La Taberna Lúpulo** (151 Calle San Sebastián, 787/721-3772, Mon.-Thurs. 6pm-2am, Sat. 1pm-2am, Sun. noon-2am), and **La Factoria** (148 Calle San Sebastián, no phone, daily 6:30pm-4am). Look for the multiple hidden bars inside La Factoria.

CASINOS

All of the island's casinos are located in hotels, and many of them are operational 24 hours a day. Dressy attire is recommended, but coat and tie are not required. All the casinos have banks of slot machines, blackjack tables, and roulette wheels. Most have craps tables, Caribbean stud poker, and three-card poker. Some have mini-baccarat, let it ride, progressive blackjack, and Texas hold 'em.

Condado

Casino del Mar (1077 Ave. Ashford, 787/977-3210, http://casinodelmarpr.com, daily 24 hours) is an elegant gaming room at La Concha Resort featuring 360 slot machines, black jack, craps, roulette and baccarat. **San Juan Marriott Resort & Stellaris Casino** (1309 Ave. Ashford, 787/722-7000, www.marriott.com, daily 24 hours) has 462 gaming machines and 26 table games.

Isla Verde

There are two casinos in Isla Verde: **Casino del Sol** (7012 Boca de Cangrejos Ave., Carolina, 787/791-0404, daily 24 hours) at the Courtyard by Marriott Isla Verde Beach Resort, and the casino at **Embassy Suites by Hilton Hotel** (8000 Calle Tartak, 787/791-0505, daily 10am-4am).

Miramar

Casino Metro (Sheraton Puerto Rico Hotel & Casino, 200 Convention Blvd., 787/993-3500, www.casinometro.com, daily 24 hours) features more than 400 slot machines and 16 table games, including blackjack, roulette, baccarat, pai gow poker, and three-card poker. The Mezzanine Stage features live entertainment most nights of the week, and players receive complimentary snacks and beverages. Take a break from the action in the Metro Lounge, where you can enjoy a specialty cocktail and watch the game on one of 12 high-definition TVs.

MOVIE THEATERS

Puerto Rico gets all the major Hollywood releases, as well as a steady offering of Spanish-language films that don't make it to the States. Offering a modern megaplex experience is **Caribbean Cinemas Fine Arts Miramar** (654 Ave. Ponce de León, 787/721-4288, www.caribbeancinemas.com), showing a variety of English and Spanish films, most of which are subtitled. Additional locations are at **Plaza Las Americas** (525 Ave. Roosevelt, 787/767-4775) and **Popular Center** (Torre Norte, 208 Ave. Juan Ponce de León, Hato Rey, 787/765-2339).

HORSE RACING

Just 20 minutes east of San Juan, **Hipódromo Camarero** (PR 3, km 15.3, Canóvanas, 787/641-6060, http://hipodromo-camarero.com, races Thurs.-Sun. 3pm-6pm, free) is a modern upscale racetrack with a restaurant, sports bar, and clubhouse with a panoramic view of the track.

FESTIVALS AND EVENTS

San Juan loves a festival. It seems as though there's one going on every weekend. Some have traditional origins, and others are products of the local tourism department, but they all promise insight into the island's culture and are loads of fun.

Held in June, **Noche de San Juan Bautista** is the celebration of the island's patron saint. Festivities last several days and include religious processions, concerts, and dance performances. But the highlight of the event is on June 24, when celebrants from all over the island flock to the beach for the day for picnics and recreation. Then at midnight, everyone walks backward into the ocean three times to ward off evil spirits.

Street festivals don't get any livelier than **Festival de la Calle de San Sebastián** (787/724-0910), held in January on Calle San Sebastián in Viejo San Juan. For five days the street is filled with parades, folkloric dances, music, food, and crafts. As many as 100,000 people flood the streets of Viejo San Juan, and the later it gets, the younger the crowd becomes.

In 2008 the Puerto Rico Hotel & Tourism Association launched the annual **Saborea Puerto Rico** (http://saboreapuertorico.com), a four-day culinary festival held in April, featuring dinners, cooking demonstrations, tastings, entertainment, and more with local and visiting celebrity chefs. **Taste of Rum** (www.tasteofrums.com) is an annual festival held in March at Bahia Urbana, Pier 6, in Viejo San Juan. The one-day event features tastings of Puerto Rican rums, educational seminars, competitions, live music, dancing, and food vendors.

Founded in honor of the renowned cellist and composer Pablo Casals, the **Casals Festival** (787/918-1106, www.facebook.com/festivalpablocasals) is held in early spring and features a slate of classical music concerts with world-renowned guest artists.

Santurce es Ley (www.facebook.com/santurceesley) is an annual independent artists street festival on Calle Cerra during the summer. Area galleries and design studios throughout Santurce stay open until late, hosting art exhibitions and musical performances featuring the work of more than 100 emerging local artists. The event also features the creation of elaborate murals on sides of buildings.

The Puerto Rico Tourism Company presents an annual three-day arts festival in May called **Feria de Artesanías** (787/723-0692, www.gotopuertorico.com). More than 200 artisans fill the walkways along Paseo La Princesa and Plaza de la Dársena, and the days are filled with music and dance performances as well as a folksinger competition.

Less an actual festival and more a cultural series, **La Casita Festival** takes place every Saturday 5:30pm-7:30pm year-round in Plaza de la Dársena by Pier 1 in Viejo San Juan. Musicians and dance groups perform, and artisans sell their wares.

Shopping

In the current era of globalization, shopping is fast becoming similarly homogenized the world over, and Puerto Rico is no different. The island is rife with shopping malls and chain stores selling the same brands you could buy at Anywhere, USA.

But there is also a strong culture of design and artisanship in Puerto Rico, and many stores sell locally designed jewelry and clothing, contemporary artwork, and traditional crafts. Viejo San Juan, with its high-end jewelry stores, clothing boutiques, and gift shops, is the place to go for the most eclectic selection of stores and merchandise.

VIEJO SAN JUAN

Visitors love to shop in Viejo San Juan because it offers the widest variety of unique shopping options in one pedestrian-friendly place. This is the place to go for fine jewelry, imported clothing and furnishings, cigars, folk art, and tourist trinkets.

Antiques and Collectibles

Thrift-store shoppers and collectors of vinyl will love **Frankie's Vintage Store** (363 Calle San Francisco, 787/722-6691, www.facebook.com/FrankieVintage, daily 10am-6pm). Come here to peruse the enormous used-record collection, from 1980s kitsch to fresh electronica. There's even a turntable available, so you can listen to the stock before you buy. This cluttered labyrinth of rooms is packed with the widest assortment of junk and collectibles you could ever imagine: decorative items, old photographs, dishes, toys, clothes—you name it.

Books

Libreria Laberinto (251 Calle de la Cruz, 787/724-8200, daily 9am-7pm) is a well-stocked bookstore selling titles related to history, politics, literature, children's literature, cookbooks, and more. Most books are in Spanish, but there are some English-language books available.

Arts and Crafts

For visitors seeking high-quality crafts by local artisans, **Puerto Rican Arts and Crafts** (204 Calle Fortaleza, 787/725-5596, puertoricanart-crafts.com, daily 9:30am-6pm) is your one-stop shopping spot. This large two-level store has everything from original paintings and prints to ceramics, sculpture, jewelry, and more.

For a small selection of exquisitely made, authentic Caribbean crafts, stop by **Tienda**

de Artesanías in the Museo de las Americas (Ballajá Barracks, Calle Norzagaray beside Quincentennial Plaza, 787/722-6057, www.museolasamericas.org, Tues.-Fri. 9am-noon and 1pm-4pm, Sat.-Sun. noon-5pm). It has a nice but small selection of quality baskets, shawls, pottery, jewelry, santos, art posters, and CDs.

Máscaras de Puerto Rico (La Calle, 105 Calle Fortaleza, 787/725-1306, http://home.coqui.net/chilean, Mon.-Sat. 10am-6:30pm, Sun. 10:30am-5:30pm) is a funky, narrow shop in a covered alleyway selling quality contemporary crafts, including masks and small reproductions of vintage *cartel* posters. In the back is Café El Punto restaurant, serving traditional Puerto Rican cuisine.

Haitian Gallery (367 Calle Fortaleza, 787/721-4362, www.facebook.com/haitian.gallery.puertorico, daily 10am-9pm) sells a large selection of Haitian folk art, including brightly colored primitive-style paintings and tons of woodwork, from sublime bowls to ornately sculpted furniture. There's a small selection of Indonesian imports, too.

Spicy Caribbee (154 Calle del Cristo, 888/725-7529, www.spicycaribbee.com, Mon.-Sat. 10am-6pm, Sun. 11am-5pm) sells

Viejo San Juan

Caribbean sauces, spice mixes, coffees, soaps, fragrances, candles, cookbooks, and more.

Mundo Taíno (256 Calle San Justo, 787/721-1722, daily 10am-6pm) is your source for traditional crafts by local artisans. Look for *vejigante* masks, wood carved santos, paintings, jewelry made from seeds and beads, reproductions of Taíno artifacts, coffee, honey, candy, and T-shirts.

La Calle (105 Calle Fortaleza, daily 10am-8pm) is a narrow passageway lined with mini shops selling local crafts, fine art, and clothing. In the back is Café El Punto, serving local Puerto Rican cuisine.

The Poets Passage (203 Calle Cruz, 787/567-9275, www.poetspassage.com, daily 10am-6pm) is owned by local poet and artist Lady Lee Andrews, who sells her whimsical fine art prints and painted tiles, many featuring inspirational sayings. There's small stage in the back for poetry events and a café selling coffee and light fare such as pastries and sandwiches.

Cigars and Rum

Like Cuba, Puerto Rico has a long history of hand-rolled cigar-making, and you can often find street vendors rolling and selling their own in Plaza de Hostos's Mercado de Artesanías, a plaza near the cruise-ship piers at Calle Recinto Sur. There are also several good cigar shops selling anything you could want—except Cubans, of course. The biggest selection is at newly renovated **The Cigar House** (257 Calle Fortaleza, 787/725-0652, www.facebook.com/thecigarhouse, daily 10am-10pm) with an inviting smoking lounge. Trinidad, Monte Cristo, Padron 1926 and 1964, Cohiba, Perdomo, Macanudo, Partagas, Romeo and Julieta, and Puerto Rican cigars aged in rum are among those sold.

For a more intimate setting, visit **El Galpón** (154 Calle del Cristo, 787/725-3945 or 888/842-5766, www.elgalpon.net, daily 10am-6pm). This small, selective shop sells a variety of quality cigars, Panama hats, masks, art prints, and superb vintage and contemporary santos.

Billing itself as a "rum boutique," **Casa Melaza** (74 Caleta de San Juan, 787/462-4782, www.casamelaza.com, daily 11am-7pm) is a small store, but it sells a big selection of Puerto Rican rums, including locally made craft varieties Rum Caray made in Juncos and Trigo from Bayamón, and limited reserve varieties from major distilleries Don Q and Bacardi. You'll also find locally produced sangrias and coffees. Owner Antonio Lizardi is a fountain of information about local rums.

Clothing and Accessories

Coco Cabana (105 Calle Fortaleza, 787/723-5888, Sun.-Thurs. 10am-9pm, Fri.-Sat. 10am-10pm) is the source for men and women's cruise wear, including graphic T-shirts, Hawaiian shirts, Panama hats, sundresses, and straw bags.

Veari (250 Calle Tanca, 787/724-4624, www.veari.com, Tues.-Thurs. and Sat.-Sun. 10am-6pm) is an upscale leather boutique selling shoes, boots, belts, handbags, and more. It specializes in crocodile skins and Western-style boots.

Costazul (264 Calle San Francisco, 787/722-0991 or 787/724-8085, Mon.-Sat. 9am-7pm, Sun. 11am-5pm) sells a great selection of surf and skate wear for men and women, as well as tropical clothing including T-shirts, shorts, rompers, sundresses, flip-flops, and bathing suits. Brands include Havianas, Reef, Columbia, Salt Life, Lush, and Hommage.

Lucia Boutique (254 San Justo, 787/725-1699, Mon.-Sat. 10am-7pm, Sun. 11am-7pm) sells beaded jewelry, hats, purses, and floaty, linen dresses favored by mature women.

Valija (209 Calle San Francisco, 787/626-0281, www.valijagitana.com, Mon.-Sat. 9am-7pm, Sun. 11am-7pm) sells contemporary women's clothing for the young and slim. Cotton rompers, long, flowy skirts, crop tops, purses, and jewelry, mostly imports from Indonesia, sell for $50 or less. There are additional stores at Plaza Rio Hondo in Bayamón and Plaza Las Americas.

Collective Request (159 Calle de la

Luna, 787/977-7707, http://collectiverequest. com, daily 10 am-7pm) is an elegant, high-end women's boutique selling clothing lines by Endless Rose, After Market, and The Fifth; sunglasses by Le Specs of France; and jewelry and accessories by local designers.

Two stores in one, **Pure Soul** (258 Calle San Justo, 787/724-0424, www. puresoulboutique.com, Mon.-Sat. 10am-6pm, Sun. 11am-6pm) has two entrances. Inside one entrance is a gift shop featuring home decor items like candles, serving dishes and utensils, coasters, and small objets d'art. Inside the other is a women's clothing store selling long, flowy linen and cotton dresses and tunics, jewelry, handbags, and leather shoes from Turkey.

Concalma (207 Calle San Francisco, 787/342-9757, www.shopconcalma.com or www.concalmalinea.com, Mon.-Sat. 9:30am-7pm, Sun. 10am-6pm) is a chic shop specializing in locally made tote bags, purses, and pouches. The variety of fabrics and patterns range from playful to sophisticated.

Almacenes Fernandez (262 Calle San Francisco, 787/724-8085 or 787/722-0991, www.facebook.com/almacenesfernandezoldsanjuan, daily 9am-6pm) has been selling men's fine clothing since 1917. The store specializes in exquisite linen shirts, guayaberas, Panama hats, and Sperry Topsider shoes. Look for brands by Cubavera and Spazio.

Since 1977, **Olé** (105 Fortaleza, 787/724-2445, www.olepuertorico.com, Mon.-Thurs. 10am-6:30pm, Fri.-Sat. 10:30am-6:30pm, Sun. 10am-6pm) has been selling quality Panama hats made in Ecuador. For $80, shoppers can select a style, have it fitted, and pick a band to finish it off. The store also stocks new and vintage carved wood santos from Puerto Rico, Ecuador, and Chile.

Imports

San Juan has several Indonesian import shops. **Eclectika** (204 Calle O'Donnell, Plaza de Colón, and 205 Calle de la Cruz, 787/721-7236 or 787/725-3163, daily 10am-7pm) has a huge array of budget-priced Indonesian imports specializing in home decor, purses, and jewelry.

Jewelry

Local jewelry designer Laura Lugo sells contemporary, architectural pieces at her boutique **Luca** (58 Calle Taft, 787/525-8291, http://shop-luca.com, Mon.-Sat. 10am-6pm, Sun. 11am-3pm), along with a small selection of sophisticated women's clothing and jewelry from designers in Australia, Japan, Italy, and Puerto Rico.

Origin (251 Calle de San Jose, 787/721-2081, daily 10am-6pm) features high-end handcrafted jewelry, both locally made and imported, as well as fine art and antiques.

Viejo San Juan is home to a dozen or so fine jewelry stores selling high-end watches and jewelry made from precious stones and metals. Many of them can be found along **Calle Fortaleza,** including **Blue Diamond** (250 Calle Fortaleza, 787/977-5555, www.facebook.com/bluediamond.luxury, daily 10am-6pm), which carries designs by Kabana, Gucci, Le Vian, and Movado.

Craft Markets

Artisans markets, selling locally crafted jewelry, leather goods, gourd art, musical instruments, paintings, and cigars, are often held at two plazas in Viejo San Juan—**Plaza Dársenas** (Calle Comercio by La Casita) and **Plaza Eugenio María de Hostos** (between Calle San Justo and Calle Tizol). Don't be surprised if there's also live entertainment and a food truck or two.

PUERTA DE TIERRA

Paseo Caribe (15 Ave. Luis Muñoz Rivera, 787/724-2400, www.paseocaribepr.com/el-mercado, Sat.-Thurs. noon-6pm, Fri. noon-9pm) is a modern residential/retail/dining complex near Caribe Hilton. Shops include It Girl and Dua Style, selling women's clothing and accessories; Media Luna, offering accessories and trendy jewelry; Sumaq fine jewelry store; and DiMare swimwear boutique. When hunger strikes, El Mercado is a food hall featuring dozens of food vendors serving everything from Thai food to fresh seafood.

CONDADO

Once a mecca for high-end shoppers seeking designer labels and European haute couture, Condado has lost some of its luster as a shopping district. But there are still a few quality shops selling clothing, jewelry, and imports. Don't be surprised if you try to enter a storefront along Condado and find the door locked during regular business hours. Just ring the doorbell and the proprietor will buzz you in.

Clothing and Accessories

If you don't mind dropping $400 for a tank top, **Olivia Boutique** (1400 Ave. Magdalena, 787/722-6317, http://shop-olivia.com, Mon.-Sat. 10am-6pm) sells high-end designer leisurewear and beachwear for women. Labels include Ulla Johnson and Veronica Beard. Don't miss the shoes—they're works of art from Italy and Spain.

Monsieur (1126 Ave. Ashford, 787/722-0918, www.monsieurpuertorico.com, Mon.-Sat. 10am-6:30pm, Sun. 11am-5pm) sells casual designer menswear for the young and clubby. Labels include Thomas Dean, Stone Rose, Ballin, Alberto, and Robert Graham.

Charmé (1374 Ave. Ashford, 787/723-9065, www.facebook.com/charmecondado, Mon.-Sat. 10am-6pm) is packed to the rafters with flowing resort wear for mature women, including the Flax Designs linen clothing line.

Jewelry

Cartier (1054 Ave. Ashford, 787/722-5879, http://stores.cartier.com, Mon.-Sat. 10am-6pm) is the place to go for high-end jewelry, watches, sunglasses, and more.

Imports

Mozaik World Village Bazaar (1300 Ave. Ashford, Condado, 787/995-7088, www.facebook.com/mozaikbazaarpr, Mon. 9am-4pm, Tues.-Sat. 10am-9pm, Sun. 10am-8pm) bills itself as a world village bazaar, although its goods are primarily from Turkey and Puerto Rico. But that's okay because it offers a well-curated selection of exceptionally well-made and unique fair-trade products including shoes, purses, clothing, lamps, jewelry, toys, candles, incense, wall art, and food items.

OCEAN PARK

Tres Palmas Surf Shop (1911 Calle McLeary, Ocean Park, 787/728-3377, www.trespalmaspr.com, Mon.-Sat. 10am-7pm, Sun. 10am-6pm) is the source for all your surfing needs, including surfboards, board shorts, flip-flops, sunglasses, T-shirts, bathing suits, and more. Daily rental rates are $30 for surfboards, $35 for fun boards, $40 for long boards, and $25 for body boards.

LOÍZA
Clothing and Accessories

Len T. Juela (1852 Calle Loíza, http://shop-lentejuela.com, Mon.-Sat. 11am-7pm) stocks a youthful, tropical-style collection of curated vintage clothing and vintage-inspired new clothing, as well as jewelry and accessories including purses and sunglasses.

Electroshock (1811 Calle Loíza, 787/727-5428, Mon.-Thurs. 11am-5pm, Fri.-Sat. 11am-6pm, Sun. noon-5pm) is a funky, budget-friendly thrift shop specializing in well-curated vintage and secondhand clothing, plus new graphic T-shirts by local artists.

Sixne Concept Store (1752 Calle Loíza, no phone, www.facebook.com/SixneConceptStore, Tues.-Sat. 11am-7pm) sells casual men's clothing by local designers for the young and hip. There's also a barber chair if you need a trim.

Moni & Coli (1762 Calle Loíza, 787/727-6839, http://moniandcoli.com, Mon.-Sat. 11am-7pm) sells retro-style sundresses and other light and breezy tropical wear for women. There's also a well-curated selection of jewelry and handbags by local designers, and a selection of cat-eye sunglasses.

Nude (1750 Calle Loíza, 787/728-7074, www.shopnude.com, Mon.-Sat. 10am-6pm) sells sophisticated, contemporary tropical sundresses, rompers, shorts, tops, bathing suits, and accessories, including shoes, handbags, and jewelry.

SANTURCE

Librería Libros AC Barra & Bistro (1510 Ave. Ponce de Leon, 787/998-5132, www.facebook.com/librosac, Sun.-Mon. 10am-6pm, Tues.-Sat. 10am-9pm) is a bookstore, as well as a restaurant and bar with musical performances, poetry readings, and more.

GREATER SAN JUAN

For all your American chain store needs, **Plaza Las Americas** (525 Ave. Franklin Delano Roosevelt, 787/767-5202, www.plazalasamericas.com, Mon.-Sat. 9am-9pm, Sun. 11am-7pm) is a two-level mall with more than 300 stores, including Macy's, JCPenney, Victoria's Secret, Ann Taylor, Foot Locker, Gap Kids, and Sears. There are also several local stores, including Hecho a Mano.

Opened in 2015, **The Mall of San Juan** (1000 The Mall of San Juan Blvd., 787/759-6310, www.themallofsanjuan.com, Mon.-Sat. 10am-9pm, Sun. 11am-7pm) is a 650,000-square-foot, multilevel shopping mecca. Stores include Nordstrom, H&M, Diesel, Free People, Salvatore Ferragamo, Gap, Louis Vuitton, Kate Spade, Ann Taylor, Gucci, and more. Dining options include Krispy Kreme Doughnuts, Starbene Coffee, and Burger & Beer Joint.

Food

San Juan's dining scene is as sophisticated and unexpected as the city itself. There are plenty of old-school purveyors of traditional Puerto Rican cuisine—called *cocina criolla*—built upon the staples of rice, beans, plantains, pork, and chicken. But more restaurants are bringing a fresh, farm-to-table approach to the cuisine and creating new interpretations of familiar dishes. The city is rife with high-profile celebrity chefs. Many restaurants are reflecting an infusion of global flavors. Through it all, there is still a strong street food presence that's nearly as old as the island itself.

VIEJO SAN JUAN
Puerto Rican

★ **Punto de Vista** (Hotel Milano, 307 Calle Fortaleza, 787/307-2970, www.facebook.com/pdvosj, Sun.-Mon. noon-9:30pm, Tues.-Wed. 11:30am-9:30pm, Thurs.-Fri. 11:30am-10pm, Sat. noon-10pm, $11-18) is the place to go for a casual meal of exceptional traditional Puerto Rican cuisine, especially the moist, flavorful mofongo stuffed with your choice of pulled pork, churrasco, or shrimp and topped with either a creamy garlic sauce or a criolla sauce made with fresh tomatoes and mangos. The views of other rooftops are not that stellar, but it's lovely at night when the city is lit up. Reservations are not accepted, and you can expect a wait unless you're willing to sit at the bar, which isn't a bad option. Otherwise, a greeter at the entrance will put your name on the wait list, and you can wander around the city until they call your cell phone when your table is almost ready. The restaurant is not wheelchair-accessible.

The hokey theme setting of **Restaurante Raíces** (315 Calle Recinto Sur, 787/289-2121, www.restauranteraices.com, Mon.-Sat. 11am-11pm, Sun. 11am-10pm, $14-30) threatens to undermine just how good the traditionally prepared *comida criolla* is here. Based on a Disneyfied interpretation of the *jíbaro* (hillbilly) lifestyle, the sprawling restaurant comprises multiple rooms tricked out like palm-thatched huts from the mountain region. Female servers wear long white dresses and turbans; male servers wear guayabera shirts and Panama hats. Drinks are served in tin cups. If you can look past the artifice, you can expect to dine on generous servings of expertly prepared rice and beans, mofongo, churrasco, *escabeche, alcapurrias,* and *chuleta can can,* an enormous fried pork chop with ribs. The original location is in Caguas (Urb. Villa Turabo, 787/258-1570).

Cinema Bar 1950 (Cuartel de Ballajá, Calle Norzagaray at Calle Morovis, 1st Fl., 787/708-6113, www.cinemabar1950.com, Tues. noon-8pm, Wed.-Thurs. and Sun. noon-9pm, Fri.-Sat. noon-11pm, $10-24) serves standard Puerto Rican fare and an array of fruit-flavored mojitos in a restaurant decked-out like a turn-of-the-century parlor. Occasional plays and independent movies are presented in the theater next door. One of the best reasons to go here is to enjoy a cocktail on the patio overlooking the grounds of El Morro.

For a more authentic experience, **La Fonda El Jibarito** (280 Calle Sol, 787/725-8375, daily 11am-9pm, $6-18) is one of the best bets for authentic Puerto Rican cuisine, including codfish stew, fried pork, fried snapper, great rice and beans, and mofongo (cooked and mashed plantain seasoned with garlic), sometimes stuffed with meat or seafood. Patrons share tables in this casual restaurant designed to look like a traditional country house. Between the blaring TV and tightly packed crowds, the noise level can be overwhelming. Thank goodness there's a full bar. Expect a wait during prime dining time.

Café Puerto Rico (208 Calle O'Donnell, 787/724-2281, www.cafepuertorico.com, Mon.-Sat. 11:30am-3:30pm and 5:30pm-11pm, Sun. noon-9pm, $9-24) has rich, dark wood paneling and a tile bar with tastefully lit contemporary artwork hanging on the walls. The coffee is outstanding, and the Puerto Rican cuisine is good solid fare. You can get everything from *asopao* and mofongo to paella and steak.

Barrachina (104 Calle Fortaleza, 787/721-5852 or 787/725-7912, www.barrachina.com, Sun.-Tues. and Thurs. 10am-10pm, Wed. 10am-5pm, Fri.-Sat. 10am-11pm, $14-49) is one of two places in Puerto Rico (the Caribe Hilton being the other) that claims to have

invented the piña colada, which is served here from a slushy-style machine, but is surprisingly tasty.

Tucked in the back of a gift shop, **Café El Punto** (105 Calle Fortaleza, 787/646-4943, www.cafeelpunto.com, Tues.-Sun. 10am-8pm, $8-15), serves authentic *criolla* cuisine accompanied by fresh salads and tropical fruit shakes. *Tostones* (fried plantains) stuffed with shrimp or chicken are popular, as is the avocado stuffed with shrimp salad. And if you've had your fill of fried foods, try the baked empanadas. The flan comes highly recommended, too.

It's hard to tell that **Los Yeyos House of Mofongo** (353-2 Calle San Francisco, 787/725-9362, daily 10am-6pm, $8) is a restaurant. It looks more like a dim, blue hallway covered with graffiti. There is a small sign outside, a couple of small tables inside, and seemingly just one employee, a friendly but slightly harried woman who takes the orders and serves up delicious mofongo, crab stew, and *carne guisado* on sectioned, school cafeteria-style plates, with plastic utensils and sodas in a can.

Casual, open-air restaurant **Princesa Gastrobar** (Paseo La Princesa, 787/723-7878, www.princesapr.com, Tues.-Thurs. 11am-10pm, Fri. 11am-midnight, Sat. 10am-midnight, Sun. 10am-10pm, $13-32) is a romantic spot, especially at night when all the twinkle lights are illuminated. Although it's located right on a busy pedestrian stretch of Paseo La Princesa, the restaurant is surrounded by tall, potted plants that help make the restaurant feel like a private oasis. The menu is extensive. Among the entrées are crab risotto, fettucine in blue cheese sauce, breadfruit mofongo stuffed with lobster, and grilled lamb chops.

Seafood

El Asador Grill (350 Calle San Francisco, 787/289-9966, www.elasadorpr.com, daily 8am-1am, $16-28), located in a contemporary hacienda-style setting, specializes in grilled fish, ceviche, mofongo, linguine, and risottos.

At night, it turns into a club atmosphere with techno music and dancing. The breakfast menu ($3-10) includes omelets, pancakes, and *mangu*, a traditional Dominican dish of cooked, pureed green plantains topped with onions. Cream-colored stucco walls, dark wood beams, terra-cotta tile floors, and dramatic archways create an inviting environment, especially at night.

Located near Plaza del Quinto Centenario, **Ostra Cosa @ Totem** (corner of Calle del Cristo and Calle San Sebastián, 787/722-2672 or 787/724-5475, daily 11am-11pm, $12-26) is an alfresco restaurant with a club vibe, thanks to the loud techno music, serving a menu featuring lobster risotto, ceviche, and coconut mojitos.

International

For traditional French cuisine in a classic elegant setting featuring an enormous crystal chandelier and walls surrounded by long white flowing drapes, there's **311 Trois Cent Onze** (311 Calle Fortaleza, 787/725-7959, www.311restaurantpr.com, Wed.-Fri. noon-3pm, Tues.-Thurs. 6pm-10:30pm, Fri.-Sat. 6pm-11:30pm, $24-35). This is the place to go for snails and foie gras. Check out their highly lauded wine-pairing dinners.

Bodega Chic (313 Calle Fortaleza, 787/721-6083, http://bodegachicpr.com, Wed.-Sat. 5pm-midnight or later, Sun. 11:30am-midnight or later, $18-28) serves sophisticated, carefully crafted traditional French cuisine in a stylishly casual setting. Appetizers include salmon tartare and bleu cheese soufflé. Mussels, braised lamb shank, and sole are featured entrées. They're known for their roasted chicken breast in banana curry. A prix fixe brunch menu ($19) is served starting at 11:30am on Sunday.

At **Istanbul Turkish Restaurant** (325 Calle Recinto Sur, 787/722-5057, www.istanbulturkishrestaurant.com, Sun.-Thurs. 11am-9:30pm, Fri.-Sat. 11am-10:30pm, $13-18), dine on heaping platters of dolma (stuffed grape leaves), kebabs, lamb chops, and baklava. In addition to a full bar, beverage offerings include traditional Turkish coffee.

Eclectic

Carli's Fine Bistro & Piano (Banco Popular building, corner of Recinto Sur and Calle San Justo, 787/725-4927, www.carlisworld.com, Mon.-Sat. 3:30pm-11:30pm, music starts at 8:30pm, $16-34) is a romantic, sophisticated lounge and restaurant serving a variety of dishes, including risottos, raviolis, quesadillas, and Caribbean-inspired tapas. The owner, jazz pianist Carli Muñoz, performs nightly with a changing array of guest musicians. It's also a great place to just sit at the bar and enjoy one of a large selection of specialty cocktails. There's alfresco dining on the sidewalk, too.

★ **Marmalade** (317 Calle Fortaleza, 787/724-3969, www.marmaladepr.com, Mon.-Sat. 5pm-10pm, tasting menus $75-95, wine pairings extra) beckons likes a fanciful oasis with its romantic bar, dramatically lit and draped with swaths of organza. In the back is an elegant, sophisticated restaurant. But that's all just packaging. It's the impressive wine list; the creative cocktails made from fresh juices, herbs, and flowers; and the changing seasonal menu of small plates and entrées with touches of molecular gastronomy that attract return visits. Offerings include braised lamb tagine and wild sea bass with pineapple-ginger relish. Order à la carte or enjoy a tasting menu of four, five, or six courses, with or without wine pairings.

Dark red tiles, upholstered banquettes, and a large, arched window overlooking Plaza Colon give **Café Berlin** (407 Calle San Francisco, 787/722-5205, www.cafeberlinpr.com, daily 9am-10pm, $16-25) a moody, romantic atmosphere. The diverse menu features Puerto Rican, European, vegetarian, and gluten-free dishes. It's a great stop for a hearty breakfast of banana raisin walnut pancakes or spinach quiche. Lunch features a variety of soups, salads, and sandwiches. Dinner ranges from pasta to mofongo, but the house specialty is dorado (mahi-mahi) in coconut sauce. There's a full bar, a small wine list, a children's menu, and outdoor dining.

Verde Mesa (107 Calle Tetuan, 787/390-4662, www.facebook.com/verdemesa, Tues.-Sat. noon-3pm and 6pm-10pm, Sun. noon-3pm, $13-18) features an eclectic, shabby-chic interior and specializes in botanical cocktails and a plant-forward menu of locally sourced dishes including Moroccan beef stew, eggplant with yogurt and sumac, and a barley stew made with duck and pumpkin.

Breakfast and Lunch

Open since 1902, ★ **La Bombonera** (259 Calle San Francisco, 787/705-3370, www.facebook.com/labombonerasanjuan, Tues.-Sun. 8am-5pm, $8-20) is an old-school diner and bakery serving a wide array of traditional Spanish and Puerto Rican dishes, including breakfast, sandwiches, tapas, and entrées such as arroz con pollo and lamb chops. But the highlight, besides an outstanding cup of coffee served from a gleaming, silver, Rube Goldberg kind of machine, is a pressed ham and cheese sandwich served on one of the best *mallorcas* found on the island. The light, airy pastry is flaky, rich, and slightly sweet, providing the perfect base for a superb breakfast sandwich. If you like things sweet, say yes to the offer of a sprinkle of powdered sugar. Service is typically very slow and perfunctory.

Cafeteria Mallorca (300 Calle San Francisco, 787/724-4607, daily 7am-6pm, $6-18) is a no-frills diner best known for its *mallorca* ($3-7), a light, flaky swirl of delicately sweetened pastry split open and stuffed with your choice of ham, cheese, egg, or bacon, then heated on a grill press and dusted with powdered sugar. The menu also features standard Puerto Rican dishes, including rice and beans, roast pork, *chicharrones de pollo* (fried chunks of chicken on the bone), and an array of baked goods.

Although it serves three meals a day, breakfast is the reason to visit ★ **Caficultura** (401 Calle San Francisco, 787/723-7731, info@caficulturapr.com, Mon.-Thurs. 8am-5pm, Fri. 8am-10pm, Sat.-Sun. 8am-8pm, $15-20).

Enjoy mocha pancakes, sweet potato crepes stuffed with chicken *longaniza*, or baguettes filled with smoked ham, cheddar cheese, egg, and house-made mayonnaise. Consider a mimosa, daquiri, or sangria made with fresh fruit juice.

Providing a welcome departure from more filling fare is **St. Germain Bistro & Café** (156 Calle Sol, 787/725-5830, Tues.-Sat. 11:30am-3pm and 6pm-10pm, Sun. 10am-3pm and 6pm-10pm, $7-15, $17 Sun. brunch), serving a large selection of soups, salads, sandwiches, pita pizzas, quiches, and desserts. There's a full bar, and a prix fixe brunch menu is served on Sundays.

Maví (366 Calle San Francisco, 787/725-0271, Mon.-Thurs. 9am-8pm, Fri.-Sat. 9am-6pm, Sun. 10am-4pm, $5) is a perfect spot for a quick, light lunch on the go. Big baked empanadas stuffed with your choice of spinach, broccoli, turkey, or beef, among other options, is the specialty, but you can also get sandwich wraps, fruit salads, and hummus.

Café Manolín (251 Calle de San Justo, 787/723-9743, www.cafemanolinoldsanjuan.com, Mon.-Fri. 6am-4:30pm, Sat. 7am-4:30pm, Sun. 8am-5pm, $9-20) is an old-school diner that has been serving breakfast and lunch since the 1940s. It's a good place to go for mofongo stuffed with chicken, pork, or shrimp. Be sure to ask for the house-made pique, a vinegar-based hot sauce.

At popular, fast-casual **Stuffed Avocado Shop** (209 Calle San Francisco, 787/722-0124, www.stuffedavocadoshop.com, Mon.-Fri. 11am-8pm, Sat.-Sun. 11am-9pm, $9-14) diners can build their own rice bowls (or switch out rice for kale, greens, or *mamposteao*) by picking their protein (salmon, tuna, chicken, beef, pork, or peas) and choosing from a list of toppings that include edamame, ginger, pineapple, corn, and avocados, of course, then selecting a sauce, including wasabi cream, ponzu, and spicy shoyu. For dessert, there is chocolate mousse or brownies, both made with avocado. Beverages include beer, fruit juices, and flavored waters.

Coffee and Tea

Café Cuatro Sombras (259 Calle Recinto Sur, 787/724-9955, http://cuatrosombras.com, Mon.-Thurs. 7am-8pm, Fri.-Sun. 7am-9pm, $2-10) is a micro-roastery that serves a variety of coffee drinks ranging from espressos to latte frappes made from beans grown on the island in the mountains of Yauco. It also serves a small menu of sandwiches and salads, including smoked salmon with cilantro mayonnaise and egg salad with asparagus. Coffee beans whole or ground are sold by the bag.

Café Finca Cialitos (267 Calle San Francisco, 939/207-9998, www.fincacialitos.com, Tues.-Fri. 7:30am-4:30pm, Sat.-Sun. 8:30am-5:30pm, $2-10) serves a variety of hot and cold coffee drinks, pastries, quiches, and sandwiches in a rustic space with a folk art vibe.

Catering to the literary minded, **Poetic Café** (203 Calle Cruz, 787/721-5020, daily 8am-9pm, $2-6) is a clever coffeehouse associated with the Poets Passage next door. Drink names sport literary references, such as the haiku espresso and couplet double espresso, and paper and pencil are provided on each table in case the writing muse strikes while you sip your metaphor café latte. A limited menu offers sandwiches and pastries, and there is a small bar.

Dessert

Get your chocolate fix at ★ **Casa Cortés ChocoBar** (210 Calle San Francisco, 787/722-0499, www.casacortespr.com, daily 8am-8pm, cocktails $10-15, desserts $7-12), which serves up a menu of sweet and savory dishes, as well as cocktails, all made from chocolate. Try the sundae made with coconut ice cream, chocolate sauce, pineapple marshmallow sauce, and toasted coconut. There's also a bakery case and small selection of chocolate bars, truffles, and drink mixes for sale.

For a refreshing treat on a hot afternoon, nothing satisfies like a fresh and fruity frozen pop on a stick. **Señor Paleta** (153 Calle Tetuan, 787/328-5878 or 787/724-2337, www.srpaletapr.com, daily 10:30am-10pm, $3) and **Los Paleteros PR** (366 Calle San Francisco, 787/559-3521, Tues.-Fri. noon-6pm, Sat.-Sun. noon-8pm, $3) serve them plain and blinged-out with your choice of sauces and toppings. Flavors range from lemonade, Oreo chocolate brownie, and passion fruit-melon to strawberry-kiwi and coconut mojito. Sugar-free varieties are available, too.

Farmers Markets and Groceries

Mercado Agricola Natural (150 Calle Norzagaray, Sat. 8am-1pm), also known as **San Juan Farmer's Market,** is appropriately located in the courtyard of San Juan's former marketplace, built in 1857. The building is also home to the Museo de San Juan. On Saturday mornings, it's the place to go for locally grown, organic fruits and vegetables, baked goods, fresh-squeezed juices, and more.

The best source for groceries in Viejo San Juan is **SuperMax** (201 Calle Cruz, 787/725-4839, daily 6am-midnight), a petite version of the modern, well-stocked chain of grocery stores found elsewhere on the island. It's conveniently located at Plaza de las Armas and carries a large selection of spirits and local coffees.

PUERTA DE TIERRA

El Mercado de Paseo Caribe (15 Ave. Luis Muñoz Rivera, 787/724-2400, www.paseocaribepr.com/el-mercado, Sun.-Tues. 8am-9:30pm, Wed.-Thurs. 8am-11pm, Fri.-Sat. 8am-midnight, vendors' hours vary) is a vibrant food hall at the Paseo Caribe residential/retail complex featuring a dozen or so vendors serving everything from pizza to popsicles, coffee to cocktails, tacos to Thai dishes. Favorite spots include Pesca'o del Dia, offering fresh seafood prepared to order from oysters on the half shell and mussels steamed in beer to whole fried snapper, and Barra Cocina, serving Spanish-inspired

---

1: Café Berlin in Viejo San Juan **2:** empanadas, *alcapurrias,* and other *frituras* **3:** Latin Star Restaurant in Condado

dishes. There's live music on Thursday, Saturday, and Sunday nights, and a DJ after party following Paseo Caribe's Friday night concert series.

CONDADO
Puerto Rican

Named one of the 30 best restaurants in the world by *Food & Wine* and *Travel + Leisure* magazines in 2019, ★ **Jose Enrique** (1021 Ave. Ashford, 787/705-8130, http://joseenriquepr.com, Tues.-Sat. 6:30pm-11pm, $16-28) is sleek and sophisticated. Famed chef Jose Enrique produces straightforward, traditional Puerto Rican cuisine, like *baccalaito,* mofongo, *carne guisado,* and fried yellow tail tuna that has been expertly sourced and prepared. The restaurant doesn't take reservations, so expect to wait for an hour or more to get in. The bar service is solid.

Mario Pagan Restaurant (1110 Ave. Magdalena, 787/522-6444, www.mariopaganrest.com, Tues.-Fri. noon-11pm, Sat. 6pm-11pm, $28-48) serves a locally sourced, seasonal menu divided by the size of the serving, ranging from small bites to shareable dishes, all beautifully plated. Nibble on starters like lamb *alcapurrias,* octopus tacos, or *pionono* of duck confit and plantain with foie gras sauce. Progress to larger servings of spiny lobster Thermidor or rabbit ravioli in smoked ripe plantain crema with arugula almond pesto. The space features a bright and airy bar and a dark and cozy dining room. The bar service is also outstanding, and there's valet parking.

★ **Cocina Abierta** (58 Calle Caribe, 787/946-1333, www.cocinaabierta.com, Mon.-Wed. 11am-11pm, Thurs.-Fri. 11am-midnight, Sat. 10am-midnight, Sun. 10am-11pm, $16-39) serves a seasonal menu of small plates rooted in Puerto Rican cuisine but reinterpreted using flavors and techniques from around the globe. Offerings include entrées such as Lamb Wellington, mofongo with Peking duck, octopus terrine, and an *empanadilla* stuffed with short rib and butternut squash. Creatively plated dishes are served in a hip, industrial space that places the focus squarely on the cuisine. Reservations are recommended.

The late-night party crowd likes **Latin Star Restaurant** (1128 Ave. Ashford, 787/724-8141, daily 24 hours, $11-40) less for the food and more for the fact that it's open 24-7. It serves a huge menu, including authentic local dishes such as goat or rabbit stew, tripe soup, and brandied guinea. There's indoor and sidewalk dining, and if you want to keep the party going, Dom Perignon is on the wine list. Breakfast and daily specials are also served.

Orozco's Restaurant (1126 Ave. Ashford, 787/721-7669, Wed.-Mon. 8am-11pm, Tues. 4pm-11pm, $11-25) serves traditional Puerto Rican cuisine featuring mofongo, grilled steak, pork, and chicken, plus daily specials. There is a full bar; try the house-made sangria. There's also live music on Fridays and Saturdays.

Seafood

Oceano (2 Calle Vendig, 787/724-6300 or 787/724-6315, www.oceanopr.com, Mon.-Thurs. 5pm-10pm, Fri.-Sat. noon-4pm and 5pm-11pm, Sun. 11am-3pm and 5pm-10pm, $18-36) is a glamorous, multilevel, beachfront restaurant with romantic views of the ocean, serving creative seafood fare, including shrimp mofongo with passion fruit reduction, blackened swordfish, and diver scallops with sweet potato puree and baked prosciutto di parma.

Waikiki Caribbean Food & Oyster Bar (1025 Ave. Ashford, 787/977-2267, daily 11am-late, $12-35), a casual oceanfront restaurant, features a long pinewood bar, sidewalk dining, a stone-grotto-style dining room inside, and a wood deck on the beach for alfresco dining. Dishes include mahi-mahi nuggets, crab-stuffed mushrooms, lobster tail, ossobuco, and seafood *criolla.*

International

Ropa Vieja Grill (Condado Palm Inn & Suites, 55 Ave. Condado, 787/725-2665, Sun.-Wed. 11am-10:30pm, Thurs. 11:30am-11pm, Fri. 11:30am-midnight, Sat. 6pm-midnight,

$15-25) is an upscale Cuban restaurant that also serves Puerto Rican and Italian cuisine. Specialties include risotto with *longaniza*, filet medallions in Roquefort sauce, and grilled sea bass in pesto sauce.

Via Appia's Deli (1350 Ave. Ashford, 787/725-8711, http://viaappiacondado.com, daily 11:30am-11pm or midnight, $11-20) serves standard Italian dishes, including pasta, sandwiches, and pizzas. It has indoor and sidewalk dining.

Turkish and Middle Eastern cuisine is on the menu at **Ali Baba** (1214 Ave. Ashford, Condado Village, 787/722-1176, www.facebook.com/AliBabaRestaurantPR, Tues. 4pm-9pm, Wed. 4pm-9:30pm, Thurs.-Fri. 4pm-10pm, Sat. noon-10pm, Sun. noon-9:30pm, $11-30). Service can be slow, but the grape leaf dolmas, chops, kebabs, and gyros are pretty good. There's a full bar.

Serving basic Tex-Mex cuisine, **Tijuana's Bar & Grill** (1350 Ave. Ashford, 787/723-3939, www.tijuanasbarandgrill.com, daily 24 hours, $8-25) serves nachos, tacos, quesadillas, enchiladas, burritos, and fajitas indoors or on an outside terrace. Specialties include shrimp diablo and Mexican lasagna. It has a full bar. Another location is in Viejo San Juan (Calle Marina, Pier No. 2, 787/724-7070).

Eclectic

Dine on pancakes for breakfast, a Mexicana pizza for lunch, fettuccine alfredo at night, and then dance off the calories at the nightclub upstairs at glamorous **Di Zucchero Lavazza Restaurant & Lounge** (1210 Ave. Ashford, 787/946-0835, www.facebook.com/dizucchero, Mon.-Thurs. 8am-8pm, Fri.-Sat. 11am-midnight, $14-19).

Classic American

For an American-style sports bar with a big beer selection, **The Place at Condado** (1378 Ave. Ashford, 787/998-4209 or 787/998-4204, http://theplacepr.com, Sun.-Thurs. 11:30am-10pm, Fri.-Sat. 11:30am-midnight, $3-16) is the place to feel like you never left the United States. Dine on burgers, pizza, and chicken wings surrounded by TVs, loud rock music, and a staff with attitude. There's a full bar.

At tiny, divey **Punk Burger & Bistro** (1129 Ave. Ashford, 787/723-4750, www.facebook.com/punkburgerbistro, daily 24 hours, $2-9), the people-watching is great as you nosh on eggs and bacon at breakfast or burgers made from beef, salmon, or turkey for lunch. Plus, there's a full bar.

Breakfast and Lunch

Kabanas Restaurant & Bar (1104 Magdalena Ave., 787/419-1016, www.facebook.com/kabanasrest, Mon.-Thurs. 9am-11pm, Fri.-Sat. 8am-1am, Sun. 8am-11pm, $10-24) is a casual spot serving hefty portions of burgers, tacos, fajitas, and nachos, as well as standard breakfast items, including eggs Benedict and whole-grain waffles served with fresh fruit. Check out the daily specials, like $6 martinis and Moscow mules after 5pm on Mondays and a bucket of Medalla beer and two burgers for $20 on Thursdays.

Fruit bowls and smoothies that promote energy and healthy skin are served up fresh and fast at **Crush Juice Bar** (1703 Ave. Ashford, 939/644-8672, daily 8am-10pm, $6-8). Yogurt and granola are also available.

Groceries

Freshmart (1310 Ave. Ashford, 787/999-7800, www.freshmartpr.com, daily 7am-11pm) is a bright, clean, modern grocery and deli specializing in organic produce, grass-fed beef, free-range chicken, and chemical-free vitamins and supplements. There's also a large selection of freshly prepared foods, including gourmet pizzas, pastas, and salads.

H & R Food & Liquors (1050-1052 Ave. Ashford, 787/721-7588, Sun.-Thurs. 8am-midnight, Fri.-Sat. 8am-1am) sells snacks, sundries, liquor, wine, and a surprising selection of craft beers.

Eros Food Market (1357 Ave. Ashford, 787/722-3631, Mon.-Sat. 7:30am-10pm, Sun. 8am-9pm) is a convenient place to stock up on provisions, including the essentials: coffee and rum. It includes a good supply of canned goods, health and beauty items, snacks, beverages, cigarettes, and more.

OCEAN PARK

Seafood

Marisquería Atlantica (2475 Calle Loiza, Punta Las Marías, 787/728-5444 or 787/728-5662, www.marisqueriaatlantica.com, Mon.-Thurs. noon-10pm, Fri.-Sat. noon-11pm, Sun. noon-9:30pm, $18-49) is a longstanding, high-quality, upscale seafood restaurant, serving everything imaginable from the sea, including *asopao*, grilled lobster, fresh fish including *chillo* and dorado, and a variety of ceviches and paellas. There's also a fresh seafood market (Mon.-Sat. 9am-8pm, Sun. 10am-3pm) where you can pick up fresh seafood to prepare at home.

New American

Uvva (Hostería del Mar, 1 Calle Tapia, 787/727-3302, www.hosteriadelmarpr.com, daily 8am-10pm, $21-38) is a casual beachside restaurant decked out in warm woods and rattan furnishings serving pan-seared duck breast in fig sauce and salmon in coconut ginger broth for dinner. Lighter fare, including burgers and beer-batter fried fish, is available for lunch.

Mexican

La B de Burro (2000 Calle McLeary, 787/242-0295, Mon.-Wed. 11am-10pm, Thurs.-Sat. 11am-midnight, Sun. noon-10pm, $4-11) is a funky little joint serving all varieties of tacos, tostados, burritos, quesadillas, and chimichangas. But they also serve lettuce tacos and an assortment of *aguas frescas* and fresh-made fruit juices, which the staff will whip up into margaritas. Try a tamarind margarita and the spicy house salsa served with crispy corn tortilla halves while you peruse the menu and check out all the Mexican Day of the Dead decor.

Eclectic

Tiny **Niche Bistro** (Acacia Boutique Hotel, 8 Calle Taft, 787/268-2803 or 787/725-0668, http://nichebistro.com, Mon-Fri. 7am-1pm, Sat.-Sun. 7am-3pm, daily 6pm-10:30pm, $27-38) is the place for an intimate, romantic dinner for two in dimly lit space constructed of stone and polished wood, and illuminated in alternating shades of purple, blue and pink lights. The menu is just as creative as the space, running the gamut from Mallorca pistachio French toast to *pastelón* with duck leg confit in ginger sauce. Reservations are recommended for dinner.

Pizza

Pirilo Pizza Rustica (2000 Calle McLeary, 787/268-2346, www.pirilopizza.com, Sun.-Wed. 11:30am-Midnight, Thurs.-Sat. 11:30am-2am. 11:30am-Midnight, $12-26) specializes in thick, loaded pizzas. Varieties include the Seven Cheeses; the Tripleta, topped with pork, cubed steak, ham and potato sticks; and the signature Pirilo, featuring ground beef and sweet plantain. For lighter appetites, try the tapas featuring empanadas, sandwiches and a hummus plate. There's another location in Viejo San Juan.

Breakfast and Lunch

Despite its name, ★ **Kasalta Bakery** (1966 Ave. McLeary, 787/727-7340 or 787/727-6593, www.kasalta.com, daily 6am-10pm, $12-25) is much more than a bakery. This large, professionally run operation sells piping hot *empanadillas, pastelillos,* and *alcapurrias,* and super-thick toasted sandwiches, including exceptional *cubanos, medias noches,* and a variety of breakfast sandwiches. In addition to a variety of soups and salads, lunch features hot daily specials (Mon.-Fri. 11:30am-3pm), including dishes such as asparagus risotto and pork tenderloin. At night, table service is offered for dinner entrées, including grilled skirt steak and seared ahi tuna. But Kasalta is still a bakery, so be sure to check out case after glass case of freshly made cookies, pastries, and slices of cheesecake. It also sells whole cakes and has an excellent wine and liquor selection. Order at the counter and grab a seat at shared tables to feast. If you drive, there's a free parking lot next door, but be prepared to wait for a parking space and stand in line to order on the weekends.

LOÍZA
Puerto Rican

Tántalo (1912 Calle Loíza, 787/249-7988, www.facebook.com/TantaloLoiza, Mon.-Wed. 4pm-midnight, Thurs.-Fri. 4pm-2am, Sat. noon-2am, Sun. 10am-midnight, $12-22) is a large, colorful, high-energy restaurant that turns into a hip club at night. The menu ranges from small bites like calamari, wings, and *pastelillos* to entrées of burgers, *pastelón,* and chicharron-encrusted salmon. Sunday brunch features live music and a menu of steak and eggs, s'mores pancakes, and bloody Mary ceviche.

★ **Molini's Native Cuisine** (1902 Calle Loíza, 787/726-2024, Mon.-Sat. 7am-10pm, $9-19) is a tiny, bare-bones diner that serves solid, inexpensive traditional Puerto Rican fare. Check the chalkboard for the daily menu, which is likely to include *sancocho* (beef stew), chicken fricassee, and whole fried snapper. Service is slow and perfunctory.

Jauja Street Food & Spirits (1810 Calle Loíza, 787/665-5270, Mon.-Thurs. noon-12:30am, Fri. and Sun. noon-1am, Sat. noon-2am, $1-10) is a casual spot serving a menu of Puerto Rican and Peruvian dishes, including mofongo, ceviche, *chaufa* (fried rice), tacos, *arepas,* and *pinchos.* Order and pick up your food at the counter, then find a table in the open-air dining area surrounded by colorful murals.

The entrance to **Azucena** (1804 Calle Loíza, 787/919-0315, Mon.-Wed. 11am-11pm, Thurs.-Sat. 11am-midnight, $22-30) is so understated and set back from the street, it's easy to walk past without even noticing it. That would be a shame because this restaurant serves a fresh, creative menu of Puerto Rican-inspired dishes such as mofongo with cod, pork cheek empanadas, and whole fried snapper inside a simple, minimalist dining room that puts the emphasis on the cuisine.

Seafood

Get your seafood fix at **La Cueva del Mar** (1904 Calle Loíza, 787/726-8700, http://cueva.r-leon.info, Sun.-Thurs. 11am-9:30pm, Fri.-Sat. 11am-11pm, $10-20). Tricked out in a 1980s-era nautical theme complete with fishing nets and wooden ship wheels, this popular spot with locals serves a huge variety of Puerto Rican-style seafood dishes from conch salad to *mofongo relleno de camarones* (mashed, garlicky plantains stuffed with shrimp). Seafood stuffed tacos, *empanadillas,* and salads, as well as salmon, mahi-mahi, and grouper dishes round out the menu. But the house specialties are Arroz con Mariscos La Cueva, featuring seasoned rice and a variety of seafood, and flan de Nutella. There's a full bar, a kids' menu, and weekly specials. There are additional locations in Viejo San Juan and Guaynabo.

International

A hip Mexican restaurant and self-described dive bar, **Panuchos** (1762 Calle Loíza, 787/545-2845, Mon.-Fri. 11am-11pm, Sat.-Sun. noon-11pm, $5-15) serves everything from tacos to tuna steak. Specialties include *ropa vieja* enchiladas with sweet plantains and a variety of tortas. Spice it up with the house-made hot sauces and wash it down with a margarita while you check out the pink-and-black-stenciled wall featuring repeated images of Frida Kahlo, mustachioed skulls, and banditos.

Diners get to enjoy a variety of banchan (side dishes) and watch servers grill thinly sliced cuts of beef and chicken at the table at **Ujeong Korean BBQ** (1916 Calle Loíza, 939-325-5247 or 939/640-1016, www.facebook.com/ujeonkoreanbbq, Tues.-Sat. 5:30pm-10pm, Sun. 3:30pm-10pm, $10-40). Entrées include sirloin bulgogi, bibimbap, and bokkeum. There are two full bars, one in the front and one in the back.

El Viejo Almacen (1503 Calle Loíza, 787/985-9122, Mon.-Thurs. 5pm-10pm, Fri. 5pm-midnight, Sat. noon-midnight, Sun. noon-10pm, $14-20) is an authentic old-school

Argentinian restaurant specializing in hearty entrées like a 16-ounce ribeye or chicken breast stuffed with ham and cheese wrapped in bacon and served with a mushroom sauce. It also serves a variety of traditional Italian dishes, including shrimp risotto and ravioli stuffed with lamb. The dining room is cozy and atmospheric, ideal for a romantic dinner for two.

Street art meets Korean-style fried chicken at **Volando Bajito** (101 Calle Ismael Rivera at Calle Loíza, 939/338-0182, www.facebook.com/pg/VolandoBajitoLoiza, Mon. and Thurs.-Fri. 5pm-10pm, Sat.-Sun. noon-10pm, $5-9), a hip, casual space specializing in wings and drumsticks tossed in your choice of sauce—sweet or spicy Korean, buffalo, or Boricua, a combo of beer and mojo sauce. Other options include veggie summer rolls, veggie patty sliders, and fries tossed with truffle oil, parmesan, and cilantro. The space doubles as an art gallery for local muralists, illustrators, and graphic designers.

Unassuming and low-key **Nonna Cucina Rustica** (103 Calle Jorge, 787/998-6555, Sun.-Thurs. noon-10pm, Fri.-Sat. noon-11pm, $13-38) is an oasis of calm in a city filled with splashy, high-energy eateries. Dine on traditional southern- and northern-style Italian cuisine, including squid ink linguine, short ribs with saffron risotto, goat cheese and ricotta ravioli in mushroom sauce, and a variety of pizzas. On the weekends, groups can enjoy the four-course family-style special for $35 per person. There's also a large selection of Italian and Spanish wines.

New American

★ **Sabrina Brunch & Bistro Bar** (1801 Calle Loíza, 939-399-3049, www.facebook.com/sabrinabistro, Tues.-Wed. 11am-10pm, Thurs. 11am-11pm, Fri.-Sat. 11am-midnight, Sun. 10am-5pm, $20-30) has a light, airy vibe combined with a splash of 1940s-era Hollywood glamour. The place is decorated with potted plants, a hibiscus wall mural, banquettes, and a pink neon sign. The inventive cocktails have names like 8am Call Time,

Starring Role, and Sofia Loren, and the food is creative and well prepared. Consider the cinnamon and bacon pancakes with coffee syrup or smoked bacon mac and cheese. For dinner, the New York strip loin is served in a tamarind and Barrilito rum glaze, and the wahoo comes with grape risotto.

Classic American

The Mac'n Cheese (1916 Calle Loíza, 939/325-5247, www.facebook.com/themacncheesepr, $11-30) is a bright, cheerful, fast-casual place serving baked tins of macaroni and cheese in small, medium, and large portions. In addition to traditional mac and cheese made with a combination of mozzarella, cheddar, gruyere, and parmesan, there are more creative varieties like chicken parmesan, bacon cheeseburger, spicy Korean bulgogi, and traditional Puerto Rican tripleta. Beer, house wine, and a limited liquor selection is available.

Pizza

Loíza 2050 (2050 Calle Loíza, 787/726-7141, Wed.-Sat. 6pm-midnight, Sun. 6pm-4am, $5-19) is a petite pizza pub that gets crowded at night. It specializes in thin crust pizza made with fresh herbs. For something different, try the pumpkin crust pizza.

More glamorous than your typical pizza restaurant, **Si No Corro Me Pizza** (1917 Calle Loíza, 787/998-2925, www.facebook.com/sinocorromepizza, Mon.-Thurs. noon-10pm, Fri.-Sat. noon-11pm, $12-21) serves a high quality rustic-style pizza, house-made focaccia, and pasta dishes such as gnocchi, lasagna, carbonara, and ravioli. The stylish space has red walls, ornate antiques, and vintage headshots of Italian movie stars.

Breakfast and Lunch

Located in a bright yellow shipping container, the kitchen at **Tresbé** (1765 Calle Loíza, 787/294-9604, www.cafetresbe.com, daily 11am-midnight, $4-12) turns out made to order marlin *pinchos* (kabobs), breadfruit *tostones*, tamarind chicken wings, burgers, tacos, and ceviche. Order at the window and find a seat at the metal picnic table beneath a shade tree.

★ **Café D'Luna** (1966 Calle Loíza, 787/666-9837, Thurs.-Sun. 9am-2pm, $1.50-5) is a quirky spot with a New Age vibe that serves outstanding creative, made-to-order *pastelillos* (empanadas). In addition to the traditional cheese, chicken, and beef varieties, these savory hand pies come stuffed with corned beef or coconut curry chicken. The Cubano *pastelillo* is filled with ham, roast pork, Swiss cheese, and pickles. The Puerto Rican variety is filled with Spam, cream cheese, and pineapple. For dessert, try a banana chocolate *pastelillo* or one stuffed with sweet potato and marshmallow sauce. There's also a full breakfast menu of eggs, pancakes, omelets, and French toast. Everything is cooked to order by one person in a tiny kitchen, but it's worth the long wait.

As if the big, bright dining room wasn't enough to beckon diners, **Tostado** (1805 Calle Loíza, 787/523-6902, daily 8am-3pm, $4-11) serves an outstanding menu of health-conscious, locally sourced breakfast and lunch options, including hearty coconut-pumpkin pancakes, grass-fed beef burgers, eggs Benedict, pulled pork sandwiches, coffee drinks, and fruit juices. There's a parking lot out front; there's a fee charged, but the restaurant validates. A second location is at 610 Calle Condado.

Dessert

Double Cake Baking Studio (1852 Calle Loíza, 787/998-9368, www.facebook.com/doublecake, Mon.-Sat. 9am-6pm, Sun. noon-7pm, $1.50-3) specializes in cupcakes in a variety of flavors including dulce de leche and Nutella. Breads, cookies, coffee drinks, and lemonade are also on the menu.

SANTURCE
Puerto Rican

★ **Lote 23** (1552 Ave. Ponce de Leon, www.lote23.com, Tues.-Wed. 7:30am-10pm, Thurs.-Fri. 7:30am-midnight, Sat. 8am-midnight,

Sun. 8am-10pm, $3-15) is a fun, inexpensive way to sample a variety of dishes by some of Puerto Rico's up-and-coming chefs. A hybrid food truck park and food hall, the outdoor space is where to dine on a pulled pork sandwich from Pernileria Los Proceres, sip a frosty cocktail made with fresh fruit juice by the bartenders at Caneca Cocteleria Movil, or indulge with a strawberry cheesecake popsicle by Señor Paleta. But it's not just about dining at Lote 23. There's also live music, film screenings, yoga classes, and a weekly arts and crafts bazaar. Check out the Facebook page for details.

El Coco de Luis (1348 Calle Morales, corner of Plaza del Mercado, 787/721-7595, http://el-coco-de-luis.business.site, Sun.-Wed. 6am-11pm, Thurs.-Sat. 6am-2am, drinks $1-8, food $4-10) is a casual, happening spot in the corner of Plaza del Mercado, famous for its mojitos and house cocktail, whiskey and coconut water. The menu includes ceviche, fresh fish, and *frita carne*.

Check out **Boronia** (Calle Capital at La Placita, 787/724-0636, www.boroniarestaurante.com, daily noon-10pm, $9-20), a modest, casual spot serving traditional *cocina criolla* cuisine with a few surprises, such as mashed celery root with codfish for an appetizer and rabbit fricassee. There's live music on weekends.

Located on the 1st floor of a four-story apartment building, **Bebo's Café** (1600 Calle Loíza, 787/726-5700, daily 7am-11pm, $6-25) is a casual restaurant serving an exhaustive menu of traditional *cocina criolla* cuisine. Literally, just about anything you can think of is served here: Cuts of chicken, pork, and beef are prepared fried, breaded, grilled, stuffed, or stewed. Shrimp, crab, octopus, and conch are served in salads or stuffed in mofongo. All varieties of fritters, sandwiches, soups, fish, and flan are also represented, as are fruit shakes and frappes. Check the daily specials for delicacies such as stewed oxtail, goat fricassee, and *pastelón*, a dish similar to lasagna that uses plantain or breadfruit in place of pasta. This place is the real deal.

★ **La Casita Blanca** (351 Calle Tapía, 787/726-5501, www.facebook.com/lacasitablancapr, Mon.-Thurs. 11:30am-4pm, Fri.-Sat. 11:30am-9pm, Sun. 11:30-5pm, $7-15) is a warm and endearingly rustic restaurant decorated like a 1950s-era living room serving some of the best traditional Puerto Rican cuisine found in San Juan. The menu changes daily but typically includes classics such as *arroz con pollo, carne guisado, pastélon con carne, amarillos, tostones,* and *picadillo.* All meals end with a tasty complimentary shot of *chichaito,* made from rum and anisette.

El Patio de Solé (718 Cale Cerra, 787/225-0967, www.facebook.com/sole5454, Mon.-Sat. 8am-4pm, $2-10) is a funky, bohemian spot marked by eye-popping murals on the outside and a charming patio inside where visitors dine on traditional Puerto Rican cuisine, including pancakes, Spanish tortillas, chicken stew, grilled fish, and churrasco.

Breakfast and Lunch
Kudough's Donuts & Coffee Bar (622 Calle Cerra, 787/995-7060, www.facebook.com/KudoughsDonuts, Tues.-Thurs. 8am-8pm, Fri. 8am-9pm, Sat.-Sun. 9am-9pm, $4-12) is a modern, cheerful shop selling a variety of doughnuts, including s'mores, passion fruit, and bacon with maple glaze varieties. There are also vegan options, a full breakfast menu, and after 3pm, a pub menu of wings, burgers, beer, and wine.

International
★ **Lima 634** (corner of Calle Cerra and Ave. Fernandez, 347/801-6038, http://lima634.com, Tues.-Thurs. 5:30pm-10pm, Fri.-Sat. 5:30pm-11pm, Sun. 1pm-10pm, $19-24) is a beautiful corner restaurant with a romantic bar hung with ornate brass light fixtures that add a splash of drama to the white tile and green-walled dining room thick with trailing green plants. It's the perfect setting for the fresh, clean burst of flavors of the bountiful

1: Lote 23 food truck park in Santurce 2: Tresbé in Loíza

Peruvian-style ceviches, lomo saltado, chaufa, and tiradito.

Axolote (622 Calle Cerra, 787/724-6296, www.facebook.com/ElAxoloteSanturcino, Mon.-Sat. 11am-11pm, Sun. noon-11pm, $10-18) is a rustic wood and tile structure with a large, covered patio, specializing in quality Mexican dishes ranging from tacos (carnitas, *nopales,* fish) to pozole, *carne asado,* ceviche, and *elotes* (Mexican street corn). The bar serves a variety of refreshing tequila and mezcal drinks, as well as beer and wine.

Located across from the Museo de Arte de Puerto Rico, **Bistro de Paris** (310 Ave. de Diego, 787/998-8929 or 787/721-8925, www.bistrodeparispr.com, Wed. 11am-10pm, Thurs. 11am-11pm, Fri.-Sat. 10am-midnight, Sun. 10am-10pm, $25-37) specializes in authentic French nouvelle cuisine, including shrimp flambé and filet mignon topped with sautéed duck liver. Globe light fixtures and art posters create a cozy ambiance in the dining room, while more casual dining is available on the patio.

Set in a colonial mansion appointed with stained-glass windows, archways, patios, intricate tile work, and lush landscaping, **La Casona** (609 Calle San Jorge, corner of Ave. Fernández Juncos, 787/727-2717 or 787/727-3229, http://restaurantelacasonapr.com, Mon.-Fri. noon-3pm and 6:30pm-11:30pm, Sat. 6pm-11:30pm, $25-35) serves a menu of classic Spanish dishes. An extensive wine list complements the paella, rack of lamb, and pâté. It's a popular spot for business lunches, banquets, receptions, and other private parties.

Eclectic
★ **Vianda** (1413 Ave. Ponce de León, 939/475-1578, www.viandapr.com, Wed.-Thurs. and Sun. 5:30pm-10pm, Fri.-Sat. 5:30pm-11pm, $15-34) opened in 2017 and has already made a big name for itself. Owned and operated by chef Francis Guzmán and his wife, Amelia Dill, who runs the front of the house, it was a semifinalist for the James Beard Award for Best New Restaurant in 2019. The casual, minimalist dining room

is simply appointed with a few potted plants and a verdant plant mural, providing the ideal setting for the seasonal, locally sourced, plant-forward menu. Small dishes may include pumpkin fritters, watermelon gazpacho, and a papaya slaw with pork belly and tamarind. Among the large plates are eggplant tikka masala and gnocchi with stewed goat. If you're lucky, the passion fruit Pavlova will be on the menu. The cuisine is complemented by a robust selection of creative cocktails, mocktails, craft beers, and wines.

The menu is always changing, from Southern cuisine to Italian to Puerto Rican at **Gallo Negro** (1107 Ave. Juan Ponce de León, 787/554-5445, www.facebook.com/gallonegrosanturce, Tues. 11am-2:30pm and 6pm-midnight, Wed.-Thurs. 11am-3pm and 6pm-midnight, Fri. 11am-3pm and 5pm-1am, Sat. 6pm-midnight, Sun. 11am-3pm, $14-28). Depending on the day, you might dine on baby back ribs with Carolina Gold sauce, churrasco with rice and beans, or chicken Alfredo. Lunch offerings may include tacos and hamburgers, and Sunday brunch goes international with Mexican *chilaquiles*, vegetarian bibimbap, or Puerto Rican-style eggs Benedict, featuring *sofrito* hollandaise sauce and smoked ham. If you're really thirsty, order a Man-Mosa, a 16-ounce glass of OJ and cava. The space is casual, crowded, and convivial.

Travel is the theme at ★ MUSA (613 Calle Cerra, 787/366-2300, www.facebook.com/musapuertorico, Mon. 9am-3pm, Tues.-Fri. 9am-3pm and 6pm-10pm, Sat. 6pm-10pm, Sun. 10am-3pm, $19-28), a trendy, popular spot serving a creative menu of seasonal, globally influenced cuisine and cocktails in a bright, playful space decorated with oversized passport stamps and vintage luggage. For breakfast try the *tres leches* French toast or *tripleta* omelet. In the afternoon nosh on selections from tapas menu, like mac and cheese with *ropa vieja* or gnocchi in pesto sauce, accompanied by a cocktail chosen from a drink menu fashioned like a passport. The Smokey Rose, featuring mezcal, pink grapefruit juice, and lime is highly recommended. Dinner

entrées include *pastelón* with truffle sauce, *lomo saltado*, and snapper filet in wine sauce.

Chef-owner José Santaella, who trained with Ferran Adrià at el Bulli and Eric Ripert, started out as a caterer before opening **Santaella** (219 Calle Canals, 787/725-1611, www.santaellapr.com, Tues.-Fri. 11:30am-11pm, Sat. 6pm-11pm, $26-36), a sleek, low-lit, upscale restaurant serving up a creative menu of braised pork shank and roasted sea bass. Save room for the Nutella sandwich with Frangelico whipped cream for dessert. Consider starting your meal with craft cocktails such as the ginger margarita or rum mango julep.

Farmers Markets

Plaza del Mercado (Calle Dos Hermanos and Calle Capital, Mon.-Sat. 6am-6pm, Sun. noon-6pm), also known as **La Placita,** is a picturesque, colonial-style, open-air farmers market built in 1910, where shoppers can pick up a wide variety of fruits, vegetables, fresh meats, frozen fruit frappes, and herbal remedies. At night the markets close up, sidewalk bars open, a live band plays, and the surrounding neighborhood turns into a lively street party.

MIRAMAR
Puerto Rican

From the same folks who run the popular Casita Blanca in Santurce, the equally popular ★ **Casita Miramar** (605 Ave. Miramar, 787/200-8227, Mon. and Wed.-Thurs. 5pm-10pm, Fri.-Sat. 11:30am-11pm, Sun. 11:30am-10pm, $18-32) serves traditional Puerto Rican cuisine in a two-story colonial building with a 2nd-floor patio. The menu changes daily based on what's fresh and in season. Be prepared to wait up to two hours if you go at prime time. The space is romantically appointed with twinkle lights and potted plants.

On the second level of the building, above another restaurant, ★ **Soda Estudio de Cocina** (909 Ave. Juncos, 787/940-2653 or 787/998-9920, www.facebook.com/SodaEstudioDeCocina, Tues.-Thurs.

5pm-10pm, Fri.-Sat. 5pm-11pm, $7.50-17) is a super-casual gastropub serving generously portioned dishes packed with bold, robust flavors like skillet-cooked mac and cheese with local *longaniza* sausage, egg rolls stuffed with *bistec encebollado* (vinegar-marinated steak and onions), and *mamposteao* (a thick stew of rice and red beans). Other menu options might include coconut *arepas* stuffed with *ropa vieja,* and fried dumplings filled with duck and pork belly. For a refreshing beverage, try the blackberry mojito made from plump fresh fruit and a fistful of fresh mint.

French

Formerly called Augusto's, **Ariel** (801 Ave. Ponce de León, 787/725-7700, www.marriott.com, Tues.-Fri. 6:30am-10am, noon-3pm, and 7pm-10pm, Sat. 7am-10:30am and 7pm-10pm, Sun. 7am-3pm, $26-40) is located in the Courtyard by Marriott hotel, but it's far from a generic hotel restaurant. The venerable French-influenced fine dining restaurant is the place to go to don your evening finery and enjoy white tablecloth service while you select a prime vintage from the extensive wine list and dine on scallops with sunflower seed puree and duck roasted with lavender and coriander.

Breakfast and Lunch

At **Abracadabra Counter Café** (1661 Ave. Ponce de León, 787/200-0447, www.facebook.com/abracadabrapr, Tues.-Fri. 8:30am-3pm, Sat.-Sun. 9am-3pm, $5-15), bright yellow-and-white striped wallpaper and vintage photographs cover the walls of this whimsical bistro frequented by a hip, young clientele, as well as families attracted by the local coffee and the fresh, organic menu. Breakfast and brunch dishes are its specialties, including the caprese omelet, Nutella-filled croissants, and bacon maple cupcakes. Live entertainment runs the gamut from magic shows to film nights to live musical performances. A full bar and free wireless Internet are available.

Al Gusto Deli (950 Ave. Ponce de León, 787/723-4321, Mon.-Fri. 7:30am-3:30pm,

$6-9) serves breakfast sandwiches and burritos, as well as deli sandwiches, wraps, salads, soups, and quesadillas. Neon green walls and bright orange chairs create a cheery place to start the day.

Groceries

Supermax (113 Ave. de Diego, 787/723-1611, www.supermaxpr.com, daily 24 hours) is a modern, full-service grocery store with a bakery, a deli, a fresh meat counter, and a produce section. It carries a large selection of spirits and a wide variety of local coffees, but you'll have to get a clerk to unlock the case for you.

ISLA VERDE
Puerto Rican

Alambique Beach Lounge (5803 Calle Tartak, 787/253-5806, www.facebook.com/elalambiqueislaverde, daily 9am-3am, $9.50-22) is a popular, casual restaurant and bar serving ceviche, sandwiches, burgers, fish tacos, mofongo, and churrasco in an open-air space directly across the street from the beach. The wraparound bar serves a variety of fruity cocktails including margaritas and piña coladas, as well as 20 varieties of beer, mostly by the bottle but a few on tap. Walk-up cup service is available for taking your drink to the beach.

True to its name, **Ceviche House** (79 Ave. Isla Verde, 787/726-0919, daily 11:30am-10pm, $14-28) serves a variety of fresh, flavorful ceviche in small and large sizes, as well as a full menu of seafood and Puerto Rican dishes, including paella, whole fried snapper, and churrasco.

Despite its location in an aging shopping center, **Mi Casita** (La Plazoleta de Isla Verde, 6150 Ave. Isla Verde, 787/791-1777, daily 7:30am-10:30pm, $5-18) is a homey oasis of authentic Puerto Rican cuisine amidst Isla Verde's flashier restaurants. Designed to look like a cozy dining room of someone's house, complete with china plates hanging on the walls, the restaurant serves a menu featuring outstanding *cocina criolla*, including a moist mofongo, *asopao*, churrasco, *chillo*, and mahi-mahi.

Located on the bottom floor of Coral by the Sea hotel, **Platos Restaurant** (2 Calle Rosa, 787/791-7474 or 787/721-0396, www. facebook.com/platosrestaurantandbar, Sun.-Thurs. 11am-10pm, Fri.-Sat. 11am-2am, $17-23) is not named after the Greek philosopher but rather the Spanish word for "plates." This bright, touristy spot specializes in candy-colored tropical drinks and a menu offering something for everyone, including mofongo, steaks, pasta, and fish.

Pa' Pical (63 Ave. Isla Verde, 787/448-0526, daily 11am-2am, $4-9) is a hopping little dive bar/restaurant serving tasty empanadas, tacos, and a $5 lunch special featuring ribs, fried pork chops, and chicken breast in garlic sauce. The drinks are strong here.

Seafood

Mar del Caribe (2444 Calle Loíza, 787/545-5025, Wed.-Sat. noon-10pm, Sun. noon-8pm, $15-32) is a casual but elegant bistro that serves outstanding seafood dishes ranging from paella and grouper with chickpeas and chorizo to shrimp risotto and lobster in garlic sauce. There are plenty of traditional Puerto Rican-style beef, chicken, and pork dishes for landlubbers, too.

Catering to the late-night party crowd, **Kintaro Sushi & Chinese Cuisine** (5970 Ave. Isla Verde, 787/726-3096, www.facebook.com/KintaroSushiRestaurant, daily 5pm-4am, $8-20) is a small, atmospheric eatery serving primarily sushi, but also tempura, noodle, and rice dishes.

International

Decor is secondary at the crowded, casual Cuban restaurant chain **Metropol** (6600 Ave. Isla Verde, 787/791-4046, www.metropolpr.com, Sun.-Thurs. 11am-10pm, Fri.-Sat. 11am-11pm, $9-40, most dishes $10-15). The house specialty is *gallinita rellena de congri*—succulent roasted Cornish hen stuffed with a perfectly seasoned combination of rice and black beans. The presentation is no-nonsense

and the service expedient, designed to get you in and out so the folks lining up outside can have your table. There are additional locations, including Hato Rey (244 Ave. Roosevelt, 787/751-4022) and Guaynabo (Jardines Reales, Ave. Las Cumbres, 787/272-7000).

With a modest location on a busy thoroughfare, the long-standing Italian favorite **Italian House and Grill—Il Nonno** (41 Ave. Isla Verde, 787/728-8050, www.facebook.com/italianhousepr, Sun.-Thurs. noon-10pm, Fri. 11am-11pm, Sat. noon-11pm, $14-36) steadily remains, serving well-executed dishes of gnocchi gorgonzola, halibut in wine sauce, and ossobuco in a warm, intimate setting.

The casual, modern, Argentine-Italian restaurant **Ferrari Gourmet** (3046 Ave. Isla Verde, 787/982-3115, 787/993-1758, www.ferrarigourmet.com, Mon.-Thurs. noon-10pm, Fri.-Sat. noon-11pm, Sun. 12:30pm-10pm, $13-36) specializes in grilled meats including Black Angus beef and chorizo, and a wide variety of creative pizzas featuring unusual toppings such as asparagus, blue cheese, and Argentinian sausage.

Eclectic

Set in a Wyndham property, ★ **Emigrante Gastrobar** (Tryp by Wyndham, 4820 Ave. Isla Verde, 787/728-1300, www.trypislaverde.com/taste/emigrante-gastrobar, daily 6:30am-10:30am, 11:30am-3pm, and 5:30pm-11pm, $9-24) is not your average hotel restaurant. The decor is elegant and dramatic, with floor-to-ceiling windows, bright white tile floors, leather couches, an L-shaped bar with black leather upholstered stools, and a colorful mural of birds. The cocktails are inventive and original. Try the Tryp Old Fashioned, made with aged rum, tamarind juice, and rosemary, or the Sexy White Dress, a potent combination of rum, vodka, coconut cream, and fresh lime. The weekday lunch specials feature soup of the day or hearty options like ribs and chicken pad Thai. For dinner, go small with a selection from the tapas menu, like the spring roll stuffed with ground beef, cheddar cheese, and sweet plantains, or go big with an entrée, such as roast quail with guava sauce, *chuleta can-can*, snapper filet, and churrasco. Save room for the house-made ice cream in flavors that include cinnamon, olive oil, coconut flan, and Nutella.

Pizza

Pizza City (5950 Ave. Isla Verde, 787/726-0356, www.pizzacityislaverde.com, daily 24 hours, $3-24) is an open-air restaurant best known for its tasty thin-crust pizza sold by the slice or pie. It also serves breakfast, sandwiches, seafood salads, and mofongo. It has a full bar.

Breakfast and Lunch

Piu Bello (2 Calle Rosa, 787/791-0091, www.facebook.com/PiuBelloGelatoPR, Mon.-Thurs. 6am-10pm, Fri.-Sun. 6am-11pm, $7-13) is a large, modern, retro-style diner with indoor and outdoor dining. The menu includes sandwiches, burgers, pizza, breakfast dishes, and gelato. There is a second location (Ave. Ashford) in Condado. There's free wireless Internet.

Bistro Café (29 Calle Jupiter at Ave. Isla Verde, 787/603-5757, Mon.-Sat. 7am-3pm, Sun. 8am-3pm, $6-18) packs in a crowd of hungry diners eager to chow down on enormous platters of omelets, pancakes, waffles, sandwiches, and salads. There's also a full bar and a wide variety of coffee drinks available.

Accommodations

Eleven major hotels in Puerto Rico underwent significant renovations after Hurricane Maria hit in 2017. Some closed completely during construction but have since reopened. Most are back in business, and a few brand-new hotels have debuted in the meantime.

In addition to an enormous array of chain and independent hotels offering every level of guest room imaginable, from budget to luxe, Puerto Rico has a healthy offering of guesthouses and inns, featuring cozier

The parking lot fills up quickly, and street parking can be hard to find.

Groceries

Super Max (Ave. Isla Verde at PR 26, 787/268-3084, http://supermaxpr.com, daily 24 hours) is a full-service grocery store with fresh meats and baked goods.

GREATER SAN JUAN

It's not necessarily worth a special trip, but if you take the ferry to Cataño to visit the Casa Bacardí Visitor Center, you might want to stop by **S.O.S. Burger** (36 Ave. Las Nereidas, Cataño, 787/788-3149, www.facebook.com/sosburger, Wed.-Thurs. noon-7:30pm, Fri.-Sun. noon-11pm, $3-15). The psychedelic-colored structure with a palm-frond roof is the quirky domain of Sammy Ortega Santiago (his initials inform the establishment's name), who sports waist-length dreadlocks and an infectious smile. As the name implies, the short menu serves a variety of burgers. But the real reason to go here is to kick back with some ice-cold Medalla beers and to nosh on the variety of tasty *pastelillos*, thin, crisp turnovers stuffed with meat, cheese, or seafood. Here they come stuffed with everything from crab, lobster, and *chapín* (boxfish) to cheese, beef, and pepperoni with tomato sauce. There's live music on weekends.

accommodations with fewer services. There are also *paradores*, government-sponsored properties that typically serve budget travelers and large families, and are especially popular with Puerto Rican travelers. Airbnb and VRBO have increased their presence in the private vacation rental market.

Tax rates vary depending on the type of property. *Paradores* and Airbnb properties are taxed 7 percent; hotels are 9 percent; and hotels with casinos are taxed 11 percent. Prices listed here are based on high-season rates and do not include taxes and fees.

VIEJO SAN JUAN

Aside from a Sheraton located near the cruise-ship docks, accommodations in Viejo San Juan are small boutique hotels. No matter where you stay in Viejo San Juan, you're within easy walking distance to some of the city's finest restaurants, shops, and cultural sights.

$100-150

Da House Hotel (312 Calle San Francisco, 844/468-3577, www.dahousehotel.com, $90-120, two-night minimum) features 27 small units, some with balconies, in a historic colonial building artfully decorated with an eclectic mix of art and furnishings that beautifully melds vintage and contemporary aesthetics. Rooms come with air-conditioning, private baths, pillow-top mattresses, free high-speed Internet, and concierge service. There are no TVs and no elevator, so be prepared to walk up as many as four flights to your room—carrying your own luggage.

A dramatic lobby and bar drenched in red velvet, crystal chandeliers, Moroccan lanterns, and pop art paintings create a hip vibe at the 35-room ★ **Casablanca Hotel** (316 Calle Fortaleza, 844/468-3577, http://hotel-casablancapr.com, $109-129, $179 suite), managed by the folks at Da House Hotel and Villa Herencia Hotel. Accommodations range from very small standard rooms to more spacious superior rooms complete with sitting area and balcony, each room uniquely decorated. There's a glass elevator with a view of the city. All rooms have air-conditioning, pillow-top mattresses, flat-screen or satellite TVs, high-speed Internet, and private baths.

$150-250

A classic colonial home built in the 1700s has been converted into ★ **Villa Herencia Hotel** (23 Caleta Las Monjas, 787/722-0989 or 844/468-3577, www.villaherencia.com, $179-209), a stunning eight-room guesthouse

featuring antique furnishings and huge, original pop art paintings by Puerto Rican artist Roberto Parrilla. A manager is on-site during the day only, and amenities are limited to an honor bar, a rooftop terrace, and some gorgeously appointed common areas. Amenities include pillow-top mattresses, high-speed Internet, air-conditioning, satellite TV, private baths, and complimentary breakfast. It's hard to find such high style in Viejo San Juan at this price.

On the edge of Viejo San Juan, overlooking the Atlantic Ocean, is ★ **The Gallery Inn** (204 Calle Norzagaray, 787/722-1808, www.thegalleryinn.com, $175-260, $325 suite), a hotel like no other. Artist Jan D'Esopo has transformed this 17th-century labyrinthine mansion into part art gallery, part concert venue, part guesthouse. There structure boasts seven levels of courtyards, patios, balconies, interior gardens, and more than 20 unique, antiques-filled guest rooms, some with private terraces and gardens. Everywhere you look are paintings, sculptures, fountains, and plants. On-site is The Cannon Club (daily 5pm-midnight, kitchen open until 11pm), a gorgeous, antiques-filled piano bar dominated by a massive crystal chandelier and two Steinways, featuring live jazz and classical music performances. There's also a pool and rooftop deck.

For modern accommodations in an excellent, central location, **Hotel Milano** (307 Calle Fortaleza, 787/729-9050, www.hotelmilanopr.com, $148-175) provides 30 clean, corporate-style rooms appointed with queen-size beds, air-conditioning, satellite TV, hair dryers, and mini refrigerators. Under separate management is Café El Punto, an excellent rooftop restaurant and bar serving *cocina criolla*.

Stay the night in an 18th-century colonial home in Viejo San Juan at **Casa Sol B&B** (316 Calle Sol, 787/399-0105, www.bedandbreakfast.com, $168-238). All five guest rooms have private bathrooms, air-conditioning and ceiling fans. Breakfast is included in the rate.

Monastery Art Suites (250 Calle del Cristo, 786/496-3516, https://monastery. club, $160-200, $245-280 suite) is a former Masonic temple that's been transformed into an eye-popping, pop art-meets-Baroque-style guesthouse featuring Louis XV-style furnishings painted bright white and upholstered in bold colors like fuchsia and turquoise. There are seven guest rooms and suites, some with kitchenettes and balconies with views of the city or ocean. Amenities include private bathrooms, refrigerators, Apple TV, wireless Internet, and sunset yoga on the rooftop. The front desk is open from 9am to 9pm.

Over $250

Spend the night in a former Carmelite convent completed in 1651 by order of King Phillip IV of Spain. ★ **Hotel El Convento** (100 Calle del Cristo, 787/723-9020, 787/721-2877, or 800/468-2779, www.elconvento.com, $245-305, $505-1,005 suite) is now a 58-room hotel in a four-level colonial structure built around a beautifully landscaped courtyard. Common areas are filled with Spanish antiques and reproductions. Rooms come with flat-screen TVs, refrigerators, wireless Internet, and goose-down pillows. Amenities include a private beach club, fitness center, plunge pool, whirlpool, and Patio del Níspero, an open-air restaurant serving three meals a day.

In 2019 all 240 guest rooms were renovated at the **Sheraton Viejo San Juan Hotel** (100 Calle Brumbaugh, 787/721-5100, www.sheratonoldsanjuan.com, $309- $329 suite). The high-rise hotel by the cruise-ship docks features all the comforts one expects from the chain. Amenities include flat-screen TVs, high-speed Internet, a rooftop pool, and a health club. There are two dining options: Palio, serving Puerto Rican cuisine, and Aroma Wine & Coffee Lounge.

Located in an 18th-century colonial building said to have once housed members of the Spanish Armada, **352 Guest House** (352 Calle San Francisco, 787/367-0636, www.352guesthouse.com, $240-270) features eight small, simply appointed guest rooms with private baths, a rooftop bar, a terrace with a hot tub, an elegant lobby, and a full-service restaurant. Rooms come with high-speed Internet and mini refrigerators.

PUERTA DE TIERRA
Over $250

★ **Caribe Hilton** (1 Calle San Geronimo, 787/721-0303, www.hiltoncaribbean.com, $370-420, $460-570 suite) debuted a $150 million renovation in 2019 that preserves the integrity of this stunning display of modernist architecture and design, built in the late 1940s. The historic, 17-acre resort features tropical gardens, a bird sanctuary, and a secluded beach. Amenities include a fitness center, pool, spa, tennis courts, and eight dining options, including Morton's The Steakhouse and Starbucks. The Caribe Hilton is one of two places in Puerto Rico (the other being Barrachina in Viejo San Juan) that claims to have invented the piña colada, so be sure to try one before you go, with rum or without.

CONDADO
$100-150

Located in the heart of Condado and two blocks from the beach, **Coral Princess Hotel** (1159 Ave. Magdalena, 787/977-5959 or 787/977-7700, www.coralpr.com, $99-135) is a compact, 25-room hotel with a small pool, complimentary continental breakfast, free Internet, flat screen TVs with cable, and a rooftop whirlpool tub.

For clean, modern, no-frills accommodations at a budget rate, **El Canario** (1317 Ave. Ashford, 787/722-3861, $105-135) offers a pleasant lobby and 25 small units.

$150-250

A seven-story hotel overlooking the Condado Lagoon, **The Wave Hotel** (76 Ave. Condado, 787/721-9010, http://thewavehotel.com, $159-179) offers rooms with queen, king, and double twin beds. Amenities include flat screen TVs, high-speed Internet, a rooftop terrace with hot tub, complimentary continental breakfast, and concierge service.

Over $250

The **Condado Plaza Hilton** (999 Ave. Ashford, 787/721-1000 or 866/316-8934, www.condadoplaza.com, $240-285, $332-420 suite) is a 21st-century modernist's dream with its minimalist aesthetic and a tastefully rendered nod to pop art sensibilities, featuring a blindingly white lobby appointed with touches of brilliant orange. The hotel underwent significant renovations following Hurricane Maria. Amenities include a fitness center, a business center, and two pools, one of which is filled with saltwater.

Olive Boutique Hotel (55 Calle Aguadilla, 787/705-9994, www.oliveboutique-hotel.com, $250-330) is a small, all-suite boutique hotel designed in a rustic Mediterranean style. Ideal for couples, the hotel features a rooftop bar with a view of the Condado Lagoon and Sage Steak Loft on the first level. Rooms come with high-speed Internet, flat-screen TVs, and see-through rain showers. Some rooms have private terraces.

Built in 1958, ★ **La Concha Resort** (1077 Ave. Ashford, 787/721-7500, www.laconcha-resort.com, $269-299, $314-379 suite) is a sprawling, shimmering example of modernist architecture from the era. Accommodations are provided in standard guest rooms and suites with European-style kitchens in two towers, the Ocean Tower and the Suite Tower. Entertainment options include Casino del Mar, located in the lobby and open 24 hours a day, and Fifty Eight, a nightclub featuring DJs and dancing. Food and beverage service is provided by a lobby bar, coffee shop, poolside bar and grill, and Serafina, an Italian restaurant. Tee times can be arranged at the golf course on sister property Bahía Beach Resort in nearby Río Grande. Other amenities include multilevel swimming pools with waterfalls and a sandy beach with food and beverage service.

Located across the street from the beach, **Condado Palm Inn** (55 Ave. Condado, 787/721-9500, www.condadopalm.com, $229-249, $339-389 suite) is a Best Western Plus property with resort-like amenities, including a swimming pool with poolside services, a fitness center, concierge service, cocktail lounge, free continental breakfast, and two restaurants, including Nestle Toll House Café and Ropa Vieja Grill, a Cuban restaurant.

Chic **Serafina Beach Hotel** (1045 Ave. Ashford, 787/625-6000, www.serafinabeachhotel.com, $255-287) is a mid-century modern-inspired, 92-room beachfront boutique hotel with ocean and lagoon views. Accommodations include standard guest rooms, penthouse rooms, and terrace suites. Amenities include infinity pool, beach access, fitness room, flat-screen Smart TVs, PiñaCo lobby bar, and aMare Restaurant, serving a menu of seafood and Mediterranean dishes.

Minimalist decor provides the setting for the contemporary art on display in the common areas of the **AC Hotel** (1369 Ave. Ashford, 787/827-7280, www.marriott.com, $240-270, $300-340 suite). Accommodations are provided in standard guest rooms and suites, some with balconies. Amenities include high-speed Internet, flat-screen TVs, fitness center, rooftop pool, and multiple dining options, including a rooftop tapas bar.

For your standard corporate stay, **San Juan Marriott Resort @ Stellaris Casino** (1309 Ave. Ashford, 787/722-7000, www.marriott.com, $349-489) is a high-rise hotel on the ocean offering spectacular views. Amenities include six restaurants and lounges, a swimming pool, fitness room, and a casino.

★ **Condado Vanderbilt Hotel** (1055 Ave. Ashford, 787/721-5500, www.condadovanderbilt.com, $350-365) is perhaps the most elegant hotel in Puerto Rico. Originally opened in 1919 by Frederick William Vanderbilt, it was designed by the architects for Grand Central Station in New York City. The hotel closed in the '90s, but was restored and reopened in 2012. Accommodations are provided in the original Spanish Revival building from 1919, or two

---

1: Hotel El Convento in Viejo San Juan **2:** one of San Juan's many cats **3:** La Concha Resort in Condado

towers built in 2012. Options include standard guest rooms, one- and two-bedroom suites, and a presidential suite. Amenities include three pools, a spa and fitness center, and seven restaurants and lounges, including Restaurant 1919, a fine dining restaurant.

For the ultimate in luxury and glamour, **OLV 55 Hotel** (55 Calle Barranquitas, 787/705-8423, http://olvhotel.com, $484-909) brings a sleek, modern aesthetic to its suites, appointed with king- or queen-size beds, custom-made furnishings, leather wall treatments, and marble bathrooms. Some rooms have balconies and views of Condado Lagoon. The hotel is home to celebrity chef Mario Pagán's **Raya** Caribbean Asian restaurant, and **Arya Rooftop** (Tues.-Thurs. 5:30pm-10pm, Fri.-Sat. 5:30pm-11pm), a lounge with stunning views of the Condado Lagoon and where Pagán oversees brunch service (Sat.-Sun. 7am-4pm).

OCEAN PARK

Ocean Park is primarily a gated residential community located on a long stretch of beach free of high-rise developments. There has also been an influx of small guesthouses, making the neighborhood more self-contained for visitors who want a low-key getaway.

$100-150

It's at the far eastern end of Condado, several blocks from the nearest restaurant or shop, but **At Wind Chimes Inn** (1750 Ave. McLeary, 787/727-4153, www.atwindchimesboutique-hotel.com, $120-205, $250 suite) is just a block from the beach. Two Spanish-style haciendas have been combined to create a quaint, artful, 22-room boutique hotel. Each room has air-conditioning, TV, and wireless Internet; some rooms have kitchenettes. Rooms are tastefully decorated with high-quality furnishings and bright, cheery bedspreads. Amenities include a small pool and rooftop terrace.

Tucked inside the gated residential neighborhood of Ocean Park is **Dreamcatcher Guest House** (2009 Calle España, 787/455-8259, www.dreamcatcherguesthouse.com, $134-209, $207-299 suite), an 11-room guesthouse with a bohemian, Zen vibe. Decorated with India print wall hangings, candles, ornate mirrors, wind chimes, and dreamcatchers, each room is different. Some are suites, and all but one has a private bath. All rooms have air-conditioning and wireless Internet, but no TVs. Guests are welcome use the communal kitchen, but it's strictly vegetarian.

The modern minimalist design and orange exterior of **Dream Inn** (2009 Calle McLeary, 787/200-6729, www.dreaminnpr.com, $119-180) gives this 13-room guesthouse a tropical industrial vibe. Amenities include wireless Internet, refrigerators, air-conditioning, private bathrooms, and beach chairs. Some rooms have balconies. There's a small lap pool and a charming rooftop terrace where yoga classes are occasionally held.

Two side-by-side houses connected by a courtyard create **Tres Palmas Guest House** (2212 Park Blvd., 787/727-4617, www.trespalmasinn.com, $108-126, $140-162 suite), containing 18 modest guest rooms, offering possibly the most economical stay you can find this close to the beach in greater San Juan. Amenities include a tiny pool and a rooftop terrace with a hot tub overlooking the ocean, which is about 15 steps away. Rooms come with air-conditioning, satellite TV, wireless Internet, refrigerators, private entrances, and complimentary continental breakfast.

Hostería del Mar (1 Calle Tapia, 787/727-3302, www.lahosteriadelmar.com, $99-239) is a compact oceanfront hotel with a small lobby featuring a Polynesian-style bar and restaurant filled with warm woods and rattan furnishings. The wooden, top-hinged windows open out from the bottom, revealing the sand and sea just a few steps away. The restaurant, Uvva, serves traditional Puerto Rican and Mediterranean-inspired dishes daily from 8am-10pm. The small, basic guest rooms have air-conditioning, cable TV, and wireless

Internet. Online booking is unavailable; call or submit a reservation query on the website.

$150-250

Acacia Boutique Hotel (8 Calle Taft, 787/268-2803, www.acaciaboutiquehotel.com, $135-260) is a small property half a block from the beach, run by the folks at the nearby At Wind Chimes Inn. Modern rooms have air-conditioning and TVs; some have balconies. Petite Niche Bistro is a destination restaurant serving a well-executed eclectic menu.

Numero Uno Beach House (1 Santa Ana, 787/726-5010 or 866/726-5010, www.numerounobeachhouse.com, $249-394) is a small, well-maintained guesthouse with attentive service. There's no lobby to speak of, just a tiny reception office beside a petite black-bottomed pool. But the 11 compact rooms are elegantly and simply decorated with comfort in mind. Amenities include air-conditioning, wireless Internet, satellite TV, and mini refrigerators. There is one wheelchair-accessible room on the 1st floor. On-site is Numero Uno Beach Bar, open daily at 8am, and Kite Puerto Rico, a kiteboarding outfitter that offers lessons, as well as equipment rental and sales.

ISLA VERDE

When it comes to accommodations, Isla Verde is best known for its luxury resorts operated by major hotel chains, such as Intercontinental and Hilton. But there are also a handful of small, independent hotels.

$100-150

In a cheerful yellow faux hacienda-style building two blocks from the beach, **Hotel Villa del Sol** (4 Calle Rosa, 787/791-2600 or 787/791-1600, www.villadelsolpr.com, $100-130) has 24 units with air-conditioning, cable TV, and mini refrigerators. Some rooms are starkly furnished; others are a little nicer, and wheelchair-accessible options are available. Amenities include a tiny pool, restaurant, bar, free parking, and free wireless Internet in the common areas. Vias Car Rental service

is on-site. Online booking is not available; call or submit a reservation query on the website.

$150-250

Catering to business travelers and families, pet-friendly **Verdanza Hotel** (820 Calle Tartak, 855/222-5956, www.verdanzahotel.com, $168-188) is not located on the beach, but it's not a far walk. The 220-room hotel offers all the amenities visitors could want, including a swimming pool with food and beverage service, a children's play area, a business center, a fitness center, two restaurants, and a café.

If you want to stay in Isla Verde but you don't want to shell out for the high-end resorts, you can't go wrong with ★ **Tryp by Wyndham** (4820 Ave. Isla Verde, 787/728-1300, www.trypislaverde.com, $180-190, $210-299 suite). Although it is a corporate chain hotel, it has a boutique vibe and the service is friendly and attentive. Amenities include wireless Internet, large flat-screen HDTVs, a swimming pool, and Emigrante Gastrobar, an outstanding lounge and restaurant. It's hard to spot, but beach access is directly across the street at the end of a short, narrow path between high-rise buildings.

Mare St. Clair (6165 Ave. Isla Verde, 787/791-5151, www.marestclair.com, $189-381, $759 suite) is a beachfront tower that serves as both a timeshare property and a hotel. All rooms have kitchens and balconies or terraces. Amenities include a pool, game room, bar, and restaurant.

Over $250

Located across the street from the beach, **San Juan Water Beach Club Hotel** (2 Calle Tartak, 787/728-3666 or 888/265-6699, www.waterbeachhotel.com, $319-349, $379 suite) is a modern, high-design boutique hotel offering luxe accommodations for the young and trendy crowd. The hotel's 75 rooms come with air-conditioning, satellite TV, high-speed Internet, and pillow-top beds. Some rooms have balconies and ocean views. Water is the theme of this stark white-and-aqua property: Bubbles float in Lucite countertops at the reception desk, and water features abound. Mist Rooftop Bar + Grill is the place to go for lunch, Sunday brunch, and an evening of craft cocktails and techno music set against a gorgeous ocean view. Zest Puerto Rican Grill Room in the lobby serves local cuisine and sushi. Spend the day at the beach beneath one of the hotel's bright blue umbrellas and enjoy food and drink service.

Equally elegant is ★ **Hotel InterContinental San Juan Resort** (5961 Ave. Isla Verde, 787/791-6100, www.ichotelsgroup.com, $269-359, $404 suite), a classic, oceanside hotel built in 1963. The lobby features long, low archways, burnished wood accents, marble tile floors, and subdued lighting that casts a flattering warm glow. There are 398 rooms, including junior and executive suites, and each one features a curved balcony that creates an undulating effect reminiscent of a waterfall on the building exterior. The grounds are lushly landscaped around a free-form, lagoon-style pool featuring waterfalls and a swim-up bar. Hotel amenities include a spa, fitness center, business center, and bar. There are two restaurants, including Saki, which serves Asian fusion cuisine that incorporates tropical flavors.

After Hurricanes Irma and Maria, ★ **El San Juan Resort & Casino** (6063 Ave. Isla Verde, 787/791-1000 or 888/579-2632, www.elsanjuanresort.com, $345-491, $691-702 suite) underwent a $65 million renovation. The lobby has been restored to its original grandeur, featuring rose marble floors, hand-carved cherry mahogany woodwork, and a massive oval-shaped, hand-blown chandelier from Czechoslovakia. Built in the late 1950s by Pan Am Airlines, the sprawling 388-room resort is steeped in old-school luxury and consummate service. There are five restaurants, including Caña, serving traditional Puerto Rican cuisine with international flourishes, and Meat Market steakhouse. Brava is one of the hottest nightclubs in Isla Verde. There are also four pools, a spa, fitness center, tennis courts, a mini-mall of shops selling clothing, shoes, sunglasses, jewelry, and sundries, and a gorgeous stretch of beach with food and beverage service.

LOÍZA
Under $100

Nomada Urban Beach Hostel & Rooftop Camping (2062 Calle Loíza, 787/470-2328, http://nomadahostel.com, $36 dorm, $58-62 tent, $68-84 room) is a large, multilevel building with 13 private and semi-private rooms, a dormitory, and rooftop tents with mattresses. Bathrooms and showers are shared, and common areas include a kitchen, computer workstation, game room with a pool table, video games, foosball, books, and board games. All rooms have air-conditioning, but none are wheelchair-accessible.

Santurcia Hostel (353 Ave. de Diego, 787/585-1690, 787/378-2519, or 787/385-3599, santurciahostel.com, $35 dorm, $75 room) bills itself as a boutique hostel, featuring vibrant, modern decor and a rooftop bar, which hosts a variety of nighttime events, including movie screenings, DJs, and yoga. There are four dormitory rooms with lockers, three coed and one for women only. There's also a private room with one queen-size bed. Bathrooms and showers are shared. Communal spaces include a fully equipped kitchen, dining room, and living room. There's also free wireless Internet.

Conturce Hostel (1507 Calle Loíza, 787/520-8854, www.conturcehostel.com, $33 dorm) has seven dormitories, three coed, three for men, and one for women. All rooms have air-conditioning, lockers, mini refrigerators, and wireless Internet. Bathrooms and showers are shared. Common areas include a kitchen, dining room, and rooftop terrace.

MIRAMAR
$150-250

Hotel Miramar (606 Ave. Ponce de León, 877/647-2627, www.hotelmiramarpr.com, $170-189) is a modest high-rise hotel of 50 guest rooms featuring cable TV, air-conditioning, microwaves, mini refrigerators, and free wireless Internet in the rooms. Other amenities include a fitness center, business lounge, café, and rooftop terrace. Wheelchair-accessible rooms are available. A continental breakfast is included in the rate. **Hyatt House San Juan** (615 Ave. Fernandez Juncos, 787/977-5000, www.hyatt. com, $216-226, $231-246 suite) provides accommodations in standard guest rooms, or studios and suites with fully-equipped stainless steel kitchens. Some rooms have views of San Juan Bay. Amenities include an outdoor pool, fitness center, business center, wireless Internet, a full-service bar serving light fare, a self-serve food market, and a complimentary omelet bar.

Over $250

Rooms at the **Sheraton Puerto Rico Hotel & Casino** (200 Convention Blvd., 787/993-3500, www.marriott.com, $209-279, $942-1,308 suite) run the gamut from standard guest rooms to a variety of multiroom suites, each one featuring large flat-screen TVs with cable, high-speed Internet, and iPod docking station radio. Microwaves and mini refrigerators are available upon request. Amenities include a fitness center, full-service spa, a 4th-floor infinity pool with whirlpool tub, wading pool and sun deck, and a casino. There are six dining options, including District Lounge & Sushi Bar, Texas de Brazil steakhouse, and Metropol Cuban restaurant.

Ciqala Luxury Suites (752 Ave. Manuel Fernández Juncos, 787/998-1159, www.ciqalasuites.com, $245-350) is a 34-room hotel of standard rooms and suites with kitchenettes, wireless Internet, flat-screen TVs, a small rooftop pool, a fitness center, business center, and restaurant. Additional amenities include free parking and a full complimentary breakfast.

Transportation and Services

GETTING THERE
Air
Luis Muñoz Marín International Airport (SJU, Isla Verde, 787/791-4670 or 787/791-3840, www.aeropuertosju.com), located 14 kilometers (9 mi) east of San Juan, is a full-service airport with four terminals offering service on 20 airlines. More than 21,000 passengers pass through the airport every day. Amenities include luggage storage, ATM, restaurants, bars, shops, and the **San Juan Airport Hotel** (787/791-1248, http://airporthotelpr.com), which can be found in Terminal D on the second level. For transportation into the city, there are several car-rental agencies on the first level, where you can catch a taxi, bus, Uber, or hotel shuttle. From the airport, take Baldorioty de Castro Avenue west toward Isla Verde, Ocean Park, and Condado and into Viejo San Juan.

Airline ticket prices fluctuate throughout the year, but the cheapest rates can usually be secured during the off-season, May-September, which is the rainy season. Note that late summer through early fall is also hurricane season.

These major airlines service San Juan from the United States:

- **American Airlines** (800/433-7300, www. aa.com)

- **Delta Air Lines** (800/221-1212 or 800/325-1999, www.delta.com)

- **Frontier Airlines** (800/401-9000, www. flyfrontier)

- **JetBlue Airways** (800/538-2583, www. jetblue.com)

- **Southwest Airlines** (800/826-6667, www. southwest.com)

- **Spirit Airlines** (800/772-7117, www.spiritairlines.com)

- **United** (800/864-8331, www.united.com)

Regional airlines serving Puerto Rico and the Caribbean include:

- **Air Flamenco** (787/724-1818, www.airflamenco.net)
- **Air Sunshine** (800/327-8900, www.airsunshine.com)
- **Cape Air** (800/227-3247, www.airflamenco.net)
- **Vieques Air Link** (888/901-9247, www.viequesairlink.com)

For regional transportation throughout the island and the Caribbean, **Isla Grande Airport** (Aeropuerto de Isla Grande, SIG, end of Ave. Lindberg, Miramar, 787/729-8790) is a single runway airport served by three airlines. More than 100,000 travelers pass through the airport annually. Amenities are limited. Service is provided by:

- **Air Flamenco** (787/724-1818, www.airflamenco.net)
- **M&N Aviation** (720/979-0312, www.mandnaviation.com)
- **Vieques Air Link** (888/901-9247, www.viequesairlink.com)

Cruise Ship

San Juan is the second-largest port in the western hemisphere, and it is a port of call or point of origin for nearly two dozen cruise-ship lines. The cruise-ship docks are at the piers along Calle La Marina in Viejo San Juan.

Some of the most popular cruise-ship lines serving San Juan include:

- **Carnival Cruise Lines** (866/299-5698 or 800/327-9501, www.carnival.com)
- **Celebrity Cruises** (800/647-2251, 800/722-5941, or 800/280-3423, www.celebritycruises.com)
- **Holland America Line** (877/724-5425, www.hollandamerica.com)
- **Norwegian Cruise Line** (800/327-7030, www.ncl.com)

- **Princess Cruises** (800/774-6237 or 800/421-0522, www.princess.com)
- **Radisson Seven Seas Cruises** (877/505-5370 or 800/285-1835, www.rssc.com)
- **Royal Caribbean International** (866/562-7625, 800/327-6700, or 305/539-6000, www.royalcaribbean.com)

GETTING AROUND
Taxis and Ride-Hailing Services

Taxis are a common way to get around San Juan. In Viejo San Juan, there are **taxi stands** just south of Plaza de Colón at Calle Tetuán and Calle Recinto Sur, at the Sheraton Old San Juan, and by the cruise-ship piers. In Condado and Isla Verde, go to any major hotel to catch a taxi or call one on the phone. Licensed taxi services are well regulated in Puerto Rico. Operators include **San Juan Taxis** (877/288-8294, www.sanjuantaxis.com), **Metro Taxi** (787/945-5555), and **Rochdale Radio Taxi** (787/721-1900, www.taxiprrochdale.com).

Fares between the airport and key tourist areas have fixed rates. From the airport, the rates are $12 to Isla Verde; $17 to Condado, Ocean Park, Miramar, and Santurce; $21 to Viejo San Juan and the piers; and $17 to Isla Grande Airport and the Puerto Rico Convention Center. Additional charges include a $1 late-night fee and a $3 airport fee. There is a $1.50 gas surcharge, and each piece of luggage is $1. Metered fares are $3 minimum, $1.75 initial charge, and $0.10 every 19th of a mile. Customers pay all road tolls.

Uber (www.uber.com) is the only major ride-hailing service available in San Juan. Drivers can drop off departing passengers at the airport, but they cannot pick up arrivals.

Bus

The public transportation system has undergone some reduction in service in recent years due to budgetary constraints and hurricane damage. As a result, the San Juan public bus system, called **Autoridad Metropolitana de Autobuses (AMA)** (www.fortaleza.pr.gov) has experienced flux in its routes and

Day Trips from San Juan

Many surprising and delightful charms are just a short drive away from the city.

PIÑONES
(page 110)
Just east of San Juan, in the area known as **Piñones,** you can explore miles of primitive beach, bike the **Paseo Piñones** boardwalk, kayak in **Laguna de Piñones** or **Laguna La Torrecilla,** and dine on seafood, fritters, and *pinchos* at the kiosks and *chinchorros* at **Boca de Cangrejos.**

To get to Piñones, take PR 26 and PR 187 east for a total of 11 kilometers (7 mi) from San Juan. Get an early start on weekends and holidays or it could take you an hour or more to get there with traffic. Pack bug spray. Sand fleas are ferocious in the afternoons.

EL YUNQUE NATIONAL FOREST
(page 114)
On a visit to nearby **El Yunque National Forest,** stop at **La Coca Falls** and climb **Yokahu Tower.** Hike **Angelina Trail** (0.8 km/0.5 mi, 20 minutes), a moderate hike to a river, or **La Coca Trail** (2.9 km/1.8 mi, 1.5 hours), a challenging and steep hike that crosses two rivers and ends at a third river.

Allow 40 minutes to drive 40 kilometers (25 mi) east from San Juan along PR 26, PR 66, and PR 3 to El Yunque.

LUQUILLO
(page 124)
In the town of Luquillo, dip into the tranquil waters of palm-shaded **Playa Luquillo.** Or rent a surfboard and ride the waves at **La Pared.** When hunger strikes, hit the vendors at the **Luquillo** *kioskos* and dine on fritters and traditional Puerto Rican dishes, or try one of the new upscale kiosks serving creative Caribbean cuisine.

Allow 50 minutes to drive 45 kilometers (28 mi) east from San Juan along PR 26, PR 66, and PR 3 to Luquillo.

FAJARDO
(page 131)
Head to the bustling seaside town of Fajardo to spend the day swimming at **Balneario Seven Seas** or snorkeling around the small islands that make up **Reserva Natural La Cordillera.** Dine on grilled fish at **La Estación,** and take a nighttime kayak tour of **Laguna Grande,** the bioluminescent bay in **Reserva Natural Las Cabezas de San Juan.**

Allow an hour to drive 55 kilometers (34 mi) east from San Juan along PR 26, PR 66, and PR 3 to Fajardo.

frequency in recent years. The main terminal, **Covadonga Bus Terminal,** at the corner of Calle la Marina and Calle J. A. Corretjer in Viejo San Juan near the cruise-ship piers, is where you can theoretically get bus schedules and maps, but they may not be current.

Bus fare is typically $0.75. Exact change or a magnetic fare card, available at Covadonga Bus Terminal and Tren Urbano stations, are required. Express routes include **E10** (Sagrado Corazón Tren Urbano station to Covadonga Terminal in Viejo San Juan, Mon.-Fri. 5am-8pm) and **E40** (Piñero Tren Urbano station in Hato Rey to Luís Muñoz Marín International Airport, Mon.-Fri. 5am-8pm, Sat.-Sun. and holidays 6am-8pm). Local routes with multiple stops include **T21** (Sagrado Corazón Tren Urbano station to Covadonga Terminal in Viejo San Juan via Condado, Mon.-Fri. 5am-9pm, Sat. and holidays 6am-8pm) and **T5** (Covadonga Terminal in Viejo San Juan to Luís Muñoz Marín International Airport, Mon.-Fri. 5am-9pm, Sat. and holidays 6am-8pm). Bus stops are marked with green signs that say *"Parada,"* except in Viejo San Juan, where you have to catch the bus at Covadonga Bus Terminal. When waiting for a bus at a *parada,* it is necessary to wave to get the driver to stop.

Train

Tren Urbano (www.trenurbanoapp.com) is an automated rapid transit system serving San Juan, Guaynabo, Río Piedras, and Bayamón. There are 16 stations on the route, starting in San Juan at Sagrado Corazón near Hato Rey and ending in Bayamón. Many of the train stations sustained damage during Hurricane Maria, and efforts to repair them have been slow. Some elevators, escalators, and automated ticket entries may not be functioning, but riders are assured access and the trains are running. Designed to serve residential commuters, the train does not go to the airport, but it does connect with a bus at Sagrado Corazón station that provides express service to Luis Muñoz Marín International Airport. The train runs daily 5:20am-11:30pm. Fares are $1.50 for two hours, including transfers. Discounts are available for students and senior citizens. A Tren Urbano smartphone app helps riders navigate the system.

Ferry

AcuaExpreso Cataño (Calle Marina, Pier 2, Viejo San Juan, 787/729-8714 or 787/788-0940) provides ferry service between Viejo San Juan and Cataño, home of Casa Bacardí, for $0.50 each way. The 10-minute ride operates daily 6am-9:40pm. Frequency is every 30 minutes except Monday-Friday 6am-10am and 3:45pm-7pm, when they run every 15 minutes except on holidays.

Público

Públicos (aka *carros públicos* or *guaguas*) are privately owned, government regulated transport services that operate passenger vans along local and intercity routes in San Juan and around the island. This is a very slow but inexpensive way to see the island. *Públicos* typically wait in a town square until they fill to capacity with riders before departing for their destinations. The central terminal is **Terminal de Carros Publicos de Este** (164-166 Calle Arzuaga, San Juan, Mon.-Sat. 4am-6pm). Providers include **Blue Line** (787/765-7733) to Río Piedras, Aguadilla, Aguada, Moca, Isabela, and other areas; **Choferes Unidos de Ponce** (787/764-0540) to Ponce and other areas; **Lina Boricua** (787/765-1908) to Lares, Ponce, Jayuya, Utuado, San Sebastián, and other areas; **Linea Caborrojeña** (787/723-9155) to Cabo Rojo, San Germán, and other areas; **Linea Sultana** (787/765-9377) to Mayagüez and other areas; and **Terminal de Transportación Pública** (787/250-0717) to Fajardo and other areas.

Car

Driving a car in San Juan can be a nerve-rattling experience for drivers not accustomed to inner-city traffic. The sheer volume of cars on the road at any given time can be daunting, creating a slow slog of traffic in congested areas throughout San Juan and along the northern coast. But renting a car is one of the best ways to explore the city and its outlying areas. In addition to most major car-rental agencies, several local companies provide comparable services.

Charlie Car Rental (6050 Ave. Isla Verde, Isla Verde, 800/289-1227 or 787/728-2418 and 1110 Ave. Ashford, across from La Concha hotel, 800/289-1227 or 787/728-6525, www.charliecars.com) is a cheap, reliable alternative to the national agencies. Drivers must be at least 21, and those younger than 25 must pay an additional $10 per day surcharge. Free pickup and drop-off at the airport, hotels, and cruise-ship port is available. There are also locations in Caguas, Aguadilla, and Rincón. Or try **Vias Car Rental** (Hotel Villa del Sol, 4 Calle Rosa, Isla Verde, 787/796-6404, www.facebook.com/viascarrental), with additional locations in Dorado and Humacao.

Bicycle

San Juan has become decidedly more bicycle friendly than it once was. Bike lanes and signage are prevalent, especially in tourist areas such as Condado, Ocean Park, and Isla Verde. There are bike rental outfitters, including **San Juan Bike Rental** (787/554-2453, www.sanjuanbikerentals.com, Mon.-Fri. 7am-6pm, Sat. 9am-6pm, from $22.50 for four hours), a mobile service that delivers road, mountain, hybrid, and cruiser bikes anywhere in Viejo San Juan, Condado, Ocean Park, Isla Verde, and Miramar.

SERVICES
Tourist Information

Puerto Rico Tourism Company (La Princesa, 2 Paseo Princesa, Viejo San Juan, 787/721-2400, www.seepuertorico.com, daily 9am-5:30pm) is located across the street from Pier 1.

Emergency and Medical Services

The central hospital serving San Juan's tourist areas is **Ashford Presbyterian Community Hospital** (1451 Ave. Ashford, Condado, 787/721-2160, www.presbypr.com), which is commonly referred to as El Presby. The emergency room is open 24 hours a day. Dial **911** in case of emergency to contact the police, fire department, or ambulance.

There are several chain pharmacies including **Walgreens** (1130 Ave. Ashford, Condado, 787/725-1510, www.walgreens.com) and **CVS** (1307 Ave. Ashford, Condado, 787/289-2510, and 105 Gilberto de Concepcíon, Viejo San Juan, 787/725-2500, www.cvs.com), as well as

independent pharmacies such as **Puerto Rico Drug Co.** (157 Calle San Francisco, Viejo San Juan, 787/725-2202).

Newspapers and Magazines

Published five days a week, the *San Juan Star* (www.sanjuanweeklypr.com) is San Juan's only English language newspaper, featuring locally produced content and wire stories from the *New York Times*. *The Weekly Journal* (www.theweeklyjournal.com) is an online English-language newspaper with a weekly print edition that specializes in investigative reporting. *El Nuevo Día* (www.endi.com) is the island-wide Spanish-language daily newspaper, with an English version online only.

The free bimonthly *Qué Pasa?* (www.quepasapr.com) is an English language travel magazine published by the Puerto Rico Tourism Company. The magazine's current issue is available online, and the publishing company's website is an exhaustive source of information about the entire island.

Banks and ATMs

There is no shortage of banks and ATMs in San Juan, including **Banco Popular** (206 Calle Tetuán, Viejo San Juan, 787/725-2636, www.popular.com) and **First Bank of Puerto Rico** (1476 Ave. Ashford, Condado, 787/268-1661, www.1firstbank.com).

Post Offices and Laundry Services

U.S. Post Office facilities are numerous, including locations in Viejo San Juan (100 Centro Gubernamental, 787/726-8008) and Condado (68 Ave. Condado, 787/400-6130).

Self-service laundries are available at **Laundromat Sol** (201 Calle Sol, Viejo San Juan, 939/262-6656, http://laundromat-sol.business.site, Mon.-Sat. 10am-6pm) and **Lavandería PR** (2002 Calle Loíza, 939/204-5377, www.lavanderiapr.com, daily 8am-9pm).

El Yunque and the East Coast

Puerto Rico's east coast is rich in natural won-ders, making it the most popular destination for day-trippers from San Juan.

Less than an hour's drive from the island's capital are three quintessential Puerto Rican sights: El Yunque National Forest, Playa Luquillo, and Bosque Estatal de Piñones, all on the north end of the east coast. Farther east is Fajardo, the island's boating center, renowned for its water activities and the bioluminescent lagoon Laguna Grande, and Ceiba, where visitors going to Vieques or Culebra can catch a plane or ferry.

The southern side of the east coast is less developed and lacks the big-draw tourist attractions found farther north, but its sleepy towns

Highlights

Look for ★ to find recommended sights, activities, dining, and lodging.

★ **Bosque Estatal de Piñones:** This untouched parcel of natural beauty features several long stretches of **wilderness beach,** salt flats, mangroves, lagoons, and tropical forest (page 111).

★ **Drive or hike through El Yunque National Forest:** The 28,000-acre reserve encompasses a rainforest, hiking trails, observation towers, waterfalls, and natural pools (page 114).

★ **Playa Luquillo:** The main island's most beautiful beach, formally known as **Balneario La Monserrate,** features gentle waters, a wide crescent-shaped strip of sand, and a palm grove (page 125).

★ **Sample regional cuisine at the Kioskos de Luquillo:** Dine on fritters, fresh seafood, mofongo, and more at some of the 50-plus food vendors that line the street at this destination dining spot (page 127).

★ **Kayak through Laguna Grande:** This **bioluminescent** lagoon glows at night and is best seen by kayak (page 131).

and beaches offer a quiet getaway for those wanting to escape the bustle and crowds.

The east coast is also home to several spectacular resorts, including St. Regis Bahía Beach Resort in Río Grande and Palmas del Mar in Humacao, as well as several luxury health spas and world-class golf courses.

There are two officially designated scenic drives in the east coast. The *Ruta Flamboyan* (along PR 30 from PR 52 to Humacao) affords a lovely view of the spectacular *flamboyan* trees that bloom throughout the summer. These huge trees, also known as royal poinciana, have a broad, umbrella-shaped canopy that blooms a brilliant orange-red from June to early August. *Ruta Coqui* doesn't necessarily get you closer to its namesake, the coqui tree frog, but the route (along PR 3 from San Juan to Humacao) passes by the east coast's most popular attractions—Playa Luquillo and El Yunque—and the town of Fajardo.

PLANNING YOUR TIME

Three of the east coast's most spectacular natural sights—Piñones, El Yunque, and Playa Luquillo—are located within 50 kilometers (30 mi) of San Juan, making them easy day trips for short-term visitors. Drive-by tourists could check out each one in a day, but a full day at each attraction is recommended. Also, traffic can be heavy, especially on weekends and holidays and during rush hour on weekdays, so travel can be slow and frustrating if you try to rush it.

When it comes to natural treasures, **El Yunque National Forest** is Puerto Rico's shining jewel. One of the world's most accessible rainforests, it offers hours of hiking, swimming, and bird-watching in a lush, tropical

setting. It's located 45 kilometers (28 mi) east of San Juan on PR 3 to PR 191. It takes about 30 minutes to drive, but can take 45 minutes to an hour on weekends and holidays.

Coming in a close second as Puerto Rico's most popular attraction is **Playa Luquillo,** officially named **Balneario La Monserrate.** This is what picture postcards are made of: a long crescent of pristine sand shaded by a thick grove of palm trees and gently lapped by the Atlantic Ocean. Located 50 kilometers (31 mi) east of San Juan, Playa Luquillo is off PR 3 at PR 193. Allow 40 minutes to get there from San Juan, and up to an hour on weekends and holidays.

If you're pressed for time, Luquillo and El Yunque are 8 kilometers (5 mi) apart, a 10-minute drive on PR 3, so they can easily be visited in the same day.

Bosque Estatal de Piñones, one of the most beautiful stretches of wilderness coastline on the island, is 15 kilometers (9 mi) east of San Juan, about a 20-minute drive on PR 26 to PR 187 during the middle of a weekday. But on weekends and holidays, it could take an hour or more due to the volume of traffic. Getting there before 10am is recommended. It's easy to spend a whole day here hiking or biking through the mangrove forest along a bike path, kayaking through its lagoons, and swimming in the Atlantic surf beside palm-lined beaches.

Spending at least one night in Fajardo is recommended because its bioluminescent lagoon, **Laguna Grande,** must be experienced after dark. The journey is 65 kilometers (40 mi) east of San Juan from PR 26 to PR 3 to PR 193. The drive takes about an hour, but allow an extra 15 minutes on holidays and weekends.

Previous: El Yunque National Forest; Yokahu Tower in El Yunque; The New Reef restaurant in Piñones.

El Yunque and the East Coast

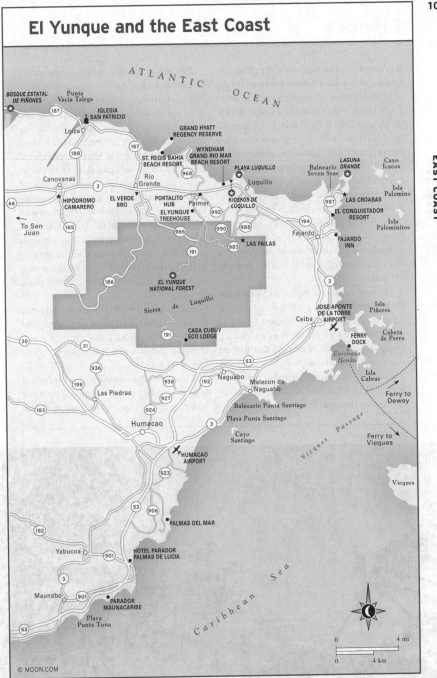

ATLANTIC OCEAN

BOSQUE ESTATAL DE PIÑONES
Punta Vacia Talega
IGLESIA SAN PATRICIO
187
Loiza
188
GRAND HYATT REGENCY RESERVE
187
ST. REGIS BAHIA BEACH RESORT
WYNDHAM GRAND RIO MAR BEACH RESORT
968
PLAYA LUQUILLO
Balneario Seven Seas
LAGUNA GRANDE
Cayo Icacos
Canovanas
3
Río Grande
Luquillo
Isla Palomino
66
HIPÓDROMO CAMARERO
EL VERDE BBQ
PORTALITO HUB
Palmer
KIOSKOS DE LUQUILLO
987
LAS CROABAS
To San Juan
185
EL YUNQUE TREEHOUSE
992
990
988
EL CONQUISTADOR RESORT
Isla Palominitos
966
983
LAS PAILAS
194
Fajardo
FAJARDO INN
191
EL YUNQUE NATIONAL FOREST
186
Sierra de Luquillo
3
JOSE APONTE DE LA TORRE AIRPORT
Ceiba
Isla Piñeros
FERRY DOCK
Cabeza de Perro
191
CASA CUBUY ECO LODGE
Ensenada Honda
30
31
53
Isla Cabras
936
938
192
Naguabo
Ferry to Dewey
198
Las Piedras
927
Malecon de Naguabo
924
Balneario Punta Santiago
183
Humacao
3
Playa Punta Santiago
Vieques Passage
Ferry to Vieques
Cayo Santiago
HUMACAO AIRPORT
923
Vieques
53
906
PALMAS DEL MAR
182
Yabucoa
901
HOTEL PARADOR PALMAS DE LUCIA
Maunabo
901
3
PARADOR MAUNACARIBE
Caribbean Sea
53
Playa Punta Tuna

0   4 mi
0   4 km

© MOON.COM

Piñones

It's remarkable that just east of the glitzy metropolis of San Juan is one of the most beautiful and pristine wilderness areas in all of Puerto Rico. Piñones is not a town; there is no plaza or city center. It is miles of undeveloped beach backed by palm groves, mangrove forests, canals, and lagoons. Running through it is PR 187, a narrow roadway lined with *kioskos* and *chinchorros* serving up fresh fritters, many of them cooked over open flame, as well as a wide variety of fish and other seafood. Tucked between the thick clusters of palms along the coastal side of the road are unmarked sandy cuts in the brush where you can park and walk over the dunes down to the water.

Much of Piñones is protected by **Bosque Estatal de Piñones,** a 1,560-acre forest reserve that features 11 kilometers (7 mi) of wooden boardwalk for walking and biking along the coastline. **Boca de Cangrejos** at the western entrance to Piñones features a small private marina, a place to rent bikes and kayaks, and a dense concentration of casual seafood restaurants.

Piñones is located in the municipality of **Loíza,** a tight-knit community rich in African-Caribbean history and culture. If you drive eastward along PR 187 through Piñones, you will arrive at the city center of Loíza. The town was originally settled by freed Yoruba enslaved people from Nigeria, who were brought over by the Spanish to work the island's sugar and coffee plantations. One of the island's most festive Carnaval celebrations takes place in Loíza. **Fiestas Tradicionales de Santiago Apóstol** (St. James Carnival) is a week-long celebration in late July with a complex history that dates to the Spanish Inquisition and is feted with parades, music, dance, food, and elaborately costumed street theater.

Loíza is also the heart of *bomba* and *plena* music, traditional forms of drumming and dancing rooted in African culture. Some of the most celebrated artists of *bomba* and *plena* are from Loíza.

Accommodations in this region are limited to a few privately owned vacation rentals and home shares in Loíza, and dining options are

Paseo Piñones

best in Piñones, which has a dizzying array of terrific roadside food kiosks and several decent restaurants specializing in seafood.

SIGHTS

★ Bosque Estatal de Piñones

There's no other place in Puerto Rico like the spectacular **Bosque Estatal de Piñones** (along PR 187 between San Juan and Loíza, 787/999-2200, ext. 5422, 5156, or 5120, office Mon.-Fri. 7:30am-4pm). Stretching from the eastern tip of Isla Verde, San Juan, to the town of Loíza, this pristine reserve is a natural wonderland of deserted beaches; mangrove, pine, and palm forests; sand dunes; coral reefs; bays; salt flats; and lagoons. An important part of the island ecosystem, Piñones is home to 46 species of birds, including a variety of herons and pelicans.

Boca de Cangrejos

Boca de Cangrejos (5 km/3 mi east of the Luis Muñoz Marín International Airport in San Juan, across PR 187 from Cangrejo Yacht Club), also known as **Punta Cangrejos,** is the gateway to Piñones from San Juan. Venturing into Boca de Cangrejos for the first time can be a daunting experience, especially on weekends and holidays when it is a chaotic tangle of automobile traffic and pedestrians. People flock here to eat at their favorite seafood restaurant or kiosk, of which there are dozens. This is some of the best and cheapest local food you'll find on the island.

RECREATION

Just past Boca de Cangrejos is **Aviones,** a popular place for **surfing.** The best area for **swimming** is around kilometer 9, where the reef recedes from the beach. Another option for a good swimming spot is **Vacia Talega,** a small, unmarked crescent beach visible from the road on PR 187 just before you cross the river into Loíza. It has a small, sandy parking

lot but no facilities. This is also a good **fishing** spot.

Another major draw for Piñones is the **Paseo Piñones Bike Path,** an 11-kilometer (7-mi) system of paved trails and boardwalks, which provides an excellent way to explore the forest.

Venture away from the coast into the forest's interior and you encounter two lagoons, **Laguna de Piñones** and **Laguna la Torrecilla.** The best way to explore these rich mangrove ecosystems is by **kayak.** To reach the launch site, turn inland off PR 187 at kilometer 9 and follow the sign pointing to the Bosque Estatal de Piñones office. Bikes and kayaks are available for rent at **Copí** (PR 187, Boca de Cangrejos, 787/253-9707, daily 9am-5pm).

Cangrejos Yacht Club (PR 187, Boca de Cangrejos, 787/791-1015, www.cangrejosyachtclub.com) is a small private marina with eight docks and 200 slips with a 50-foot capacity. There is a restaurant, pool, and a fueling station.

Fishing

Caribbean Outfitters (5900 Avenida Isla Verde, 787/641-1469, www.facebook.com/www.fishinginpuertorico) offers fishing and fly-fishing charters throughout Puerto Rico, Vieques, Culebra, the Dominican Republic, and St. Thomas with Captain Omar. Three-quarter-day kayak fishing trips are $600 for one person, $750 for two, including gear and bait. Light tackle fishing ventures start at $350 per person for a half day and $450 for three-quarters of a day. Deep-sea fishing starts at $575 for a half day, $825 for three-quarters of a day, and $1,150 for a full day. Stay two nights at **Tarpon Nest Lodge** (PR 187, km 5.6, Loíza, 787/640-6848 or 787/783-7227, www.tarponnest.com) and enjoy a light tackle fishing venture ($775 half-day, $875 three-quarter day) or deep-sea fishing ($687 half-day, $787 three-quarter day). Prices include accommodations.

Magic Tarpon (Cangrejos Yacht Club, 787/644-1444, www.puertoricomagictarpon.

com) offers half-day tarpon and fly-fishing charters for $330-460 for 1-4 people.

Rental Gear and Outfitters

Copí (PR 187, Punta Cangrejos, 787/253-9707, daily 9am-5pm) rents kayaks for $15 per person per hour, and a variety of bicycles, including children's bikes and tandem bikes, for $10 an hour. Traveling east on PR 187 from San Juan toward Piñones, turn right immediately after the Cangrejos Yacht Club and look for El Faro restaurant. Copí is next door.

Caribbean Surf School (PR 187, km 6.0, Playa Aviones, 787/637-8263, www.caribbeansurfpr.com, daily 7am-10pm) offers surfboard rentals, surf tours ($30-40 per day), and surf lessons for all ages, both private and groups.

ENTERTAINMENT AND EVENTS

Boca de Cangrejos (5 km/3 mi east of the Luis Muñoz Marín International Airport in San Juan, across PR 187 from Cangrejo Yacht Club) is a sandy patch of beachfront bars, restaurants, clubs, and food kiosks. Since this is also a popular weekend beach spot, the party tends to start early and lasts late into the night. The best way to get to Boca de Cangrejos from San Juan is to drive or take a taxi, although you'll have to call one to pick you up when you're ready to leave. If you drive, be sure not to leave anything of value visible in the car; break-ins are not uncommon.

Balcon del Zumbador (PR 187, km 6.2, no phone, Wed.-Sat. 3pm-midnight) is a casual, authentic beachside bar hosting concerts by top old-school salsa artists and bands. You can also enjoy the Afro-Caribbean sights and sounds of drummers and dancers performing *bomba* and *plena* music some nights.

Fiestas Tradicionales de Santiago Apóstol (St. James Carnival) is one of Puerto Rico's liveliest and most colorful festivals, spanning about six days around July 25. Based in Plaza de Recreo de Loíza, the festival features lots of costumed parades, dances, street pageants, concerts, and traditional food vendors. Ostensibly it's a celebration of the town's patron saint, but religion takes a backseat to this raucous street party, which has origins in 13th-century Spain but is heavily influenced by African traditions. At the center of the celebration is a street pageant in which costumed caballeros (Spanish knights), masked *vejigantes* (Moors), and *locas* (trickster men dressed as old women) reenact Spain's defeat of the Moors. The colorful *vejigante* mask, made from coconut shell, wire, and papier-mâché and featuring protruding horns, has become a highly collectible, iconic symbol of the festival and Puerto Rico as a whole, and there are several local artisans in the area who produce them. St. James Carnival is also a prime place to revel in the African-influenced *bomba* music, which is performed late into the night.

SHOPPING

Artesanías Castor Ayala (PR 187, km 23.5, 787/564-6403, daily 10am-6pm) is located in a brightly colored, traditional wooden criolla house belonging to the Ayala family of renowned *vejigante* mask-makers. Inside is a modest display of family memorabilia and a few masks for sale ($30-75).

Across the street in a two-story house on a side street is **Estudio de Arte Lind** (PR 187, km 23.5, Loíza, 787/876-1494, http://samuellind.artistwebsites.com, Tues.-Sun. 9:30am-5:30pm), which is open to the public for the sale of paintings, prints, and sculptures by artist Samuel Lind, who captures images from island life in bright, tropical colors.

FOOD

At first glance, **Boca de Cangrejos** (just east of the Luis Muñoz Marín International Airport in San Juan and the Cangrejo Yacht Club) looks like a shantytown of wooden shacks and concrete sheds, but it contains some of the best and cheapest local food you'll find, from stuffed fritters to all varieties of seafood. Walk from kiosk to kiosk and try a little bit of everything. Many items cost only $1. Expect crowds and a party atmosphere on weekends and holidays. Continue east along PR 187 and encounter scores of *kioskos, chinchorros,* and bars. Some people caution against venturing here at night, but it can be a fun, adventurous immersion into the local scene if you keep your wits about you.

Choosing the best option from the scores of restaurants and fry shacks in Piñones isn't easy, but here's a tip: Skip establishments where the food is sitting under a heat lamp in a glass box and find a place where the cooks are making it while you wait.

★ **Donde Olga's** (PR 187, km 5.0, 787/791-6900, fry shack and bar Sun.-Thurs. 11am-midnight, Fri.-Sat. 11am-3am; dining room Mon.-Wed. 11:30am-3pm and 6:30pm-9:45pm, Thurs.-Sun. 11:30am-9:45pm, $2-26) is just such a place. The large, open-air dining area is located right beside the outdoor kitchen, where you can watch the cooks roll up *alcapurrias* in sea grape leaves and fry them in huge kettles over an open fire. Get in line and order your selection of fritters at the walk-up bar, where you can also get super-cold cans of Medalla beer. And don't forget to douse your piping hot goodies with a squirt or two from the spicy bottles of *pique* that dot the communal tables. If you want table service and a proper meal, go inside the dining room,

where you can order grouper casserole, paella, and lamb chops. If you're driving in from San Juan, pass the heart of Boca de Cangrejos and stay on PR 187. In a short while, you'll find Donde Olga's on the right.

One of the more pleasant places to dine in Piñones, **The New Reef** (Boca de Cangrejos, PR 187, 787/646-9933, Mon.-Thurs. noon-11pm, Fri.-Sun. 11am-2am, $12-36) features a large wooden deck with tables shaded by umbrellas right on the water, with a view of Isla Verde. Dine on a variety of fritters, as well as seafood, mofongo, and paella. There's also a large rustic bar inside.

Mi Casita Seafood (PR 187, km. 5, 787/971-1481, Mon. and Thurs.-Sat. 10am-1am, Tue.-Wed. and Sun. 10am-midnight, $10-25) serves fresh snapper, mahi-mahi, conch, lobster, and octopus in a super casual, open-air restaurant with full bar that gets hopping late at night.

El K'rajo Beach Bar (PR 187, km 8.3, 787/354-5977, ww.facebook.com/ ElKrajobeachbar, Fri.-Sun. noon-9pm, $6-12) is a fun little watering hole on a remote stretch of beach, featuring a playful pirate theme, complete with rooftop deck tricked out like a pirate's ship. This is the place to kick back in the sun with a piña colada and dine on ribs,

Donde Olga's in Piñones

ceviche, and *pinchos*. It was featured on the TV show *Bar Rescue* after it nearly closed following Hurricane Maria.

ACCOMMODATIONS

The best option for accommodations in Loíza and Piñones is a **vacation apartment rental** or **home share** in one of the many modern, gated condominium developments that have cropped up. Find listings via VRBO (www.vrbo.com) and Airbnb (www.airbnb. com).

TRANSPORTATION AND SERVICES

The best option for exploring Piñones is to drive there. Piñones is 20 kilometers (12 mi) east of San Juan. Take PR 26 east to PR 187 east. Loíza is 40 kilometers (25 mi) east of San Juan. Take PR 26 east to PR 66 east to PR 188 north. Traffic can be congested on this route, especially weekends and holidays. Expect the drive to take at least 30 minutes and possibly as long as 90 minutes. Be sure to lock your car, avoid parking in remote areas, and don't leave anything of value visible inside.

Bus service from Santurce and Isla Verde is available on bus D45.

Juan Carlos Transportation (787/876-3628 or 787/374-1056, Mon.-Fri. 8am-5pm) offers taxi service and tours around Loíza. For 24-hour service, call 787/467-1222.

For health and beauty needs, there is a **Walgreens** (Calle 1 at Calle 3, Loíza, 787/256-2626). Banking services are available at **Banco Popular** (65 Calle San Patricio, Loíza, 787/876-3535, www.bancopopular. com), and there is a **post office** (64 Calle San Patricio, Ste. 1) in town.

Río Grande and El Yunque

Although its city center doesn't hold much appeal for visitors, Río Grande boasts some of Puerto Rico's most popular attractions: the gateway to El Yunque National Forest and a trio of celebrated golf courses. The area is also home to several exclusive resorts, and it's all conveniently located just a half-hour drive east from the San Juan airport.

Río Grande is a convenient stop on the way to El Yunque, Playa Luquillo, or Fajardo. Visitors to Río Grande tend to ensconce themselves at a luxury resort and indulge in a host of amenities, including spa services, pool-side cabanas, and upscale restaurants.

In the tiny community of **Palmer**, located at the base of El Yunque, a couple of shops and restaurants have sprung up around El Yunque Portalito Hub, a temporary information center for the rainforest.

TOP EXPERIENCE

★ EL YUNQUE NATIONAL FOREST

El Yunque National Forest (787/888-1880, www.fs.usda.gov/elyunque) is a spectacular natural preserve and the crown jewel of Puerto Rico's natural treasures. The name El Yunque refers to the forest's second-highest peak (3,469 ft.). It is the only tropical forest in the U.S. National Forest System. This ecologically diverse place is home to hundreds of native plant and animal species. Some of the only virgin forest remaining on the island is located within El Yunque.

The name El Yunque is believed to be a Spanish derivation of the Taíno Indian name for the area, Yuke ("white earth"). The name comes from the clouds that often encase the mountaintops. The Taíno believed that El Yunque was a sacred place and home to their gods. They visited the forest to harvest trees, vines, and palm fronds to make canoes, baskets, and roofing thatch, and to gather its abundant fruits, roots, and medicinal plants. Religious ceremonies and rituals were often held here, and petroglyphs can be found carved into rocks and boulders throughout the forest.

Hurricane Recovery

In 2017 Hurricanes Irma and Maria severely damaged much of El Yunque, shuttering the park for a year and half. Following an extensive recovery effort led by the U.S. Forest Service, the park reopened in 2019, though restoration work will continue for some time. Most notably, the architecturally striking **El Portal Forest Center** closed for repairs; it's expected to reopen in 2021. For now, visitors can go to **Portalito Hub** in the town of Palmer to pick up maps and brochures, use restroom facilities, and stock up on water.

Immediately after the storms ended, the vegetation on El Yunque began replenishing itself. While much of its old growth—some of it 1,000 years old—is gone, the environment has returned to its lush, green state. One of the unexpected benefits of the sparser tree canopy is the dazzling views of the Atlantic Ocean from the mountainside.

Flora

More than 240 inches of rain—100 billion gallons!—fall annually in the forest, making it a rich habitat for moisture-loving flora and fauna. It is home to more than 1,000 plant species, including 50 types of orchids, 150 ferns, and 240 species of trees, 23 of which are endemic only to El Yunque.

El Yunque National Forest is located in the Sierra de Luquillo, and its mountains range in height from 600 feet to more than 3,500 feet above sea level. The area encompasses four distinct forests. Most of it is *tabonuco forest,* found in areas up to 2,000 feet above sea level. This is the most dramatic part of the

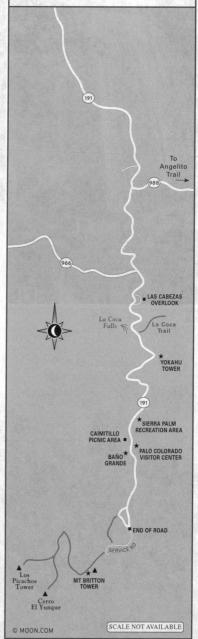

El Yunque National Forest

forest and site of the true rainforest. The dominant tree species is the *tabonuco*, which grows up to 125 feet in height and is distinguished by its huge dark-green canopy and straight trunk, which has a smooth whitish bark.

The **sierra palm forest** is found along steep slopes and near rivers and creeks more than 1,500 feet above sea level. Its dominant tree, the sierra palm, is identified by the thick skirt of exposed roots around its base, which is an adaptation that allows it to thrive in wet soil. The *palo colorado* **forest** is found in valleys and slopes at an altitude between 2,000 and 3,000 feet. The dominant tree is the *palo colorado*, also known as swamp cyrilla, characterized by its thick twisted trunk and red bark.

On the uppermost peaks of El Yunque, between 2,500 and 3,500 feet above sea level, is the **cloud forest**, also known as the dwarf forest. This is an otherworldly environment where constant wind and moisture have stunted and twisted the dense vegetation. Roots snake across the windswept ground in thick tangles, and the trees, which don't exceed 12 feet in height, are covered with moss and algae. Here you also find many species of ferns and bromeliads, which bloom with brilliant red flowers. The air is cool, and visibility is often obscured by misty cloud covering.

Fauna

The majority of El Yunque's wildlife falls into three categories: **birds, reptiles,** and **amphibians.** There are more than 50 species of birds in the forest; the rarest and most beloved is the **Puerto Rican parrot,** which is classified as endangered. Today there are about 35 Puerto Rican parrots living in El Yunque. You're highly unlikely to spot one, but just in case, keep your eyes peeled for a foot-long, bright green Amazon parrot with blue wing tips, white eye rings, and a red band above its beak. When in flight, it emits a repetitive call that sounds like a bugle.

Other species of birds found in El Yunque include the sharp-shinned hawk, the broad-winged hawk, the bananaquit, the Puerto Rican tody, the red-legged thrush, the Puerto Rican lizard-cuckoo, the green mango, the Puerto Rican emerald, the Puerto Rican woodpecker, the elfin-woods warbler, the Puerto Rican bullfinch, and the stripe-headed tanager.

Even more beloved than the Puerto Rican parrot is the tiny **coqui tree frog.** There are 16 varieties of the species on the island, 13 of which live in El Yunque. You're only slightly more likely to see a coqui than a Puerto Rican parrot, but you're sure to hear its distinctive "co-QUI" call, particularly after a rain or at dusk. Even more elusive is the **Puerto Rican boa,** a nonpoisonous snake that reaches lengths exceeding six feet.

Probably the most likely creature to be spotted in El Yunque is one of its many species of lizards. They are as common as ants at a picnic. The large **Puerto Rican giant green lizard,** which can grow as big as a cat, is commonly found along the limestone hills, and the smaller **anoli,** of which there are eight species, are ubiquitous.

The only mammals native to Puerto Rico are **bats,** of which there are 11 species in El Yunque. Rats and mongooses have been introduced to the island and now live in the forest. The rats were inadvertently brought over on trade ships and thrived on the island's sugar plantations. The mongooses were imported in a misguided attempt to control the rat population. They can be aggressive, so give them a wide berth if you encounter them.

Orientation

The main thoroughfare through El Yunque is **PR 191.** The road once bisected the forest from north to south, but recurrent landslides convinced engineers that the soil was too unstable to sustain a roadway at the forest's highest peaks. The forest is still accessible from the north and south on PR 191, but its midsection has been permanently closed.

Most visitors to El Yunque drive in from

1: La Coca Falls in El Yunque National Forest **2:** hikers on a trail in El Yunque **3:** Yokahu Tower

One Day in El Yunque

The beaches may be Puerto Rico's most popular attraction, but to truly appreciate the island's charms, you need to experience the unique beauty of the tropical rainforest. One of the things that makes El Yunque unique is its accessibility. All of its trailheads and observation areas are located along PR 191, which snakes 13 kilometers (8 mi) from the base at Portalito Hub to less than 2 kilometers (1 mi) from the summit.

PLANNING YOUR TIME

It's possible to take a drive-by tour of El Yunque in about an hour, but spending the day immersed in this natural wonderland is recommended. To ensure you get the most out of your adventure, make sure you're prepared. Wear sturdy, closed-toe shoes with good tread. Trails can be rocky and slippery. Bring light rain gear and plenty of water, as well as sunscreen and bug spray.

Allow at least five hours to complete the hike to the **summit of El Yunque,** more if you take the short spur to **Mount Britton,** an observation tower that affords views of both the Atlantic Ocean and Caribbean Sea.

Be sure to be back down at the base of the mountain by 6pm when the park gates at Coca Falls close.

MORNING

Fuel up on bacon waffles or frittata at **Lluvia,** preferably while sitting on the back patio where you can enjoy the view of El Yunque. Then stroll across the street to **Portalito Hub,** the National Forest Service visitors center, to pick up a map, see the educational exhibits, and check on current conditions.

Begin your tour of the park by driving 8 kilometers (5 mi) south on PR 191 just past the park gate (opens daily at 7:30am) to km 8.1 where you can view **Coca Falls,** visible from the road. The dramatic waterfall is a popular spot to take pictures, so proceed with caution. There is often a tangle of traffic here and lots of people milling about.

Proceed to drive up PR 191 a short distance to **Yokahu Tower** and climb up the spiral steps of the 69-foot observation tower for a 360-degree view of the island.

Continue driving about 3 kilometers (2 mi) to the **Palo Colorado Information Center,** an outpost of Portalito Hub. From here you can follow the signs on a short, 2-minute walk to **Baño Grande,** a picturesque stone pool with an arched bridge constructed in the 1930s. (Swimming is prohibited.)

AFTERNOON

Grab some snacks from the Palo Colorado Information Center, then drive south for 1.3 kilometers (0.8 mi) to the closed gate and park. Look for the Mount Britton trailhead on the right. The strenuous 45-minute hike on **Mount Britton Trail** ends with 360-degree views from high up on El Yunque. If you have time, continue another hour to the **summit of El Yunque.** Allow 4-5 hours for this round-trip hike.

EVENING

If you're famished after all that hiking, return to Palmer via PR 191, then drive 5 kilometers (3 mi) east on PR 3 to the **Kioskos de Luquillo,** where more than 50 food vendors sell everything from fritters like empanadas and *alcapurrias* to fresh seafood dishes including stuffed mofongo and a whole fried snapper.

GETTING THERE

To get to El Yunque from the San Juan airport, drive 44 kilometers (27 mi) east on PR 26 to PR 66 east to PR 3 east to Río Grande. Turn right on PR 191 at the community of Palmer and travel 8 kilometers (5 mi) to the beginning of the park's recreation area. The drive takes about 35 minutes.

the north end of PR 191 because it is easily accessible from San Juan. From Palmer, it's possible to drive 13 kilometers (8 mi) south on PR 191 before reaching the end of the road at PR 9938.

The forest stretches far beyond Río Grande into the municipalities of Ceiba, Canóvanos, Fajardo, Naguabo, Luquillo, and Las Piedras. Many locals prefer the southern and western sides of the forest because they're less likely to attract busloads of tourists and they feature plenty of waterfalls and natural pools for swimming. To explore the western side, take PR 186 south from PR 3. To explore the southern side from Naguabo, proceed west on PR 31 and go north on PR 191.

Visitors Centers

The official entrance to the forest is **El Portal Tropical Forest Center** (PR 191, km 4, www.fs.usda.gov/elyunque), which was severely damaged during Hurricanes Irma and Maria. It is expected to reopen in 2021 after restoration work is complete. It is a striking piece of architecture designed by the local firm Sierra Cardona Ferrer. A modern interpretation of the traditional pavilion-style structure seen throughout the island, it has an elevated walkway that leads visitors to an open-air interior filled with interactive educational displays. There's also a gift shop, bathroom facilities, and a small screening room that continuously shows a film about the forest alternately in English and Spanish.

Portalito Hub (54 Calle Principal, Palmer, 787/809-0534, daily 9am-5pm) is a temporary visitors center to replace El Portal while it's closed. Located in the town of Palmer, it's where visitors can pick up maps and brochures, use restroom facilities, and stock up on water, T-shirts, and hiking gear. It is also a source of educational information on El Yunque and its long-range restoration plans, presented in exhibits, videos, and ranger talks (Sat.-Sun. 11am and 2pm).

Driving Tour

From Portalito Hub, proceed south on PR 191 and through the **park gate** (daily 7:30am-6pm). The first stop is **La Coca Falls** (PR 191, km 8.1), the most accessible and photographed waterfall in the forest. It has an 85-foot drop and a constant flow of rushing water. There's plenty of parking space and a small snack bar nearby. This is also the trailhead for **La Coca Trail.**

The next stop on the route is **Yokahu Tower** (PR 191, km 8.8), a 69-foot-high observation tower built in 1963. Climb its steps to get terrific views of the forest and the Atlantic Ocean.

Farther south is **Sierra Palm Recreation Area** (PR 191, km 11.3), offering more food concessions, restrooms, and a picnic area. Across the street is the Caimitillo Trailhead.

The next stop is **Palo Colorado Visitors Center** (PR 191, km 11.8), an information center with still another snack bar and picnic area. Across the street is a short hike to **El Baño Grande,** a picturesque stone pool built in the 1930s by the Civilian Conservation Corps (CCC).

Just before you reach the end of PR 191, the road intersects at kilometer 12.6 with a small loop road called PR 9938. This road takes you to the trailhead for Mount Britton Trail, which leads to **Mount Britton Tower,** built by the CCC. If visibility is good, you can see the south coast from here. From Mount Britton Trail, you can pick up the Mount Britton Spur Trail to the observation deck on the peak of El Yunque and **Los Picachos Tower,** another CCC tower.

Hiking

The best way to fully appreciate El Yunque's beauty and majesty is to park the car and hike into the jungle. It doesn't take more than a couple of dozen steps to become completely enveloped by the dense, lush foliage. One of the greatest joys of hiking in El Yunque is the sound. Here the aural assault of the 21st century is replaced by a palpable hush and the comforting, sensual, eternal sounds of water dripping, gurgling, rushing, raining.

There are 12 trails spanning about 23

kilometers (14 mi) in El Yunque. Many of the trails are paved or covered in gravel because the constant rain and erosive soil would require continuous maintenance to keep them passable. Nonetheless, hiking boots with good tread are a necessity. Even paved trails can be slippery and muddy. The warm air and high humidity also require frequent hydration, so bring plenty of water. And naturally, it rains a lot, so light rain gear is recommended. Avoid streams during heavy rains, as flash floods can occur. Primitive camping is permitted in some areas. Permits are required and can be obtained at El Portal Tropical Forest Center.

The following trails are found in El Yunque. All trail lengths and hiking times are approximate.

Angelito Trail (0.8 km/0.5 mi, 15 minutes, easy, clay and gravel) crosses a stream and leads to Las Damas, a natural pool in the Mameyes River. To get to the trailhead, proceed south on PR 191 just past El Portal and turn left on PR 988, less than a kilometer past Puente Roto Bridge.

La Coca Trail (3 km/2 mi, 1.5 hours one way, strenuous, gravel) starts across the street from La Coca Falls. The steep and muddy trail requires navigating over rocks and through streams to access a natural pool.

El Yunque Trail (4 km/2.5 mi, 2 hours one way, moderate, paved and gravel) is one of the forest's longest and most strenuous hikes. It starts a little north of the Palo Colorado Visitors Center and climbs to an altitude of 3,400 feet. Along the way it passes several rain shelters, traverses through the cloud forest, and ends at the peak of El Yunque. The lower part of the trail is accessible from Caimitillo Trail and Baño de Oro Trail. The higher reaches of the trail connect with Mount Britton Trail and Los Picachos Tower Trail.

Mount Britton Trail (1.5 km/1 mi, 45 minutes, strenuous, paved) starts at PR 9938, a loop road at the end of PR 191. It is an uphill hike through *tabonuco,* sierra palm, and cloud forests. The trail crosses two streams and runs along a service road for a short distance—if you're not sure which way to go, just keep heading straight up. It ends at the Mount Britton Tower, built in the 1930s by the Civilian Conservation Corps (CCC).

Mount Britton Spur (1.5 km/1 mi, 30 minutes, moderate, paved) connects Mount Britton Trail to El Yunque Trail.

Los Picachos Trail (0.4 km/0.25 mi, 25 minutes, strenuous, unpaved and steps) is a steep ascent from El Yunque Trail to an observation deck built by the CCC.

El Yunque

The forest's remaining two trails are outside El Yunque Recreation Center on the western side of the forest. The trails are unpaved, muddy, not maintained, and often overgrown in parts. Long sleeves and pants are recommended for protection against brush, some of which can cause skin irritation on contact. These trails are for adventurous hikers who really want to get away from it all.

Trade Winds Trail (6 km/4 mi, 4 hours, strenuous, primitive) is the forest's longest trail. To reach the trailhead, drive all the way through El Yunque Recreation Area to the end of PR 191 where the road is closed. Be mindful not to block the gate. Walk past the gate to the trailhead. The trail ascends to the peak of El Toro, the highest peak in the forest, where it connects with the El Toro Trail.

El Toro Trail (3 km/2 mi, 3 hours, difficult, primitive) starts at PR 186, kilometer 10.6, and traverses *tabonuco*, sierra palm, and cloud forests. It connects with the Trade Winds Trail.

Four of the park's trails suffered significant hurricane damage and are expected to reopen in 2021. **La Mina Trail** (0.8 km/0.5 mi, 25 minutes, moderate, paved and steps) starts at Palo Colorado and follows the La Mina River, ending at La Mina waterfall, where it connects with Big Tree Trail. **Big Tree Trail** (1.5 km/1 mi, 35 minutes, moderate, paved and steps) is an interpretive trail with signs in Spanish and English. It passes through *tabonuco* forest, over streams, and ends at La Mina waterfall, where it connects to La Mina Trail. The trailhead is by a small parking area at PR 191, kilometer 10.2. **Caimitillo Trail** (0.8 km/0.5 mi, 25 minutes, easy, paved and steps) begins at Sierra Palm Recreation Area and crosses a stream. Along the way you'll pass a picnic area and structures used by the Puerto Rican parrot recovery program. It connects to the Palo Colorado Visitors Center and El Yunque Trail. **Baño de Oro Trail** (0.4 km/0.25 mi, 20 minutes, moderate, paved and gravel) starts just south of the Palo Colorado information center and passes by Baño de Oro before connecting with El Yunque Trail.

Getting There

El Yunque is about 35 minutes east of San Juan. From the San Juan airport, proceed east on PR 26, PR 66, and PR 3 to Río Grande. Turn right on PR 191 at the community of Palmer and travel south for 8 kilometers (5 mi) of twisty road up the mountain to access the recreation area where trailheads, observation areas, and picnic shelters are located.

RÍO GRANDE
Recreation
GOLF

What made Río Grande a fertile, well-hydrated place for growing sugarcane and coffee back in the day has made it an excellent place for golf courses today.

Wyndham Grand Río Mar Beach Resort (PR 968, km 1.4, 800/474-6627, teetime-riomar@wyndham.com, www.wyndhamhotels.com) has two courses. The Ocean Course, built in 1975 by George and Tom Fazio, is a 6,716-yard course offering excellent views of the Atlantic Ocean and one of the best-rated holes (16) on the island. The River Course, an 18-hole grass course with water in play, built in 1997 and designed by Greg Norman, runs along the Río Mameyes. There's also a 35,000-square-foot clubhouse and golf clinic. Golf club rentals are available.

Coco Beach Golf and Country Club (100 Club House Dr., Río Grande, 787/657-2000, www.cocopuertorico.com, daily dawn-5pm) offers 36 holes of oceanside golf on courses designed by Tom Kite and Bruce Besse. Food and beverage service is provided on the course and in the clubhouse, which also has a pro shop. The club has a putting green and driving range as well. It has hosted the PGA Tour's Puerto Rico Open on multiple occasions.

St. Regis Bahía Beach Resort (PR 187, km 4.2, Río Grande, 787/809-8920, www.marriott.com) is home to the **Robert Trent Jones Jr. Golf Course**, a par 72, 6,979-yard course that meanders around saltwater lagoons and oceanfront views, with El Yunque rainforest visible in the distance.

TENNIS

Wyndham Grand Río Mar Beach Resort (6000 Río Mar Blvd., Río Grande, 787/888-7066, www.wyndhamriomar.com) features 11 Har-Tru surface courts and two hard courts, four equipped with lights for nighttime play. There's also a 35,000-square-foot clubhouse and a pro shop. Lessons, clinics, and packages are available.

Entertainment and Shopping
CASINOS

Wyndham Grand Río Mar Beach Resort (PR 968, km 1.4, 787/888-6000, www.wyndhamriomar.com) features a 7,000-square-foot **casino** (Sun.-Thurs. noon-2am, Fri.-Sat. noon-3am) with 152 slots and video poker games, blackjack, roulette, craps, Caribbean poker, Texas hold 'em, and three-card poker. Enjoy a complimentary cocktail while you play, or watch the big game on 50-inch HDTV plasma screens in the Players Club sports bar.

HORSE RACING

Hipódromo Camarero (PR 3, km 15.3, Canóvanas, 787/641-6060, hipodromo-camarero.com, Thurs.-Sun., admission free, betting starts at $10) is technically in the municipality of Canóvanas, just east of Río Grande. The first race begins at 2:45pm except on Sunday, when it begins at 2:15pm; the last race is at 6pm. Watch the races with food and beverage service from the grandstand, the clubhouse, or the Terrace Room restaurant. You can also watch the action on live monitors in the Winners Sports Bar.

SOUVENIR SHOPS

Caribbean Trading Company (4 Calle Principal, Palmer, 787/888-2762 or 800/576-1770, www.caribbeantrading.com, daily 10am-6pm) is a great place to stock up on the flavors of the island. The shelves are stocked with local spices, hot sauces, coffees, and cigars, as well as CDs, books, and bath products.

Food

★ **El Verde BBQ** (PR 3, km 24.7, 787/887-0958, daily 9am-midnight, $10) serves some of the best mofongo and ribs around. This popular roadside spot specializes in a variety of grilled meats and *cocina criolla* served cafeteria-style from a steam table.

Accommodations
$150-250

Spend the night high up in the jungle at eco-friendly **Rainforest Inn** (PR 186, km 22.1, Río Grande, 787/378-6190 or 800/672-4992, www.rainforestinn.com, $165-170). Rooms come with porches, kitchenettes, free wireless Internet, and vegetarian breakfast. No children under 12 are permitted. Villa Hermosa ($475) has five bedrooms, 4.5 baths, and a swimming pool. Children are permitted in the villa. Enjoy the yoga studio, book a massage, or take the private trail (a difficult trek that requires signing a waiver) to a waterfall and swimming hole. There's a three-night minimum.

Dos Aguas (PR 3, km 24.9, Río Grande, 787/585-7010, www.dosaguasriogrande.com, $225) is a small, ecofriendly boutique hotel offering contemporary accommodations featuring air-conditioning, microwaves, and complimentary breakfast. The Bamboo Suite V is a spacious, spa-like room with kitchenette and 180-degree views of the Espíritu Santo river. Book a massage, take a yoga class, or rent a kayak or paddleboard and ride the river to a private beach.

OVER $250

Hyatt Regency Grand Reserve (200 Coco Beach Blvd., 787/657-1234, www.hyatt.com, $364-524) is a Hyatt property featuring 579 suites with balconies or terraces. Amenities include access to the Coco Beach Golf Club, a spa, three restaurants, a lagoon-style pool, and beach access.

Coco Beach Golf Resort & Residences (200 Coco Beach Blvd., PR 3 at PR 955, 787/657-2005, ext. 1000, www. cocoresidencespr.com, $400) offers three-bedroom villas with 3.5 baths, a two-car parking garage, free wireless Internet, and access to the Coco Beach Golf Club, pool area, and gym. The resort is within walking distance to the beach.

Wyndham Grand Río Mar Golf & Beach Resort (6000 Río Mar Blvd., Río Grande, 787/888-6000, www.wyndhamrio-mar.com, $338-528, $560 suite) is a massive property with nearly 700 rooms and suites appointed with lots of amenities, including 42-inch flat-screen HDTVs, high-speed Internet, cable TV, mini bar, air-conditioning, coffee-maker, and refrigerator upon request. Pets up to 20 pounds are permitted. Resort amenities include two oceanfront pools, a mile of secluded beach, eights restaurants and bars, a casino, spa, tennis center, and two 18-hole golf courses.

★ **St. Regis Bahía Beach Resort** (PR 187, km 4.2, Río Grande, 787/809-8000, www.marriott.com, $1,200-1,350, $1,489-1,889 suite) is a tropical oasis of moneyed luxury. The 483-acre seaside property boasts a golf course designed by Robert Trent Jones Jr.; over a mile of pristine sandy beach; two restaurants and a bar. With only 139 units, there is plenty of space to get away from it all in style. Other amenities include a terraced, oceanfront swimming pool with cabanas, walking trails, kayaking, snorkeling, sailing, diving, windsurfing, fishing, a tennis center, a spa, and the Iguana Kids Club for children ages 5-12.

Transportation and Services

Río Grande is 30 kilometers (19 mi) east of the San Juan airport. Take PR 26 east to PR 66 east to PR 3 east. The drive takes 25-35 minutes, depending on traffic.

Luquillo Taxi (787/513-7685, www.luquillotaxi.com) provides one-way transportation from the San Juan airport for $69 for up to four passengers, including luggage and tolls. Advance reservation is required. **Río Grande Taxi Service** (787/635-0836, www.riograndeprtaxi.com) also provides transfer services to and from and San Juan airport and the piers in Viejo San Juan.

For pharmaceutical needs, there is a **Walgreens** (PR 3, km 23.9, 787/887-0237, daily 8am-10pm). Banking services are available at **Banco Popular** (Centro Comerical Villas de Río Grande, 99 Calle Pimental, 787/887-2316, www.bancopopular.com). In the same shopping center, there's a **post office** (Centro Comerical Villas de Río Grande, 99 Calle Pimental).

PALMER
Recreation
ZIPLINING

At **Rainforest Zipline Park** (PR 191, km 1.1, 787/370-1010, www.rainforestzipline.com, $99 adults, $79 children 8-15) you can zoom between trees and over the forest canopy on this 2,300-foot-long ride featuring eight ziplines. The tour lasts 90 minutes to two hours. Participants must be in good health, able to climb up ladders, walk 10 minutes uphill over uneven ground, and weigh 250 pounds or less.

JungleQui Zipline Park (PR 191 at PR 990, 787/500-7555, www.junglequipr.com) has an 11-zipline ride and two 45-foot freefall rappels at El Yunque. Tours last 2.5 hours and include a nature walk and tour of three natural pools where visitors are free to swim at their own risk. Cost is $85 for adults and $75 for children ages 7-12. Weight limit is 275 pounds.

Food

Lluvia (52 Principal Calle, 787/657-5186, www.lluviapr.com, daily 7am-3pm, $6-14) is a bright, contemporary breakfast-lunch spot decked out in shades of lime green and orange that serves frittatas, waffles, flatbread pizzas, and salads, as well as coffee drinks and a small selection of cocktails. For a snack on the go, select a cupcake or blondie from the small bakery case. Be sure to check out the landscaped garden out back with a view of El Yunque.

Antojitos Puertorriqueños (60 PR 968, Barrio Las Coles, 787/888-7378, Mon. and Wed.-Thurs. 7:30am-10pm, Tues. 7:30am-3pm, Fri.-Sun. 7:30am-10:30pm, $9-20) serves local cuisine, including stuffed mofongo and *tostones,* rice and crab, *chillo* in garlic sauce, and salmon. Don't stop here if you're in a hurry. Service can be very slow.

After building up an appetite on El Yunque, ★ **El Yunque Treehouse** (PR 191, km 1.4, 939/640-0384, www.facebook.com/elyunquetreehouse, Sun.-Wed. 11am-7pm, Thurs. 11am-9pm, Fri.-Sat. 11am-11pm, $13-39) is a welcome sight. The large covered patio strung with twinkle lights beckons the tired and hungry to dine on outstanding selections of traditional Puerto Rican cuisine, including stuffed Cornish hen, *chuleta can can, sanchoco* stew, and mofongo. The service is warm and attentive. There's live jazz music on the weekends.

Señor Carrucho (Calle Principal, 787/426-2675, Fri.-Sun. 11am-5pm, $1-7.50, cash only) is a food kiosk in the heart of Palmer serving *arepas* and *pastelillos* stuffed with octopus, shrimp, conch, lobster, or a combination.

Luquillo

Luquillo attracts visitors from far and wide for two reasons. One is its beautiful public beach, commonly referred to as Playa Luquillo, although its proper name is Balneario La Monserrate. Many consider it one of the finest beaches on the main island. The other reason is for the Luquillo *kioskos,* more than 50 food vendors serving some of the very best street food available in Puerto Rico.

Luquillo's town center has an uncommonly large, modern plaza with very little charm, so there's not much reason to tarry here. Instead, head over to the coastal side of town along La Pared, the seawall. On the street side is a cluster of restaurants and bars. On the sea side is a popular surfing spot.

SIGHTS
Las Pailas

Las Pailas (also spelled **Las Paylas,** PR 983, $5 parking) is a natural waterslide located in a mountain stream behind a residential neighborhood near El Yunque. It's a lot of fun for those adventurous enough to give it a try. Take note, though: This not an official attraction and there are no safety measures in place, so go at your own risk. The slide is formed by a river that cascades over a smooth but rocky descent that bottoms out in a chest-deep pool of crystal-clear water. Some locals even slide down on their bellies or on their feet.

From San Juan, take PR 3 east to Luquillo, turn right on PR 992, left on PR 991, and then right on PR 983. The drive is about 50 kilometers (31 mi) from San Juan, but it will take 60 to 90 minutes, depending on traffic. Look for a chain-link fence posted with signs that say "Las Paylas" and "Finca Privada." Pull in to one of the two parking areas in front of a private home, and pay the attendant $5 to park (cash only). Walk through the carport, where you can use the bathroom for $0.25 or buy fruit-flavored *limbers* (Italian ice) for $1. To reach the slide, walk about 10 minutes along an uneven path riddled with rocks and tree roots. Once you reach the water, there are large boulders big enough to spread out picnics and watch the action.

BEACHES

Although Playa Luquillo gets all the accolades and attention, it isn't the only beach in Luquillo. **La Selva Natural Reserve** (PR 193, just east of Luquillo), a designated nature

Luquillo

© MOON.COM

preserve, is a 3,240-acre tract of land comprising wetlands, mangroves, coastal forest, and pristine beaches ideal for swimming and surfing—just beware of the reefs. This is an important nesting site for leatherback turtles.

In the town of Luquillo, along PR 193, is **Playa Azul,** a sandy crescent beach great for swimming and snorkeling. Parking is limited, and there are no facilities besides a few street vendors selling snacks. Farther east on Calle Herminio Diaz Navarro is **La Pared,** a great surfing spot adjacent to a picturesque seawall, just one block from Luquillo's central plaza.

★ Playa Luquillo

Playa Luquillo, or **Balneario La Monserrate** (PR 3, east of San Juan, 787/889-5871, www.drdpuertorico.com, daily 8:30am-6pm, $5.50/vehicle), is the kind of place people dream of when they envision an island paradise. A thick grove of tall, shady coconut palm trees sways in the breeze over a mile-long wide crescent of pristine sand gently lapped by the Atlantic Ocean. The only signs of civilization are a clean modern complex of bathrooms and showers, some covered picnic shelters, and a couple of snack bars serving fritters and piña

coladas. **Camping** (787/889-5871 for reservations, $10, $17 with electricity) is permitted in a grassy area with picnic tables and grills on the western side.

The only drawback to this idyllic spot is that it gets packed with beachgoers on weekends, holidays, and during the summer, when beach chairs and umbrellas are available for rent and lifeguards keep an eye on things. If you want solitude, visit on a weekday during the low season, and you'll practically have the place to yourself.

On the far eastern side of the beach is **Mar Sin Barreras** (Sea Without Barriers), a staffed, **wheelchair-accessible beach** that caters to visitors with disabilities. In addition to a system of ramps that permits those in wheelchairs to roll right into the water, there are accessible bathrooms, showers, parking, and picnic shelters. The facility also rents special wheelchairs for entering the water.

RECREATION

Surfing Puerto Rico (La Pared, 787/501-7873, www.surfingpuertorico.com, Mon.-Sat., $60 two-hour session) provides instruction for beginners and intermediate surfers at La Pared in Luquillo. Children must be at least 8 years old for a lesson.

Carabalí Rainforest Adventure Forest (PR 3, km 32.4, 787/889-5820, 787/889-4954, or 787/889-2682, www.carabalirainforestpark.com) is a 600-acre ranch offering one- and two-hour guided ATV ($55-99) and UTV ($110-195) off-road adventures and horseback tours ($39-99) along mountainside and beachfront trails. Participants must be at least 16 years old, 60 inches or taller, and have a license to drive an ATV or UTV. Other attractions include go-karts, hayrides, and luxury yacht rental. A bar and grill provides food and beverage service.

1: Las Pailas water slide near Luquillo **2:** La Pared, a popular surf spot in Luquillo **3:** Playa Luquillo

SHOPPING

The **Kioskos de Luquillo** include some retail shops. The best of the bunch is **Studio Coco** (kiosko #13, PR 3, 787/615-0892, www.cherifordblack.com, daily noon-6pm), featured copper enameled and sea-glass pendants and earrings made by Cheri Ford Black. If business is slow, they sometimes close, so call ahead before making a special trip.

FOOD

★ Kioskos de Luquillo

The **Kioskos de Luquillo** (PR 193 at PR 3) are nearly as popular an attraction as Playa Luquillo. Along PR 3 just before you reach Luquillo from San Juan, this long stretch of 50-plus side-by-side kiosks is one of the best places to experience Puerto Rico's array of traditional fritters. Shaped like discs, halfmoons, cigars, boats, and balls, these crispy deep-fried goodies come stuffed with a varied combination of meat, fish, crab, poultry, or cheese. Most kiosks serve similar fare at stand-up bars where you can eat on your feet or seated at a table nearby. Pick one of each (they're only $1-3 apiece) and wash it all down with a cold beer, a cocktail, or *coco frio* (icecold coconut water served from the shell). Be sure to buy a bag of *coco dulce*—sinfully rich patties of sugary coconut—for later. This place can get packed on the weekends and holidays, and the atmosphere can get rowdy at night. Despite the area's rustic nature, most kiosks accept credit and debit cards.

Puerto Rico's emergence as a culinary destination has not been lost on the kiosk proprietors in Luquillo. Many of the tried-and-true purveyors of Puerto Rican street food and home-style *cocina criolla* dishes are still here of course, and thank goodness. But among them have cropped up outlets that are serving some of the finest, most creative cuisine on the island, with an emphasis on fresh, seasonal ingredients. In addition to jazzing up the cuisine, these newcomers have created

Kiosk Cuisine

The roadways all over Puerto Rico are dotted with countless lean-tos, shacks, pavilions, tents, and trucks where enterprising cooks sell a variety of mostly fried local delicacies called *frituras*. For the uninitiated, the assortment of fried food can be daunting. But if you want a truly traditional Puerto Rican experience, pop an antacid and dive into an adventurous array of some of the tastiest food on the island.

Items sell for as little as a dollar apiece, are served in napkins, and are often eaten standing up. There are two commonly served condiments: a homemade vinegar-based hot sauce called *pique* or mayo ketchup, a pink sauce that combines the two condiments. Nothing washes it all down better than an ice-cold Medalla beer.

Luquillo and Piñones are famous for their concentration of food kiosks, but kiosks can be found all over, typically near beaches, parks, and tourist sites, including Plaza de Hostos in Viejo San Juan, Punta Sardinera beach in Isabela, and Jardín de Atlantico park in Aguadilla.

Some of the most common items include:

- *alcapurria:* Mashed yuca (also called cassava), yautia (taro root), and/or green banana is stuffed with crab or beef and deep-fried. They are elongated but fat in the middle. They look like a thin sweet potato or fat cigar.

- *aranitas:* Little haystacks of shredded green plantain, deep-fried, of course.

- *arepa:* South American in origin, it's a small, round patty of cornmeal batter fried, split open on one side, and stuffed with meat or seafood. It looks like a small, fried hockey puck.

- *bacalaito:* A codfish fritter that looks like a giant, irregularly shaped, deep-fried pancake.

- *barcazas:* Whole plantains are sliced lengthwise, stuffed with ground beef, and topped with cheese. They look like banana boats.

- empanada or *empanadilla:* A savory circle of pastry is stuffed with meat, crab, lobster, shrimp, or fish, folded into a half-moon, thickly crimped along the rounded side, and deep-fried. It looks like an apple turnover.

more aesthetically pleasing environments for their diners, painting their kiosks in tropical colors and creating alfresco dining areas out back, facing the ocean. The following are some favorites.

La Parrilla #2 (787/889-0590, www.laparrillapr.com, Sun.-Thurs. noon-9:30pm, Fri.-Sat. noon-10:30pm, $17-38) is a full-blown, upscale restaurant with patio dining and an upstairs deck with an ocean view. They specialize in mofongo stuffed with grouper, mahi-mahi, or snapper, grilled pork chop stuffed with cheese and topped with a teriyaki sauce, and chicken breast stuffed with sweet plantains and mozzarella, wrapped in bacon and glazed in *guayaba*

sauce. There's also a full bar serving a variety of frozen cocktails.

At **El Jefe Burger & Mojito Factory #12** (787/604-0644, www.facebook.com/jefeburgershackmojitofactory, Sun.-Tues. and Thurs. noon-9pm, Fri.-Sat. noon-10pm, $9-14), burgers come in two sizes or stuffed with your choice of chorizo, beer-braised short ribs, or jalapeños and green chiles. Other gut-busters include bacon and cheese fries, beer-battered onion wedges and buckets of shrimp, and chicken or tilapia grilled or fried and served in your choice of sauce. The ginger mojito is outstanding.

Started by a pair of tattoo artists but now run by a pair of musicians and a mixologist,

one of more than 50 food kiosks and restaurants in Luquillo

- *papa rellena:* A big lump of mashed potatoes is stuffed with meat and deep-fried. It looks like a fried baseball.

- *pastelillo:* The same thing as an empanada or empanadilla: a savory hand pie.

- *pinchos:* Chunks of chicken, pork, or fish are threaded on a skewer and grilled kebab-style. They're often served with a brush of barbecue sauce and slice of bread stuck on the point of the skewer.

- *pionono:* A ball of seasoned ground beef is wrapped mummy-style in slices of plantain and deep-fried. Sometimes it also contains egg. It looks like a craggy, deep-fried softball.

- *sorullito:* Small, cigar-shaped nosh is made from cornmeal and cheese.

Tattoo Tavern #17 (787/889-1189, www.tattootavern.com, Mon. and Wed.-Thurs. 5pm-midnight, Fri. 5pm-2am, Sat. 1pm-2am, Sun. 1pm-midnight, $2.40-10.50) is a pub that doubles as a dive bar at night featuring live rock music. Burgers, nachos, and chicken wings comprise the menu.

Peruvian cuisine is on the menu at **Ceviche Hut #42** (787/355-1200, www.facebook.com/cevichehutkioskosluquillo42, Wed.-Sat. 11am-10pm, Sun.-Mon. 11am-9pm, $11-26), but the fresh seafood ceviche is the reason to go.

Rustic Bar & Grill #21 (787/556-2802 or 787/959-6094, Sun. and Wed.-Thurs. 10am-10pm, Fri.-Sat. 10am-midnight, $15-30) serves a variety of *pastelillos,* and entrées including *arroz con* corned beef, whole snapper stuffed with conch salad, and *trifongo* (mofongo made with green plantain, sweet plantain, and yuca). There's often live music, pay-per-view parties to watch boxing and MMA matches, as well as an '80s party every last Saturday of the month. The bar stays open late if the crowd lingers.

Puerto Rican

Carnivores will delight in the meaty offerings at **Brasas y Cultura** (PR 3, km 32.9, 787/239-6722, www.facebook.com/brasasycultura, Mon.-Tues. 11am-6pm, Wed.-Sat. 11am-10pm, Sun. 11am-9pm, $9-29), specializing in grilled and smoked meats including pork ribs, churrasco, and chicken. They also serve stuffed mofongo, burgers, and *chuleta can can*.

Mediterranean

Latin Gyros (352 Calle Fernandez Garcia at the intersection of PR 992 and PR 193, right by PR 3, 787/889-4801, www.facebook.com/LatinGyros, Mon.-Thurs. 7am-6pm, Fri.-Sat. 7am-9pm, Sun. 7am-4pm, $4-12) is an excellent place to get a good, cheap Mediterranean-, American-, or Puerto Rican-style breakfast or lunch. This little corner deli serves gyros, burgers, lamb barbecue, Cuban sandwiches, *tortilla española* omelets, French toast, and more. It also sells chorizo and Serrano ham by the pound.

Mexican

Lolita's Mexican Restaurant (PR 3, km 41.8, 787/889-0250, Sun.-Thurs. 11am-9pm, Fri.-Sat. 11am-10pm, $3-17) is the place to go when you have a hankering for margaritas, tacos, burritos, and chiles rellenos.

Classic American

As the name suggests, **Boardriders Surf Bar** (25 Calle Miguel Veve Calzada at La Pared, 787/355-5175, http://boardriderssurfbar.com, Sun.-Thurs. noon-10pm, Fri.-Sat. noon-11pm, $9-29) is a haven for surfers, but even landlubbers are made to feel welcome at this casual restaurant and bar located across the street from Luquillo's celebrated La Pared surf spot. Nosh on fish tacos, ribs, burgers, salads, and wraps and get the lowdown from the friendly, no-attitude staff on where the best surf breaks are. Live music on weekends features roots, rumba, jazz, and reggae.

Dessert

Located in front of the Plaza de Luquillo, **Chachi's** (119 Calle Fernandez Garcia, 787/536-9147, Sun.-Thurs. 3pm-9pm, Sat. 7pm-11pm, $2-8) serves ice creams and sorbets in a variety of tropical flavors, including coconut, pineapple, almond, tamarind, passion fruit, and corn. You can order coffee drinks, fruit frappes, and milkshakes, too.

ACCOMMODATIONS

Despite Luquillo's popularity as a tourist destination for locals and international travelers alike, it has a dearth of overnight accommodations. **Luquillo Sunrise Beach Inn** (A2 Ocean Blvd., 787/889-1713, www.luquillosunrise.com, $135-150, $140-250 suite) is a modest 18-room guesthouse conveniently located across the street from the surf beach La Pared and two blocks away from the town center. The rooms are very basic but clean and come with air-conditioning, satellite TV, and free wireless Internet. Some rooms have balconies, microwaves, and refrigerators.

TRANSPORTATION AND SERVICES

Luquillo is 40 kilometers (25 mi) east of San Juan. Take PR 26 east to PR 66 east to PR 3 east. The drive typically takes 30-45 minutes, depending on traffic. **Luquillo Taxi** (787/513-7685, www.luquillotaxi.com) provides one-way transportation from the San Juan airport for $79 for up to four passengers, including luggage and tolls. Advance reservation is required.

For health and beauty needs, visit **Walgreens** (889 Calle 2, 787/889-3107). **Banco Popular** (PR 193 and Calle B, 787/889-2610, www.bancopopular.com) provides banking services, and there is a **post office** (160 Calle 14 de Julio) in town.

Fajardo

Fajardo is a bustling little seaside town notable for its marinas and launch site for private or chartered boat rides to Caribbean points east, including Vieques, Culebra, St. Thomas, and beyond. Although it has a town proper, with the requisite plaza and church, the heart of Fajardo is along the coast, where hundreds of vessels dock and dozens of seafood restaurants vie to serve the day-trippers who flock here for the superb diving, fishing, sailing, and golf.

Fajardo is also home to one of the island's bioluminescent lagoons, Laguna Grande, in Reserva Natural Las Cabezas de San Juan. Here you can kayak at night and marvel at the phosphorescent microorganisms that light up the water with a sparkling green glow.

SIGHTS

Balneario Seven Seas

Balneario Seven Seas (PR 987, beside Las Cabezas de San Juan, Las Croabas, 787/863-8180, Sept.-Apr. Wed.-Sun. 8:30am-6pm, May-Aug. daily 8:30am-6pm, $5 per vehicle) is a great beach for swimming and snorkeling. For underwater action, check out the reef on the far eastern end of the beach. Facilities include restrooms and picnic shelters. Camping (787/863-8180 for reservations) for RVs and tents is also available, although quarters are close, so don't expect much privacy.

Parque Las Croabas

Parque Las Croabas (PR 987) is a pleasant waterside park overlooking Bahía Las Croabas, dotted with moored fishing boats. From here you can see the island of Vieques. There are several concrete picnic shelters, poorly maintained bathroom facilities, and a small boat launch. Across the street are several bars and restaurants serving seafood. At dusk the park hums with activity because this is the launch site for kayak outfitters offering guided bio-bay tours in Laguna Grande.

Reserva Natural La Cordillera

Reserva Natural La Cordillera, comprising Icacos, Diablo, Palomino, and Palominitos, is a protected string of small, sandy islands just north and east of Fajardo with lots of great snorkeling and diving spots around them. Bring plenty of water and sunscreen—there are no facilities or stores on the islands. To get here, go to the dock in Las Croabas and arrange a ride with one of several water taxis that operate there. They'll drop you off and return later to pick you up. The cost ranges from $25-45. Be aware that the islands can get crowded on weekends and holidays.

★ Bioluminescent Laguna Grande

Laguna Grande is a mangrove lagoon filled with dinoflagellate, a microscopic bioluminescent organism that glows white, green, or blue at night when motion is sensed. Several outfitters in the area offer nighttime kayak tours that launch from Parque Las Croabas and pass through a mangrove canal before opening up into the lagoon. The best time to go is when there is little or no moon visible in the sky. No kayak experience is required, but participants must be able to paddle themselves into the lagoon and back out again. Tours last about an hour.

Laguna Grande is located inside **Reserva Natural Las Cabezas de San Juan** (PR 987, km 5.9, 787/860-2562, 787/722-5882, or 787/722-5834, www.paralanaturaleza.org or www.pln.org), a 316-acre nature reserve containing a variety of natural habitats, including coral reefs, turtle grass, sandy and rocky beaches, lagoons, a dry forest, and a mangrove forest. It is home to many endangered wildlife species, including the osprey and the sea turtle. Artifacts of the Igneri Indians, precursors to the Taínos, have been excavated here. In addition to Laguna Grande, the reserve is home to a neoclassical lighthouse, built by

Fajardo

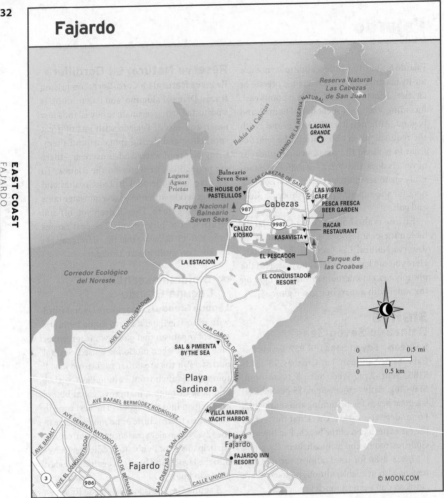

Reserva Natural
Las Cabezas
de San Juan

Bahía las Cabezas

LAGUNA
GRANDE

CAMINO DE LA RESERVA NATURAL

Laguna
Aguas
Prietas

CAR CABEZAS DE SAN JUAN

Balneario
Seven Seas

THE HOUSE OF
PASTELILLOS

Cabezas

LAS VISTAS
CAFE

PESCA FRESCA
BEER GARDEN

Parque Nacional
Balneario
Seven Seas

987

9987

CALIZO
KIOSKO

KASAVISTA

RACAR
RESTAURANT

LA ESTACION

EL PESCADOR

Parque de
las Croabas

Corredor Ecológico
del Noreste

EL CONQUISTADOR
RESORT

CAR CABEZAS DE SAN JUAN

AVE EL CONQUISTADOR

SAL & PIMIENTA
BY THE SEA

0   0.5 mi

0   0.5 km

Playa
Sardinera

AVE RAFAEL BERMÚDEZ RODRÍGUEZ

VILLA MARINA
YACHT HARBOR

AVE GENERAL ANTONIO VALERO DE BERNABÉ

AVE BARALT

AVE EL CONQUISTADOR

Playa
Fajardo

FAJARDO INN
RESORT

Fajardo

3

986

CALLE UNIÓN

© MOON.COM

the Spanish in 1880. The reserve was severely damaged by hurricanes in 2017 and is closed indefinitely for restoration. Luckily, Laguna Grande is still accessible, though only by kayak from Parque Las Croabas.

GUIDED KAYAK TOURS

Kayaking Puerto Rico (PR 987, km 5, Las Croabas, 787/742-0523 or 787/245-4545, www. kayakingpuertorico.com) offers two nightly bio-bay kayak tours ($48) at Laguna Grande. These easy tours launch from Las Croabas,

last two hours, and are suited for ages 6 and older. They also offer island-hopping and snorkel tours (3.5 hours, from $65), which launch from **Puerto Chico Marina** (PR 987, km 2.4).

Puerto Rico Access Tours (PR 987, Las Croabas, 787/421-1800 or 787/463-1940, www. accesstourspr.com) offers two-hour bioluminescent bay tours of Laguna Grande (Sun.-Fri. 6pm and 8pm, $50 pp). It's possible to add on transportation to and from San Juan ($100), or a tour of El Yunque rainforest and a stop at Kioskos de Luquillo ($154). Tours are wheelchair-accessible and adaptive for those who have special needs.

Eco Adventures (787/206-0290, www. ecoadventurespr.com) offers bio-bay tours for $48 per person. Tours last about two hours and launch from Las Croabas. Children must be at least 5 years old to participate.

Yokahu Kayaks (PR 987, km 6.2, Las Croabas, 787/604-7375, www.yokahukayaks. com, $48 pp) offers two-hour kayak tours to Laguna Grande in Las Cabezas de San Juan with licensed guides and equipment included. Reservations are required.

Las Tortugas Adventures (4 Calle La Puntilla, San Juan, 787/657-5274 or 787/637-8356, www.kayak-pr.com) offers a variety of half- and full-day snorkeling and kayak tours on the east coast, launching from Bahía Las Croabas in Fajardo. Tours include Las Cabezas de San Juan in Fajardo, the bioluminescent lagoon, the mangrove forest in Piñones, and excursions to Cayo Icacos, Cayo Diablo, and Monkey Island. No experience is necessary, and all equipment is provided. Reservations are required.

Island Kayaking Adventures (787/444-0059 or 787/225-1808, www.ikapr.com) offers bio-bay kayak tours to Laguna Grande for $45 per person with a six-person minimum. Rainforest and bio-bay combo tours cost $100 per person.

RECREATION

Located on the grounds of Fajardo Inn, **Coco's Park** (52 Parcelas Beltrán, 888/860-6006, www.fajardoinn.com, 10am-5pm, $20) is a family recreation area open to the public for a fee, featuring a swimming pool, swim-up bar, whirlpool, slide, miniature golf course, tennis court, half basketball court, playground, and gift shop.

Snorkeling, Diving, and Sailing

Most water-sports outfitters offer a variety of snorkeling, diving, and sailing opportunities to the northeast coast's natural attractions, as well as to Vieques and Culebra.

Sail Getaways (Villa Marina Yacht Harbor, 200 Ave. Marina View, 787/860-7327, http://sailgetaway.com) provides beach snorkeling tours, sailing trips, and private charters to Culebra's Playa Flamenco and Icacos Island. Take a seven-hour powerboat excursion to Culebra ($112 adults, $95 children 6-12), which includes snorkel gear, lunch, and drinks. It's not suitable for pregnant women or people with back injuries. Catamaran sailing excursions and sunset sails are also available.

Caribe Bliss (Puerta del Rey Marina, slip 8102, 787/439-1672 or 772/333-9383, www. caribebliss.com) offers snorkeling tours to Culebra ($115 adults, $90 children 3-11). The tour includes lunch, drinks, snorkel gear, and flotation devices. The five-hour tour starts at 9:30am.

In nearby Ceiba, **Pure Adventure** (Roosevelt Roads Marina, 787/202-6551, www.pureadventure.com) provides snorkel tours to Vieques ($69 pp, four hours), dive tours to Culebra ($92 pp, seven hours), bioluminescent bay tours at Laguna Grande in Fajardo ($48 pp, two hours), and more.

S. S. Tobias Snorkel and Beach Tours (787/567-4495, www.snorkelandbeachtour. com) offers 6.5-hour snorkel tours to Culebra ($103 adults, $85 children under 12, includes lunch) from Villa Marina in Fajardo, as well as sailing tours, Laguna Grande bio-bay tours, and more.

Sea Ventures Dive Center (Marina Puerto del Rey, PR 3, km 51.2, 787/739-3483 or 800/863-3483, www.divepuertorico.com) offers dive and snorkel trips to local reefs. A two-tank dive for certified divers is $120, including gear. A two-tank dive for beginners is $160, including gear and instruction. Beginners must be at least 10 years old and strong swimmers. Tours last about 5.5 hours. Snorkel tours are $60, including gear.

Salty Dog (787/717-6378 or 787/717-7259, www.saltydreams.com) offers catamaran snorkeling tours, including all-you-can-eat lunch buffet and unlimited rum drinks for $70 per person. A sunset cruise with cocktails and light snacks costs $45 per person and lasts about two hours.

East Island Excursions (Puerto Del Rey Marina, 787/860-3434 or 787/409-2485, www.eastwindcats.com) offers sailing and snorkeling trips aboard a 62-foot sailing catamaran with a glass bottom and a slide, a 65-foot power catamaran, or a 45-foot catamaran. Excursions are available to Vieques, Culebra, Culebrita, and St. Thomas. Reservations are required.

Caribbean School of Aquatics (Villa Marina, 787/728-6606, http://funcatpr.com) offers snorkeling, diving, and sailing trips to Vieques and Culebra aboard catamarans and sailing sloops. Reservations are required.

Boating and Fishing

One of the largest marinas in the Caribbean, **Marina del Rey** (PR 3, km 51.4, 787/860-1000, www.puertodelrey.com) has more than 1,000 slips that can accommodate boats up to 180 feet long, dry storage, a restaurant, a market, and boat repair, rescue, and fueling services. There's also a heliport, a U.S. Customs office, and overnight accommodations provided in one- and two-bedroom apartments. Yacht charters and several tour operators are based on-site.

Puerto Chico Marina (PR 987, km 2.4, 787/863-0834) is a commercial marina on Bahía Sandinera with 279 docks, dry boat storage, fuel service, a seafood restaurant, and several tour operators, including Kayaking Puerto Rico and 787 Fishing Charter.

Villa Marina Yacht Harbor (PR 987, km 1.3, Avenida Marina View, 787/863-5131, www.facebook.com/villamarinapr) is a private marina with docks, dry boat storage, fuel service, and a bar and grill.

787 Fishing (Marina Puerto Chico, PR 987, km 2.4, 787/347-4464, http://787fishing.com, $350-450 half-day for 4-6 people) offers fishing excursions on 22-foot and 26-foot catamarans or 17-foot skiffs.

FOOD

The dining scene is on fire in Fajardo. The number of exceptional restaurants, especially seafood spots, keeps increasing. It's worth staying in the area for a few days just to try all the great restaurants.

Puerto Rican

The House of Pastelillos (Balneario Seven Seas, PR 987, 787/268-2222, Sat.-Sun. 10am-6pm) is a *chinchorro* serving stuffed *arepas* and mofongo, seafood salad, and, of course, *pastelillos* filled with options like chicken, beef, pepperoni, mofongo, or Nutella. The selection of fruity cocktails is generously proportioned. Because of its location beside Balneario Seven Seas, this is a great place to fuel up while spending a day at the beach.

Barbecue

★ **La Estación** (PR 987, km 3.5, next to El Conquistador Resort, Las Croabas, 787/863-4481, www.laestacionpr.com, Mon. and Thurs. 5pm-10pm, Fri.-Sat. 5pm-11pm, Sun. 3pm-9pm, $9-22), owned and operated by Kevin Roth from Brooklyn, New York, and Idalia Garcia from Puerto Rico, is a super-casual oasis of convivial fun and outstanding, freshly prepared cuisine. The kitchen is located in a converted gas station, but the sprawling dining areas are on open-air patios appointed with awnings, padded lawn furniture, butterfly chairs, and tabletops surrounded by tiki torches and festive strings of lights. There's also a partially enclosed bar with a jukebox filled with contemporary Latino rock and reggaetón tunes and a pool table. The vibe is akin to hanging out in your coolest friend's basement. But it's the food that really puts this place on the map. Everything—fresh fish of the day, shrimp, *churrasco,* strip steaks, chicken, and burgers—is charcoal-grill smoked right outside, where you can watch the action. The green papaya salad makes for a refreshing starter. And many of the ingredients are locally sourced.

1: Balneario Seven Seas **2:** Parque Las Croabas

Be sure to start with a cocktail made with fresh-squeezed fruit juices.

Seafood

There is a small, intimate indoor dining room at **Calizo Seafood Bar & Grill** (PR 987, km 5.9, Las Croabas, 787/863-3664, Mon.-Fri. 5pm-10pm, Sat. 1pm-11pm, Sun. 1pm-10pm, $17-30), but why go there when you can dine alfresco on the large, romantic patio or at the lively outdoor bar? It's an ideal setting for the creative tropical cuisine coming out of this kitchen. The restaurant specializes in interesting sauces—a ginger lime sauce for the frog legs in panko; a spicy red pepper sauce for the sautéed prawns—and those are just appetizers. For entrées, sautéed grouper is served in a cilantro Manchego sauce and baby back ribs are cooked in a guava sauce. Other selections include fried or steamed whole snapper, mofongo stuffed with Angus skirt steak and chimichurri sauce, and paella. The menu is conveniently printed in Spanish and English.

Restaurante Ocean View (PR 987, km 6.8, 787/863-6104, Wed.-Mon. noon-11pm, $10-40) is right across the street from Parque Los Croabas and is a festive, casual place to dine on fresh seafood under an open-air pavilion. It serves excellent combination seafood platters, mofongo, and paella, and it has a full bar.

Inside Parque Las Croabas, ★ **El Pescador** (PR 9987, km 7, Las Croabas, 787/972-1501, Mon. 9am-5pm, Tues.-Sat. 4pm-10pm, Sun. 1pm-9pm, $14-29) is an oasis of calm in a rustic but elegant setting. The exterior looks like a wood shack, but inside driftwood light fixtures, polished tree trunk slab tables, jute chairs, and romantic lighting create an artfully eclectic vibe. The menu is presented on a plank of wood. There is a large craft cocktail list of drinks heavy on fresh fruit juices and a daily sangria. Entrées include grilled whole or shelled lobster (market price), whole snapper grilled or fried, arepa sandwiches, and mofongo stuffed with churrasco. The service is welcoming and attentive.

Pesca Fresca Beer Garden (PR 987, km 6.7, Las Croabas, 787/610-0542, www. facebook.com/pescafrescabeergarden, Mon.-Thurs. 3pm-10pm, Fri.-Sun. noon-10pm, $12-32) is a trendy, black-and-turquoise restaurant serving cocktails in mason jars and a wide variety of seafood and Puerto Rican cuisine, including mofongo, whole fried snapper, empanadas, and stuffed *arepas*. There's a rooftop bar and walk-up window for to-go orders. Service can be slow.

Located beside Reserva Natural Las Cabezas de San Juan, **Rincón del Faro** (PR 987, km 5.9, 787/863-0028, Sun.-Mon. and Thurs. 11am-9pm, Tues. noon-8pm, Fri.-Sat. 11am-10pm, $8-27) looks like a casual, open-air *chinchorro*, but the menu is more extensive, specializing in seafood and Puerto Rican dishes including mofongo, whole fried snapper, paella, and lobster, as well as burgers and *chuleta can can*.

By day **Kasavista** (PR 9987, Las Croabas, 787/655-7070, www.kasavista.com, Tues.-Wed. and Fri. 4pm-9pm, Sat. 3pm-9pm, Sun. 1pm-9pm, $13-27) is a light, airy, casual bistro, and at night it feels more upscale. No matter what time you go, though, expect to dine on fresh seafood well prepared, including grilled dorado with tropical chutney and coconut rice, stuffed mofongo, coconut curry shrimp, and seafood paella for two. There's a second location in Naguabo.

★ **Sal & Pimienta by the Sea** (PR 987, km 2.7, 787/534-3477, www.facebook.com/salypimientapr, Tues.-Thurs. 4pm-10pm, Fri.-Sat. noon-10pm, Sun. 11am-9pm, $19-30) specializes in creative seafood dishes like calamari in ginger sauce, spicy crab salad, and fish, shrimp, or lobster in choice of sauce, such as *criolla* or cilantro and roasted garlic. Dine inside or on the terrace overlooking the ocean. The stuffed mofongo and fish with octopus salad are exceptional.

Conveniently located near Parque Las Croabas, a waterside park popular with kayakers, **Racar Seafood** (PR 987, Las Croabas, 787/801-0413, daily 8am-8pm, $13-36) is a reliable source of good, solid Puerto Rican cuisine, including mofongo, seafood platters, and rice dishes.

Cuban

Metropol (Punta del Este Sur Court at the intersection of PR 3 and PR 194, 787/801-2877 or 787/801-2870, www.metropolpr.com, daily 11:30am-10:30pm, $10-36) is a modest, casual restaurant serving excellent Cuban cuisine. The house special is *gallinita rellena de congri*—succulent roasted Cornish hen stuffed with a perfectly seasoned combination of rice and black beans. The presentation is no-nonsense and the service expedient.

Breakfast and Brunch

★ **Las Vistas Café** (83 Calle 2, Las Croabas, 787/655-7053, www.lasvistascafepr.com, Thurs.-Mon. 8am-2pm, $8-14.50) is a cheerful rooftop restaurant in a residential neighborhood with stunning panoramic views of the ocean. Both service and food are exceptional. Breakfast and brunch options include buttermilk pancakes with choice of fresh bananas or coconut, eggs Benedict, and penne pasta with choice of marinara or pesto sauce with chicken or shrimp. Reservations and walk-ins accepted.

Café Playero (PR 987, km 6.8, Las Croabas, 787/534-8213, Thurs. 8:30am-9pm, Fri.-Sat. 8am-9pm, Sun. 8am-7pm, $6-12) is a cute little seaside spot that looks like a wooden trailer with orange umbrella tables out front, serving a full menu of breakfast dishes including pancakes, waffles, and omelets, as well as a long list of sandwiches, from Cubanos to clubs. There are coffee drinks and pastries, too.

Dulce Aroma (100 Calle Union, 787/657-5173, Mon.-Sat. 7:30am-4pm, $3-8) serves sandwiches, pastries, and coffee drinks.

ACCOMMODATIONS
$100-150

The Fajardo Inn (52 Parcelas Beltrán, 787/860-6006, www.fajardoinn.com, $140-190) is a large, adobe-colored complex with 97 units high on a hill, affording gorgeous views of the ocean from one side and the mountains from the other. The guest room furnishings are severely outdated, and the low-budget mattresses leave a lot to be desired. But there's air-conditioning, cable TV, and some rooms have kitchenettes, balconies, mini refrigerators, and whirlpool baths. Amenities include two restaurants and a sprawling family recreation area called Coco's Park, featuring a swimming pool, swim-up bar, whirlpool, slide, miniature golf course, tennis court, half basketball court, and gift shop. The park is also open to the public for a fee.

Siete Mares Bay Inn (83 Calle 2, Las Croabas, 787/655-7053, $95) is a small, tidy guesthouse with three units featuring cable TV, air-conditioning, free wireless Internet, private baths, and private entrances. Upstairs is Las Vistas Café, serving breakfast and brunch Thursday through Monday.

Over $250

El Conquistador Resort & Las Casitas Village (1000 Conquistador Ave., 787/863-1000, www.elconresort.com, $299, $324-399 suite) is a behemoth property with 750 rooms in five complexes perched atop a dramatic cliff with a stunning panoramic view of the ocean. There are more than a dozen restaurants and bars, as well as a casino, fitness center, full-service spa, seven swimming pools, an oceanside water park, seven tennis courts, an 18-hole golf course, and a 35-slip marina. Every room has air-conditioning, satellite TV, telephone, mini bar, marble bathroom, and coffeemaker. Snorkeling, scuba diving, and fishing tours and equipment are available on-site. There's also transportation available to the more secluded beaches on nearby Palomino Island. In addition to the hotel accommodations, Las Casitas Village offers luxury apartment stays with full kitchens in a separate complex with its own swimming pools, restaurants, and butler service.

TRANSPORTATION AND SERVICES

Fajardo is 50 kilometers (31 mi) east of the San Juan airport. Take PR 26 east to PR 66 east to PR 3 east to PR 194 north. The drive takes about 45 minutes to an hour, depending on traffic. **Luquillo Taxi** (787/513-7685, www.luquillotaxi.com) provides one-way transportation from the San Juan airport for $89 for up to four passengers, including luggage and tolls. Advance reservation is required.

Air

The area's airport is **José Aponte de la Torre Airport** (NRR, PR 3, 787/863-4447 or 787/729-8462, $8.50 per day parking) on the former Roosevelt Roads Naval Base in Ceiba. The airport is a small operation that provides transportation to the coast's neighboring islands. **Vieques Air Link** (888/901-9247, www.viequesairlink.com) flies to Vieques, Culebra, and St. Croix. Charter air service is available through **Air Flamenco** (787/901-8256). Don't expect much in the way of services. There's no food or beverage service, and the ATM has been broken for years. The airport is 60 kilometers (37 mi) southeast of the San Juan airport and takes about an hour to drive. From San Juan, take PR 66 east to PR 3 east, which turns into PR 53. In Fajardo, take Exit 2 toward Puerto del Rey Marina and follow the signs to the airport, eventually turning left on Tarawa Drive. Pass the guard house and continue following the signs.

Ferry

Located at the former Roosevelt Roads Naval Base in Ceiba, the **Ceiba Ferry Terminal** (Marina Dr., 787/863-0852, 787/860-8618, or 800/981-2005, www.porferry.com, daily 8am-11am and 1pm-3pm) operates daily ferry service to Vieques and Culebra. This is an economical mode of transportation, but it can be irregular with schedules subject to change with little notice. Be sure to check the website regularly for updates.

Tickets can be purchased in advance online, and travelers are highly advised to do so. But buying a ticket ahead of time does not guarantee you a seat. If there isn't enough space to accommodate passengers, locals with a Puerto Rico ID card get priority and visitors will be bumped. Passengers often line up hours before scheduled departures, especially on holiday weekends, in hopes of getting aboard. Boarding begins one hour before departure.

There are two types of ferries: passenger and cargo. Passengers are permitted to ride on both ferries, but seating is limited on cargo ferries, which are used to transport vehicles and other large cargo between islands. Note that car rental agencies in Puerto Rico do not permit their automobiles to leave the main island, so it will be necessary to leave your car in Ceiba and rent another car at your destination.

Passage takes between 1-1.5 hours. The fare is $4 per person to Vieques round-trip, and $5 per person to Culebra round-trip.

Water Taxi

Several companies offer **water taxi service** from Fajardo to some of the small islands in the Reserva Natural La Cordillera. The fee is typically $25 to Icacos and $40-45 to Palomino, and may require a minimum number of riders. **Puerto Rico Water Taxi** (787/231-9365, www.prwatertaxi.com) and **Mandibula Water Taxi** (PR 987, km 6.9, Las Croabas, 787/909-0226 or 787/556-6091, www.facebook.com/alexmandibula, daily 8am-5pm) provide water taxi service to Icaco and Palomino.

Emergency and Medical Services

In Fajardo, **HIMA-San Pablo Hospital** (404 Av. General Valero, 787/655-0505, www.himasanpablo.com) offers emergency medical services. For pharmacy needs, there is a **Walgreens** (4203 Calle Marginal, 787/860-1600).

Banks

Bank service is available at **Banco Popular** (Centro Comercial Plaza, Fajardo Mall, PR 3, km 4.2, 787/860-5353, www.bancopopular.com).

Humacao and Naguabo

The central stretch of Puerto Rico's east coast is dominated by Palmas del Mar, a luxury residential, recreation, and vacation development in Humacao. Downtown Humacao is anchored by a charming shady plaza flanked by a church and *alcaldía* (town hall) and surrounded by a bustling commercial district of shops and restaurants. On the coast is Balneario Santiago public beach.

Naguabo's *malecón,* a seaside promenade several miles south of the town plaza on PR 3, is a lively social center on weekends and holidays, attracting throngs of visitors who gather here to eat fresh seafood, drink, dance, shop, and people-watch. In contrast, the town center is on the shabby side, with many empty shopfronts surrounding the plaza.

SIGHTS

Balneario Punta Santiago (PR 3, km 72.4, Humacao, 787/852-1660 or 787/852-3066, www.drdpuertorico.com, Mon.-Fri. 7:30am-3:30pm, Sat.-Sun. and Mon. holidays 7:30am-5pm, $3 cars, $2 motorcycles, $4 vans, $5 buses, camping $25-40) is a great stretch of publicly maintained beach and vacation center with a swimming pool and modest overnight accommodations, camping facilities, bathrooms, and picnic shelters. Adjacent to the *balneario,* along about kilometer 68.3, is a large, shady **wilderness beach** that is unfortunately heavily littered and crawling with feral dogs. On the weekends you can find vendors there selling beverages, trinkets, oysters, and other food items. From here you can see **Cayo Santiago,** also known as Monkey Island because of the large population of rhesus monkeys placed there by animal researchers. Visitors are not allowed on the island, but they're welcome to dive and snorkel around its edges and watch the primates from a distance.

Reserva Natural de Humacao (PR 3, km 74.3, Humacao, 787/852-6058, May-Aug. Mon.-Fri. 7:30am-3:30pm, Sat.-Sun. and Mon.

holidays 7:30am-6pm, Sept.-Apr. Sat.-Sun. and Mon. holidays 7:30am-5:30pm, free) is a lovely natural reserve containing 3,186 acres of swamps, marshes, channels, and an interconnected lagoon system perfect for kayaking. It also has 10 kilometers (6 mi) of walking and bike trails. Sights along the way include an antique water-pumping station and bunkers constructed during World War II. Morrillo Cycle (787/559-7280, $7-15 an hour) rents bikes on-site for exploring the reserve's trails.

Iglesia Dulce Nombre de Jesus (3 Ave. Font Martelo, Humacao, 787/852-0868), located on the main plaza in downtown Humacao, is a Spanish colonial-style church built in 1793.

Malecón de Naguabo took a beating from Hurricanes Irma and Maria, but it has since been beautifully restored. The seaside promenade that stretches along PR 3 is the center of the city's social scene on weekends and holidays. Friends and families flock here in droves to dine at the seafood restaurants and fritter shacks across the street, shop, sun, stroll, and listen to music, most often recorded and played at earth-shaking decibels, but occasionally live.

Bosque de Pterocarpus (5 Academy Dr., Humacao, 787/285-6425, www.pterocarpus.org, daily 6am-6pm, free) is a 51-acre swamp forest home to 44 species of flora and 52 species of fauna. Take a self-guided tour or schedule a guided tour (in Spanish only) along a 1.2-kilometer (0.75-mi) boardwalk that takes about 45 minutes.

RECREATION

Palmas Athletic Club (Palmas del Mar, Country Club Dr., Humacao, 787/656-3000, www.talgracefeeds.com/palmas) has two 18-hole, 72-par courses: Golf Club was built in 1974 by Gary Player; and Flamboyan, considered one of the island's most challenging, is a newer course designed by Rees Jones. There

are also 20 tennis courts—both hard and clay surfaces, some lit for nighttime playing—a beach club with an enormous pool, a fitness center, and a modest spa.

Rancho Buena Vista (Palmas Dr., Palmas Del Mar Resort, Humacao, 787/479-7479, www.ranchobuenavistapr.com) is an equestrian center offering horseback riding on the beach and pony rides for children.

Water Sports & Ecotours (Playa de Humacao, PR 3, km 75.7, Humacao, 787/397-1900, Wed.-Sun. 9am-3:30pm) rents kayaks and paddleboards ($15/hour) for self-guided tours through the canals of the Reserva Natural de Humacao, as well as a one-hour guided pedal boat or walking tour ($10).

Monkey Island Kayak & Snorkel Tour (Barefoot Travelers Guesthouse, corner of Calle 2 and Calle 3, Punta Santiago, Humacao, 787/850-0508, www.barefoottravelersrooms. com, $65) takes groups of people from age 5 and older on a three-hour tour to Cayo Santiago to view from a safe distance the rhesus monkeys that live there. Beginning kayakers are welcome.

FOOD
Puerto Rican
Pura Vida (Palmanova Plaza, 295 Palmas Inn Way, Humacao, 787/914-0316, Sun. and Tues.-Thurs. 6pm-midnight, Fri.-Sat. 6pm-2am, $13-20) serves mofongo, churrasco, and seafood.

Seafood
Restaurante El Rincón Playero (PR 3, Malecón de Naguabo, 787/874-0045, Fri.-Sun. 11am-8pm or 9pm, $8-23) is a casual, open-air restaurant serving a variety of seafood fritters, mofongo with shrimp, snapper, or lobster, and an array of rice dishes, including paella.

Bobby's Place (PR 3, Malecón de Naguabo, 787/874-0335, Wed.-Thurs. 10am-6pm, Fri.-Sat. 10am-10pm, Sun. 10am-8pm, $5-24) offers carry-out service from a window

---

1: Malecón de Naguabo 2: Ikakos restaurant in Naguabo

piled high with fried seafood. Place your order for seafood fritters, mofongo, or whole fried snapper and take it to one of the nearby picnic tables to dine.

★ **Kasavista** (PR 3, km 66.5, Malecón de Naguabo, 787/655-7070, www.facebook.com/ Kasavista, Thurs.-Sun. noon-9pm, $13-27) is a modern bistro serving an outstanding menu of fresh seafood, including grilled dorado with tropical chutney and coconut rice, stuffed mofongo, coconut curry shrimp, and seafood paella for two. Service is exceptional, too. There's a second location in Fajardo.

For upscale ambience, **Ikakos** (PR 3, Malecón de Naguabo, 787/874-6122, http:// ikakospr.com, Sun. and Tues.-Thurs. 11am-midnight, Fri.-Sat. 11am-1:30am, $12-27) boasts a blue-tiled bar with pendant lighting, stacked stone walls, and exposed wood ceiling in the main dining room, and a private dining room featuring a modern chandelier, original oil paintings, and ambient blue lighting. The extensive menu features stuffed arepas, fried calamari, *pastelillos,* mofongo, whole fried snapper, and churrasco. The house specialties include snapper stuffed with shrimp, octopus, and conch ($38) and grilled lobster tail with shrimp, octopus, conch, and fish ($65).

Los Makos Restaurant (PR 3, Malecón de Naguabo, 787/874-2353, Mon.-Wed. 11am-8pm, Thurs. and Sun. 11am-10pm, Fri.-Sat. 11am-11:45pm, $10-40) is a large, modern restaurant with dining indoors and out, and a separate bar. It specializes in seafood, and its big seller by far is the local lobster, served in salads, soups, creole sauce, charbroiled, in garlic butter, or "Makos"-style, accompanied by octopus, conch, and shrimp.

International
The venerable **Chez Daniel** (Anchor Plaza, Harbour Dr., Humacao, 787/850-3838, www. chezdanielpr.com, July-May Wed.-Sun. 6pm-10 pm, $14-34) has been serving classic French cuisine in the Palmas del Mar community since 1985. An elegantly simple spot on a pier overlooking a marina, the restaurant serves crab crepes, seared duck liver, frog legs,

mahi-mahi in lobster sauce, and roasted rack of lamb. For a splurge, order the sautéed Dover sole in lemon butter sauce ($54). Next door is **Tapas Bar at Chez Daniel** (http://chezdanielpr.com/tapas-bar-palmas-del-mar), a casual restaurant with patio dining serving a variety of paellas and churrasco, as well as tapas such as white anchovies and *tostones* stuffed with crab.

Bocata by Campillo (Calle Dr. Vidal, PR 3, Humacao, 787/850-4429, http://bocatabycampillo.com, Mon. 11am-8pm, Tues.-Sat. 8am-10pm, Sun. 8am-8pm, $6-13) serves Spanish-style tapas, sandwiches, and paella. The wine selection is excellent, service is attentive, and there's occasionally live music.

ACCOMMODATIONS

Palmas del Mar (PR 3, km 86.4, Humacao, 787/852-8888, www.palmasdelmar.com) is a 2,700-acre planned community that includes residential and resort developments. For vacation rentals in Palmas del Mar, visit www.prwest.com. Police, fire, postal, banking, and medical services are all available at Palmas del Mar.

Under $100

Barefoot Travelers Rooms and Adventure Guesthouse (corner of Calle 2 and Calle 3, Punta Santiago, Humacao, 787/850-0508, www.barefoottravelersrooms.com, $77-88) features three guest rooms, one with an en suite bathroom and two that share a bath. Amenities include a shared kitchen, living room, TV, pool, and wireless Internet. The proprietors operate a number of adventure tours, including hang gliding, paragliding, and kayak tours to Cayo Santiago, aka Monkey Island.

Centro Vacacional de Humacao Villas Punta Santiago (PR 3, km 72.4, Punta Santiago, Humacao, 787/622-5200, www.drdpuertorico.com, $65-71 cabanas, $109-115 villas, two-night minimum) is a government-maintained and -operated vacation center

patronized mostly by Puerto Rican visitors, but anyone looking for basic, economical accommodations on the ocean is welcome. The gated property features a yellow-and-adobe-colored complex containing 99 cabanas and villas. Only the villas are air-conditioned, but both cabanas and villas have full kitchens. Linens, towels, and cooking utensils are not provided. Amenities include tennis courts, a playground, a pool with a waterslide, and lovely shady grounds featuring almond trees, palms, and *flamboyans*.

$100-150

Casa Cubuy Eco Lodge (PR 191, km 8.7, Naguabo, 787/291-9507, 787/455-2630, or 787/539-4192, www.casacubuy.com, $99-$130, includes breakfast, two-night minimum) is a small, low-key lodge on the quiet, less-visited southern side of El Yunque. Perched on a hill above a gurgling stream, this is definitely the place to go to get away from it all. Amenities are few (no TV!) beyond balconies and hammocks. But you're a short hike away from waterfalls and a natural pool where you can take an invigorating dip. A restaurant is on-site. In-room massages are available.

Plaza Suites (235 Harbour Dr., Palmas del Mar, 817/983-0664 or 800/997-9138, www.theplazapr.com, $129-209) is a 31-room condo hotel with a pool, 12 tennis courts, and a spa. Rooms come with a refrigerator, microwave, flat-screen TV, and complimentary wireless Internet.

$150-200

Wyndham Candelero Beach Resort (170 Candelero Dr., Humacao, 787/247-7979, www.wyndham.com, $169-314) features 107 guest rooms with air-conditioning and cable TV. Attractions include several miles of beach, an 8,000-square-foot pool, and access to a 200-slip marina, two golf courses, tennis courts, a fitness center, a spa, and eight restaurants. Both all-inclusive and room-only packages are available.

TRANSPORTATION AND SERVICES

Humacao is 55 kilometers (34 mi) southeast of the San Juan airport, which takes about an hour to drive. Take PR 52 south to PR 30. Naguabo is 70 kilometers (43 mi) southeast of the San Juan airport. Take PR 52 south to PR 31 east. For taxi services, call **Humacao Taxi** (787/852-6880).

Emergency medical services are available at **Ryder Memorial Hospital** (355 Calle Font Martelo, Humacao, 787/852-0768, hryder.org). **Walgreens** (477 PR 3, Humacao, 787/852-1330) has a full pharmacy.

Banking services are available at **Banco Popular** (PR 3, km 83.6, St. Triumph Plaza, Humacao, 787/852-8000), and there is a **post office** (122 Calle Font Martelo) in Humacao.

Yabucoa and Maunabo

Often bypassed by visitors, Yabucoa and Maunabo are quiet, low-key, seaside municipalities in the southeastern corner of Puerto Rico that offer a tranquil getaway from the crowds, traffic, and U.S. influence found elsewhere on the island. Nevertheless, the area is home to several modest hotels and restaurants that serve travelers who aren't looking for a lot of excitement or nightlife.

Unlike the island's southwestern corner, the vegetation here is emerald-green thanks to the convergence of several rivers from the Cordillera Central, and its beaches are mostly narrow and rocky. Primarily an agricultural community, Maunabo boasts stunning views

along the coastline where the mountains meet the sea. Yabucoa historically has been a center of industry. During the height of sugar production, it was home to six sugar mills. Today it is a manufacturing center, producing electronics, clothing, and cigarettes. Its coastline is home to a large oil refinery.

For stunning bird's-eye views of the ocean's horizon from a dramatic vantage point where the mountains meet the sea, take a **scenic drive** from Yabucoa to Maunabo along PR 901. Part of **La Ruta Panorámica,** the celebrated panoramic route that runs through the central mountain region of the island from east to west, this leg takes a half-hour

the coast of Maunabo

to travel the 18 kilometers (11 mi) of twisty roadway, and the vistas are breathtaking. Stop at **Restaurante El Nuevo Horizonte** and enjoy an empanada while admiring the scenery. If that leaves you wanting more, continue onto PR 3 to Patillas for another 30 minutes, stopping at **Paisajes Curet** for lunch. You can see **Faro de Punta Tuna** lighthouse from the outdoor dining area.

SIGHTS

The primary reason to visit the area is for its long stretches and private pockets of deserted beaches gently lapped by the Caribbean Sea. The most popular one is **Playa Punta Tuna** (PR 760, km 3, Maunabo), where the low-lying hills of the Cordillera Central kiss the sea. In addition to a nice, wide, mile-long beach and great surfing, this is where you'll find picturesque Faro de Punta Tuna, a lighthouse perched atop a hilly point that juts into the water.

Other beaches in Maunabo are **Los Bohios** (PR 760, Bordaleza), which offers a wonderful view of the Punta Tuna lighthouse and great surfing, and **Los Pinos** (PR 901), northwest of Playa Punta Tuna. **Playa Lucía** (PR 901, km 4) is a small beach in Yabucoa.

Faro de Punta Tuna (follow the signs from PR 760, Maunabo, 787/861-0301, Wed.-Sun. 9am-4pm, free) is a neoclassical-style lighthouse built in 1863. Stop by the office for information on the history of the lighthouse and the surrounding community, available in English and Spanish, then stroll the short, shady path toward the octagonal tower high on a cliff offering 180-degree views of the ocean and mountains.

ENTERTAINMENT AND EVENTS

If you want something to do besides loll around on the beach all day, visit during festival time when things get lively. In Maunabo, the big draw is **Festival Jueyero** (Sept.), a celebration that fêtes the land crab, held in the town plaza on Calle Santiago Iglesia. All sorts of crab dishes are on the menu, in addition to a parade, crab races, and more. Maunabo is also home to **Fiestas del Pueblo** (June), a town celebration held in the plaza featuring music, dance, rides, games, and food kiosks. Yabucoa has a **Patron Saint Festival** (late Sept.-early Oct.), in Parque Felix Millan, to commemorate Saint Angeles Custodios.

FOOD

Restaurante El Nuevo Horizonte (PR 901, km 8.8, Yabucoa, 787/893-5492, Sun. and Wed.-Thurs. 11am-8pm, Fri.-Sat. 11am-10pm, $13-29) offers inside dining on seafood and Puerto Rican cuisine while enjoying the ocean view from high up on a mountain peak. Outside is a kiosk serving empanadas and other Puerto Rican-style fritters and beers.

Rincón Familiar (PR 901 at PR 760, Maunabo, 787/861-4045, www.facebook.com/rinconfamiliar, Fri.-Sun. 11am-8pm, $6-24) is a casual *chinchorro* serving traditional Puerto Rican cuisine, including some less-commonly served dishes, such as *arroz con jueyes* (rice and land crab) and *guanimes con bacalo* (codfish stew with corn dumplings).

Paisajes Curet (PR 3, km 109, Maunabo, 787/861-2752, www.facebook.com/restaurantepaisajescuret, Mon.-Thurs. 11am-8pm, Fri.-Sat. 11am-10pm, Sun. 11am-9pm, $9-25) is a terrific full-service restaurant high up on a mountaintop, with a gorgeous view of the ocean and Faro de Punta Tuna. The menu includes mofongo, *chuleta frita*, churrasco, grilled duck breast, and an array of seafood dishes. Next door is Kiosko Curet, selling *pastelillos* and *alcapurrias*.

Palmas de Lucía (Hotel Parador Palmas de Lucía, PR 901 at PR 9911, Playa Lucía, Yabucoa, 787/893-4423, www.tropicalinnspr.com, Sun.-Thurs. 8am-9pm, Fri.-Sat. 8am-10pm, $11-17) serves three meals a day. Lunch consists of burgers, ribs, and chicken fingers; dinner specializes in a variety of fresh seafood, including halibut, shrimp, and lobster, as well as Puerto Rican dishes such as mofongo and *asopao*.

ACCOMMODATIONS

Hotel Parador Palmas de Lucía (PR 901 at PR 9911, Playa Lucía, Yabucoa, 787/893-4423, www.tropicalinnspr.com, $54-63, $101 s/d all-inclusive) is a modern motel-style property with a petite pool and a small, sandy beach half a block away. It has 34 simple, comfortable rooms featuring air-conditioning, satellite TV, refrigerators, microwaves, coffeemakers, and balconies. There's a restaurant on-site serving breakfast, lunch, and dinner.

Located along the eastern leg of La Ruta Panorámica, **Parador MaunaCaribe** (PR 901, km 1.9, Barrio Emajagua, Maunabo, 787/861-3330, www.paradorinns.com, $54) is part of the Tropical Inns chain of economical, well-maintained, and well-managed properties on the southeastern coast. The oceanfront property has 52 rooms featuring air-conditioning, satellite TV, telephones, and wireless Internet. Amenities include a large infinity pool overlooking the Caribbean with bar service, a fitness room, a video game room, wireless Internet, and a restaurant serving breakfast, lunch, and dinner. All-inclusive packages are available.

TRANSPORTATION AND SERVICES

For transportation services, call **Yabucoa Taxi** (787/266-4047) or **Mauna Coqui Taxi** (787/317-7258) in Maunabo. Yabucoa is 64 kilometers (40 mi) southeast of San Juan. Take Highway 52 south to Highway 30 south to PR 921 south to PR 908 south. Maunabo is 80 kilometers (50 mi) southeast of San Juan. Take Highway 52 south to Highway 30 to Highway 53.

Walgreens (302 Ernesto Carrasquillo, Yabucoa, 787/893-4410) provides pharmaceutical services. Banking services are available at **Banco Popular** (561 PR Ernesto Carrasquillo, Yabucoa, 787/266-2600). There is a **post office** (184 Ave. Calimano) in Maunabo.

Ponce and the South Coast

The south coast stands in stark contrast to

Puerto Rico's north coast.

Instead of lush, rocky coastlines, rough Atlantic waters, mountainous karst country, and a dense population, the south coast features a flat, dry topography and considerably less commercial development. It's a great place to go if you want to escape the traffic and U.S. influence found elsewhere on the island. And there are many great historic and cultural sights to explore.

Historically, the south coast was a major player in the island's sugar industry. It was once dotted with enormous sugarcane plantations, as well as sugar refineries, rum distilleries, and shipping operations. As that industry died out, the south coast turned its economic

Highlights

Look for ★ to find recommended sights, activities, dining, and lodging.

Jayuya

Barranquitas

Aibonito

Cayey

Coamo

Hacienda Buena Vista ★ ★ **Centro Ceremonial Indígena de Tibes**

Ponce ★ —**Castillo Serrallés**

Aguas de Termales ★ **de Coamo**

Patillas

Salinas

Guayama

Arroyo

Guánica

Museo de Arte de Ponce

Punta Brea

Cayos de Barca

Cayos Caribes

Caribbean Sea

© MOON.COM

★ **Museo de Arte de Ponce:** With arguably the finest art collection in Puerto Rico, this museum features significant Italian baroque and British pre-Raphaelite work, as well as a solid body of work by Puerto Rican artists (page 153).

★ **Castillo Serrallés:** This four-story Spanish Revival mansion was built in 1934. Take a tour to see the luxe furnishings and elaborate decor (page 154).

★ **Centro Ceremonial Indígena de Tibes:** Once the ceremonial grounds to two indigenous groups, the Igneri and the Pre-Taínos, this site contains several ceremonial *bateyes* (ball fields), plazas, and petroglyphs (page 157).

★ **Hacienda Buena Vista:** The 19th-century coffee plantation has been painstakingly restored and turned into a working museum that still produces coffee and cocoa (page 157).

★ **Take a dip in the Aguas de Termales de Coamo:** These natural hot springs have been a tourist attraction since Spanish colonial days (page 165).

Ponce and the South Coast

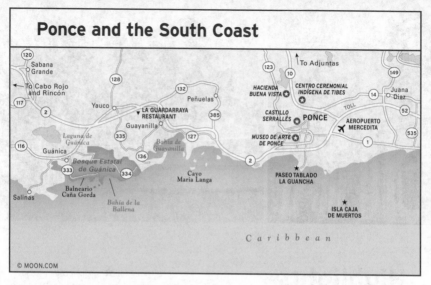

© MOON.COM

development toward the manufacturing of goods, although it hasn't come close to restoring the area to the level of wealth it once enjoyed.

Ponce is the south coast's biggest city, and what a city it is. It has a large, lovely central plaza that bustles with activity night and day, and it rivals San Juan as the island's cultural, historical, and architectural center. Home to the founders of Don Q rum, Ponce was once a very wealthy city, which is apparent in its many beautiful buildings, museums, and elaborate festivals.

The south coast was home to a significant Taíno community, established in the 1200s, that stretched from Guánica to Ponce. At the time of Columbus's arrival, its chief was Cacique Agüeybaná, who is believed to have been the island's most powerful leader at that time. But the south coast's indigenous history predates the Taíno culture. Just north of Ponce, Centro Ceremonial Indígena de Tibes is one of Puerto Rico's most significant historical sites. Many ceremonial ball fields, plazas,

and petroglyphs have been discovered on this site, which archaeologists have attributed to Pre-Taíno and Igneri cultures that date back as far as 300 BC.

East of Ponce is Baños de Coamo, a natural hot springs near the center of the region. Believed to contain restorative powers, Baños de Coamo has been a tourist attraction since colonial times, and it remains one today.

The southeastern corner of Puerto Rico is the least populated part of the island. Tourist sights are few, but there is a wealth of terrific seafood restaurants, a couple of modest hotels, and the clear blue waters of the Caribbean that beckon visitors eager to escape the hubbub of San Juan. This region is where Hurricane Maria made landfall in 2017, causing tremendous damage. Nevertheless, businesses are back up and running.

In late 2019 and early 2020, the region experienced a series of earthquakes measuring more than 5 on the Richter scale. The quakes caused a few deaths and some structural damage.

Previous: downtown Ponce; Catedral de Nuestra Señora de Guadalupe in Ponce's Plaza Las Delicias; Paseo Tablado La Guancha in Ponce.

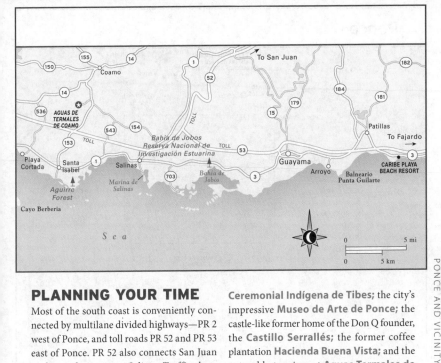

PLANNING YOUR TIME

Most of the south coast is conveniently connected by multilane divided highways—PR 2 west of Ponce, and toll roads PR 52 and PR 53 east of Ponce. PR 52 also connects San Juan to the south coast near Salinas. Traffic along the south coast is generally pretty light, so all in all, getting around the area is fairly easy.

Ponce is 130 kilometers (81 mi) away from San Juan and takes about 1.5 hours to drive. You can get there and back in a day, but you'd be hard-pressed to see it all in that short span of time. Better to stay a weekend or longer, so you're sure to have time to visit the **Centro** **Ceremonial Indígena de Tibes;** the city's impressive **Museo de Arte de Ponce;** the castle-like former home of the Don Q founder, the **Castillo Serrallés;** the former coffee plantation **Hacienda Buena Vista;** and the natural hot springs at **Aguas Termales de Coamo.**

Salinas, on the other hand, is close enough to drive to from San Juan for dinner. Maunabo is the kind of place where you want to kick back and chill out for a while. It's a great place to spend the weekend if you want to do nothing more than sunbathe, swim, and dine on fresh seafood.

Ponce and Vicinity

TOP EXPERIENCE

Elegant, cultured Ponce was an economic and cultural rival to San Juan back in the day. It experienced great growth and wealth during the 18th and 19th centuries thanks to its international shipping trade, which brought in an influx of European immigrants who established lucrative rum distilleries and plantations growing coffee and sugarcane. All that wealth translated into the construction of hundreds of gorgeous, ornate homes and buildings that combine rococo, neoclassical, and Spanish Revival architectural elements with traditional *criolla* building styles, distinguished by broad balconies, large doorways, and open-air patios. Unfortunately, many of them fell into disrepair over the course of the 1980s and 1990s due to economic hard times.

Ponce

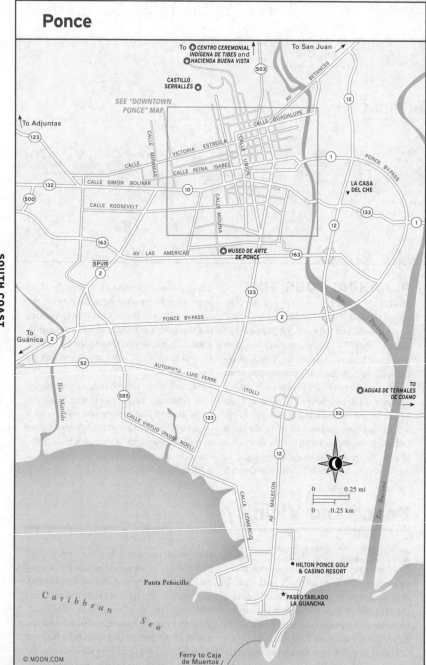

© MOON.COM

But things are on an upswing, and many of the city's stunning buildings have been restored to their former glory.

At the city's core is Plaza las Delicias, an enormous, shady plaza anchored by a massive fountain, Fuentes de Leones, and the impressive Catedral de Nuestra Señora de Guadalupe. The streets around the plaza are lined with many thriving businesses, and during the day, sidewalks are filled with shoppers, tourists, and street vendors. At night there are often live concerts.

Several miles south of the city is Paseo Tablado La Guancha, Ponce's waterfront entertainment district. Although the wooden boardwalk is closed due to hurricane damage, the bars and restaurants are still open.

Ponce has a petty street crime problem, so stick close to Plaza Las Delicias at night if you're on foot, and take taxis to restaurants and casinos.

If you're traveling by car, beware of Ponce drivers. They're arguably the worst on the island.

SIGHTS

Led by Ponce locals, **Isla Caribe Tours** (6953 Calle Isabel at Calle Munoz Rivera, 939/265-5691, www.islacaribepr.com) is a great introduction to the city. Daily two-hour **walking tours** (Mon.-Sat. 10:30am, Sun. 11am, $20 adults, $10 children 6-12, free for children 5 and younger) start at the souvenir shop **Utopia** (14 Calle Isabel). Other options include coffee, salsa, and art tours.

Plaza Las Delicias

Plaza Las Delicias (bounded by Calles Isabel, Atocha, Unión, and Simon Bolívar) is a bustling Spanish colonial plaza surrounded by many lovely 19th-century buildings, many of them containing banks, but there is a bar and a couple of fast-food joints. Although it looks like one large plaza, Plaza Las Delicias is in fact composed of two smaller plazas: Plaza Degetau and Plaza Luis Muñoz Rivera. Together they create a central gathering spot for Ponce residents, especially on the weekends.

During the day, the sidewalks along Calle Isabel and Calle Atocha are lined with dozens of brightly colored umbrellas, under which vendors sell hot dogs, silk flowers, lottery tickets, gift wrap by the yard, electronics, sneakers, jewelry, and more. At night, live bands give concerts, attracting multigenerational families, troops of preening teenagers, and love-struck couples who stake out cuddling

Fuentes de Leones in Plaza Las Delicias

Downtown Ponce

Map labels: CALLE BERTOLY, CALLE ARENAS, CALLE TRIOCHE, CALLE GUADALUPE, CALLE PROTESTANTE, CALLE ROSICH, Nuevo Plaza de Mercado Isabel II, CALLE LEON, CALLE MAYOR, CALLE SALUD, ESTRELLA, CALLE CASTILLO, Río Portugués, CALLE VICTORIA, CALLE MÉNDEZ VIGO, CALLE UNION, CALLE ATOCHA, CALLE SOL, CALLE VIVES, PASEO ATOCHA, CASA WIECHERS VILLARONGA, CHEF'S CREATIONS, MUSEO DE LA HISTORIA DE PONCE, CASA DE LAS TIAS, MUSEO DE LA MÚSICA PUERTORRIQUEÑA, Plaza de las Delicias, VISTAS, CALLE REINA ISABEL, PONCE PLAZA HOTEL & CASINO, PARQUE DE BOMBAS, CALLE CRISTINA, HOTEL BÉLGICA, CATEDRAL DE NUESTRA SEÑORA DE GUADALUPE, HOTEL MELIA, CALLE COMERCIO, CALLE VILLA, CALLE LUNA, CALLE AURORA, CALLE JOBOS, MUSEO DE LA MASSACRE DE PONCE, CALLE MOLINA, Parque Dora Colón Clavell, CALLE CONCORDIA, CALLE HOSTOS, CALLE MARINA, KING'S CREAM, CALLE FERROCARRIL, © MOON.COM, 10, 0 800 yds, 0 800 m

corners on park benches. Street preachers are known to get up on the soapboxes here, projecting their sermons through public address systems.

The plaza contains two enormous fountains, including the elaborate **Fuentes de Leones** (Fountain of Lions). This is also where you'll find the stunning **Catedral de Nuestra Señora de Guadalupe** (787/842-0134, office: Mon.-Fri. 9am-1:30pm; services: Mon.-Fri. 7am, 9am, and 12:05pm, Sat. 7am, 4pm, and 7pm, Sun. 7am, 9am, 11am, 4pm, and 7pm), a gorgeous French neoclassical-style edifice reconstructed in the 1930s and featuring two bell towers, stone tile floors, and a sky-high arched ceiling painted a robin's-egg blue and hung with 20 crystal chandeliers. Check out the religious statuary, including

one of Mary dressed in a pale blue robe with a gold halo above her head, and the bloodied body of Christ in a glass coffin.

But by far the most exceptional structure in Plaza Las Delicias is **Parque de Bombas** (787/284-3338, daily 9am-5pm, free), a startlingly whimsical black-and-red-striped pavilion built in 1882 to provide exhibition space for the Exhibition Trade Fair. A year later it became home to the city's fire station. Today it is a museum honoring the history of the city's firefighters. It contains portraits of past fire chiefs, exhibits of fire helmets, hats, axes, hose nozzles, and a fire truck.

Casa Wiechers-Villaronga

Looking like a pink-and-white-frosted wedding cake, **Casa Wiechers-Villaronga** (50

Calle Isabel, generally Wed.-Sun. 8am-noon and 1pm-4:30pm, but posted hours often are not observed) is a stunning example of Classical Revival architecture, designed by celebrated Ponce architect Alfredo B. Wiechers. The house museum contains period furnishings and photographs of notable architects from the island and some of their designs. Even if the museum is closed, it's worth the short walk from Plaza Las Delicias to see the eye-popping exterior.

★ Museo de Arte de Ponce

The **Museo de Arte de Ponce** (2325 Blvd. Luis A. Ferre Aguayo, 787/848-0505 or 787/840-1510, www.museoarteponce.org, Wed.-Mon. 10am-6pm, $6 adults, $3 children), the crown jewel of Puerto Rico's cultural institutions, contains more than 3,000 pieces of European, North American, and Puerto Rican art from the 14th century to the present. In addition to its renowned collection of Italian baroque and British Pre-Raphaelite work, Puerto Rican artists are also represented with works by painters José Campeche (1759-1809) and Francisco Oller (1822-1917), as well as photographer Jack Delano (1914-1997), a member of a distinguished group of photographers who worked for the Farm Security

Administration during the Depression and documented the island's people and places for more than 50 years.

The most celebrated piece in the museum's collection is *Flaming June*, an 1895 classicist painting of a slumbering woman in a brilliant orange gown by Briton Lord Fredric Leighton. It may seem an unlikely symbol of Ponce's cultural heritage, but once you witness the power of the large gilt-framed painting in the Museo de Arte de Ponce, you can begin to understand why the image has not only been plastered on coffee cups, T-shirts, and mouse pads in the museum store but has been appropriated by local contemporary artists who've taken the liberty of altering her image in various ways, including wrapping her in the Puerto Rican flag.

Museo de la Música Puertorriqueña

Museo de la Música Puertorriqueña (Calle Isabel at Calle Salud, 787/290-1530, 787/669-1866, or 787/848-0505, Wed.-Sun. 8am-4pm, 30-minute guided tours by appointment, free) is a tribute to the rich history of Puerto Rican music in a lovely neoclassical home built in 1912. Designed by architect Alfredo Wiechers Pieretti of Ponce, the

Parque de Bombas in Plaza Las Delicias

home's stained-glass windows, stone tiles, and brass-embossed walls are reason enough to tour the museum.

Each room is dedicated to a different musical style and the vintage instruments used to create it. In the *danza* room are cellos, violins, and French horns; in the salsa room are bongos, bells, maracas, trumpets, trombones, timbales, and *güiros* (gourds); in the *bomba y plena* room are tambourines, *güiros,* and accordions. There's also a room devoted to Taíno ceremonial instruments, including a drum made from a tree trunk, wooden maracas, conch shell horns, flutes made of royal palm and bamboo, and ocarinas (seeds made into flutes). Another room is devoted to the art of making bongos from wooden barrels. Free classes in bongo-making are held in June and July.

Museo de la Historia de Ponce

Museo de la Historia de Ponce (53 Calle Isabel, corner of Calle Mayor, 787/844-7071 or 787/842-7042, Tues.-Sat. 9am-4pm, free) is more than just a monument to the city's history. Its construction served to preserve and adapt two historic neoclassical homes, Casa Salazar and Casa Zapater, and thanks to the Ernesto Ramos Antonini auditorium, it is also a cultural center for the local arts community. Permanent exhibits focus on ecology, pre-Hispanic times, politics, economic development, and architecture. Wall text and exhibit information are in Spanish only.

Parque Dora Colón Clavell

Built in 1995, the $11-million **Parque Dora Colón Clavell** (between Calle Marina and Calle Concordia) is a gorgeous city park with lacy wrought ironwork and glass pavilions and pergolas, landscaped walkways, and an amphitheater. Five kiosks sell breakfast, lunch, and dinner, as well as wine, beer, and coffee. It's four blocks south of Plaza Las Delicias.

Museo de la Masacre de Ponce

Museo de la Masacre de Ponce (corner of Calle Marina and Calle Aurora, 787/844-9722, by appointment only, free) has a modest exhibit in Spanish dedicated to the memory of a bloody incident on Palm Sunday in 1937 when local police were ordered to fire on Puerto Rican nationalists demonstrating for Puerto Rico's independence from the United States. Nineteen people were killed and more than 200 were injured.

★ Castillo Serrallés

Set high on a hill overlooking Ponce is a startling reminder of the height of the city's flourishing sugar industry, when its port was the busiest on the island. **Castillo Serrallés** (17 Calle El Vigía, 787/259-1774, 787/259-1775, or 800/981-2275, www.castilloserralles.org, Thurs.-Sun. 9:30am-5pm, $13 adults, $6 children, $7 seniors) was built in 1934 for Eugenio Serrallés, a leader in the local sugarcane industry and founder of the still-operating Serrallés Rum Distillery, maker of the island's premier rum, Don Q.

Designed by architect Pedro Adolfo de Castro, the four-story Spanish Moroccan-style mansion was last inhabited in 1979 by Serrallés's daughter. It became a museum in 1991.

The house contains many of the Serrallés family's original furnishings, several of them made by Puerto Rican artisans or imported from Europe, the oldest piece being a small 16th-century table in the foyer. No cost was spared in the construction of the house. The parquet wood floor in the parlor was imported from Brazil; the dining room, which took 18 months to build, features a painted, hand-carved ceiling made of oak, mahogany, and ceiba woods; and the black-and-cream bathrooms are designed in an art deco style. The building was technologically advanced for the times: It even has an intercom system with 14 receivers as well as an elevator. In the kitchen is a 1929 GE side-by-side refrigerator that still works. One room in the house has

---

1: Centro Ceremonial Indígena de Tibes **2:** *piragua* vendor in Ponce **3:** Castillo Serrallés

been converted into an exhibition space that explains and illustrates sugarcane processing and rum-making.

There are also three gardens on-site that can be toured for an additional fee, as well as the Butterfly Nursery.

Across the street from Castillo Serrallés is **Cruceta del Vigía** ($10 adults, $6 students and seniors, includes admittance to Castillo Serrallés), an enormous concrete cross with an observation deck built in 1984. It marks the site of a Spanish lookout station established in 1801 to watch over the Ponce harbor. At that time, a crude wooden cross was erected on the site that remained there until it was destroyed in 1998 by Hurricane Georges. The cross was used as a flag-signaling system to alert troops to the arrival of merchant ships in the harbor. If a white flag was raised, it meant the harbor was under possible attack.

Paseo Tablado La Guancha

Commonly called **La Guancha** (Calle C), this waterfront entertainment district compensates for the fact that although Ponce is on the coast, little of it is suitable for recreational use.

The broad wooden waterfront promenade at the heart of this entertainment district was damaged during Hurricane Maria and has been closed indefinitely. But many of the restaurants, bars, and kiosks selling beach gear remain open, as is the covered viewing area at the end, where visitors can feed the tarpon and get up close and personal with the pelicans. Other attractions include a large children's playground and a small beach.

There are several water sports outfitters, including **Caribe Rentals** (787/433-7079, www.facebook.com/CaribeRentalspr, Mon.-Fri. by appointment, Sat.-Sun. 11am-8pm), offering hourly rentals of paddleboards, kayaks, and pedal boats; **Island Venture Water Excursions** (787/842-8546, www.islandventurepr.com) and **East Island Excursions** (787/860-3434, www.eastislandpr.com), providing day-long outings by catamaran to Isla Caja de Muertos; and **WaterLand Adventure** (787/556-1568 or 787/432-9882, www.waterlandadventure.com), which provides daily transportation and tours of Isla Cardona.

La Guancha is pretty sleepy during the week, but it comes alive on weekend nights. To get here, take PR 12 south to the end and turn left on Calle A, then right on Calle B, which ends at the parking lot for La Guancha.

Cruceta del Vigía

It's a 10-minute drive of 6 kilometers (4 mi) from central Ponce.

★ Centro Ceremonial Indígena de Tibes

In 1975 the remains of two indigenous civilizations were discovered a couple of miles north of Ponce on what is now called the **Centro Ceremonial Indígena de Tibes** (PR 503, km 2.5, 787/840-2255, www.nps.gov, Tues.-Sun. 9am-3:30pm, $3 adults, $2 children, $1.50 seniors and visitors with disabilities). The Igneri reigned over the region from 300 BC to AD 600. On the same location, a pre-Taíno culture thrived from AD 600 to 1200. Excavation of the site is still underway, but among the structures uncovered and restored are seven *bateyes,* or ball fields, and two rectangular stone-rimmed ceremonial plazas, around which you can spot faint petroglyphs carved into the rock.

The vegetation is rich with many of the same plants used by native cultures for medicinal and other purposes, including the *cohoba* tree (its red berries were used to induce hallucination and communication with the gods), the calabash tree (its gourd-like fruit was hollowed out and dried to make bowls), and the *mavi* tree (its bark was used to make a fermented drink).

A small museum contains artifacts from both cultures found on the site, including *cemies,* amulets, vomit spatulas, *dujos* (stools), idols, necklaces, a mortar and pestle, flints, blades, and stone collars. In addition, there are the human remains of a woman, possibly sacrificed, found among 187 bodies discovered buried under one of the *bateyes.* There's also a gift shop selling literature about the native cultures and traditional crafts made by local artisans.

★ Hacienda Buena Vista

Hacienda Buena Vista (PR 123, km 16.8, 787/722-5882, www.paralanaturaleza.org, Wed.-Sun. by reservation only, $12 adults, $9 children and seniors, accessibility is limited) is a carefully restored 19th-century coffee plantation about 15 kilometers (9 mi) north of Ponce on PR 123.

Established in 1833, Hacienda Buena Vista was one of the most successful of the 50 plantations around Ponce. It was founded by a Venezuelan, Salvador de Vives, who began growing corn, plantains, yams, pineapples, and coffee. Eventually he added a corn mill, a rice husker, a cotton gin, and a coffee depulper to the operation. As Puerto Rico's coffee industry boomed, so did Hacienda Buena Vista, due in large part to the labor of as many as 57 enslaved people.

When the island's coffee industry went bust in 1897, the plantation was converted into orange groves and remained operational until the 1950s. Termites destroyed most of the original buildings, and the farm machinery was left to rust for many years, but in 1984 the Conservation Trust of Puerto Rico began an extensive restoration project using 19th-century construction techniques.

In addition to the restored structures, mill, and machinery, the plantation's lush natural setting is worth a visit. On the Canas River, the property features mature vegetation home to a variety of birds, including the mangrove cuckoo and Puerto Rican screech-owl, as well as plenty of coquí frogs and lizards. In October, coffee beans from the property are processed and sold by the bag. The Conservation Trust leads occasional guided hikes and bird-watching expeditions in Spanish. Check the website for details.

Access to Hacienda Buena Vista is available by guided tour only. Tours last 1.5 hours and are offered in Spanish or English. Because the tour requires climbing lots of steps and traversing uneven ground and boardwalks, it is not wheelchair-friendly and may not be appropriate for those with mobility issues. Tour reservations should be made at least 48 hours in advance (earlier for a weekend or holiday). Check the website for availability.

From Plaza Las Delicias in Ponce, it takes about 30 minutes to drive the 15 kilometers (9 mi) to Hacienda Buena Vista. Look for a black metal gate with a guard shack, pull off the road onto the narrow shoulder, and wait for the gate to open at the appointed time.

Isla Caja de Muertos

Isla Caja de Muertos is a small, uninhabited island 8 kilometers (5 mi) south of Ponce featuring beautiful **Playa Pelicano,** hiking trails through a semiarid forest containing a variety of cacti, and a lighthouse built in 1887. The snorkeling is great, too.

To access the island, book a tour with **East Island Excursions** (787/860-3434, www.eastislandpr.com) or **Island Venture Water Excursions** (787/842-8546, www.islandventurepr.com), both of which launch daily from La Guancha, and plan to spend the whole day.

RECREATION
Rental Gear and Outfitters

Island Venture Water Excursions (La Guancha, 787/842-8546, www.islandventurepr.com) offers 6.5-hour, all-inclusive high-speed catamaran tours to Isla Caja de Muertos ($70 adults, $60 children 4-10). The cost includes lunch, snacks, drinks, beer, kayaks, paddleboards, and snorkel equipment. Children under 4 are not permitted. Excursions depart at 9:30am and return at 4pm.

Caribe Rentals (La Guancha, Calle C, 787/433-7079, www.facebook.com/CaribeRentalspr, Sat.-Sun. 11am-8pm, by appointment on weekdays) rents pedal boats, one- and two-person kayaks, and paddleboards.

East Island Excursions (La Guancha, Calle C, 787/860-3434, www.eastislandpr.com) offers day-long catamaran tours to Isla Caja de Muertos (once daily, $70 pp). Children under 4, pregnant women, and people with back or neck injuries are not permitted. The tour includes a buffet lunch, beverages (including beer), snorkel gear, shared kayaks, and a tour of the lighthouse on Caja de Muertos. Participants should bring sunscreen, a hat, sunglasses, a towel, water shoes, and sturdy shoes with tread for the lighthouse tour. Tours depart at 9:30pm and return at 4pm.

WaterLand Adventure (La Guancha, Calle C, 787/556-1568 or 787/432-9882, www.waterlandadventure.com) provides daily excursions to Isla Cardona, a small, uninhabited island just a 10-minute ride away. All-inclusive tours include a guided snorkeling tour with equipment, a tour of an abandoned lighthouse, lunch, and use of a beach chair and umbrella. The transportation-only option costs $23 per person.

Ponce Yacht Club (787/842-9003 or 787/840-4388, www.ponceyachtclub.com) is a full-service marina with an enormous activities pavilion, including a bar and restaurant (seafood and Puerto Rican cuisine, daily noon-10pm). Visiting boaters who pay a dockage fee can use the facilities (showers, cafeteria, restaurant, bar). Registration at the office (Mon.-Fri. 8am-5pm, Sat. 8am-3pm) is required.

Costa Caribe Golf and Country Club (Ponce Hilton Golf and Casino Resort, 1150 Ave. Caribe, 787/259-7676, www.costacariberesort.com, www.ponce.hilton.com) is a 27-hole course designed by Bruce Besse on what was once sugarcane fields. It offers spectacular views of the Caribbean and Puerto Rico's central mountain region. The signature hole is number 12, featuring an island green.

ENTERTAINMENT AND EVENTS
Nightlife

There are three gambling options in Ponce. **Holiday Inn and Tropical Casino** (3315 Ponce Bypass, 787/844-1200, www.ihg.com, daily 24 hours) is a 9,800-square-foot casino with 346 slot machines plus blackjack, craps, roulette, let it ride, poker, three-card poker, and triple shot. **Ponce Hilton and Casino Resort** (1150 Ave. Caribe, 787/259-7676, www.ponce.hilton.com, daily 24 hours) is a large casino with 330 slot machines plus blackjack, craps, roulette, Caribbean stud poker, Texas hold 'em, and three-card poker. **Casino de la Plaza** (Ponce Plaza Hotel & Casino, Calle Isabel at Calle Unión, Plaza de Las Delicas, 787/813-5050, ext. 7606 or

7607, www.ponceplazahotelandcasino.com, daily 24 hours) features more than 260 slot machines, live blackjack, craps, roulette, and bingo. There's also live entertainment nightly and craft cocktails available at the casino's bar, Viva.

Che Che Cole (3 Calle Union, Plaza Las Delicas, no phone, Fri. 6pm-2:30am, Sat. 7pm-2:30am, $8-14) is a weekend bar where salsa music blasts from the speakers at an ear-splitting volume and the booze is cheap and plentiful. The bar specializes in fruit-flavored mojitos including mango, melon, and passion fruit. The cocktails ($4) are very strong and served in 16-ounce plastic cups. Food is provided by the Mexican restaurant next door and includes fish tacos, burritos, and fajitas. If the music is too loud, you can take your drink with you and stroll around the plaza, where the people-watching is always entertaining.

4 Palos Tasca Boricua (7037 Calle Mende Vigo, 787/242-9607, Tues.-Fri. 5pm-11pm, Sat. 5pm-2am, $2-3) is the polar opposite of Che Che Cole. This small, chill space 1.5 blocks from the plaza is an ideal spot to kick back with a couple of beers or cocktails in the cool interior or at a sidewalk table and soak up the elegant ambience of Ponce.

Festivals and Events

Río de Janeiro's celebration may be the world's most famous, but Ponce's **Carnaval** is no slouch. In February, during the five days preceding the first day of Lent, Plaza Las Delicias is filled with festivities. Elaborate masquerade dances and parades are held each day, during which revelers show off their elaborate costumes and play out a symbolic battle between the Christians and the Moors. Traditional costumes include *caballeros,* who represent Spanish knights; *vejigantes* (horned entities), who represent the Moors; and the evil trickster spirits of the *viejos* (old men) and *locas* (crazy women).

In dramatic contrast to the frivolity of Carnaval is **Las Mañanitas** (787/841-8044). Every December 12 beginning at 5am, a religious procession marches from Calle Lolita Tizol to Plaza Las Delicias. Leading the way are mariachis who sing songs honoring the city's patron saint, Our Lady of Guadalupe.

Semana de la Danza (787/841-8044) features a weeklong series of events celebrating *danza,* a turn-of-the-20th-century ballroom dance that originated in Ponce, and one of its most beloved composers, Juan Morel Campos. Held mid- to late May, the festival features conferences, concerts, parades, and dance competitions. A melding of Caribbean and European styles, the formally structured musical style is often described as an Afro-Caribbean waltz. Puerto Rico's national anthem, "La Borinqueña," was originally written as a *danza.*

In early April, Ponce hosts **Las Justas,** a massive athletic event that started as an intercollegiate track and field competition but now embraces all varieties of sporting events, including swimming, baseball, basketball, judo, table tennis, and cheerleading. Each year the event attracts more than 100,000 people, drawn as much by the athletic competition as by the nightly concerts featuring the island's biggest reggaetón stars. If this isn't your thing, stay far away from Ponce during Justas. Many businesses, including restaurants and hotels, not only close down but board up their windows; the heavy-drinking crowds are known to get rowdy.

SHOPPING

Paseo Atocha is a pedestrian part of Calle Atocha between Calle Isabel at Plaza Las Delicias and Calle Vives. The sidewalk is lined by a variety of shops selling shoes, clothing, jewelry, electronics, discount housewares, sewing notions, and tourist trinkets. On weekends (Friday-Sunday), the sidewalk fills with street vendors selling flowers, lottery tickets, gift wrap and cards, sewing notions, tourist trinkets, and more.

The renovated **Nueva Plaza de Mercado Isabel II** (corner of Paseo Atocha and Calle Victoria, Mon.-Fri. 6am-5pm, Sat. 6am-4pm, Sun. 6am-noon) is a thriving marketplace filled with vendors selling everything from fresh fruits, vegetables, meats, and seafood to souvenirs, lottery tickets, clothing, and more. There are also several small eateries serving good, cheap *criolla* cuisine.

Pick up a bag of locally grown coffee roasted on the premises at **Torrefacción Mayor** (2638 Calle Mayor at Calle Aurora, 787/812-1941, www.facebook.com/cafemayorpr, Mon.-Fri. 8am-5pm). Three roasts are available, but the French roast is the best.

Mi Coqui (9227 Calle Marina, facing Plaza Las Delicias, 787/841-0216, daily 9am-7pm) is a two-level wonder. Downstairs is a large, densely packed trinket shop where you can find some low-end, locally made crafts, as well as bottles of rum and bags of coffee. But request access to go upstairs and you'll find a large gallery filled with original artwork, both traditional and contemporary, including oil paintings; *vejigante* masks; and the highly collectible santos, small hand-carved saints.

Utopia (14 Calle Isabel, 787/848-5441, Mon.-Fri. 7am-6pm, Sat. 8am-6pm, Sun. 11am-6pm) is a huge souvenir and import gift shop selling T-shirts, jewelry, and beachwear. A small lunch counter serves coffee and sandwiches.

El Candil (93 Calle Union, 787/242-6693, www.elcandil.com, Mon.-Sat. 9am-5pm, Sun. noon-4pm) is a large, bright bookstore with a small café selling coffee, cookies, sandwiches, beer, and wine. Children's events are held every Sunday at 1pm. Most books are Spanish language, but there are a few English-language books available, as well as CDs.

For all the latest in contemporary fashions and accessories, **Plaza del Caribe** (2050 Plaza del Caribe, Ponce Bypass, PR 2, 787/259-8989, www.plazadelcaribe.net, Mon.-Sat. 9am-9pm, Sun. 11am-7pm) is a mall that has you covered. You'll find familiar American chains, as well as local chains including Valija Gitana.

FOOD
Puerto Rican

Order your food at the counter and dine on home-style Puerto Rican cuisine in the courtyard at **Sabor Rumba** (66 Calle Reina Isabel, 787/843-3003, Mon.-Thurs. 9am-10pm, Fri. 9am-11pm, Sat. 11am-11pm, Sun. noon-6pm, $10-19). Order your mofongo made with choice of yuca, green plantain or yellow plantain, or a combination of all three, and stuff it with your choice of chicken, shrimp, or churrasco. Other options include calamari, ceviche, grilled mahi-mahi, and pork loin ribeye. Enjoy a fresh fruit frappé to wash it all down.

Enter the lobby at 76 Calle Cristina and take the elevator to the top floor to enter ★ **Vistas** (76 Calle Cristina, 939/350-2407, www.facebook.com/vistasponce, Tues.-Thurs. 4pm-10pm, Fri.-Sat. 4pm-11pm, Sun. 2pm-8pm, $16-29), a chic, upscale restaurant with fantastic views of the city, serving a robust menu of creative dishes inspired by Puerto Rican cuisine. Start with shrimp in *bacalao* batter or fry bread topped with shredded pork and chicharrón, then dig into entrées ranging from pan-seared mahi-mahi with crab stew or lamb shank fricassee. The house-made sangria is highly recommended.

It's not easy to find, but ★ **La Casa del Chef** (Callejon Fagot, 787/843-1298, Sun.-Mon. noon-9pm, Tues.-Thurs. noon-10pm, Fri.-Sat. noon-11pm, $11-29) is worth the trouble of seeking it out. A favorite among business workers for lunch, the enormous menu specializes in expertly prepared Puerto Rican cuisine, including stuffed mofongo, churrasco, and fried pork, as well dishes like lobster alfredo and steak Diane. The service is excellent. It's located in a blue building in the parking lot of Centro del Sur mall across from Marshall's. To gain entry, ring the bell and get buzzed in.

Seafood

Pura Vida (9 La Guancha, Calle C, 787/400-8420, Sun.-Thurs. 11am-midnight, Fri.-Sat. 11am-2am, $8-20) is a lively open-air restaurant overlooking the water at La Guancha,

1: Utopia gift shop in Ponce **2:** Hotel Bélgica
3: shopping along Paseo Atocha

serving stuffed mofongo, whole fried snapper, churrasco, and burgers.

La Monserrate Sea Port Restaurant (PR 2, km 218, 787/841-2740, daily 11am-10pm, $12-35) offers oceanfront terrace dining and a menu featuring every type of seafood imaginable, including lobster, conch, octopus, red snapper, mahi-mahi, grouper, and shrimp.

Eclectic

The menu is as eclectic as the decor at ★ **Chef's Creations** (100 Calle Reina, 787/848-8384, Mon.-Wed. 11am-2pm, Thurs.-Fri. 11am-2pm and 6pm-10pm, Sat. 6pm-10:30pm, $16-25). Tricked out in rustic wood and stone walls draped with twinkle lights and Mexican blankets, this festive, bohemian eatery serves a changing menu that combines elements of Puerto Rican, Mediterranean, Southwestern, and Creole cuisines. Dishes include quesadilla *tripleta,* churrasco with potatoes in a sauce of ancho chiles and cilantro, and chicken breast stuffed with cheese and chorizo.

Breakfast and Lunch

Melao Coffeeshop (corner of Calle Reina and Calle Union, 787/813-5050, ext. 7582, Sun.-Wed. 7am-9pm, Thurs.-Sat. 7am-10pm, $7-22) serves breakfast all day long, as well as burgers, sandwiches, and pizzas. There's a kid's menu and play area, too.

Proscenium Café Teatro (Calle Isabel, corner of Atocha, 787/840-3315, www.facebook.com/Prosceniumponce, Mon.-Thurs. 7am-2pm, Fri. 8am-11:45pm, Sat. 9am-11:45pm, Sun. 9am-7pm, $10-20) serves breakfast and lunch during the week, and on the weekends it turns into a supper club with live shows featuring music, comedy, and dance. The menu runs the gamut from French toast and acai yogurt parfaits in the morning to Monte Cristo and Philly cheesesteaks mid-day to shrimp scampi and risotto at night.

Dessert

King's Cream (61 Calle Vives, 787/378-7137, daily 9am-10pm) is a no-frills operation serving soft ice cream in a variety of flavors. There's no seating on the premises, so plan to take your treat to go. The fresh fruit flavors are the best.

ACCOMMODATIONS

The elegant **Meliá Century Hotel** (75 Calle Cristina, 787/842-0260, www.meliacenturyhotel.com, $95-140) was established in 1900 as a world-class European-style hotel. After Hurricane Maria, it underwent a dramatic renovation that turned its lobby, pool, and courtyard area into a hip, high-concept space featuring shiny white walls, enormous crystal chandeliers, and oversized baroque chairs lacquered in shades of electric blue and yellow. Unfortunately, the rooms retain the dated, budget-corporate look of a business traveler's motel. Rooms come with air-conditioning, phones, satellite TV, wireless Internet, and bathtubs (a rarity!). Amenities include a pool, a business center, and laundry service.

Charming, authentically vintage ★ **Hotel Bélgica** (122 Calle Villa, off Plaza Las Delicias, 787/844-3255, www.hotelbelgica.com, $90-105) has been a continuously operating hotel since its construction in 1872. The 21 very clean, simple rooms have been modernized and feature air-conditioning, satellite TV, mini refrigerator, and wireless Internet. Some rooms have shared balconies for no additional cost. The rooms are comfortably appointed with quality furnishings, and the staff is small but attentive. There is no restaurant or bar onsite, but complimentary coffee is served in the lobby. Proximity to the plaza means it can be a bit noisy at night if there's an event going on.

Right on Plaza Las Delicias is ★ **Ponce Plaza Hotel & Casino** (Calle Reina at Calle Unión, Plaza Las Delicias, 787/813-5050, www.ponceplazahotelandcasino.com, $129-139, $150 suite), which features 69 rooms in an 1882 building. The hotel's casino has 260 slot machines, blackjack, craps tables, roulette, and bingo. Rooms come with TVs, air-conditioning, and wireless Internet. Other amenities include a pool, fitness room, coffee shop, and bar.

Hilton Ponce Golf and Casino Resort (1150 Caribe Ave., 787/259-7674, www.hilton-ponceresort.com, $220-250) is a beachside resort with 259 rooms and suites and a lot of amenities, including a 27-hole golf course on a former sugar plantation, a casino (daily 24 hours), tennis courts, miniature golf, fitness center, swimming pool, three restaurants, and two bars.

TRANSPORTATION AND SERVICES

Ponce is 115 kilometers (71 mi) southwest of San Juan on PR 52. Plans are underway to expand and renovate **Mercedita International Airport** (PSE, 787/842-6292) to better accommodate bigger commercial jets. Currently there are two passenger terminals and one cargo terminal. JetBlue offers direct flights to Ponce from JFK airport in New York City and from Orlando, Florida. All other U.S. airline companies go through San Juan's Luis Muñoz Marín International Airport, where you can catch a plane to Ponce on one of several daily flights by Cape Air.

There is no public transportation service available from the airport, but you can catch a taxi waiting at the airport. There are several car-rental agencies at the airport, including Avis, Hertz, L&M, Budget, and **Charlie Car Rental** (2395 Ponce Bypass/PR 2, 787/651-4121, www.charliecars.com), a locally owned, budget rental car agency with locations in San Juan, Aguadilla, and Caguas.

Taxi service is provided by **Best Union Taxi** (787/840-9126), **Borinquen Taxi Cab** (787/843-6000 or 787/843-6100), and **Ponce Taxi** (787/840-0088).

Medical services are available at **Hospital San Lucas** (917 Ave. Tito Castro,

787/844-2080, www.sanlucaspr.com). There's a 24-hour pharmacy at **Walgreens** (2979 Ave. Fagot, 787/841-7400). The U.S. **post office** has branches at 93 Atocha (787/842-2997, 787/842-8303, or 787/284-2186) and PR 100, km 123.3 (787/812-0206, 787/812-0207, or 787/812-0208).

GUAYANILLA

The southwestern town Guayanilla is primarily a residential community that doesn't often attract visitors, but it is home to an outstanding restaurant and a modern hotel and casino. The island's popular Festival del Café is held every year in the nearby town of Yauco.

Festivals and Events

Festival del Café is an annual weeklong celebration of the coffee harvest held in March in the nearby town of Yauco. Festivities take place in Plaza Fernando de Pacheco and include parades, award ceremonies, dance and musical performances, arts, crafts, and food vendors. Yauco is less than 10 kilometers (6 mi) west of Guayanilla.

Food and Accommodations

In 1957 Don Juan Vera-Martinez fulfilled a special request for a patron by deep-frying a pork chop specially cut so that it retained a thick rind of fat and part of the ribs. When cooked, the rind of fat curled in a way that recalled the petticoats of a can-can dancer, and *chuleta can can* was born. Now as much a tradition as mofongo, it's found on most every menu serving *cocina criolla*. But the best is served by Don Juan's descendants at ★ **La Guardarraya** (PR 127, km 6.0, 787/856-4222, www.laguardarraya.com, Wed.-Sun. 11am-7:30pm, closed the last two weeks of Dec., $6-16), a destination restaurant halfway between Guánica and Ponce. Built in 1993, the restaurant is a large, lovely *criolla*-style wood structure with shuttered doors and windows tucked in the woods, and the service is professional. The house sangria made from fresh juices is outstanding and strong. The $6 weekly lunch specials are a steal. The restaurant can be a challenge to find. From Ponce, go west on PR 2, take exit 205 for Penuelas/Guayanilla, and turn left. Turn right at McDonald's, then take an immediate left onto PR 127 and cross the bridge. The restaurant is on the right. The drive takes about 30 minutes.

Costa Bahia Hotel, Convention Center & Casino (PR 127, km 8.6, 787/835-3335, www.costabahiahotel.com, $120) is modern 136-room hotel. Guest rooms feature satellite TV, mini refrigerators, and free Internet. Amenities include a complimentary breakfast, swimming pool, fitness center, business center, and the Blue Dolphin Casino.

Transportation

Located on PR 2, Guayanilla is 145 kilometers (90 mi) southwest of San Juan and 25 kilometers (16 mi) west of Ponce.

Coamo and Salinas

Coamo is a growing community in the hilly terrain just south of the island's majestic Cordillera Central mountain range. Its claim to fame, the Aguas de Termales de Coamo, is a natural hot springs reputed to have restorative powers. About 30 kilometers (19 mi) to the south, Salinas is a fishing village best known for its concentration of fresh seafood restaurants. This is an ideal area for a day trip from Ponce.

SIGHTS

Bahía de Jobos Reserva Nacional de Investigación Estuarina (PR 705, km 2.3, Salinas, 787/853-4617 or 787/864-0105, Mon.-Fri. 7:30am-noon and 1pm-4pm, Sat. 7:30am-noon and 1pm-3pm) is a 2,800-acre reserve of mangrove forests and freshwater wetlands, pocketed with lagoons, salt flats, and mud beds. This is a great spot for kayaking, although rentals are not available on-site. Guided tours can be arranged in advance.

Albergue Olímpico (PR 712, km 0.3, Salinas, 787/824-2200, http://albergueolimpico.com, May 16-31 Sat.-Sun. 10am-5pm, June-July daily 10am-5pm, $18) is the place to go for some outdoor family fun. In addition

Aguas de Termales de Coamo

to a sprawling waterpark with waterfalls and slides, there is a miniature golf course and a rock-climbing wall. Don't miss the museum (daily 10am-5pm), featuring exhibits devoted to Puerto Rico's Olympic athletes including tennis player Monica Puig, the island's first gold medal winner. These attractions are part of a 1,500-acre complex that also contains athletic training facilities for swimming, tennis, boxing, fencing, track, and a school for athletically gifted 7th-12th graders.

★ Aguas de Termales de Coamo

Aguas de Termales de Coamo (PR 546, km 1.7, Coamo, 787/803-1070, 787/803-1072, or 787/803-1074, daily 6am-pm, $1-3.35) may well be Puerto Rico's very first tourist attraction. The hot springs, which retain a constant 110°F temperature and are rich in minerals, were first discovered by the Taíno people, who shared their find with the Spanish colonists. By the mid-16th century, visitors were making their way here in a steady stream, and in the 17th century, a resort was built that operated until the 1950s. Wealthy visitors from all over the world visited Coamo, including the most illustrious U.S. proponent of hot springs himself, President Franklin D. Roosevelt. Today the complex is modern and pleasant, and there's plenty of parking. There are two pools about 2.5 feet deep. The smaller one is filled with water directly from the thermal spring, and it is the warmest. The larger one is diluted with cooler water. Amenities include a bathhouse, snack bar, gift shop, picnic tables, and massage service. It can get crowded on weekends and holidays. It is advised that time in the springs be limited to 15 minutes.

RECREATION

Marina de Salinas (end of PR 701, 787/752-8484 or 787/824-3185, www.marinadesalinas.com) accommodates 103 vessels and provides guests with water, electricity, ice, gas and diesel, private showers, laundry facilities, and a convenience store.

EVENTS

Maratón de San Blas de Illesca (Coamo, 787/825-1370) is an internationally renowned half marathon held in early February.

FOOD

El Balcon del Capitan (A-54 Calle Principal, PR 701, Salinas, 787/824-6210, daily 11am-10pm, $12-24) is a small casual waterfront restaurant with a blue-green exterior, and both indoor and outdoor dining spaces appointed with brightly colored chairs. Dine on the large selection of *empanadillas*, stuffed with everything from lobster and beef to octopus and shrimp. Other specialties include lobster, paella, *arroz con jueyes,* and mofongo stuffed with lobster or mixed seafood.

La Barkita (Camino de la Playa at Calle E, Salinas, 878/824-4918, Sun.-Thurs. 9am-10pm, Fri.-Sat. 9pm-midnight, $7-28) is an open-air seafood restaurant specializing in paella.

P'al Hamburger (PR 153, just north of PR 154, Coamo, 787/803-8300, www.facebook.com/pg/palhamburgercoamo, Sun. and Thurs. noon-9am, Fri.-Sat. noon-10pm, $5-12) is the place to go for double-decker burgers, loaded fries, tacos, and wings.

Coamo Golf Bakery (PR 153, km 11.5, Coamo, 787/803-1377, daily 5am-10pm, $3-12) is a great place to pick up a quick sandwich, pastry, or breakfast sandwich.

TRANSPORTATION AND SERVICES

North of PR 52 on PR 138, Coamo is 105 kilometers (65 mi) southwest of San Juan and 40 kilometers (25 mi) east of Ponce.

Just off PR 52 near the split with PR 53, Salinas is 105 kilometers (65 mi) south of San Juan and 45 kilometers (28 mi) east of Ponce.

Walgreens (106 Calle Piel Canela, Coamo, 787/803-6802) provides pharmaceutical services. **Banco Popular** (7 Calle Mario Braschi Bajos, Coamo, 787/825-1135) provides banking services, and the **post office** (100 Calle A, Suite 1) provides postal services.

Guayama and Patillas

It's not easy to go someplace that feels remote on this island. But the towns of Guayama and Patillas, located in the southeastern corner of Puerto Rico on the Caribbean Sea, fit the bill. They are devoid of traffic, tourists, and U.S. influence. Granted, the beaches are narrower and thicker with vegetation than the broad sandy beaches around San Juan, but the water is clear blue and calm, and you're likely to find a whole stretch to yourself. Fishing is a primary industry in the area, so there are several excellent seafood restaurants serving fresh catch. But the main reason to come here is to get some serious R&R. It's ideal for a day trip from San Juan or Ponce.

GUAYAMA

Guayama features a lovely central plaza, **Plaza de Recreo Cristóbal Colón,** distinguished by rows of unique umbrella-shaped trees and **Iglesia San Antonio de Padua,** a neo-Roman-style church with twin towers. Across the street is **Casa Cautiño,** an architectural vision of white lacy ironwork on a cream-colored *criolla*-style house with colonial details. Just east of town is the **Bellas Artes building,** another 19th-century architectural gem. The rest of the town is a gritty jumble of densely packed homes and businesses, many of which are in need of repair, and steady streams of traffic slowly navigating the narrow one-way streets lined with parked cars.

Sights

Centro de Bellas Artes de Guayama (Calle McArthur, 787/864-7765 or 787/864-0600, ext. 2306, Wed.-Sat. 9am-3:30pm, free) is an art center in a restored 19th-century building. It contains 11 exhibition galleries devoted to art and history.

Museo Casa Cautiño (1 Calle Palmer, 787/864-9083, www.nps.gov, Tues.-Sat. 9am-4:30pm, Sun. 10am-4pm, free) is on the main plaza in Guayama in a lovely 19th-century neoclassic *criolla*-style home distinguished by an ornately decorated exterior and lacy ironwork. The one-story, U-shaped house was built in 1887 and belonged to wealthy landowner General Cautiño Vázquez. During the Spanish-American War, the home served as headquarters for American forces. The home contains the family's original, locally made furnishings and artwork.

Bosque Estatal de Aguirre (PR 7710, south of PR 3, 787/864-0105, daily 7am-3:30pm, free) is a pristine piece of undeveloped paradise containing mangrove forest, tidal flats, and large populations of birds and manatees. A wooden boardwalk provides easy access. Camping is not allowed.

Recreation

El Legado Golf Resort (Hwy. 52, 787/866-8894, www.ellegadopuertorico.com) is an 18-hole course designed by local legend Chi Chi Rodriguez in a residential condominium community. It includes several lakes, a waterfall, and a putting green shaped like the island.

Club Náutico de Guayama (end of PR 7710, 939/244-2257) is a private marina that accepts visitors.

Entertainment and Events

Q'ltura (1 North Calle Calimano, 787/486-9352, Sun. and Thurs. 4pm-midnight, Fri.-Sat. 4pm-2am) is a late-night spot to come and watch sports on big-screen TVs or dance to DJs and occasionally live salsa bands. There's a patio out back and a light menu of bar snacks.

Feria Dulces Sueños (787/864-7765) is a Paso Fino horse competition held at the fairgrounds in early March with food kiosks and music. **Fiesta de Reyes** (787/864-7765) is

---

1: Iglesia San Antonio de Padua in Guayama
2: Museo Casa Cautiño in Guayama

held every year on January 6 to celebrate the traditional Puerto Rican holiday Three Kings Day. The royal pilgrims visit each barrio in the municipality before proceeding to Plaza de Recreo Cristóbal Colón for music, games, and more.

Food

With an interior decorated like an eastern European castle, **Kasón Restaurante** (2 Calle Baldorioty, 787/548-6034, Wed.-Fri. 11am-2pm and 4pm-10pm, Sat. 4pm-10pm, Sun. noon-8pm, $11-29) is a unique setting for a terrific selection of Puerto Rican cuisine, including *chuleta can can* and a variety of seafood ranging from shrimp and salmon to grouper and mahi-mahi served in a choice of sauces. The dark wood bar and ceiling give the place an old-world ambience, and every inch of wall space is filled with paintings by local artists. In the back is **Kasón Lounge** (Sat. 8pm-midnight, $5) that caters to a younger crowd with DJs, live rock, and salsa music.

Cowboy-themed **Restaurant Libras Steakhouse & Steaks** (PR 7710, km 0.67, 787/240-4007, www.facebook.com/RestauranteLibrasSeakhouseSeafood, Sun.-Thurs. 11am-9pm, Fri.-Sat. 11am-10pm, $10-28) serves an extensive menu featuring whole fried snapper, pasta seafood dishes, paella, churrasco, *chuleta can can,* stuffed mofongo, steak, burgers, and pizza. Brunch is served Friday-Sunday 9am-2pm, and happy hour is Monday-Friday 1pm-6pm. Service tends to be very slow, so expect to linger for a while.

Rex Cream (2 Calle Calimano, 787/864-1608, Mon.-Fri. 11am-8pm, Sat. 11am-9pm, Sun. noon-9pm, $2-3.50) serves a variety of fruit-flavored ice creams, including coconut, pineapple, corn, tamarind, passion fruit, and guava, in cups, cones, and sundaes.

Accommodations

Casa Pura Bed & Breakfast (PR 7710, Punta Pozuelo, 787-221-2626 or 787/866-0539, $80) is a casual, bohemian-style B&B, café, bar, and acoustic music venue that also offers sailing tours of the Caribbean. Amenities including air-conditioning, Internet, and breakfast.

Transportation

Guayama is off PR 53, 90 kilometers (56 mi) south of San Juan.

PATILLAS

Patillas is a small town about 4 kilometers (2.5 mi) north of the Caribbean coast. This corner of the island is often overlooked by visitors—it doesn't have the wide, sandy beaches or the flashy restaurants, clubs, and shops found on the Atlantic side—but that is its draw for those who want to escape the more touristy parts of the island and enjoy a low-key getaway on the Caribbean side of the island. The area's attractions are concentrated in two coastal neighborhoods, Barrio Guardarraya and Barrio Bajo.

Patillas was ground zero when Hurricane Maria hit Puerto Rico in September 2017. It's not uncommon to still see homes covered with blue tarps here, but the tourist infrastructure has bounced back admirably. The community's outstanding seafood restaurants, many of them right on the water, continue to thrive and beckon day-trippers. Food service is leisurely here.

Sights

Parroquia Inmaculado Corazón de María (Patillas plaza, 787/839-5333, daily mass) is a modest mission-style church containing a stunning turquoise nave with a gorgeous, white, gilt-trimmed altarpiece. A spiral staircase leads to balcony seating, and 10 round stained-glass windows look down on a painted tile floor.

Food

★ **Mustafá Restaurant** (PR 3, km 114, Barrio Guardarraya, 787/839-5428 or 787/644-5193, Mon.-Thurs. 11am-8pm, Fri.-Sun. 11am-10pm, $10-22) offers open-air dining so close to the water's edge that the sea practically laps at your feet. Sit at the outdoor bar or take a seat inside the enormous pavilion lined with coconut palms, where you can dine on an extensive *cocina criolla* menu heavy on seafood dishes. Specialties include land crab stew; lobster stuffed with octopus, conch, and shrimp; and *chillo* fried whole or filleted and stuffed with shrimp. For landlubbers there is *chuleta can can* and mofongo stuffed with chicken. There's live entertainment on the weekends and karaoke on Thursday nights. Service can be excruciatingly slow, so order a drink first and prepare to kick back and enjoy the view.

A neighborhood restaurant in the truest sense, **Lordemar Restaurant** (PR 3, km 112.5, Barrio Guardarraya, 787/839-7692, Fri.-Sun. 11am-9pm, $7-27) is located on the covered patio in back of a small green house among a cluster of modest waterfront homes. The menu includes *asopao,* churrasco, mofongo, and crab stew. It has a full bar.

Cayo Lindo (PR 3, km 115.9, Barrio Guardarraya, 787/803-8102, Mon.-Thurs. noon-8pm, Fri.-Sat. noon-10pm, Sun. noon-9pm, $9-18) serves Puerto Rican-style seafood including shrimp in garlic sauce, on a pretty patio overlooking the Caribbean.

Mar de la Tranquilidad (PR 3, km 120.8, Barrio Bajo, 787/839-6469, www.facebook.com/MarDelaTranquilidad21, Fri.-Sun. 10am-7pm, $11-30, cash only) is a casual, oceanfront restaurant serving seafood and Puerto Rican cuisine, including stuffed *arepas,* mofongo, and piña coladas.

El Paraiso Bar & Restaurant (PR 3, km 20.7, Barrio Bajo, 787/803-8586, Mon.-Thurs. 11am-10pm, Fri.-Sun. 11am-midnight, $12-18) is a large corner restaurant with a big wraparound patio for outdoor dining on stuffed mofongo, fish, and lobster, as well as a variety of *pastelillos* filled with fish, lobster, crab, shrimp, and octopus.

Transportation and Services

Patillas is 105 kilometers (65 mi) south of San Juan. Take PR 52 south to PR 53 east to PR 3 east. From Ponce, it's 78 kilometers (48 mi) to Patillas. To get there, take PR 52 north to PR 53 east to PR 3 east.

Walgreens (1 Calle Marginal, Suite 2, Guayama, 787/864-5800) provides pharmaceutical services. **Banco Popular** (33 Calle Rivera, Patillas, 787/839-2130) provides banking services. There is a **post office** (101 PR 3) in Patillas.

Rincón and the West Coast

The west coast of Puerto Rico—with its craggy cliffs, protected coves, vast salt flats, and underwater walls—is a wild and woolly region of untamed natural beauty.

Visitors to the island are increasingly bypassing San Juan altogether and flying straight to the west coast, thanks to the expansion of Rafael Hernández International Airport in Aguadilla, which offers direct flights from New York City; Newark, New Jersey; and Orlando, Florida. As a result, tourism has flourished, and loads of hotels, restaurants, and attractions have cropped up to serve year-round visitors.

The region is known among surfers for its stellar waves, and divers are drawn here for the underwater attractions. But the west coast has more to offer than water sports: It encompasses a huge range of

Highlights

Look for ★ to find recommended sights, activities, dining, and lodging.

★ **Stroll along the Paseo Real Marina:** This modern promenade along the waterfront in the center of Aguadilla is a popular destination for dining, drinking, and people-watching (page 183).

★ **Surfing in Rincón:** Novice surfers can hone their skills at Sandy Beach, while experienced surfers hit the waves at Steps Beach (page 191).

★ **Balneario de Boquerón:** One of the island's loveliest public beaches features a long, wide crescent of sand (page 214).

★ **Porta Coéli:** A rare example of Gothic architecture in the New World, this chapel contains a collection of 18th- and 19th-century religious paintings and sculpture (page 220).

★ **Bosque Estatal de Guánica:** This 10,000-acre subtropical dry forest features hiking trails, caves, beaches, the ruins of a Spanish fort, and great bird-watching (page 225).

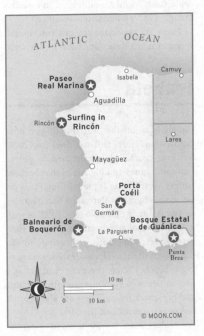

environments within just an 80-kilometer (50-mi) range.

In addition to the surf towns of Rincón, Isabela, and Aguadilla, the region also boasts the colonial city of Mayagüez, the fishing village of Boquerón, the mountain town of San Germán, the phosphorescent bay in La Parguera, the salt flats of Cabo Rojo, and the 10,000-acre subtropical dry forest in Guánica.

Most notably, the west coast is about as far away as you can get—both literally and figuratively—from San Juan. The fast-paced, high-stress urban environment in the island's capital is replaced here with a slow-paced, nature-loving vibe.

PLANNING YOUR TIME

The entire west coast could be driven from tip to tail in less than two hours, but who would want to? There's so much to do and see, you could easily spend a month here. In a pinch, though, a **long weekend** will suffice.

There are two main reasons you should spend as much time as possible on the west coast. For one, most of the charms are to be found by taking up some form of water sport, and that takes time. Whether it is mastering the art of surfing on the beaches in **Isabela, Rincón,** or **Aguadilla,** taking a diving expedition to **Desecheo Island,** paddling a kayak through the mangrove channels, taking a stand-up paddleboard tour, or going on a boat ride through the **Bahía Fosforescente** in La Parguera, you've got to get in the water to appreciate all the west coast has to offer.

The other reason you'll want to linger here is that there is a laid-back, easygoing rhythm to life on the west coast that compels you to slow down, take your time, have another beer, and watch the sunset. And if you don't let yourself be a part of that magic, you'll miss the whole reason for visiting.

To fully explore the west coast, **a car is essential.** If you're arriving via San Juan, it's about a 160-kilometer (99-mi) drive and takes 2-4 hours, depending on time of day and road construction projects along the way. It's also possible to fly into Aguadilla and rent a car.

Isabela

Isabela is an off-the-beaten-path gem of a destination. Here, cliff-top dwellings look out over coastal plains rimmed by petrified sand dunes and big swells that beckon surfers. At its center is the bustling Plaza de Isabela anchored by Parroquia San Antonio de Padua and the *alcaldía* (city hall), as well as a number of restaurants and stores that cater to residents. Visitors gravitate to PR 466, which stretches alongside the town's gorgeous beaches where there are plenty of opportunities to go swimming, surfing, diving, and horseback riding. There are also several hotels, restaurants, and bars, too.

Condominium developments have started to encroach in the area, but there are still long stretches of undeveloped land thick with palm groves and flat, grassy plains where cattle graze. Beyond the plains is a long cliff that runs parallel to the beach, creating a dramatic backdrop to the pastoral scene. A paved 12-kilometer (7-mi) bike path provides an ideal way to take in the natural beauty.

The area known today as Isabela was once ruled by Cacique Mabodamaca, one of the island's most powerful Taíno chiefs. Legend has it that when faced with capture by the Spanish colonists, he leapt to his death off the cliffs. When his body was recovered, the medallion that signified his lofty place in the hierarchy of Taíno culture was missing from around his neck and is still sought among the cliffs

---

Previous: Playa Crash Boat in Aguadilla; Playa Villa Pesquera in Isabela; Porta Coéli chapel in San Germán.

Rincón and the West Coast

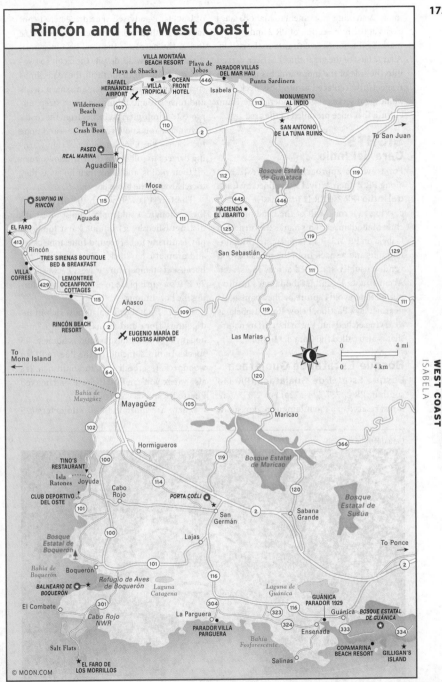

VILLA MONTAÑA BEACH RESORT
Playa de Jobos
PARADOR VILLAS DEL MAR HAU
Playa de Shacks
OCEAN FRONT HOTEL
VILLA TROPICAL
RAFAEL HERNÁNDEZ AIRPORT
Punta Sardinera
Isabela
446
MONUMENTO AL INDIO
113
Wilderness Beach
107
SAN ANTONIO DE LA TUNA RUINS
Playa Crash Boat
110
To San Juan
2
PASEO REAL MARINA
112
Bosque Estatal de Guajataca
119
Aguadilla
Moca
445
HACIENDA EL JIBARITO
446
SURFING IN RINCÓN
115
111
EL FARO
Aguada
125
129
413
Rincón
San Sebastián
TRES SIRENAS BOUTIQUE BED & BREAKFAST
111
VILLA COFRESÍ
429
LEMONTREE OCEANFRONT COTTAGES
115
111
Añasco
109
119
RINCÓN BEACH RESORT
2
Las Marías
EUGENIO MARÍA DE HOSTAS AIRPORT
341
To Mona Island
64
120
Bahía de Mayagüez
Mayagüez
105
102
Maricao
Hormigueros
366
TINO'S RESTAURANT
100
119
Bosque Estatal de Maricao
Isla Ratones
Joyuda
114
Cabo Rojo
PORTA COÉLI
120
Bosque Estatal de Susúa
CLUB DEPORTIVO DEL OSTE
101
San Germán
2
Sabana Grande
Bosque Estatal de Boquerón
100
Lajas
To Ponce
101
2
Bahía de Boquerón
Boquerón
Refugio de Aves de Boquerón
116
BALNEARIO DE BOQUERÓN
Laguna Cartagena
Laguna de Guánica
GUÁNICA PARADOR 1929
El Combate
301
304
Bosque Estatal DE GUÁNICA
Cabo Rojo NWR
323
324
Guánica
333
La Parguera
116
334
Salt Flats
PARADOR VILLA PARGUERA
Ensenada
COPAMARINA BEACH RESORT
EL FARO DE LOS MORRILLOS
Bahía Fosforescente
Salinas
GILLIGAN'S ISLAND

0   4 mi
0   4 km

© MOON.COM

today. A striking monument to Mabodamaca exists at the intersection of PR 2 and PR 113, marking the northern entrance to the region. A large bust of the great chief has been carved into the side of the mountain, his medallion respectfully replaced around his neck. The monument serves as a reminder of the Taíno culture that once prevailed in the area.

SIGHTS
Cara del Indio

For travelers approaching the west coast along PR 2, their arrival is heralded by **Cara del Indio** (PR 2 at PR 113), a massive modern carving in a rock wall of the head of Taíno chief Mabodamaca. This marks the turnoff to Isabela on PR 113. It's a popular stop for photographs and a snack from the roadside food vendor usually stationed across the street. According to legend, Mabodamaca leapt to his death to avoid capture by the Spanish. At nearby Playa Pastillo, below Royal Isabela, is a carving etched into the rocky cliff by nature that is also called the Cara del Indio.

Bosque Estatal de Guajataca

Bosque Estatal de Guajataca (PR 446 south of PR 2, 787/724-3724) is a 2,357-acre forest reserve in a mountainous region south of Isabela. Be advised: The drive here is not for the fainthearted. The closer you get to the forest, the narrower the road becomes until it's just one car wide, despite the fact it's a two-way road. Adding to the thrill, the road climbs steadily upward and takes many sharp twists and turns around mountains with steep, unprotected drop-offs just inches from the road's pavement. You know you're close—and none too soon—when you encounter a sign warning drivers to roll down their windows, turn off their radios, and honk their horns as they travel around the blind curves.

The forest is well worth the drive to get there, though. A subtropical moist forest, it's distinguished by its unique karst topography featuring underground limestone caves and dramatic haystack hills called *mogotes*. Because its temperature wavers between 75-79°F, it's a great place to escape the heat during the hot summer.

Bosque Estatal de Guajataca is rich in indigenous flora and fauna, Honduras mahogany and teak hibiscus, and is home to 45 species of birds, including the Puerto Rican woodpecker, screech-owl, and bullfinch. It's also where you can find the rare, endangered Puerto Rican boa constrictor.

There are more than 40 kilometers (25

Cara del Indio

mi) of trails in the forest, but the one that's well marked and most often used is a moderate hike from the trailhead by the park office (PR 446, km 9) to **El Viento Cave** (4 km/2.5 mi). The route begins on the interpretive trail, then branches off onto Trail #1, which leads to the mouth of the cave. From there, descend some 40 steep and slippery steps into the cave. A strong flashlight with backup batteries is required. There are no lights inside the cave, and there are holes and slippery spots where injuries could easily occur. Proceed with caution, allowing about two hours for the hike and cave exploration.

Primitive camping is allowed, but a permit is required.

Cuevas Las Golondrinas

Located at Playa Pastillo is **Cuevas Las Golondrinas** (end of Calle El Pastillo at PR 113, km 5.1), a large, arched opening in a rock wall on the far western end of Playa Pastillo that brings to mind a cathedral carved by nature. Here, swallows roost and can be seen flying in and out. The cave is typically only accessible during the summer, and when the tide is low and the waves are small. Swimming is not advised at any time at Playa Pastillo because of rough waters and strong currents.

To get here, take PR 113 to km 5.1 and turn onto Calle El Pastillo. Drive to the end and park on the side of the street. If you're facing the ocean, turn left and walk on the beach about 20 minutes to reach the cave.

Ermita de San Antonio de Padua de la Tuna

Ermita de San Antonio de Padua de la Tuna (Calle Ermita, off PR 2, 787/872-0059, 787/370-6235, or 787/306-3724) is the ruins of a church founded in 1730 in what was the first Spanish settlement in the northwest corner of the island, called Tuna. In the early 1800s, the community relocated closer to the coast and became known as Isabela. The ruins are visible behind a locked chain-link fence. Next door is the office of Casa Tuna, the nonprofit organization that protects and studies the ruins. Call to schedule a guided tour inside the gates.

The ruins are located in a residential neighborhood. Traveling west from Quebradillas on PR 2, drive 2.5 kilometers (1.5 mi) past the turn off to PR 113 and Cara del Indio, and watch for signs. Turn left on Calle Cerro de Los Pineiros. Stay left at the fork and travel about 2 kilometers (1 mi), then turn left on Calle Ermita. The ruins are on the right.

Gozalandia Cascadas

Gozalandia Cascadas (off PR 446, daily 9am-5pm, $5 parking) is an off-the-beaten path, hidden gem of natural beauty tucked in a tropical forest near San Sebastian, 27 kilometers (17 mi) south of Isabela. There are a number of waterfalls in Puerto Rico, but Gozalandia is double the fun because it has two waterfalls: one upriver and one downriver, each with a rope swing and a natural pool. Anyone is free to try their rope-swinging skills, but there are no lifeguards or other security measures. On-site are bathrooms and a *chinchorro* serving beer, cocktails, and Puerto Rican cuisine.

From the parking lot, walk downhill. The concrete path to the right is a moderate, 15-minute uphill hike to the smaller, upriver waterfall. The path to the left leads to a steep, 10-minute hike down wooden steps to the larger, downriver fall.

To get to Gozalandia, travel south from Isabela on PR 112 to Moca and turn left onto PR 446, then left at the homemade sign that says "*Cataratas*/Waterfall." (If you reach PR 445, you've gone too far.) Proceed less than half a kilometer and turn left through the gate and proceed another half-kilometer to the parking lot. Allow about 40 minutes for the drive.

RECREATION

Surfing is a big draw in Isabela, which hosts the Corona Pro Surf Circuit annual competition in October.

Beaches
PLAYA DE JOBOS
Ground zero for experienced surfers is **Playa de Jobos** (PR 466 just east of PR 4466). The point break off Punta Jacinto is renowned for its right-breaking tube.

Carefully walk eastward on the point's rocky coral reef to see a blowhole, where the ocean waves rush underneath and spray water into the air through a hole in the reef. It's a fantastic sight and a great place for photos.

There are no facilities at the beach. Parking is limited to the shoulders of the road or the occasional house where you can pay a small fee.

PLAYA VILLA PESQUERA
East of Playa de Jobos, **Playa Villa Pesquera** is a scruffy, secluded beach tucked into a densely vegetated area that's popular with locals. There's a modest recreation area featuring playground equipment, a basketball court, a pavilion, and a cluster of kiosks selling fritters and booze. Salsa bands play on weekends and holidays.

To get here from Isabela, drive north on PR 112 about a quarter-mile and fork right onto Calle Francisco Camacho at the big condominium development. At the bottom of the hill, fork right, proceed one-quarter mile, and you've arrived. If you proceed another eighth of a mile, you'll come to **Playa Sardinera,** a small cove protected by petrified sand dunes. For a spectacular show, watch the waves crash against them during high tide. If you fork left at the bottom of the hill, you'll come to an even more secluded wilderness beach area obscured by brush. There's no parking, but there are sandy pull-ins where you can park your car and walk down to the sea.

PLAYA DE SHACKS
Playa de Shacks (PR 4466 in front of Villa Tropical) not only has good surfing and kite-surfing, it also has excellent snorkeling and diving. **Blue Hole** is touted as one of the area's best snorkeling spots. It's located in the surf just outside the office at Villa Tropical and about 500 meters east of Villa Montaña.

There are also underwater caverns accessible from the reef. Several dive shops offer excursions in the area, and horseback riding can be arranged at the resort. There are no facilities, and parking is limited to the shoulders of the road or the occasional house where you can pay a small fee.

one of the waterfalls at Gozalandia Cascadas

Water Sports

For expert advice on the best surf spots, visit **Hang Loose Surf Shop** (PR 4466, km 1.2, Playa de Jobos, 787/560-0181, http://hang-loose-surf-shop.business.site, Sun.-Mon. 10am-3pm, Tues.-Sat. 10am-4pm, board rentals $30/day). This is the place to buy or rent boards or get private surfing lessons. The shop also sells beachwear and accessories, including towels, sunblock, sunglasses, sandals, bathing suits, beach chairs, snorkeling equipment, and souvenirs.

WRV Surf Shop (PR 466, Playa Jobos, 787/669-3840, www.waveridingvehicles.com, daily 9am-6pm) rents surfboards (from $20 for 4 hours) and stand-up paddleboards (from $25 for 4 hours). Surf lessons are $35 an hour. This shop is a great source for wave conditions and information on currents, as well as beachwear and gear.

Volcom Surf School Puerto Rico (Uma's, PR 4466, km 7.2, Playa Jobos, 787/510-3164, daily 9am-5pm) offers surf lessons to beginners and experienced surfers. A 1.5-hour class is $75. Multi-lesson packages are also available.

Biking

Paseo Lineal is a wide, well-maintained 12-kilometer (7-mi) bike path, part paved asphalt and part wooden boardwalk, that stretches along the coast from Playa Jobos to Playa Villa Pesquera at Punta Sardinera. The mostly flat path has a total ascent of 33 feet, and walkers and joggers are welcome to use it as well. The path passes by stunning views and runs through a wooded area near Cuevas Las Golondrinas. Isabela also boasts a protected paved bike path along PR 466.

In addition to being a bike rental shop, **Pedalea** (Centro Empresarial, Villa Pesquera, *kiosko* A-5, 787/908-1807, 787/658-6557, or 787/367-9288, http://pedaleaisabela.com, Sat.-Sun. 9am-6pm) doubles as a café (Mon. and Thurs. 4pm-9pm, Fri. 4pm-11pm, Sat. 9am-7pm, Sun. 9am-9pm) serving coffee drinks, cocktails, and a light menu of snacks. Rentals are available beyond regular shop hours via online reservation. Bike rentals are $15 for three hours, $25 for six hours, and $40 for a full day.

Golf

The Links at Royal Isabela (396 Noel Estrada Ave., 787/609-5888 or 855/609-5888, www.royalisabela.com, $150-200 greens fees) is a spectacular 18-hole course designed to showcase the island's natural beauty on a cliff overlooking the ocean at this luxury resort. Caddies are also available.

Horseback Riding

Isabela has great beaches for horseback riding, and **Tropical Trail Rides** (PR 4466, km 1.8, 787/872-9256, www.tropicaltrailrides.com, daily rides at 9am and 3:30pm, $55 pp for 2 hours) offers guided tours along tropical trails on Paso Fino horses through an almond forest, along secluded beaches, and to cliffside caves. It includes a stop for a swim or exploring the caves. There's also a sunset tour available. Private rides can be arranged.

ENTERTAINMENT AND EVENTS
Nightlife

La Central (35 Calle Barbosa, Plaza de Isabela, 787/543-2796, Wed.-Thurs. 6pm-10pm, Fri.-Sat. 6pm-2am, Sun. 3pm-10pm, $6-11) is a large, dark urban bar on the plaza in downtown Isabela, serving local craft beers on draft and creative cocktails like a spicy passion fruit margarita or a white Negroni. Listen to an eclectic mix of vintage salsa, pop, and acoustic music spun on vinyl or performed live while you dine on a menu of small bites like black-eyed pea hummus, *bacalao croquetas* (cod croquettes), mahi-mahi tacos, a bacon burger, and steak frites.

Beer Box (PR 110, km 31.6, 787/291-3963, www.facebook.com/beerboxpr, Mon. 3pm-10pm, Wed.-Thurs. 3pm-11pm, Fri. 3pm-midnight, Sat. 1pm-midnight, Sun. 1pm-9pm, $5-12) is a beer garden serving a wide variety of local and imported craft beers, as well as cocktails and a menu of bar bites, including

A Closer Look at Paso Fino Horses

Paso Fino horses

Although not indigenous to Puerto Rico, the Paso Fino horse is closely associated with the island because it was here and in the Dominican Republic where the Spanish conquistadors first introduced the mixed-breed horse. Sharing a family tree with the Moorish Berber, Spanish jennet, and Andalusian breeds, the Paso Fino is a superb saddle horse thanks to its unusual gait. Unlike other horses, its feet fall in a natural lateral pattern instead of a diagonal pattern, which creates a smoother ride for its passenger.

Puerto Rico's Paso Fino horse is typically smaller than horses in the United States, coming in somewhere between 13 and 16 hands high. Their body shape varies from stocky to lithe, and they can be found in every equine color except the Appaloosa pattern. Besides their unusual gait, Paso Finos are characterized by a high level of endurance, great agility, and remarkable obedience.

Juan Ponce de Léon reportedly first introduced the horse to the island in 1521, bringing with him 50 specimens of the mixed breed from Spain. They were quickly put into service working farms, providing transportation, and participating in military maneuvers.

In 1610 the San Juan Races were established as part of the city's patron saint festivities. As a testament to their smooth gait and obedience, the horses were raced without the use of reins. In fact, riders reportedly crossed their arms over their chests and smoked tobacco while their steeds raced to the finish line.

Through the careful selection of mares and stallions that best embodied the horses' unique traits, a specific breed began to develop by the 1700s, although it wasn't until the mid-1800s that the Spanish government officially recognized the breed.

Today, there are about 8,000 registered purebred Puerto Rican Paso Fino horses. They're still used for transportation in rural parts of the island—most notably in Vieques and Culebra, where they also roam and graze freely throughout the islands.

Guided trail rides on Paso Finos are available along beaches and through tropical forests with **Tropical Trail Rides** (787/872-9256, www.tropicaltrailrides.com) in Isabela, **Pintos R Us** (787/516-7090, www.pintosrus.com) in Rincón on the west coast, and **Carabalí Rainforest Adventure Park** (787/889-5820 or 787-889-4954, http://carabalirainforestpark.com) in Luquillo on the east coast.

pimento cheese puffs, hot pretzels, quesa-dillas, frittatas, wings, and burgers. Special events include takeover nights by local restaurants and beer yoga.

Launched in 2017, **Boxlab Brewing Company and Taproom** (PR 111, km 0.1, 787/551-3150, www.facebook.com/boxlabatdelbarril, Fri. 5pm-11pm, Sat. 2pm-11pm, Sun. 2pm-9pm, $5-12) produces an American IPA, English oatmeal stout, American pale ale, and New England IPA, among other beers. The taproom is open to the public Friday through Sunday for tastings.

SHOPPING

Located on the marginal road along PR 2, just east of PR 4470, is **La Tiendita Tipica** (3560 Ave. Militar, 787/609-6273, daily 9am-6pm including holidays). This little store stands out in more ways than one. It looks like a modest *jíbaro* house, like the kind you would see in the mountains, but it is surrounded by fast-food outlets and strip malls. Inside you will find every kind of traditional Puerto Rican sweet you can imagine, including candies, cakes, ice cream, puddings, fruit frappés, and local cheeses.

FOOD
Puerto Rican

★ **Jota** (Royal Isabela, 396 Ave. Noel Estrada, 787/609-5888, http://royalisabela.com, Mon.-Thurs. 9am-9pm, Fri.-Sat. 9am-10pm, Sun. 9am-6pm, $26-32) is the romantic centerpiece of Royal Isabela, a stunning, private, low-key resort. The restaurant features breathtaking clifftop views of the sea and cuisine by chef Jeremie Cruz, celebrated for his creative Puerto Rican dishes including seared dorado with yautía and spiced coconut sauce, shrimp risotto, and a sublime chocolate mousse.

Sonido del Mar (PR 466, km 7.4, Playa Jobos, 787/609-6004, www.facebook.com/sonidodelmarpr, Mon.-Thurs. 11am-midnight (kitchen closes 11pm), Fri.-Sat. 11am-2am (kitchen closes 1am), $10-25) is a massive, lively, beachside *chinchorro* at Playa Jobos serving a huge selection of appetizers including empanadas, nachos, burritos, mini pizzas, and octopus cocktail, as well as a large menu of Puerto Rican entrees like mofongo and churrasco.

Al Gusto (PR 2, km 112.9, 787/872-9926, Mon.-Wed. 10am-10pm, Thurs.-Sat. 10am-2am, Sun. 10am-midnight, $12-29) specializes in Puerto Rican dishes including mofongo, *chuleta can can,* empanadas, and *alcapurias.* Stop by on Sunday for whole roast pig.

Ocean Front Restaurant (Ocean Front Hotel, PR 4466, km 0.1, 787/872-0444 or 787/872-3339, www.facebook.com/OceanFrontPlayaJobosIsabela, Sun. and Wed. 11:30am-9pm, Tues. 11:30am-10pm, Fri.-Sat. 11:30am-2pm, $8-22) serves creative Puerto Rican cuisine with an emphasis on seafood, including mofongo, lobster, and ceviche.

Eclectic

Uma's (PR 466, km 7.2, Playa Jobos, 917/865-6261, daily noon-9:30pm, bar open until 11pm, $14-20) is a fun, seaside spot with a large, open-air bar right on the beach, serving Puerto Rican and global-inspired seafood dishes including *pinchos,* black fin tuna poke, coconut lentil soup, and ceviche. This is the Caribbean outpost for the original Uma's at Rockaway Beach in Queens, New York.

Ola Lola's Tiki Bar (PR 4466, near Playa Shacks, 715/303-9938, www.facebook.com/olalolagardenbar, Mon.-Tues. and Thurs.-Sat. 4pm-10pm, $6.50-9.50) is a charming, remote spot on a farm-like setting serving cocktails, burgers, and poke bowls in a laid-back environment at an open-air bar and a covered patio. From Playa Jobos, travel west on PR 4466 for about 2.5 kilometers (1.5 mi) and right before the big curve in the road that takes you up the cliff, turn right and go about 300 yards, bearing left at the fork. The restaurant is on the left. Look for signs for the restaurant, as well as signs for Villa Montaña and Tropical Rides. They're all located in the same vicinity. The restaurant accepts payment by cash and Venmo only.

★ **La Vista Smokehouse** (PR 466, km 6.3, 787/609-6044, www.facebook.com/

lavistasmokehouse, Tues.-Sun. 11am-10pm, $11-25) blends the culinary traditions of Puerto Rico and North Carolina to produce an outstanding selection of smoked meats like ribs, chicken, brisket, pulled pork, sausage, and fish, accompanied by a choice of seven barbecue sauces, including mango, tamarind, and Lowcountry gold. Sides include rice and beans, sweet plantains, macaroni and cheese, baked beans, and slaw. Located atop the cliff that looms over Playa Jobos, the restaurant has spectacular views, making it a great place just to sip a refreshing glass of sangria and listen to live music on Sundays, starting at 6:30pm.

Two-time winner of the Wine Spectator Award of Excellence, ★ The Eclipse (Carr. 4466 Int., km 1.9, 787/872-9554, www.villamontana.com, daily 7am-11am, noon-5pm, and 6pm-10pm, $22-35) at Villas Montaña Beach Resort is an elegantly beautiful, open-air beachside restaurant serving wood-fired pizzas, catch of the day, lamb chops, wild game, and churrasco. For the complete experience, go for the chef's menu ($65-75), which features four or five courses.

Sushi

Aqua (PR 4466, km 0.1, Playa Jobos, 787/689-3200, www.facebook.com/aquasakesushi, Thurs. 5pm-10pm, Fri.-Sat. 5pm-11pm, Sun. 4pm-9pm, $6-16) is a small, casual, lively sushi restaurant specializing in creative rolls. Check the blackboard for daily specials.

Bakeries

El Maná Bakery (PR 466, 787/872-1475, www.facebook.com/elmanabakeryisabela, daily 6am-10pm, $5-16) is a fast-casual full-service bakery and deli, offering generously stuffed sandwiches, a selection of hot Puerto Rican dishes including roast chicken, pork, rice and beans, and an assortment of pastries, cheesecakes, and cookies.

Ricomini (PR 2, km 111, 787/830-3860, daily 5am-midnight, $3-8) is a full-service

bakery serving coffee drinks, pastries, bread, and a variety of sandwiches.

Food Trucks

Jobos Food Stop (PR 4466, km 0.8, 787/609-6660, Sun. and Tues.-Thurs. 3pm-9pm, Fri.-Sat. 3pm-10pm) is a food truck park that's located in an asphalt parking lot lined with cement picnic tables overlooking the ocean. Among the vendors serving *pinchos,* mofongo, stuffed roasted potatoes, and pizza is The Blue Box Café (787/366-1271), located in a blue storage container, serving *empanadillas* stuffed with a variety of fillings including churrasco, *longaniza,* rabbit, lobster, and cod.

ACCOMMODATIONS
$100-150

The Perch Hotel (51D Calle Jose Gonzalez, Villa Pesquera, 787/291-4675 or 939/228-0581, http://hotelperch.com, $85-120) is a small, modest, family-run guesthouse. The rooms are compact but comfortable and a tastefully decorated. Each one comes with air-conditioning, private bath, and cable TV. Some rooms have coffeemakers, toaster ovens, and microwaves. Services are limited, but the owners are very accommodating and will happily arrange excursions and provide chairs and coolers for the beach. Check in at the on-site restaurant and bar Deep Roots, which serves a menu of pizza, burgers, and pasta dishes on weekends. Light sleepers take note: When the bar is open, the music can be loud, and across the street is a cluster of restaurants and bars that party late into the night on weekends and holidays.

Villa Tropical (Playa de Shacks, 326 Barrio Bajuras, 787/872-7172, www.villatropical.com, $95-330) manages 28 oceanfront, fully equipped apartment units in various buildings on Playa de Shacks. Each apartment is different, but they all come with full kitchens, satellite TV, air-conditioning, and free parking. Apartment sizes range from studios to three bedrooms.

Pelican Reef Apartments (PR 4466, km 0, Playa de Jobos, 787/872-6518, www.

1: Ermita de San Antonio de Padua de la Tuna
2: Paseo Lineal in Isabela 3: the Royal Isabela resort

pelicanreefapartments.com, $110-115 studio, $125 one-bedroom) is a salmon-colored condo on the beach that rents studio and one-bedroom apartments by the day, week, or month. Accommodations are simple, clean, and modern. Rooms come with air-conditioning, cable TV, microwaves, refrigerators, and stovetops. All are oceanfront, although there's no beach, and have balconies. The building is purely self-serve; there are laundry facilities on-site and wireless Internet.

$150-250

Parador Villas del Mar Hau (PR 466, km 8.3, Playa Montones, 787/872-2021 or 787/872-2045, www.hauhotelvillas.com, $170-240) is a casual paradise. Tucked away from civilization on a gorgeous stretch of beach, the property runs wild with bougainvillea, hibiscus, begonias, and sea grapes. At the center is a large cove protected by petrified sand dunes. Along the water's edge, shaded by palms, are individual cabanas, some with porches, and small clusters of studio apartments. This is a rustic, well-worn property full of authentic, old-school charm. Apartments come with air-conditioning and cable TV. Other amenities include barbecue grills, a pool, a basketball court, laundry facilities, snorkel-equipment rental, and horseback riding. The on-site restaurant Olenas y Arenas is best for breakfast and cocktails. Apartment sizes range from studios to three bedrooms.

Over $250

★ **Villa Montaña Beach Resort** (PR 4466, km 1.9, 787/872-9554 or 888/432-4667, www.villamontana.com, $212-233, $327 suite, $531-697 villa) is an exclusive gated resort with meticulously landscaped grounds and posh accommodations decorated in an antique Caribbean style. The 35-acre property has 35 villas and 52 rooms with air-conditioning, phones, cable TV, kitchens or kitchenettes, and terraces. Some have whirlpool baths, roofless showers, and laundry facilities. There are two swimming pools, a fitness room, a rock-climbing wall, and spa services. Mountain-bike and sea-kayak rentals are available on-site. The Eclipse, the on-site restaurant and bar, serves Caribbean-Asian fusion cuisine with an emphasis on seafood.

Located high up on a bluff overlooking the beach is ★ **Royal Isabela** (396 Ave. Noel Estrada, 787/609-5888 or 855/609-5888, www.royalisabela.com, $499-599), a luxurious,

Parador Villas del Mar Hau in Isabela

environmentally conscious resort consisting of 20 separate casitas appointed with natural woods and Spanish tiles, each one featuring a private plunge pool, large spa bath, two LCD TVs, Frette linens, and wireless Internet, situated on 400 pastoral acres. Amenities include a large pool, a lap pool, spa, 21-hole golf course, a restaurant, and an outdoor bar with a 360-degree view of the coast.

TRANSPORTATION AND SERVICES

Isabela is 115 kilometers (71 mi) west of San Juan, and 15 kilometers (9 mi) northeast of Aguadilla. From San Juan, take PR 2 west to PR 22 west to PR 113 west. From Aguadilla, take PR 2 north to PR 459 northeast.

Aguadilla Taxi (787/318-9546) provides taxi service in Isabela.

Banco Popular (Plaza de Isabela, corner of PR 4 and PR 4494, 787/830-1555, www.popular.com) has an ATM. For pharmacy needs, try **Isabela Farma Express** (1-350 G. Ave. Noel Estrada, 787/872-1930, http://isabelafarmaexpress.com).

Jobos Beach Liquor Store Mini Market (PR 466, km 9.4, 787/551-4882, Sun.-Thurs. 10am-midnight, Fri.-Sat. 10am-2am) is a good source for beer, wine, liquor, cigarettes, and beach gear.

Aguadilla

Once a bit of a rough-and-tumble town, Aguadilla is becoming a vacation destination in its own right. A gateway to the island's west coast, the city offers tourist attractions and trendy restaurants and bars that make it a place worth lingering in.

Unlike most coastal towns in Puerto Rico, Aguadilla's city center is on the ocean. It boasts several plazas, a bustling commercial district, an oceanfront promenade, and a massive public art project that has turned a row of modest houses into one of the largest murals in the world.

North of downtown is Playa Crash Boat, a popular place to swim and surf, and Rafael Hernández International Airport.

SIGHTS

★ Paseo Real Marina

Paseo Real Marina (Calle Jose de Jesus Esteves) is a wide, modern promenade that stretches along the waterfront for 16 kilometers (10 mi) from Calle Fuerte south to Parque Colón in the heart of Aguadilla. Not only does it significantly beautify the city, but it is also a central gathering place on weekends, holidays, and evenings for locals and visitors drawn to the food kiosks, public artwork, and ocean views. There is also a boat ramp, parking, and access to a small, sandy beach.

Plazas

Aguadilla's central plaza, **Parterre J. de Jesus Esteve** (Calle José de Diego) was built in 1851. It is an elegant and shady park featuring balustrades, statuary, arched bridges, and benches. At its center is Ojo de Agua, a natural spring that flows into Aguadilla Bay.

Behind the plaza, in the hills overlooking the ocean, is an eye-popping, colossal public art project called **Pintalto Casas de Colores** (Barrio Cerro Cabrera, Calle José C. Barbosa), created in 2018 by Samuel Gonzalez, a young architect from Manatí. More than a dozen tightly packed houses have been painted with geometric designs in tropical shades of pink, blue, green, and yellow to create one massive, contiguous mural.

Plaza Placido Acevedo (PR 442, km 4.2) is a multipurpose park featuring a skate park, a running track, and a couple of snack bars. Boxing matches are often held here.

Coloso Central Sugar Mill

Eight kilometers (5 mi) south of Aguadilla on PR 2 are the massive, ghostly ruins of the **Coloso Central Sugar Mill** (PR 418, Aguada), once the largest and longest-running sugar processing operations on the island. Turn right on PR 418 to get a close-up view through a chain-link fence. There is no public access, but for fans of industrial-era antiquities, it's worth checking out and makes for great photos. It began as a cattle-driven sugar mill in the 1820s, capable of producing 100 barrels of sugar a day. It was updated and mechanized over the years into a refinery that ultimately employed 1,500 people and produced 5,000 tons of sugar a day. The mill ceased operation in 2003. It has been declared a historic monument and is administered by the Institute of Puerto Rican Culture.

RECREATION
Beaches
Playa Rompeolas (Calle Jose de Jesus Esteves, off PR 111) is a small beach right downtown that is popular with locals, especially during summer months. There are no facilities, but there is free parking.

Wilderness Beach (from PR 107, Ramey) is also called El Natural. This remote beach is accessible by several small roads that branch off in different directions, but they all dead-end at the same place—a lovely patch of sand and sea. The beach is just past **Las Ruinas,** the ruins of the Punta Borinquen lighthouse, which was destroyed by a tsunami in 1918. There are no facilities at Wilderness Beach and minimal space for parking. To get here, turn west on a narrow, unmarked road that passes through the Punta Borinquen Golf Club. Continue down the bumpy, rutted road past Wilderness Beach to reach the big waves at **Surfer's Beach.** This is where you'll find the popular surfing spots Table Top and Survivor.

PLAYA CRASH BOAT
Playa Crash Boat (PR 458, km 1.4, daily 8am-5pm, parking $4-5) is a unique and popular beach for swimming and sunning. The beach was once part of the now-shuttered U.S. Air Force base, Fort Ramey. The remains of an abandoned concrete pier, painted bright blue and yellow, stretches far into the ocean, where it once connected with docks that served military ships. The beach is actually two beaches divided by a small river. The first beach is publicly owned and operated with a parking lot that has a snack bar and bathroom facilities. The beach is accessed by a short walk down a steep, paved incline.

The second beach is accessible over a

Pintalto Casas de Colores, a public art project by Samuel Gonzalez

footbridge, or by a road that dead-ends at a parking lot that is privately owned and operated. There are no facilities here, but there are lots of vendors selling food and handicrafts.

Strategically located by the river between the two beaches is **West Paradise Water Sports** (787/549-9304 or 787/549-4008, http://westparadisepr.com), offering snorkel gear and personal watercraft rentals, as well as banana boat rides and deep-sea fishing trips.

Water Sports

Aguadilla has several fantastic **surfing** spots, especially along the former Ramey Air Force Base. As you travel north from Playa Crash Boat to Punta Agujereada, the island's farthest northwestern point, surf sites include (in order) Gas Chamber, Wishing Well, Wilderness, Ponderosa Ruins, Surfer's Beach, and Table Top. There are several surf shops in the area, which are great sources for surfing tips and advice on when and where to hit the best swells. They can provide you with maps to all the great sites.

West Paradise Water Sports (Playa Crash Boat, PR 458, km 1.4, 787/549-9304 or 787/549-4008, http://westparadisepr.com) offers snorkel gear ($20/day), stand-up paddleboards ($25/hour), and personal watercraft rentals (from $65/half-hour), as well as banana boat rides ($12 for 15 minutes) and deep-sea fishing trips (from $595).

Surf Zone (704 Cliff Rd., Ramey, 787/890-5080, http://surfzonepuertorico.com, Mon.-Sat. 9am-6pm, Sun. 7am-4pm) is a surf and skate shop that's been around since 1985. It carries an extensive selection of athletic and street wear for men and women, including labels by O'Neill, Vans, Roxy, Billabong, Volcom, and Patagonia. Surfboard rentals are $30 for 24 hours and $150 a week. An expansive separate room in the back handles skateboard sales and repairs.

El Rincón Surf Shop (703 Belt Rd., Ramey Shopping Center, Ramey, 787/890-3108, Mon.-Sat. 9am-6pm, Sun. 11am-5pm, board rentals $25-35/day) rents and sells surfing, sailboarding, and snorkeling equipment. It

has an excellent selection of quality bathing suits, sandals, sunglasses, and other beach accessories.

Aquatica (PR 110, km 10, Gate 5, Ramey, 787/890-6071, Mon.-Sat. 10am-5:30pm, Sun. 9am-3:30pm, www.aquaticapr.com, board rentals $25/day) offers stand-up paddleboard lessons and tours for $75 per person, as well as dive and snorkeling trips and surf instruction. A two-tank dive is $95 per person. A two-hour guided snorkel tour is $75 per person. Surfing instruction is $65 for 90 minutes. Rental equipment is available.

Golf

Punta Borinquen Golf and Country Club (Ramey Base, 787/890-2987, www.puntaborinquengolfclub.org) is one of only a handful of courses in Puerto Rico that are not associated with a resort. Designed by Fred Garbin, it opened in 1940 to serve the military base. When the base closed, the course was opened to the public. It features 18 holes with straight and open fairways overlooking the ocean.

ENTERTAINMENT AND EVENTS

Cuchi's Beach Bar (Plaza Placido Acevedo, PR 442, km 4.2, 787/932-6741, www.facebook.com/CuchisBeachBar, Sun.-Thurs. 11am-midnight, Fri.-Sat. 11am-2am, $2-12) is a lively, casual outdoor bar overlooking Paseo Real Marina, perfect for drinking beer and shots on a hot day while people-watching on weekends.

FOOD
Puerto Rican

The oceanside rooftop bar at **Sal de Mar** (69 Paseo Real Marina, 787/589-3838, www.facebook.com/SalDeMarBeachRestaurant, Sun.-Thurs. 11am-midnight, Fri.-Sat. 11am-2am, $10-32) is a popular gathering spot, especially on nights and weekends when the action on Paseo Real Marina is hopping. In addition to a full bar specializing in big fruity cocktails, there is an extensive menu of Puerto Rican

dishes with an emphasis on seafood, including fresh fish, steak, mofongo, and paella.

Popular with locals, **Rompeolas Bar and Grill** (Playa Rompeolas, PR 111R at Calle Stahl, 787/891-6831, www.facebook. com/rompeolasrestaurante, Tues. 4pm-11pm, Wed.-Sun. 11am-11pm, $5-22) is an open-air, beachside *chinchorro* serving frosty adult beverages to accompany the traditional Puerto Rican cuisine, including mofongo, shrimp in criolla sauce, churrasco, and whole fried snapper. Entertainment includes karaoke and televised sporting events.

Seafood

Peña Blanca (61 Calle Stahl, 787/235-6545, www.facebook.com/penablancaaguadilla, Sun.-Thurs. 11:30am-10pm, Fri.-Sat. 11:30am-midnight, $14-27) is an upscale seafood restaurant decked out in cool shades of blue, green, and white and murals of beach scenes. The menu features whole fried snapper, *asopao* made with shrimp or lobster, and the house special, dorado Peña Blanca, featuring mahi-mahi topped with octopus, shrimp, and squid in a *criolla* sauce. There's also a robust menu of cocktails that won't break the bank ($4-7.50) and a terrific offering of *cocina criolla* lunch specials for $6-11.

Eclectic

★ **Marina's** (27 Paseo Real Marina, 787/472-6062, Tues.-Wed. 11am-9pm, Thurs.-Sat. 11am-midnight, Sun. 11am-6pm, $16-28) doesn't look like much. The spartan dining room is devoid of decor and furnished with well-worn wooden tables and chairs and utilitarian pedestal fans. But the creative, robust dishes that fuse Puerto Rican and Asian flavors produced by chef-owner Carlos Rosario make up for what the place lacks in ambience. The menu changes often but might include parmesan and chorizo encrusted New York strip steak with mushroom sauce, ribs glazed in coconut sauce, octopus salad, and

paella. The house-made bread is outstanding, and desserts, including key lime pie and Nutella semifreddo, are worth saving room for. Portions are generous and prepared with care, but because the food is made to order, service is slow. Don't come if you're in a hurry.

Octopus salad, fish tacos, and roast pork loin with coconut and pineapple salsa are on the menu at **Textura Restaurante** (PR 2, km 120.8, 787/431-2687 or 787/436-5953, Wed.-Thurs. 4pm-9pm, Fri.-Sat. 4pm-10pm, Sun. 2pm-9pm, $15-18), a small, contemporary restaurant with atmosphere and good service.

Breakfast and Lunch

Cafelados (4 Paseo Real Marina, 787/675-4323, www.cafelados.com, Mon.-Fri. 11am-10pm, Sat. noon-10pm, Sun. 1pm-10pm, $2-12) is a kiosk with outdoor seating that serves coffee drinks, frappés, sandwiches, pizzas, and pastries.

Muelle de Azúcar (29 Calle Stahl, 787/819-1411, Tues.-Thurs. 7:30am-4pm, Fri.-Sun. 7:30am-8pm, $5-13) is an inviting little downtown eatery serving eggs, pancakes, and waffles for breakfast, and quesadillas, nachos, and mofongo for lunch. Quench your thirst with a frappé or a variety of fresh fruit juices. There are also daily specials. There's a small parking lot across the street.

Panadería Borinqueña (PR 107, Ramey, 787/882-4141, daily 5:30am-10pm) and **El Ramey Bakery** (Belt Rd., Ramey Shopping Center, Ramey, 787/890-2768, daily 6am-8:30pm) serve pastries, sandwiches, and hot Puerto Rican fare from a steam table. You can also pick up essentials such as ice, toilet paper, and water.

Located in an oceanside kiosk, **Gylro** (6 Paseo Real Marina, 787/229-4713, Wed.-Thurs. 4pm-midnight, Fri. 4pm-2am, Sat. noon-2am, Sun. noon-midnight, $4-8) serves up fresh and flavorful gyros made from chicken, pork, beef, or lamb, and home-style fries accompanied by an array of dipping sauces.

1: Peña Blanca restaurant **2:** Aguadilla Food Truck Park

Food Trucks

Aguadilla Food Truck Park (Carr. 110, km 30.4, 787/464-4808, www.facebook.com/aguadillafoodtruckpark, Tues.-Thurs. 4pm-9pm, Fri. 4pm-11pm, Sat. 2pm-11pm, Sun. 4pm-8pm) is the site of several outstanding food vendors operated by young, up-and-coming chefs, including **Blue Fin** ($12-16), dishing up burgers, fresh grilled tuna, and fish tacos; **Ribs Smoke Shack** ($5-11), serving ribs, pulled pork, chili, and macaroni and cheese; and **Tuk Tuk** ($5-11), offering fried wontons, noodle dishes, and curries.

ACCOMMODATIONS

One area in which Aguadilla could use some improvement is its options for overnight accommodations. There are few to choose from, and the best bets are a couple of corporate hotels on the former Air Force base.

Courtyard Marriott Aguadilla Hotel & Casino (200 W. Parade, Belt Rd., 787/658-8000 or 787/891-9191, www.courtyardaguadilla.com, $199-213, $249-259 suite) offers lots of modern amenities, including two pools, a restaurant, bar, poolside grill, wireless Internet, video game room, and 24-hour casino.

Punta Borinquen Resort (90 Wing Rd., 787/890-9000, www.bqnresort.com, $130-160) offers modern accommodations in king and double queen rooms and suites appointed in neutral shades of browns and grays with pops of bright blue highlights. Suites have a lounge area, microwave, and mini refrigerator. Amenities include a restaurant and swimming pool.

Parador El Faro (PR 107, km 2.1, 787/882-8000, www.farohotels.net, $99-104) is a modest budget hotel featuring 64 guest rooms with air-conditioning, satellite TV, free Internet, swimming pool, and room service. Pets are allowed for a $25 non-refundable fee.

TRANSPORTATION AND SERVICES

Aguadilla is 130 kilometers (81 mi) west of San Juan. From San Juan, take PR 22 west to PR 2 west.

Rafael Hernández International Airport (BQN, north of PR 2 on PR 110, between Isabela and Aguadilla, 787/891-2286) boasts the longest runway in the Caribbean. Several airlines offer direct flights here from the United States, including JetBlue, Spirit Airlines, and United. Several national car rental agencies operate out of the airport, including **Avis** (787/890-3311), **Budget** (787/890-1110), **Hertz** (787/890-5650), and **L&M** (787/890-3010), as well as the locally based **Charlie Car Rental** (787/890-8929, www.charliecars.com). Taxi service is available via **Mega Taxi** (787/819-1235).

The **tourism office** (787/890-3315, Mon.-Fri. 8am-5pm) is in Rafael Hernández International Airport. There are several banks, including **Banco Popular** (PR 2, km 129.2, 787/891-9500) and **Banco Santander** (Ave. Kennedy, 787/891-2190).

Walgreens (PR 2, km 129.7, 787/882-8005) operates a 24-hour pharmacy. Medical services are available at **Hospital Buen Samaritano** (PR 2, km 141.7, 787/658-0000).

Rincón

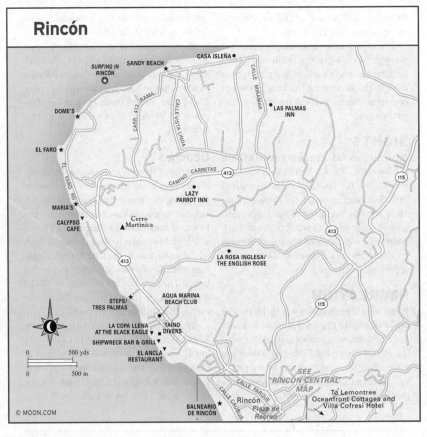

© MOON.COM

Rincón

Rincón is a fun-loving bohemian surf town, and the kind of place where people come to visit and never leave. Local lore says 80 percent of the beachfront property is owned by people from the States, and there are so many mainlanders here that it's often referred to as "Little America."

Starting in the late 1960s, tourism in Rincón catered primarily to surfers with cheap bare-bones accommodations, casual restaurants, and beachfront bars. But the rest of the world has discovered this little burg's unparalleled charms. More upscale accommodations have set up shop, and restaurants that

combine fine dining with a casual atmosphere are following suit.

Rincón has several distinct barrios (neighborhoods), each with its own characteristics. To the north is **Puntas,** a hilly point overlooking some of the area's best surf spots. It is home to restaurants, bars, and hotels that cater to the party-hearty crowd. Slightly south is **Ensenada,** where the Steps Beach/Tres Palmas surf spot is located. Farther south is Rincón's town center, **Pueblo,** featuring the plaza and several good restaurants. Nearby is the public beach, **Balneario de Rincón.** Farther south are the barrios of **Parcelas** and

Barrero, and the town of **Añasco,** home to several restaurants and hotels.

The high season in Rincón is December through April, when the swells reach their peak for optimum surfing. Some businesses close in the summer or limit their hours of operation. February is peak season for whale-watching tours.

SIGHTS

A terrific park has been built around **El Faro** (El Faro Rd., PR 4413 off PR 413, Barrio Puntas, 787/823-5024), a lighthouse built in 1892. You can't go inside, but the tower provides a lovely backdrop to the landscaped grounds complete with picnic tables, shelters, restrooms, and an observation deck offering gorgeous views of the coastline. There's plenty of parking on-site.

RECREATION

Water-sports enthusiasts will think they've died and gone to heaven in Rincón. Not only is it world-renowned for its outstanding surfing, but the diving and fishing are stellar. The water along the west coast can be choppy, if you plan to go boating, take a motion-sickness pill the night before you go out, and then take

another the next morning. Local pharmacies sell the pills for $0.10 apiece.

Many of the water-sports outfitters operate from the beach at the end of Calle Black Eagle, an area that locals call **Black Eagle** or **Black Eagle Marina,** although take note: There is no marina there. It's just a shallow put-in for kayaks and an anchorage area for boaters.

Beaches

The size of Rincón's waves and its sharp, craggy reefs make its coastline better suited for surfing than swimming, but sandy beaches suitable for sunbathing and swimming can be found. **Balneario de Rincón** (off PR 413, south of downtown behind the junior high school and across from Costa Ensenada condominiums) offers a wide, sandy swimming beach. The facilities are temporarily closed due to damage from Hurricane Maria, but the beach is still open to the public.

Options in Barrio Puntas include **Sandy Beach** (off PR 413 Int., west of Casa Isleña guesthouse), and **Antonio Beach** (east of Casa Isleña). There is also a small stretch of sand at **Black Eagle** (off PR 413 Int. at Calle Black Eagle). There are no public facilities.

Rincón

Rincón Central

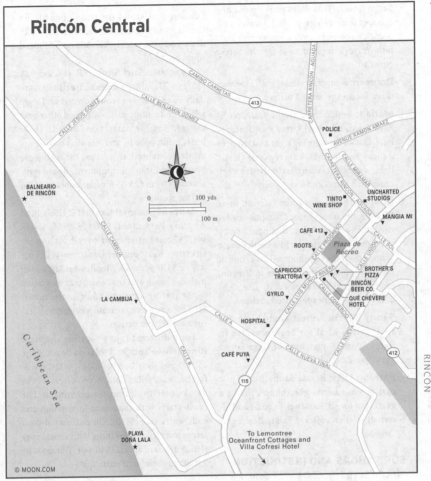

On the southern end of Rincón, you'll find **Playa Córcega,** a small, sandy beach at the end of Calle 11 in Barrio Parcelas. Amenities include a playground, baseball field, basketball court, covered picnic shelters, restrooms, and a small pizzeria.

Playa Doña Lala (intersection of Calle Cambija and PR 115) is a partially shady beach behind Ventana del Mar shopping center less than a kilometer southeast of the main plaza. It is named after a local woman who was known for wearing colorful clothes, flowers in her hair, and bright red lipstick while she danced in the plaza. There are no facilities or services here.

★ Surfing

The beaches in Rincón are known for surfing, thanks to the water's great breaks and long tubes, especially around the lighthouse during high season, December to April. Area surf shops can provide maps and tips on current conditions. The following is a list of hot surf spots in order of location if traveling north along PR 413 from Rincón:

- **Steps Beach/Tres Palmas:** For pros only, this spot features long, powerful waves with occasional breaks over a rocky reef bottom. Waves can get up to 25 feet. It's rarely crowded.

- **Dogman:** A superior winter spot, Dogman is not for inexperienced surfers.

- **María's:** Beside the Calypso Café, on El Faro Road, off PR 413, this spot features long, fast waves running right and left over a rocky reef bottom. This regional classic is for experienced surfers only. It's very crowded on weekends.

- **Domes:** This spot is often referred to as BONUS, the acronym for the name of a retired nuclear power plant distinguished by two green domes that sit idle on the shore just north of the lighthouse. This is one of the most popular surfing sites in Rincón, and it can get quite crowded. The right point break is for experienced surfers.

- **Sandy Beach:** A great sandy-bottomed spot, this is ideal for beginners. It's in Barrio Puntas, just west of Casa Isleña guesthouse.

- **Parking Lots:** Beside Sandy Beach just east of Casa Isleña guesthouse, this is a great spot for six-foot swells and a good alternative when adjacent Sandy Beach gets crowded.

SURF SHOPS AND INSTRUCTION

Rincón Surf School (787/823-0610, www. rinconsurfschool.com) conducts a surf school for beginners and experienced surfers looking to up their game. You can choose a variety of outings depending on your ability or the surfing experience, such as dawn patrol and sunset sessions. Sessions are three hours long and include board rental. Choose a group session ($95), private lessons and guided adventures ($120), or the Solo Project, with one-on-one, three-hour sessions ($165).

Azul Surf Shop (PR 413, km 4.4, Barrio Puntas, 787/823-5692 or 787/214-7224, daily 8am-5pm) rents long boards, short boards, and stand-up paddleboards by the day and week. Surfboards rent for $25 daily and $150 weekly. Guided paddleboard tours cost $40.

Desecheo Surf Shop (PR 413, km 2.0, 787/246-7755, http://desecheosurfshop.com, daily 9am-6pm) is a family-owned surf shop selling and renting surfboards and other gear for enjoying the water. Long boards, short boards, fun boards, and learning boards are available, as well as leashes, racks, boogie boards, and snorkel equipment. Board rentals range from $25-35 for four hours to $150-210 for the week.

Surf 787 Summer Camp (PR 115, behind Angelo's Restaurant, 787/448-0968, www. surf787.com) offers year-round surfing instruction. Kids Summer Day Camp is $75 per day or $350 per week Monday-Friday, which includes lunch and snack and transportation to the surfing location. Adult instruction is $105 for a two-hour private lesson; group lessons are $80 per person.

For a different type of surfing, **Radical Rincón Kite and Surf** (Mango Beach Shop, PR 413 in Sandy Beach, 787/431-6329, www. facebook.com/RadicalRincon) offers a two-day kitesurfing camp for beginners. The camp starts with classroom instruction and ends with a ride ($450). The outfitter also offers private lessons for those with some experience in board sports ($40-60). You must be a strong swimmer to participate.

Stand-Up Paddleboarding

Rincon Paddleboards (Black Eagle beach, south of El Ancla, 787/546-9545 or 787/323-6977, http://rinconpaddleboards.com, daily 9am-5pm) specializes in paddleboard lessons, guided tours, and equipment rental. But they also offer surfing lessons and rentals and kayak tours and rentals. If you prefer an adventure after dark, LED nighttime paddleboard tours and nighttime kayak and snorkel tours are also available. A paddleboard lesson and tour is $75 per person. Lessons and tours last about two hours.

Diving and Snorkeling
DESECHEO ISLAND

Not only does the west coast have lots of great reef diving along its shore, but there is a small uninhabited island 20 kilometers (12 mi) offshore that offers exceptional diving spots in pristine waters.

From a distance, **Desecheo Island** looks like a gray mountain in the sea. Its tall peaks once served as a hideout for pirate ships that would lie in wait for unsuspecting cargo ships to pass by. Today the island is a protected wildlife refuge, and no one is allowed to enter it. But everyone's welcome to don a mask and explore its reefs. You can see all kinds of colorful marine life, including rays, parrot fish, grunts, porkpie fish, sharks, coral formations, and more.

There is no regularly scheduled transportation between Desecheo Island and Rincón, but all the tour operators in town offer snorkeling and scuba trips to its shores.

DIVE SHOPS

Taíno Divers (564 Calle Black Eagle off PR 413, Barrio Ensenada, 787/823-6429, www.tainodivers.com, daily 9am-6pm) offers daily snorkeling and dive trips. Trips to Desecheo Island leave at 8am and return at 2pm. The cost for these excursions is $95 for snorkeling, $120 for a two-tank dive, and $170 for a Discover dive. Taíno also offers **whale-watching cruises** (late Jan.-mid-Mar.), as well as fishing charters and sunset cruises. Private excursions to Desecheo Island can be arranged. There is also equipment for rent or sale.

Rincón Diving & Snorkeling (PR 115, km 12.0, 787/506-3483, www.rincondiving.com, daily 9am-5pm) offers a variety of snorkel and dive lessons and tours for all levels from beginning to experienced. The guided snorkel tour lasts about four hours and is suitable for all ages and experience levels. For children under 8, call to make special arrangements. The fee is $50 plus tax and fees, and includes all equipment. Novice divers age 10 and up can take a Discover scuba tour and dive down 40 feet underwater. The fee is $125 for one dive and $185 for two dives, plus fees and taxes, including all equipment. Participants must complete a PADI medical questionnaire upon signing in and can't fly within 18 hours of diving.

413 Divers (Ventana del Mar shopping center, PR 115, km 12.9, 787/400-2359, http://413divers.com, Tues.-Sun. 9am-5pm) offers shore dives in Rincón and Aguadilla, ideally suited for beginning snorkelers and divers. Two-hour tours including gear cost $99 to dive and $39 to snorkel. You can also rent paddleboards ($25 for 2 hours, $75 for the day), and boogie boards ($10/day).

Boating
Katarina Sail Charters (Calle Black Eagle, PR 413, Rincón, Barrio Ensenada, 787/823-7245, www.sailrinconpr.com) takes guests on snorkeling trips ($75 adults, $37.50 under age 12), sunset tours ($55 adults, $27.50 under age 12), and full-moon sails ($55 adults only) aboard a 32-foot catamaran.

Rincón Capital Watersports (Calle Cambija, beside Balneario de Rincón, 787/718-7771, 787/345-5665, or 787/823-3635, www.facebook.com/rinconxtreme) rents Jet Skis and kayaks. They also rent out beach chairs.

Fishing
Taíno Divers (Calle Black Eagle, PR 413, Barrio Ensenada, 787/823-6429, www.tainodivers.com, daily 9am-6pm) offers half-day offshore fishing charters including tackle, bait, lunch, and soft drinks for $1,200. It also offers snorkeling, dive, and whale-watching tours.

Makaira Fishing Charters (787/299-7374, fishrinconpr.com, $625-675 half-day charter, $900-975 full-day charter) offers half-day and full-day charters aboard a 34-foot 2006 Contender. Rates include tackle and refreshments; there's a six-passenger maximum. Half-day charters are 7am-1pm and 1pm-7pm. Full-day charters are 7am-4:30pm.

Mona Island

Oh, the tales it could tell if Mona Island could speak. The small uninhabited island, which is located halfway between Mayagüez and the Dominican Republic, has seen much drama through the years. It has been home to a thriving Taíno village, a stopover for pirates, the site of a guano mining operation, and the final resting place for many a ship sent careening into its unforgiving cliffs by rough waters and winds.

Today, Mona Island is a protected wildlife refuge. A limited number of visitors per day are permitted to hike its trails, explore its ruins, camp on its beaches, dive or snorkel its crystal-clear shoreline, and fish its waters as long as permission is obtained from the **Department of Natural Resources** (787/722-1726 or 787/999-2200, ext. 2100). But it's not for the faint-hearted. The jagged and rocky terrain is challenging to navigate, and the climate is hot and dry. Access requires a three- to four-hour boat ride from Rincón or Mayagüez across the rough waters of Mona Passage. There are no facilities or commercial operations on the island, so all supplies, including fresh water, must be brought in.

But for the hale and hearty who are capable of strenuous hiking expeditions and roughing it overnight, Mona Island offers the kind of stunning natural beauty only found in remote corners of the world. Mona is a semiarid subtropical island with around 30 kilometers (19 mi) of coastline, most of it vertical cliffs rising from the sea to heights of more than 200 feet. The cliffs are penetrated by an intricate marine cave system that extends 150-800 feet under the island's surface in some places.

The surface of the island is mostly flat coastal plain with little vegetation, but it is home to a rich diversity of wildlife, most notably the world's only indigenous population of Mona iguanas. This prehistoric-looking reptile grows up to four feet long and wields its massive tail like a billy club. It has an aggressive appearance, thanks to a horned snout and jagged bony crest down its back, but it's a harmless vegetarian that can survive as long as 50 years. Mona is also an important habitat for the inch-long *geco oriundo* lizard, hawksbill and leatherback sea turtles, and the red-footed booby, among other sea birds.

There are a number of trails on the island that connect to three sandy beaches and a lighthouse, which is on the eastern point. In addition to enjoying the island's great hiking, diving, and bird-

Horseback Riding

Pintos R Us (PR 413 at Calle Black Eagle, Barrio Ensenada, 787/516-7090, www.pintosrus.com, no credit cards accepted) leads daily rides starting at 8:30am and 4pm on Paso Fino horses for beginners and advanced riders. The trail takes you alongside lovely beaches, cliffs, and tropical trails. Pintos R Us also offers riding lessons, trail rides, and full-moon rides. Private rides are $90 per person. Two-hour guided tours are $70 per person. Pony rides for children ages 2-8 costs $20 for 20 minutes.

Whale-Watching

Migrating humpback whales can be spotted off the coast of Rincón during the winter, and several local operators offer boat tours

to see them, including **Taíno Divers** (564 Calle Black Eagle, PR 413, Barrio Ensenada, 787/823-6429, www.tainodivers.com, daily 9am-6pm).

Yoga

Centro La Paz (PR 115, km 14, 787/823-2885, www.lapazrincon.com, $15 drop in) offers private and group yoga classes, Pilates classes, massage, reiki, meditation classes, and more.

ENTERTAINMENT AND EVENTS
Nightlife

In addition to water sports, Rincón is equally renowned for its hard-partying ways. Nothing complements a day spent surfing or diving like a pub crawl, and Rincón has no shortage

Mona iguanas are indigenous to Mona Island.

watching, visitors can explore the faint remains of the Taíno civilization. Petroglyphs, stone walls, and graves are enduring reminders of Mona's colorful past.

Individuals who secure their own permits and have access to a private boat can visit on their own. But most visitors go with outfitters that organize three-night camping trips, including gear, meals, and guided tours for around $650 per person. Outfitters include **Mona Island Tours** (24 El Retiro, Mayagüez, 787/501-7333) and **Acampa** (517 Ave. Andalucia, San Juan, 787/706-0695, www.acampapr.com). Participants must be between the ages of 16 and 62, and their weight cannot exceed 230 pounds.

of great bars and watering holes for partying into the wee hours.

Every Thursday between 5pm and 10pm, the main plaza becomes a hub of festivities for **Rincón Artwalk.** Dozens of artisans and vendors set up booths and sell their wares while hundreds of patrons peruse the goods and purchase one-of-a-kind souvenirs, including jewelry, coffee, and soaps. There's often live music, and there's always good people-watching. Most of the shops and restaurants around the plaza stay open late on Thursdays, too.

The food and service can be inconsistent, but when **Roots** (4 Calle Progreso, on the plaza, 787/823-2886, Mon.-Tues. 5pm-midnight, Wed. and Sun. 11am-3pm and 5pm-midnight, Thurs. 4pm-midnight, Fri.

11am-3pm and 5pm-2am, Sat. 5pm-2am, $5-25) is on, it's really on point. For your best bet, go for the fresh fruit cocktails and the fish tacos.

Rincón Beer Co. (15 Calle Muñoz Rivera, on the plaza, 787/280-8866, Mon.-Wed. 4pm-11pm, Thurs. 4pm-midnight, Fri. 4pm-1am, Sat. noon-1am, Sun. 9am-11pm, $5-18) features 16 taps and more than 50 varieties of bottled beer, including microbrews from around the island. Cocktails and pub food including burgers, fish tacos, ribs, and wings are also available. There's also live music on the weekends, big-screen TVs for watching sports, and a Sunday Hangover Brunch (9am-1pm) featuring music.

For the latest in tropical-inspired craft cocktails, go to **Gylro** (20 Calle Muñoz Rivera, on the plaza, 787/229-4713, www.facebook.com/gylro, Mon.-Fri. 4pm-midnight, Sat. 1pm-2am, Sun. 1am-midnight, cocktails $8-11, bar snacks $7-17), an eclectic space featuring black-and-white tile floors, walls covered in graffiti and street-art murals, a large, chunky wood bar, and an arresting mix of modern and vintage pendant lighting fixtures. Try the Old Papaya, a twist on an old-fashioned, featuring Jack Daniels and papaya syrup, or La Cacula, featuring white rum, Campari, and grapefruit juice. The menu features above-average bar snacks, like Greek-style nachos made with pita chips and tzatziki sauce, and lamb burger sliders. There's often live salsa music on Thursdays and Saturdays.

Pool Bar & Sushi (PR 413 Int., Barrio Puntas, 787/823-2583, www.poolbarsushi.com, Dec.-Apr. daily 5pm-10pm or later, depending on crowd, May-Nov. Wed.-Sun. 5pm-10pm) is a fun, laid-back, outdoor bar by the pool at Pools Beach Cabanas. Surf movies, music videos, and blockbusters are projected on a 20-foot-high screen by the pool, and sushi is on the menu.

At **Calypso Cafe** (on El Faro Rd., off PR 413, María's Beach, Barrio Puntas, 787/823-1626, daily 11:30am-10pm, bar Sun.-Thurs. until 11pm, Fri.-Sat. until 2am), a funky laid-back spot on the water at María's Beach, happy hour (5pm-7pm) happily coincides with sunset every day. Everyone in town seems to start the evening here, sipping $2.50 rum punch and Coronas while they watch the glorious pink and orange sunset. The menu includes fish ceviche, grilled dorado burritos, and churrasco. There's live music on weekends.

Villa Cofresí Patio Bar (Villa Cofresí Hotel, PR 115, km 12, Barrio Parcelas, 787/823-2450, www.villacofresi.com, daily 10am-midnight) is named after Puerto Rico's claim to piracy fame—Roberto Cofresí, a seafaring Robin Hood who terrorized passing ships and stole their goods until he was captured and executed in 1825. This beachside bar is off the lobby of Villa Cofresí Hotel, and it's a popular spot for vacationing Puerto Ricans, who come to play pool, dance to live music or the jukebox, and break away for romantic walks on the beach. The patio bar is a great place to wrap up the night with the bar's drink special, called Pirata (pirate). The sweet, potent concoction features three kinds of rum, coconut juice, crème de cacao, and cinnamon, and it's served in a freshly cracked coconut.

Festivals and Events

Rincón honors Santa Rosa de Lima with its **Patron Saint Festival** (787/823-5024) on the plaza in late August or early September with music, games, and food.

SHOPPING

Surf Town Rincón (PR 115, km 12.5, 787/823-2515, http://surftownrincon.com, Mon.-Sat. 9am-6pm, Sun. 10am-6pm) sells surfboards, longboards, T-shirts, swimwear, shoes, and hats from brands like Billabong, Polaroid, Sector, and Arbor.

El Bazar (PR 115, km 14.1, 787/245-9976 or 787/532-7757, Mon., Wed., and Sat. 10am-5pm, Thurs. 10am-2pm and 6pm-10pm, Fri. noon-5pm, Sun. 10am-3pm) is a thrift store selling used clothes, books, toys, and jewelry, as well as new graphic T-shirts.

The Uncharted Studio (6 Calle Sol, 939/697-8177, www.unchartedstudio.com, daily 11am-6pm) is an apparel shop selling silkscreened T-shirts in unique designs, locally designed bikinis, hats, soaps, artwork, and books.

Ocean State of Mind (4 Calle Progress, on the plaza, 808/384-1950, Sun.-Mon. and Wed. 10am-3pm, Thurs. 10am-10pm, Fri.-Sat. 10am-5pm) started on Etsy. Now it has a shop in the heart of Rincón, where it sells a large selection of tie-dyed dresses and jumpers, batik sarongs, crystals, and jewelry made by local designers, as well some from Hawaii.

Mango Beach Shop (PR 413, across the street from Sandy Beach, 787/823-2100, http://mangobeachshop.jimdo.com, daily

10am-6pm) is a small roadside gift shop selling T-shirts, sea-glass jewelry, and beachwear. They also rent surfboards and beach chairs.

Part art gallery, part gift shop, **Playa Oeste Tropical Surf Art Gallery & Gift Shop** (PR 413, km 0.5, 787/823-4424, www.playaoestegallery.com, winter Tues.-Sun. 11am-5pm, summer Thurs.-Mon. noon-5pm) specializes in collectible surf art by renowned artists, including John Severson, Ken Auster, and Wade Koniacowsky. It's also a great place to pick up imported batik sundresses, artisan-made jewelry, and local coffees.

Caribbean Trading Co. (23 Calle W. Muñoz Rivera, 787/888-2762, http://caribbeantrading.com, Thurs. 9am-10pm, Fri.-Wed. 9am-7pm) sells locally made T-shirts, jewelry, candies, hot sauces, soaps, cigars, and handicrafts.

Tinto Wine Shop (176 Calle Sol, 787/823-4773, www.facebook.com/TintoWineShop, Tues.-Wed. noon-7pm, Thurs.-Sat. noon-10pm, Sun. 11am-5pm) is a boutique wine shop that also serves vino by the glass and a small menu of tapas.

FOOD

The dining options keep getting better and better in Rincón, but be prepared to pay top dollar even at the most casual places. And if you're traveling off-season, expect your options to be fewer. Many restaurants close or reduce their hours May through November.

Puerto Rican

Dine on fish tacos, lobster *empanadillas,* ceviche, and whole fried snapper at **La Cambija** (17 Calle Cambija, 787/823-1118, www.facebook.com/lacambija1, Thurs.-Fri. 4pm-9:30pm, Sat. noon-9:30pm, Sun. noon-9pm, $8-25) at this lively *chinchorro* conveniently located between Playa Doña Lala and Balneario de Rincón.

Excellent coffee and a stellar Cubano sandwich make ★ **Café Puya** (PR 115, 43 Calle Muñoz Rivera, 787/618-8780, Mon.-Fri. 6am-4pm, Sat. 7am-3pm, $3-10) worth a stop. This small, casual diner serves a full breakfast menu and a rotating roster of daily specials such as rice and beans, *pastelón,* and shrimp in garlic sauce.

Red Flamboyán (PR 413, km 3.3, 787/823-4508, www.redflamboyan.com, Wed.-Thurs. 5pm-9pm, Fri. 5pm-9:30pm, Sat. 1pm-9:30pm, Sun. 1pm-8:30pm, $5-24) serves an encyclopedic menu of Puerto Rican dishes including *chuleta can can,* churrasco, whole fried snapper, and stuffed mofongo. It's also a popular watering hole featuring different drink specials Wednesday through Friday from 5pm to 7pm and from 1pm to 5pm on Saturday and Sunday.

El Ancla (PR 413, km 1.0, at Black Eagle, 787/823-6200, winter Wed.-Sun. noon-7pm, summer Wed.-Sun. noon-5pm, $7-19) is a secluded beachside *chinchorro* serving cheap drinks in plastic cups and a menu of Puerto Rican dishes with an emphasis on seafood, including whole fried snapper and grilled lobster.

New American

Enjoy creative Caribbean flavors at ★ **La Copa Llena at The Black Eagle** (Calle Black Eagle, PR 413, 787/823-0896, www.attheblackeagle.com, mid-Dec.-Apr. Wed.-Sat. 5pm-9pm, Sun. 10am-2pm, $24-36). Sip craft cocktails like a hibiscus margarita and dine on creative cuisine made with the freshest local ingredients. Small plates include chargrilled octopus and quinoa fritters. Entrées include coriander-encrusted pork tenderloin in a tamarind glaze. Dine inside or on the large, oceanside patio. This is a popular spot to watch the sunset.

International

Decorated with luchador masks, fun and funky **Nacho Libre** (PR 115, km 11.6, 787/551-7000, www.facebook.com/nacholibrerincon, Sat.-Tues. 4pm-midnight, Fri. 4pm-2am, $5-12) serves potent margaritas and robust plates of tacos, enchiladas, fajitas, and chilaquiles. All of the sauces, beans, and rice are vegan, and all dishes can be made vegan by request. Breakfast is available all day, and there's a full

bar. This place turns into a popular watering hole at night.

Owned by chef Rebecca White, winner of the Food Network show *Cooks vs. Cons*, Italian restaurant **Mangia Mi** (4 Calle Munoz Rivera East, on the plaza, 787/823-4812, www.facebook.com/mangiamirincon, Sun.-Tues. 4:30pm-9pm, Thurs.-Sat. 4:30pm-10pm, $12-17) serves fresh pasta dishes and grilled pizza featuring local fish and produce.

Capriccio Trattoria (corner of Calle Comercio and Calle Muñoz Rivera, on the plaza, 787/823-3030, Tues.-Sat. noon-10pm, Sun. noon-9pm, $12-32) serves a large menu of solid Italian fare from your basic pasta dishes featuring alfredo, carbonara, and Bolognese sauces, to hearty meat dishes like beef tenderloin in gorgonzola sauce, to a variety of shrimp and lobster dishes. There's also a selection of soups, salads, and creative pizzas, like one featuring sweet plantain, chorizo, and a blend of mozzarella, cheddar, and goat cheeses.

The likelihood of finding an Irish pub in a tropical locale seems slim, but here it is: **Finn and Ollie's Pickle Barrel** (1 Calle Muñoz Rivera, on the plaza, 787/658-6090, www.facebook.com/picklebarrelpr, Thurs.-Sat. 5pm-10pm, Sun. 4pm-10pm, $10-16) is a dark and cavernous pub serving steak and Guinness pie, bangers and mash, and fish-and-chips, as well as burgers, soups, salads, and a full Irish breakfast all day long.

Seafood and Steak

The Beach House (PR 413, km 2.8, 787/823-1990, www.thebeachhouserincon.com, Sun.-Thurs. 7am-midnight, Fri.-Sat. 7am-2am, $6-28) is a large and lively casual restaurant in the hills of Rincón with a great view of the ocean and a varied menu of Puerto Rican and American dishes that are consistently well prepared. The lengthy appetizer menu includes *pinchos*, ceviche, and fish tacos. Entrées include catch of the day and churrasco. Check

out the drink specials on Taco Tuesday and the special late-night menu of bar snacks.

A funky, casual, open-air tiki bar and eatery, **Shipwreck Bar & Grill** (beside Taíno Divers at Black Eagle, off PR 413, Barrio Ensenada, 787/823-0578, www.rinconshipwreck.com, winter daily 11am-late, summer Mon.-Tues. 5pm-late, Sat.-Sun. noon-late, $10-28) looks like something Gilligan might have built, complete with gravel floor and tin-roofed bathrooms. It serves excellent, freshly prepared food ranging from mussels to poached halibut. But it's the laid-back beach-bum vibe that invites visitors to tarry longer than they planned, sipping cocktails, noshing on fried shrimp with coconut curry dipping sauce, and chatting up the colorful characters who hang out here—especially during happy hour, 3pm-6pm.

Meat lovers will find plenty to choose from at **Cowboys Cantina** (PR 115 Int., km 11.6, 787/370-5835, www.cowboysrincon.com, Wed. 5pm-9pm, Thurs.-Fri. 5pm-10pm, Sat. 1pm-10pm, Sun. noon-9:30pm, $12-36). Steaks, chops, ribs, and burgers dominate the menu at this large, open-air restaurant overlooking a rodeo ring. If you time your visit right, you might get to see some riding and roping action.

Parrillería Vacas Gauchas (PR 115, km 11.8, 787/529-1200, www.facebook.com/vacasgauchasrinconpr, Wed.-Thurs. 4pm-9pm, Fri. 4pm-10pm, Sat. 3pm-10pm, $14-35) specializes in grilled meats, including chorizo, ribeye, rack of lamb, pork tenderloin, duck breast, Cornish hen, and tuna. The service is friendly and attentive.

Burgers and Light Bites

With its rough-hewn wooden walls, surfboard decor, and lofty location up a flight of stairs, **Kahuna Burger Bar** (PR 413, across from Casa Verde, Barrio Puntas, Sandy Beach, Mon.-Thurs. 4pm-midnight, Fri.-Sun. noon-midnight, kitchen closes 10pm nightly, $8-12) feels like a cool treehouse where you can chow down on the namesake burger, featuring pineapple and ham, or the bikini burger, made

---

1: beach at Black Eagle in Rincón **2:** La Copa Llena restaurant

with a veggie patty and pepper jack cheese. Sliders, wings, and a chicken sandwich are also available. There's also a full bar, making this place a lively hot spot at night.

Decked out in eye-popping shades of red, blue, and orange, **Café 413** (157-B Calle Progreso, on the plaza, 939/697-8188, www.facebook.com/cafe413, Mon.-Tues. and Thurs. 7am-11:45pm, Fri. 7am-1:45am, Sat. 8am-1:45am, Sun. 8am-11:45pm, $4-13) is a large, cheerful coffee shop and sports bar serving bagels, salads, burgers, tacos, sandwiches, coffee, and cocktails.

Breakfast and Lunch

Ask anyone in town who serves the best breakfast, and they will probably send you to ★ **The English Rose** (PR 413 Int., km 2.0, Barrio Puntas, 787/823-4032 or 787/207-4615, www.larosainglesa.com, Mon.-Tues. and Thurs.-Fri. 8am-noon, Sat.-Sun. 8am-1pm, $9-14). The steep drive up to this mountaintop B&B is a bit of a fright, but it's worth it to dine on the Dead Elvis, French toast with caramelized bananas, or The Full Monty, a traditional English breakfast. Breads are baked on the premises, sausages are stuffed in-house, and fruit juices are squeezed fresh every day.

Casa Isleña Restaurant (Casa Isleña, PR 413 Int., km 4.8, Parking Lot Beach, Barrio Puntas, 787/823-1525 or 888/289-7750, www.casaislena.com, daily 8am-1pm, $4-20) is a great breakfast or lunch option for overnight guests of the eponymous inn, as well as beachgoers, thanks to its seaside location.

Ricomini Bakery (Rincon Plaza Shopping Center, PR 115, km 13.2, 787/823-5117, http://ricominipr.com, daily 6am-11pm, $2-8) is a large, bright, modern bakery in the Rincon Plaza Shopping Center featuring seven large glass cases containing a tempting array of donuts, cookies, pies, cakes, and pastries. But Ricomini is much more than a bakery. It also serves a full breakfast menu, a large variety of sandwiches, and daily lunch specials of hot Puerto Rican dishes, such as ribs, roast chicken, *longaniza*, and *mechado*. There's also

a small market selling milk, juice, bread, and coffee.

Sana Farm to Table (PR 115, km 14.4, 787/823-7621, Tues.-Thurs. 10am-3pm, Fri.-Sat. 10am-9pm, $9-14) is a roadside restaurant specializing in locally grown, organic produce. Try the tuna or vegan poke bowl, fish or vegan tacos, pad Thai, and veggie burger sliders. Fresh fruit juices, smoothies, coffee drinks, signature cocktails, beer, and wine are also available. There's also a vegetable stand here.

The colorful lighting and upscale vibe beckon visitors to **El Patio** (corner of Calle Sol and PR 115, Mon. and Thurs. 5pm-midnight, Fri.-Sat. 5pm-2am, Sun. 1pm-10pm, $7-12) for fruity cocktails, live music, and a light menu of wraps, salads, churrasco, and avocado stuffed with shrimp, chicken, or steak.

Food Trucks

Gastro Park @ 115 (PR 115, km 12.4, 787/431-9034, Wed.-Sat. 4pm-midnight, Sun. noon-10pm, $4-13) is a food truck park with a large covered shed for shady dining. Trucks here include Platano Loco (burgers, mofongo, and plantain soup), Torina (sushi), Bocas (pizza, with options like Thai style, *ropa vieja,* carbonara, and margherita), and Bat's Cave (cocktails made from Bacardí rum).

A roadside food truck, **Jack's Shack** (PR 4413, km 2.5, 787/246-6180 or 939/274-8066, www.facebook.com/jacksshackpr, winter Mon.-Fri. 8am-5pm, Sat.-Sun. 8am-9pm, $5-10) serves fresh, local, organic cuisine, including fish tacos and chicken burritos, as well as vegetarian options.

Kabanas at Steps Beach (PR 413, km 1.7, no phone, daily 10am-6pm, $3-10) is a convenient beachside food truck with covered seating, serving up a quick lunch of burgers, *pinchos,* tacos, nachos, *empanadillas,* and salads to surfers and sun worshippers spending the day at Steps Beach.

Dessert

Coconut Ice Cream (Calle Cambija, 787/229-8963, www.facebook.com/

coconuticecreamrincon, Mon.-Wed. noon-8pm, Thurs.-Fri. noon-9pm, Sat.-Sun. 11:30am-9pm, $1-8) serves a light, icy version of the frozen confection popular on the island, using fresh fruits. Lemon, pineapple, Nutella, and the eponymous coconut are typical flavors.

Farmers Markets

Rincón Farmer's Market (Rincón plaza, Sun. 9am-2pm) is a great source for local, organic, and pesticide-free fruits and vegetables, as well as baked goods, honey, jam, and goat cheese.

ACCOMMODATIONS

Accommodations run the gamut in Rincón, from cheap, basic crash pads for surfers and midrange B&Bs to upscale resorts and an exclusive enclave for the rich and famous.

$100-150

Qué Chévere Hotel (17 Calle Muñoz Rivera, on the plaza, 787/823-6452, http://quecheverepr.com, $100-150) is a delightful budget hotel with 13 Ikea-furnished rooms right on the central plaza with balconies and free wireless Internet, but no TVs. There's a common room with a microwave and honor refrigerator, a backyard patio, and a rooftop garden.

Punta Taino Guest House (corner of Calle Vista del Mar and Calle Juan Hernandez, off PR 413 near Sandy Beach, 347/236-9858 or 787/823-0228, www.rinconpuertoricoguesthouse.com, $80-120) is a modern Spanish hacienda-style guesthouse that provides basic accommodations in one- and two-bedroom studios with air-conditioning, ceiling fans, microwaves, mini refrigerators, coffeemakers, and wireless Internet. There's also a three-bedroom villa ($225), complete with full kitchen, two bathrooms, a hot tub, and two balconies.

Casa Verde Hotel (PR 413, Barrio Puntas, Sandy Beach, 787/823-3756, www.casaverdehotel.com, $140) is a pleasant, convenient place to stay if you want to be close to popular bars, restaurants, and surfing spots.

Amenities include a swimming pool, free wireless Internet, plus casual dining at Big Kahuna Burger. Sandy Beach is a short walk away.

Owned and operated by the folks at Casa Isleña Inn, **Las Palmas Inn** (PR 413, Rincón, 787/823-1530, palmasinnpuertorico.com, $145-155) is a self-serve inn featuring 10 spacious, well-appointed guest rooms in a three-story structure on a hillside not far from the beach. Each room has a kitchenette with mini refrigerator and microwave, satellite TV, and super-comfy beds. The suite ($210) on the 3rd floor offers an ocean view. There is a small swimming pool but no restaurant, bar, or reception desk. Check-in at Casa Isleña Inn.

★ **The English Rose** (PR 413 Int., km 2.0, Barrio Ensenada, 787/207-4615, http://rinconpuertoricobedandbreakfast.com, $90-150, breakfast extra, two-night minimum, three-night minimum during holidays) is an idyllic three-unit guesthouse located high on a mountaintop with great views of the ocean. Comfortable accommodations come with air-conditioning, private baths, kitchenettes, satellite TV, and wireless Internet. There's a small pool, and the on-site restaurant serves the best breakfast in town. Depending on which way you approach The English Rose, you may encounter the steepest drive up a hill you've ever seen. Don't be intimidated. Once you do it a time or two, you won't even notice its dizzying height.

Surf 787 Resort (PR 115, 787/448-0968, www.surf787.com, $110-160) is a modern eight-bedroom villa that can be rented by the room from October through April, or in its entirety ($575-795). Amenities include a yoga studio, game room, swimming pool, and air-conditioning.

Villa Cofresí Hotel and Restaurant (PR 115, km 12, 787/823-2450, www.villacofresi, $115-180) has 80 modern oceanside units with air-conditioning, mini refrigerators, coffeepots, telephones, and TV. Some rooms have balconies, whirlpool baths, kitchens, and bathtubs. The large lobby contains an enormous, popular bar. Amenities include a pool, a game room, a gift shop, and a restaurant. Personal-watercraft and kayak rentals are available on-site.

$150-250

Casa Verde (PR 413, km 4.4, Barrio Puntas, Sandy Beach, 787/823-5600, $138-182, two-night minimum) started out as a modest crash pad for surfers with few amenities, but it has since expanded into a big, Spanish hacienda-style guesthouse with all the modern conveniences, including air-conditioning, mini refrigerators, wireless Internet, and coffeemakers. On-site is **Sandy Beach Café** (hours and days vary throughout the season, closed Sept.-early Nov.), serving breakfast and lunch.

Lazy Parrot Inn (PR 413, km 4.1, Barrio Puntas, 787/823-5654 or 800/294-1752, www.lazyparrot.com, $143-192) is a 23-unit, fun-loving hotel. Stay in the original part of the hotel and you get a simple, modestly furnished, no-frills room. Or stay in the newer poolside suites, which are roomier and more nicely furnished. Either way, you get air-conditioning, a mini refrigerator, a microwave, free continental breakfast buffet, and free wireless Internet by the pool. The pool and its recently renovated grotto-style grounds are the best part.

Rustic **Pools Beach Cabanas** (PR 413, Barrio Puntas, 787/398-3314, www.poolsbeach.com, $137-197) offers four very basic, bohemian accommodations in a thickly wooded site across the street from the beach. The Love Shack is a small, secluded house on a bluff overlooking the ocean, accessible by a path. Two- and four-bedroom bungalows sleep 4-8 people and come with a kitchenette, air-conditioning, and TV. A two-bedroom A-frame apartment sleeps six and comes with a kitchen, air-conditioning, cable TV, laundry facilities, and porch. Amenities include pool, bar, and wireless Internet at the pool.

Lemontree Oceanfront Cottages (PR 429, km 4.1, Barrio Barrera, 787/823-6452, www.lemontreepr.com, $275-298) features six simply furnished units appointed with rattan furniture and whimsical art glass. Amenities include flat-screen TV, wireless Internet, air-conditioning, and private bathrooms. Some of the rooms have oceanfront balconies. The property is located on a swimmable beach, and beach chairs, floats, and a grill are available for use. Rates are as low as $80 per night during the off-season.

Casa Isleña Inn (PR 413 Int., km 4.8, Sandy Beach, Barrio Puntas, 787/823-1525 or 888/289-7750, www.casaislena.com, $150-240) is a well-maintained modern property designed to resemble a Spanish hacienda, complete with imported tile and mission-style furniture. There are only nine units, and each one comes with air-conditioning, cable TV, and a mini refrigerator. Some have whirlpool baths and balconies. Other amenities include a pool and a beachfront view.

★ **Aqua Marina Beach Club** (556 Calle Black Eagle, off PR 413, 787/823-2593, www.aquamarinabeachclub.com, $215-270, $270 suite) is an elegant, beachfront property featuring eight luxury rooms, each one appointed with a private entrance, a patio or terrace, flat-screen TV with digital cable, air-conditioning, fresh flowers, and custom tile work. Lushly landscaped grounds feature a pool with fountains, underwater bar stools, a hot tub, and a fire pit. This is a truly exceptional property.

Over $250

★ **Tres Sirenas Boutique Bed & Breakfast** (26 Sea Beach Dr., off PR 413, 787/823-0558 or 787/918-5118, http://tressirenas.com, $225-350, 4-night minimum) is an elegant, oceanfront B&B offering just five exclusive accommodations with private baths, air-conditioning, flat-screen cable TV, and wireless Internet. Rooms range from a standard room with kitchenette and private veranda to a two-bedroom penthouse suite with wraparound balcony. A full breakfast is included.

TRANSPORTATION AND SERVICES

Rincón is 155 kilometers (96 mi) west of San Juan. It is a straight shot west along PR 22 to PR 2 to Aguadilla. From the Rafael Hernández International Airport in Aguadilla, Rincón is 30 kilometers (19 mi) southwest on PR 2 to PR 115.

Borinquen Taxi (787/431-8179, www.aguadillaborinquentaxi.com) serves all airports and major hotels, can carry up to seven passengers, and can transport surfboards. Other taxi services include **AA Taxi Service** (787/823-0454), **Aguadilla Taxi** (787/318-9546), and **Point to Point Taxi** (787/431-7768).

Located in a modern facility near the plaza, **Costa Salud Community Health Center** (28 Calle Muñoz Rivera, 787/656-6000, www.costasalud.com, Mon.-Fri. 8am-4:30pm, Sat.-Sun. 8am-4pm) is a clinic that offers emergency services (Mon.-Fri. 7am-11pm, Sat.-Sun. 8am-4pm).

Banking services can be found at **Banco Popular** (PR 115, km 12.4, Calle Albizu Campus, 787/823-2260, www.popular.com). There is a **post office** (100 PR 115) in town.

AÑASCO

Añasco used to be little more than a crossroads located halfway between Rincón and Mayagüez, easily overlooked as travelers zoomed past in their cars. But it has experienced prosperity in recent years. Several large, modern gas stations and convenience stores line PR 2, making it an ideal spot to stop and gas up. If hunger strikes, there are a variety of restaurant options. And if you decide to stay a while, there is a pleasant public beach and a full-service hotel in the area.

Sights

Balneario Tres Hermanos (PR 401 at Calle Los Robles, Wed.-Sun. 8:30am-5pm, $2-4 per vehicle) is a publicly maintained beach with restrooms, showers, picnic shelters, and a campground with tent sites ($10-17).

Food

An array of rainbow-colored mojitos served in large plastic cups is the main attraction at **Mahi Mahi** (PR 402, km 4, 787/826-5500, www.facebook.com/MahiMahiRest, Mon.-Thurs. noon-10pm, Fri.-Sun. noon-midnight, $12-28), as well as the fresh mahi-mahi and mofongo on the dinner menu.

Sharanas (Carr. 402, km 4.3, 787/229-1092, Mon.-Sat. 8:30am-3:30pm, Sun. 9am-3pm, $2-12) is an excellent coffee shop and breakfast spot serving up generous helpings of pancakes, omelets, waffle fries, French toast, and pasta dishes.

Kaplash (PR 115, km 7, Curvas de Rincón, 787/826-4582, Sun.-Thurs. 11am-10pm, Fri.-Sat. 11am-11pm, $1-3) serves a simple menu featuring nothing but beer and *empanadillas*—lobster, conch, crab, shark, grouper, shrimp, seafood combo, pizza, lasagna, and meat. The bright orange exterior welcomes visitors into a small bar inside, decorated with Pedro Albizu Campos posters and kitschy beach tchotchkes. Upstairs are two levels of outside seating overlooking the ocean. The rooftop floor has its own bar.

Brasas Restaurant (Rincón Beach Resort, PR 115, km 5.8, 787/589-9000, www.rinconbeach.com, Mon.-Fri. 7am-10:30am and 5pm-11pm, Sat.-Sun. 7am-11am, 12:30pm-4:30pm, and 5pm-11pm, $18-29) offers fine dining in a dramatic setting featuring dark woods, adobe accents, a massive wrought-iron chandelier, and an open kitchen. Outside dining is available on the terrace. Entrées include tuna tartare, rack of lamb, and duck breast glazed with honey and Grand Marnier.

Accommodations

Rincón Beach Resort (PR 115, km 5.8, 787/589-9000 or 866/589-0009, www.rinconbeach.com, $245-265, $350-660 suite) is a 136-unit upscale oceanfront resort with a huge open-air lobby featuring high ceilings, a wrought-iron chandelier, and pink and adobe tile floors. On one end is a full bar; on the other is the reception desk. Outside the lobby is an open courtyard with patio umbrellas, tables, and chairs surrounded by *flamboyan* trees overlooking a long scalloped-edge pool with a swim-up bar and a hot tub. Other amenities include a boardwalk along a sandy beach, a playground, an exercise room, meeting rooms, and a gift shop, plus fine dining at Brasas Restaurant and casual dining at Pelican Grill.

Transportation and Services

Añasco is 16 kilometers (10 mi) from Rincón via PR 115 and PR 402. It's 13 kilometers (8 mi) from Mayagüez via PR 2 and PR 109.

Mayagüez

Mayagüez is a lovely colonial city and a bustling mini-metropolis that has resisted the siren's call of tourism and mainland influence. Mayagüez is home to the University of Puerto Rico of Mayagüez, the second-largest campus in the university system, which gives the city a college town vibe, especially the Barcelona neighborhood along Calle Dr. Basora, which is lined with dance clubs, late-night bars, coffee houses, and trendy restaurants. The heart of the city is stately Plaza Colón, a large, thriving central town square.

SIGHTS

Plaza Colón (on Calle de la Candelaria) is a lovely, large, shady Spanish-style plaza. There is an outdoor café in the plaza where you can sip a *café con leche* and people-watch for a while.

Located on the plaza is **Catedral Nuestra Señora de la Candelaria** (Plaza Colón, 67 Calle de la Candelaria, 787/831-2444), a beautiful cathedral featuring marble floors, a wood-beamed ceiling, and stunning religious statuary. The first church on the site was a wooden structure built in 1763. Seventeen years later it was replaced with a masonry structure that was damaged in the 1918 earthquake and rebuilt in 1922. In 1976 the Diocese of Mayagüez was established and the church was rededicated as a cathedral. The church underwent a $3.5 million reconstruction in 2004. In the 18th century, the church's baptismal font (since replaced) was used to baptize

Plaza de Colón and Catedral Nuestra Señora de la Candelaria in Mayagüez

Mayagüez

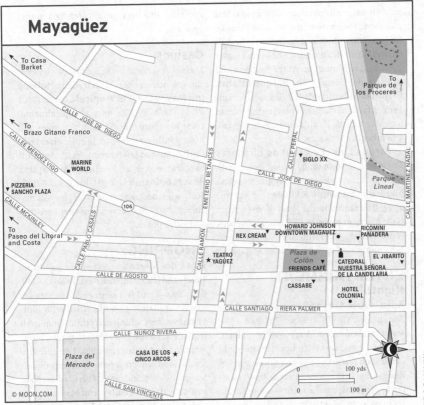

enslaved people after they were bought by abolitionists who set them free. Listen for the church bells when they ring every day at 6am and 6pm.

Declared a National Historical Landmark in 1976, the **Teatro Yagüez** (Calle de la Candelaria, 787/834-4484) is a stunning example of baroque architecture built in 1920 and still active as a cultural venue hosting operas, plays, and concerts. The original wooden structure was built in 1909 and was lavishly appointed with carpets from Spain and ceilings from Italy. It was destroyed in 1919 by a fire in which 150 people perished.

Museo Casa Grande (104 Calle Méndez Vigo) is an outstanding example of the city's turn-of-the-20th-century architecture; its interior is closed indefinitely for renovation. Though not open to the public, **Casa de los**

Cinco Arcos (Calle Betances between Calle San Vicente and Calle Muñoz Rivera) is worth a drive-by. It's a striking example of *criolla* architecture. The home was built in 1865, and its name means House of the Five Arches.

Parks

Mayagüez is graced with several urban parks. Established in 1977, **Parque de los Proceres** (corner of PR 108 and PR 65, daily dawn-dusk) is a picturesque park along Río Yagüez featuring formal gardens, a wrought-iron gazebo, walking paths, and plaques commemorating historic figures. It connects to **Parque Lineal** (Calle Martínez Nadal, daily dawn-dusk), a nicely landscaped walking path that runs along the riverbank.

Built in 2010, **Paseo del Litoral** (PR 102, south of Calle Méndez Vigo, www.

paseolitoral.com) contains walking paths that run along the shore of the bay and Plaza de las Banderas, which commemorates the XXI Central American and Caribbean Games 2010, held in Mayagüez. At the southern end of Paseo del Litoral is the **Parque Infantil El Nuevo Milenio** (PR 102, Tues.-Sun. 9am-6pm), a fanciful children's playground built to look like a castle, with swings, jungle gyms, and other fun activities.

Parque Lineal y Carril de Bicicletas Cacique Urayóan (daily 5:30am-6pm, parking $1/hour) is a pleasant shady greenway and bike path that runs 0.8 kilometers (0.5 mi) along Río Yagüez in the heart of town, from Calle Martínez Nadal to PR 2 Ramal. The park is dedicated to the Taíno chief Urayóan, who is memorialized with a large bronze statue.

ENTERTAINMENT
Nightlife
Aura Club Mayagüez (103 E. Calle Antonini, 787/579-1198 or 787/243-3370, www.facebook.com/AuraClubPR, Thurs. and Sat. 9pm-3am) is an upscale late-night dance club featuring DJs and bottle service. Reservations are recommended. Avoid wearing baggy jeans, caps, athletic wear, or sneakers in order to meet the dress code.

La Cuevita de Tarugos (64 Calle Dr. Basora, 787/986-1313, Mon.-Sat. 3pm-1:45am, Sun. 8pm-1:45am, $1-8) is a small no-frills college bar with colorful murals on the wall. This spot serves local beers and boasts a full bar, drink specials, and pizza. The crowds grow bigger the later it gets.

The Black and Blue Club (65 Calle Dr. Betances, 787/981-1036, www.facebook.com/theblackandblueclub, Tues.-Sun. 9pm-2am, $2-10) is a late-night dance club featuring drink specials and DJs spinning electronica and reggaetón. "Urban casual" is the recommended dress code.

El Garabato (73 Calle Dr. Betances, 787/834-2524, Mon.-Fri. 3pm-2am, Sat.-Sun. 5pm-2am, $1-10) is a bare-bones college bar where ice cold beer, televised sports, drink specials, and beer pong cater to a young crowd.

Casinos
Mayagüez is home to the west coast's only casinos, which are open 24 hours daily. **Holiday Inn Mayagüez & El Tropical Casino** (2701 PR 2, 787/265-4200, www.eltropicalcasino.com) has more than 350 slot machines and nine gaming tables, including blackjack, Caribbean stud poker, craps, let it ride, mini-baccarat, poker, and roulette. **Mayagüez Resort & Casino** (PR 104, km 0.3, 787/832-3030, www.mayaguezresort.com) has slot machines, blackjack, craps, roulette, baccarat, and video poker.

SHOPPING
Plaza del Mercado (corner of Calle Pablo Casals and Calle Muñoz Rivera, 787/832-9240, daily 5am-6pm) is a large enclosed farmers market containing booths filled with individual vendors selling everything from fresh fruits, vegetables, and meats to plants, birds, vitamins, and herbal remedies. There are also several food vendors serving fruit frappés, coffee, sandwiches, and more. This is a great place to get a real feel for daily life in Mayagüez.

Marine World Surf Shop (53 Calle Méndez Vigo, 787/833-5735, Mon.-Sat. 10am-6pm, Sun. noon-5pm) sells beach, surf, and skate wear, including brands by Quiksilver, Billabong, and Crocs, as well as backpacks and skateboards.

Complices (68 Calle Bosque, 787/235-2640, www.facebook.com/complicespr, Mon.-Fri. 9am-5:30pm, Sat. 9am-1pm) is a women's clothing boutique selling rompers, crop tops, lingerie, accessories, and jewelry.

Clandestina Book Bar (68 Calle Bosque, 939/289-2316, Mon. 9am-6pm, Tues.-Thurs. 9am-8pm, Fri. 9am-5pm, $3-9, cash only) is a bookstore and bistro that doubles as an art gallery and a venue for live music and readings. The menu features flatbreads, macaroni and cheese, sandwiches, desserts, coffee drinks, beer, wine, and cocktails.

FOOD

Puerto Rican

Cassabe (Plaza Colón, 107 E. Calle Antonini, 787/805-1888, Sun.-Thurs. 11am-10pm, Fri.-Sat. 11am-11pm, $10-25) is a pretty, elegant restaurant with high ceilings, white walls, a polished mahogany bar, and a large window-front overlooking the plaza. In addition to traditional Puerto Rican dishes such as *chuleta can can,* whole fried snapper, and churrasco, the menu also features chicken breast stuffed with sweet plantains and cheese, chorizo and cream cheese, or serrano and swiss cheese, with a choice of sauce, including mushroom, wine, chimichurri, and guava.

La Jibarita (109 Calle Martínez Nadal, 787/476-0056, www.facebook.com/LaJibaritaMayaguez, Mon. 11am-10pm, Tues.-Fri. 11am-2am, Sat. 10am-3pm, Sun. 10am-10pm, $4-18) is a popular corner pub with a large patio and L-shaped bar serving pizza, burgers, pasta, and steaks. Brunch is served Saturday and Sunday from 10am to 3pm, featuring French toast, chicken and bacon waffles, and croque madame.

Office workers and students alike flock to **Pizzeria Sancho Panza** (87 Calle de la Candelaria, 787/833-0215, daily noon-11pm, $5-20) to eat their weekday lunch. The very large, very casual open-kitchen eatery serves a long list of Puerto Rican dishes, including mofongo, churrasco, and shrimp in garlic sauce. They also serve thin-crust pizza, a few basic Italian dishes, and a few dishes that blend cuisines, such as churrasco parmesan, and unexpected pizza toppings like pastrami and chorizo. Every meal starts with a basket of garlic bread.

Siglo XX (9 Calle Peral, at Calle de Diego, 787/833-1370, Mon.-Sat. 6am-8:30pm, $7-15) is a small, old-fashioned, downtown diner serving cheap, home-style Puerto Rican cuisine including fried pork, *carne guisada,* snapper fillet, and churrasco.

Hacienda Latina (PR 64, km 1.1, 787/833-2041, Tues.-Sun. 11am-10pm, $15-20) is a cute, rustic spot with a *jibaro* theme, featuring servers dressed in traditional Puerto Rican dress and the restaurant tricked out in natural woods and corrugated tin like a mountain shack. The food is traditional, too, featuring mofongo, *chuleta can can, tostones, maduros,* and rice and beans. The restaurant is at the northern edge of Mayagüez.

Seafood

Gonzalez Sea Food Restaurant (PR 102, km 6.6, 787/265-7497, Tues.-Sun. 11am-10:30pm, $20-25) is a casual, home-style eatery serving up lobster empanadas, crab stew, fried whole *chillo,* and other traditional Puerto Rican seafood dishes.

Eclectic

Costa (Plaza de las Banderas, Paseo del Litoral, 939/272-9095, www.facebook.com/CostaRestaurant, Mon.-Wed. 4pm-9pm, Thurs. 4pm-10pm, Fri.-Sat. 11am-11pm, Sun. 10am-3pm, $7-29) is a striking gray modernist structure perched on a cliff with a stunning view of the ocean, where visitors can soak in the beauty while they sip a cocktail and dine on tapas like bruschetta, tacos, and sliders, and entrées including moussaka, churrasco, and risotto.

D'Calle Street Food Market (23 Calle de la Candelaria, www.facebook.com/DCalleStreetFoodMarket, Mon.-Fri. 7:30am-9pm, Sat. 10am-9pm, $3-16) is a petite food hall featuring a handful of vendors serving everything from tacos and ribs to burgers and hot dogs. There's live music on the weekends.

Mexican

Brightly colored and decked out in skulls and *luchador* masks, **Cinco de Maya** (85 W. Calle de la Candelaria, 787/978-3007, daily 11:30am-10pm, $8-15) is a lively Mexican restaurant serving nachos, tacos, quesadillas, and burritos.

Breakfast and Lunch

Cabra Tostá Coffee House (68 Calle Dr. Basora, 787/804-3055, Mon.-Fri. 8am-8pm, Sat.-Sun. 9am-3pm, $4-8) is a hipster coffee

shop with an industrial vibe serving coffee drinks, sandwiches, and breakfast dishes.

LuJe's Café & Bistro (64 Calle Dr. Basora, 787/659-7055, www.facebook.com/LuJesCafe, Mon.-Wed. and Fri. 8am-4pm, Thurs. 8am-4pm and 9pm-1:45am, Sun. 9pm-1:45am, $2-12) is a café by day, serving coffee drinks, pastries, breakfast dishes, tapas, and desserts. By night it's a bistro serving wine, cocktails, and daily specials like ribs, shrimp and rice, and churrasco.

★ **Casa Barket** (70 Calle Bosque, 787/652-4232, Mon.-Thurs. 9am-7pm, Fri.-Sun. 9am-3pm, $4.50-14) is a charming 1939 Spanish hacienda trimmed in purple wrought iron with a Spanish tile roof. It's run by an eager young staff serving sweet and savory breakfast dishes, avocado toast, and burgers.

Ricomini Panadería (131 Calle Méndez Vigo, 787/832-0565 or 787/831-3217, daily 5:30am-midnight, $4.50-9.50) is much more than a bakery. This large, modern, fast-food-style restaurant serves eggs, ham, and *tortilla española* omelets for breakfast, as well as overstuffed hot sandwiches, barbecued chicken, stews, salads, and more. Plus there are five glass cases offering a huge selection of cakes and pastries. Buy a couple of gift boxes of *brazo gitanos* for souvenirs. The jelly rolls, traditional to Mayagüez, are stuffed with a variety of fruits and cream cheese.

Friends Café (Plaza Colón, Mon.-Fri. 8am-11pm, Sat. 8am-midnight, Sun. noon-10pm, $2-5) is a pleasant sidewalk café serving coffee drinks, fruit frappés, croissants, bagels, pastries, and Argentine meat pies. Take the food to go or enjoy it at one of the umbrella tables on the plaza.

Before the beverage known as Sangria Fido was bottled and distributed throughout Puerto Rico and beyond, it was mixed up behind the bar of Fido's, a hole-in-the-wall bar and liquor store established in 1970 by Wilfrido Aponte. The original establishment burned down, but **Fido's Sangria** (78 Calle Fido/Calle Dulievre, 787/833-4192, Sun.-Mon. 9am-6pm, Wed.-Sat. 11am-midnight, $5-16) lives on. Stop in to try the powerful concoction of fruit juices, Bacardi 151 rum, and red wine. A mural depicts the original Fido's with Aponte at the helm. A small menu of sandwiches and tapas, including chorizo in wine and calamari Francesca, is served.

Dessert

Brazo gitano is a fruit-filled jelly roll cake brought to Mayagüez in the 1850s by a Spanish company called E. Franco & Co. **Brazo Gitano Franco** (276 Calle Méndez Vigo, 787/832-0070, daily 7am-5pm, $6-11) produces more than 20 varieties of the cakes, including guava and pineapple.

Rex Cream (60 Calle Méndez Vigo, 787/832-8544, daily 9am-11pm, $1.50-4) is a popular ice cream chain based in Mayagüez that sells a soft ice cream in cones, cups, pints, and quarts. Flavors include chocolate, strawberry, pineapple, and coconut.

ACCOMMODATIONS

The **Hotel Colonial** (14 Calle Iglesia Sur, 787/833-2150, www.hotelcolonial.com, $65-108) is in a former convent built in 1920 that housed the nuns from Catedral Nuestra Señora de la Candelaria. If you can overlook the shabby neighborhood, this well-maintained, well-run property is the best deal in town. Continental breakfast and wireless Internet are free. If you don't mind the lack of windows, ask for room 23—it's in what was once the top of the chapel and features a fantastic dome ceiling.

Holiday Inn El Tropical Casino Hotel (2701 PR 2, 787/833-1100, www.holidayinn.com/mayaguezpr, $118-127, $155 suite) sits on a bluff overlooking the west coast. Amenities include a pool, a children's pool, a restaurant, and a casino. Smoking rooms are available.

Mayagüez Resort and Casino (PR 104, km 0.3, 787/832-3030, www.mayaguezresort.com, $195-285, $365 suite) is an independently owned, modern hotel with a pool, casino, and restaurant on-site.

WEST COAST
MAYAGÜEZ

1: Costa restaurant in Mayagüez **2:** Casa Barket restaurant

Rooms at **Howard Johnson Downtown Mayagüez** (70 Calle Méndez Vigo, 787/832-9191, www.hojo.com, $99-120, $140 suite) have air-conditioning, cable TV, coffeemakers, and hair dryers. The suite has a kitchenette. There's a modest diner with a large wine list in the lobby, as well as a tiny pool oddly located inside a glassed-in courtyard. The property is a bit run-down, the decor is outdated, and the elevator has a musty odor. Light sleepers beware: Noise from nearby nightclubs may last until 2am.

TRANSPORTATION AND SERVICES

Mayagüez is 190 kilometers (118 mi) west of San Juan along PR 52 south to PR 2 west. It is 25 kilometers (16 mi) south of Aguadilla on PR 2.

Mayagüez is served by **Eugenio María de Hostos Airport** (north of town, PR 341, km 148.7, 787/265-7065). It is serviced primarily by **Cape Air** (800/352-0714, www.flycapeair.com), which provides several daily flights from San Juan. There are no direct flights from the United States to Mayagüez. Several car-rental agencies service Eugenio María de Hostos Airport, including **Avis** (787/833-7070), **Budget** (787/832-4570), **Hertz** (787/832-3314), and **Thrifty** (787/834-1590).

There are several taxi services in Mayagüez, including **City Taxi** (787/265-1992), **Taxi Western Bank** (787/832-0563), and **White Taxi** (787/832-1154).

Medical services are available at **Hospital San Antonio** (18 N. Calle Dr. Betances, 787/834-0050) and **Hostos Medical Services** (28 Calle José de Diego, 787/833-0720 or 787/265-2929). **Walgreens** (Mayagüez Mall, Ave. Hostos, 787/831-9251) operates a 24-hour pharmacy.

Banks in town include **Banco Popular** (1 Calle Suau, 787/831-6845, and 975 Ave. Hostos, 787/834-4790).

The **Tourist Office** (Plaza Colón, 51 Calle de la Candelaria, 787/832-5882, turismo@amayguezpr.gov, Mon.-Sat. 8am-4:30pm) has a helpful staff and lots of brochures on local sights, but most of them are in Spanish.

Cabo Rojo

Because of its remote location and unusual topography, the municipality of Cabo Rojo is quite unlike anywhere else on the island. For one thing, it is hotter and more arid than the rest of the island, and the foliage gets scrubbier and browner the farther south you travel. Its geography is distinguished by two unique environments: more than 1,000 acres of natural salt flats along Bahía Salinas, and the red limestone cliffs along its southernmost tip that inspired the municipality's name, which means "red cape."

Most visitors to the island don't make the trek this far southwest, but Cabo Rojo's charms include its three major points of interest: Joyuda, a fishing village with scores of terrific seafood restaurants; Boquerón, a popular summertime vacation town; and the Cabo Rojo peninsula, site of the island's most picturesque lighthouse.

JOYUDA

Joyuda is home to a preponderance of fresh seafood restaurants. Many of them are open-air and located right on the water, with terraces perched on pilings in the sea. Locals often throw bits of their dinner over the railing to feed the enormous tarpon fish that come here to compete for snacks. The majority of the restaurants serve the same basic menu of seafood dishes prepared *criollo* style, and most of them are very casual—some perhaps more casual in cleanliness than one might like, so select your dining spot with care. The best rule of thumb is to look for the restaurants with the most cars, but be prepared to wait for your food. Even when restaurants aren't busy, service is exceedingly slow.

There are numerous hotels and guesthouses in Joyuda, but they are all fairly basic with limited services. Joyuda caters to Puerto Rican vacationers, who tend to travel with extended family members, so a big selling point is how many people can fit in a single unit. Kitchenettes are also popular. High season spans from Mother's Day to Labor Day, and it peaks in July.

Recreation

Pelayo Marine (PR 102, km 12.3, 787/547-6084, daily 7am-6pm) is a modest marina with a rustic dock that can accommodate small boats. It also sells gasoline and boating supplies.

Club Deportivo del Oeste (PR 102, km 15.4, 787/851-8880) is a private country club with a marina, tennis courts, and a hilly 18-hole golf course with a practice putting green, a driving range, and club rentals. It also has a golf shop and full-service restaurant.

Isla Ratones is a tiny island off the coast of Joyuda, managed by the Department of Natural and Environmental Resources. Its sandy beach and clear waters make it an excellent place to swim and snorkel. Unfortunately, the pier was destroyed by Hurricane Maria, so it is only accessible by private boat or water taxi ($5) from the dock beside Island View Restaurant (PR 102, km 13.7). For information about traveling to Isla Ratones call 787/999-2200.

Food

Tino's Restaurant (PR 102, km 13.6, 787/851-2976, Mon.-Tues. and Thurs. 11am-10pm, Fri.-Sat. 11am-11pm, Sun. 11am-9pm, $13-32) is a slightly upscale eatery serving Puerto Rican seafood dishes and specializing in mofongo. The decor is simple, punctuated with stuffed fish hanging on the wall. It also offers monthly wine specials.

El Gato Negro (PR 102, km 13.6, 787/851-2966, Sun.-Mon. and Wed.-Thurs. 11am-9pm, Fri.-Sat. 11am-11pm, $13-22) is an enormous, rustic restaurant right on the water, serving a huge menu of *criolla*-style seafood in a myriad of ways, including stewed, fried, grilled, or in salads, stews, and garlic sauce. It also serves a large selection of *empanadillas.* There is patio dining out back, overlooking the water. The restaurant hosts karaoke on Thursday nights.

★ **Mao's Seafood House** (623 PR 102, 787/255-1801, Tues.-Thurs. noon-10pm, Fri.-Sat. noon-11pm, Sun. noon-9:30pm, $12-21)

Cabo Rojo

is a homey, casual, oceanside restaurant serving outstanding whole fried snapper, stuffed mofongo, and paella.

Accommodations

Hotel Costa de Oro Inn (PR 102, km 14.7, 787/851-5010, $69 and up per couple, $75 double) is a small, homespun guesthouse with a tiny pool and lobby and super-clean little rooms to match.

Parador Perichi's (PR 102, km 14.3, 787/851-3131 or 800/435-7197, www.hotelperichi.com, $85-117) has a bright perky exterior, but the rooms in the main building are drab. Some overlook the pool; others overlook the parking lot. All rooms have air-conditioning, cable TV, bathtubs or showers, and hair dryers. A better option is the higher-priced "hacienda" rooms, in a separate building at the back of the property. They have spiffier decor, refrigerators, and wireless Internet. Other amenities include a large pool with umbrella tables, wheelchair-accessible rooms, a restaurant, and a cocktail lounge.

Transportation and Services

Joyuda is 40 kilometers (25 mi) south of Aguadilla, and 190 kilometers (118 mi) west of San Juan. From Aguadilla take PR 2 south and PR 100 west. From San Juan take PR 52 south to PR 2 west and PR 100 west.

Your best bet for tourist information, banking, or health care is the town of Cabo Rojo, on PR 101, east of PR 100. Just outside of town is the **tourism office** (PR 100, km 13.7, Cabo Rojo, 787/851-7015, Mon.-Fri. 8am-4:30pm), which has tons of brochures and a helpful staff. In town you can find a hospital, **Hospital Metropolitano Cabo Rojo** (108 Muñoz Rivera, Cabo Rojo, 787/851-2025), and a pharmacy, **Farmacia Encarnación** (45 Muñoz Rivera, 787/851-1250). For banking services, **Western Bank,** which has an ATM, is on the corner of PR 100 and PR 102, on the way to Joyuda.

BOQUERÓN

Traveling south from Joyuda to Boquerón along PR 100 is a beautiful drive through lush green hills and traffic medians filled with flowering plants. To the east is a lovely pastoral valley with mountains visible in the distance, and to the west is the sea. This is one of the last sights of greenery you'll see as you continue south to El Combate, where the topography turns desert-like.

Boquerón is a sleepy little fishing village that explodes in the summer into a popular

Boquerón

The Pirate Cofresí

The west coast of Puerto Rico abuts the 3,000-foot-deep Mona Passage, an important shipping lane since the early days of colonialism. The area was a popular hideout for pirates lying in wait for passing ships filled with goods traveling between Europe and the New World.

Among historical records are reports of pirate activity in Mona Passage that include the capture of a frigate in 1625 by the African pirate Mateo Congo. And in 1637, Dutch pirate Adrian Cornelis led 14 ships in the capture of an African ship carrying a load of cedar. It is believed that English pirate William Kidd hid out on Mona Island after capturing an Armenian vessel carrying goods worth 100,000 sterling pounds—some believe that treasure may still be found within Mona's intricate cave system.

Born more than 100 years later but likely inspired by tales of those notorious pirates, Roberto Cofresí took up the piracy game as a young man and gained hero status among many Puerto Ricans along the way.

off the coast of Boquerón

Roberto Cofresí was born in Cabo Rojo in 1791, and as a young boy he had a small boat called *El Mosquito* that he used to putter around the shore of his hometown. For a brief time he was employed as a corsair, licensed to bring in foreign ships seeking authorization to dock. But he soon turned his attentions to raiding passing ships for their riches.

Acquiring a schooner he dubbed *Ana*, Cofresí and his men raided eight ships, including one from the United States, and crew members were killed in the process. Because he often shared his ill-gotten goods with fellow townspeople, he quickly gained a reputation as a Puerto Rican Robin Hood who robbed the exploiters and gave back to their victims. In collaboration with the United States, Spain set a trap for Cofresí and his men. Using as bait a U.S. Navy ship disguised as a commercial vessel, they captured Cofresí and his men, who were incarcerated at Castillo San Felipe del Morro in San Juan. Cofresí was tried by the Spanish Council of War and found guilty. He was executed at El Morro on March 29, 1825, and buried just outside the confines of the historic Old San Juan Cemetery.

Cofresí's legend has grown with time, and his memory is still celebrated in songs, books, and dance. A statue by artist José Cuscaglia Guillermety in Cabo Rojo's Boquerón Bay stands in monument to the notorious and beloved El Pirata Cofresí.

family beach destination. Puerto Rican families flock here to swim, fish, dine on seafood, browse souvenir shops, and bar-hop late into the night. Book early if you plan to come during a holiday. Boquerón gets really packed then, and the traffic getting into and out of town can be fierce. Because Boquerón primarily attracts Puerto Rican tourists, hotels and guesthouses cater to families who bunk together in single units. Many rooms sleep up to eight people and are priced accordingly. High season is April through August.

Boquerón's streets are lined with vendors selling T-shirts, hammocks, shell crafts, fresh oysters, and more. PR 101 Int. turns into **Calle José de Diego** as it passes through the heart of town, called Poblado de Boquerón. José de Diego is closed to automobile traffic Friday through Sunday, turning the road into a pedestrian promenade.

Sights

The **Refugio de Aves de Boquerón** (PR 301, km 8.8, 787/851-7260, daily sunrise-sunset, free) is a bird sanctuary that's home to more than 60 species. There is a short, well-maintained boardwalk through a mangrove swamp ideal for bird-watching. Keep an eye out for the endangered *mariquita,* a medium-size bird with black plumage and a yellow spot on the shoulder.

★ BALNEARIO DE BOQUERÓN
Balneario de Boquerón (PR 101, km 18.1, Apr.-Aug. daily 8:30am-6pm, Sept.-Mar. Wed.-Sun. 8:30am-5pm, $5.50/vehicle) is one of Puerto Rico's most beautiful public beaches. The beach is a very long white crescent gently lapped by calm waters. Dozens of sailboats moored in the distance provide a picturesque sight. The property is very shady, thanks to all the palm trees and sea grapes that grow in the area. The facilities include an activities pavilion, picnic tables, baseball field, cafeteria, and restrooms. They're all open, but some look heavily battered due to damage from the hurricanes in 2017. There are three large parking lots.

Recreation
Light Tackle Adventure (Boquerón pier, 787/849-1430 or 787/547-7380) specializes in light tackle and fly-fishing excursions. Excursions for two people are $340 for four hours, $450 for six hours. A $150 reservation deposit is required. This company also provides kayak trips to the Cabo Rojo salt flats, Boquerón Bay, Joyuda, and La Parguera. Bird-watching tours in Cabo Rojo salt flats are also available.

Boquerón Kayak Rental and Banana Boat (15 Calle José de Diego, 787/255-1849, www.facebook.com/pimienta158, Sat.-Sun. and Mon. holidays 10am-5pm in winter, daily 10am-5pm in summer) offers banana boat rides ($10-15), kayak rentals ($10 per hour), and guided kayak expeditions through mangrove channels ($45-65).

Puerto Rico Adventure Water Sports (Balneario de Boquerón, 787/567-4386, www. facebook.com/puertoricoaws) offers Jet Ski rentals ($90 for 1 hour, $50 for 30 minutes), Jet Ski tours for up to two passengers per vehicle ($120 for 1 hour, $210 for 2 hours), and kayak rentals ($20/hour). Three-hour kayak tours with snorkeling are $50 per person.

Entertainment and Events
There is no shortage of bars in Boquerón. During the weekends, when the main street is closed to car traffic, partiers freely stroll from bar to bar, drink in hand.

El Schamar (20 Calle José de Diego, beside Boquerón pier, 787/851-0542, Mon.-Thurs. 11am-midnight, Fri.-Sat. noon-1am) is a big popular beer hall with a full bar, pool tables, and a jukebox. This is the place to go for long happy hours and karaoke on Friday and Saturday nights. A small counter outside serves breakfast items, sandwiches, tacos, pizza, and fritters ($5-10). Grab a cold Medalla beer from the bar, an *empanadilla* from the food counter, and walk out back to sit by the water.

Shopping
Red Sun (10 Calle José de Diego, 787/254-3136, www.facebook.com/RedSunSurf, Mon.-Wed. 9am-6:45pm, Thurs. and Sun. 9am-9:45pm, Fri.-Sat. 9am-10:45pm) is a great source for fun women's beachwear and tropical clothing, as well as T-shirts, jewelry, sarongs, sunglasses, and flip-flops. Labels include Roxy, Billabong, and Quiksilver. There's another location in La Parguera.

Orobela Boutique Café (22 Calle José de Diego, 551/697-6815, www.facebook.com/ Orobelacafeboutique, Apr.-Aug. Wed.-Thurs. 8am-8pm, Fri.-Sat. 8am-11pm, Sun. 8am-9pm, Sept.-Mar. Fri. 4pm-11pm, Sat. 9am-11pm, Sun. 9am-9pm) is a café on one end and a boutique on the other, selling bohemian-style tropical wear including dresses, rompers, sarongs, shirts, jewelry, purses, and more. Handcrafted items by more than a dozen local artisans are among the merchandise, as are Indonesian imports.

Food

★ **Terramar Restaurant** (9 Calle José de Diego, 787/645-3996, Sun.-Thurs. noon-10pm. Fri.-Sat. noon-11pm, $7-24) is a warm, casual, stone-walled eatery that takes the flavors of Puerto Rico and turns them into creative pizzas, like the Mar y Tierra, topped with churrasco, lobster, and bacon, and other unexpected dishes like churrasco that's stuffed with cheese, plantains, and chorizo, then wrapped in bacon, and pistachio flan.

The café side of **Orobela Boutique Café** (22 Calle José de Diego, 551-697-6815, www.facebook.com/Orobelacafeboutique, Apr.-Aug. Wed.-Thurs. 8am-8pm, Fri.-Sat. 8am-11pm, Sun. 8am-9pm, Sept.-Mar. Fri. 4pm-11pm, Sat. 9am-11pm, Sun. 9am-9pm) serves coffee drinks, cocktails, and a light menu of nachos, tacos, sandwiches, pastries, flan, and fruit-flavored *limbers,* like a Popsicle in a cup. The other part of the space is a clothing boutique.

101 West Kitchen and Bar (PR 101, km 15.7, 787/649-4320, www.facebook.com/101westpr, Wed.-Thurs. noon-10pm, Fri.-Sun. noon-midnight, $10-26) is a cheerful, colorful restaurant serving craft cocktails and a creative menu featuring house-smoked pork belly, almond-crusted salmon, lobster macaroni and cheese, and chicken gorgonzola.

El Bulgao (35 Calle José de Diego, 787/547-5020, Wed. 3pm-midnight, Thurs. 8pm-1am, Fri.-Sat. 3pm-3am, Sun. 1pm-midnight, $5-16) is a kitschy tiki bar that serves local snails—*bulgao.* More bar than restaurant, its cocktails are made with fresh fruit juices, but the limited menu includes burritos and salads made with lobster, octopus, shrimp, chicken, and, of course, snails.

Accommodations

Aquarius Vacation Club (PR 101, km 18, 787/999-6330, http://boqueron.aquariusvacationclub.com, $144) is part time-share, part hotel. It provides a beautifully landscaped, well-appointed resort-like setting for a budget price. Amenities include a swimming pool, café, a children's water play area, and a fitness center. The towels are thin and services are limited, but the ocean views and lagoon pool are top-notch.

Parador Boquemar (Calle José de Diego, Poblado de Boquerón, 787/851-2158, www.boquemar.com, $107-128, $133 suite) is a modern three-story hotel with 75 guest rooms with air-conditioning and cable TV. Each room can sleep up to four people, and some have small

oyster vendor in Boquerón

balconies. Amenities include a pool, wireless Internet in the lobby, and a restaurant and bar.

One of the better options for accommodations in Cabo Rojo is **Apartamentos Adamaris** (Calle Gil Boyet at Calle José de Diego, 787/851-6860, www.facebook.com/AdamarisAPT, $85 studio, $142 one-bedroom). The modest little complex of apartments offers neat, modern rooms with air-conditioning, wireless Internet, and cable TV. All but the studios have full kitchens. There's no pool or restaurant, but the beach is across the street, and restaurants and bars are within walking distance.

Boho Beach Hotel (PR 101, km 18.1, Balneario de Boquerón, 787/851-7110 or 787/851-7100, www.bohobeachclubpr.com, $79-149) is a 75-suite budget hotel with a pool and restaurant. Rooms come with TVs and mini refrigerators.

Cofresí Beach House (57 Calle Muñoz Rivera, 787/254-3000, www.cofresibeach.com, $129-219) has a modernist, art deco exterior with clean, simply furnished rooms. It offers 16 one-, two-, and three-bedroom apartments with air-conditioning, cable TV, and fully equipped kitchens. Some rooms have balconies.

Transportation

Boquerón is 185 kilometers (115 mi) west of San Juan and 50 kilometers (31 mi) south of Aguadilla. From San Juan take PR 52 south to PR 2 west to PR 117 west to PR 101 west. From Aguadilla take PR 2 south to PR 100 south.

CABO ROJO PENINSULA

The Cabo Rojo peninsula has such a dramatically different topography from the rest of Puerto Rico that you might think you've left the island altogether. The northern region of the peninsula features vast, rolling, grassy hillsides. But the closer you get to the southwestern tip, the flatter, drier, and more barren the terrain gets. There are few gas stations—or any other businesses, for that matter—in the area, so be sure to gas up before you leave Boquerón.

The only commercial district in the region is **El Combate,** a small fishing village that transforms into a popular vacation destination for locals on weekends, holidays, and throughout the summer. Here you'll find a variety of options for dining, drinking, and modest overnight stays. But best of all, there is a beautiful stretch of undeveloped beach and a buzzy energy emanating from the sun worshippers and outdoor adventure seekers who flock here to experience the rugged beauty of this remote corner of the island. Because it's so flat, biking is a popular pastime, as is hiking, kayaking, fishing, and riding personal watercraft.

South of El Combate are more than 1,000 acres of salt flats, which have been mined for centuries. This area is also a protected habitat for shorebirds. At the farthest tip of the island's southwest corner is the Cabo Rojo lighthouse, which sits atop dramatic red limestone cliffs that contain an intricate system of caves once frequented by the pirate Roberto Cofresí.

Sights

Faro Los Morrillos (end of PR 301, 787/357-0066 or 787/255-1560, Wed.-Sun. 9am-4:30pm, $3) is the only lighthouse in Puerto Rico that allows visitors partial access. Inside, on the ground level, are historic photographs on display, and a spiral staircase provides access to an observation deck directly behind the lighthouse. Getting to the lighthouse requires a moderate hike of just over a kilometer on a paved path with a slight incline. En route, take a short detour on a path to the right to see **El Puente del Piedra,** an unusual sea stack with a thin natural bridge spanning from the tip of the stack to the cliffs on shore. After you tour the lighthouse, you can go back the way you came, or proceed eastward for five minutes on a rocky, unpaved trail with a steep decline behind the lighthouse to reach **Playuela** (also called **Playa Sucia**), a gorgeous long, thin crescent of sandy beach surrounded by the dramatic red cliffs and sea stacks of Cabo Rojo.

Five kilometers (3 mi) south of El Combate, the landscape turns extremely flat and barren as you approach the 1,200-acre **Cabo Rojo salt flats** (PR 301, km 11). Touted as Puerto Rico's first industry, the salt was mined during pre-Taíno times, and the area is still mined today for industrial use. Visit the **Centro Interpretativo los Salinas de Cabo Rojo** (PR 301, km 11, 787/851-2999, Fri.-Sun. 8:30am-4:30pm, free), an educational information center featuring exhibits, videos, and brochures. There's also an observation tower across the street for a bird's-eye view of the salt flats.

The salt flats are part of the **Cabo Rojo National Wildlife Refuge** (Camino Mediano Rodríguez, off PR 301 at km 5.1, 787/851-4795, www.fws.gov, Mon.-Sat. 9am-4pm, free), a wildlife refuge encompassing more than 400 acres of non-contiguous mangrove wetlands. These protected parcels of land are an important breeding ground for birds, sea mammals, and fish. The refuge's interpretive center has a few small exhibits featuring stuffed birds and a freshwater aquarium. Signage is in Spanish only, as are most of the printed educational materials. Several hiking trails start here. Birds to look for in the refuge include the yellow warbler,

bananaquit, black-necked stilt, and marquita, a yellow-shouldered blackbird.

Recreation
BEACHES

There are two beaches in El Combate. **Playa El Combate** (next to Annie's Restaurant, PR 3301, km 3) is a miles-long, narrow crescent of sandy beach rimmed by calm, crystal-clear water and backed by a thick forest of trees that provide shade to those who get there before the crowds arrive. On weekends and holidays, locals often set up tents, awnings, tables, and grills, and spend the whole day here.

Combate Playa Bohio (PR 3301, Calle 2) is a small, publicly maintained beach with dedicated parking less than a mile north from the hubbub of Playa El Combate.

WATER SPORTS

BAMA Boqueron Aqua Marine Adventures (PR 3301, Playa El Combate, 787/472-1321, http://bamapr.com, daily 8am-5pm) offers Jet Ski rentals (from $65 for 30 minutes) and tours (from $70 for 30 minutes). Kayak and paddleboard rentals are $25 for one hour and $15 for each additional hour.

Combate Beach Resort Kayak and Bike Rentals (PR 3301, km 2.7, 787/254-2358,

Faro Los Morrillos

www.combatebeach.com) rents single kayaks for $20 an hour and double kayaks for $25 an hour. Bike rentals start from $25 for two hours. Reserve your bike or kayak no later than 5pm the day before.

HORSEBACK RIDING
Hacienda Paraíso (PR 303, km 9.3, 787/399-7039, www.facebook.com/haciendaparaiso303) offers horseback riding (from $25 for 30 minutes) on the grounds of a hacienda. Riders must wear long pants and closed-toe shoes, and not exceed 250 pounds. Reservations are required. No experience is necessary.

BIKING
Puerto Rico Bike Adventures (Playa El Combate, PR 3301, km 2.7, 787/381-4596, www.facebook.com/puertoricobikeadventures) rents mountain bikes (from $25 for two hours), with overnight rental options. Guided tours are $65.

Food
Annie's Place (PR 3301, km 3.0, 787/254-2553, 787/487-2990, or 787/613-2990, Mon.-Thurs. 11am-9pm, Fri. 11am-midnight, Sat. 10am-midnight, Sun. 10am-10pm, $8-27) is a slick, upscale but casual open-air restaurant just steps away from Playa El Combate. Seated at the long bar, in the large covered dining room, or on the small, outdoor patio, diners can feast on a smorgasbord of fritters, including *sorullitos, alcapurrias,* empanadas, and stuffed *tostones,* as well as Puerto Rican entrées like stuffed mofongo, churrasco, and *asopao.* The full bar serves frosty piña coladas and mojitos, as well as buckets of Medalla beer on ice.

Small, casual **Los Chapines** (PR 3301, Calle 3, 787/254-9556, 787/646-9936, or 787/640-8173, www.loschapines.com, Fri. noon-midnight, Sat. noon-1am, Sun. 10:30am-9pm, $8-27) serves an extensive menu of Puerto Rican dishes with an emphasis on seafood. Try the octopus salad or paella. There's also a good selection of fish, including red snapper, mahi-mahi, salmon, and halibut, served in a choice of sauce. Carnivores can choose from churrasco, *chuleta can can,* veal chops, and chicken alfredo.

Shiny, modern **Fogota del Mar** (PR 3301, km 2.9, 787/256-0574, www.facebook.com/fogatadelmar, Mon. 11am-9pm, Fri.-Sat. 11am-midnight, Sun. 11am-10pm, $7-28) turns out a wide variety of Puerto Rican seafood dishes like whole fried snapper and stuffed mofongo, as well as a selection of refreshing cocktails, including a frozen sangria.

Dine on two-fisted burgers and mounds of chili cheese fries at **Señor Burger** (PR 3301, km 2.0, 787/448-0540, www.facebook.com/senorburger2018, Fri. 5pm-1am, Sat. 1pm-2am, Sun. 1pm-8pm, $3-12), a casual walk-up restaurant with an outdoor dining area with umbrella-shaded tables.

Luichy's Restaurant (PR 3301, km 2.9, 787/931-7690, http://luichys.com, Mon.-Fri. 9am-6pm, Sat. 9:30am-6pm, $9-25) is a casual spot serving stuffed mofongo, churrasco, *chuleta can can,* and chicken breast stuffed with sweet plantains. There's also a guesthouse here if you want to stay the night.

Supermercado Mr. Special (Ritamar Plaza, PR 100, km 6.7, 787/851-1334 or 787/851-1339, Mon.-Sat. 6am-10pm, Sun. 7am-7pm) is a modern, full-service grocery store complete with a bakery and deli.

Accommodations
Combate Beach Resort (PR 3301, km 2.7, 787/254-2358, www.combatebeach.com, $109-179, $115-239 suite) is a modern, well-maintained, two-level motel. There are 47 simple, clean rooms featuring air-conditioning, satellite TV, and mini refrigerators. Amenities include a small pool, basketball court, volleyball court, gift shop, and beach access. A café serves breakfast daily from 7:30am to 10:30pm.

Luichy's Guest House (PR 3301, km 2.9, 787/931-7690, http://luichys.com, $135-145, $165-225 suite) provides modest, centrally located rooms with flat-screen TVs, free wireless Internet, air-conditioning, and private bathrooms. Some rooms have kitchenettes with microwaves and toasters. Accommodations include standard rooms with two double beds or one queen bed with a view, and one- and two-bedroom suites. Amenities include a restaurant on-site and proximity to the beach.

Los Chapines Apartments (787/646-9936 or 787/640-8173, www.loschapines.com) books vacation rentals at a variety of apartments around Combate, ranging from basic beachfront studios to two-bedroom villas with a swimming pool.

Transportation and Services

El Combate is 195 kilometers (121 mi) southwest of San Juan, and 60 kilometers (37 mi) south of Aguadilla. From San Juan, take PR 52 south to PR 2 west to PR 116 west to PR 305 west to PR 301 south. From Aguadilla take PR 2 south to PR 100 south to PR 301 south.

Farmacía El Combate (PR 3301, km 2, Playa El Combate, 787/851-8120, 787/851-8123, or 787/851-8129, Mon.-Thurs. 9am-8pm, Fri.-Sat. 9am-9pm, Sun. 9am-2pm) is the source for prescriptions, as well as health and beauty aids.

San Germán

Established in 1573, San Germán is the second-oldest colonial city in Puerto Rico. It's a lovely town where the streets are lined with grand 18th- and 19th-century homes painted pastel shades of blue, pink, and green, and decked out with verandas, columns, and intricate wrought-iron work. San Germán has two plazas. The older and smaller of the two, **Plazuela Santo Domingo,** is home to many historic houses

and Porta Coéli, one of the oldest churches in the Americas. The larger plaza is **Plaza Francisco Mariano Quiñones;** here you'll find the *alcaldía* (town hall) and Iglesia San Germán de Auxerre.

Accommodations are limited in San Germán, but the drive is a pleasant and shady route through winding mountain roads, making it an ideal option for a leisurely day trip from Ponce or Mayagüez.

Plazuela Santo Domingo

SIGHTS

Call the **Oficina de Turismo** (2nd Fl., Casa Alcaldía Antiqua, Plaza Francisco Mariano Quiñones, 787/892-7195, Mon.-Fri. 8am-noon and 1pm-4pm) to schedule a free walking or trolley tour of San Germán.

★ Porta Coéli

Porta Coéli (corner of Calle Ramos and Calle Dr. Santiago Veve, south end of Plazuela Santo Domingo, 787/892-5845, Wed.-Sun. 8am-noon and 1pm-4pm, $3) is one of the few examples of Gothic architecture built in the "New World," and it's the oldest chapel in Puerto Rico, having been established in 1606. The original structure, now razed, was completed in 1607 as a chapel for the convent of Santo Domingo. It was rebuilt in 1692, and although many of its components have been rebuilt and restored over the years, it retains the original characteristics, featuring interior columns and a roof made from tile and wood, as was common in construction in the 17th and 18th centuries. Set high up on a hill overlooking Plazuela Santo Domingo, the structure appears to live up to its name, which translates to "gateway to heaven." Its primitive, dark sanctuary contains a fantastic collection of 18th- and 19th-century religious paintings and sculpture, including striking primitive-style wood carvings of the 12 stations of the cross. Beside the chapel are the brick ruins of a monastery.

San Germán de Auxerre Parish

Built in 1739, **San Germán de Auxerre Parish** (Plaza Francisco Mariano Quiñones, 787/892-1027) has been restored and rebuilt multiple times over the years, but it retains the sublime beauty of its neoclassical origins. The sanctuary contains three naves, 10 altars, two chapels, and a belfry tower, which was rebuilt after it was damaged in the 1918 earthquake. The ceiling and archways feature trompe-l'oeil painting made to resemble wood coffers, and in the choir loft is a painting by José Campeche, a renowned rococo artist

from Puerto Rico, as well as 18th-century wood carvings.

RECREATION

Fun in the sun is the order of the day at **Surf N Fun Waterpark** (PR 2, km 174.2, 787/659-7440, http://surfandfunwaterpark.com, summer daily 10am-6pm, $20 adults, $16 children ages 3-12), where attractions include a wave pool, bumper boats, a lazy river, a rock-climbing wall, bungee jumping, and more.

FESTIVALS AND EVENTS

La Fiesta del Acabe del Café celebrates the end of coffee harvest season in mid-February at a three-day celebration in Maricao, 20 kilometers (12 mi) north of San Germán. Festivities include musical performances, crafts, and food vendors.

FOOD AND ACCOMMODATIONS

★ **Tierra Viva Bistro** (13 Calle Carro, corner of Calle Dr. Santiago Veve, 787/634-4331 or 787/629-9789, www.facebook.com/tierravivasangerman, Sun.-Mon. 10am-5pm, Wed. 10am-7pm, Thurs. 10am-9pm, Fri.-Sat. 10am-10pm, $8-24) is a delightful contemporary restaurant serving a seasonal and locally sourced menu of simple but creative dishes, including shrimp scampi with mofongo, stuffed *tostones*, burgers served on house-made buns, passion fruit crème brûlée, and melon mojitos.

Located on the plaza across from the Porta Coéli chapel, **Lupito's Comida Mexicana** (60 Calle Dr. Santiago Veve, 787/603-1296, Wed.-Thurs. 11:30am-9pm, Fri. 11:30am-11pm, Sat. 1pm-11pm, Sun. noon-9pm, $2-17) is the place to go for frosty margaritas and spicy Mexican cuisine, from quesadillas and burritos to chicken mole and mahi-mahi in cilantro sauce.

Wakey Monkey (89 Ave. Universidad Interamericana, 787/659-7027, www.facebook.com/wakeymonkey, daily 8am-8pm, $9-15) is a hip, youthful coffee shop, café, and bar, serving a full breakfast and daily dinner specials that include ravioli Florentine, stuffed chicken breast, salmon with risotto, and churrasco.

A romantic little jewel of a spot, ★ **Tapas Café** (50 Calle Dr. Santiago Veve, 787/264-0610 or 787/370-5227, Wed.-Thurs. 5pm-10pm, Fri.-Sat. 5pm-11pm, Sun. 11am-9pm, $2-15) features a blue-tiled bar and tabletops, giving the place a Mediterranean vibe and providing the perfect setting for a menu of expertly prepared Spanish dishes. As its name implies, the menu primarily serves tapas, including *piquillo* peppers stuffed with tuna, sardine spread with mussels over toast, chorizo in red wine, and *tortilla española*. A variety of paellas are available, which serve two or more diners.

Spend the night in a restored 1917 home at **A2 Tiempo AyS Bed & Breakfast** (Calle Dr. Santiago Veve, 787/476-1027, $90-110).

There are five guest rooms that share three bathrooms, and a made-to-order breakfast is served every morning. Services are limited, and there is no air-conditioning.

TRANSPORTATION AND SERVICES

San Germán is 175 kilometers (109 mi) southwest of San Juan, and 50 kilometers (31 mi) south of Aguadilla. From San Juan, take PR 52 south to PR 2 to PR 362 north. From Aguadilla, take PR 2 south to PR 360 east to PR 396 west. Ponce is 60 kilometers (37 mi) east of San Germán via PR 2, and Mayagüez is 22 kilometers (14 mi) northwest on PR 2.

Hospital Metropolitano de San Germán (8 Calle Javilla CDT, 787/892-5300, http://hospitalmetrosangerman.com) supplies medical services to San Germán, and **Walgreens** (10 Ave. Fenwal, 787/892-4482) has a pharmacy.

La Parguera

The village of La Parguera is a popular vacation destination for Puerto Rican travelers. Much of what makes La Parguera special—its mangrove canals, coral reefs, and coastal forest—are part of La Parguera Natural Preserve, which is managed by the Department of Natural Resources. While there is plenty of swimming to be had in La Parguera, it's typically done from the bow of a boat because there isn't much in the way of sandy beaches. Be sure to get on a boat while you're here to experience the real La Parguera. Its main attraction is Bahía Fosforescénte, a bioluminescent bay that's home to glowing microscopic organisms. Unfortunately, the use of gas-powered boats, coupled with light pollution, has greatly diminished the bay's glow. But that doesn't stop visitors from flocking to the town's docks to catch boat rides to the bay after dark.

La Parguera is also the site of the famous La Pared, an underwater wall that is one of the most renowned diving spots on the island. Other popular activities include deep-sea fishing and boat rides through mangrove channels, where enormous sea stars, sea anemones, blowfish, and manatees live.

The town of La Parguera is a dense cluster of seafood restaurants, bars, and boating outfitters set around a plaza and the waterfront docks. Radiating from there are private homes—some situated on pilings in the water, where instead of cars there are boats floating in the garages. On the hills overlooking the town are several lavish, architecturally daring homes. This popular vacation town gets very crowded, especially during the summer high season and on holidays.

SIGHTS
Plaza San Pedro

Plaza San Pedro (PR 304) is the central plaza in La Parguera, located between the waterfront and the town's central business district. There are several food vendors, tables with umbrellas for dining, restroom facilities, and, up a flight of stairs, a viewing platform offering great vistas of the water and the town. It is often the site of special events like live concerts, dancing, and festivals. Behind the plaza is Plaza de La Parguera, lined with shops selling souvenirs and handcrafted jewelry and shell art. Steps away are the docks, where local boating outfitters offer rides on the water.

La Pared

La Pared is an underwater coral reef wall that runs parallel to the coast from Guánica to Cabo Rojo and is a world-class dive site. The wall drops from 55 feet to more than 1,500 feet in depth, and the water visibility ranges 60-150 feet. There are also plenty of other outstanding dive sites in the area, where you can see rays, moray eels, parrot fish, grunts, sharks, rare black corals, and more.

Los Canales Manglares

Los Canales Manglares are an intricate series of canals that wind around 30 mangrove cays off the coast of La Parguera. On weekends and holidays, locals boat to their favorite spots and anchor for a day of swimming and fishing in shallow, crystal-clear waters. Go to the boat docks in the heart of town to arrange a trip with one of several boating outfitters. Ask to see the enormous Mona iguanas that live on one of the cays, and watch the water for sea stars, sea anemones, blowfish, manatees, and more.

You can also explore some of the cays, referred to collectively as **Los Cayos.** They are ideal spots to swim, fish, and snorkel. Each cay has its own personality. The most popular is **Caracoles,** which can get crowded with revelers. **Enrique, Medialuna,** and **Majimo** are the best options for primitive camping. **Isla Cuevas** is inhabited by rhesus monkeys, placed there by the now-closed La Parguera Primate Facility, so proceed with caution. They can be aggressive.

Isla Mata La Gata

Isla Mata La Gata is one of several uninhabited islets in La Parguera Nature Preserve, and it's the only one with facilities for visitors. In addition to a dock, there are restrooms and changing rooms, covered and uncovered picnic areas with grills, a boardwalk for nature hikes, and a protected swimming area where the water is calm enough for young children to play. The island is only accessible by boat, and there are no shops, so visitors must bring everything they'll need, including sunscreen, snacks, and plenty of drinking water.

Bahía Fosforescénte

Puerto Rico is home to several bioluminescent bays and lagoons. These warm bodies of water contain millions of dinoflagellates, unique microorganisms that emit a glow when they sense motion. The only way to see them is to take a boat ride on the water after dark, preferably when the moon is not visible (ambient light diminishes their brilliance). Under the right conditions, it can be a spectacular sight. Notably, La Parguera's **Bahía Fosforescénte** permits swimming and motor boats, which has significantly diminished the bioluminescence.

Nevertheless, if you're in La Parguera, there are worse ways to spend an evening than taking a nighttime boat ride into sparkly waters. Several tour operators offer nightly rides into the bay on motorboats and a double-decker catamaran, beginning at 7:30pm from the docks in La Parguera. Kayaking into the bay is an option for experienced kayakers who can endure the 8-kilometer (5-mi) round-trip journey.

RECREATION
Beaches

Playita Rosada (Camino Paseo de la Guayacanes, Tues.-Sun. 9am-5pm, $2) is a publicly maintained, vast saltwater swimming pool that was created in the ocean using underwater fencing and a rectangular floating dock. This is a great way to go swimming without having to go out on a boat. From La

Parguera, take PR 304 to the end and turn right onto Calle 6. Follow it to the end and turn right onto Calle 7, which turns into Camino Paseo de la Guayacanes. The facilities, which are fully accessible, include bathrooms, showers, picnic areas, and pavilions.

Diving and Snorkeling

Paradise Scuba Snorkeling and Kayaks (PR 304, km 3.2, 787/899-7611, www.paradisescubasnorkelingpr.com) offers standard scuba tours (from $100), Discover scuba tours (from $130), snorkeling tours (from $40), sunset snorkeling and bio bay tours ($65), gear rental, and dive instruction.

West Divers (PR 304, km 3.1, 787/899-3223, www.westdiverspr.org) offers snorkeling and diving tours, night dives, and bio bay tours, as well as kayak rentals and boat charters.

Boating

Along the docks in the heart of La Parguera are several boat operators that provide walk-up service for renting 10- and 12-foot skiffs; guided tours of the bio bay, the mangrove canals, and the keys; and water taxi service to Isla Mata La Gata.

Gina at Johnny's Boats (787/460-8922, Sun.-Thurs. 8am-9pm, Fri. 8am-10:30pm, Sat. 8am-11pm, cash only) offers guided tours of the mangroves and keys for $45 an hour; 30-minute nighttime tours of the bio bay for $10 per person; and $5 water taxi service to Isla Mata La Gata. Boat rentals are available for $35 an hour, no training or boat captain license required for non-Puerto Rico residents. Reservations are recommended.

Aleli Tours (PR 304, km 3.2, 787/899-6086, www.alelitours.com) provides sailing, snorkeling, and mangrove channel tours around La Parguera and Guánica on a catamaran. It also has kayaks for rent. Bio bay power boat tours for up to six people cost $120 and have no time limit.

Fondo de Cristal III (end of PR 304, 787/899-5891 or 787/344-0593, Mon.-Thurs. 8:30am-9:30pm, Fri.-Sun. 8:30am-11:30pm, $8-12) offers 30-minute nighttime tours of the bio bay on a 72-foot bi-level glass-bottomed catamaran that is wheelchair-accessible. On busy nights, the boats are so crowded than only a few people can see out the glass bottom portals, and even then, you can't see much. In addition, the loudspeaker system blares loud dance music the whole time. This tour is best suited for families with children who just want to enjoy a nighttime boat ride, or the party-hearty crowd who want to drink and dance their way across the water. Fondo de Cristal III also provides transportation to Isla Mata La Gata, rents boats, and offers smaller bio bay tours on motorboats. No reservations are required.

Fishing

Parguera Fishing Charters (PR 304, 787/382-4698, www.puertoricofishingcharters.com) offers half-day ($550) and full-day ($950) trips to fish for dorado, tuna, blue marlin, and wahoo on a 31-foot, twin diesel Bertram Sport Fisherman. Trips include bait, tackle, beverages, snacks, and lunch. It also offers light-tackle reef fishing, half-day snorkeling trips, and customized charters.

Water Sports

Parguera Watersports (787/646-6777, www.prkbc.com) provides kiteboard, wakeboard, and paddleboard rental and instruction starting at $95 an hour.

FOOD

Moons Bar and Tapas (PR 304, km 3.2, 787/920-4273, www.facebook.com/moonsparguera, Thurs. 3pm-midnight, Fri. 3pm-2am, Sat. 8am-2am, Sun. 8am-midnight, $7-19) is a casual, open-air restaurant serving small plates of fish tacos, churrasco, fried calamari, and *chorizos tostados*. There is live music here.

El Karakol (in front of the boat dock, 787/899-5582, www.facebook.com/elkaracolpr, Mon.-Tues. 10am-9pm, Wed.-Thurs. and Sun. 10am-10pm, Fri.-Sat. 10am-2pm, $11-28) has two sides. One room offers a casual, fast-food vibe, but the other is a proper dining room with nice furnishings and decor. The menu includes fried seafood, paella, churrasco, *chuleta can can,* and pasta dishes. It's known for its excellent Coño sangria, a refreshing treat.

La Casita Seafood (PR 304, km 3.3, 787/899-1681, Tues.-Thurs. 4pm-10pm, Fri.-Sat. 11am-10pm, $8-25) is a large, casual, family-oriented restaurant serving Puerto Rican cuisine and seafood. Its specialties include whole fish and *asopao,* a seafood stew featuring octopus, lobster, or shrimp.

Craft beer fans will love **Isla Cueva** (PR 304, Plaza San Pedro, 787/920-4274, www.islacueva.com, Sun.-Thurs. noon-midnight, Fri.-Sat. noon-2am, $7-26) and its 80 varieties of beer. There's also a hearty menu of burgers, tacos, and ribs to soak up the suds. Service can be slow.

Located in the center of town, **Puerto Parguera** (Calle Lopez, 787/808-1640, daily 8am-11pm, $8-34) is a casual restaurant with indoor and outdoor seating, serving traditionally Puerto Rican cuisine, including stuffed mofongo, paella, shrimp salad, *empanadillas,* and *asopao.*

For the money, you can't beat **M&M Bakery and Deli** (PR 304 between Calle 1 and Calle 2, 787/899-1415, Sun.-Thurs. 6:30am-7pm, Fri.-Sat. 6:30am-8pm, $2-7), serving breakfast, sandwiches, pastries, and hot daily specials.

ACCOMMODATIONS

Accommodations in La Parguera are budget oriented, so don't expect any frills. Services are limited and furnishings are basic at best.

Parguera Plaza Hotel (PR 304, km 3.2, 787/920-4275, www.pargueraplaza.com, $125-140) is a compact lodging wedged into the dense downtown area, across the street from the water. Amenities include free wireless Internet, satellite TV, outdoor pool, pool bar, and coffee shop.

In the heart of La Parguera, **Nautilus Hotel** (PR 304, 787/899-4565, www.nautiluspr.com, $98-158) has 22 no-frills hotel rooms with air-conditioning and TVs. Amenities include laundry facilities and a pool with a hot tub.

Turtle Bay Inn (153 Calle 6, 787/508-9823 or 787/899-6633, www.turtlebayinn.com, $90-125) is a small, budget two-story inn with 12 petite rooms appointed

Parador Villa Parguera

with satellite TV, wireless Internet, and air-conditioning.

Parador Villa Parguera (PR 304, 787/899-7777, www.villaparguera.net, $117-171) is a sprawling, old-fashioned waterfront *parador* (rural inn) that was quaint at one time, but it hasn't been updated in decades and has grown tired and shabby with age. Service is practically nonexistent. The grounds are nice, and there is a pool and restaurant.

Guánica

The region encompassing the town of Guánica has a very different landscape from the rest of Puerto Rico. The flat, dry, desert-like landscape is so unusual, in fact, that a large part of the municipality has been designated a United Nations Biosphere Reserve in an effort to preserve and study its unique environment. Called Bosque Estatal de Guánica, the 10,000-acre reserve contains hiking trails, caves, beaches, and the ruins of a Spanish fort, among other sights. The coast offers great snorkeling and diving.

Guánica has an expansive, modern plaza surrounded by several historic buildings, including the original *alcadía* (city hall), and Parroquia San Antonio Abad, a mission-style church built in 1976.

In late 2019 and early 2020, Guánica experienced a series of earthquakes measuring more than 5 on the Richter scale. The quakes caused a few deaths and some structural damage.

It is commonly believed that Christopher Columbus first disembarked on the island of Puerto Rico in 1493 at **Bahía de Guánica,** which is also the site of the skirmish that ended the Spanish-American War in 1898. A **monument** to the war can be found on the *malecón* (Calle Beverly) overlooking the bay, a picturesque sight if it weren't for the industrial grain storage operation located on the opposite shore.

TRANSPORTATION AND SERVICES

La Parguera is 175 kilometers (109 mi) southwest of San Juan, and 60 kilometers (37 mi) from Aguadilla. From San Juan, take PR 52 south to PR 2 west to PR 116 south to PR 324 west. From Aguadilla, take PR 2 west to PR 114 south to PR 116 south to PR 304 south.

An **ATM** (PR 304) is located at Parador Villa Parguera.

TOP EXPERIENCE

★ BOSQUE ESTATAL DE GUÁNICA

The primary draw for visitors to Guánica is the astounding landscape of **Bosque Estatal de Guánica** (PR 334, 787/821-5706, 787/724-3724, or 787/721-5495, Mon.-Fri. 9am-5pm, free). This 10,000-acre subtropical dry forest sits atop petrified coral reefs millions of years old and features a variety of environments. On the southern side you'll find the dry scrub forest, featuring sun-bleached rocky soil, cacti, and stunted, twisted trees. There are also patches of evergreen forest along the upper eastern and western parts of the forest, where you can find Spanish moss, mistletoe, bromeliads, and orchids.

The rest of the forest has deciduous growth, where 40 percent of the trees lose their leaves between December and April. Agave and *campeche* trees, a source of red and black dye once exported to Europe for hundreds of years, are common to the area. Other flora among the forest's 700 species includes prickly pear cactus, sea grape, milkweed, mahogany, and yuca. Be sure to avoid the poisonous *chicharrón*, a shrub with reddish piney leaves that can irritate the skin on contact.

WEST COAST
GUÁNICA

Wildlife

Guánica is of special interest to bird-watchers. More than 80 species have been identified here, including the pearly-eyed thrasher, a variety of hummingbirds, the Puerto Rican mango, and the Puerto Rican nightjar, a bird that nests on the ground and remains nearly motionless all day until dusk. Other species of wildlife include the crested toad, a variety of geckos and lizards, land crabs, and green and leatherback turtles. Mongooses are also present in the area, having been introduced to the island many years ago to kill rats on the sugar plantations. The vicious little varmints are to be avoided at all costs.

Hiking

There are nearly 60 kilometers (37 mi) of trails in the forest. From the main entrance off PR 334, follow the long narrow road to the **information center,** where you'll find the trailheads and where you can obtain trail maps and tips from the helpful English-speaking rangers. The most popular hikes include: a trek to the ruins of **Fuerte Capron** (5 km/3 mi, 1.5 hours), once a lookout tower for the Spanish Armada and the site of an observation tower built by the Civilian Conservation Corps in the 1930s; a 40-minute loop trail ideal for bird-watching; a 35-minute hike to see an ancient *guayacán* tree (either 300 or 1,000 years old, depending on the source); and a 2-hour hike to underground caves, which requires special permission from the information center and accompaniment by a guide.

If you're planning to hike in the forest, be sure to wear sturdy shoes or hiking boots and bring a hat, insect repellent, sunscreen, and plenty of fresh drinking water.

Driving Tour

For a breathtakingly beautiful drive through the forest, take the **PR 333 scenic route,** which starts in the town of Guánica and traverses eastward for 10.5 kilometers (6.5 mi) along the southern rim of the forest. The curvy road snakes up the side of a steep incline that grows thick with cactus and bougainvillea. When the road crests, prepare yourself for a stunning bird's-eye view of the ocean and Bahía de Guánica. Continue eastward and you pass the ruins of a **Spanish lighthouse** on the left. On the right is the **Area de Pesca Recreativa,** a shady, remote patch of beach and a fishing spot with no facilities except for one picnic shelter. The road

monument to the Spanish-American War

leading to the recreation area is bumpy and deeply rutted, but it is possible to travel without a four-wheel drive if you proceed with caution.

Continue eastward along PR 333 and you encounter **Balneario Caña Gorda** (PR 333, km 5.8), a large, modest, shady public beach with bathrooms, covered picnic shelters, a roped-off swimming area, and a wheelchair-accessible area. The facilities are fairly worn but well maintained. Other features include a basketball court and lots of parking.

Continue east for 1 kilometer (0.5 mi) to **Punta San Jacinto,** where you can catch a **ferry** (PR 333, km 6.8, 787/821-4941, Tues.-Sun. 9am-5pm, every hour on the hour, $10 round-trip) to **Gilligan's Island** (also called Gulligan's Island and Cayo Aurora), a small *cayo* just a few hundred yards offshore featuring a beach, pavilions, changing rooms, and compostable toilet. If you plan to spend a while here, be sure to bring bug spray, sunscreen, a hat, and plenty of water. There is nowhere to purchase supplies.

Proceed east 3 kilometers (2 mi) to the end of PR 333 and park your car. Walk 1 kilometer (0.5 mi) west to **Bahía de la Ballerna,** a lovely sandy beach area and a great snorkeling and diving spot known as Submarine Gardens.

To re-enter civilization, you'll have to drive back the way you came. The whole drive can be done in 30 minutes or less, but you'll want to allow extra time to linger at some of the attractions along the way.

RECREATION

San Jacinto Boats and Seafood (PR 333, 787/821-4941) operates a **ferry** (Tues.-Sun. 9am-5pm, $10 round-trip) to Gilligan's Island. It also serves traditional Puerto Rican fare for carryout.

Island Scuba (392 Calle Marina Ensenada, end of PR 325, 787/309-6556 or 787/473-7997, www.sanjuandiver.com) provides daily dive and snorkeling trips, scuba diving for first-timers, and diving certification.

FOOD

Alexandra (Copamarina Beach Resort, PR 333, km 6.5, 787/821-0505, Mon.-Thurs. 7am-9:30pm, Fri.-Sun. 7am-10pm, $24-29) is that rare thing in Guánica: an upscale fine dining establishment. The lovely enclosed oceanside restaurant features floor-to-ceiling windows hung with sheer white curtains that set an elegant, romantic mood for your meal. The menu offers classic continental and new American cuisine, including lamb lollipops glazed in mustard and za'atar, black squid risotto, and crab cakes.

Las Palmas (Copamarina Beach Resort, PR 333, km 6.5, 787/821-0505, www.copamarina.com, daily 11am-5pm and 6pm-9:30pm, bar daily 7am-10pm, $8-21) is a casual seaside restaurant at Copamarina Beach Resort serving sandwiches, pizza, salads, mofongo, churrasco, and snapper fillet.

Located on the *malecón,* **Capronne Pizza Bar & Tapas** (59 Ave. Esperanza Idrach, 787/821-2155, www.facebook.com/capronnepizza, Thurs. 11:30am-3pm, Fri.-Sun. noon-10pm, $8-18) is a super-casual restaurant specializing in wood-fired pizza, including chorizo, bacon, and churrasco varieties, as well as pasta dishes, burgers, and stuffed *tostones.* Lunch specials are available Thursday and Friday, starting at $6.

Trasiego Sea Food (Ave. Esperanza Idrach, 787/821-0073, Mon.-Thurs. noon-10pm, Fri.-Sat. noon-midnight, Sun. noon-11pm, $14-28) has a slick, upscale vibe with a large and lively bar. The seafood dishes are plentiful, and include grilled lobster, whole fried fish, and mofongo stuffed with shrimp or octopus. There are options for landlubbers, too, like chicken *asopao* and *chuleta can can.*

ACCOMMODATIONS

Guánica Parador 1929 (PR 3116, km 2.5, Ave. Las Veteranos, 787/821-0099, www.guanica1929.com, $100-110) is a two-story Spanish colonial-style structure built in 1929 on Ensenada Bay. The simply furnished rooms come with air-conditioning, private bath, wireless Internet, TV, coffee maker, and microwave. There's a small swimming pool and restaurant on-site. All-inclusive packages are available.

★ **Copamarina Beach Resort** (PR 333, km 6.5, 787/821-0505 or 800/468-4553, www. copamarina.com, $149-189, $750 suite, $1,399 villa) is a secluded full-service luxury resort featuring large, comfortable rooms appointed with lovely, thick pine furniture, Dutch doors, and plantation windows that look out over the water. There is an excellent white-linen restaurant, Alexandra, serving seafood and Puerto Rican cuisine, as well as a casual, waterside eatery and bar, Las Palmas. The beautifully landscaped beachfront grounds feature two pools, two children's pools, two whirlpool baths, lighted tennis courts, and a lovely white-sand beach with a pier and a small boat dock. Other amenities include a spa and a fitness room.

TRANSPORTATION AND SERVICES

Guánica is 160 kilometers (99 mi) southwest from San Juan, and 75 kilometers (47 mi) south of Aguadilla. From San Juan take PR 52 south to PR 2 west to PR 116 south to PR 3116. From Aguadilla, take PR 2 south to PR 116 south to PR 3116.

Banco Santander Puerto Rico (Calle 25 de Julio) has a branch in Guánica. There is a **post office** (39 Calle 13 de Marzo, Suite 101) in town.

North Coast

The north coast of Puerto Rico is a wild expanse of rocky coastline and gorgeous ocean views, hilly karst country, and green farmland.

It's also thick with industrial plants, shopping centers, fast-food restaurants, road construction, and traffic. Despite the urban sprawl, though, the north coast has a lot going for it.

Picturesque rocky shores and rough waters with strong currents can make finding the ideal swimming spot a challenge on the north coast. Many beaches are better for looking at and walking along than going swimming. But there are a few spectacular oceanside jewels worth seeking out—at the resorts in Dorado, at Punta Cerro Gordo in Vega Alta, and at Playa Mar Chiquita in Manatí. Meanwhile, the powerful

Highlights

Look for ★ to find recommended sights, activities, dining, and lodging.

★ **Golf like a pro in Dorado:** The course at Dorado Beach Resort has hosted many tournaments, including the PGA Puerto Rico Open, the Senior PGA Tour Championship, and the World Cup (page 235).

★ **Play in the sand at Balneario Cerro Gordo:** This idyllic beach is a great spot to sun, swim, and surf (page 239).

★ **Playa Mar Chiquita:** Tucked down at the bottom of a cliff, this small protected cove in Manatí offers calm waters for swimming and an intricate system of **limestone caves** where you can find Taíno **petroglyphs** (page 240).

★ **Cueva del Indio:** Explore petrified sand dunes, natural arches, blow holes, and ancient Taíno **petroglyphs** (page 244).

★ **Observatorio de Arecibo:** Check out the largest and most sensitive radio telescope in the world. The 18-acre dish is in a natural sinkhole created by the hilly karst landscape (page 244).

waves along the north coast make for excellent surfing, especially around Manatí and Arecibo. The major sport in the area, though, is golf. Dorado is home to two classic courses.

There are two major attractions on the north coast. First are the world-class golf courses in Dorado, just 30 minutes from San Juan. The other is the Observatorio de Arecibo, which is the world's largest radio telescope. The observatory is about a 30-minute drive south of Arecibo into the island's mountainous karst country. The unusual topography alone is worth the drive. An intricate system of underground limestone caves creates enormous sinkholes and haystack hills—called *mogotes*—on the earth's surface. It's a stunning sight completely unlike anywhere else on the island—and nearly the world.

PLANNING YOUR TIME

Puerto Rico's north coast is a great place for a day trip, an overnight stay, or a long weekend. Thanks to two major roadways, it's easily accessible whether you're approaching it from San Juan or from the west coast.

Despite what you might think, PR 22, a multilane divided toll road with six tollbooths between San Juan and Arecibo, is the best route along the north coast. Although construction projects and commuter rush hours can slow your progress, it is the most expeditious route. The alternative is PR 2, a congested multilane commercial route that bisects the island's longest, most unsightly stretch of urban sprawl. It should be avoided when possible.

Dorado is the farthest eastern municipality, about 17 miles and 30 minutes from San Juan. A popular vacation spot, it has lovely beaches, luxurious resorts, and world-class golf courses. Farther westward are the municipalities of Vega Alta and Manatí, which have some spectacular beaches—**Balneario Cerro Gordo** and **Playa Mar Chiquita,** respectively—that are ideal for swimming.

One of the most popular sights along the north coast is the **Observatorio de Arecibo,** about 1.5 hours from San Juan. While in the municipality of Arecibo, check out **Cueva del Indio,** an amazing geological and archaeological wonder featuring petrified sand dunes and Taíno petroglyphs.

The best selection of hotels and restaurants can be found at either end of the north coast. To the east is Dorado, where the accommodations are upscale resorts and pricier restaurants, and to the west is Hatillo, home to more budget-minded hotels and eateries.

Toa Baja and Toa Alta

To many travelers, Toa Baja and Toa Alta are municipalities you have to blow through to get to points farther west. But these communities have their charms. There are some good swimming and fishing spots to be found. The town of Toa Alta boasts the Parroquia San Fernando Rey, a church built in 1752, and the beloved *bala de cañon* tree, which bears fruit that looks like cannonballs. The best reason to stop, though, is to dine at Millie's Place.

SIGHTS
Isla de Cabras

Located on an islet in San Juan Bay, but accessible by car via a narrow roadway, **Parque Nacional de Isla de Cabras** (Calle Manuel Enrique, PR 870, Toa Baja, 787/788-0440 or 787/622-5200, www.drdpuertorico.com, May-Aug. daily 8:30am-6pm, Sept.-Apr. Wed.-Sun. 8:30am-5pm, $4 parking) is a pleasant park with terrific views of the bay and San Juan's

Previous: Cueva del Indio; Antigua Central Plazuela in Barceloneta; Fort San Juan de la Cruz on Isla de Cabras.

North Coast

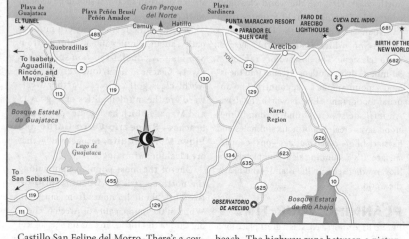

Castillo San Felipe del Morro. There's a covered pavilion, picnic tables, and a beach for sunbathing, although swimming is prohibited due to strong currents.

On the southern tip of Isla de Cabras, visible on the right just after you cross the roadway that connects the main island to the islet, is **Fort San Juan de la Cruz,** a small part of the Spanish fortification system. It was originally built from wood in 1610. After it was destroyed during a battle with the Dutch, it was reconstructed in the 1670s.

Past the park, on the right, is a police department firing range. If you follow the road to the end, park your car, and follow the path a short distance on foot uphill, you'll see the stone ruins of **Lazaretto,** a leper colony that operated here from 1883 until 1923. The grounds are not maintained, so explore at your own risk.

RECREATION

The lovely drive along PR 165 east from Dorado toward **Balneario Punta Salinas** (787/795-3325, Wed.-Sun. 8:30am-5pm) is reason alone to visit this publicly maintained beach. The highway runs between a picturesque stretch of roadway that divides an undeveloped palm grove from the rocky coastline. The beach lies on both sides of an isthmus that juts into the Atlantic and offers a great view of Viejo San Juan. The facilities include picnic shelters, bathrooms, and a snack bar. A space age-style geodesic dome sits on a hill overlooking the beach that houses the 140th Air Defense Squadron.

Area Recreativa de Lago La Plata (PR 824, km 4.9, Toa Alta, 787/723-6435, Wed.-Sun. 6am-6pm) is a recreation area popular with freshwater anglers. It features bathroom facilities, picnic shelters, and barbecue grills. The lake is stocked with fish, including largemouth bass, by the Maricao Fish Hatchery.

FOOD

It's well off the beaten path, but ★ **Millie's Place** (377 Calle Parque at Acueducto, Barrio Sabana Seca, Toa Baja, 787/784-3488, Wed.-Thurs. noon-4pm, Fri. noon-7pm, Sat.-Sun. noon-6pm, $16-45) is well worth the trip. People travel from far and wide to dine on Millie's magnificent land crabs. The trick

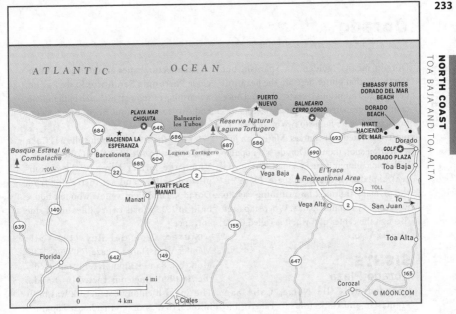

is finding this modest blue concrete structure, across the street from a neighborhood ballpark. From San Juan, travel west on PR 22, and then go north on PR 866, which takes several turns. The road dead-ends at a T intersection in front of a pharmacy. To the left is PR 187, but you'll want to turn right. Go less than half a kilometer and turn left onto Acueducto, beside the El Semaforo auto parts store. Millie's Place is on the left across from the baseball field. If you get lost, just call. The English-speaking staff gives great directions.

At a sharp bend in the road between Dorado and Punta Salinas is **El Caracol** (PR 165, km 20.2, Toa Baja, 787/604-5409, Mon.-Wed. 10am-8pm, Thurs.-Sun. 10am-11pm), a large, very casual open-air restaurant and pool hall right on the beach. In addition to selling bottles of beer for $1 during its "permanent happy hour," it has a great selection of fried fare, including empanadas, *pastelillos,* and *taquitos.*

Café El Boricua (PR 870, Isla de Cabras, Toa Baja, 787/485-2938, Wed.-Sun. 10am-10pm, $10-20) serves traditional Puerto Rican cuisine including mofongo, seafood in garlic or *criolla* sauce, fried chicken and steak, and stewed rice dishes with lobster, shrimp, or crab.

TRANSPORTATION

Toa Baja and Toa Alta are 30 kilometers (19 mi) west of San Juan. Take PR 22 west and go north on PR 693 to Toa Baja and PR 165 south for Toa Alta.

Dorado

Dorado means "golden" in Spanish, but the things that glitter here are the beautiful beaches and luxurious resorts. The land once contained grapefruit and pineapple plantations, but now it's home to two of the island's most celebrated golf courses. More than just a vacation spot, though, Dorado is a popular bedroom community to San Juan. The town's central plaza has charm to spare. PR 693 is the primary thoroughfare running east to west across the municipality. Where it passes through the center of town, it is called Calle Méndez Vigo.

SIGHTS
Dorado Plaza

Bounded by Calle Norte, Calle San Francisco, and Calle Jesus T. Pinero, the **central plaza** in Dorado is a lovely place for a stroll. In the center is *El Monumento a las Raíces Puertorriqueñas,* a statue depicting three figures: a Taíno Indian, an African, and a Spaniard, honoring the three groups that came together to create Puerto Rican culture.

Architectural sites around the plaza include **Parroquia San Antonio de Padua,** a charming mission-style church built in 1848, and **Anfiteatro Angel Hernández,** a concert hall.

Across the street from the plaza is **Casa Marcus Juan Alegría** (192 Calle Méndez Vigo), the former home of the accomplished painter and art instructor from Dorado. The bright yellow wooden house built in 1913 sports twin gables and a side entrance.

Museo Casa del Rey (292 Calle Méndez Vigo, Dorado Plaza, 787/796-5740, Mon.-Fri. 8am-4:30pm, free) is reportedly the first building constructed in Dorado. The Spanish colonial structure was built in 1823, first as an inn that housed Spanish government personnel. It became a private residence in 1848 and was home at one time to the notable author Manuel Alonso y Pacheco.

Museo de Arte e Historia de Dorado (Calle Méndez Vigo at Calle Juan Francisco, 787/796-5740, Mon.-Sat. 9am-3:30pm, free)

ruins at Isla de Cabras

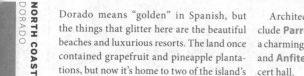

has three galleries featuring displays of art, archaeological artifacts, and illustrations depicting the city's history.

El Dorado Gran Parque Agroturístico Ecológico Recreativo

El Dorado Gran Parque Agroturístico Ecológico Recreativo (PR 165 at PR 693, south of Dorado, no phone, Mon.-Fri. 6am-6pm, $1 Mon.-Thurs., $2 Fri.) is an 850-acre park designed to educate and entertain the public with agricultural attractions and events. The majority of the acreage is used to grow crops to sell, but visitors can stroll among experimental plantings of various strains of coffee, bananas, star fruit, tamarinds, and more. Features include a horse corral and ring for riding, a children's playground, picnic shelters, and walking trails.

RECREATION
Beaches

El Ojo del Buey (Calle 13, end of PR 698, Barrio Mameyal) is a primitive recreation area along the rocky coast with terrific views of the water. It's great for hiking, but be sure to wear sturdy shoes such as sneakers or hiking boots to help you navigate the hills and craters. And be sure to follow the path through the thick sea-grape bushes to the site's namesake—El Ojo del Buey (The Ox's Eye)—an impressive rock formation that resembles the head of an ox. Legend has it that the Puerto Rican pirate Roberto Cofresí buried his treasure here. Unfortunately, the beach is often strewn with litter. To get here from the Dorado plaza, travel north on PR 693 and turn right on Calle Pedro Albizu Campos. Pass Boston Scientific on the right, then fork left. Once you pass the school, turn right on Calle 13 and follow it to the end.

Much of the coastline along Dorado is rocky, except for that occupied by the resorts, but you can find a nice little patch of sandy beach with restrooms at **Balneario Nolo Morales** (Calle A, end of PR 697, daily 8:30am-5pm, free) in town.

Heading east on PR 165, just before you cross the border into Toa Baja, is **Reserva Natural Playa Grande El Paraíso,** a gorgeous stretch of protected wilderness beach where sea turtles often lay their eggs.

★ Golf

Dorado Beach Resort (PR 693, west of Dorado, 787/626-1010, www.dorado-beach.com) is home to two championship Tournament Players Club courses managed by the PGA. Among the tournaments to have been played here are the Senior PGA Tour Championship, the Chi Chi Rodriguez Pro Am Golf Classic, the Johnnie Walker International Pro Am, and the World Cup. The 72-par **East Course** was designed and built in 1958 by Robert Trent Jones Sr., modified in 1999, and restored to Jones's original vision by his son, Robert Trent Jones Jr., in 2012. It was named the top golf course in Puerto Rico by *Golf Digest* in 2016. It features panoramic views of the ocean and natural sand bunkers. Even more challenging is the **Sugarcane Course,** which also offers views of lakes and rivers. The practice range opens Tuesday and Friday at 8am, and the rest of the week at 7am.

FOOD
Puerto Rican

One of the few restaurants open on Mondays in Dorado, **Katrina** (Calle A, 939/268-5372, Sun.-Thurs. 11am-10pm, Fri.-Sat. 11am-midnight, $8-36) is a large, open-air restaurant with a nautical-themed bar and sidewalk dining across the street from Balneario Nolo Morales. It serves a solid and extensive menu of Puerto Rican dishes, including stuffed mofongo. Specialties include churrasco stuffed with shrimp or lobster, served with choice of criolla, cream garlic, or butter sauce. There's karaoke 7pm-11:30pm on Friday and Saturday.

Also located across the street from Balneario Nolo Morales is **Villa Dorado D'Alberto** (Calle A, 787/278-1715, Sun.-Tues. 11am-9pm, Wed.-Thurs. 11am-10pm, Fri.-Sat. 11am-midnight, $12-28), an upscale seafood

restaurant with attentive service, specializing in whole fried snapper and mofongo stuffed with lobster.

The venerable **El Capitán** (511 Calle Extension Sur, 787/278-0011, Thurs.-Sun. noon-9:30pm, $9-24) serves an extensive menu of mofongo, seafood, churrasco, and rice dishes.

La Terraza (PR 693, km 8.1, Calle Marginal, Costa de Oro, 787/796-1242 or 787/796-7114, www.laterrazadorado.com, Sun.-Thurs. 11:30am-10pm, Fri.-Sat. 11:30am-11pm, $16-28) is a restaurant on an open-air terrace decked out in a cheery nautical theme. The rooftop bar (Sun.-Thurs. 5pm-midnight, Fri.-Sat. 5pm-2am) stays open late and serves a separate bar menu. The menu features mostly traditional Puerto Rican cuisine; its specialty is mofongo stuffed with everything from octopus to lobster to chicken. Other menu items include whole snapper, shrimp brochette, picadillo, and *chuleta can can.*

Cuban

★ **Metropol** (Plaza Dorado Shopping Center, PR 698, Calle Méndez Vigo, 787/278-5500 or 787/278-2600, www.metropolrestaurant.com, daily 11am-10:30pm, $10-15) is a popular local chain of casual restaurants serving outstanding Cuban cuisine. The house specialty is *gallinita rellena de congri—* succulent roasted Cornish hen stuffed with a perfectly seasoned combination of rice and black beans. The presentation is no-nonsense and the service expedient, designed to get you in and out so the folks lining up outside can have your table.

Italian

Grappa (247 Calle Méndez Vigo, 787/796-2674, Wed. 6pm-10pm, Thurs.-Sun. 5pm-10pm, $12-32) offers Italian staples and daily specials, including lamb ravioli, lasagna, pizza, and a variety of risottos in an intimate setting with excellent service.

Seafood and Steak

★ **El Ladrillo** (334 Calle Méndez Vigo, 787/796-2120, www.elladrillorest.com, Tues.-Thurs. and Sun. 5pm-10pm, Fri.-Sat. 11:30am-3pm and 5pm-10pm, $12-38) is a lovely Old World fine dining restaurant that has been serving expertly prepared steaks, seafood, and Puerto Rican cuisine to locals and visitors alike since 1975. Redbrick arches and colorful paintings by local artists contribute to the warm atmosphere. Specialties include plantain soup, rice dishes, and a variety of lobster dishes and steaks. It has a full bar and a well-stocked wine cellar.

Breakfast and Lunch

Punta Plena (279 Calle Méndez Vigo, Dorado Plaza, 787/359-4893, Thurs. and Sun. 11am-10pm, Fri.-Sat. 11am-midnight, $2-6) is a friendly, family-run bar serving a variety of *frituras* (fritters) including stuffed arepas, *alcapurrias,* and empanadas.

ACCOMMODATIONS

In addition to private residences, ★ **Dorado Beach, A Ritz-Carlton Reserve** (100 Dorado Beach Dr., 787/626-1001 or 787/253-1700, www.ritzcarlton.com, $1,799-2,499, $2,749-5,248 suite) offers 115 ultra-luxury guest rooms, some with private plunge pools, on 50 acres of a former pineapple plantation. There are three restaurants, including Coa, specializing in seasonal dishes prepared in a wood-fire oven and with a wine cellar containing more than 690 labels. There's also a culinary center where guests can take cooking classes. Other amenities include a spa, two PGA golf courses, and a mile-long stretch of pristine beach.

Embassy Suites Dorado del Mar Beach & Golf Resort (201 Dorado del Mar Blvd., 787/796-6125, www.embassysuites3.hilton.com, $270-290) has 175 suites featuring cable TV, microwave, refrigerator, and high-speed Internet. Amenities include a lagoon pool overlooking the beach, a whirlpool bath, tennis courts, a fitness room, two

1: Balneario Nolo Morales 2: Katrina restaurant

restaurants, and a bar. Rates include a complimentary breakfast.

TRANSPORTATION AND SERVICES

Dorado is 35 kilometers (22 mi) west of San Juan. Take PR 22 west to PR 165 north.

The **police department** (787/796-2020 or 787/796-1212) is at kilometer 7.2 of PR 693/ Calle Méndez Vigo. For emergencies call **911. Dorado Community Health Center** (PR 698, Barrio Mameyal, 787/278-3330, http://emergenciaspr.com) provides 24-hour emergency care.

Walgreens (PR 693, 787/796-5811) is open 24 hours. **Banco Popular** (787/278-1171) has an **ATM** in the **Grande supermarket** (787/278-2400) on Calle Méndez Vigo.

Vega Alta and Vega Baja

Vega Alta and Vega Baja are on fertile low-lying land divided by Río Cibuca. Today, visitors come to the Vegas to enjoy Punta Cerro Gordo, a gorgeous piece of coastline that boasts one of the island's best publicly maintained beaches and a great camping area.

SIGHTS

Believed to have been built around 1776 (when Vega Baja was established), **Museo de Arte Casa Alonso** (34 Calle Betances, Vega Baja, 787/855-1931, Mon.-Fri. 9am-3pm, free) is a two-story neoclassic *criolla*-style home constructed of wood, brick, and stone. The interior has been restored and now serves as an art and history museum, displaying, among other objects, many of the artifacts recovered from the home, including ceramics, tiles, stoneware, and coins. In the 1st-floor courtyard is a 40-foot well, which provided water to the home's residents, the first of whom was Vega Baja mayor Pablo Soliveras. In addition to a collection of 19th-century furnishings, the house contains a room devoted to Puerto Rican popular music that includes photographs, phonographs, records, and radios.

RECREATION

Puerto Nuevo (PR 686, km 12, at PR 692, Vega Baja, 787/858-6447) has two parts to it.

view from the campsites at Balneario Cerro Gordo in Vega Alta

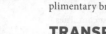

One part is a *balneario*, a free, city-maintained recreation area with a lovely natural lagoon. Facilities include covered picnic shelters, outdoor showers, a playground, and a variety of food vendors selling fried snacks. Directly east of the *balneario* is a narrow road that takes you to the other part: a spot of wild coast where rocky outcroppings and soft patches of beach compete for space. Sandy pull-offs into the low-lying shrubs and trees line the beach in some places; the area is something of a lovers' lane at night. But on weekend days and holidays, it's a popular party beach for teenagers and young adults. There are no facilities, and the property is not well maintained, as evidenced by the amount of litter.

El Trece Recreational Area (PR 160, km 13, Vega Baja) is a 13-acre city-maintained sports and recreation park on the Indio River, where visitors can swim in natural pools of fresh river water. There are also hiking trails, picnic shelters, bathroom facilities, a handball court, and a grass volleyball court.

Reserva Natural Laguna Tortuguero (PR 687, km 1.2, Vega Baja, 787/858-6617 or 787/858-5020, Wed.-Sun. 6am-5pm) is a long lagoon surrounded by swamps, marshlands, and karst mountains. A fishing dock provides a great place to angle for tilapia. In addition to fish, the lagoon is home to an estimated 1,000 caimans, a species of crocodile. They grow to six feet and can be vicious, but they're typically out at night, when the lagoon is closed. The **Vega Baja Eco-Tourism Office** (Laguna Tortuguero, PR 687, km 1, 787/807-1822, Mon.-Fri. 8am-3pm) offers guided nature tours through the lagoon. It also operates tours at El Trece Recreational Area, among others. Advance reservations for tours are required.

★ Balneario Cerro Gordo

Even if there weren't a shortage of beaches suitable for swimming on the north coast,

Balneario Cerro Gordo (PR 690, Vega Alta, 787/883-2730 or 787/883-2515, Wed.-Sun. 8:30am-6pm, parking $4 cars and vans, $2 motorcycles) would still be a wildly popular place to plunk down in the sun or frolic in the surf. It is a large, drop-dead gorgeous spot of forested coastline with dramatic cliffs, a rocky peninsula, and a palm-lined beach. There's a large protected cove that's perfect for swimming, and on the other side of the point are rougher waters ideal for surfing.

Facilities include bathrooms, showers, food vendors, lifeguards, and picnic tables. On the eastern end, on a shady mountaintop, are some great **campsites** ($13 per person) with ocean views. Expect a crowd on weekends and holidays.

ENTERTAINMENT AND EVENTS

It's all about the celebration of food in the Vegas. In mid-July, Vega Alta heralds the versatility of breadfruit with the **Festival de Panapén** (787/883-5900). In addition to performances by musicians and dancers, there are arts and crafts booths, food kiosks, and a breadfruit-cooking contest.

In Vega Baja, it's all about syrup at the **Festival del Melao Melao** (787/858-6617) held in early October. Artisans and food vendors line the Plaza de Recreo, where wood-carving competitions are held.

TRANSPORTATION AND SERVICES

Vega Alta is 40 kilometers (25 mi) west of San Juan. Take PR 22 west to PR 690 south. Vega Baja is 50 kilometers (31 mi) west of San Juan. Take PR 22 west to PR 2 west.

Vega Baja Casa de Cultura y Turismo (Calle Betances at Tulio Otero, Vega Baja, 787/858-6447, Mon.-Fri. 8am-4:30pm) offers information on the history and culture of the area and provides tours upon request.

Manatí and Barceloneta

Once known for their grand sugar plantations and haciendas, Manatí and Barceloneta's economies now revolve around pharmaceutical manufacturing and pineapple farms. Manatí's town center features a large, modern plaza and a striking cultural center located in a historic building that once housed the city's marketplace. It's also home to several modern health facilities.

Along the coast north of Manatí is a wonderland of rolling green hills and delightful beaches ideal for swimming and surfing. The thick vegetation and elevation make it a cool enclave for the fabulous homes and condos that have cropped up here.

Barceloneta is a small, bustling town with a modern plaza featuring a kinetic, modern art sculpture and a contemporary *alcadía*. It is also home to the restored ruins of Central Plazuela, a sugar mill dating back to 1907. The town is notable as the starting point for a spectacular scenic drive to Arecibo and as home to the Bosque Estatal de Combalache, a small forest popular for its wooded mountain bike trails.

SIGHTS

A **scenic drive** from **Barceloneta to Arecibo** is an excellent reason to venture off PR 22. This 16-kilometer (10-mi) stretch along PR 684 north and PR 681 is like Puerto Rico's own little version of California's Pacific Coast Highway, rich in gorgeous views of the ocean with lots of spots to pull over and go for a swim. There's also a great surf break at Machuca's Garden at La Boca off PR 684.

Hacienda La Esperanza

Hacienda La Esperanza (PR 616, Manatí, 787/722-5882, http://paralanaturaleza.org, $12 adults, $9 seniors and students) was one of the biggest, richest sugar plantations in Puerto Rico in the late 19th century. Take a 90-minute guided tour of the restored manor house, the sugar mill, sugarcane fields, and an extensive machete collection. Offered in Spanish only, tours are for ages 6 and up. Times and dates vary, so check the schedule on the website.

★ Playa Mar Chiquita

If you're anywhere near Manatí, don't pass by without stopping at **Playa Mar Chiquita** (end of PR 648, off of PR 685, north of Manatí), an enchanting wonderland of natural beauty. Tucked down in the base of a wooded cliff is a perfectly formed natural pool almost completely enclosed by two long reaches of rocky coral that embrace a pristine crescent of sandy beach and crystal-clear water ideal for taking a dip.

The formation of Playa Mar Chiquita is so picture-perfect that a legend has grown up around it to explain its creation. As the story goes, a beautiful woman went to Mar Chiquita and fell into the ocean. She began to drown, but then the sea opened up and the waves washed her ashore. A few days later she returned to Mar Chiquita and was surprised to discover that the lovely fan-shaped pool had formed.

There's more to Playa Mar Chiquita than its baby-safe beach, though. The mountain base contains an intricate **cave system,** where the adventurous can discover stalagmites and stalactites, as well as **petroglyphs** left behind by indigenous people. Mangrove trees and sea grapes grow thick and low throughout the area, creating their own cave-like nooks where lovers park for a rendezvous. Crumbling ruins of small buildings and walls add a bewitching quality. And set high into a cliff wall is a tiny shrine containing a likeness of the Virgin Mary, who looks down on all the mysterious beauty below.

1: Centro de las Artes Joaquín Rosa Gómez 2: Playa Mar Chiquita in Manatí

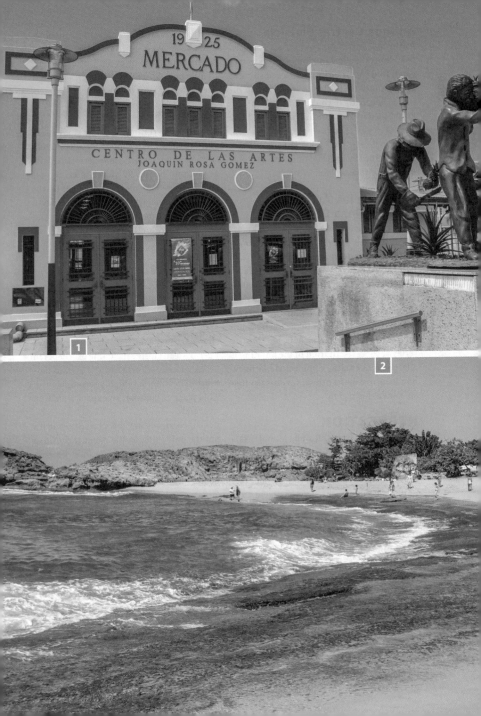

Antigua Central Plazuela

Antigua Central Plazuela (Ave. Plazuela, Barceloneta, daily 7am-7pm, free) is where you'll find the beautifully restored ruins of an old sugar mill. This is worth a trip off the beaten path if you're into antiquities. Established in 1907, the mill produced 2,000 tons of sugar at its height of production. Operations ceased in 1963. Today the property is maintained by the Departamento de Obras Públicas (Office of Public Works).

Centro de las Artes Joaquín Rosa Gómez

What once served as Manatí's central marketplace, built in 1925, is now **Centro de las Artes Joaquín Rosa Gómez** (1 Calle Padial, Manatí, 787/851-6118, www.facebook.com/CentrodeArtesManati), a beautifully restored and striking marigold-colored colonial structure that contains a performing arts center. It is home to the town's youth orchestra and children's choir, and hosts a series of concerts. In front of the building is a large bronze statue of pineapple farmers, honoring one of the primary industries that sustained this region.

RECREATION

Playa Los Tubos (PR 686, Manatí) is a beautiful wilderness beach popular with experienced surfers. Los Tubos is not for the inexperienced surfer. Swimming is not recommended due to the strong currents. Do not leave valuables visible inside your car; this is a popular spot for smash and grab thefts.

Mountain bikers will want to check out **Bosque Estatal de Cambalache** (PR 682, km 6.3, beside the Job Corps facility, Barceloneta, 787/999-2200, ext. 5610 or 5613, 787/881-1004 or 787/469-8027, Sat.-Sun. 9am-5pm, free), a small, wooded recreation area where trails meander through a 1,000-acre subtropical forest reserve distinguished by its dramatic, hilly karst formations. There are also 6 kilometers (4 mi) of hiking trails, a wheelchair-accessible trail, and camping for up to 40 people. Call ahead (Wed.-Fri. 8am-4pm) to obtain permits to camp or cycle. Unfortunately, there's no bike rental outfitter, so you'll need to bring your own gear.

SHOPPING

Puerto Rico Premium Outlets (1 Premium Outlets Blvd., Barceloneta, 787/846-5300, www.premiumoutlets.com/puertorico, daily 11am-7pm) boasts 90 stores offering discounts of 25-65 percent off designer labels, including Ann Taylor Factory Store, Calvin Klein, Izod, Kenneth Cole, Michael Kors, and Nautica. There are also restaurants and fast-food outlets.

FOOD AND ACCOMMODATIONS

Salt and Pepper (Calle Marginal 8, Manatí, 787/854-4422, Tues.-Fri. 11am-10pm, Sat. 3pm-10pm, Sun. noon-8pm, $15-28) is a simple, casual spot serving contemporary Puerto Rican cuisine including excellent red beans and rice, churrasco, and stuffed mofongo. The sangria is highly recommended. This place is popular, so expect a wait on weekends.

Grilled steaks are the specialty, but it's not the only thing on the menu at **Su Casa Steakhouse** (PR 670, km 1.0, at PR 668, Manatí, 787/884-0047, Wed.-Thurs. 11:30am-9pm, Fri. 11:30am-10pm, Sat. 4:30pm-10pm, Sun. 11:30am-3pm, $12-28). You can also get grilled pork chops in mango salsa and churrasco in mushroom sauce, among other hearty dishes.

Strawberry and Coffee Lovers and More (Barceloneta plaza, 787/846-5133, www.facebook.com/StrawberryCoffeeLoversAndMore, Tues.-Wed. and Fri. 10am-5pm, Thurs. 11am-8:30pm, Sat. 11am-9pm, Sun. 2pm-9pm, $4-12) serves breakfast, lunch, coffee, and smoothies, but it's famous for its over-the-top frappés and milkshakes adorned with bouquets of skewered fresh fruit and chocolate candy.

Frances Marie Bakery (corner of Ave. Palmas Atlas and Calle Nueva, Barceloneta, across from the ball field, 787/846-3296, www. facebook.com/francesmariepr, daily 6am-10pm, $2-4) serves a variety of sandwiches, including *tripleta, cubano,* and *media noche,* prepared with bread made right on the premises. There's also a huge glass case of tempting cheesecakes, doughnuts, cookies, and pastries.

Hyatt Place Manatí (corner of PR 2 and PR 149, Manatí, 787/854-1000, www. hyatt. com, $129-134, $149 suite) is an extended-stay hotel catering to business and medical tourism clients. Amenities include free wireless Internet, a 24-hour fitness center, swimming pool, and a fee-based shuttle service.

TRANSPORTATION AND SERVICES

Manatí is 50 kilometers (31 mi) west of San Juan at the intersection of PR 22 and PR 149. Barceloneta is 60 kilometers (37 mi) west of San Juan at the intersection of PR 22 and PR 140.

Doctors' Center Hospital (PR 2, km 47.7, 787/854-3322, http://tuhospitalfamiliar.com) provides 24-hour medical emergency services. Other health facilities include **HealthSouth Rehabilitation Center Hospital** (PR 2, km 47.7, 787/621-3800, www.healthsouth-manati.com) and **Manatí Medical Center** (PR 674, 787/525-0046 or 787/621-3700, w2.manatimedical.com).

Banco Popular (Villa Maria Shop, PR 2, Manatí) has an **ATM.**

Arecibo

Arecibo is the most populated municipality on the north coast, with about 100,000 residents. It has a bustling plaza, a vibrant restaurant scene, and a large, historic promenade overlooking the harbor and the Río Grande de Arecibo. There are several popular attractions in the area, most notably the world-famous Observatorio de Arecibo, located in the mountainous karst country south of town. On the coast is Cueva del Indio, a geographic wonder of petrified sand dunes that double as a natural repository for Taíno petroglyphs. Nearby is *Birth of the New World,* a massive, modern sculpture depicting Christopher Columbus. And for children, there's the Faro de Arecibo Lighthouse and Historical Park, with its themed playgrounds and welcoming patch of beach.

SIGHTS
Casa Ulanga
Built in 1854, **Casa Ulanga** (51 Calle Gonzalo Marín, 787/878-8015, Mon.-Fri. 8am-noon and 1pm-4:30pm) is one of the oldest structures in Arecibo. Francisco Ulanga, a Spanish industrialist who brought the steam engine

to Puerto Rico, built the home as his primary residence. It later was used as a court and a jail. Today it houses the Arecibo department of culture. After the city's art museum was damaged by Hurricane Maria, the institution's art collection was relocated here.

Paseo Las Damas
Also known as Paseo Victor Rojas or El Fuerte, **Paseo Las Damas** (Calle Gonzalo Marín at Ave. José de Diego) is a rectangular, oceanfront promenade built in 1881 on the ruins of Fuerte San Miguel, using stones from the 18th-century fort for its construction. Listed in the U.S. National Register of Historic Places, it overlooks the harbor and Río Grande de Arecibo. Food trucks are often parked nearby.

Faro de Arecibo Lighthouse and Historical Park
Families will enjoy **Faro de Arecibo Lighthouse and Historical Park** (PR 655, Barrio Islote, 787/880-7540 or 787/880-7560, www.arecibolighthouse.com, Mon.-Fri. 9am-6pm, Sat.-Sun. 10am-7pm, $12 adults,

$10 children 12-2, free for children under 2, $3 parking). Built in 1898, the neoclassical lighthouse is on top of Punta Morrillo, a rocky mountain overlooking the north coast, and offers spectacular views of the Atlantic Ocean and surrounding area. The lighthouse is still operational, and inside are historical displays and artifacts of curiosities found in the ocean, including a 1910 diving suit.

Road-tripping families will want to stop here to let their young children burn off some energy in the surrounding historical park. Representing the island's historical eras are interactive, kid-sized reproductions of a Taíno village; Columbus's ships the *Niña*, the *Pinta*, and the *Santa María;* living quarters for enslaved African people; Blackbeard's pirate ship, the *Queen Anne's Revenge;* and a spooky pirate's cave containing tanks of sharks, turtles, and alligators. There's also a small saltwater aquarium, a water park, a playground with swings and slides, and a well-maintained beach with picnic shelters and bathrooms.

Birth of the New World

Taller than the Statue of Liberty by 59 feet, *Birth of the New World* (PR 681, km 9.5), locally known as **La Estatua de Colón,** is a 360-foot sculpture made of bronze, steel, and copper that commemorates Christopher Columbus's first voyage. It was designed by Georgian artist Zurab Tsereteli, who offered to donate it to several U.S. cities; it was rejected until it found a home in Arecibo. At the time of its installation in 2016, it was the tallest structure in North America. Plans to construct a welcome center and parking lot have been delayed indefinitely.

★ Cueva del Indio

A trip to **Cueva del Indio** (PR 681, km 7.9, 787/220-3330, daily 9:30am-5pm, $5) starts with a short trek through scrubby, prickly brush until the topography gives way to what looks like a moonscape rising out of the sea. The massive, rocky outcropping is a petrified sand dune that has been carved over time by

the pounding sea at its base. Visitors are free to wander the surface.

To the west is a large hole in the surface that leads down into a cave, which bottoms out on the sea floor. On its interior walls are faint **petroglyphs**—a sun, an owl, human faces—believed to have been made by Taíno people more than 500 years ago. To the east are huge natural arches where the sea has cut through the mass. During high tide, waves crash into it with such force that water shoots 20-30 feet in the air.

Hiking shoes or sturdy sneakers are a must. The surface of the dune is rough and uneven, and there are no railings, so proceed with caution. This is not recommended for young children or people with mobility or balance issues. Sunscreen and a hat are recommended. Payment is accepted by cash or Venmo only.

Cueva del Indio is 75 kilometers (47 mi) west of San Juan via PR 22 and PR 681, and it's 13 kilometers (8 mi) east of Arecibo on PR 681.

★ Observatorio de Arecibo

You know you're headed someplace unique as you travel south from the town of Arecibo toward the Observatorio de Arecibo (end of PR 625, 787/878-2612, www.naic.edu, mid-Jan.-May and Aug.-mid-Dec. Wed.-Sun. 10am-3pm, June-July and mid-Dec.-mid-Jan. daily 10am-3pm, $12 adults, $8 seniors and children), the world's largest and most sensitive radio telescope. The bustle of commerce, industry, expressways, and road-construction projects eventually gives way to a bright green, grassy landscape dotted with dramatic haystack-shaped hills called *mogotes.* Passing cars become few as the curvy road winds upward around the hills, past sprawling cattle farms and errant chickens.

As you trek uphill from the parking lot, you'll get your first glimpses of the radio telescope's suspension apparatus, a startling sight. Its metal construction is a sharp contrast to the wilderness that surrounds it.

1: *Birth of the New World* in Arecibo **2:** Callejón del Beso restaurant

The highlight of a visit here is the observation deck, from which you can peer over the side of the massive dish. In addition to gawking at the telescope dish, visitors can explore the observatory's education center featuring two levels of informative displays and interactive exhibits on the finer points of the study of space and the atmosphere. A short film on the telescope is screened throughout the day in both English and Spanish.

There's also a snack bar and a gift shop that sells all kinds of great educational books, models, and toys. It's a good source for maps of the island, too. Thirty-minute VIP tours for up to seven people are available with advance reservations. Entry to the observatory requires a half-mile hike—mostly up stairs—from the parking lot to the entrance, and there's little shelter along the way. Visitors unable to make the journey by foot can get permission from the guard to drive up to the entrance. Be sure to bring sturdy walking shoes.

The observatory is 25 kilometers (16 mi) south of Arecibo. Take PR 129 south to PR 134 east to PR 635 east to PR 625 south. From San Juan it's 100 kilometers (62 mi) east via PR 22 to PR 129 south to PR 134 east to PR 635 east to PR 625 south.

ENTERTAINMENT

In continuous operation since 1957, **Auto Cine Santana** (PR 662, km 0.5, 787/881-7869, www.facebook.com/AutoCineSantanaArecibo, Mon. and Wed.-Thurs. 8pm, Fri.-Sun. 7:30pm and 9:30pm, $3.50 pp) is a family-friendly drive-in movie theater playing first-run Spanish- and English-language movies with Spanish subtitles.

FOOD AND ACCOMMODATIONS

★ **La Buena Vida** (65 Calle Gonzalo Marín, 787/650-8773, www.facebook.com/LaBuenaVidaArecibo, Mon.-Wed. 5pm-10pm, Thurs. 5pm-midnight, Fri.-Sat. noon-midnight, Sun. 2pm-11pm, $7-11) is a hip, casual place serving a small but delicious menu of tapas and pasta dishes in a warm, friendly atmosphere. Tapas are served on slices of toasted bread; toppings include various combinations of smoked oysters, smoked salmon, pesto, brie, sun-dried tomatoes, bacon, anchovies, and hummus. Pasta dishes are served on your choice of noodle, with or without chicken, salmon, or bacon, and there is a variety of creative sauces from which to choose. The Pasta Salá features fresh anchovies, cayenne pepper, and parmesan. The Pasta Fariara features smoked oysters, bacon, sriracha, and parmesan in a white sauce. There are plenty of vegetarian options and a long list of craft beers available. On weekend nights, there's live music featuring salsa bands and DJs that create a street party vibe outside the entrance.

With an eye-catching exterior painted like the Puerto Rican flag, you can't miss **Callejón del Beso** (5 Calle Gonzalo Marín, 787/650-3872, www.facebook.com/callejondebesopr, Thurs. 3pm-11pm, Fri.-Sat. 3pm-1am, Sun. noon-9pm, $7-17). But that doesn't prepare you for what's inside: a romantic, Spanish-style wine bar serving a menu of tapas and paellas with a long list of wine and sangria. Dine inside, in the charming alley, or on the sidewalk.

Owned by the same folks behind Callejón del Beso, **Guajira** (1 Calle Gonzalo Marín, 787/881-9200, www.facebook.com/guajirapr, Thurs. 3pm-10pm, Fri.-Sat. 3pm-2am, Sun. 1pm-10pm, $5-16) is a Cuban restaurant that serves tapas, sandwiches, and entrées like grilled mahi-mahi in a lemon cilantro sauce, roast pork, and *ropa vieja* made with chicken. There's live entertainment on the weekends, featuring salsa bands and stand-up comedians.

Located next to a boat ramp, overlooking Arecibo's harbor, **Carbón y Leña** (PR 655, km 0.2, 939/256-7083, Mon.-Thurs. 11am-9pm, Fri.-Sat. 11am-10pm, $10-17) is a sprawling restaurant serving Puerto Rican cuisine. Dine inside or out on mofongo, *chuleta can can,* and whole fried snapper. There's also a location in Quebradillas.

Look to the Stars

large radio telescope at the Observatorio de Arecibo

Built in 1963, the **Observatorio de Arecibo** is a curved dish telescope set into the earth on what was once a coffee plantation in the upper regions of Puerto Rico's karst country. The landscape is distinguished by an underground system of limestone caves that has transformed the topography into clusters of fertile green hills and sinkholes. It is because of the landscape's natural depressions, which were big enough to contain the telescope's dish, that the observatory was built here.

To convey a sense of its immensity, consider these statistics: The aluminum-lined dish is 1,000 feet wide from rim to rim. The receiver is on a 900-ton platform suspended 450 feet above the dish on a 304-foot moveable arm. Cornell University managed the observatory for four decades until 2011, when the National Science Foundation took over operations. The observatory employs about 120 scientists and engineers from around the world.

Many significant astronomical discoveries have been made at the observatory in the last four decades. Joseph Taylor won the Nobel Prize in 1993 for discovering the first binary pulsar from Arecibo. Other discoveries include polar caps on Mercury and the existence of planets around a pulsar.

But Arecibo's most infamous contribution to science has been as the center of operations for the Search for Extraterrestrial Intelligence Institute's Phoenix Project, which monitored the telescope for signs of intelligent life in the universe. A respected organization made up of some of the world's foremost scientists, including three Nobel Prize winners, the SETI Institute and its Arecibo research project were funded through grants by NASA for many years before the organization became private in 1993. The project is not as "ET" as it sounds, though. The telescope doesn't so much "seek" intelligent life as listen for radio signals that might indicate its presence. Nevertheless, its otherworldly visage has made it a popular backdrop for filmmakers, including the Jodie Foster movie *Contact* and the James Bond movie *GoldenEye*.

There's one more thing about the Arecibo Observatory that is unique, and that is its longevity. Most major telescopes become obsolete after about 10 years as technological advancements are made, but not Arecibo. Multimillion-dollar upgrades have been made through the years that have extended its viability for more than 50 years.

Salitre Meson Costero (PR 681, km 3.8, 787/816-2020, www.salitre.com, Sun.-Mon. and Wed.-Thurs. noon-8pm, Fri.-Sat. noon-9pm, $14-36) is an oceanfront restaurant serving a large menu of Puerto Rican cuisine with an emphasis on fresh seafood. The mofongo here is made with yuca and comes stuffed with octopus, lobster, conch, chorizo, crab, or the local specialty, ceti, a tiny, transparent fish that's eaten whole. A variety of fileted fish and paellas are also available, as well as churrasco, steaks, ribs, and pork chops. Adjacent to the restaurant is an eight-room B&B ($93-108, $158 suite) that can be rented by the room or as an entire villa. Each room has its own bathroom, air-conditioning, and high-speed Internet. There's also a swimming pool.

TRANSPORTATION AND SERVICES

Arecibo is 80 kilometers (50 mi) west of San Juan, north of PR 22 at the convergence of PR 2, PR 10, and PR 129.

Taxi service is provided by **Arecibo Taxi Cab** (787/878-2929). Other services include the **police department** (Ave. Hostos, 787/878-2020), **Hospital Pavía Arecibo** (PR 129 and Ave. Rotario, 787/878-7272, daily 24 hours), and **Banco Popular** (614 Ave. San Luis Arecibo, 787/878-4949), which has an **ATM.**

CAMUY

Camuy is a small, sleepy coastal town northwest of Arecibo. Its main attraction was the Cavernas del Río Camuy, a fantastic nature park in the island's karst country where visitors could once explore the massive subterranean cave system beneath the island's surface. Unfortunately, the park was damaged by Hurricane Maria in 2017, and remains closed indefinitely.

Sights
PLAYA PEÑÓN BRUSI/ PEÑÓN AMADOR

Spend the day swimming, fishing, and hiking at **Playa Peñón Brusi/Peñón Amador** (PR 485, km 2.1), a lovely spot of natural beauty featuring a crescent of beach, a dingy dock, and mounds of petrified coral reef providing gorgeous panoramic views of the northern coast. Just be sure to bring a sturdy pair of lace-up shoes; the coral is sharp. Curiosities to explore include a six-foot wooden tiki totem on one reef and a cross planted on another. Lore has it that a grieving father made the cross from the wood of an old church and put it there to commemorate his daughter, who died at sea. Some people believe a 20-foot shark lives under the reef. There's also a terrific little food vendor called **El Pescadería Peñón** that serves up fresh seafood dishes.

Food

It looks like a snack bar, but **El Pescadería Peñón** (Playa Peñón Brusi/Peñón Amador, PR 485, km 2.1, 787/356-3589, Wed.-Thurs. 9am-3pm, Fri.-Sun. 9am-5pm, $1-20) serves excellent *pinchos, pastelillos,* and whole fried snapper.

Transportation

Camuy is 105 kilometers (65 mi) west of San Juan. Take PR 22 west to PR 2 west.

Hatillo

The town of Hatillo has a charming central plaza distinguished by brightly colored buildings in shades of purple, orange, yellow, and green. On the streets surrounding the plaza are a library, pharmacy, theater, tourism office, and the Museo de Arte y Historía Oscar Colón Delgado, which honors the Hatillo-born artist. The commercial district along PR 2 is a thick tangle of urban sprawl.

Milk production drives the local economy. Hatillo produces one-third of the milk consumed on the island. A bronze statue of a farmer holding a calf in the split between PR 2 and PR 485 is a testament to the community's reverence for the industry.

Hatillo is the site of the annual Festival de la Máscaras, a three-day celebration that culminates on December 28, when hundreds of elaborately costumed and masked people dance through the streets, gathering at the town plaza at 3pm for a parade.

SIGHTS

Museo de Arte y Historia Oscar Colón Delgado (Hatillo plaza, corner of Ave. Roosevelt and Calle Padre Delgado, 787/898-3840, ext. 1284, Mon. 8am-4:30pm, Tues.-Fri. 8am-5pm, Sat. 9am-1pm, free) features three galleries: one devoted to the history of Hatillo, one featuring the work of artist Oscar Colón Delgado (1889-1968), and one for changing exhibitions.

Located on the border of Hatillo and Camuy, **El Gran Parque del Norte** (PR 119, 787/820-6229, daily 6am-9pm, free) is an 18-acre waterfront park built in 2011. A wooden boardwalk runs along the beach and the mouth of Río Camuy, where it spills into the ocean. Swimming is not recommended due to strong currents, but it's a popular place to kayak. Other attractions include playgrounds, picnic shelters, a basketball court, grass and sand volleyball courts, and a soccer field. There are also modern restroom facilities and a full-service restaurant. On the weekend there are train rides for the kids.

RECREATION

They're not necessarily worth going out of your way for, but if you're in the area and want to get to a beach, there are a couple of options. **Paseo del Carmen** (PR 119) is a small patch of beach by a shady pull-over in town. A bright blue balustrade lines a short sea walk that ends at a matching pavilion. The other option is **Playa Sardinera** (at PR 2, km 84.6, turn beside entrance to Punta Maracayo Resort). This is the site of the **Luis Muñoz Marín Vacation Center** (787/820-0274, Mon.-Fri. 8am-4:30pm, Sat.-Sun. 8am-5pm, $3), which features a protected lagoon and a well-maintained beach lined by a wooden boardwalk. Facilities include bathrooms, a pool, a playground, a basketball court, a volleyball court, and a cafeteria, as well as a campground and villa rentals. The main drawback is that there's not a lick of shade in sight.

El Gran Parque del Norte in Hatillo

ENTERTAINMENT AND EVENTS

Festival de la Máscaras

Hatillo hosts one of the island's most celebrated annual festivals. Originating in 1823 with the Spaniards who settled this part of the island, **Festival de la Máscaras** is a three-day costumed celebration held December 26-28. Originally it was meant to retell the story of King Herod's attempt to kill the infant Jesus by ordering the death of all male babies. Men would don elaborate costumes and masks and travel house-to-house on horseback. After playfully harassing the residents and demanding money, which was donated to the church or a civic organization, they would receive homemade treats and beverages. Today, festivities revolve around street parades, music, dance, food, and crafts on the main plaza. The last day is reserved for **Día de Inocentes,** a festival specifically for children.

FOOD AND ACCOMMODATIONS

Don Kike's BBQ (PR 2, km 84.5, 787/820-5754, www.facebook.com/Donkikesbbqhatillo, daily 8am-8pm, $5-12) is a super-casual cafeteria serving roast pork, chicken, rice, beans, and *tostones.* There's also a location in Camuy.

El Mampasteao (PR 2, km 85, 787/820-2264, www.facebook.com/elmamposteaorestaurante, Mon. 11am-9pm, Tues.-Thurs. and Sun. 11am-10pm, Fri.-Sat. 11am-11pm, $5-18) is famous for its namesake dish, a thick combination of rice and beans with a crispy crust. It's served alone or as an accompaniment to roasted or fried chicken, pork, and beef.

Marilyn's Bar & Restaurant (PR 2, km 84.6, 787/610-3763, www.facebook.com/marilynsbarandgrill, Sun. and Tues.-Wed. 10am-10pm, Thurs.-Sat. 10am-2am, $6-24) is a casual, oceanfront restaurant with a large deck serving ribs, wings, burgers, and mofongo. Daily lunch specials ($7) are offered Tuesday through Friday.

The prices are low and the atmosphere is pleasant at **El Truco de Güin** (141 Ave. Pablo Aguilar, 787/544-7659, www.

Playa de Guajataca with El Tunel in the background

facebook.com/El.Truco.de.Guin.Rest, daily 6am-2am, $10-18), an open-air restaurant specializing in pastrami, which comes stuffed in mofongo or a sandwich. Other offerings include quesadillas, wings, and churrasco. There is a $6 lunch special Monday through Friday.

El Rancho del Norte (PR 119, in El Gran Parque del Norte, 787/234-1460 or 787/630-3715, www.facebook.com/ElRanchoHatillo, Wed.-Sun. 11am-2am, $9-27) is a casual, open-air *chinchorro* serving Puerto Rican cuisine, including *frituras,* mofongo, and whole fried snapper, as well as wings, nachos, and burgers.

For breakfast, **El Buen Café** (PR 2, km 84, 381 Calle Carrizales, 787/898-3495, www.paradorelbuencafe.com, daily 5:30am-10pm, $4-20) is a good option. The cafeteria serves bacon and eggs, as well as sandwiches, soups, and heartier fare such as chicken and rice, mofongo, roast pork, and more. Other than breakfast and sandwiches, the food is only fair and it's a bit pricey for what it is. Across the street is **Parador El Buen Café** (PR 2, km 84, 381 Calle Carrizales, 787/898-1000, $90-120, $195 suite), offering 33 modern, clean rooms with air-conditioning, satellite TV, and mini refrigerators. There's also a tiny pool.

Punta Maracayo Resort (PR 2, km 85, 787/544-2000 or 877/887-0100, www.hotelpuntamaracayopr.com, $100, $210 suite) is a three-floor hotel in the middle of an enormous parking lot right on travel-clogged PR 2. The rooms are clean and modern with air-conditioning, mini bars, and cable TV. Amenities include a pool and a restaurant. Although the hotel isn't directly on the ocean, it is within walking distance to Playa Sardinera, and rooms on the 2nd and 3rd floors have ocean views.

TRANSPORTATION AND SERVICES

Hatillo is 90 kilometers (56 mi) west of San Juan just south of PR 2 at Calle 1.

For taxi service, call **Plaza del Norte Taxi** (787/879-3370).

Quebradillas

Notorious as a pirate's lair during the 17th century, Quebradillas is not an affluent town. It was once a leader in textile production, but manufacturers pulled out of the area in the 1990s, and tourist traffic typically bypasses the community. But in a way, that is a part of the charm of its town center, which looks much the same as it did 150 years ago, and it's one of the few places you'll see wood buildings in town.

SIGHTS

The drive westward on PR 2 at Quebradillas provides one of the most dramatic views in all of Puerto Rico as you crest a high mountain that gives way to a steep decline, revealing a panoramic view of the Atlantic Ocean. **Guajataca Mirador** (PR 2, km 103.7) is an observation tower that provides an ideal spot to pull over and take in the view. And there's a snack bar serving fritters and frozen drinks.

Puente Blanco (Calle Panorámico) is a picturesque, reinforced concrete railway bridge that spans a gorge on the coast of Quebradillas. Built in 1922, it was part of the now defunct American Railroad Company transportation system that traversed the island. The bridge was restored by the municipality of Quebradillas and listed in the National Register of Historic Places in 1984. To get here from San Juan, go west on PR 2 and look for the Quebradillas Plaza Shopping Center on the left. Just past it, turn right on PR 485. Go about 3 kilometers (2 mi) and turn left on Calle Panorámico. Go about 3 kilometers (2 mi) to the dead end, then walk about five minutes through the woods to the bridge. This is not an official tourist site. There are no facilities or safety measures, so proceed at your own risk.

The simplicity of **Iglesia San Rafael** (110 Calle San Carlos, 787/895-2035), a mission-style church built in 1828, gives it a graceful beauty that sets it apart from the island's more opulent houses of worship. The interior features an unusual stamped ceiling. It's on Plaza de Luis Muñoz Rivera. Next door is **La Casa del Rey** (Plaza de Luis Muñoz Rivera), a yellow, three-story wood structure built in 1857 to accommodate the town hall, the Guard Corps, and a jail. It is not open to the public at this time. Nearby is **Teatro Liberty** (157 Calle Rafols), a small Spanish revival theater built in 1921 and in the National Register of Historic Places.

RECREATION

Playa de Guajataca (PR 2, km 103.8) is a primitive patch of sand with no facilities, tucked down between two escarpments. The tide is too rough for swimming, but it's a popular surf spot that's great for beginners. The western escarpment bears a reminder of the sugarcane train that once connected one side of the island to the other: **El Tunel** is an abandoned train tunnel that can be seen disappearing into the mountain.

Merendero de Guajataca (PR 2, km 103.5, daily 9am-5pm) is a fantastic little nature park that also offers dramatic views of Playa de Guajateca. Paved trails cut through the thick brush to stone picnic shelters and gorgeous views of the ocean. There are also

clean, modern bathroom facilities and plenty of parking.

Located halfway between Camuy and Quebradillas, **Puerto Hermina** (PR 485 at Camino de la Cruz and El Pozo del Mago) is a tiny wedge of pretty beach between cliffs that served as a hideout for 17th-century pirates. The waters are too rough for swimming here.

FOOD

Carbón y Leña (PR 2, km 100.4, 787/229-4596, Sun.-Tues. 11am-8pm, Wed.-Thurs. 11am-9pm, Fri.-Sat. 11am-10pm, $10-17) is a casual restaurant serving Puerto Rican cuisine, including mofongo, *chuleta can can,* and whole fried snapper. There's also a location in Arecibo.

Located near the historic railway bridge, **Restaurante El Historíco Puente Blanco** (PR 4484, km 1.9, Calle Estacíon, 787/895-1934, Sun.-Thurs. 11am-8pm, Fri.-Sat. 11am-10pm, $9-18) is a sprawling, casual eatery serving traditional Puerto Rican cuisine.

La Casona (105 Calle Ramon Savedra, Plaza de Luis Muñoz Rivera, 787/895-2717, Mon.-Fri. 6:30am-3pm, Sat.-Sun. 6:30am-10pm, $5-15) is a modest, homey place serving eggs, sandwiches, and *cocina criolla,* including *carne guisada* and arroz con pollo, from a steam table. It has a full bar.

TRANSPORTATION

Quebradillas is 105 kilometers (65 mi) west of San Juan. It straddles PR 2 just west of PR 481/PR 484.

Cordillera Central

It's hard for some visitors to wrap their heads

around the idea of spending their time in Puerto Rico not in the water but in the mountains. That's what makes the Cordillera Central, Puerto Rico's central mountain region, one of the island's greatest hidden gems.

Thousands of acres of undeveloped land thick with tropical jungle, high mountain peaks, waterfalls, rivers, caves, and canyons comprise the interior of the island, but the natural beauty isn't the only reason to visit. This is the place adventure junkies come to go hiking, rappelling, spelunking, and ziplining, and it's where history buffs go to explore the island's Taíno Indian roots.

Accommodations tend to be more rustic here than in San Juan, and

Highlights

Look for ★ to find recommended sights, activities, dining, and lodging.

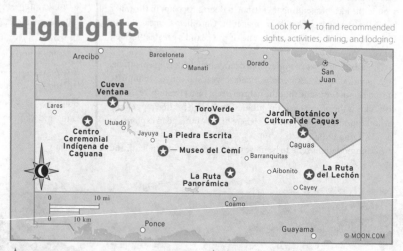

© MOON.COM

★ **Drive La Ruta Panorámica:** The well-marked scenic route runs through the Cordillera Central from east to west, offering **stunning views** of mountains and coast. In some spots, you can see the Atlantic and the Caribbean at the same time (page 256).

★ **Jardín Botánico y Cultural de Caguas:** Tour the ruins of Hacienda San José, a former sugar plantation and rum distillery with recreated slave quarters (page 257).

★ **Cruise along La Ruta del Lechón:** This scenic drive through the mountains features spectacular views. Plan a tasting tour of the *lechoneras* along the way, which serve roast pork and other traditional delicacies (page 258).

★ **ToroVerde:** This world-class adventure park features **ziplining, rappelling,** and more (page 263).

★ **Museo del Cemí:** Shaped like a Taíno amulet, this unique museum in Jayuya contains artifacts of Puerto Rico's indigenous culture (page 269).

★ **La Piedra Escrita:** This boulder covered with Taíno **petroglyphs** is in a river by a large natural pool ideal for swimming (page 269).

★ **Centro Ceremonial Indígena de Caguana:** Tour this significant Taíno **archaeological site,** which dates to AD 1100. Many artifacts, petroglyphs, and ceremonial ball fields have been excavated here (page 271).

★ **Cueva Ventana:** Take a 30-minute hike that ends in a limestone cave and enjoy stunning views of the northern karst country from the other side (page 271).

the service may not be up to some travelers' standards. But there are some unusual and unique places to stay, like a coffee plantation dating back to 1858 in Jayuya and a 107-acre nature retreat among the peaks of Utuado. And the restaurants may not be on the cutting edge of the latest culinary trends, but you can dine on some of the best pit-cooked pork you'll ever taste at restaurants called *lechoneras,* which specialize in the delicacy.

The Cordillera Central was hit especially hard during Hurricane Maria in 2017. A lot of the old-growth trees that towered over this region were toppled, making many roads unnavigable for months. All major roads have since reopened.

Some of the communities here were the last on the island to have their electricity restored, a year after the storm. Nevertheless, the people in this region are resilient and accustomed to getting by with few resources.

Those feeling the storm's long-lasting effects most are the region's coffee growers, whose crops were destroyed. The industry has been set back three or four years—that's how long it takes for new coffee trees to produce berries.

PLANNING YOUR TIME

One of the great things about the Cordillera Central is that it's possible to get a taste of its charms on a day trip from just about anywhere on the island.

On the east side of the island, **PR 52** travels south from San Juan through Cayey to Salinas on the south coast. On the west side of the island, **PR 10** runs south from Arecibo through the mountain towns of Utuado and Adjuntas, ending in Ponce on the south coast.

Ambitious travelers who want to journey the whole length of the Cordillera Central can drive **La Ruta Panorámica,** a designated route following a series of well-marked secondary roads that travel along the highest peaks, offering stunning views of mountains and sea. Due to the sometimes narrow, twisty roads and scenic points along the way, it can take the better part of the day to drive the 270-kilometer (165-mi) route one way.

The greatest number of dining options can be found on the eastern side of the mountain region along the **Pork Highway,** in Barrio Guavate, in the municipality of **Cayey,** where there is a high concentration of *lechoneras* roasting whole pigs over open fires. A number of *chinchorros*—casual, open-air restaurants serving cheap food and beer—proliferate in the side-by-side towns of **Morovis** and **Orocovis,** which are also rich in outdoor adventure activities, including **ziplining** and **canopy tours.** Near the center of the region is **San Cristóbal Cañon,** a verdant canyon between Aibonito and Barranquitas, another popular spot for thrill-seekers who are into challenging **hikes** and **rappelling.**

Jayuya is home to the island's highest peaks, but it's best known as a center of Taíno culture, evident at **La Piedra Escrita,** a natural pool in Río Saliente featuring large boulders covered in Taíno petroglyphs, and **Museo del Cemí,** a unique museum shaped like a Taíno amulet containing Indian artifacts found in the area. Nearby in **Utuado** is **Centro Ceremonial Indígena de Caguana,** a major Taíno archaeological site dating to AD 1100, and **Cueva Ventana,** a cave with a large opening in the back offering a spectacular view of the valley below.

Recommended accommodations are few in the Cordillera Central, but there are two worth seeking out, one a former **coffee plantation** in Jayuya and the other an off-the-grid **yoga retreat** in Utuado.

It **rains** often in the mountains and can be cool at night, so pack accordingly. And keep an eye on the weather. Heavy rains occasionally result in **mudslides** and **flooding,** which could close some roads. As you're driving, watch out for livestock. It's not unusual to see a cow or horse tied up to a house right beside the road, and chickens are forever crossing the asphalt.

Previous: jungle in central Puerto Rico; Cueva Ventana in Utuado; Salto de Doña Juana, south of Jayuya.

Cordillera Central

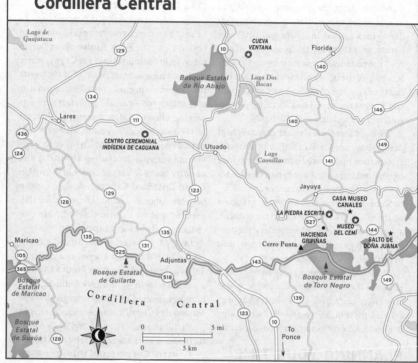

★ La Ruta Panorámica

You couldn't ask for a better way to explore Cordillera Central than to drive this 270-kilometer (165-mi) route from Mayagüez on the west coast to Yabucoa on the southeast coast. The route takes visitors to breathtaking heights on the island's highest peaks, revealing panoramic views of both the Atlantic and the Caribbean, as well as the dramatic mountains and valleys that make up the island's spine. Parts of the route are so remote you may not see another car for miles.

The well-maintained, well-marked, two-lane route traverses a network of secondary roads beginning on PR 105 in Mayagüez and ending on PR 182 in Yabucoa. It's clearly marked on most maps, including the ubiquitous tourist map (www.travelmaps.com) available at businesses throughout the island.

From end to end, the journey takes about six hours, not including stops, so plan to spend two days to see all the landscape has to offer.

Highlights along the way include **Reserva Forestal de Carite** in Cayey, **Mirador Piedra Degetau** in Aibonito, **Mirador Orocovis-Villalba, Bosque Estatal de Toro Negro** in Jayuya, and **Bosque Estatal de Maricao.**

Most towns have at least one gas station. Cayey, Orocovis, Morovis, Jayuya, Utuado, and Adjuntas are the best bets for dining. Accommodations are hard to come by; Jayuya and Utuado have the best options.

If you only want to explore part of the route, drive the PR 143 leg between Adjuntas and Barranquitas, which traverses the island's highest mountains. The 68-kilometer (42-mi) route takes about 1.5 hours to drive.

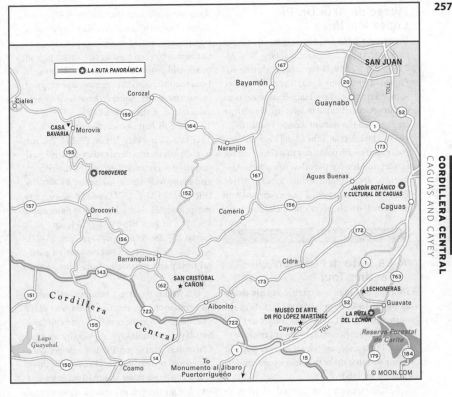

Caguas and Cayey

The eastern mountain towns of Caguas and Cayey have plenty to offer in the way of attractions. Caguas has a thriving town center with lots of interesting restaurants and a lively nightlife scene. It is also home to the impressive botanical gardens at Jardín Botánico y Cultural de Caguas. Cayey is graced with a dozen or so *lechoneras,* casual eateries that specialize in open-pit roasted pork. Many locals make a day of visiting the area to dine at all-you-can-eat buffets, dance to the live bands, and shop at roadside vendors, who sell everything from local crafts to homemade cheeses and sweets to gallons of *mavi,* a traditional Taíno beverage made from fermented tree bark of the *mavi* tree.

SIGHTS
★ Jardín Botánico y Cultural de Caguas

Jardín Botánico y Cultural de Caguas (PR 156, km 56.5, Caguas, 787/653-0470, www.jardinbotanicoycultural.org, Wed.-Sun. 10am-4pm, $5 adults, $3 ages 7 and younger and 60 and older) is a gorgeous oasis of natural beauty that was once the site of Hacienda San Jose, a sugar plantation and rum distillery established in 1825. Ruins of the home still remain on the grounds, as do remnants of the rum distillery and sugar mill, including an iron sugarcane press and brick smokestacks. The well-maintained grounds also house a re-created *jíbaro* farmhouse and Taíno *batey* (ceremonial ball field).

Museo de Arte Dr. Pío López Martínez

Museo de Arte Dr. Pío López Martínez (205 Ave. Antonio R. Barceló, Cayey, 787/738-2161, ext. 2209, https://cayey.upr.edu/museo-dr-pio-lopez-martinez, Mon.-Fri. 8am-4:30pm, holidays 11am-5pm, free) is an art museum dedicated to local artists with an emphasis on the work of Ramon Frade (1875-1954), who celebrated the island's agricultural community with paintings that dignified the farmer and his contribution to society. Also featured are changing exhibitions of *cartels*, Puerto Rico's renowned poster art used to publicize festivals, plays, and social concerns.

TOP EXPERIENCE

★ La Ruta del Lechón Tasting Tour

South of San Juan is a terrific **scenic drive** along **PR 184** through Barrio Guavate in the municipality of Cayey. Not only does this route provide spectacular views of the mountains, but it also passes by the many popular *lechoneras* that make this area a popular destination for foodies.

Specializing in pork cooked whole hog-style over a wood fire, *lechoneras* are casual, open-air restaurants that also serve other authentic Puerto Rican dishes such as *guineitos en escabeche,* a salad made from pickled green bananas, *arroz con gandules* (rice with pigeon peas), and *pasteles,* a tamale-like dish made from mashed plantain or cassava and wrapped in banana leaves. Some *lechoneras* have live salsa music on the weekends.

From San Juan, proceed south on PR 52. Take exit 32 and turn left on PR 184. For the next 15 kilometers (9 mi) you will drive past stunning panoramic views of the mountains and many *lechoneras,* including **El Mojito** (PR 184, km 32.9, 787/738-8888, www.guavatepr.com/ElMojito.htm, daily 8am-8pm, $5-22) and **Los Pinos** (PR 184, km 27.7, Cayey, 787/286-1917, daily 7am-7pm, $5-22). A good end point is **Charco Azul,** a natural freshwater swimming hole with a small waterfall.

On weekends, street vendors sell crafts, homemade cheese, candied fruits, and *mavi* champagne along the roadside. On Saturdays, Sundays, and holidays, especially around Christmas, traffic on PR 184 can get congested and restaurants are crowded. Without stops, the drive takes about 30 minutes one way, but for the best experience, devote a full day to the drive.

Jardín Botánico y Cultural de Caguas

Charco Azul

The **Reserva Forestal de Carite** (PR 184, km 17.8, Cayey, 787/747-4510 or 787/747-4545, Tues.-Sun. 6am-6pm, free) is classified primarily as a subtropical humid forest rich in vegetation, including Honduran mahogany, hibiscuses, eucalyptus, giant ferns, and several varieties of palm. Its main attraction is the striking, deep-blue **Charco Azul,** a natural freshwater swimming hole fed by an eight-foot waterfall.

There are also a few picnic tables, grills, bathrooms, and campsites for tents. To secure a camping permit, call 787/999-2200, extension 5157, at least 15 days before arrival. Access to Charco Azul requires a half-mile hike on a level, paved path.

Monumento al Jíbaro Puertorriqueño

Technically located in the municipality of Salinas, **Monumento al Jíbaro Puertorriqueño** (PR 52, km 49.0, accessible only from the southbound lane) is located just south of Cayey and honors the Puerto Rican farmer. It's easy to spot from the highway as you drive along PR 52. If you want a closer look, there is an exit just past the statue, which ends at a parking lot. From there you can take the quarter-mile hike to the base of the large white statue depicting a hard-working man of the land, his solemn wife, and their infant child, created by sculptor Tomás Batista of Luquillo.

ENTERTAINMENT

The casino at **Four Points by Sheraton Caguas Real Hotel & Casino** (500 Alhambra en Granada Blvd., Caguas, 787/653-1111, www.fourpointscaguas.com) has 570 video slot machines, a craps table, two roulette tables, one mini baccarat table, and six blackjack tables.

Located near Caguas's central plaza, **La Azateo** (11-17 Calle Padial, Caguas, 939/414-9383, www.facebook.com/laazoteakitchenandbar, Tues.-Sun. 5pm-2am, $2-15) is the place to go for late-night fun. Salsa bands, DJs, and drink specials keep things lively. The menu features bar fare including tacos, ceviche, and sandwiches.

FOOD

Cayey is famous for its many *lechoneras,* which are located in Barrio Guavate. From PR 52, exit onto PR 184, where you'll find many restaurants serving pit-cooked pork as well as roast chicken stuffed with plantains, *pasteles* (mashed plantain or cassava stuffed with meat and steamed in banana leaves), and more. Drive around and check them out until you find one to your liking. The ones that are most crowded are a good bet. Be sure to go there hungry and bring a cooler to carry your leftovers home.

Lechonera El Mojito (PR 184, km 32.9, 787/738-8888, www.guavatepr.com/ElMojito.htm, daily 8am-8pm, $5-22) is the first *lechonera* you encounter after exiting onto PR 184 from PR 52, and you can't miss it thanks to its bright purple exterior. This casual, family-friendly concrete-block restaurant is a gastronomic emporium of fresh roast pork and all the fixings. Take a peek at the whole pigs cooking on a spit over an open fire before taking your place in line to peruse the long steam tables piled high with sliced pork, ribs, pork skins, whole roast chickens, rice and beans, sausages, *tostones, maduras,* yuca, and more. Point out the dishes you want to sample and take a seat at the common tables and wait for a server to deliver your feast. There's a full bar, too.

★ **Lechonera Los Pinos** (PR 184, km 27.7, Cayey, 787/286-1917, daily 7am-7pm, $5-22) is famous for its woodfire-roasted whole pig, which you can see cooking at the front of the restaurant. The succulent meat is served in big juicy hunks topped with a crisp of skin. Choose your sides cafeteria style, including rice and beans, sweet plantains, *pasteles,* and more. There's a separate bar serving beer and *cuba libres,* and live music on weekends.

★ **Marcelo Restaurant** (PR 1 at Ave. Mercado, Caguas, 787/743-8801, http://marcelorestaurant.com, daily 10am-10pm, $12-29) has been serving outstanding *criolla* fare and more since 1969. The low-slung building decorated in shades of beige looks like it hasn't been redecorated since the day it opened, but that's part of its charm. The reason to go is the house specialty—smoked chicken, an unusual offering that is delectably moist and packed with so much flavor, you'll want to lick your plate. Other dishes include baked chicken stuffed with shrimp, shrimp stuffed with cheese, lamb chops, fettuccine, mofongo, and paella. The service is professional in an old-school way, and there's a full bar, of course. Check out the dessert case at the entrance, filled with cakes and flans.

Located off PR 52 at exit 21, **Restaurante Raíces** (H-31 Ave. Pino, across the street from Plaza del Carmen Mall, Villa Turabo, Caguas, 787/258-1570 or 787/705-9333, www.restauranteraices.com, Mon.-Wed. 11am-8pm, Thurs.-Sat. 11am-10pm, Sun. noon-8pm, $12-39) serves excellent *criolla* cuisine, specializing in mofongo, churrasco, and *chuleta can can.*

Enjoy a fine dining experience in a casual setting at ★ **Orujo** (80 Ave. Gautier Benitez, Caguas, 787/508-0038, www.facebook.com/orujotaller, Tues.-Sun. 5pm-11pm, $18-45). The gastropub serves creative interpretations of Caribbean cuisine ranging from tapas like grilled octopus and foie gras to entrées like macadamia-crusted salmon with black rice and dry-aged rib eye with asparagus tempura.

ACCOMMODATIONS

Billing itself as a culinary farm lodge, ★ **El Pretexto** (PR 715, Cayey, no phone, www.elpretextopr.com, $125-175) is a serene, secluded bed and breakfast that offers three spacious, tastefully designed villas on a picturesque mountaintop surrounded by spectacular views of the island's interior. All villas have kitchens or kitchenettes, and balconies or terraces. One villa has a living room and dining room. Breakfast is included, and guests have the option to dine on a four- or five-course dinner for $50 per person with advance reservations. Non-guests are welcome at occasional pop-up dinners, which are prepared by a notable chef.

Four Points by Sheraton Caguas Real Hotel & Casino (500 Alhambra en Granada Blvd., Caguas, 787/653-1111, www.marriott.com, $179, $215 suite) is a business hotel with seven meeting rooms, an outdoor pool, fitness center, casino, and restaurant. Rooms

Lechonera Los Pinos on La Ruta del Lechón

come with complimentary high-speed wireless Internet and flat-screen TVs.

TRANSPORTATION AND SERVICES

Caguas is 30 kilometers (19 mi) south of San Juan on PR 52. Cayey is 55 kilometers (34 mi) south of San Juan on PR 52.

Cayey has two taxi services, **Cayey Metro Taxi** (787/738-8001) and **Cayey Taxi** (787/738-4343). **Charlie Car Rental** (PR 183, km 2.4, Caguas, 787/743-2336, www.charliecars.com) is a budget car rental agency with additional locations in San Juan, Ponce, and Aguadilla.

The hospital in Cayey is **Hospital Menonita de Cayey** (PR 14, km 0.3, Cayey, 787/535-1001, http://sistemamenonita. com). For your banking needs, go to **Banco Popular** (Centro Comercial Sierra de Cayey, Ave. Antonio R. Barceló, PR 14, km 70.6, 787/738-2828). For pharmacy needs, visit **Walgreens** (Cayey Shopping Center, 5800 Ave. Jesus T. Pinero, 787/263-5166).

Aibonito and Barranquitas

Of these two mountain towns, Barranquitas offers the more charming plaza and city center. The plaza features a beautiful wrought-iron gazebo in the middle, and the streets around it are lined with bustling shops and museums. Both municipalities have much to offer visitors in search of spectacular natural beauty, history, and annual festivals.

SIGHTS

Museo Luis Muñoz Rivera (10 Calle Muñoz Rivera, Barranquitas, 787/857-0230, Wed.-Sun. 8:30am-4:20pm, $1) is dedicated to one of Puerto Rico's most celebrated native sons, Luis Muñoz Rivera, a poet, journalist, politician, and defender of the island's independence both under Spanish and American rule. Inside this traditional Puerto Rican-style home built in 1857 are many artifacts of Rivera's life, including newspaper clippings, his impressive two-sided walnut desk from 1893, his death mask, and the 1912 Pierce-Arrow that transported his body from his funeral services to his burial site in **Mausoleo Luis Muñoz Rivera** (Calle Padre Berrios, Tues.-Sat. 8am-4:30pm).

Casa Museo Joaquín de Rojas (Calle Barceló, Barranquitas, 787/857-6293, Mon.-Fri. 8am-4:30pm, free) is a museum with a mishmash of interesting items that include vintage farm tools, *mundillo* lace, and newspaper clippings about the town's history. Most interesting is a large photograph of Barranquitas taken in 1950. Contemporary artists maintain studios here.

Mirador Piedra Degetau (PR 7718, km 0.8, Aibonito, Wed.-Sun. 9am-6pm) is a new, pristinely landscaped park thick with blooming bougainvillea in a riot of colors. There are picnic shelters, bathrooms, a playground, and snack machines, but the focal point of the roadside attraction is the observation tower, which offers an amazing view of the mountains and even the sea when visibility is clear.

RECREATION
San Cristobal Cañon

San Cristóbal Cañon (PR 162/PR 725, between Aibonito and Barranquitas) is reportedly the biggest canyon in the Caribbean at 4.5 miles long and 500-800 feet deep. It's hard to believe this beautiful deep hole in the earth, now filled with verdant green vegetation, was once a garbage dump. Today it's a popular site for adventure seekers who want to get away from it all and witness the canyon's natural beauty, including a spectacular river, waterfalls, and shoals. It is not advisable to enter the canyon without a trained guide.

Montaña Explora (PR 191, km. 27.9, Camino Viejo, Charco El Hippie, 787/516-6194, www.facebook.com/mexplorapr)

provides guided extreme adventure tours of San Cristóbal Cañon. A challenging six-hour hiking and rappelling tour is $175 and is only for the physically fit and truly adventurous, although no previous rappelling experience is required. Gear is provided. Other tours include hiking and swimming in a freshwater pond on the less-touristy southern side of El Yunque.

ENTERTAINMENT AND EVENTS

Aibonito is known as the City of Flowers because every year it bursts into a riot of color and floral scents for the **Festival de las Flores** (PR 722, km 6.7, 787/735-4070, $6-7 adults, $2 children), held from the last weekend of June through the first weekend of July. On 25 acres of land, the festival grounds are filled with horticulture and landscaping exhibitions and more than 50 vendors selling flowers and plants, as well as pottery and garden accessories. There's also live music, and vendors sell food and crafts.

Feria Nacional de Artesanías (23 Calle Muñoz Rivera, Barranquitas, 787/857-6293), held in mid-July, features more than 200 artisans from all over the island who flock here to sell local arts and crafts, including wood carvings, musical instruments, ceramics, hammocks, and more.

TRANSPORTATION AND SERVICES

Aibonito is 75 kilometers (47 mi) south of San Juan. Take PR 52 south to PR 14 west. Barranquitas is 55 kilometers (34 mi) south of San Juan. Take PR 2 south to PR 167 south to PR 147 south to PR 152 south.

Taxi service is provided by **Aibonito Taxi** (787/735-7144).

Banking services are available at **Banco Popular** branches in Aibonito (PR 14, km 51, 787/857-0520) and Barranquitas (San Cristobal Shopping Center, PR 156, 787/857-4380). Health care is provided by **Mennonite General Hospital Aibonito** (Calle José at Calle Vazquez, Aibonito, 787/735-8001).

Orocovis, Morovis, and Ciales

Orocovis and Morovis are small mountain towns 16 kilometers (10 mi) apart that offer a great immersion into the beauty and adventure of Cordillera Central. Orocovis features the popular extreme adventure park ToroVerde and several excellent restaurants. Ciales is a charming mountain town where dramatic outcroppings of exposed limestone called *mogotes* tower overhead and the rivers Toro Negro, Yunes, Grande de Manatí, and Cialitos converge both above and below ground, creating an intricate cave system.

SIGHTS

Mirador Orocovis-Villalba (PR 143 between Orocovis and Villalba, Wed.-Sun. 9am-5pm) is a park and overlook 2,000 feet above sea level. From here you can see

both the island's north and south coasts. Amenities include a children's playground and picnic tables.

The biggest draw to Ciales is its underground rivers, rock walls, and caves, including **Yuyu, La Virgen, Las Archillas,** and **Las Golondrina,** where you can find sea fossils, stalactites, and columns. **21 Climb & Tour** (Calle 6A, Vega Baja, 939/218-7887, http://21climbandtour.com) offers guided tours.

In addition to its spectacular caves, Ciales has several modest sights worth seeking out if you're in the area. **Museo del Café** (42 Calle Palmer at Paseo del Aroma, Ciales, 787/313-0925, www.facebook.com/museodelcafepr, Tues.-Fri. 8am-3pm, Sat.-Sun. 9am-5pm, free) is a hands-on facility, demonstrating how coffee is grown, harvested, and prepared in a variety of tasty coffee drinks, which visitors can purchase along with an assortment of fresh-made pastries.

★ ToroVerde

ToroVerde (PR 155, km 32.9, Orocovis, 787/944-1196, 787/944-1195, or 787/867-6606, www.toroverdepr.com, Thurs.-Sun. 8am-5pm, $65-200, reservations required) has become one of the most popular tourist attractions in Puerto Rico. This adventure lover's dream come true features a variety of extreme activities including ziplines, suspension bridges, and free falls.

Claiming to be the longest zipline in the Americas, the **Monster** ($73 pp) is 1.5 miles long. The tour takes 60-80 minutes. Participants must be at least 7 years old, 4 feet tall, and 100 pounds. The upper weight limit is 270 pounds.

Escape If You Can ($50 pp) is a 3- to 4-hour tour featuring four suspension bridges, two ziplines, and a 131-foot free fall. Participants must be at least 12 years old and 5 feet tall. The upper weight limit is 250 pounds.

A **day pass** ($99 pp) gets you access to all the park's attractions. Closed-toe shoes and advance reservations are required. You must be at the park at least 45 minutes before your reservation time.

RECREATION

21 Climb & Tour (Calle 6A, Vega Baja, 939/218-7887, http://21climbandtour.com) leads a variety of hiking, rock climbing, and camping tours around Puerto Rico, including a **rock-climbing tour** ($95 adults, $50 children 9 and under, 3-person minimum) of Ciales that can be adapted for everyone from beginners to experienced climbers. This tour starts at 10am and lasts five hours. They also offer tours of the Ciales caves, San Cristóbal Cañon, El Yunque National Forest, and more.

Certified guides at **Aventuras Tierra Adentro** (268-A Ave. Jesus T. Piñero, San Juan, 787/766-0470, www.aventuraspr.com, Fri.-Sat. 6am-5pm) lead **Río Camuy cave tours** ($175 pp) that include rappelling and swimming across an underground lake. Tours are offered every weekend and last 11 hours. Participants must be 18 or older, in excellent physical condition, and a strong swimmer.

ENTERTAINMENT AND EVENTS

Festival de Cuatristas y Trovadores (Plaza de Recreo, Morovis, 787/862-2155)

El Descuadre, a *chinchorro* in Orocovis

is a celebration of traditional Puerto Rican music and art held in August. Local artisans who make *cuatros,* stringed guitar-like instruments, demonstrate their craft. *Cuatro* musicians and troubadours perform as well.

Festival de Pastel (Orocovis, 787/867-5000, ext. 2295) is a culinary festival held in late November for three days, from noon to midnight, in honor of the *pastel,* a Taíno dish traditionally eaten during the Christmas holidays. Similar to a tamale, it's made of mashed, seasoned plantain filled with fried pork that's wrapped in a banana leaf and steamed. Festivities include live music and artisan vendors.

FOOD

★ **Casa Bavaria** (PR 15, km 38.3, Morovis, 787/862-7818, www.casabavaria.com, Thurs. 10am-8:30pm, Fri.-Sat. 10am-10:30pm, bar until 2am, Sun. 10am-8:30pm, bar until 10pm, $9-17) marks the unlikely intersection of Puerto Rican and German culture. In a two-story, open-air structure plastered with beer signs and banners, Casa Bavaria serves outstanding Puerto Rican and German cuisine. Alongside the usual mofongo, shrimp, lobster, and chicken, you can dine on heaping platters of bratwurst, wiener schnitzel, and sauerkraut. Cocktails are a mere $3.50, and there's an extensive wine list with offerings from Italy, Spain, Chile, and Germany. Dine in the crowded, pleasantly raucous bar, or go around back and take a seat in the quiet dining room overlooking a gorgeous mountain view. There's live music on Saturdays. Oktoberfest is celebrated the first and second weekends of October with live bands all weekend long. Be forewarned: There's an infectious party atmosphere here that will have you drinking shots of Jägermeister before you know it!

Located in a valley, **La Playita** (PR 155, km 42.6, Morovis, 787/485-1837 or 939/276-1586, Tues.-Thurs. 10am-7pm, Fri. 10am-10pm, Sat.-Sun. 9am-10pm, $9-19) is lively *chinchorro* serving fried chicken, shrimp,

and churrasco on platters with *tostones* and choice of potatoes or mofongo. Get *arroz con longaniza* (rice with chicken or pork sausage) with beans for $5 on Saturday and Sunday. There's karaoke on Sundays.

Pal Campo (PR 155, km 39.1, Morovis, 787/975-2337, Thurs.-Sat. noon-11pm, Sun. 11am-11pm, $10-15) is a *chinchorro* that opened in 2018. It serves *longaniza* (sausage) made from chicken, as well as grilled chicken, garlic shrimp, and wings.

Hipper than your average *chinchorro* and popular with motorcycle enthusiasts, **El Descuadre** (PR 155, km 35.6, Orocovis, 787/323-3887, www.facebook.com/jimnezcolon, Thurs.-Sun. noon-1am, $7-14) is run by a young couple who have created a Wild West vibe complete with saloon doors and saddle stools. The menu features smoked pork, octopus salad, and chicken *longaniza* (sausage).

★ **Roka Dura Wine and Grill** (PR 155, km 32.2, Orocovis, 787/867-4680, Wed.-Thurs. 10am-10pm, Fri.-Sat. 10am-midnight, Sun. 10am-8pm, $13-26) is an upscale but still casual *chinchorro* offering fantastic mountain views, an extensive wine list, and a long list of traditional Puerto Rican and Cuban dishes, including fried whole snapper, *ropa vieja,* stuffed mofongo, chicken wings, grilled steaks, and churrasco. Its specialty is chicken or pork *longaniza* (sausage), served as an appetizer or entrée. There's also an extensive dessert list. On holiday Mondays, Roka Dura is open 10am-8pm.

Morovis is known for its *pan de la patita echá,* a delicious, braided bread. It's served at any number of the many *panaderías* (bakeries) found here, but the best-known place is **Panadería La Patria y Repostería** (20 Calle Ruiz Belvis and PR 155, Morovis, 787/862-2867, daily 8am-6pm). Believed to be one of the oldest bakeries in Puerto Rico, it was established in 1862. Another option is **Panadería y Repostería Barahona** (PR

1: Pal Campo *chinchorro* in Morovis **2:** Casa Bavaria in Morovis

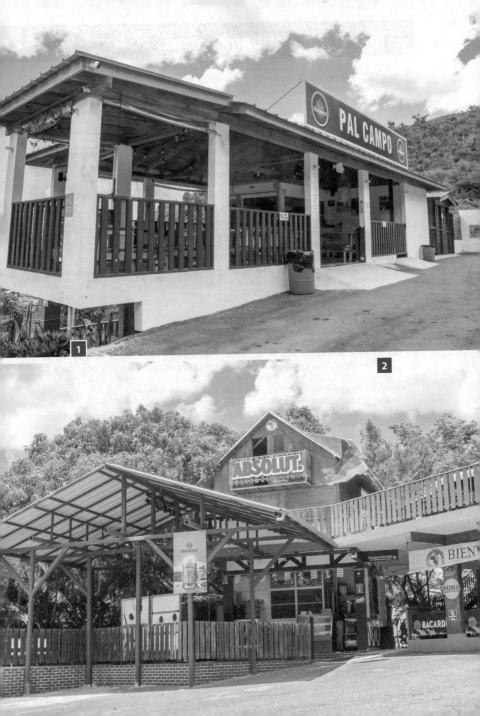

Take a Tour of *Chinchorros*

Chinchorros are casual, open-air roadside restaurants that serve simple, traditional Puerto Rican food, as well as ice-cold beer and a full array of cocktails, all on the cheap. The layout is often large and rambling, and they may look a little shabby. Often their only decor is big flashy banners advertising Medalla beer or Bacardi rum. There may be a pool table, televised sports, or live music on the weekends. But the primary reason to visit a *chinchorro* is to eat and drink among friends without spending much money.

When it comes to the bounty of creative dining options in Puerto Rico, the *chinchorro* is often overlooked. But it recently has enjoyed a renewed sense of appreciation, particularly among locals who long for food the way their *abuelas* made it. *Chinchorro* tours have become a popular way to socialize on weekends or holidays. Groups of friends and family convene in the morning and spend the day driving along a predetermined route, stopping at the *chinchorros* along the way to sample the food and beverages at each. There are even tour companies like **Chinchorreo Bus** (787/998-5466, www.chinchorreobuspr.com) that provide transportation for large groups.

Roka Dura in Orocovis

Chinchorros can be found anywhere on the island, from the beach to the mountains. PR 155 through Orocovis and Morovis is a *chinchorro* route that guarantees spectacular mountain views and an array of cheap, filling local cuisine including *longaniza,* a delicious sausage made from pork or chicken that is a specialty of the area.

Start your tour at **La Playita** (PR 155, km 42.6, Morovis), where you can get a plate of *arroz con longaniza* with beans for just $5 on the weekends. Entertainment includes a pool table and karaoke on Sundays. Proceed to **Pal Campo** (PR 155, km 39.1, Morovis), a *chinchorro* that opened in 2018, and dine on chicken wings and garlic shrimp. Next up is **Casa Bavaria** (PR 15, km 38.3, Morovis) where, in addition to traditional Puerto Rican dishes, you can dine on German fare such as wiener schnitzel, spaetzle, and bratwurst. Next up is **El Decuardre** (PR 155, km 35.1, Orocovis). Tricked out like a biker bar with a Wild West saloon vibe, it serves smoked pork and octopus salad. End your journey at **Roka Dura** (PR 155, km 32.2, Orocovis). It's more upscale than the typical *chinchorro* and a little pricier, but it has beautiful views and outstanding food. It's famous for its *longaniza* and also serves whole friend snapper and *chuleta can can.*

Cell phone and GPS service can be spotty in the mountains, so plot your route before you go. If you plan to go with a large group, call each restaurant at least one day in advance to give the owners and staff fair warning. And be sure to have a designated driver who can safely navigate the curvy roads.

155, km 4.1, Morovis, 787/862-2538, daily 8am-10pm).

TRANSPORTATION AND SERVICES

Morovis is 60 kilometers (37 mi) southwest of San Juan. Take PR 22 west to PR 137 south. Ciales is 74 kilometers (46 mi) southwest of San Juan. Take PR 22 west of PR 149 south. Orocovis is 87 kilometers (54 mi) southwest of San Juan. Take PR 22 west to PR 137 south.

Banking services are available at **Banco Popular** (6623 PR 155 Int., 787/862-2160) in Morovis. For pharmacy needs, visit **Walgreens** (200 PR 137, 787/862-0104) in Morovis.

Jayuya

Visit the Jayuya municipality to experience gorgeous mountain scenery and some of the highest peaks on the island, where it's possible to see both the Atlantic Ocean and the Caribbean Sea, as well as vegetation thick with sierra palms, bamboo, banana trees, and brilliantly colorful impatiens. This is also the place to get a glimpse of vestiges of Taíno culture in the environment where the culture once had deep roots. The central town of Jayuya offers little of interest to visitors.

SIGHTS

Cacique Jayuya Monument

The **Cacique Jayuya Monument** (58 Calle Torrado, Jayuya) honors the great cacique who once ruled the Taíno people that lived in the area now named in his memory. In addition to a sculpture of Cacique Jayuya by Tomás Batiste, here you'll see La Tumba del Indio, a tomb containing the remains of a Taíno Indian along with soil from all 78 of the island's municipalities.

Bosque Estatal de Toro Negro

If you want to see thick, virtually uninhabited tropical jungle as far as the eye can see and travel so high up in the mountains that you can see both coasts, **Bosque Estatal de Toro Negro** (along Ruta Panorámica on PR 143, south of Jayuya) is the place to go. From these heights you can see clouds drift between the peaks below, and you're surrounded by tangles of wild bamboo, banana trees, hibiscus, enormous ferns, impatiens, elephant ears, *flamboyan* trees, and miles of sierra palms, distinguished by their long straight trunks and pale green foliage towering 30-50 feet high. The roads are steep and twisty, putting a strain on small engines and inducing dizziness or—worse—motion sickness. But it's one of the most exotic sights you'll see on the island and well worth the effort.

The highest peaks in Puerto Rico can be found in Toro Negro, the tallest being Cerro Punta (4,390 feet). Driving through these mountains along La Ruta Panorámica, you can often catch a glimpse of the ocean off the southern coast. If visibility is clear, you can see the north coast, too.

Around kilometer 21 on PR 143, there is a small, rustic park on Cerro Maravillas where you can park and take in a stunning panoramic view of Ponce and the Caribbean Ocean. Unfortunately, the picnic shelters and other structures are poorly maintained and marred with anti-American and anti-Semitic graffiti. It's hard to say if it's the work of rebellious teens or something more sinister. This was the site of a notorious incident in 1978 when police officers killed two *independistas* suspected of planning to sabotage a television transmission tower on the mountain's summit.

In Toro Negro you can also see one of the island's highest waterfalls, **Salto de Doña Juana** (PR 149, km 41.5). It can be viewed from the road (it's on the left if you're traveling south) if you look way up high. Although it's not particularly wide, the water propels off the mountaintop with great force, making it a spectacular sight.

The highest peaks of Toro Negro Forest contain dwarf or cloud forest, where the foliage has been stunted from the constant moisture in the atmosphere. The southern part of the forest features many rugged rock cliffs, jagged peaks, and waterfalls. Much of the forest has been subjected to clearing by the logging industry, but long-term reforestation efforts have helped repair some of the damage.

There are 10 trails in the forest, most of which originate from the **Doña Juana Recreation Center** (PR 143, km 32.4, 787/724-3724, daily 7:30am-4pm). One trail is a 10-minute walk to a natural freshwater **pool** (Apr.-Sept. Sat.-Sun. and Mon. holidays 9am-5pm $1 adults, children under 10 free).

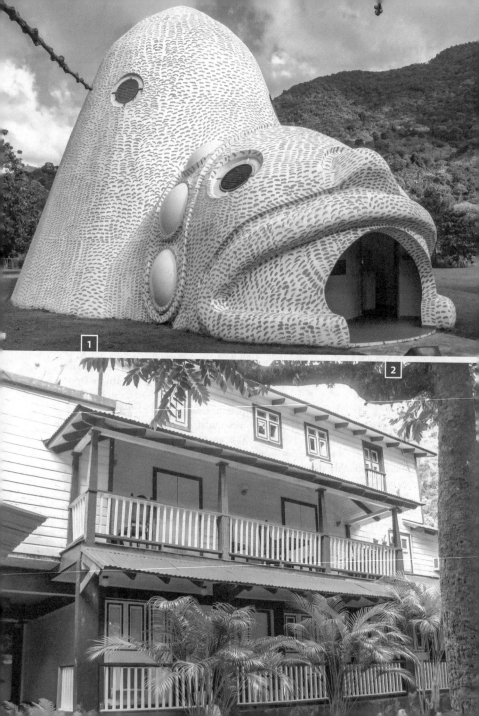

Another hike is a 3-kilometer (2-mi) trek to **Torre Observación** lookout tower. A camping area with toilets and showers (but no electricity) is a 550-yard hike away.

★ Museo del Cemí

Museo del Cemí (PR 144, km 9.3, 787/828-1241 or 787/828-4618, daily 10am-12:30pm and 1pm-3:30pm, $2 adults, $1 children age 5-15) makes quite a statement for itself as you drive along PR 144. Museo del Cemí is shaped like a huge *cemí*—a triangular artifact with animal characteristics made by the Taíno Indians. Its significance is unknown, but it's believed to have represented a deity and to have contained many powers.

Downstairs is a small collection of Taíno artifacts: necklaces of stone and shells, ritual vomit spatulas, ceremonial maracas, a *dogolito* (a phallic symbol of power for caciques), and the mysterious stone collar/belt, the purpose of which is unknown. Upstairs are poster-size photographs of petroglyphs found in Jayuya, Comerio, Utuado, Naguabo, Luquillo, Corozal, and Río Piedras.

Next door is **Casa Museo Canales** (PR 144, km 9.3, 787/828-4618 or 787/828-1241, daily 11am-4pm, $1 adults, $0.50 children ages 5-15, free for children under 5), a replica of the home of the celebrated author Nemesio R. Canales (1878-1923) and his revolutionary sister Blanca Canales (1906-1996). This traditional *criolla*-style wood frame structure contains many of the Canales's furnishings and a room devoted to the nationalist revolt Blanca led against the United States, the Jayuya Uprising, aka El Grito de Jayuya, in October 1950. One of several revolts orchestrated around the island that day, Blanca Canales's group attacked the police station, killing one policeman, and burned down the post office. The United States retaliated with infantry troops, mortar fire, and grenades. Blanca was arrested and sentenced to a life sentence plus 60 years. She was pardoned in 1967. Objects on view include revolvers used in the revolt and a card identifying Blanca as a member of the Nationalist Party. Unfortunately, the wall text is in Spanish only.

★ La Piedra Escrita

La Piedra Escrita (PR 144, km 7.3, free) is one of Puerto Rico's most revered reminders of the island's Taíno culture. The enormous granite boulder measures 32 feet high and 13 feet wide and is located smack-dab in the middle of Río Saliente, creating a natural pool where visitors can go for a swim.

But it's what's on the boulder that is of interest to historians and archaeologists. On the rock's surface are 52 petroglyphs that were carved into the rock by members of indigenous groups sometime between AD 600 and 1200. Some of the symbols clearly depict faces of humans and animals while others are geometric or abstract in shape. Because of the quantity of petroglyphs on the rock, some believe La Piedra Escrita was an important ceremonial site, but its significance is ultimately unknown.

La Piedra Escrita is a popular tourist sight. A long series of wheelchair-accessible switchback ramps descends from the stone escarpment overlooking the river down to the water where visitors can get a close-up look at the rock and go for a dip. It's a popular picnic spot on weekends.

ArqueoTours Coabey (787/718-1838, www.facebook.com/arqueotour, $65 adults, $20 children age 5-12, free for children 4 and under) offers family-friendly hiking tours to La Piedra Escrita guided by a historian and archaeologist. They also run tours to other Taíno archaeological sites.

Hacienda Pomarrosa

Hacienda Pomarrosa Coffee Lodge (PR 511 at PR 143, near Jayuya, 787/844-3541, http://pomarrosacoffeelodge.com, $20 adults, $10 children 10 and younger, reservations required) is a working coffee plantation offering two-hour tours (11am Tues.-Sat.) that teach

---

1: Museo del Cemí **2:** Hacienda Gripiñas

you about their production process. Two modest B&B-style rooms are available for overnight stays for $125-150, including breakfast.

ENTERTAINMENT AND EVENTS

Festival Nacional Indígena de Jayuya (Plaza Nemesio R. Canales, Calle Nemesio R. Canales and Calle Figuera, 787/828-1241) is an annual three-day celebration of the Taíno culture, beginning November 19. Participants don Taíno-style clothing, prepare traditional foods, and perform traditional music and dances. More than 100 artisans sell handmade crafts as well, and many demonstrations and ceremonies are held.

Other festivals include **El Festival del Pueblo del Tomate,** held in mid-April to celebrate the municipality's production of tomatoes. Festivities include games, music, and food kiosks. The **Jayuya Patron Saint Festival** honors the Virgen de la Monserrate with religious processions, music, and food kiosks in early September.

Christmas is celebrated with a **Magic Forest** featuring large holiday dioramas and storytelling December 1-January 15, and **Three Kings Day** on January 5 features traditional Christmas foods, music, and children's activities. All of Jayuya's festivals are held on the fairgrounds at Complejo Deportivo Filiberto García on PR 144 at the entrance to Jayuya.

FOOD AND ACCOMMODATIONS

Restaurante La Casona (PR 144, km 1.2, 787/828-3346, Mon. 11am-2pm, Tues. 11am-7pm, Wed. 11am-8pm, Thurs. 11am-9pm, Fri. 11am-10pm, Sat.-Sun. 2pm-10pm, $8-28) is a warm, rustic restaurant serving generous platters of mofongo, stuffed chicken breast, churrasco, red snapper, and other traditional Puerto Rican dishes. They have both indoor and outdoor dining areas.

Café Hacienda San Pedro Tienda y Museo (PR 144, km 8.4, Jayuya, 787/828-2083, www.cafehsp.com, Fri.-Sun. 10am-5pm, free) serves coffee drinks and sells bags of whole beans and ground coffee to take home. Also on-site is a coffee museum that features exhibits of coffee-processing equipment dating back to the plantation's origins in 1931. Farm tours are available on weekends by reservation only.

★ **Hacienda Gripiñas** (PR 527, km 2.5, 787/828-1717, 787/828-1718, or 787/828-1719, www.haciendagripinas.net, $75-105), built in 1858, was once one of the island's most prosperous coffee plantations. Today, its white wooden structures with green trim and red tin roofs are a unique lodging surrounded by the majestic mountains of the Cordillera Central. The rooms are rustic but comfortable and include modern bathrooms, excellent beds, air-conditioning, local TV, and amazing mountain views. Some rooms have private balconies, but for those that don't, there is a lovely large common porch with rocking chairs and hammocks overlooking the lush grounds thick with birds and coquí tree frogs. Amenities include a swimming pool and restaurant. All-inclusive packages are available.

TRANSPORTATION AND SERVICES

Jayuya is 100 kilometers (62 mi) southwest of San Juan. Take PR 22 west to PR 149 south.

Banking services are available in Jayuya at **Banco Popular** (84 Guillermo Estates, 787/828-4120).

Utuado

Utuado is one of the most accessible of Puerto Rico's mountain towns, via PR 10 from Arecibo. The wide multilane thoroughfare is well-marked and well-maintained, and it offers a spectacular ascent into Puerto Rico's Cordillera Central, where you can see massive mountain peaks towering overhead. The road has been cut right through the mountains in some places, creating dramatic profiles that stand in testament to the engineering feat it took to build the passage. Note, though, that the narrow winding roads that lead off PR 10 are not for the fainthearted. Proceed on them with caution, especially if it's raining, because mudslides and flooding are not uncommon. Otherwise, don't be deterred from venturing into this region. Its natural beauty is breathtaking, and Utuado is home to the island's most significant Taíno Indian archaeological site.

SIGHTS

★ Centro Ceremonial Indígena de Caguana

Centro Ceremonial Indígena de Caguana (PR 111, km 12.5, between Utuado and Lares, 787/669-1866, 787/894-7325, or 787/894-7310, daily 8am-4:30pm, $5 adults, $4 children 6-13 and seniors 60 and older) is one of the island's most significant archaeological sites.

Taíno Indians did not live on the site in Caguana, but dating back to AD 1100 they congregated here for religious ceremonies and ball games, leaving behind 12 ceremonial ball fields called *bateyes*, two of which have yet to be excavated. All but one are rectangular fields rimmed with stones and small monoliths, some of which have animal faces and spiral symbols carved into their sides. One is an atypical horseshoe shape. *Bateyes* were central to Taíno culture. This is where men competed with neighboring Taíno groups in a game similar to soccer, played with a ball made from rubber plants and reeds.

There is a small museum of artifacts, including *cemíes* (amulets) and stone collars, as well as a gift shop.

Excavation first began on the park in 1915, and it has undergone various stages of excavation and restoration over the years, including a $500,000 overhaul in 2005 that made it more tourist-friendly through the planting of a promenade of palm trees at the entrance and the creation of picnic areas and attractive stone walkways through the park.

The best way to get here is to take PR 10 south from Arecibo to PR 111, which is a tight, windy road featuring hairpin curve after hairpin curve. Beware of livestock on this road: Horses and cows can frequently be seen tied up to houses that hug the road, and chickens wander freely.

★ Cueva Ventana

Its name translates as Window Cave, which suits this gorgeous natural wonder perfectly. **Cueva Ventana** (PR 10, km 75, border of Utuado and Arecibo, 787/322-3554, www.cuevaventanapr.com, daily 10:30am-4:30pm, $17-19 nonresidents, $9-10 residents of Puerto Rico with ID, children under 5 not permitted) is an easy-to-access limestone cave that provides a stunning view of the region's karst country through the cave's gaping back window. Guided tours last 90 minutes and include a 45-minute moderate hike along a dirt path through the woods and up concrete stairs.

Lago Dos Bocas

Lago Dos Bocas (Embarcadero Lago Dos Bocas, PR 123, Utuado) is a manmade lake created in 1942 to generate hydroelectric power. It is also a potable water reservoir for the island. There are two lakeside restaurants accessible by a free boat ride from the *embarcadero* (pier) on weekends. The restaurants ferry diners from the pier to the restaurants, but the government also operates a small ferry primarily for residents. If there is availability, visitors can take the 45-minute ride around the lake. To reach the pier, travel south from Arecibo on PR 10 toward Utuado; turn left on PR 621; turn right on PR 123; the pier will be on the right. Boat rides are free.

Bosque Estatal de Río Abajo

Bosque Estatal de Río Abajo (PR 621, km 4.4, just west of PR 10, 787/880-6557 or 787/724-3724) is a 5,000-acre mostly subtropical humid forest in the heart of Puerto Rico's karst country, spanning the municipalities of Utuado and Arecibo. Once heavily deforested by industry, the reserve was founded in 1943 and continues to undergo reforestation efforts.

The forest is home to 175 endangered plant species, 47 of which are in danger of extinction, and 34 species of birds. Although it is not open to the public, the forest contains an aviary where the indigenous Puerto Rican parrot is raised in captivity and released in hopes of restoring the endangered species to the island habitat. Recreational facilities include hiking trails and campgrounds, which require a permit. Secure one by calling 787/999-2200, extension 5156, 5110, or 5158, at least 15 days in advance of your arrival.

RECREATION

Lago Dos Bocas (PR 123, north of Utuado, 787/894-3505) is a large artificial mountain lake perfect for kayaking and fishing for sunfish, largemouth bass, catfish, and tilapia. Boats are available from the municipal dock to take visitors to lakefront restaurants on weekends only.

For a truly unique experience, tube through caves as long as 1,000 feet with **Río Tanamá Adventures** (PR 111, km. 48.4, Barrio Caguana, Utuado, 787/462-4121, www.tanamariveradventures.com). The moderately difficult tour takes three hours and includes hiking and lunch for $89. Other tours include an easier, family-friendly, two-hour option for $65 and a moderately difficult, four-hour cave-tubing/hiking/rappelling experience for $79. More challenging rappelling tours are also available for experienced climbers.

ENTERTAINMENT AND EVENTS

The municipality of Utuado commemorates San Miguel Arcángel each year with a **Patron Saint Festival** (787/894-3505) in late September to early October. In addition to the usual religious processions, music, and food kiosks, there are amateur boxing matches,

Cueva Ventana

softball games, and domino competitions. It's held in Luis Muñoz Rivera Plaza.

FOOD AND ACCOMMODATIONS

Some of the tastiest and cheapest food in Puerto Rico can be purchased from street vendors, and the town of Utuado is a great place for just that. All along PR 111 going into and out of town, there are vendors selling grilled *pinchos* (meat kabobs), *pollo al carbón* (barbecue chicken), *grandules* (pigeon peas), and fresh fruit.

Don't let the rustic appearance dissuade you from stopping at **Hijos del Josco** (PR 123, km 58, 787/201-1218, www.facebook.com/hijosdeljosco, Sun.-Thurs. 11am-10pm, Fri.-Sat. 11am-midnight), home of the popular tacolao, a tortilla stuffed with bacalao, and mason-jar mojitos. There's a great view of the river, too.

Casa Grande Mountain Retreat (PR 612, km 0.3, at the intersection of PR 140, Barrio Caonillas, 787/894-3939 or 888/343-2272, www.hotelcasagrande.com, $136) is a 107-acre property that features freestanding monastic cabins surrounded by a lush, verdant forest. Amenities include a small pool, yoga classes, hiking trails, and restaurant. The property sustained some damage from Hurricane Maria, but has since renovated and reopened.

TRANSPORTATION AND SERVICES

Utuado is 110 kilometers (68 mi) southwest of San Juan. Take PR 22 west to PR 10 south.

Banking services are available at **Banco Popular** (59 Calle Dr. Cueto, 787/894-2700). For pharmacy needs, visit **Walgreens** (PR 123, Edificio 940, 787/894-0574).

Adjuntas

Situated along La Ruta Panorámico, Adjuntas is known as the "Switzerland of Puerto Rico" because of its cool temperatures. The municipality maintains an average 72 degrees year-round thanks to the high altitude. Adjuntas is also known as the "City of the Sleeping Giant," named after the shape of the mountain range. The sleepy little agricultural town has a pleasant central plaza lined with a couple of pizza restaurants, a bakery, a souvenir shop, and a general store, selling everything from guitars to electric generators. An easy 32-kilometer (20-mi) drive up PR 10 from Ponce, Adjuntas is a great, centrally located place to explore the Cordillera Central for budget travelers looking for low-cost accommodations.

SIGHTS

Bosque Estatal de Guilarte (intersection of PR 518 and PR 131, 787/724-3647 or 787/829-5767, Mon.-Fri. 7am-3:30pm, Sat.-Sun. 9am-5:30pm) is a 3,600-acre subtropical wet forest reserve featuring Monte Guilarte, one of the highest peaks on the island at 3,953 feet above sea level. A marked trail leads the way on a 35-minute uphill hike to the mountain's summit. The forest has 26 bird species and 105 species of trees, including a eucalyptus grove.

Casa Pueblo (30 Calle Rodofo Gonzáles, 787/829-4842, www.casapueblo.org, daily 8:30am-3pm, free) is a 19th-century house that has been transformed into a community center that features an exhibition space, a small butterfly garden, a lending library, a solar-powered movie theater, and a gift shop selling local coffee. It's also home to a radio station, WOQI 1020 AM. The center is managed by a nonprofit environmental group that also oversees **Bosque del Pueblo** (PR 605), a forest reserve that was once pit mined for copper. The reserve features hiking trails and primitive campgrounds (permit required). Casa Pueblo was instrumental in providing aid to survivors of Hurricane Maria by providing solar lights and refrigerators. Now the organization is working with local businesses and agencies to make Adjuntas the first all-solar town in Puerto Rico.

Hacienda Tres Angeles (PR 129, km 38.4, 787/360-0019, www.haciendatresangeles.com, Fri.-Sat. 8am-5pm, Sun. 11am-5pm) is an agro-tourism site that encompasses a working coffee farm and roastery, with a café serving its locally produced coffee and light fare, including pastries and Puerto Rican cuisine. Visitors are welcome to stroll around the farm and admire the mountain views from the expansive patio, or take a guided tour (Sat. 10am), which is available by reservation only.

If you don't mind the heart-clutching drive to get there, **Puente La Hamaca** (PR 518) is a picturesque hanging pedestrian bridge that spans a cove on Lago Garzas. To get there from Adjuntas, drive the steep, narrow, and twisty route along PR 518, part of La Ruta Panorámica, to **La Belotta Restaurante & Bar** (PR 518, km 7.3). Park and walk across the street to a gated road. Pedestrians are permitted to shimmy around the gate post and take a strenuous, half-mile hike up two steep inclines along a rocky, uneven surface to reach the narrow, crude bridge made from cables strung across the cove. Cross at your own risk.

Set in the mountains, **Charco El Ataúd** (PR 123/PR 522) is an idyllic freshwater swimming hole fed by the two-tiered **Las Garzas waterfall.** It's popular with locals on weekends and holidays. It's off the beaten track, and there aren't any signs to point the way. Start at **Parador Sotomayor** (PR 123/PR522, km 36.6) and proceed along the road left of the hotel. The road will grow narrow and you'll encounter some forks along the way, but stay on the main, wider road. Look for a bridge on your left and take it over the river and continue about a mile or so until you see cars parked along the roadside and an unmarked trail. That trail leads to the top of the falls. From here you can climb down to the pond. Swim at your own risk, and note that the trail and the rocks can be slippery.

RECREATION

Lago Garzas (PR 518, south of Adjuntas), a 91-acre artificial lake, is primarily used to generate electricity. But it's also a great little fishing spot for largemouth bass, sunfish, catfish, and shad. Take a two-hour guided kayak tour of the lake with **Giant Kayaks** (787/384-2218, $25).

Casa Pueblo in Adjuntas

FOOD AND ACCOMMODATIONS

★ **El Campo es Leña** (PR 521, km 7.8, no phone, www.facebook.com/elcampoeslena, Fri. 3pm-10pm, Sat. 2pm-10pm, Sun. 1pm-9pm, $5-15) is a rustic, bohemian restaurant and bar in a rambling, multilevel structure made from wood and corrugated metal serving artisanal, wood-fired pizzas made from locally sourced ingredients, some grown right on the grounds. Colorful murals, live music, great food, and gorgeous views make this a place you want to hang out for a while.

Restaurante El Boricua (PR 5516, km 0.4, 787/829-1956, Mon.-Tues. 10:30am-8pm, Wed.-Thurs. and Sun. 10:30am-midnight, Fri.-Sat. 10:30am-2am, $5-15) is a huge, rambling roadside restaurant featuring an enormous bar, pool tables, big-screen TVs, and a moderately priced menu serving everything from fried pork chops to crab stew to octopus salad. In typical fashion, there is a full bar and the restaurant is family friendly.

La Terraza by the River Cantina (PR 123/PR 522, km 36.6, 787/665-0305, www.facebook.com/laterrazaadjuntas, Thurs. 3pm-10pm, Fri.-Sat. noon-1am, Sun. 11am-11pm, $5-18) is more bar than restaurant, but it's a great place to hang out on the deck overlooking the river and knock back a few cold beers or mojitos. The menu features pub fare like burgers, fries, and stuffed *tostones*. On special occasions there's a pig roast, and there's karaoke and live music at night.

Traditional *criolla* cuisine is on the menu at **Restaurante Las Garzas** (Parador Villas Sotomayor, PR 123/PR 522, km 36.6, 787/829-1717 or 787/829-1774, www.paradorvillassotomayor.com, Sun.-Thurs. 8am-10pm, Fri.-Sat. 8am-midnight, bar open until 10pm Sun.-Thurs., until midnight Fri.-Sat., $5-23), and the selections are surprisingly diverse for such a small operation. There are several rabbit dishes as well as octopus salad, plantain soup, and mofongo stuffed with choice of octopus, churrasco, shrimp, chicken, or pork.

Catering to Puerto Rican families, **Parador Villas Sotomayor** (PR 123/PR 522, km 36.6, 787/829-1717 or 787/829-1774, www.paradorvillassotomayor.com, $126-250) offers a modest place to stay for a modest price. The 14-acre grounds have 36 cabin-style accommodations including studios, suites, and two-bedroom apartments. Rooms come with air-conditioning, satellite TV, microwaves, coffeepots, and mini refrigerators. Larger rooms have full refrigerators and a stovetop. Amenities include a swimming pool, tennis courts, game room, and playground. Horses, bikes, kayaks, and grills are available for rent. A restaurant and bar are on-site. All-inclusive packages are available.

TRANSPORTATION AND SERVICES

Adjuntas is 125 kilometers (78 mi) southwest of San Juan. Take PR 22 west to PR 10 south to PR 123 south. Adjuntas is 30 kilometers (19 mi) north of Ponce on PR 10.

Medical services are provided by **Hospital Castañer** (PR 125, km 64.2, 787/829-5010). Banking services are available at **Banco Popular** (12-21 Calle San Joaquín, 787/829-2120).

Lares and Maricao

Lares is considered the birthplace of Puerto Rican nationalism because it played a much-revered role in Puerto Rico's independence movement. Today, it is best known for its production of Alto Grande coffee, a highly prized variety.

Home to one of the island's oldest forest reserves, Maricao is a major producer of coffee and host of an annual festival celebrating the crop.

SIGHTS

Bosque Estatal de Maricao (PR 120, km 13.2, Maricao, 787/838-1040, Tues.-Sun. 7:30am-4pm) encompasses 10,000 acres ranging from the Tetas de Cerro Gordo in San Germán (2,870 feet above sea level) to Río Cruces (49 feet) and is home a wide diversity of vegetation including 91 species of orchid. There is a recreation area with bathrooms, picnic areas, hiking trails, and overnight accommodations.

Centro 23 del Septiembre Plaza (Calle Dr. Pedro Albizu Campos, off PR 111) is the central plaza in Lares, and it is a testament to the town's independence from Spain's rule. In the plaza is a tamarind tree that was planted by beloved independence leader Dr. Pedro Albizu Campos in soil from several independent Spanish-speaking countries. Legend has it that when the tree bears an abundant amount of fruit, Puerto Rico will be free again.

Montoso Gardens (PR 120, km 18.9, Maricao, 787/838-0318, http://montosogardens.com, Sat.-Sun. 9am-5pm, $5, reservations required) is a 90-acre botanical garden and tropical plant nursery devoted to preserving and cultivating more than 600 species of tropical fruit, nut, spice, and ornamental plants.

EVENTS

Since the 1800s, Maricao has been celebrating the end of coffee harvest, which occurs in mid-February. The tradition continues with **La Fiesta del Acabe del Café,** a three-day celebration featuring food vendors, musical performances, crafts, rum, and coffee.

FOOD AND ACCOMMODATIONS

Located in Lares, on the town's plaza, **Heladería Lares** (2 Calle Vilella, 787/378-4288, Mon.-Fri. 10am-5pm, Sat.-Sun. 10am-6pm, $2-3.50) has been serving exotic ice cream flavors since 1968. In addition to tropical fruit flavors like coconut, mango, guava, and pineapple, there are unusual flavors such as rice and beans, corn, and sweet potato. Like most ice creams in Puerto Rico, these confections are lighter with an icier texture than commercial brands.

Cabaños Monte del Estadol (787/873-5632, www.parquesnacionalespr.com, sugerencias@cpnpr.gobierno.pr, $60) offers basic brick cabins with fireplaces (bring your own wood). Just down the road is **Parque Ecológico Monte del Estado** (787/873-5652, ext. 5632, $15), a well-appointed campground with fireplaces, barbecues, bathrooms, and showers.

TRANSPORTATION AND SERVICES

Lares is 115 kilometers (71 mi) southwest of San Juan. Maricao is 140 kilometers (87 mi) southwest of San Juan.

Banking services are available at **Banco Popular** (562 Ave. Patriotas, Lares, 787/897-2525). For health services, go to **Lares Medical Center** (PR 111, km 2.9, Lares, 787/897-1444).

1: river in Adjuntas **2:** Puente La Hamaca near Adjuntas

Vieques and Culebra

Vieques and Culebra are two island municipali-

ties a mere 8 and 17 miles, respectively, off the east coast of Puerto Rico, but the lifestyle there is light-years away from that of the main island.

Referred to as the Spanish Virgin Islands, Vieques and Culebra are often described as "the way Puerto Rico used to be." The pace of life doesn't just slow down, it comes to a screeching halt. There are no fast-food restaurants or high-rise hotels, no golf courses or casinos, virtually no nightlife, and few tourist sights. And the only way to reach the islands is by plane or ferry. But what they do have are stunning beaches, world-class water sports, and lots of opportunity for R&R.

The small Spanish fort and museum El Fortín Conde de Mirasol on Vieques and the Museo Histórico de Culebra are the closest things to

Highlights

Look for ★ to find recommended sights, activities, dining, and lodging.

★ **El Fortín Conde de Mirasol:** Tour the last fort built by colonial Spain and see the 4,000-year-old remains of a man exhumed from an archaeological site in Vieques (page 284).

★ **Mosquito Bay:** Take a guided kayak or electric pontoon boat to Vieques's **bioluminescent bay,** which glows an electric blue at night (page 284).

★ **Balneario Sun Bay:** Vieques's mile-long, sandy, crescent-shaped beach borders crystal-blue waters (page 289).

★ **Playa Flamenco:** This stretch of white sand is celebrated as one of the most beautiful beaches in the United States (page 304).

★ **Diving and snorkeling in Culebra:** Culebra is surrounded by 50 dive sites, and excellent snorkeling can be found right off its beaches (page 304).

© MOON.COM

Vieques

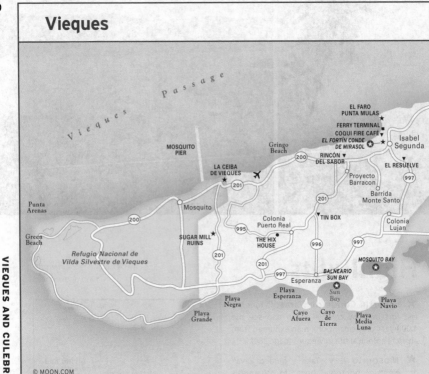

VIEQUES AND CULEBRA

cultural attractions the islands have to offer. Instead, one of the main reasons to go is the islands' wide sandy beaches, the most popular being Balneario Sun Bay in Vieques and Playa Flamenco in Culebra. In addition to its beaches, Culebra and Vieques offer fantastic opportunities for diving and snorkeling. If you don't want to go on a group tour, excellent snorkeling from the beach at Playa Carlos Rosario in Culebra is easily accessible. And visitors to Vieques would be remiss not to visit the bioluminescent Mosquito Bay, which requires an overnight stay.

For the most part, Culebra escaped the wrath of Hurricane Maria in 2017, but Vieques was severely damaged by the storm and in some ways is still struggling to recover. It was one of the last municipalities to have its power restored after nearly a year without it. Most of the hotels are back in business, and there's even a new one under construction in Esperanza. Several restaurants have closed, but a few new ones have opened. Meanwhile, the beaches are still as gorgeous as always, and the bioluminescence of Mosquito Bay is more brilliant than ever.

PLANNING YOUR TIME

To get to Vieques and Culebra, you can fly from either the Isla Grande Airport or the Luis Muñoz Marín International Airport in San Juan, or the José Aponte de la Torre Airport in Ceiba on the east coast. Another option is to take the Puerto Rico Port

---

Previous: wild horses on the beach at Vieques; coastline of Vieques; Fulladoza Bay in Culebra.

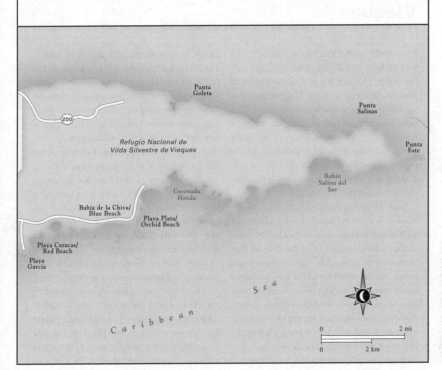

Authority Passenger Ferry from Ceiba, but the service can be unreliable. If you're short on time, flying is recommended.

Although it's possible to get to your hotel and some of the islands' beaches using *públicos* (shared vans that carry multiple fares at a time), to fully explore the islands' remote beaches, a **rental car** or, in Culebra, a **rental golf cart,** is recommended. Book early though, because they go fast.

Vieques and Culebra are such small islands that it's possible to **spend a day and a night on each** one to get a cursory feel for them both. But the reason most people go is to experience the islands' unparalleled natural beauty and soak up plenty of R&R. To do those things properly, it takes a few days to reset your internal clock to "island time" and achieve a blissful state of total relaxation.

Vieques

In a world where change is constant, it's nice to be reminded that some things stay the same. That is a big part of the charm of Vieques. Granted, a couple of new businesses have opened and a couple of have closed. This hotel has changed names, and that one has a new coat of paint. But all in all, it's still just a sleepy little island where life moves at a snail's pace, cats and horses wander the island freely, and the only alarm clock you need is the crow of the roosters that run the place.

Just 21 miles long and 5 miles wide, Vieques is a natural wonderland. It is rimmed with wilderness beaches, untouched by commercial development, and coral reefs that teem with undersea life. Among the island's mangrove forests is **Mosquito Bay,** one of the world's most spectacular bioluminescent bays. No visit to Vieques would be complete without a nighttime boat ride through luminescent blue waters. Inland Vieques is thickly forested hills and arid stretches of desert-like land. Bats are the only mammal native to Vieques, but other wildlife commonly found includes geckos, iguanas, frogs, pelicans, seagulls,

egrets, herons, doves, and horses, of course. Horses are a common mode of transportation in Vieques, and they can be seen following the same traffic laws as automobiles, stopping at four-way stops and so on. But they also graze and roam freely. The waters around the island are home to several endangered species, including the manatee and a variety of sea turtles, which nest on the beaches at night. About 60 percent of the island once belonged to the U.S. Navy, which used it for a training base. The Navy left in 2003, and the land was converted into a protected wildlife sanctuary—**Refugio Nacional de Vida Silvestre de Vieques**—managed by the U.S. Fish and Wildlife Service. Some of the island's most beautiful wilderness beaches are located here.

There are two primary communities on Vieques. On the north coast is **Isabel Segunda,** a.k.a. Isabel II, a traditional Puerto Rican town with a central plaza, an *alcaldía* (town hall), a post office, a grocery store, and a couple of banks and gas stations. It is also where the ferry from Ceiba docks. There are a few shops, restaurants, and hotels here that

fishing boats on the beach near Esperanza on Vieques

cater to visitors, but Isabel Segunda is primarily a town where the island's residents conduct their daily business.

On the south coast is **Esperanza,** a funky, bohemian enclave of residential homes, guest houses, restaurants, and bars where tourists gravitate. It is home to **Sun Bay,** one of the most gorgeous publicly maintained beaches in all of Puerto Rico. The main hub of Esperanza is along the oceanfront stretch of Calle Flamboyán, distinguished by the picturesque *malecón,* a boardwalk with balustrades, benches, and pavilions. From here you can also see Cayo Afuera, a small islet in

spitting distance with excellent snorkeling on the western side. On the opposite side of the street is an inviting array of casual open-air bars and restaurants that overlook the water and grow lively with tourists and locals as sundown approaches. There are also a handful of boutiques and a couple of guesthouses in the area, as well as the Vieques Conservation and Historical Trust, a modest institution but a great source of information on the island.

There are a few things travelers should know when visiting Vieques. The island has one of the highest unemployment rates in the United States, and petty theft from parked cars is a problem. When in town, visitors are encouraged to keep their cars locked at all times and never leave anything visible inside. The greatest threat to car break-ins is at the beach. Drivers are encouraged to leave all the windows rolled down and the sunroof and glove box open to avoid having to pay the cost of replacing a broken window. And always park your car as close to you as possible—preferably away from any bushes and within sight range.

There is a rustic quality to life here. Restaurants tend to be open-air, even nice ones, so don't expect a respite from the heat and humidity at dinner. When using public facilities, plumbing issues require toilet paper be disposed of in trash receptacles instead of flushed, which can make for an odorous experience during the heat of the day. And if you think restaurant service is slow on the main island of Puerto Rico, you haven't seen anything yet. Many businesses close or curtail hours during low season. Just when "low season" is can be a topic of debate. To be safe, assume it's anything that isn't high season, which everyone seems to agree is mid-November through April. In fact, assume all hours of operation are more suggestions than fact. The secret to enjoying Vieques is to chill out and let things unfold in their own way and time.

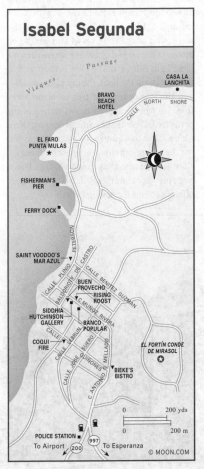

Isabel Segunda

VIEQUES AND CULEBRA
VIEQUES

SIGHTS

★ El Fortín Conde de Mirasol

Built between 1845 and 1855, **El Fortín Conde de Mirasol** (PR 989, Isabel Segunda, 787/741-1717, www.vieques.com/fortin-spanish-fort, Wed.-Sun. 8:30am-4:30pm) was the last fort built by the Spanish in the New World. Never attacked or used in battle, it originally housed Spanish troops and later became a jail and execution site. Among those incarcerated here were fugitive enslaved people from local sugar plantations and political prisoners who sought Puerto Rico's independence from Spain. Later it was used as a municipal jail until the 1940s, when it was closed and fell into disrepair. In 1989 the Institute of Puerto Rico began restoration of the fort, which still has its original brick floors, exterior walls, and hardwood beams.

The fort has been beautifully restored, and the views from its elevated site are gorgeous. Inside are a few exhibits dedicated to the island's indigenous people, its historic sugarcane industry, and local artists. It also contains the Vieques Historic Archives.

★ Bioluminescent Mosquito Bay

Mosquito Bay (off PR 997, near Esperanza) is a naturally occurring bioluminescent bay that attracts visitors to Vieques from around the world. The only way to see the bioluminescence for yourself is to paddle a kayak into the bay at night or take an electric boat ride. Several outfitters in town provide guided tours. The kayak tour is easy, even for beginners and kids. Swimsuits, shorts, and swim shoes are recommended because you will get wet. Tours should be booked at least one day in advance. For best results, plan your trip during a new moon, when the bay glows brightest.

Tours last around 90 minutes to two hours. Each begins after the sun goes down, with a 20-minute, bumpy ride in a van on a dirt road through a thick forest. From the edge of the water, you board your vessel and paddle or motor to the far end of the bay where the ambient light is lowest. The glow is most visible in the wake of the boat, the dip of the paddle, and the zigzag trails of fish scooting away from your boat's approach. Swimming is not permitted. Despite the name of the bay, there isn't a lot of mosquito activity on the water, but the no-see-ums may come out on shore for a few hours right after sundown. DEET-free bug spray is recommended. Many outfitters offer discounts for paying in cash.

El Fortín Conde de Mirasol

TOUR OPERATORS

Jak Water Sports (787/644-7112 or 787/447-8697, www.jakwatersports.com) provides guided bio-bay tours (2 hours, $50-56 pp) in two-person, clear-bottom kayaks for optimum viewing. A Visa or MasterCard is required to book a spot. The pickup point for the tour is in the dirt parking lot across from El Blok in Esperanza.

Taíno Aqua Adventures (787/349-6964, www.tainoaquaadventures.com, $55-60 pp) hosts bio-bay tours in clear-bottom double kayaks (450-pound weight limit). The tour lasts two hours, and the skill level is easy. Kayakers meet 15 minutes prior to tour time at El Blok in Esperanza. Call ahead to arrange a private tour or if you're a group of 10 or more.

If kayaking isn't your thing, **El Viequesnse Sea Tours** (787/644-7112, www.elviequenseseatours.com) offers guided electric boat tours of the bay for $50 per person. The tour lasts about an hour.

Melaya's Tours (787/222-7055, www.melayasours.net) offers guided bio-bay tours in two-person, clear-bottom kayaks for $65 per person. The weight limit is 250 pounds per person. Kids 3 years and older are welcome.

Travesias Isleñas Yaureibo (787/447-4104 or 939/630-1267, www.viequesoutdoors.com) offers nightly bio-bay tours (2 hours, $45 pp). The kayaking skill level is easy. Meet on the *malecón* in Esperanza across from Tradewinds. They also offer extended kayak tours (3 hours, $65 pp), historical walking tours (3 hours, $30 pp) and snorkel tours (2.5 hours, $20 pp).

El Faro Punta Mulas

Built in the late 1800s, **El Faro Punta Mulas** (Calle Plinio Peterson, north of Isabel Segunda, 787/741-3141) looks less like a lighthouse and more like a modest, rectangular government building with a large light on top of it. It's still operational today, but visitors can't enter the lighthouse.

Site of Hombre de Puerto Ferro

Often referred to as Vieques's Stonehenge, this archaeological site on the south side of the island off PR 997 was discovered to contain the 4,000-year-old remains of a man who became known as **Hombre de Puerto Ferro.** The remains originally were displayed at El Fortin Conde de Mirasol, but have since been moved. To access the site, drive a half-kilometer east of the entrance to Sun Bay, and turn inland onto a dirt road that takes you to the fenced-off site. Giant boulders mark the spot where the remains were excavated in 1990. Some believe the boulders were placed around the grave; others say it's a natural phenomenon.

La Ceiba de Vieques

After Hurricane Maria decimated so much of Vieques in 2017, it was feared that the beloved, mighty **ceiba tree** that had stood near Mosquito Pier for more than 275 years had been destroyed. Its leaves were gone and its limbs were ravaged. But it became a beacon of hope for the people of Vieques when it miraculously recovered and now stands larger and prouder than ever. It's now a popular tourist sight, and a park has been built in the vicinity. There's also a narrow sandy beach ideal for picnicking and swimming. From the airport, drive three minutes west on PR 201, then turn right on PR 200; the tree is on the right.

Vieques Conservation and Historical Trust

Tucked between the bars and restaurants across from the *malecón* in Esperanza, **Vieques Conservation and Historical Trust** (138 Calle Flamboyán, Esperanza, 787/741-8850 or 787/741-2844, www.vcht.org, Mon.-Fri. 8am-4pm, free but donations accepted) is a small institution with a big mission to help protect and preserve the island's natural habitat. It has been involved in a research project with the Scripps Institute of Oceanography in San Diego, California, on the effect of light pollution on Mosquito Bay. It also runs a children's summer camp and

The Electric-Blue Waters of Mosquito Bay

In 2013 Vieques's world-renowned bioluminescent Mosquito Bay went dark. It was a shocking turn of events that set the entire tourism industry on edge. Theories about what caused it included global warming, shifting tides, silt run-off, and pollution. In early 2014 the National Guard arrived and cleared debris from 10 acres around the lagoon, and by the end of the year, the glow had begun to return. It was a chilling reminder of the importance of protecting this remarkable natural phenomenon.

So just what is it that makes the bioluminescent lagoon in Mosquito Bay glow? The mangrove bay's rich nutrients and clean, warm water create the perfect environment for sustaining the zillions of microscopic organisms called **dinoflagellates** that wash into the bay during high tide and remain trapped there when the tide recedes. The single-celled creature contains properties similar to both plants and animals. But more notably, when it senses motion, it experiences a **chemical reaction** that creates a burst of light not unlike that of a firefly.

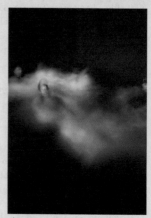

glowing waters in a bio-bay

Puerto Rico is said to have as many as seven bays rich in dinoflagellates, although only three are commonly known: **Bahía Fosforescénte in La Parguera** (page 222) on the southwest coast of Puerto Rico, **Laguna Grande in Fajardo** (page 131) on the east coast, and **Mosquito Bay in Vieques** (page 284).

Mosquito Bay is touted as one of the most spectacular bioluminescent bays in the world because of its high concentration of dinoflagellates and the absence of pollution and ambient light. The brilliance of the bioluminescence varies, depending on weather conditions and how bright the moon is. The darker the sky, the brighter the bioluminescence.

leads tours to the Sugar Mill Ruins. Stop in to take a look at the aquariums containing local sea creatures or pick up some information on the island.

TOP EXPERIENCE

Vieques National Wildlife Refuge

The **Vieques National Wildlife Refuge** (PR 997, halfway between Isabel Segunda and Esperanza, 787/741-2138, www.fws.gov/caribbean/Refuges/Vieques, daily 6am-sunset, field office Mon.-Fri. 8am-3pm, free) was once the Camp Garcia defense testing site for the U.S. Navy. Parts of it were swept clean of live artillery when it transitioned into a national wildlife refuge following the Navy's departure

in 2003. Note: Much of the area has not been cleared, so it is essential that visitors **stay on marked paths and roads.**

The largest wildlife refuge in the Caribbean, encompassing 60 percent of the island, the 17,770-acre refuge contains a variety of natural habitats, including wilderness beaches, mangrove forests, subtropical dry forest, and Mosquito Bay. It is home to four endangered plants and 10 endangered animals, including the brown pelican and several species of sea turtles. Some of Vieques's finest wilderness beaches are located in the refuge, including Playa Caracas/Red Beach, Playa Pata Prieta, La Chiva/Blue Beach, and Playa Plata/Orchid Beach.

For spectacular views of the ocean and some cool ruins, don't miss the **Puerto**

Esperanza

Ferro Lighthouse, established in 1896 by the Spanish and abandoned in 1926. As soon as you turn into the refuge from PR 997, take an immediate right onto a gravel road and follow it for about 5 kilometers (3 mi) to the end. Leave your car in the small parking lot and walk about 200 yards to the lighthouse and some breathtaking views of the sea.

The refuge is a protected area. No camping, fires, unleashed pets, or drones are permitted.

BEACHES

There are small, remote beaches tucked into the island's south-central coastline, which are part of the refuge. From the entrance to the refuge, located on PR 997 halfway between Isabel Segunda and Esperanza, there are four main wilderness beaches, and all of them are extraordinary.

Each one is a crescent of white, powdery sand, lapped by pale turquoise waters and rimmed with thick, lush vegetation. Measuring their distance from the entrance, they are **Playa Caracas/Red Beach** (3.9 km/2.4 mi), **Playa Pata Prieta** (4.3 km/2.7 mi), **La Chiva/Blue Beach** (4.8 km/3 mi), and **Playa Plata/Orchid Beach** (7.1 km/4.4 mi).

Playa Grande Sugar Mill Ruins

The **Playa Grande Sugar Mill Ruins** (off PR 201 near Playa Grande, west of Esperanza, 787/741-8850 or 787/741-2844, www.vcht.org, free) are what is left of one of four sugar mills that operated in Vieques beginning in the 1830s. It was closed in the early 1940s when the Navy arrived, and much of what was left has begun to be reclaimed by Mother Nature, but there are still about a half-dozen buildings remaining. Long pants, hiking shoes, and bug spray are recommended. Much of the site is thick with vegetation.

From the airport, drive west on PR 200 for about three minutes. After you pass Mosquito Pier on your right, turn left on the next unmarked road. Drive to the end and look for a handwritten sign marking the site. Explore on your own or take a guided tour with the **Vieques Conservations and Historical Trust** (138 Calle Flamboyán, Esperanza, 787/741-8850 or 787/741-2844, www.vcht.org).

RECREATION
Beaches

Aside from Mosquito Bay, the main reason to come to Vieques is to enjoy the staggering beauty of its miles of remote, pristine beaches

1

2

and clear, turquoise waters. Each beach has its own unique characteristics—some are calm and shallow, others have big crashing waves, and still others offer spectacular snorkeling. Several are accessible only from dirt trails, off-road or by foot, so bring sturdy shoes. And don't forget the bug spray and sunscreen.

Playa Negra is a black-sand beach containing minute particles of lava, a reminder of the island's volcanic origins millions of years ago. To get there from the *malecón* in Esperanza, go west on PR 996 and turn left on PR 201. When you reach the sign for Oro gallery, pull off the road and park. Look for the bridge in the road and hike down into the dry creek bed beneath it. Follow the creek bed through a thickly wooded forest to the ocean.

Playa Grande is a long, thin strip of beach that curves around the southwestern tip of the island and is a great spot for walking and hunting for shells. Go when it's breezy because it can be buggy with sand fleas. It's located west of Esperanza off PR 201.

Green Beach is on Punta Arenas at the farthest most southwestern tip of the island, and it features a shallow reef, making it ideal for snorkeling. Look for "flamingo tongues," a brightly colored sea snail that lives here. Nearby is Kiani Lagoon, a mangrove bay accessible by a wooden boardwalk that is rich with starfish. Green Beach is best visited early in the day or when it's breezy because it can be buggy with sand fleas. To access it, take PR 200 as far west as possible, then follow the dirt road to the end.

Esperanza Beach is a fairly unremarkable beach along Esperanza's strip of restaurants and guesthouses. But it's within walking distance if you're staying in town and offers excellent snorkeling, especially around Cayo Afuera, a tiny islet just offshore.

A note of caution: Although violent crime is uncommon in Vieques, the island has a petty theft problem, which can be avoided if you use caution. Don't bring anything of value to the beach if you can avoid it. And if you can't, have someone you trust watch your things, or bring a waterproof dry bag, available at dive shops, to contain your valuables. Don't leave anything inside your car and be sure to roll all your windows down and open the glove box so it's apparent nothing is inside.

★ BALNEARIO SUN BAY

The island's best beaches are on the southern coast. The most spectacular is the long white crescent and calm waters of **Balneario Sun Bay** (PR 997, east of Esperanza, 787/741-8198, daily 8:30am-6pm, $4 vehicles, $2 motorcycles), also known as Balneario Sombé. It's the only publicly maintained beach in Vieques. Surrounded by a tall cyclone fence, it has plenty of modern, fairly clean facilities, including bathrooms, showers, changing rooms, a snack bar, and guards. Camping (787/741-8198) is permitted for $10 a day; reservations are required. Adding to the charm of the place is the herd of horses that grazes here.

The Balneario Sun Bay complex also encompasses two smaller, more secluded beaches farther eastward along a sandy road. The first one you'll encounter is **Media Luna,** a protective cove where the water is shallow. Farther eastward is **Navio Beach,** which sometimes has large waves and is popular with gay beachgoers.

Water Sports

Vieques Sailing Charters (787/435-4858 or 939/332-5778, www.viequessailingcharters.com) offers half-day sailing trips and snorkeling tours twice a day for $150 per person (up to 8 people, ages 12 and up). Private half-day tours for up to four people are offered for $750 (ages 6 and up).

Jak Water Sports (787/644-7112 or 787/447-8697, www.jakwatersports.com) provides guided Mosquito Bay tours (2 hours, $50-56) in clear-bottom kayaks for optimum viewing. A Visa or MasterCard is required to make a reservation. They also offer motorboat snorkeling, nighttime snorkeling, and

1: La Ceiba de Vieques 2: Puerto Ferro Lighthouse in the Vieques National Wildlife Refuge

paddleboarding tours, as well as bike, paddleboard, snorkel, and kayak rentals.

El Viequesnse Sea Tours (787/644-7112, www.elviequenseseatours.com) offers guided electric boat tours of Mosquito Bay for $50 per person. The also offer fishing, snorkeling, and beach-hopping charters.

Blackbeard Sports (575 German Rieckehoff, Isabel Segunda, 787/300-0155 or 787/966-7540, www.scallywagsvieques.com or www.facebook.com/BlackBeardSports) offers dive and snorkel tours, paddleboard and kayak tours, and more.

Go inshore fishing for kingfish, amberjack, barracuda, pompano, and tarpon with **Caribbean Fly Fishing** (787/450-3744, www.facebook.com/cffcinc). A full-day outing is $650 and a half-day is $375, including gear and tackle (2-person maximum).

Fun Brothers Hut (grass hut on the *malecón* across from El Quenepo, 787/435-9372 or 787/741-0151, www.funbrothersvieques.com) rents Jet Skis ($70 for 30 minutes, $110 for 1 hour), kayaks ($20/hour), and glass-bottom bio-bay tours ($60 pp).

Horseback Riding

Explore the island atop a locally bred Paso Fino horse with **Esperanza Riding Company** (787/435-0073, www.esperanzaridingcompany.com/vieques, cash only, reservations required). Two-hour guided tours through hills, meadows, riverbeds, and beaches cost $80. A private guided tour is $110. Children 7 and younger can take a 20-minute, hand-led pony trail ride for $15. Due to the small stature of the breed, there is a weight limit of 225 pounds for riders. Long pants and closed-toe shoes are recommended.

Jurutungo Farms (PR 997, 787/307-1998, www.jurutungo.com) offers 1.5-hour guided horseback riding tours to Playa Negra for groups of four or less for $80 per person. Private tours and combo horseback riding and snorkel tours are available. No previous horseback riding experience is necessary. Children who can sit in a saddle and follow instructions are permitted. Long pants or leggings and closed-toed shoes are recommended.

Yoga

Hix Island House (PR 995, km 1.5, 787/435-4590, www.hixislandhouse.com) offers 90-minute yoga classes ($15) daily in its beautiful outdoor pavilion. Call in advance to confirm your spot.

Bananas Guesthouse, Beach Bar & Grill in Esperanza

Spa

Beatriz Beauty Boutique (349 Calle Antonio G. Mellado, Isabel Segunda, 787/556-8662, www.facebook.com/thenewspa) is a full-service salon that offers massage, facials, manicures and pedicures, hair and scalp treatments, and waxing.

ENTERTAINMENT AND EVENTS

Bars

If partying into the wee hours is your idea of the perfect vacation, Vieques may not be the place for you. There are no nightclubs, discos, or casinos on the island, and many of the restaurants close by 10pm. There are a couple of watering holes that stay open late, though. Salty sea dogs gravitate to the no-frills **Bananas Guesthouse, Beach Bar & Grill** (142 Calle Flamboyán, Esperanza, 787/718-6349, www.bananasvqs.com, daily 11am-10pm, bar stays open later), a delightfully funky oceanfront bar and restaurant where happy hour is held twice a day every day, from 11am-12:30pm and 5pm-7pm. There's also a robust menu of sandwiches, salads, seafood, and mofongo, as well as a rooftop terrace open Thursday-Sunday from 4:30pm-10pm. There are four small guest rooms on-site if you need a place to crash.

Saint Voodoo's Mar Azul (577 German Rieckehoff, Isabel Segunda, 787/741-3400, Sun.-Tues. 9am-midnight, Thurs.-Fri. 4pm-midnight, Sat. 9am-2am) is purple and has a lot of goth touches. It's a dive bar in all the best ways, and it boasts unparalleled views of the sunset. Happy hour is every night 5pm-7:30pm, and there's karaoke starting at 9pm on Saturdays. A light menu of bar grub is served, including burgers, fries, and fish tacos, plus daily specials.

Lazy Jack's Pub (corner of Calle Orquideas and Calle Flamboyán, on the *malecón*, Esperanza, 787/741-1447, www.lazyjacksvieques.com, Sun.-Thurs. 8:30am-1am, Fri.-Sat. 8:30am-2:30am, kitchen open daily until midnight, $8-16) serves food, but the reason to come is the well-stocked bar, featuring a huge list of beers and specialty cocktails such as strawberry daiquiri, Jack's Rum Punch, and a Lazy Lime Killer. It also serves a robust menu of pizzas, salads, wraps, burgers, wings, and fish tacos. There's a hostel, too.

Duffy's Esperanza (140 Calle Flamboyán, on the *malecón*, 787/435-6585, www.duffysesperanza.com, daily 11am-11pm or later, kitchen 11am-10pm, $3-16) is primarily a great open-air bar where you can down a few cold ones, rub elbows with the locals, and watch the ocean waves roll in. The bar serves a selection of craft beers and a menu of creative cocktails, including the Viequense, a combination of vodka, passion fruit liqueur, orange juice, and cranberry juice. The menu features pub fare including burgers, wraps, nachos, and wings. Flamboyán Guesthouse is located upstairs.

Festivals and Events

There are two major festivals in Vieques. The biggest one is **Fiestas Patronales de Nuestra Señora del Carmen** (787/741-5000), which is held on the plaza of Isabel Segunda Wednesday-Sunday during the third weekend of July. Attractions include parades, religious processions, a small carnival, and lots of live salsa music and dancing. Entertainment usually starts around 9pm and lasts until the wee hours of the morning. Festivities are fueled by *bili*, a traditional beverage made from a local fruit called *quenepa* mixed with white rum, cinnamon, and sugar.

The other big event is the **Cultural Festival** (787/741-1717), sponsored by the Institute of Puerto Rican Culture at El Fortín Conde de Mirasol in Isabel Segunda after Easter. Festivities include folk music and dance performances, a craft fair, and a book fair.

SHOPPING

At first glance you might think **Vieques Flower and Gifts** (134 Calle Flamboyán, Esperanza, 413/522-6590, Nov.-May daily 9am-6pm, June-Oct. daily 10am-5pm) is another souvenir shop selling T-shirts and tchotchkes, but you'll also find artisan-made *vejigante* masks and pottery by local artists.

Siddhia Hutchinson/Glen Wielgus Gallery Vieques (123 Calle Muñoz Rivera, Isabel Segunda, 787/741-1343, www.hutchinsonwielgusgallery.com, Nov.-Apr. Mon.-Sat. 9am-5pm, May-July Mon.-Sat. 9am-3pm) represents more than a dozen contemporary Caribbean artists working in a variety of mediums.

Oro (PR 201, km 7.1, Playa Negra, no phone, http://orovieques.com) is a large fine art gallery with beautiful grounds that represents more than 20 Puerto Rican artists and artisans. It also hosts changing exhibitions and special events, including performing arts and weddings.

Mama Playa Himalaya (350 Calle Antonio G. Mellado, Isabel Segunda, 787/548-1010, Mon.-Sat. 10am-5pm) sells imported Indian and Caribbean women's tropical clothing, including floral dresses, sarongs, and bags, as well as original designs by owner Ute Hanna.

Scallywags (575 German Rieckehoff, Isabel Segunda, 787/966-7540, www.scallywagsvieques.com, Mon.-Sat. 10am-6pm, Sun. 10am-3pm) sells beachwear, bathing suits, jewelry, and more. The shop also rents beach chairs, umbrellas, snorkel gear, paddleboards, and kayaks. You can also book snorkel trips and dives with Blackbeard Sports here.

FOOD
Puerto Rican

It doesn't get any more casual than ★ **El Guayacán** (134 Calle Flamboyán, Esperanza, Wed.-Sun. 5pm-midnight, $15-20). This one-man operation offers just a couple of tables on a street-front patio and a limited menu of dishes, but the food is consistently outstanding. Except for the *tostones*, options change daily and may include whole fried snapper in pesto sauce, chicken stew, mofongo, and pork chops.

For breakfast sandwiches, mofongo, rice and beans, and other traditional Puerto Rican

fare, ★ **El Resuelve** (PR 997, km 1, Isabel Segunda, 787/741-1427, Thurs.-Sat. 9am-9pm, Sun. 9am-6pm, $2-12, cash only) serves it fresh and cheap in a small, modest spot with patio dining in a residential neighborhood. Stop by and pick up a bag of empanadas for $2 apiece on your way to the beach.

Restaurante Bili (144 Calle Flamboyán, 787/741-1382 or 787/402-0357, www.facebook.com/RestauranteBili, Thurs.-Sat. 5pm-11pm, Sun.-Mon. 5pm-10pm, $10-29) is a veteran restaurant that has been in business for many years. The menu serves Puerto Rican cuisine with an emphasis on seafood, including whole fried snapper. The fresh and fruity cocktails are superb. Beware, though: Service can be slow to nonexistent.

Bieke's Bistro (787/741-6381, 34001 Calle Antonio Mellado, Isabel Segunda, www.biekesbistro.com, Tues.-Sat. 10:30am-9:30pm, $18-29) serves a slightly upscale version of *criolla* cuisine, featuring churrasco, mofongo, fried snapper, and lobster tail.

★ **El Quenepo** (148 Calle Flamboyán, Esperanza, 787/741-1215, www.elquenepovieques.com, mid-Nov.-Aug. Tues.-Sat. 5:30pm-close, $20-32) is hands-down the finest restaurant in Vieques. Owner-chef Scott Cole creates sublime new interpretations of *criolla* cuisine, and his wife, Kate, who runs the front of the house, knows how to provide the kind of service diners expect from a top-dollar establishment. Together they have created a casually elegant oasis of fine dining. Open to the sea on one side, the interior is hung with long white sheers, and wall sconces provide just enough lighting to make everyone look more attractive than they really are. Soft jazz noodles in the background. The effect is instantly calming. And then there is the food. The menu changes but may include calabaza gnocchi pan-seared in brown butter and served with toasted pumpkin seeds, goat cheese, and pomegranate molasses; jasmine rice-crusted calamari, Peking duck pad Thai; and breadfruit mofongo stuffed with lobster.

La Placita (El Blok, 158 Calle Flamboyán, Esperanza, 787/741-6020, www.elblok.com,

Wed.-Sun. 5pm-10pm, $20-35) is a fine dining restaurant specializing in generous servings of creative Caribbean cuisine including house-cured anchovies, grilled swordfish with yuca mofongo, ceviche, *tostone* sliders, and lobster pasta. The industrial-chic dining room provides a sophisticated backdrop to an exquisite meal. There are lots of vegetarian options, too.

Locals' favorite **El Yate Bar & Restaurant** (Calle Rieckehoff across from the ferry dock, Isabel Segunda, 787/741-4191, daily 8am-10pm, $8-25) is tiny bare-bones restaurant located in the middle of a fork in the road, serving traditional Puerto Rican cuisine from empanadas to mofongo.

The main reason to go to **El Local** (51 Calle Antonio G. Mellado, Isabel Segunda, 787/245-0936, www.ellocal00765.com, Mon.-Sat. 5pm-11pm, $17-28) is to sit under the *quenepa* tree on the large, lovely patio at night and sip on outstanding craft cocktails like the El Pilon, made with gin, fresh lime, and guava juice. The dinner menu features upscale variations on Puerto Rican dishes including churrasco, whole fried snapper, and shrimp in garlic or *criolla* sauce.

Taste a smorgasbord of Puerto Rican flavors at **Vieques Food Park** (PR 200, km 0.6, 939/358-1783 or 787/219-3030, Mon.-Thurs.

6am-9pm, Fri.-Sat. 6am-10pm, Sun. 6am-5pm, $8-15), a food truck park with outdoor dining. One of the best trucks here is ★ **Rincón del Sabor** (939/358-1783, Mon.-Thurs. 11am-9pm, Fri.-Sat. 11-10pm, Sun. 11am-5pm), specializing in fresh seafood and mofongo.

International

Coqui Fire is the name of a popular, locally made hot sauce ubiquitous in gift shops across the island. The sauce's creator also has a restaurant called ★ **Coqui Fire Café** (421 Calle Carlos Lebrum, Isabel Segunda, 787/741-0401, www.facebook.com/CoquiFire, Mon.-Fri. 5pm-9pm, $8-30). Located in a small yellow house, the casual eatery serves Caribbean-inspired Mexican cuisine. This is a popular spot, so reservations are highly recommended. Between the crowds and the open kitchen, the dining room can feel hot and chaotic, but it's worth it for the food, especially the blackened shrimp with coconut mole and cherry almond cayenne cheesecake.

Taverna (453 Calle Carlos LeBrum, Isabel Segunda, 787/438-1100, www.facebook.com/tavernavieques, Jan.-Apr. Sun.-Thurs. 5:30pm-9pm, $9-28) serves up generous portions of traditional Italian-American cuisine from

Scallywags in Isabel Segunda on Vieques
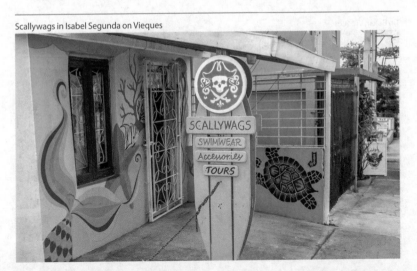

brick oven pizzas to spaghetti Bolognese to crème brûlée.

Located in the lower level of the bright pink Baroque building in downtown Isabel Segunda, ★ **Roy's Martinis & Tapas** (355 Calle Antonio G. Mellado, Isabel Segunda, no phone, Sun.-Mon. 4pm-10pm, $5-16) is a delightful patio restaurant tricked out in mismatched tables and chairs, tons of potted plants, and large portraits of celebrity icons such as Bette Midler, Elvis, and Mary Tyler Moore. While recordings of 1930s-era chanteuses play softly in the background, sip on a crisp, dry martini and dine on small plates of shepherd's pie or gnocchi in a marinara sauce with bacon, ricotta, and Parmesan cheese. But don't get too attached to a dish; the menu changes on the whim of this creative proprietor.

Seafood and Steak

★ **Tin Box** (PR 996 at PR 201, 787/435-6064, www.facebook.com/TinBoxVQS, Wed.-Sun. 4pm-9pm, $16-28) is a rustic open-air spot constructed of corrugated metal with a beautiful deck in back overlooking the forest. The menu specializes in smoked meats and seafood, including ribs, tacos, steaks, and po'boys.

Trade Winds Restaurant (Calle Flamboyán, Esperanza, 787/672-9927 or 787/436-7889, www.tradewindsvieques.com, daily 7:30am-9pm, $16-34) is a casual open-air restaurant that overlooks the water and serves grilled fish, steak, lobster, pork loin, pasta, mofongo, and coconut curry. For dessert, try the piña colada bread pudding with warm rum sauce. Reservations are recommended. There are 10 small guest rooms behind the restaurant.

Café del Mar (150 Calle Flamboyán, Esperanza, 787/248-2097, Wed.-Sat. 8am-11am and 5pm-10pm, Sun. 9am-2pm and 5pm-10pm, 787/248-2097, $10-26) is an inviting open-air restaurant on the main strip through Esperanza serving whole fried snapper, ceviche, and pasta dishes. Sunday brunch (9am-2pm) features churrasco and eggs, huevos rancheros, and banana or blueberry pancakes.

Classic American

Bananas Guesthouse, Beach Bar & Grill (142 Calle Flamboyán, Esperanza, 787/718-6349, www.bananasvqs.com, daily 11am-10pm, bar stays open later, $5-17) is a casual drinking hole serving mostly American pub fare, including burgers, wings, and hot dogs, as well as jerk chicken, ribs, and grilled fish.

Tin Box in Vieques

Breakfast and Lunch

Rising Roost Market & Cafe (110 Calle Muñoz River, Isabel Segunda, Thurs.-Mon. 7:30am-12:30pm, $2-12) is a bohemian-style breakfast and brunch spot in a pink house, serving eggs, hash browns, avocado toast, smoothies, juices, coffee, and more. There's also a market selling locally made souvenirs, food items, and gift baskets.

Carambola (Inn at the Blue Horizon, Calle Flamboyán, west of Esperanza, 787/741-3318, www.innonthebluehorizon.com, Sat.-Sun. 7am-2pm, $6-16) is the place to go for brunch with a view. Dine on omelets, pancakes, frittatas, or huevos rancheros while admiring the ocean view.

With its eye-popping colors of pink, yellow, and turquoise, you can't miss **D'Frozz** (105 Calle Muñoz Rivera, Isabel Segunda, 787/239-4081, www.facebook.com/downtowncreamfactory, Mon.-Thurs. 7am-9pm, Fri.-Sun. 7am-10pm, $6-9). It bills itself as an artisanal ice cream and coffee bar, but it serves a large menu of breakfast dishes and sandwiches, too, including bacon and eggs, pancakes, wraps, and quesadillas. Ice cream flavors include red velvet cake, Nutella, almond, and *malanga* (taro).

Locals know to call their orders in ahead of time because service is excruciatingly slow, but the Cubano sandwich is worth the wait at ★ **Panadería La Viequense** (352 Calle Antonio Mellado, Isabel Segunda, 787/741-8213, Mon.-Sat. 6am-4pm, Sun. 6am-2pm, $5-11). Coffee drinks, egg dishes, and a large glass case of pastries round out the menu.

Farmers Markets and Groceries

For a nice selection of fresh local produce, visit **Vieques Farmers Market** (PR 201, just south of PR 200, Isabel Segunda, 787/407-0392, Tues. and Fri. 7:30am-6pm) and **Vieques Fruit Truck** (intersection of PR 997 and PR 200, Isabel Segunda, daily until 5 or so). Try the green speckled oranges. They are sweet and juicy.

Buen Provecho (123 Calle Muñoz Rivera, Isabel Segunda, 787/529-7316, Mon.-Sat. 10am-6pm) is a gourmet market selling organic goods, fresh produce, butcher-cut meats, and specialty food items, including artisan cheeses and live lobsters. There's a small counter in the back, serving breakfast, salads, and sandwiches ($10-12), as well craft beer and cocktails.

They're more modestly stocked than the grocery stores on the main island, but you can find most anything you need to cook a meal at **Superdescuentos Morales** (PR 200, near the gas station, 787/741-6701, Mon.-Sat. 7am-7pm, Sun. 7am-noon) and **Supermercado Morales** (Calle Baldorioty de Castro, downtown Isabel Segunda, 787/741-2251, Mon.-Sat. 7am-5pm, Sun. 8am-noon).

The Green Store/La Tienda Verde (corner of Calle Flamboyán/PR 996 and Calle Robles, Esperanza, 787/741-8711, daily 9am-9pm) is a convenience store selling all the dry goods and beverages you'll need to set up house for a week—coffee, toilet paper, bug spray, beer, water, etc.

ACCOMMODATIONS

There are a large number of privately owned guesthouses, vacation rentals, and house shares in Vieques. If you want to live like a local, check out the options at Airbnb.com, HomeAway.com, or Vrbo.com.

Under $100

Overnight camping is permitted in a small, lightly shaded area at **Balneario Sun Bay** (PR 997, east of Esperanza, 787/741-8198, parking $4 vehicles, $2 motorcycles) for $10 a night. Tents are permitted but not required. Facilities include picnic tables, grills, toilets, and outdoor showers.

Located on the grounds of Lazy Jack's Pub, **Lazy Hostel** (corner of Calle Orquideas and Calle Flamboyán, on the *malecón*, Esperanza, 787/741-5555, www.lazyhostel.com) offers basic accommodations in mixed gender and female-only dorms ($25) and private bedrooms ($55-65), some with en suite bathrooms. Amenities include free wireless Internet in common areas and a shared kitchen. Located across the street from the ocean, Lazy Hostel offers a work-stay program for guests who want to extend their stay. **Villa Coral Guesthouse** (485 Calle Gladiolas, Esperanza, 787/981-741-6335, www. villacoralguesthouse.com, $89, $160-185 suite) is a clean, comfortable six-room guesthouse in a residential neighborhood several blocks from the *malecón*. Rooms come with a queen bed, window air-conditioning unit, ceiling fan, a mini refrigerator, and a coffeepot. There's a covered porch with wireless Internet, board games, magazines, and a microwave, plus a rooftop terrace with a view of the ocean. The owners also have a one-bedroom cottage with a full kitchen and satellite TV a couple of blocks away that rents for $795-895 a week.

Just want a cheap place to crash? If you don't plan to spend much time in your room, **Bananas Guesthouse, Beach Bar & Grill** (142 Calle Flamboyán, Esperanza, 787/741-8700, www.bananasvqs.com, $70-100) may meet your needs. In the back of the popular Bananas bar and restaurant, this bare-bones guesthouse has four basic rooms with deck flooring. There's no TV or telephone, but some rooms have air-conditioning, screened porches, and mini refrigerators.

$100-150

If you don't mind the noise of late-night partiers downstairs, **Flamboyán Guesthouse** (140 Calle Flamboyán, on the malecón, 787/435-6585, www.flamboyanvqs.com, $102-120) offers four guest rooms above Duffy's Esperanza. All rooms come with air-conditioning, private bathrooms, and a patio overlooking the ocean.

Trade Winds Guest House and Restaurant (Calle Flamboyán, Esperanza, 787/741-8666, www.tradewindsvieques.com, $115-140) is a simple, basic guesthouse conveniently situated in the middle of Esperanza and across the street from the *malécon* (sea walk). The 10 rooms are small, windowless, and spartan, but they're clean and have firm mattresses. Rooms come with mini refrigerators, wireless Internet, and continental breakfast. There's no TV or telephone, but some rooms have air-conditioning. The rooms open onto a scrappy courtyard with plastic patio furniture, and there's a restaurant and bar upstairs.

$150-250

For a unique experience that is both rustic and stylish, **Finca Victoria** (PR 995, km 2.2, 787/646-0011, www.lafinca.com, $139-199) is a beautiful three-acre spread located in the island's interior on one of its highest points. Accommodations are provided in a variety of individually decorated and innovatively designed structures that contain suites, apartments, lofts, and tiny houses. Vintage furnishings, elegant lighting, and original artwork fill the rooms, which come with bathrooms, outdoor showers, mini refrigerators, terraces, and hammocks. Some have kitchenettes. Amenities include a saltwater pool, common kitchen, complimentary vegetarian breakfast, yoga, and all the fruit you want from the garden. There is no air-conditioning, TV, or wireless Internet.

If you like the convenience of staying in the heart of town, **The Wave Hotel** (571 Calle Plinio Peterson, Isabel Segunda, 787/741-1793 or 314/481-0317, www.thewaveveiques.com, $100-270) offers modest, oceanfront accommodations with private bathrooms, and wireless Internet in the lobby. Some rooms have terraces.

Bravo Beach Hotel (1 N. Shore Rd., Isabel Segunda, 939/260-0110, www.bravobeach-hotel.com, $90-189, $202 suite, two-night minimum) features nine guestrooms and a two-bedroom apartment ($315) in a cluster of small bungalows. Each room is different, but the spacious interiors all feature stark white walls and dark mahogany furnishings. Some rooms have oceanview balconies and floor-to-ceiling windows, and there's one suite with 180-degree windows and a king-size four-poster bed. Across the street is Casa Roja, which has one- and two-bedroom apartments ($104-180). Amenities include satellite

TV, air-conditioning, a mini refrigerator, and wireless Internet. Although it's on the ocean, the hotel doesn't have a swimmable beach, but there are two swimming pools, one oceanside.

There's something positively Mediterranean about the exterior appearance of **Casa La Lanchita** (374 N. Shore Rd., Isabel Segunda, 845/891-1502 or 787/741-5139, www.casalalanchita.com, $135-180, $210 suite). The bright white four-story structure with archways and balustrades is built right on the sandy beach of a brilliant blue sea and is surrounded by flowering bougainvillea. Despite the posh exterior, the rooms are modestly appointed with dated furnishings, but each room has a private terrace, living room, and kitchen.

★ **Malecón House** (105 Calle Flamboyán, Esperanza, 939/239-7113, www.maleconhouse.com, $180-210) is a modern two-story guesthouse overlooking the *malecón*. It was built in 2010 and has brought a new level of sophistication to the area. Rooms come with air-conditioning and ceiling fans; some rooms have mini refrigerators and balconies. Amenities include a small pool, rooftop deck, wireless Internet, and continental breakfast.

Over $250

Tropical Victorian elegance is the theme at **Hacienda Tamarindo** (Calle Flamboyán, just west of Esperanza, 787/741-8525, www.haciendatamarindo.com, $219-265, $392 villa). Built around a 245-year-old tamarind tree that's rooted in the lobby and shades the 2nd-floor breakfast room, this beautifully appointed hotel is furnished in a tasteful combination of antique Caribbean and Victorian styles. Folk art, wall murals, and vintage circus posters provide playful touches. There are 17 guestrooms and suites. Each one is different, but they all contain basket-weave furnishings, brightly colored bedspreads, and air-conditioning. Rooms have neither TVs nor telephones, but each one comes with folding chairs, oversize towels, and coolers for the beach or pool. The hotel doesn't have a restaurant per se, but it does serve a free breakfast, and a box lunch can be prepared if requested the night before. There's a 24-hour honor bar and a swimming pool. Some rooms require a three-night minimum stay. No guests under age 15 are permitted during high season.

A romantic getaway doesn't get any lovelier or secluded than **Inn on the Blue Horizon** (PR 996, km 4.3, west of Esperanza, 787/741-3318 or 787/741-0527, www.innonthebluehorizon.com, $360-500, no children 16 or younger). The small, 10-room inn has undergone a complete renovation since Hurricane Maria. It is perched on a cliff overlooking the ocean and is geared primarily toward couples. Rooms are exquisitely furnished with four-poster beds, antiques, and original artwork. Amenities include a small gym, pool, lighted tennis courts, and an inviting pavilion bar. Rooms have air-conditioning but no TV or telephone. **Carambola** restaurant serves brunch on the weekends, but has plans to expand service.

Avant-garde architecture in a thickly wooded setting distinguishes the most unusual hotel in Puerto Rico, **The Hix House** (PR 995, km 1.5, 787/435-4590, www.hixislandhouse.com, $175-415, $435-455 loft). Five unpainted concrete buildings house 19 industrial-chic lofts, many with open sides, outdoor showers, terraces, and ocean views. Designed by architect John Hix to have as little impact on its 13 acres as possible, the property uses solar energy and recycles used water to replenish the vegetation. There's no TV or telephone, and wireless Internet is restricted to the lobby, but the linens are Frette, the pool is spectacular, and each morning the kitchen is stocked with juices, cereal, breads, and coffee. Yoga classes are conducted in the pavilion, and in-room or garden massages are available. New to the property is Casa Solaris, an all-solar guesthouse with one- and two-bedroom lofts.

In 2014 ★ **El Blok** (Calle Flamboyán, Esperanza, 787/741-6020, www.elblok.com, $250-290), a new 22-room luxury boutique hotel opened and brought a fresh, retro-modern style of glamour to the funky seaside strip in Esperanza. Featuring a stunning architectural design by Fuster+Architects, the four-story hotel boasts a striking curved shape and lacy concrete facade that recalls the midcentury modern design of some of San Juan's grand hotels, such as Caribe Hilton. The rooms are designed in a minimalist style featuring industrial-chic plaster walls and tile floors. All rooms have forest or ocean views, terraces, flat-screen TVs, and wireless Internet. There's a small rooftop pool, a lobby bar, and a restaurant, Placita (Wed.-Sun.), serving creative Caribbean cuisine for dinner. On weekends, you'll often find DJs or live musicians performing in the rooftop bar. It's not the place to stay if you're sensitive to noise at night. The music in the bar can get loud.

TRANSPORTATION
Air

As almost anyone who's taken the ferry from Ceiba to Vieques will tell you, the best way to get to the island is by air. Several small airlines fly to Vieques from the main island, and the flights are relatively inexpensive and short in duration.

In San Juan, flights can be arranged from

Luis Muñoz Marín International Airport near Isla Verde or from the smaller Isla Grande Airport near Viejo San Juan. Flights are about 30 minutes. But the cheapest flight is from José Aponte de la Torre Airport on the former Roosevelt Roads Naval Base in Ceiba on the east coast. The flight takes about 15 minutes.

Antonio Rivera Rodríguez Airport (VQS) near Isabel Segunda is a small, two-level structure, but a new wing was added in 2019 to service passengers on Vieques Air Link. There is no ATM or rental car agency on-site. Visitors must call their rental car companies to request pickup when they land. It may take up to an hour for them to arrive. Located outside the upper level of the main building by the back parking lot is **Isla Nena Café** (daily 9am-7pm, $3-6), which serves coffee, cocktails, beer, burgers, hot dogs, and breakfast dishes.

Vieques Air Link (787/741-8331, www.viequesairlink.com) offers flights to Vieques from San Juan International, Isla Grande, St. Croix, and Ceiba. **Seaborne Airlines** (866/359-8784, www.seaborneairlines.com) flies to Vieques from San Juan International, Isla Grande, St. Thomas, and St. Croix. **Air Sunshine** (954/434-8900, www.airsunshine.com) has flights to Vieques from San

Antonio Rivera Rodríguez Airport in Vieques

Juan International. **Cape Air** (800/227-3247, www.capeair.com) offers flights to Vieques from San Juan International.

For travel to and from Ceiba, Vieques, Culebra, St. Thomas, and Tortola, **Taxi Aero** (Jose Aponte de Torre airport in Ceiba, 787/718-8869, https://taxiaeropr.travel, daily 7am-6pm) offers on-demand charter service. Pets up to 40 pounds fly for free. One-way fares start at $180 for 1-3 people from Ceiba or $475 for 1-3 people from San Juan.

Ferry

Operated by the Puerto Rico Port Authority, the **passenger ferry** (787/497-7740, www.porferry.com, $5.35 one way) provides daily transportation between Vieques and Ceiba, as well as between Vieques and Culebra. But if your travel schedule is not flexible, flying is a better option. The ferry operation is plagued with scheduling irregularities and overcrowding. Weather conditions also affect schedules. In addition, ticket holders are not guaranteed a seat because Puerto Rican residents get priority. Note that ferries are particularly crowded on holiday weekends.

If you have flexibility on when you arrive and depart, the ferry can be a pleasant ride, lasting 30 to 45 minutes. If you do take the ferry, buy your tickets one week in advance online. Only 20 percent of tickets are sold online, so even if the ferry you select appears sold out, you may be able to buy tickets at the gate, beginning one hour prior to departure. On your day of departure, be sure to check the schedule online because it is subject to change.

There is also a **cargo ferry** with a limited amount of passenger space. Car rental companies in Puerto Rico do not permit their cars to be transported to Vieques or Culebra, so plan to park your car on the main island and rent another mode of transportation in Vieques and Culebra.

Car

To get the most out of your stay in Vieques, you're going to need a rental car or golf cart to get around, especially if you want to explore the island's remote beaches. A taxi service and *públicos* are a great way to get from the ferry or airport to your hotel, but beyond that, neither service is as reliable as the taxi service mainland Americans may be accustomed to.

If you do rent a car, book it at least a month in advance of your arrival. They get snapped up quickly, especially on holiday weekends. Rental fees start around $80 per day, and penalties can be accrued if you return it with excessive sand inside, damp seats, or less gas in the tank than when you got it. Most vehicles are four-wheel drive because many of the beaches require off-roading to reach them. Blowouts are not unusual, so make sure your car has a full-size replacement tire and the tools necessary to change it. If you need assistance changing the tire, the rental-car agency may send someone to help, but it will cost you. The seat belt law is enforced, as are speed limits, which are mostly 35 miles per hour, except in town and on beach roads, where it's 10-15 miles per hour.

Several gas stations can be found along PR 200 near Isabel Segunda, west of the plaza. Because gas is shipped from San Juan on weekdays only, gas shortages are not unusual on holiday weekends when the island is crowded. And sometimes gas stations close early on Sundays, since that's the day many people go to the beach, including the gas-station operators.

Car rental agencies on Vieques include **Martineau Car Rental** (787/500-1666 or 787/741-0078, www.maritzascarrental.com), **Vieques Car** (km 0.8, 787/742-8540, http://viequescarrental.com), **Coqui Car Rental** (787/741-0190 or 787/741-3696, www.coquicarrental.com), and **Island Jeep Rental** (787/741-0190, www.islandjeeprental.com). All provide transportation to and from the airport and the ferry dock to their rental agency offices, or will deliver their vehicles to your location. Remember that horses roam freely on Vieques. Because many roads in Vieques are unlit, it's nearly impossible to see the horses in the dark, so take extra care when driving at night.

If you want to feel the breeze in your face, **Scooters for Rent** (346 Calle Antonio G. Medallo, Isabel Segunda, 939/437-2053, www.scootersvieques.com) rents motorized two-wheelers (from $40/day), UTVs (from $75/day), and golf carts (from $65/day).

Público

Públicos are vans operated by individuals who provide transportation on the island. They are an economical way to get around, but they're not particularly expedient. Expect to share your ride with others who are going to different destinations, which can add time and distance to your journey, depending on how many stops are on the way. Fares are typically $5 around town and $10 to various sites on the island. You can usually pick up a list of *público* operators at the airport or your hotel. They include **Jose Morales** (787/435-4227), **Letty Perez Kiani Tours** (787/556-6003), and **Juanito** (787/645-2329).

Taxi and Car Service

Vieques Taxi (787/741-8294) typically provides transportation up until 10pm, but late-night service may be arranged in advance. **741Taxi** (787/741-8294, www.741taxi.com) offers taxi service throughout the island with bilingual operators driving Jeep Wranglers.

Travel can be arranged in advance through **Vieques Island Tours and Transportation** (PR 996, 787/397-2048).

SERVICES

Most services on Vieques are in Isabel Segunda. You'll find the **police station** (787/741-2020 or 787/741-2121) at the corner of PR 200 and PR 997, and the **fire department** (787/741-2111) can be reached by phone. Serving visitors' pharmacy needs is **Farmacia Rey** (52 Calle Benitez Guzman, 787/741-8397, http://farmaciareypr.com).

There are several ATMs on the island, including at **Banco Popular** (115 Calle Muñoz Rivera, 787/741-2071). Nearby, on the same street, is the **post office** (787/741-3891). **Familia Ríos** (Calle Benítez Castaño, 787/556-5518) provides a self-serve laundry service.

The island's hospital was destroyed by Hurricane Maria in 2017 and has not yet been reopened.

Culebra

As laid-back as Vieques is, it's practically Las Vegas compared to Culebra. Halfway between mainland Puerto Rico and St. Thomas, the tiny amoeba-shaped archipelago with 23 surrounding cays is just four miles by seven miles. The island is home to 3,000 residents and has one small community—**Dewey** (commonly called "Pueblo" or "Town")—on **Ensenada Honda harbor,** where the ferry docks.

Culebra has yet to be discovered by the tourism industry, but experienced divers know it as one of the best underwater spots in the Caribbean. The clear, clean waters are practically untouched by people and their polluting by-products, thanks in part to the arid island's absence of rivers or streams. The result is superb visibility and healthy, intact coral systems that support a wide variety of sea life.

In 1909, recognizing the island's vital role as a natural wildlife habitat, President Theodore Roosevelt proclaimed much of the island a National Wildlife Refuge, which today encompasses 1,568 acres. Nonetheless, in 1939 the U.S. Navy made Culebra its primary gunnery and bomb practice site and continued its operations here until 1975, when it turned its focus to Vieques.

The island is a combination of hilly terrain with dry subtropical forest and a highly irregular coastline punctuated by cliffs,

Culebra

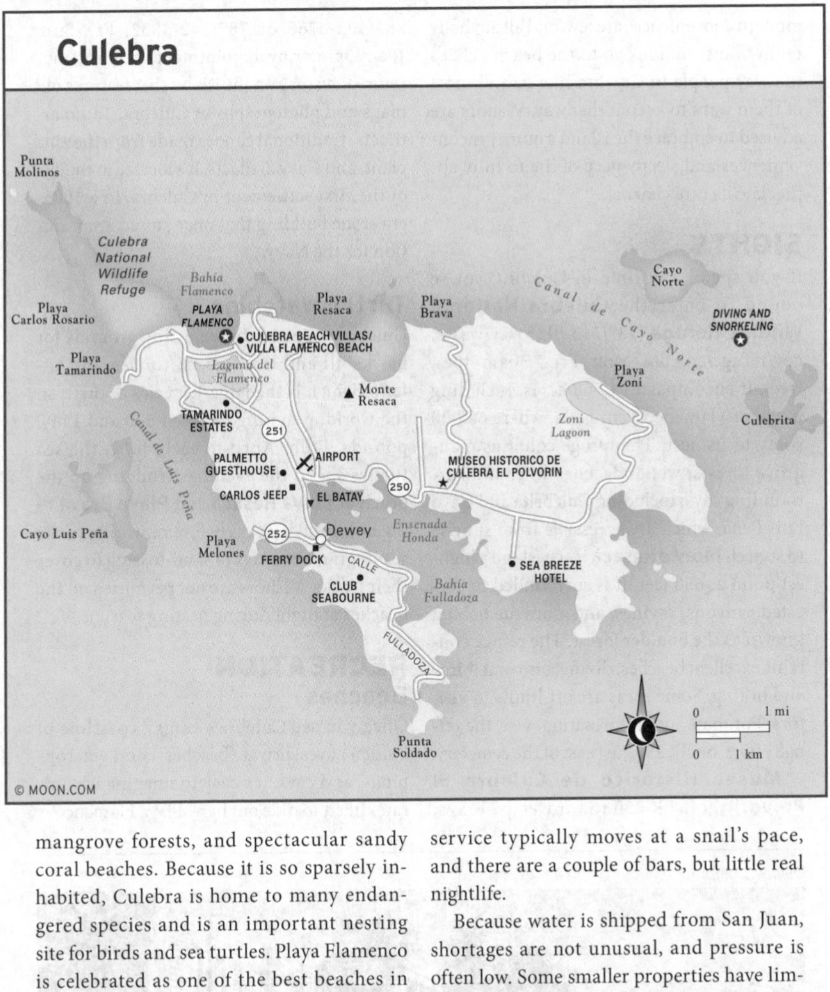
Punta Molinos
Culebra National Wildlife Refuge
Bahía Flamenco
Playa Carlos Rosario
PLAYA FLAMENCO
CULEBRA BEACH VILLAS/ VILLA FLAMENCO BEACH
Playa Resaca
Playa Brava
Canal de Cayo Norte
Cayo Norte
DIVING AND SNORKELING
Playa Tamarindo
Laguna del Flamenco
Monte Resaca
Playa Zoni
TAMARINDO ESTATES
Canal de Luis Peña
251
Zoni Lagoon
Culebrita
PALMETTO GUESTHOUSE
AIRPORT
MUSEO HISTORICO DE CULEBRA EL POLVORIN
CARLOS JEEP
250
EL BATAY
Cayo Luis Peña
252
Dewey
Ensenada Honda
Playa Melones
FERRY DOCK
CALLE
SEA BREEZE HOTEL
CLUB SEABOURNE
Bahía Fulladoza
FULLADOZA
0
1 mi
0
1 km
Punta Soldado
© MOON.COM

mangrove forests, and spectacular sandy coral beaches. Because it is so sparsely inhabited, Culebra is home to many endangered species and is an important nesting site for birds and sea turtles. Playa Flamenco is celebrated as one of the best beaches in the United States. But there are many other smaller beaches to discover, some completely deserted much of the time.

Accommodations in Culebra are mostly small mom-and-pop guesthouses, some little more than spare bedrooms. The operations here are mostly self-serve. In fact, it's not unusual for visitors to have the run of the place when owners decide to head to the beach or bar to while away the day. But a handful of small luxury hotels and condo rental units service travelers who want more modern-day amenities. At the dozen or so restaurants, service typically moves at a snail's pace, and there are a couple of bars, but little real nightlife.

Because water is shipped from San Juan, shortages are not unusual, and pressure is often low. Some smaller properties have limited hot water or none at all. Plumbing in general can be problematic—the standard practice is to discard toilet paper in the trash instead of flushing it. And alarm clocks are never necessary, because you're sure to be woken by one of the roosters that roam the island. An anomaly in the world, Culebra is virtually crime-free. Instead of petty theft, visitors need only brace themselves against the voracious mosquitoes and sand gnats that tend to invade around dusk.

Culebra is one of the last vestiges of pre-tourism Puerto Rico. Nobody is in a hurry, modern conveniences are few, and all anybody really wants to do is go to the beach. That's the way people in Culebra like it, and most of them want to keep it that way. Visitors are advised to embrace the island's quirky inconveniences and sleepy pace of life to fully appreciate its rare charms.

SIGHTS

If you spend any time in Culebra, you're bound to enter the **Culebra National Wildlife Refuge** (787/742-0115, www.fws.gov/refuge/culebra, Mon.-Fri. 7:30am-4pm, free). It encompasses 1,568 acres, including much of Flamenco Peninsula, where 60,000 sooty terns nest. The refuge contains mangrove forests, wetlands, coastline, and surrounding cays, including Culebrita and Cayo Luis Peña, which are accessible from sunrise to sunset. **Monte Resaca** is the island's highest point at 650 feet. It is surrounded by forested canyons, ravines, and a unique habitat known as the boulder forest. The refuge contains excellent beaches, diving, bird-watching, and hiking. Some areas are off-limits to visitors. For maps and information, visit the refuge office, on PR 250, just east of the cemetery.

Museo Histórico de Culebra El Polvorin (off PR 250 toward Playa Brava, 787/405-3768 or 787/742-3832, Fri.-Sun. 10am-3pm or by appointment, free) is a museum of history on the island that features old maps and photographs of Culebra, Taíno artifacts, traditional canoes made from the zinc plant, and Navy artifacts. It's located at the site of the first settlement in Culebra, in a 1905-era stone building that once stored ammunition for the Navy.

Turtle-Watching

Culebra is one of three nesting grounds for hawksbill and leatherback turtles, the latter of which is the largest species of turtle in the world, weighing between 500 and 1,600 pounds. From April to early June, the sea turtles spend the evenings trudging up the beach at **Playa Resaca** and **Playa Brava** to dig holes and lay eggs before returning to the sea in grand displays of sand-tossing to cover their tracks. Visitors are not permitted on the beaches at night during nesting season.

RECREATION
Beaches

Once you see Culebra's craggy coastline of hidden coves, private beaches, coral outcroppings, and cays, it's easy to imagine why pirates liked to hide out here. Playa Flamenco is

Dewey, Culebra

Sea Turtles

sea turtle

One of the most magnificent sights you can witness in the waters around Vieques and Culebra is a sea turtle. A chance encounter is reason enough to go diving or snorkeling in the area. Three species of sea turtles can be found in the area; all of them are endangered and protected.

The **leatherback sea turtle** is the largest species of sea turtle, weighing between 500 and 1,600 pounds and reaching lengths from four to eight feet. It is distinguished by seven pronounced ridges that run down the length of the shell, which has a rubbery texture and is primarily black with white spots. Leatherback sea turtles feed mostly on jellyfish, but they also like to eat sea urchins, squids, crustaceans, fish, seaweed, and algae. They dive as deep as 4,200 feet and can stay submerged for up to 85 minutes.

The **green sea turtle** has a hard, smooth shell mottled in shades of black, gray, green, brown, and yellow. Its head is small and its lower jaw is hooked. It tops out at 350 pounds, is around three feet long, and is the only sea turtle that eats only plants.

The **hawksbill sea turtle** is the smallest species at 180 pounds and three feet long. It is distinguished by the serrated edges of its shell, its beak-shaped mouth, and the brown-and-white pattern of its shell and skin. The hawksbill lives in coral reefs and primarily eats sea sponges but also sea anemones, jellyfish, and Portuguese man-of-wars.

Sea turtles mate every couple of years, and the females return to the beaches of their birth to lay their eggs in pits they dig in the sand. When they hatch, the tiny turtles crawl to the water, where they swim to offshore feeding sites. This is a vulnerable time in their life cycle because birds and lizards feed on the eggs and hatchlings. Nesting mostly occurs April through June, although it can be anytime between March and October, depending on the species. During that time, beaches may be closed to the public unless they are part of a turtle watch program, approved by the Puerto Rico Department of Natural and Environmental Resources.

For more information about conservation efforts and ecotourism opportunities, visit the **Wider Caribbean Coastal Sea Turtle Conservation Network**'s website at www. widecast.org.

the island's most celebrated beach, and rightly so. But there are many less-populated and more-remote beaches to be found for those willing to hike in.

If Playa Flamenco is too crowded, take a 20-minute hike from the Playa Flamenco parking lot westward over the ridge along a sandy path. Bypass the first small beach you encounter to reach the more private **Playa Carlos Rosario,** a pleasant, narrow beach flanked by coral reef and boulders. It offers excellent snorkeling around the long, vibrant stretch of coral reef not too far offshore. Other great snorkeling and diving beaches are **Punta Soldado** (south of town, at the end of Calle Fulladoza), which also has beautiful coral reefs; **Playa Melones,** a rocky beach and subtropical forest within walking distance of town; and **Playa Tamarindo,** near Tamarindo Estates off PR 251, where you'll find a diversity of soft corals and sea anemones. At the far eastern side of Culebra at the end of PR 250 is **Playa Zoni,** which features a deserted sandy beach and great views of Culebrita, Cayo Norte, and St. Thomas.

Excellent deserted beaches can also be found on two of Culebra's cays—**Cayo Luis Peña** and **Culebrita,** the latter of which is distinguished by a lovely but crumbling abandoned lighthouse and several tidal pools. To gain access, secure transportation on a water taxi. Providers include **Puerto Rico Water Taxi** (787/231-9365, www.prwatertaxi.com), **H2O Water Taxi** (787/685-5815, www.facebook.com/h2owatertaxi, daily 9am-5pm) and **Cayo Water Taxi** (787/376-9980, daily 7am-9pm). Be sure to bring water, sunscreen, snacks, a towel, and a hat. There are no facilities or stores on the islands.

Playa Brava has the biggest surf on the island, but it requires a bit of a hike to get there. To reach the trailhead, travel east on PR 250 and turn left after the cemetery, and then hike downhill and fork to the left. Note that Playa Brava is a turtle-nesting site, so it may be off-limits during nesting season from April to June.

Like Playa Brava, **Playa Resaca** is an important nesting site for sea turtles and it is ill-suited for swimming because of the coral reef along the beach. The hike to Playa Resaca is fairly arduous, but it traverses a fascinating topography through a mangrove and boulder forest. To get there, turn on the road just east of the airport off PR 250, drive to the end, and hike the rest of the way in.

★ PLAYA FLAMENCO

Named one of "America's Best Beaches" by the Travel Channel, **Playa Flamenco** (north on PR 251 at dead-end) is one of the main reasons people come to Culebra. It's a wide, mile-long, horseshoe-shaped beach with calm, shallow waters and fine white sand. The island's only publicly maintained beach, it has bathroom facilities, picnic tables, lounge-chair and umbrella rentals, and a camping area. There's a large parking lot and lots of food and beverage vendors serving sandwiches, *pinchos,* and frozen cocktails. An abandoned, graffiti-covered tank remains as a reminder of the Navy's presence. It can get crowded on summer weekends and holidays—especially Easter and Christmas.

★ Diving and Snorkeling

Culebra more than makes up for its dearth of entertainment options with a wealth of diving opportunities. There are reportedly 50 dive sites surrounding the island. They're mostly along the island's fringe reefs and around the cays. In addition to diverse coral formations, divers commonly spot sea turtles, stingrays, puffer fish, angelfish, nurse sharks, and more.

Among the most popular dive sites are **Carlos Rosario (Impact),** which features a long, healthy coral reef teeming with sea life, including huge sea fans, and **Shipwreck,** the site of *The Wit Power,* a tugboat sunk in 1984. Here you can play out your *Titanic* fantasies and witness how the sea has claimed the boat for its habitat.

Many of the best dive sites are around Culebra's many cays. **Cayo Agua Rock** is a single, 45-foot-tall rock surrounded by sand

and has been known to attract barracudas, nurse sharks, and sea turtles. **Cayo Ballena** provides a 120-foot wall dive with spectacular coral. **Cayo Raton** is said to attract an inordinate number and variety of fish. And **Cayo Yerba** features an underwater arch covered in yellow cup coral, best seen at night when they "bloom," as well as a good chance to see stingrays.

There are a number of outfitters that lead dive and snorkel tours on the island, including the veteran, **Culebra Divers** (4 Calle Pedro Marquez, across from the ferry terminal in town, 787/742-0803, www.culebradivers.com), offering daily snorkeling trips for $60, one-tank dives for $85, and two-tank dives for $125, including tanks and weights. Snorkeling and dive gear is available for rent. It's also a good place to go for advice on snorkeling from the beach.

Culebra Snorkeling & Dive Center (Kiosk #5, Plaza del Mercado, Calle Pedro Marquez, PR 251, 787/435-3662, www.culebrasnorkelingcenter.com) rents and sells gear and provides expert advice on snorkeling, diving, surfing, and paddleboarding.

Kayaking Puerto Rico (787/245-4545, http://kayakingpuertorico.com) offers daylong and half-day Aquafari tours that combine kayaking and snorkeling in Culebra. The nine-hour day tour from San Juan is $79; the four-hour half-day tour for those already in Culebra is $55. Swimming with turtle experiences are also available for $55.

Culebra Island Adventures (31 Calle 2, 787/529-3536, www.culebraislandadventures.com) leads one-hour snorkel with turtle tours for $54.

ENTERTAINMENT

Nightlife is limited on Culebra, but sometimes even nature lovers and beachcombers need to cut loose. **El Batey** (PR 250, km 0.1, 787/930-8807, Sun.-Mon. and Thurs. 11am-midnight, Tues.-Wed. 9am-midnight, Fri.-Sat. 11am-2am) provides that opportunity. Dancing is the primary attraction at this large, no-frills establishment, where DJs spin salsa, merengue, and electronic music on Friday and Saturday nights. It also serves deli sandwiches and burgers ($3-5) during the day.

La Lobina (28 Pedro Márquez, 787/556-3971, www.facebook.com/LobinaSportBar, Wed.-Thurs. 5pm-midnight, Fri.-Sat. 5pm-2am, Sun. 5pm-9pm) bills itself as a sports bar, but it also has live salsa music, DJs, and karaoke. The large deck overlooking the lagoon is the place to be if you want to dance.

abandoned tank on Playa Flamenco

Everybody who goes to Culebra ends up at ★ **Mamacita's** (64 Calle Castelar, 787/742-0090, www.mamacitasguesthouse.com, Sun.-Thurs. 4pm-10pm, Fri.-Sat. 4pm-11pm) at some point. The popular open-air watering hole right on the canal in town attracts both locals and visitors. Two side-by-side tin-roofed pavilions provide shade for the cozy oasis appointed with brightly painted tables and chairs surrounded by potted palms. The blue-tiled bar is tricked out with colorful folk art touches painted in shades of turquoise, lime green, and lavender. Behind the bar you can buy cigarettes and condoms, and you can get a spritz of bug spray free of charge when the sand gnats attack. Happy hour is 4pm-6pm daily. Try the house special cocktail, the Bushwhacker, a frozen concoction of Kahlúa, Bailey's Irish Cream, coconut cream, rum, and amaretto. Check the chalkboard for excellent daily dinner specials.

The Sandbar (ferry dock, 787/448-6050, Sun.-Thurs. 10am-midnight, Fri.-Sat. 10am-2am, no American Express or Discover) is a pleasant dive bar serving a variety of beers and cocktails in a small, cool spot with colorful paintings of sea creatures on the walls and ceilings.

SHOPPING

La Cava Gift Shop (Dewey, 787/742-0566, daily 9:30am-5pm) is a small shop selling tourist trinkets, T-shirts, jewelry, sundresses, floppy hats, and postcards.

FOOD

The concept of service is very different here from what stateside dwellers may be accustomed to. Things move at a slow, casual pace, so it's best to be patient and prepared to linger for a while. Also, note that operating hours can change unexpectedly, and some restaurants close up shop completely for weeks at a time.

Puerto Rican

The name says it all. At **Dinghy Dock** (Calle Fulladoza, south of the drawbridge, on Ensenada Honda, 787/742-0233 or 787/742-0518, daily 8am-2:30pm and 6pm-9:30pm, dinner $9-30), boats literally dock beside your table at this casual waterfront spot. Plastic patio chairs line a narrow dock under a hanging roof. The cuisine is standard Puerto Rican fare with an emphasis on seafood. Breakfast includes waffles and French toast. Check out the huge tarpon swimming in the water below, waiting for a handout. There is a full bar, which is a good thing because service takes forever.

International

Located in a brightly colored house on a dead-end street in town, ★ **Zaco's Tacos** (21 Calle Pedro Marquez, 787/742-0243, www.zacostacos.com, Mon.-Fri. noon-9pm, Sunday 9:30am-2:30pm, $3-9) serves outstanding cocktails made with fresh fruit juices and creative tacos and burritos stuffed with goodies like pork belly or blackened tofu. Order and pick up at the bar and take a seat on the covered deck out back. It also serves milkshakes and smoothies. Call before you go, since their hours may vary.

Heather's Pizza (14 Calle Pedro Marquez, 787/742-3175 or 939/731-4434, www.facebook.com/heatherpizza, Sun.-Thurs. 10:30am-10pm, Fri.-Sat. 10:30am-11pm, $2-15) is a friendly spot where locals gather to watch the game, have a drink, and chow down on pizza, served by the slice or pie. Options include unusual combinations such as the Boricua Pizza, featuring ground beef, garlic, sweet plantains, and cilantro. Panini and pasta dishes round out the menu.

Seafood and Steak

Mamacita's Restaurant (64 Calle Castelar, by the canal south of the drawbridge, 787/742-0090, www.mamacitasguesthouse.com, Sun.-Thurs. 4pm-10pm, Fri.-Sat. 4pm-11pm, $14-28) is a colorful open-air restaurant and bar serving excellent Caribbean-American-style dishes featuring snapper, churrasco, pork, mofongo, and pasta, as well as a few pub-style appetizers. The dinner menu changes nightly and includes terrific dishes like grilled dorado in cilantro lime aioli. Mamacita's doubles as a popular watering hole at night and rents rooms, too.

Susie's Restaurant (PR 250, east of town, just before the road turns right toward Museo Histórico de Culebra, 787/340-7058, www. facebook.com/susiesculebra, Fri.-Sat. 6pm-9:30pm, Sun. 6pm-10pm, $18-32) is located in a beautiful former home with patio dining in a residential neighborhood that is well suited to the upscale creative Caribbean-Asian cuisine coming out of the kitchen. Dishes include salmon filet in a creamy caper sauce and shrimp tempura in a ponzu sauce with wasabi. Reservations are recommended.

El Eden (836 Sardinas, 787/617-8517, www. eledenculebra.com, Wed.-Sat. 6pm-10pm, bar opens 4pm, $17-29) is a funky little sunbaked spot with a tiki vibe serving outstanding Caribbean-Italian cuisine, including whole grilled lobster, whole fried snapper, a variety of risottos including lobster and chorizo, seafood pasta, and more. There's also a nice selection of tapas and wines, as well as a full bar.

★ **Krusty Krab** (6 Calle Pedro Marquez, near the ferry dock, 787/435-0671, Mon. and Wed.-Sat. 6pm-10pm, Sun. 6pm-midnight, $13-25) has a new home. Formerly a food truck parked on a remote hill with a stunning ocean view, this popular operation now has a permanent home. The menu is small and it changes daily, but the seafood is guaranteed to be fresh. Dishes include whole fried snapper, crab stew, and ceviche.

From the outside, **Harspoon's** (99 Barriada Clark, Calle Luis Muñoz Marín, between the airport and town, 787/742-1891, www.facebook.com/Harspoon1, daily 5pm-10pm, $16-24) doesn't appear too inviting, but the interior conveys a modern gastropub vibe with its warm wood finishes and vintage lighting. The menu changes daily, depending on what comes out of the sea that day, but may include sesame encrusted tuna, shrimp in criolla sauce, and ceviche. For landlubbers, there is churrasco and tamarind-glazed ribs.

Located by the gas station on the lagoon in town, **Caracoles Restaurant** (655 Calle Villa Pesquera, 305/323-4216, Thurs.-Sun. 5-10pm, $21-38) defies its lackluster exterior with a lovely interior decked out in shades of dark turquoise, sporting large fish aquariums and water views. It's a great special occasion restaurant serving creative seafood dishes, including lobster bouillabaisse, shrimp curry, and halibut with prosciutto.

Breakfast and Lunch

Vibra Verde (Plaza Mercado, Calle Pedro Marquez, 787/909-4094, www.facebook. com/vibraverdeculebra, Mon.-Wed. and Fri.-Sat. 8am-2pm, Sun. 8am-1pm, $3-10) is a quick, casual spot for a healthy and delicious breakfast or light lunch, including fruit smoothies, fruit bowls, soups, salads, and sandwiches.

Pandeli Bakery (17 Calle Pedro Marquez at the corner of Calle Escudero, PR 250, 787/742-3311, Mon.-Sat. 5:30am-5pm, Sun. 6:30am-5pm, $2-6) is a modern, cozy bakery serving breakfast, sandwiches, burgers, empanadas, and pastries. There's also a small selection of dry goods and wines.

Tiki's Grill (Calle Escudero, PR 250, 787/742-0241, www.facebook.com/ tikisgrillculebrapr, hours vary, $8-12) is a food truck operation with a small deck for dining that overlooks the bay. The menu is scrawled on a blackboard and features the usual breakfast fare, wings, and coffee drinks. But the specialty is big juicy burgers fixed a myriad of creative ways.

Groceries

Colmado Milka (Calle Escudero, 787/742-2253, Mon.-Sat. 7am-8pm, Sun. 7am-1pm) is a general store selling a good selection of dry goods, meats, produce, and frozen foods. **Colmado Costa del Sol** (221 Calle 1, 787/742-0599, Mon.-Sat. 7am-9pm, Sun. 7am-noon) provides basic grocery needs, and **D's Garden** (Calle 5, near the bay, 787/435-9844, Mon.-Sat. 9am-4pm, Sun. 9am-1pm) sells fresh local fruits, vegetables, and herbs.

Dewey

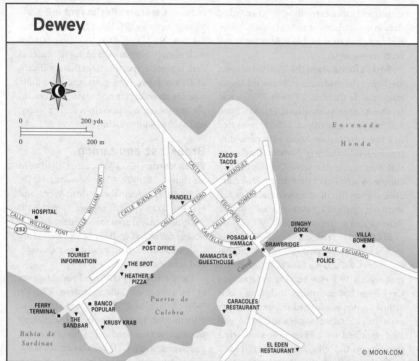

ZACO'S TACOS
CALLE MARQUEZ
CALLE PEDRO
CALLE ESCUDERO
CALLE ROMERO
CALLE BUENA VISTA
PANDELI
CALLE WILLIAM FONT
HOSPITAL
CALLE WILLIAM FONT (252)
CALLE CASTELAR
DINGHY DOCK
POSADA LA HAMACA
DRAWBRIDGE
VILLA BOHEME
CALLE ESCUERDO
POST OFFICE
TOURIST INFORMATION
THE SPOT
MAMACITA'S GUESTHOUSE
POLICE
HEATHER'S PIZZA
Canal
Puerto de Culebra
FERRY TERMINAL
BANCO POPULAR
THE SANDBAR
KRUSY KRAB
CARACOLES RESTAURANT
Bahía de Sardinas
EL EDEN RESTAURANT
Ensenada Honda
© MOON.COM

ACCOMMODATIONS

There is a large number of privately owned guesthouses, vacation rentals, and house shares in Culebra. If you want to live like a local, check out the options at Airbnb.com, HomeAway.com, and Vrbo.com.

Under $100

Playa Flamenco Campground (Playa Flamenco, 787/742-0700, $30, cash only) is a large, shady campground right on the beach and the only place on Culebra that permits overnight camping. There are 400 campsites, and it can get a bit raucous with partiers, especially on holiday weekends. But there are five sections, and section E is designated as a quiet zone for those who want a more peaceful stay. Facilities include outdoor showers, picnic tables, and toilets, although toilet paper is not provided. Officially, reservations are required, but it's possible to show up without

them. If you can't get through by phone to make your reservation, write to Autoridad de Conservación y Desarrollo de Culebra, Attention: Playa Flamenco, Apartado 217, Culebra, PR 00775.

The Spanish-style guesthouse **Posada La Hamaca** (68 Calle Castelar, Dewey, 787/742-3516, www.posada.com, $90-123) has 10 rooms that are light, airy, and tidy; each comes with satellite TV, air-conditioning, mini refrigerators, free Internet, and hot water. There's a large shady deck overlooking the canal out back with two gas grills. Beach towels, coolers, and free ice are provided for trips to the beach. It's within walking distance of the ferry dock.

$100-150

In town on Ensenada Honda is **Casa Ensenada** (142 Calle Escudero, 787/241-4441 or 866/210-00709, www.casaensenada.com, $125-175). Despite its small size and modest aesthetics, this three-room guesthouse has everything you could need. Rooms are outfitted with air-conditioning, satellite TV, VCRs, hot showers, and kitchenettes, and a telephone, high-speed Internet, and copier are on-site. For trips to the beach, towels, chairs, coolers, umbrellas, and ice are available.

Mamacita's Guesthouse (64 Calle Castelar, 787/742-0090, www.mamacitasguesthouse.com, $105-120) is a pastel-colored hodgepodge of balconies and archways squeezed between Calle Castelar and the canal. The hostel-like accommodations are strictly functional and feature air-conditioning and satellite TV in the bedrooms. It's best suited for those just looking for a place to crash and a hopping bar and excellent restaurant on-site. Laundry facilities and boat dockage are available for guests.

Palmetto Guesthouse (128 Manuel Vasquez, two blocks behind Carlos Jeep, 787/742-0257 or 787/235-6736, www.palmettoculebra.com, $110-152) is a modest six-unit property in a residential neighborhood within walking distance of the airport. The small, tidy rooms are appointed with modern furnishings, air-conditioning, and mini refrigerators. Common areas include two kitchens.

An option right on Playa Flamenco is **Villa Flamenco Beach** (Playa Flamenco, 787/742-0023, http://villaflamencobeach.com, $135-185). The two-story pink-and-green concrete structure contains six tidy, basic units. Upstairs, there are four studio apartments with kitchenettes that sleep two people. On the ground floor are two one-bedroom apartments with full kitchens that sleep four. All units have air-conditioning and hot water in the shower only. Some rooms have beachfront balconies. The place is low-key and self-serve. Bring insect repellent.

Villa Boheme (368 Calle Fulladoza, 787/742-3508, www.villaboheme.com, $125, $185-240 suite) has a lovely Spanish hacienda-style exterior and landscaped grounds overlooking the water on Fulladoza Bay. Inside are 12 simply decorated rooms with air-conditioning and hot water. Some rooms have private balconies and small kitchens; others share a communal kitchen in the patio area, which also contains satellite TV. A large terrace spans the length of the rambling property. Guests may use the dock, equipped with water and electricity, for a fee. Moorings are also available for rent.

El Navegante (Calle Pedro Marquez, no phone, http://naveguest.com, $89-129) is a modest hotel located in town, featuring eight simple rooms with private bathrooms, air-conditioning, and complimentary wireless Internet.

$150-250

Right on Playa Flamenco, **Culebra Beach Villas** (Playa Flamenco, 787/409-2599 or 877/767-7575, www.culebrabeachrental.com or www.culebrabeach.com, $125-225) offers 33 individually owned cottages and guestrooms with air-conditioning and kitchens. The rooms are fairly spartan, but the cottages have decks and covered porches. The upkeep varies from cottage to cottage; some are a bit rundown. Services are minimal, although linens and towels are provided. Request a newer unit in the back of the complex if available. And be sure to bring your insect repellent—it gets buggy.

★ **Club Seabourne** (PR 252, Calle Fulladoza on Ensenada Honda, 787/742-3169 or 800/981-4435, www.clubseabourne.com, $185-279) is a charming property with 14 units overlooking Fulladoza Bay. There is a New England vibe to the gray clapboard villas with pitched tin roofs dotted around the wooded property. The rooms are quite luxe, with super-plush canopy beds and balconies. Rooms have air-conditioning, cable TV, and free wireless Internet. A lovely landscaped pool surrounded by umbrella tables overlooks the bay. Rates include complimentary breakfast. Kayak and bicycle rentals can be arranged at the front desk. Docking and mooring services can be purchased with advance notice.

For total seclusion, you can't do much better than **Tamarindo Estates** (off PR 251, km

2.2, just south of Playa Flamenco, 787/742-3343, www.tamarindoestates.com, $149-260). The property features 12 simply furnished, hillside cottages on 60 acres overlooking the water and Cayo Luis Peña. Units look like they were furnished by a flea market, which gives them a quaint homespun vibe. Each one contains a TV, free wifeless Internet, air-conditioning in the bedroom, a fully equipped kitchen, a screened porch, and a rooftop veranda. The rocky beach directly in front of the property offers great snorkeling, and a short hike north is a sandy beach for swimming.

Over $250

Sea Breeze Hotel (PR 250, km 1.8, 855/285-3272, www.seabreezeculebra.com, $149-249) is a large complex overlooking the bay, featuring 160 units; more than half are privately owned condominium units. Suites and junior suites come with microwaves, mini refrigerators, air-conditioning, and balconies. There are no TVs or daily housekeeping services. Amenities include a swimming pool and a poolside bar and grill.

TRANSPORTATION AND SERVICES
Air

Several small airlines fly to **Benjamin Rivera Noriega Airport** (CPX) in Culebra from the main island, and the flights are fairly inexpensive and speedy. The only catch is that it's not for the faint of heart. Landing on the tiny island requires a steep descent over a mountaintop that takes your breath away.

In San Juan, flights can be arranged from Isla Grande Airport or from the José Aponte de la Torre Airport in Ceiba, on the east coast of the big island.

Vieques Air Link (787/534-4221, 787/534-4222, or 787/741-8331; for service to Culebra, call 888/901-9247) flies to and from Ceiba.

Air Flamenco (787/724-1818, 787/721-7332, or 877/535-2636, www.airflamenco.net) offers flights from Ceiba and Isla Grande. Charter flights are available.

Taxi Aero (787/602-7605, http://taxiaereopr.travel) provides on-demand charter air service to Culebra and Vieques from Ceiba and San Juan's Isla Grande airport. Pets up to 40 pounds fly for free. One-way fares start at $180 for 1-3 people from Ceiba or $475 for 1-3 people from San Juan.

Ferry

The Puerto Rico Port Authority operates a **passenger ferry service** (787/497-7740, www.porferry.com, $5.35 one way) between Culebra and Ceiba, as well as between Culebra and Vieques. But be forewarned: As bad as passenger ferry service is to Vieques, it's even worse to Culebra. Schedules change and routes are cancelled frequently. There is a cargo ferry with limited passenger space, but note that car rental agencies in Puerto Rico do not permit their automobiles to leave the main island. Also, ticket holders are not guaranteed a seat because Puerto Rican residents get priority, since they depend on the service for supplies and commuting to and from work. Note that ferries are particularly crowded on holiday weekends. But if you have flexibility on when you arrive and depart, the ferry can be a pleasant ride, lasting 30 to 45 minutes.

Car

It is possible to get around Culebra without renting a vehicle, but it is not advisable. If you want to explore the island, jeeps, scooters, and golf carts are available for rent. Just be sure to book early—2-3 months in advance is recommended.

There are few roads on Culebra, but they can be narrow, steep, and riddled with potholes. Parking and seat belt laws are strictly enforced, and for some odd reason, driving bare-chested can get you a ticket.

Note that many places don't have traditional addresses with street names and numbers. If you ask people for an address, they're more likely to describe its physical location in relation to something else, as in "beside El Batey" or "across from the ferry." Also, nobody who lives in Culebra calls Dewey by its

Ferry Riding Tips

the car ferry in Vieques

Ferry service to Vieques and Culebra has become increasingly unreliable. If you plan to take a ferry to Vieques or Culebra, here are a few things worth noting.

- Tickets should be bought at least one week in advance, but they do not guarantee space on the ferry.

- Only 20 percent of tickets are sold online. If a route is sold out, you may still be able to buy tickets at the gate starting one hour before departure.

- Check the schedule online on the day of your departure. Schedules change frequently and without notice.

- If a ferry is oversold, ticket holders with a Puerto Rico Permanent Resident Card get priority over visitors.

- The ferry is crowded on holidays and long weekends. Line up 90 minutes before departure to increase your chances of getting aboard.

- If you are prone to motion sickness, take preventive medication. The ride is sometimes choppy.

- Ferries do not always arrive or depart on time.

- There is an additional $2 charge for camping or beach equipment.

- Rental cars may not be transported on the cargo ferry.

name; it's usually just referred to as "Pueblo" or "Town."

Several agencies provide jeep rentals for about $65 per day, although some travelers report success at negotiating a better rate. Bring a copy of your insurance policy to avoid steep insurance charges. Note that

children under 12 are not permitted to ride in golf carts.

Carlos Jeep Rental (PR 250, Isabel Segunda, 787/742-3514 or 787/613-7049; airport 787/742-1111, www.carlosjeeprental. com) conveniently has an office located at the airport and has a well-maintained fleet of

2011 jeeps for $65 a day. Golf carts are $40 a day. Other rental options include **Jerry's Jeeps** (787/742-0587, 787/742-0526, 787/512-9331, or 787/512-9108, www.jerrysjeeprental.com) and **Dick and Cathie's Jeep Rental** (787/742-0062).

Público and Car Service

Públicos are vans operated by individuals who provide transportation on the island. They are an economical way to get around, but they're not particularly expedient. Expect to share your ride with others who are going to different destinations, which can add time and distance to your journey, depending on how many stops are on the way. It costs about $5 to go from the airport to town or from town to Flamenco Bay. You'll typically see *públicos* waiting at the airport or ferry dock when you arrive. If not, ask an employee for a list. Options include **Nata** (787/969-2863 or 787/972-1183) and **Raul** (787/358-4816).

Car service can be arranged through **Culebra Concierge** (787/742-3000, www.culebraconcierge.com), which also offers other services, such as arranging accommodations, meals, and activities.

Water Taxi

Puerto Rico Water Taxi (787/231-9365, www.prwatertaxi.com) provides transportation to Culebrita and Cayo Luis Peña, smaller, uninhabited islands off the coast of Culebra, for $75 per person, $225 minimum. Snorkel gear and umbrellas are available for rent. Other water taxis services include **H2O Water Taxi** (787/685-5815, www.facebook.com/h2owatertaxi, daily 9am-5pm) and **Cayo Water Taxi** (787/376-9980, daily 7am-9pm). Be sure to bring water, sunscreen, snacks, towels, and hats. There are no facilities or stores on the islands.

Services

For medical services, **Hospital de Culebra** (end of Calle William Font, in town, 787/742-0001) is a modest facility that provides emergency medical service. In addition, **Health ProMed** (44 Calle Pedro Marquez, 787/468-2966 or 787/919-3919, www.healthpromed.org) operates a nonprofit clinic and pharmacy Monday-Friday 8am-4pm. The **police department** (787/742-3501) is on Calle Fulladoza just past Dinghy Dock.

An ATM is available at **Banco Popular** (787/742-3572, Mon.-Fri. 8:30am-3:30pm) across from the ferry dock at 9 Calle Pedro Marquez. You'll find the **post office** (787/742-3862, Mon.-Fri. 8am-4:30pm) at 26 Calle Pedro Marquez, and coin **laundry facilities** (PR 250, in town) are available in the back of La Surana apartments.

You can gas up your rental car at **Dakiti Gas Station & Mini Market** (Calle Escudero, near the drawbridge, 787/742-1199, Mon.-Sat. 7am-7pm, Sun. 7am-3pm).

Background

The Landscape

GEOGRAPHY

Puerto Rico is a rectangular island, situated roughly in the middle of the **Antilles,** a chain of islands that stretches from Florida to Venezuela and forms the dividing line between the Atlantic Ocean and the Caribbean Sea. The Antilles are divided into two regions—Greater Antilles and Lesser Antilles. Puerto Rico is the smallest and easternmost island of the Greater Antilles, which include Cuba, Hispañola (Dominican Republic and Haiti), and Jamaica.

In addition to the main island, which is 111 miles east to west and 36

miles north to south, Puerto Rico comprises several tiny islands or *cayos,* including Mona and Desecheo off the west coast and Vieques, Culebra, Palomino, Icacos, and others off the east coast. The northern and eastern shores of Puerto Rico are on the Atlantic Ocean, and the southern shores are on the Caribbean Sea. To the west is Mona Passage, an important shipping lane that is 75 miles wide and 3,300 feet deep.

The island is believed to have been formed between 135 million and 185 million years ago when a massive shift of tectonic plates crumpled the earth's surface, pushing parts of it down into deep recesses below the ocean floor and pushing parts of it up to create the island. This tectonic activity resulted in volcanic eruptions, both underwater and above it.

Two significant things happened as a result of all this geologic activity. The **Puerto Rico Trench** was formed off the island's north coast. At its greatest depth, it is 28,000 feet below sea level, making it the deepest point known in the Atlantic Ocean. Secondly, it formed the mountainous core of Puerto Rico that spans nearly the entire island from east to west and reaches heights of 4,390 feet above sea level. Volcanic activity is believed to have been dormant in Puerto Rico for 45 million years, but the earth is always changing. The Caribbean plate is shifting eastward against the westward-shifting North American plate, which results in occasional earth tremors. In December 2019, there was significant, sustained earthquake activity in the southwest corner of the island around Ponce and Guánica. The island experienced a swarm of more than 1,000 earthquakes well into 2020, the largest being a 6.7-magnitude quake on January 7, 2020. One person was killed and 4,000 people were forced to seek shelter.

Puerto Rico has three main geographic regions: mountains, coastal lowlands, and karst country. More than 60 percent of the island is mountainous. The island's mountains, which dominate the island's interior, comprise four ranges: **Cordillera Central, Sierra de Cayey, Sierra de Luquillo,** and **Sierra de Bermeja.** The largest and highest range is Cordillera Central, which spans from Caguas in the east to Lares in the west. Its highest point is Cerro Punta (4,390 feet above sea level), in the Bosque Estatal de Toro Negro near Jayuya. Sierra de Luquillo is in the northeast and contains the Caribbean National Forest, home to El Yunque rainforest. These two mountain ranges feature dramatic pointed peaks and lush tropical vegetation. Sierra de Cayey, in the southeast between Cayey and Humacao, and Sierra de Bermeja, in the southwest between Guánica and the island's southwestern tip, are smaller in area and height, drier, and less forested.

The **coastal lowlands** span more than 300 miles around the rim of the island, 8-12 miles inland in the north and 2-8 miles inland in the south. Formed through time by erosion of the mountains, the coastal lowlands are important agricultural areas that benefit from the rich soil and water that wash down from the mountains. Much of the area is defined by sandy or rocky beaches and mangrove swamps, although the mangrove forests are being whittled away by development.

The island's third region is unique. The **karst region** spans the island's northern interior, from San Juan in the east to Aguadilla in the west, and the southern interior, from Ponce in the east to San Germán in the west. It can also be found in isolated pockets throughout the island, as well as on Mona Island off the west coast. The karst region is distinguished by a fascinating landscape of sinkholes, cliffs, caves, and conical, haystack-shaped hills called *mogotes.* More than 27 percent of Puerto Rico's surface is made up of limestone, and its erosion from rain helped create the beguiling patchwork of hills and holes. One of limestone's unique properties is that it re-precipitates and forms case rock

---

that is impervious to chemical and climatic change, which has basically frozen the odd formations in time. In addition, water produced by re-precipitation bubbles up to hydrate the earth's surface, and drips down, creating subterranean rivers and caves.

As a result of its karst region, Puerto Rico has some of the most significant cave systems in the western hemisphere and the third-largest underground river, Río Camuy. **Las Cavernas del Río Camuy** is a massive cave system in the municipality of Camuy.

In addition to Río Camuy, Puerto Rico's other major rivers include the north-running **Grande de Arecibo,** the island's longest; **La Plata, Cibuco, Loíza,** and **Bayamón,** which run north; and **Grande de Añasco,** which runs west. There are no natural lakes in Puerto Rico, although 15 reservoirs have been created by damming rivers. But there are several natural lagoons, including **Condado** and **San José** in San Juan, **Piñones** and **Torrecilla** in Loíza, **Joyuda** in Cabo Rojo, **Tortuguero** in Vega Baja, and **Grande** in Fajardo.

CLIMATE

Puerto Rico's climate is classified as **tropical marine,** which means it's typically sunny, hot, and humid year-round. The temperature fluctuates between 76-88°F in the coastal plains and 73-78°F in the mountains. Humidity is a steady 80 percent, but a north-easterly wind keeps things pretty breezy, particularly on the northeast side of the island.

Nobody wants rain during a tropical vacation, but precipitation is very much a part of life in Puerto Rico. Although there are periods when the deluge is so heavy that you might think it's time to buy a boat, rains are generally brief and occur in the afternoons. The average annual rainfall is 62 inches. Although it rains throughout the year, the heaviest precipitation is from May to October, which is also hurricane season. The driest period is January to April, which coincides with the tourism industry's high season throughout much of the island. Keep in mind that the north coast receives twice as much rain as the south coast, so if the outlook is rainy in San Juan, head south.

As the devastation of Hurricanes Irma and Maria in 2017 illustrated, tropical storms pose a very real threat to Puerto Rico. Much of the island was without electrical power for an entire year following Hurricane Maria, a category 4 storm that did $139 billion worth of damage to the island. An estimated 3,000 people died either as a direct result of the storm or because of medical complications due to lack of electricity.

But Hurricane Maria is a considered a "storm of the century," meaning it was highly irregular and far from the norm. The previous biggest storm was Hurricane Georges, a category 3 that struck in 1998 and did $2 billion of damage.

According to the U.S. National Weather Service, hurricane season in the Caribbean spans from June through November, but August through October is when Puerto Rico is most vulnerable.

For the latest information on weather conditions in Puerto Rico, visit the National Weather Service at www.noaa.gov/weather.

ENVIRONMENTAL ISSUES

Because Puerto Rico is part of the United States, local industry is subject to the same federal environmental regulations and restrictions as in the United States.

Puerto Rico's greatest environmental threats concern its vanishing natural habitat and the resulting impact on soil erosion and wildlife. Reforestation efforts are underway in many of the island's national parks and forest reserves, and organized efforts are underway to protect and rebuild endangered wildlife populations, especially the Puerto Rican parrot, the manatee, and the leatherback sea turtle.

Many of the island's environmental protection efforts are overseen by the Conservation Trust of Puerto Rico, whose headquarters is based in **Casa de Ramón Power y Girault**

(155 Calle Tetuán, San Juan, 787/722-5834, ext. 242, www.paralanaturaleza.org, Tues.-Sat. 9am-5pm), where visitors can peruse exhibits and pick up printed information on its projects. The organization leads a variety of educational tours throughout the island and has launched an initiative to expand protected territory through land acquisition.

In Vieques, the biggest environmental concern surrounds the ongoing cleanup of the grounds once occupied by the U.S. Navy, which stored munitions and performed bombing practice on the island.

After years of protest by local residents, the Navy withdrew in 2003, but much of its land (18,000 acres) is still off-limits to the public while efforts to clear it of contaminants and the live artillery that still litters the ocean floor are underway. The cancer rate in Vieques is 27 percent higher than that of the main island, and many blame it on the presence of unexploded artillery leaking chemicals into the water and the release of chemicals into the air when the artillery is detonated, which is the Navy's way of disposing of it.

Plants and Animals

For such a small island, Puerto Rico has a wide diversity of biological environments.

For instance, Bosque Estatal de Guánica in the southwestern corner of the island is classified as a subtropical dry forest, where cacti, grasses, and evergreen trees hosting Spanish moss and mistletoe compete for water and nutrients from sun-bleached rocky soil. On the opposite end of the island is the Caribbean National Forest, which contains subtropical moist forest, also called rainforest. Palm trees, a multitude of ferns, *tabonuco* trees, orchids, and bromeliads grow here. And along the coast are mangrove forests, where the mighty land-building trees flourish in the salty water and provide vital habitat to marine life.

The first extensive study of Puerto Rico's diverse flora was undertaken in the early 1900s, thanks to American botanists Nathaniel and Elizabeth Britton, founders of the New York Botanical Gardens. Their annual trips to the Caribbean, beginning in 1906, led to the publication in 1933 of *The Scientific Survey of Puerto Rico and the Virgin Islands*, the first systematic natural history survey in the Caribbean region.

TREES

The official tree of Puerto Rico is the **ceiba,** also called silk-cotton tree or kapok tree.

Often the tallest tree in the forest, the ceiba attains heights of 150 feet and has a ridged columnar trunk and a massive umbrella-shaped canopy. Its far-reaching limbs often host aerial plants, such as moss and bromeliads. Ceibas can live hundreds of years. Unfortunately, many of the island's old ceiba trees were destroyed by Hurricane Maria in 2017.

The ceiba was important to the island's indigenous Taínos because its thick trunks were perfect for carving into canoes. Its flowers are small and inconspicuous, but it produces a large ellipsoid fruit that, when split open, reveals an abundance of fluffy fibers, called kapok.

Arguably Puerto Rico's most beautiful tree, though, is the *flamboyan,* also known as royal poinciana. If you visit the island between June and August, you're sure to notice the abundance of reddish-orange blooms that cover the umbrella-shaped canopy of the *flamboyan*. It is a gorgeous sight to behold. The tree is also distinguished by fernlike leaves and the long brown seedpods it produces.

Probably the most plentiful and easily identifiable tree in Puerto Rico is the mighty palm, which grows throughout the island. There are actually many varieties of palm in Puerto Rico. Among them are the **coconut** palm, which has smooth gray bark marked by ring scars from fallen fronds and which bears the beloved coconut in abundance; the royal palm, distinguished by its tall, thin, straight trunk, which grows to 25 feet and sports a crown of leaves that are silver on the underside; the Puerto Rican hat palm, featuring a fat tubular trunk and fan-shaped frond; and the sierra palm, which has a thin straight trunk and thick thatch.

Puerto Rico's mangrove forests are found in swampy coastal areas throughout the island. Much of the island's coast was once covered in mangrove, but a lot of it has been destroyed to make way for commercial development. Fortunately, efforts are underway to preserve many of the island's last remaining mangrove forests in parks in Piñones, Boquerón, Fajardo, Vieques, and elsewhere.

The mangrove tree is a unique plant. For one thing, it is able to grow along the ocean's shallow edges, absorbing, processing, and secreting salt from the water. But what's truly amazing about the mangrove, and what makes it so vital to marine life, is its adaptive root system. Because the trees grow in thick, oxygen-deprived mud, they sprout aerial roots to absorb oxygen from the air and nutrients from the surface of the water. The aerial roots take many different forms, including thousands of tiny pencil-shaped roots sticking up from shallow waters; big knee-shaped roots that emerge from the ground and loop back down; and roots that sprout from branches.

Between its complex tangle of roots and its low-lying compact canopy, the mangrove forest plays several important roles in the environment, primarily by providing habitat to local wildlife. Its branches are a haven to nesting birds, and its underwater root systems protect crabs, snails, crustaceans, and small fish from predators. Mangrove forests also help protect the coastal plains from violent storms, reduce erosion, and filter the ocean waters. And finally, mangrove forests actually build land by providing nooks and crannies within their root systems that capture soil,

aerate it, and create conditions where other plants can grow.

Puerto Rico is rich in plants that have edible, medicinal, or other practical uses. For the Taíno Indians, the island's forests served as their pharmacy and grocery store.

The mamey is prized not only for the delicious fruit it bears but also for its fragrant flowers and lovely appearance. Resembling a Southern magnolia, the mamey grows to 60 feet high and features a short stout trunk and dense foliage with long, glossy, leathery dark-green leaves. The flowers feature 4-6 white petals and have a lovely fragrance. The fruit is brown and leathery on the outside, and inside it can be sweet and tender or crisp and sour, depending on the variety. Another popular tree that bears edible fruit is the mango. The ubiquitous leafy tree grows in forests, backyards, and alongside roadways, and in the summer each tree bears what appear to be hundreds of mangoes. When ripe, the fruit is covered with a thick yellow and brown skin, but inside is a soft succulent fruit similar to a peach. You'll often see locals on the side of the road selling bags of them out of their trucks.

The curious calabash tree served an entirely different purpose in Taíno culture. Its greatest value was in the large, round, gourd-like fruit that sprouts directly from the tree's trunk. After the fruit was cleansed of its pulp, the remaining shell was dried and used as a bowl for food preparation and storage. Sometimes the bowls were decorated with elaborate carvings etched into the sides before the shell dried. Carved calabash bowls are popular souvenir items today.

FLOWERING PLANTS

Like any good tropical island, Puerto Rico has a bounty of flowering plants. Probably the one most commonly encountered, particularly in gardens but also in the wild, is the beautiful sun-loving bougainvillea. The plant produces great clusters of blossoms with thin papery petals, which come in an assortment of colors, including pink, magenta, purple, red, orange, white, and yellow. The plant is actually a vine, but in Puerto Rico bougainvillea often grows freestanding, with its long thin branches hanging heavy with blooms.

The mountains are home to many varieties of flowering plants, including one that home gardeners in the States may recognize—the shade-loving **impatiens,** a lovely ground-covering plant with white blooms. They can be seen blooming in great drifts along mountain banks. Other mountain flowering plants include more than 50 varieties of **orchids,** but don't look for corsage-sized blossoms—Puerto Rico's orchids tend to be small, some the size of a fingernail. Where you find orchids, you can usually find **bromeliads,** which, like orchids, grow on other plants that serve as hosts. Bromeliads are typically distinguished by overlapping spirals of leaves with a tubular punch of color in the center, but the family includes some atypical variations, including **Spanish moss** and the **pineapple,** both of which grow on the island.

Other plants found commonly in Puerto Rico are a large variety of ferns, big and small, in the mountains. Along the beaches, the sea grape, a low-lying compact shrub that grows in clusters, creates a cave-like reprieve from the sun. Several varieties of cactus grow in the subtropical dry forest along the southwestern coast and on the islands of Vieques and Culebra.

MAMMALS

The only mammal native to Puerto Rico is the bat. Eleven species live on the island, including the **red fig-eating bat,** which roosts in the forest canopy in the Caribbean National Forest, and the **Greater Antillean long-tongued bat,** which lives in caves and feeds on fruits and nectar from flowers.

Thanks to colonial trade ships, **rats** were introduced to the island in the late 1400s. They thrived here in great abundance, causing havoc on sugar plantations. Then someone had the brilliant idea of introducing **mongooses** from India to keep the rat population down. Unfortunately, mongooses are active during the day, and rats are active at night, so the effort failed, and now there's a mongoose problem. They have no natural predators on the island, and they live up to 40 years. Mongooses are to be avoided at all costs as they are major carriers of rabies.

Paso Fino horses are a common form of transportation in rural areas of Puerto Rico, especially in Vieques and Culebra, where they roam the island freely.

Some parts of Puerto Rico also have a **feral**

brown pelican

The Coqui Tree Frog

There is one sweet sound unlike any other that you can hear throughout the island of Puerto Rico at night, and that is the song of the **coqui tree frog.** Rarely seen but often heard, these tiny translucent amphibians are the beloved mascot of the island.

The scientific name is *Eleutherodactylus,* and they differ from other frogs in two key ways: First, instead of webbed feet, they have tiny pads on their feet that facilitate climbing to the tops of trees, where they like to gather at night to mate and feed on insects, including mosquitoes, termites, and centipedes. Second, they do not begin life as tadpoles but hatch fully formed from eggs.

There are 17 varieties of coquis in Puerto Rico, but only two of them sing the famous songs: the **coqui comun** and the **coqui de la montaña,** also known as the *coqui puertorriqueño.* And only the male sings the "co-QUI!" call after dusk. Coquis can be found throughout the Caribbean and Latin America, but only those in Puerto Rico sing the song.

In recent years the coqui inadvertently has been introduced to Hawaii, hidden in plants shipped there from Puerto Rico. But while Puerto Ricans love the sound of their coqui, many people in Hawaii do not. In fact, they consider the frogs to be a scourge to the island, and the state government is trying to have them eradicated. Meanwhile, in Puerto Rico, some species of coquis have been put on the endangered list, including the tiniest one, the **coqui llanero,** which was only discovered in 2005 and whose song is so high-pitched it is barely perceivable by humans.

dog problem. It's not uncommon to see roving packs of mangy, skeletal canines rummaging for scraps in small towns and rural areas.

BIRDS AND INSECTS

Puerto Rico is a bird-watcher's paradise, but the one endemic bird you probably won't see is the **Puerto Rican parrot.** Although once prolific throughout the island, the endangered bird's population is a mere 35 or so that live in the wild today because of the loss of habitat to development. They are found in the Caribbean National Forest.

In 1987 the U.S. Fish and Wildlife Service initiated a program to raise Puerto Rican parrots in captivity and release them into the Caribbean National Forest in hopes of building up the population. Unfortunately, success has been stymied by hurricanes and predators (primarily the red-tailed hawk). But the efforts continue, and today there are about 150 living in captivity in aviaries in Luquillo and Bosque Estatal Río Abajo.

It's highly unlikely a visitor to El Yunque will see a Puerto Rican parrot, but just in case, keep your eyes peeled for a foot-long, bright green Amazon parrot with blue wing tips, white eye rings, and a red band above its beak. When in flight, it emits a repetitive call that sounds like a bugle.

Other species of birds found in more plentiful numbers in Puerto Rico include sharp-shinned hawks, broad-winged hawks, bananaquits, Puerto Rican todies, red-legged thrushes, stripe-headed tanagers, brown pelicans, lizard-cuckoos, elfin-woods warblers, hummingbirds, and nightjars, which nest silently on the ground by day and fly in search of prey at night.

At dusk, many of Puerto Rico's wilderness beaches come under attack by **sand fleas,** also called no-see-ums: vicious, minuscule buggers that have a fierce bite. If they attack, your best defense is to pack up as quickly as possible and call it a day.

REPTILES AND AMPHIBIANS

Of all the creatures that call Puerto Rico home, none are as beloved as the tiny **coqui tree frog,** the island's national symbol. A mere 1-1.5 inches long fully grown, the coqui is difficult to spot, but you can definitely hear the male's distinctive "co-QUI" call at dusk or after a rain. Despite the ubiquity of their cheerful chirp, of the 16 varieties that live in Puerto Rico, only two make the eponymous sound, which serves to attract a mate and repel reproductive competitors.

Unlike many frogs, the coqui does not have webbed appendages and does not require water to live or reproduce. In fact, coquis are never tadpoles. The female coqui lays its eggs on leaves, and tiny little froglets emerge fully formed from the eggs. Although they're born with tails, they lose them posthaste.

It is considered good luck to spot a coqui, and there are many other legends surrounding them. One is that a little boy was transformed into a frog because he misbehaved, and now he comes out and sings at sunset. Another involves a bird that was stripped of its wings but was later turned into a frog so it could climb back into the trees where it once lived.

The one creature visitors to Puerto Rico are sure to spot is a **lizard.** The island is literally crawling with them, varying in species from the ubiquitous four-inch **emerald anoli,** which is sure to slip inside the house if a window is left open, to the **Puerto Rican giant green lizard,** an imposing reptile that can grow up to 16 inches long and lives mostly in the limestone hills.

But Puerto Rico's mack-daddy lizard is the prehistoric-looking **Mona iguana,** which grows up to four feet long. Mona Island off the west coast of Puerto Rico is the only natural habitat for the Mona iguana, but there is a tiny mangrove *cayo* in the bay at La Parguera where a small population is kept for research purposes and which can be seen by boat. Although an herbivore, the Mona iguana has an intimidating appearance because of its horned snout and the jagged bony crest down its back. The Mona iguana lives up to 50 years.

Snakes are few in Puerto Rico, but they do exist. Fortunately, they are all nonpoisonous. The **Puerto Rican boa** is an endangered species. The longest snake on the island, it grows up to six feet and is quite elusive.

MARINE LIFE

Puerto Rico has an abundance of marine life. Among its endangered marine creatures is the **manatee,** a 1,000-pound submarine-shaped mammal with a tail, two small flippers, and a wrinkled, whiskered face. The slow-moving herbivore lives in shallow, still waters, such as lagoons and bays. Their only natural predators are humans, and because they often float near the water's surface, they are particularly susceptible to collision with watercraft.

Iguanas are common throughout Puerto Rico.

The U.S. Fish and Wildlife Service operates a recovery program for the manatee, and if you spot one, you're likely to see its tracking device.

Also endangered are the **hawksbill** and **leatherback sea turtles,** the latter of which is the world's largest species of sea turtle. There are several important turtle nesting sites in Puerto Rico, along the north shore and on the islands of Mona and Culebra. The turtles nest between April and June by climbing up on the beach at night and burying their eggs in the sand before returning to the sea. Unfortunately, turtle nests are vulnerable to animals and poachers, who prize the eggs. Several government agencies are involved in protecting the nesting sites.

Besides its endangered species, Puerto Rico has numerous other varieties of thriving marine life, from **rays** and **nurse sharks** to **puffer fish** and **parrot fish.** The reefs themselves are sights to behold, with their **brain coral, sea fans,** and **yellow cup coral,** which blooms at night. The exotic looking **lionfish** from the Indian and Western Pacific Oceans has become a prevalent invasive species in Puerto Rico. The fish has several spines that can puncture a predator and inject venom, but it's safe to eat and is finding its way on menus around the island.

Although typically associated with colder waters, migrating **humpback whales** can be spotted along the island's west coast between January and March.

History

INDIGENOUS CULTURES

The earliest known inhabitants of Puerto Rico were the **Archaic** or **Pre-Ceramic** cultures, which are believed to have lived on the island from 3000 BC until AD 150. They were loosely organized in small nomadic groups of about 30 who occupied encampments for brief periods. What little is known about this culture has been deduced from a couple of burial sites and a few excavated stone and shell artifacts, such as flint chips, scrapers, and pestles. They are believed to have been primarily hunters and gatherers who did not cultivate crops or make pottery. There are two main theories about the origins of the Archaic culture. It is believed they either originated in South America and migrated to Puerto Rico by way of the Lesser Antilles or they originated in the Yucatán Peninsula and crossed from Cuba and Hispañola.

The Archaic were followed by the **Arawak,** who migrated from Venezuela. The earliest Arawak were classified as **Igneri** or **Saladoid,** and they lived in Puerto Rico from 300 BC to AD 600. The Igneri were superb potters, whose ceramics were distinguished by white paint on a red background. They also produced small *cemies,* three-sided amulets believed to have religious significance. Their society was organized in villages of extended-family houses situated around a central plaza, under which the dead were buried. In addition to hunting and gathering, the Igneri cultivated crops.

Around AD 600, the Igneri culture evolved into two separate cultures that are grouped together under the name **Pre-Taíno.** The **Elenoid** lived on the eastern two-thirds of the island while the **Ostionoid** lived on the western third of the island. The Elenoid culture is identified by a coarse, thick style of unpainted ceramics. The Ostionoid produced pottery similar to the Igneri's, except that it was painted in shades of pink and lilac. Little is known about Pre-Taíno culture. Both cultures continued to hunt, fish, gather, and farm. Although they had centralized villages, there is evidence that many Pre-Taíno split into nuclear families and lived in houses separate from one another scattered throughout the island. It is during this time that many Taíno customs began to appear. The Pre-Taíno were the first to construct *bateyes* (rectangular ball courts) and central plazas, which were square or round. They produced larger *cemí* amulets than found in Igneri culture, and they began carving petroglyphs—typically human or animal faces—into stones.

The most significant Igneri and Pre-Taíno archaeological site in Puerto Rico is **Centro Ceremonial Indígena de Tibes** near Ponce. In addition to seven *bateyes* and two plazas, a cemetery containing the remains of 187 people was discovered here.

Around AD 1200, the Pre-Taíno evolved into the **Taíno** culture. Of all the indigenous groups that lived in Puerto Rico, the most is known about the Taíno, perhaps because they were the ones to greet Christopher Columbus when he arrived in 1493, and several Spanish settlers wrote historical accounts about their culture.

The Taíno society was highly organized and hierarchal. They lived in self-governing villages called *yucayeques*. Commoners lived in conical wood-and-thatch huts called *bohios*, while the chief, or cacique, lived in a rectangular hut called a *caney*. They were a highly spiritual culture and would gather on sacred grounds, distinguished by plazas and *bateyes* (ball courts), to perform their religious ceremonies and compete in ball games.

The Taínos produced highly complex ceramics, as well as wood and stone implements, such as axes, daggers, *dujos* (ceremonial stools), and stone collars, the purpose of which is unknown. In addition to hunting, fishing, and gathering, they were highly developed farmers. The Taínos were also highly spiritual, and they created many *cemí* amulets, which were much more complex than those of past cultures, and stone carvings.

The Taínos were a peaceful people, a fact that was severely challenged by the arrival of the Spanish conquistadors as well as the marauding Caribs, a highly aggressive, warrior culture that originated in Venezuela and roamed the Antilles plundering goods and capturing women. A hotly debated topic in scholarly discussions about the Caribs is whether or not they practiced cannibalism. The Taíno culture vanished around 1500 after the arrival of the Spanish conquistadors. Those not killed and enslaved by the Spanish died from a smallpox epidemic.

When the Taíno Ruled Boriken

The Taínos were an indigenous group of people who ruled the island of Puerto Rico (which they called Boriken) when Christopher Columbus and his expedition arrived in 1493. A little more than two decades later, they were virtually wiped out.

But surprising developments have recently revealed that the Taínos may live on in Puerto Rico, and not just in the vestiges of their customs, cuisine, and language that are still prevalent today. Preliminary results from DNA studies conducted at the Universidad de Puerto Rico in Mayagüez indicate that nearly half the island's Puerto Rican residents may contain indigenous DNA.

The study of Taíno history and culture is a fairly recent academic undertaking. Previously, what little was known of the peaceful, agrarian society was derived from written accounts by Spanish settlers. But the ongoing study of archaeological sites has uncovered new details about the highly politicized and spiritual society.

The Taínos are thought to have originated in South America before migrating to the Caribbean, where they settled in Puerto Rico, Haiti, the Dominican Republic, and Cuba. Taíno society in Puerto Rico is believed to have developed between AD 1100 and 1500. By the time of Columbus's arrival, the island comprised about 20 political chiefdoms, each one ruled by a cacique (chief). Unlike the laboring class, who mostly wore nothing, the cacique wore a resplendent headdress made of parrot feathers, a gold amulet, and a *mao*, a white cotton shawl-like garment that protected the shoulders and chest from the sun.

Second in power to the caciques were the *bohiques* (shamans). Ornamenting their faces with paint and charcoal, they led spiritual rituals and ceremonies, using herbs, chants, maracas, and tobacco to heal the sick. To communicate with the gods and see visions of the future, *bohiques* and caciques inhaled a hallucinogenic powder made from the bright red seeds of the *cohoba* tree. It was ingested in a ceremony that began with a ritual cleansing that involved inducing vomiting with ornately carved spatulas. The powder was then inhaled through tubes created from tubers or bones.

Of special spiritual importance to the Taínos was the enigmatic *cemí*, a three-pointed object carved from stone or wood. Its significance is a mystery, but some believe it was thought to contain the spirit of the god Yocahu. *Cemies* were plentiful, powerful objects, believed to control everything from weather and crops to health and childbirth. Most *cemies*, which were kept in shrine rooms, were representations of animals and men with froglike legs. Some were ornamented with semiprecious stones and gold and are believed to represent the *cohoba*-fueled visions of the caciques and *bohiques*.

The Taínos saw spirituality in every natural thing, even death. Laborers were buried under their houses, called *bohíos*—conical huts made from cane, straw, and palm leaves. But chiefs and shamans had special funerary rites. Their bodies were left to decompose in the open, and then their bones and skulls were cleaned and preserved in wooden urns or gourds, which were hung from the rafters. Pity the poor wives of the caciques, who were polygamists. Their favorite wives were buried alive when their husbands died.

Religious ceremonies, called *areytos*, were held in ceremonial plazas or rectangular ball courts, called *bateyes*. Lining its perimeter were monoliths adorned with petroglyphs—carvings of faces, animals, and the sun. This is where feasts, celebrations, sporting events, and ritual dances were held. Music was performed on conch trumpets, bone flutes, wooden drums, maracas, and *güiros*, a washboard-type percussion instrument made from gourds. Sometimes neighboring villagers would join in the festivities, participating in mock fights, footraces, or ball games

similar to soccer, played with a heavy bouncing ball made from rubber plants and reeds. As in our modern-day ball games, the consumption of alcoholic beverages—corn beer in Taíno times—was also a highlight of the activities.

When they weren't whooping it up at the *batey*, the Taínos were hard at work growing, gathering, and hunting food. Luckily for them, the island was rich in resources. Peanuts, guavas, pineapples, sea grapes, black-eyed peas, and lima beans grew wild. Fields were cleared for the cultivation of corn, sweet potatoes, yams, squashes, papayas, and yucas, a staple that was processed into a type of flour used to make cassava bread. Cotton was also grown for the making of hammocks. Iguanas, snakes, birds, and manatees were hunted. The sea provided fish, conchs, oysters, and crabs. Canoes, carved from tree trunks, were used to fish and conduct trade with nearby islands. Some canoes were so huge that they could hold 100 men.

The Taínos were a matrilineal society. Women held a special place in the culture because nobility was passed down through their families. The only commoners to don clothing, married women wore a cotton *nagua* (apron); the longer the *nagua*, the higher the social rank of the wearer. Women spent their time making pottery, weaving hammocks, and processing yuca, a time-consuming and complicated procedure. Babies were carried on their mothers' backs on boards that were tied to the babies' foreheads, a practice that produced the flat heads that Taínos found attractive.

Columbus's arrival marked the beginning of the end for Taíno society. They were already weakened from attacks by the Caribs, an aggressive, possibly cannibalistic indigenous group from South America who captured Taíno women and forced them into slavery. The Spanish followed suit by enslaving many of the remaining Taínos.

It didn't take long for unrest to grow among the Taínos. In 1510 Cacique Urayoan ordered his warriors to capture and drown a Spanish settler to determine if the colonists were mortal. Upon Diego Salcedo's death, the Taínos revolted against the Spanish, but they were quickly overpowered by the Spaniards' firearms. Thousands of Taínos were shot to death, many are believed to have committed mass suicide, and others fled to the mountains.

Several devastating hurricanes hit the island during the next several years, which killed many more Taínos. It has been reported that by 1514, there were fewer than 4,000 Taínos left, and in 1519 a smallpox epidemic is said to have virtually wiped out the rest of the remaining population.

In recent decades, interest in learning more about the Taínos has increased. As pride in the legacy of Taíno society grows, so do efforts to preserve its heritage.

In 2007 what experts are calling the largest and most significant pre-Columbian site in the Caribbean was discovered during the construction of a dam in Jacana near Ponce. The five-acre site contains plazas, *bateyes,* burial grounds, residences, and a midden mound—a pile of ritual refuse. After a preliminary four-month investigation that included the removal of 75 boxes of skeletons, ceramics, and petroglyphs, the site has been covered back up to preserve it until a full-scale excavation can begin. It is expected to take 15 to 20 years to unearth all the secrets the site contains.

There are two archaeological sites open to the public: **Centro Ceremonial Indígena de Caguana** (PR 111, km 12.5, between Utuado and Lares, 787/669-1866, 787/894-7325, or 787/894-7310, www.nps.gov/nr/travel/privi/pr25.htm) in Utuado and **Centro Ceremonial Indígena de Tibes** (PR 503, km 2.5, 787/840-2255, www.nps.gov/nr/travel/privi/pr15.htm) in Ponce.

And for a taste of Taíno culture, visit Jayuya in November for the Festival Nacional Indígena, featuring traditional music, dance, food, and crafts.

To learn more about Taíno history and culture, visit the websites of the United Federation of Taíno People (www.uctp.org) and the Jatibonicu Taíno Tribal Nation of Boriken (www.taino-tribe.org).

COLONIZATION

Christopher Columbus was on his second voyage in his quest to "discover" the New World when he arrived in Puerto Rico in 1493. There is debate as to where exactly Columbus, called Cristóbal Colón by the Spanish, first disembarked on the island. That momentous occasion is claimed by Aguada, on the northwest coast of the Atlantic, and Guánica, on the southwest coast of the Caribbean. Either way, he didn't stick around long enough to do much more than christen the island San Juan Bautista, after John the Baptist.

It wasn't until 1508 that Juan Ponce de León, who had been on the voyage with Columbus, returned to the island to establish a settlement. The Taíno provided no resistance to his arrival. In fact, Taíno cacique Agueybana allowed Ponce de León to pick any spot he wanted for a settlement so long as the Spanish would help defend the Taíno against the Caribs. His choice of Caparra, a marshy, mosquito-ridden spot just west of what is now San Juan, was a poor one.

Around 1521 the settlement was relocated to what is now Viejo San Juan, and in 1523 Casa Blanca was built to house Ponce de León and his family, although by that time the explorer had left for Florida, where he met his demise. Originally, the new settlement was called Puerto Rico for its "rich port." It's not clear why—possibly a cartographer's mistake—but soon after it was founded, the name of the settlement was switched with the name of the island.

San Juan quickly became a vital port to the Spanish empire. An important stopover for ships transporting goods from the New World to Europe, it soon became a target for foreign powers. To protect its interests, Spain began a centuries-long effort to construct a formidable series of fortresses to defend the harbor and the city.

Construction of the island's first Spanish fort, La Fortaleza, began in 1533. The small structure, which to this day serves as home to the island's governor, was built to store gold and protect it from Carib attacks. The port quickly grew in importance, and Spain's enemies—England, Holland, and France—began to threaten it with attacks. More elaborate defense systems were needed. To protect the city's all-important harbor, construction of Castillo San Felipe del Morro began in 1539, forming the nucleus of the city's fortifications. Through the years, it was expanded to four levels and five acres before completion in 1787.

To protect the city from attack by land, San Cristóbal castle was begun in 1634. By the time it was completed in 1783, it was the city's largest fort, spanning 27 acres. That same year began the 200-year construction of La Muralla, the massive stone wall that once encircled the city, much of which still stands. It contained five gates, which were closed at night and guarded at all times.

The English were the first to significantly damage the city. In 1595 Sir Francis Drake led 26 vessels in an attack that partially burned the city but was successfully repelled. The next English attack proved more fruitful. Led by George Clifford, the earl of Cumberland, troops landed in Santurce in 1598 and occupied the city for several months before illness and exhaustion forced them to abandon their stronghold.

The most devastating attack to date came when 17 Dutch ships led by Boudoin Hendricks attacked in 1625. And in 1797 the British, led by Sir Ralph Abercrombie, attacked again.

Meanwhile, other settlements were being established throughout the island. The area now known as Aguada was established as Villa de Sotomayor in 1508, but it was destroyed by indigenous peoples in 1511. In 1516 Franciscan friars built a monastery nearby, which was destroyed by indigenous peoples 12 years later. A new monastery was built in 1590, followed by a chapel in 1639. Also an important stopover for ships on their way to Spain from South America, it suffered attacks by the English, French, and Dutch. San

Germán was founded in 1573 and was attacked by pirates, the English, and the Dutch. Arecibo followed in 1606.

Attack by foreign powers waned in the 1800s, and the island's sugarcane and coffee plantations flourished due to an increase in the North Atlantic enslaved people trade, which brought an enslaved workforce by the boatload to the island. Most of the enslaved people were from West Africa originally, but many of them came to Puerto Rico by way of other Caribbean islands. Records are spotty on slavery in Puerto Rico, so it's not known how many lived on the island. They were promised freedom if they joined an independence rebellion that began brewing among the island's rural class in the late 1860s.

On September 23, 1868, about 500 Puerto Ricans organized a revolt called **Grito de Lares,** proclaiming the mountain town of Lares free of Spanish rule. Local stores and offices owned by Spanish merchants were looted, enslaved people were declared free, and city hall was stormed. The revolt was quickly squelched the next day, when rebel forces attempted to take over a neighboring town. Revolutionary leaders were taken prisoner, found guilty of treason and sedition, and sentenced to death. But to ease the political tension, they were eventually released. Although the revolt was unsuccessful, it resulted in Spain's giving the island more autonomy.

Colonial reforms were made, national political parties were established, and slavery was abolished. But at the same time, restrictions were imposed on human rights, such as freedom of the press and the right to gather. Meanwhile, the Spanish empire was beginning to crumble. It eventually lost all its Caribbean colonies except Cuba and Puerto Rico, and increased tariffs and taxes were imposed on imports and exports to help fund Spain's efforts to regain control of nearby Dominican Republic. Living conditions in Puerto Rico deteriorated as the economy declined. Illiteracy was high; malnutrition and poverty were rampant. Violent clashes broke out between desperate residents and Spanish merchants who monopolized trade on the island.

SPANISH-AMERICAN WAR

As the 19th century drew to a close, tensions had grown between Spain's declining empire and the rising world power of the United States, which had set its sights on the Caribbean islands to protect its growing sea trade. Under pressure from the United States, Spain granted Puerto Rico constitutional autonomy. The island established its own currency, postal service, and customs department. It was preparing to hold its first self-governing elections when the Spanish-American War was declared in April 1898.

The war was fought mostly in the waters around Cuba and the Philippines, but in May 1898, San Juan was pounded with artillery for three hours from U.S. warships led by Admiral William T. Sampson. The attack was a misguided effort to flush out a Spanish squadron commander who was not in San Juan at the time. Both of San Juan's major forts sustained damage. The top of Castillo San Felipe del Morro's lighthouse was destroyed, and several residences and government buildings were damaged.

In July 18,000 U.S. troops were sent to secure Puerto Rico. Landing in Guánica, ground troops began working their way northwest to San Juan, but before they could arrive, Spain agreed to relinquish sovereignty over the West Indies. With the signing of the Treaty of Paris in December 1898, Puerto Rico was ceded to the United States.

U.S. RULE AND THE FIGHT FOR INDEPENDENCE

For two years after the Spanish-American War, the United States operated a military government in Puerto Rico until 1900, when the first civilian government was established. The governor, his cabinet, and the senate-like Higher House of Delegates were appointed by the U.S. president. A 35-member Local House of Delegates and a resident commissioner, who represented Puerto Rico in the U.S. House of Representatives but had no vote, were elected by popular vote. In 1917 Puerto Ricans were granted U.S. citizenship by President Woodrow Wilson.

Living conditions in Puerto Rico advanced very little in the first 30 years under U.S. rule. A couple of hurricanes between 1928 and 1932 left the economy—dependent solely on agriculture—in ruins. Homelessness and poverty were rife. The unhappy state of affairs fueled the organization of the independence movement led by the Harvard-educated nationalist leader Pedro Albizu Campos. The doctor chafed against U.S. rule and asserted it had no claims to the island because it had been given its independence from Spain before the Spanish-American War broke out. Campos was named president of the island's Nationalist Party.

On Palm Sunday in 1937, a Nationalist Party demonstration was organized in Ponce to protest Campos's imprisonment for sedition. Just as the march was getting underway, police fired on the crowd, killing 19 people and injuring 200 in what went down in history as the Ponce Massacre. It was a huge blow to the independence movement, and with Campos imprisoned, it seemed as though the fight for freedom had been quelled. Instead, the incident merely drove the movement underground and possibly fueled its embrace of violent tactics.

To quell the brewing unrest, protect its interests, and benefit from the island's resources, the United States took several momentous steps beginning in the 1940s that had far-reaching effects on Puerto Rico's culture. During World War II, several large military bases were established on the island—Fort Buchanan Army Base in Guaynabo, Ramey Air Force Base in Aguadilla, Roosevelt Roads Naval Station in Ceiba, and Vieques Navy Base—which significantly boosted the economy. In 1940 a major hydroelectric-power expansion

Nationalist Hero

Dr. Pedro Albizu Campos died in 1965, but the beloved nationalist leader lives on in the memory of Puerto Ricans everywhere. Nearly every town in Puerto Rico has a street or school named after him, and local artist Dennis Mario Rivera has memorialized him with a graffiti portrait reproduced throughout the island, helping make Campos a pop-culture icon.

Born in Ponce in 1891, Campos was a brilliant man fluent in eight languages who held five degrees from Harvard University. So how did he end up spending the last 25 years of his life in and out of prison? By leading the charge for Puerto Rico's independence from the United States.

Campos was reportedly not anti-American. But he passionately believed that the 1898 Treaty of Paris, which ended the Spanish-American War, wrongfully gave the United States sovereignty over Puerto Rico. After all, Spain had granted autonomy to Puerto Rico in 1897. The island had established its own currency, postal service, and customs department. It's hard to deny Campos's belief that Spain had no authority to bequeath the island to the United States.

graffiti portrait of Dr. Pedro Albizu Campos by local artist Dennis Mario Rivera on Calle San Sebastián

A gifted orator nicknamed El Maestro, Campos joined the Nationalist Party in 1924 and toured Latin America seeking support for the independence movement. He eventually became president of the Nationalist Party, but was never able to rally more than a small minority support. Independence efforts turned violent in 1935, when four nationalists were killed by police in the Río Piedras Massacre. The next year, two nationalists killed a police officer and were arrested and executed without trial. That same year, Campos was convicted of seditious conspiracy to overthrow the U.S. government and sent to the federal penitentiary in Atlanta.

Campos returned to Puerto Rico in 1947 and is believed to have become involved in a plot to incite armed struggle against the United States. Three years later, two nationalist attacks—one on La Fortaleza, the governor's residence in San Juan, and one on Blair House, the temporary home of President Harry Truman—led to Campos's imprisonment for sedition at La Princesa in Viejo San Juan. During that time, his health took a serious decline, which he attributed to radiation experiments performed on him without his consent.

He was eventually pardoned in 1964 and died a year later following a stroke. More than 75,000 people joined his funeral procession. Although the independence movement still has little political clout in Puerto Rico today, Campos is revered as a man who dreamed of liberty but never achieved it.

program was undertaken, providing electrical power throughout the island and attracting U.S. industry. In 1947 President Harry S. Truman agreed to give Puerto Rico more control of its local government, and the next year the island chose its first self-elected governor, Luis Muñoz Marín, a member of the Popular Democratic Party.

But by this time, Campos had finished serving his time and returned to Puerto Rico, where he reinvigorated efforts to achieve independence—this time, at any cost.

On November 1, 1950, two Puerto Rican nationalists attempted to assassinate President Truman in a gun battle that left one police officer dead. Campos was again arrested and found guilty of his role in planning the assassination attempt. He spent the remainder of his life in and out of prison until his death in 1965.

In 1952 Puerto Rico adopted a new constitution, and commonwealth status was established. The island had more self-governing powers than ever before. This was the beginning of the long debate that still rages today over Puerto Rico's political status. While roughly half the population is content with commonwealth status, an equal number of residents have worked steadily toward trying to achieve statehood.

Puerto Rico's first self-elected governor, Luis Muñoz Marín, was a New Deal-style reformist with progressive ideas who served four terms as governor. In partnership with the United States, he initiated many programs that advanced economic and cultural development throughout the island and significantly improved the infrastructure. Under his leadership, an economic development program called Operation Bootstrap was successfully launched to entice global industry to the island with federal and local tax exemptions. *The Economist* described it as "one century of economic development...achieved in a decade." The standard of living leapt to new heights, and the tourist trade soon exploded. The next three decades, from the 1950s through the 1970s, were a huge period of growth and development for the island. But some believed Operation Bootstrap was a throwback to colonial ideals in which the island's resources were exploited without fair compensation, rendering the island increasingly more dependent on the United States.

Meanwhile, the independence movement was quietly gaining momentum, and peaceful protest was not part of the agenda. Two pro-independence organizations formed in the 1970s. The Popular Boricua Army, commonly known as Los Macheteros, primarily operated in Puerto Rico. The Armed Forces of Puerto Rican National Liberation (FALN) operated in the United States. The two organizations communicated their desire for independence with terrorist attacks.

One of FALN's most notorious attacks was setting off a briefcase bomb in 1975 in New York City's Fraunces Tavern, a historic landmark where George Washington delivered his farewell speech to colonial troops during the Revolutionary War. Four patrons were killed. Other bombs were detonated in a Harlem tenement, Penn Station, and JFK airport. All told, FALN set off 72 bombs in New York City and Chicago, killing 5 people and injuring 83.

In 1981 Los Macheteros infiltrated the Puerto Rican Air National Guard base and blew up 11 military planes, causing $45 million in damage. In 1983 members of Los Macheteros raided a Wells Fargo depot in Hartford, Connecticut, wounding a policeman and making off with $7.2 million, ostensibly to fund the organization's efforts.

Sixteen instigators from both organizations were eventually captured and sentenced to federal prison, bringing the terrorist acts to a halt. In 1999 President Clinton granted them clemency.

The 1980s were hard on Puerto Rico. The energy crisis and U.S. recession sent the tourist trade into decline, and many of San Juan's glamorous high-rise hotels fell into disrepair, some shuttering altogether. Hurricane Hugo, a borderline category 3/4 storm in 1989, dealt a devastating blow, and Operation Bootstrap was discontinued, which sent many manufacturers packing.

CONTEMPORARY TIMES

The dawn of a new century found Puerto Rico in a heated contest with the U.S. military over its naval base in Vieques. For years the military had been using the island for bombing practice and ammunitions storage. But in 1999, civilian David Sanes was accidentally killed by a bomb in Vieques, which set off an organized protest effort that raged for several years. The military finally relented, pulling out of Vieques in 2003. Without the base in Vieques, the U.S. Navy decided it didn't need the Roosevelt Roads Naval Station in Ceiba, and it was closed in 2004, taking with it its estimated $250 million-a-year infusion into the local economy. With Ramey Air Force Base having closed in the mid-1970s, Fort Buchanan in Guaynabo is the last remaining U.S. military base on the island.

The independence movement in Puerto Rico has long since abandoned its violent ways, and in truth, only 5 percent of the population wants independence. But every once in a while, something occurs that reminds islanders of the movement's presence and its bloody history. As recently as 2005, the FBI killed—some say ambushed—Los Macheteros organizer Filiberto Ojeda Ríos in a shoot-out at his home in Hormigueros. The 72-year-old man was the ringleader in the 1983 Wells Fargo attack and had evaded authorities ever since. To some, the fact that Ojeda was killed on September 23—a holiday honoring the independence movement's 1868 uprising against Spain—seemed to send a clear reminder to *independistas* that their past activities had not been forgotten.

The single most defining characteristic of Puerto Rico's political climate today is the decades-old debate over whether it should remain a territory of the United States or become a state. In 2012 61 percent of the voters chose statehood in a historic, non-binding referendum. Whether the island actually attains statehood remains to be seen.

The power of protest remains vital in Puerto Rico. In June 2019 Governor Ricardo Rosselló resigned following two weeks of daily mass protests outside his home at La Fortaleza. Half a million people gathered in the streets to protest government corruption and ineptitude in light of the island's debt crisis, reduction of public services, and mismanagement of recovery efforts following Hurricanes Irma and Maria.

Government and Economy

GOVERNMENT ORGANIZATION

Puerto Rico is a self-governing commonwealth of the United States. Its residents are U.S. citizens, but they can't vote for members of Congress or the president. A resident commissioner represents the island's interests in Washington but cannot vote on legislative matters. Businesses pay federal taxes, but individuals do not, although they do contribute to federal programs such as Social Security and Medicare. Individuals also pay about 32 percent of their income in local taxes.

Ever since Puerto Rico became a commonwealth in the early 1950s, its residents have debated the best course for the island's political future. A small but fervent number want independence, but the rest of the island is evenly divided between pro-statehood and pro-commonwealth factions. Statehood would mean more federal funding and a voice in national decisions.

Those opposed to statehood fear losing their Spanish language and heritage in the rush toward Americanization.

In some ways, Puerto Rico is already like a state. The United States oversees all federal affairs, including interstate trade, foreign relations, customs, immigration, currency, military service, judicial procedures, transportation, communications, agriculture, mining, and the postal service. The local Puerto Rican government oversees internal affairs. Based in San Juan, the head of government is an elected governor, and there are two legislative chambers—the House and the Senate. Because of Puerto Rico's severe debt crisis, U.S. Congress enacted the PROMESA law in 2016, creating a financial oversight board to manage Puerto Rico's operating budgets and debt restructuring.

There are 78 municipalities in Puerto Rico, and each one is governed by a popularly elected mayor and municipal assembly.

Puerto Rico Municipalities

© MOON.COM

POLITICAL PARTIES

Puerto Ricans are passionate about politics. Political rallies are frequent, and during election years, political alliances are proclaimed by flag-waving caravans that drive through towns honking their horns and broadcasting speeches from loudspeakers. Puerto Rico has one of the highest percentages of voter turnout in the United States.

There are three political parties in Puerto Rico. The **Popular Democratic Party** is pro-commonwealth, the **New Progressive Party** is pro-statehood, and the **Puerto Rican Independence Party** is pro-independence. Those who embrace independence represent only 5 percent of the population. For decades the island was fairly evenly divided between pro-statehood and pro-commonwealth factions. But a 2012 referendum indicates statehood is gaining in popularity.

JUDICIAL SYSTEM

The judicial system in Puerto Rico is structured the same as in the United States. The highest local court is the Supreme Court, consisting of a chief justice and six associate justices appointed by the governor. There is a Court of Appeals, Superior Court, a civil and criminal District Court, and Municipal Court. The U.S. Federal Court, based in San Juan, has final authority.

ECONOMY

Puerto Rico is in the midst of a debt crisis. In 2014 three major credit agencies downgraded bonds issued by Puerto Rico because the government was incapable of paying its debt. Unable to sell more bonds on the open market, the government began exhausting its savings. In 2016 the U.S. Congress enacted the PROMESA law and appointed a financial oversight board to control government spending. Forced to operate on a reduced budget, the island's government raised taxes and cut public services, which fueled unrest among residents, ultimately leading to the ouster of Governor Ricardo Rosselló in 2019 following two weeks of mass protests outside his home in La Fortaleza.

Contributing factors to the troubled economy include an end to federal exemptions for corporations; the economic depression of 2008; government cronyism, corruption, and wasteful spending; and the Jones Act, which requires all goods shipped to Puerto Rico arrive on U.S.-owned and -operated ships, a costly option. According to a study by the University of Puerto Rico, the Jones Act costs Puerto Ricans $537 million a year. The situation was bad enough when Hurricanes Irma and Maria hit, and the storms made things much worse. In addition to the emotional and financial toll the hurricanes took on residents and businesses, tourism temporarily screeched to a halt, cutting an essential revenue stream.

Currently, 46 percent of the population in Puerto Rico lives below the federal poverty level, compared to the U.S. national average of 15 percent. The island's national debt is $74 billion, it has $49 billion in unfunded pension obligations, and its public utilities like the electric power authority and transportation authority are operating under enormous deficits. But Puerto Rico cannot technically file bankruptcy because U.S. debt relief laws only apply to municipalities on the mainland. At the present, and for the foreseeable future, the Financial Oversight and Management Board is managing debt restructuring.

People who live on the island feel the pinch of Puerto Rico's financial crisis. But the average tourist is not likely to witness its affects. Despite everything, the tourist infrastructure is strong and thriving in Puerto Rico, and visitors can take comfort knowing that every penny they spend on the island helps sustain its residents.

People and Culture

POPULATION

Today more Puerto Ricans live on the U.S. mainland than in Puerto Rico. The island's population was already shrinking due to a double-digit unemployment rate prior to Hurricanes Irma and Maria in 2017. After the storms, the population dropped to a 40-year low of 2.9 million, down from 3.6 million in 2014.

NATIONAL IDENTITY

In 2005 Puerto Ricans were proclaimed the happiest people on earth, according to a highly reported study by the Stockholm-based organization World Values Survey. There does seem to be a collective, fun-loving spirit and zest for life at the heart of Puerto Rican culture, despite the challenges residents endure. Puerto Ricans tend to celebrate big and often. There are more than 500 festivals a year on the island, and everything is a family affair involving multiple generations of relatives. Music and food are at the center of most gatherings.

But don't mistake the *joie de vivre* for frivolity. There are many great thinkers and artists from Puerto Rico. Many locals tend to be very passionate about their opinions and happy to debate politics or sports for hours. They are also exceedingly proud of their island and their heritage. The Puerto Rican flag is ubiquitous on the island.

The island's culture has been significantly shaped by its history. It was originally inhabited by a society of peaceful, agriculturally based indigenous people who migrated to the island from South America. But beginning in 1508, the island became a Spanish colony, and for the next four centuries, European influence reigned. Towns were developed around central plazas and churches, according to Spanish custom. The church spread Catholicism, and Spanish became the official language.

Because the majority of colonists were men, the Spanish Crown officially supported marriage between Spanish men and Taíno women, leading to a population of mixed-race offspring. The Spanish also brought enslaved laborers to the island from Africa to work the island's many coffee and sugar plantations. They also produced offspring with the Taíno and Spanish colonists, resulting in a further blending of races.

Because of this historic mixing of races, Puerto Ricans often claim there is no racial disparity on the island, but recently there have been reports of racial profiling of those of African descent among law enforcement.

When the United States took control of Puerto Rico in 1898, the island underwent another enormous cultural transformation. Suddenly U.S. customs and practices were imposed. English became a common second

Jíbaro Culture

After the Taíno people succumbed to the Spanish conquistadors, an agrarian culture developed in the mountains of Puerto Rico. By the 19th century, wealthy Europeans arrived by ship to establish grand haciendas. Along with enslaved laborers, locals were employed to work the land, growing coffee and sugar. Isolated from developing port cities by unnavigable forest, dependent upon their own two hands to feed and shelter their families, and governed by a strict moral code informed by both Catholicism and Taíno spiritual beliefs, the early Puerto Rican mén and women were poor, hard-working people who made up for their lack of formal education with common sense. When they did venture into the cities, townspeople jeered at them for their straw hats, their neckerchiefs, and their country ways, calling them *jíbaros*, a word similar in meaning to hillbilly.

The word **jíbaro** first appeared in a song and poem in 1820, but it gained widespread acceptance in 1849 when Dr. Manuel Alonzo published his book *El Gíbaro,* a collection of folktales about rustic life. Because they had to create their own entertainment, a big part of *jíbaro* culture was music. Steeped in Spanish roots, *jíbaro* music emphasizes stringed instruments, particularly the four-string *cuatro,* similar in sound to the *guajiro* from Cuba, and is often likened to the folk music of the Appalachian region of the United States. *Jíbaro* music is still quite popular in Puerto Rico and is performed at weddings and Christmas celebrations.

Once a source of embarrassment, the *jíbaro* identity has evolved over time to become a source of Puerto Rican pride. The symbol for the Popular Democratic Party formed in 1938 is the *jíbaro's* straw hat. A monument in Salinas, depicting a man, woman, and child, pays tribute to the *jíbaro* culture. And popular restaurants, such as Raíces Resturante in Viejo San Juan, dress their servers as *jíbaros* in straw hats and neckerchiefs. To be called a *jíbaro* today is to be called a true Puerto Rican.

language, and has at times been proclaimed the official language. The U.S. dollar became the legal tender. American corporations set up shop, bringing with them an influx of mainland Americans, whose ways of dress, cuisine, and art were integrated into the existing culture. Much of this influence is from those in the military. Some people credit that influence on the relative stability and orderliness of public life on the island. Visitors will not be accosted by hordes of people hawking souvenirs in Puerto Rico, like in some islands. The island's governmental and judicial systems are organized similarly to the United States, and many U.S. social services are offered on the island.

Inroads of contemporary American culture have been made into much of island life, but Puerto Ricans are fiercely proud of their Spanish heritage. Since becoming a U.S. territory a little more than 100 years ago, Puerto Rico has undergone a seismic shift in its national identity that has divided the island politically. Puerto Ricans are U.S. citizens, and they enjoy many—but not all—the privileges

that entails. The issue of Puerto Rico's future political status has been an ongoing debate for more than 50 years, and it is as much a part of the island's national identity as its Spanish language and customs.

GENDER ROLES

When it comes to gender roles, Puerto Ricans are fairly traditional. However, as in the rest of the industrial world, women have made inroads into leadership positions in the formerly male worlds of business, politics and sports.

Those who identify as LGBTQ enjoy the same rights and privileges as heterosexual individuals. Transgender persons are permitted to change the gender on their birth certificates, and third gender is legally recognized.

RELIGION

Before the arrival of Christopher Columbus in 1493, Puerto Rico's indigenous population was composed of highly spiritual individuals who worshipped multiple gods believed to reside in nature. It was a common belief that these gods controlled everything from the success or failure of crops to one's choice of a spouse.

All that began to change when Ponce de León arrived in 1508, bringing with him several Roman Catholic priests who ministered to the new colony and set about converting the Taínos to the faith, beginning with baptisms. In 1511 Pope Julius II created a diocese in Caparra, the island's first settlement.

Today, depending on the source, Puerto Rico's population is between 75 and 85 percent Roman Catholic. Although weekly church attendance is far below that figure, the Catholic Church has great influence on Puerto Rican life. Each town has a Catholic church at its center and celebrates its patron saint with an annual festival. Although many patron-saint festivals have become much more secular over time, they typically include a religious procession and special Mass to mark the day. Images of saints are common items in traditional households.

Some Puerto Ricans practice a hybrid form of religion called *espiritismo*, which combines elements of the Catholic religion and indigenous beliefs in nature-dwelling spirits that can be called on to effect change in one's life. Similarly, some Puerto Ricans of African descent practice Santería, introduced to the island by West Africans. It also observes multiple gods and combines elements of Catholicism. Practitioners of both religions patronize the island's *botanicas,* stores that sell roots, herbs, candles, soaps, and amulets that are employed to sway the spirits to help individuals achieve success, whether it be in business, love, or starting a family.

Once the United States arrived in Puerto Rico in 1898, Protestantism began to grow on the island, and all major sects are represented. Pentecostal fundamentalism has developed in recent decades, and there is a small Jewish community on the island as well.

HOLIDAYS AND FESTIVALS

No matter when you visit Puerto Rico, there's a good chance there's a holiday or festival

going on somewhere on the island. Among the biggest festivals are San Juan's **Festival de la Calle de San Sebastián** in January; Ponce's **Carnaval** in February; the **Saborea Puerto Rico** culinary festival in April; Luquillo's **Turtle Festival** in April; Lajas's **Pineapple Festival** in May or June; San Juan's **Noche de San Juan Bautista** in June; Aibonito's **Festival de las Flores** in June-July; San Sebastián's **Festival Nacional de la Hamaca** in July; Loíza's **Fiestas Tradionales de Santiago Apóstol (St. James Carnival)** in July; Jayuya's **Festival Nacional Indígena** in November; **Discovery of Puerto Rico Day** in November; Hatillo's **Festival de Máscaras** and **Día de los Inocentes** in December; and **Santurce es Ley** in Santurce.

Being a U.S. commonwealth, Puerto Rico has adopted an American-style celebration of Christmas, but it also celebrates the more traditional **Día de los Reyes,** also known as **Three Kings Day,** on January 6. On January 5, children fill shoeboxes with grass to feed the Wise Men's camels and place them under their beds. In the morning, the grass is gone and in its place is a present.

But most notably, all 78 municipalities in Puerto Rico honor their patron saints with annual festivals called *fiestas patronales.* Although special Masses and religious processions may be a part of the celebrations, secular festivities such as musical performances, dancing, traditional foods, artisan booths, and games often take precedence. The festivals typically take place in the main plaza.

LANGUAGE

Puerto Rico has two official languages: Spanish and English. Many Puerto Ricans living in metropolitan areas are bilingual, but by far the majority of the population uses primarily Spanish. Spanish is spoken in the public school system, and English is taught as a foreign language.

In recent years, the designation of Puerto Rico's official language has been caught in a political volley between the pro-statehood and pro-commonwealth factions. In 1991

An Island Christmas

The Twelve Days of Christmas have nothing on Puerto Rico. Here, Las Navidades (the Christmas holidays) start the day after Thanksgiving and end in mid-January with the San Sebastián Festival. On any given day during the Christmas holiday period (usually after 10pm), a roving band of *parranderos*—like carolers but dressed in straw hats and playing guitars and maracas — will wake an unsuspecting friend with Christmas songs and raucous demands for food and drink. After the visitors have emptied the pantry and the refrigerator, the owners of the home close up the house and join the *parranderos* at the next house, and the next house, and so on, until dawn, when the last house serves everyone the traditional *asopao de pollo* (chicken and rice stew).

Nochebuena (Christmas Eve) is an official half-day holiday when friends and family come together over a large meal, followed by midnight Mass. Many Puerto Ricans have adopted the tradition of Santa Claus on Christmas Day, called Navidad. In addition to presents from St. Nick, the highlight is a daylong party that usually involves roasting a whole pig over wood charcoal.

On December 28, the north coast town of Hatillo commemorates Herod's slaughter of innocents in Bethlehem with Día de los Inocentes, a celebration featuring costumed parades throughout the countryside, where tricks are played on friends and family.

At the stroke of midnight on New Year's Eve or Año Viejo (Old Year), tradition dictates that locals eat 12 grapes, sprinkle sugar outside the house for good luck, and throw a bucket of water out the window to get rid of the old and make room for the new. Fireworks light up the sky at the Puerto Rico Convention Center in San Juan at midnight.

Puerto Rico's traditional Christian holiday is Día de los Reyes (Three Kings Day) on January 6. Festivities begin the night before with Víspera de los Reyes (Eve of the Epiphany of the Kings), when children fill drinking glasses with water for thirsty Wise Men and fill shoeboxes with grass for their camels. The next morning children discover that the water and grass have been consumed and find gifts that have been left beneath their beds.

The Festival de la Calle de San Sebastían in Viejo San Juan originated as a day to honor Saint Sebastian. It takes place in mid-January, which makes it a natural bookend to the island's holiday season. The four-day festival is likened to Mardi Gras without the beads, when hundreds of thousands of people descend on Viejo San Juan for parades, concerts, artisan booths, and lots of eating and drinking.

Governor Rafael Hernández Colón, a proponent of commonwealth status, declared Spanish as the sole official language. He was preceded by Governor Pedro Rosselló, a proponent of statehood who changed the official language to English. But for now, both languages enjoy official status.

EDUCATION

Puerto Rico has a 94 percent literacy rate, and its educational system is structured the same as in the United States—kindergarten through 12th grade. In addition to the public school system, the Catholic Church operates a private school system. Both systems teach in Spanish. There are also several English-language private schools on the island.

There are many institutions of higher learning in Puerto Rico, the largest one being the Universidad de Puerto Rico, with campuses in Mayagüez, San Juan, Río Piedras, and Humacao. Other schools include Universidad Polytechnica de Puerto Rico, Universidad Intermericana de Puerto Rico, Universidad Carlos Albizu, and Universidad del Sagrado Corazón. There are also two arts schools—Escuela de Artes Plásticas de Puerto Rico and Conservatorio de Música de Puerto Rico.

The Arts

Puerto Rico is a melting pot of indigenous, Spanish, and African influences, and nowhere is that more apparent than in the island's rich cultural life. Food, music, art, dance—they all reflect different aspects of the cultures that came together over time to create *la vida criolla* (the Creole life).

MUSIC

Music is a huge part of Puerto Rican life. Sometimes it seems as though the whole island reverberates to a syncopated beat, thanks to the strains of music that waft from outdoor concerts, open windows, barrooms, and passing cars. Nearly every weekend there is a holiday or festival in Puerto Rico, and at the core of its celebration is always music. During a recent stay in Viejo San Juan, each morning began with the sound of a lone elderly man walking up the deserted street singing a heartbreaking lament that echoed off the 18th-century buildings.

The island has made many significant contributions to the world of music at large, starting with the birth of a couple of uniquely Puerto Rican instruments. The national instrument of Puerto Rico is the *cuatro*, an adaptation of the Spanish guitar that features 10 strings arranged in five pairs and is typically carved from solid blocks of laurel. Several classic Puerto Rican instruments date to the indigenous people, including the popular *güiro*. Similar in principle to the washboard, the *güiro* is a hollowed gourd with ridges cut into its surface, which is scraped rhythmically with a comb-like object. Other prevalent local instruments that reflect African influence are the *barril*, a large drum originally made by stretching animal skin over the top of a barrel; the *tambour*, a handheld drum similar to a tambourine but without the cymbals; and the maraca, made from gourds and seeds.

Some of Puerto Rico's earliest known musical styles are *bomba* and *plena*, which have roots in African culture. They're both heavy on percussion and lightning-fast rhythms. *Bomba* features call-and-response vocals and is accompanied by frenzied dancing in which the dancers match their steps to the ever-quickening beat of the drum. In *plena*, the emphasis is on the vocals, which are more European in origin and retell current events or local scandals. Local *bomba* masters include Los Hermanos Ayala (traditionalists from Loíza) and the more contemporary Cepedas (based in Santurce, San Juan). Reviving interest in *plena* is the band Plena Libre.

Akin in philosophy to the origins of American country music, *música jíbara* is the folk sound of Puerto Rico's rural mountain dwellers, called *jíbaros*. Performed by small ensembles on *cuatro*, *güiro*, bongos, and occasionally clarinets and trumpets, *música jíbara* is more Spanish in origin than *bomba* or *plena*, although the Caribbean influence is unmistakable. Vocals, which play an important part in *música jíbara*, are usually about the virtues of a simpler way of life. There are two types of *música jíbara*—*seis* and *aguinalda*. *Seis* is typically named after a particular town, and the lyrics are often improvised and sung in 10-syllable couplets. *Aguinaldos* are performed around Christmas by roaming carolers. Ramito (1915-1990) is considered Puerto Rico's quintessential *jíbaro* artist.

Historically, while Puerto Ricans of African descent grooved to *bomba* and the farmers played their folk tunes, Puerto Rico's moneyed Europeans turned their attentions to classical music, eventually giving birth around 1900 to *danza*, a romantic classical style of music often described as Afro-Caribbean waltz. Originating in Ponce, *danza* was performed on piano, cello, violin, and *bombardino* (similar to a trombone) for dancers who performed structured, ballroom-style steps. The form is celebrated in Ponce with the annual Semana de la Danza in May.

The most famous composers of *danza* were Manuel Gregorio Tavarez (1843-1883) and his pupil, Juan Morel Campos (1857-1896).

In 1956 renowned Catalan cellist and composer Pablo Casals moved to Puerto Rico, and a year later Festival Casals was born. The international celebration of classical music continues today in concert halls in San Juan, Ponce, and Mayagüez every June and July. In Viejo San Juan, there is a museum dedicated to Casals, featuring his music manuscripts, instruments, and recordings.

Of course, salsa is the music most associated with Puerto Rico today. A lively, highly danceable fusion of jazz, African polyrhythms, and Caribbean flair, salsa is performed by large ensembles on drums, keyboards, and horns. When people refer to Latin music, they usually mean salsa. It is the predominant form of music heard on the island, so just stop in almost any bar or restaurant advertising live music and you're likely to hear it. Watching expert salsa dancers move to the music is as entertaining as listening to the it. Born in New York City but Puerto Rican by heritage, percussionist and composer Tito Puente (1923-2000) was a major influence on salsa music. Other masters include Celia Cruz (1924-2003), Willie Colón, and El Gran Combo de Puerto Rico. Contemporary salsa artists include Marc Anthony and the group Pirulo y la Tribu.

Reggaetón, a blend of American hip-hop, *bomba, plena,* and Jamaican dancehall, is the musical form born and bred in Puerto Rico. The first big breakout artist was Daddy Yankee, who grew up in the public housing projects of San Juan and managed to cross over into the American market. Reggaetón festivals have become a popular pastime in Puerto Rico, but you can also hear it in nightclubs and blasting from car windows. Other popular reggaetón artists include Don Omar, Tego Calderón, Ivy Queen, and Calle 13, which launched the successful solo careers of singer/songwriter iLe (Ileana Cabra Joglar), the band's solo female member, and rapper Residente (René Juan Pérez Joglar).

In 2017 singer Luis Fonsi and Daddy Yankee released the single "Despacito" with a video filmed in La Factoria bar and La Perla neighborhood in San Juan. Three months later the English remix with Justin Bieber was released. The song was a musical sensation. It won four 2018 Latin Grammy Awards, including Song of the Year, and was number one on the Billboard Hot 100 chart for 16 consecutive weeks.

Another contemporary breakout star from Puerto Rico is Bad Bunny (aka Benito Antonio Martinez Ocasio), a pioneer of Latin trap music from Vega Baja. He was working as a grocery store bagger in Arecibo while attending the University of Puerto Rico when his music was discovered on Soundcloud. He won the Artist of the 2018 Latin American Music Awards Best New Artist honor.

VISUAL ARTS

The visual arts have been a thriving art form in Puerto Rico for centuries, and its artists' output runs the gamut from historic baroque European-influenced paintings to contemporary conceptual pieces that challenge the definition of art.

Puerto Rico's best-known early artists were José Campeche (1751-1809) and Francisco Oller (1833-1917). Campeche was of mixed race, born in San Juan to a freed enslaved person, Tomás Campeche, and a native of the Canary Islands, María Jordán Marqué. He was primarily a self-taught artist, first learning the skill from his father, but he studied for a time with Luis Paret, an exiled Spanish painter who lived in Puerto Rico for a while. As was common at the time, Campeche primarily painted portraits of wealthy landowners and religious scenes in heavily ornamented detail, which was in keeping with the rococo style of the day. He painted more than 400 paintings during his lifetime, the majority of them commissions. Campeche's *Virgen de la Soledad de la Victoria* was the first acquisition of the Museo de Arte de Puerto Rico, where you can see many other examples of his work.

Oller was born in Bayamón and studied

Fiestas Patronales

The most elaborate and renowned *fiestas patronales* take place in San Juan and Loíza, but all of the municipalities' celebrations honoring their patron saints offer visitors a unique opportunity to get a concentrated dose of local culture. Here is a list of some of the island's *fiestas patronales*.

FEBRUARY

- **Manatí:** La Virgen de la Candelaria, February 2
- **Mayagüez:** La Virgen de la Candelaria, February 2
- **Coamo:** La Virgen de la Candelaria and San Blas, February 3

MARCH

- **Loíza:** San Patricio, March 17
- **Lares:** San José, March 19
- **Luquillo:** San José, March 19

MAY

- **Arecibo:** Apóstol San Felipe, May 1
- **Maunabo:** San Isidro, May 15
- **Toa Alta:** San Fernando, May 30

JUNE

- **Barranquitas:** San Antonio de Padua, June 13
- **Dorado:** San Antonio de Padua, June 13
- **Isabela:** San Antonio de Padua, June 13
- **San Juan:** San Juan Bautista, June 23
- **Orocovis:** San Juan Bautista, June 24
- **Toa Baja:** San Pedro Apóstol, June 30

JULY

- **Culebra:** Virgen del Carmen, July 16
- **Hatillo:** Virgen del Carmen, July 16
- **Morovis:** Virgen del Carmen, July 16
- **Aibonito:** Santiago Apóstol, July 25

art at the Academia de Bellas Artes in Madrid from 1851 to 1853. He also studied in Paris from 1858 to 1863, where he was a contemporary of Pissarro, Cézanne, and Guillaumins and exhibited at several Paris salons. Influenced by realist and impressionist styles, his work encompassed portraits, landscapes, and still lifes. But once he returned for good to Puerto Rico in 1884, his work became primarily realist in nature, typically rendered in

- **Fajardo:** Santiago Apóstol, July 25
- **Guánica:** Santiago Apóstol, July 25
- **Loíza:** Santiago Apóstol, July 25
- **San Germán:** San Germán, July 31

AUGUST
- **Cayey:** Nuestra Señora de la Asunción, August 15
- **Adjuntas:** San Joaquín and Santa Ana, August 21
- **Rincón:** Santa Rosa de Lima, August 30

SEPTEMBER
- **Jayuya:** Nuestra Señora de la Monserrate, September 8
- **Moca:** Nuestra Señora de la Monserrate, September 8
- **Salinas:** Nuestra Señora de la Monserrate, September 8
- **Cabo Rojo:** San Miguel Arcangel, September 29
- **Utuado:** San Miguel Arcangel, September 29

OCTOBER
- **Yabucoa:** Los Angeles Custodios, October 2
- **Naguabo:** Nuestra Señora del Rosario, October 7
- **Vega Baja:** Nuestra Señora del Rosario, October 7
- **Quebradillas:** San Rafael Arcangel, October 24

NOVEMBER
- **Aguadilla:** San Carlos Borromeo, November 4

DECEMBER
- **Vega Alta:** La Inmaculada Concepción de María, December 8
- **Vieques:** La Inmaculada Concepción de María, December 8
- **Ponce:** Nuestra Señora de la Guadalupe, December 12

somber colors. His subjects tended to focus on traditional Puerto Rican ways of life. One of his most famous paintings is *El Velorio (The Wake)*, which depicts a rural family gathered in a home for an infant's wake and can be seen in a gallery at the Universidad de Puerto Rico in Río Piedras. Oller's work has been acquired by many important museums, including the Musée d'Orsay in Paris.

Two other important early artists were

Miguel Pou (1880-1968) and Ramón Frade (1875-1954), whose paintings celebrated the dignity of *jíbaro* (peasant) life.

Another internationally recognized artist was island transplant Jack Delano (1914-1997), a significant photographer who chronicled the Puerto Rican people and way of life from 1941 until his death. Born in Kiev, Ukraine, he first came to Puerto Rico in 1941 on assignment for the U.S. Farm Security Administration in conjunction with President Franklin D. Roosevelt's New Deal programs. The program sent many famous photographers throughout the United States to document rural life. In addition to Delano, they included Walker Evans, Dorothea Lange, Marjory Collins, and Gordon Parks, among others. After the war, Delano returned to Puerto Rico in 1946, settled there permanently, and continued to photograph the island's changing culture. His work is journalistic in nature but is deeply imbued with a respect for the human condition. In addition to his photography, Delano was a musical composer of sonatas.

Beginning in the 1940s, a radical new art form exploded in Puerto Rico that reflected growing concern among artists and writers that the island's native culture was being subsumed by American influence. That sentiment was expressed in visually striking representations of graphic poster art, called *cartels*. Originally funded by the local government, artists produced colorful illustrations of important books, plays, songs, and poems, as well as political slogans and quotations. Eventually the art form evolved away from its boosterish origins. Some artists used the form to criticize the government and social issues, while others celebrated the island's natural and architectural beauty. Today it's most commonly seen advertising festivals. Among its most celebrated artists is Lorenzo Homar (1913-2004), who was a recipient of the National Medal of Honor and cofounder of the Centro de Arte de Puertorriqueño, which played an important role in advancing the graphic art form. The Museo de Arte de Puerto Rico has a gallery devoted to an excellent collection of *cartels*.

Another significant artist was Rafael Tufiño (1922-2008), whose somber paintings captured the island's people and customs, as well as its pockets of squalor. Tufiño was also a cofounder of the Centro de Arte de Puertorriqueña and a faculty member for the Puerto Rico Institute of Culture's art school, Escuela de Artes Plásticas.

Puerto Rico's arts scene continues to evolve. Recognizing the positive impact art can have on the economy, in 2001 Governor Sila M. Calderón initiated a $25 million program to fund the **Puerto Rico Public Art Project,** which put in place scores of contemporary site-specific public art installations throughout the island.

Santurce es Ley (www.facebook.com/santurceesley), a union of independent artists, was started in 2010. In addition to commissioning visually arresting mural projects throughout Santurce, it hosts an annual street festival and other events that celebrate and promote contemporary artists and DJs. The timing of the festival changes from year to year, but it's possible to see the resulting murals that have accumulated over time along Calle Loíza and Calle Cerra.

CRAFTS

Puerto Rican artisans produce a variety of crafts unique to the island's culture. The most distinctive craft is the *vejigante mask,* a brilliantly colored object made from coconut shells or papier-mâché featuring large protruding horns. The masks represent the Moors in annual festivals revolving around street pageants that reenact Spain's defeat of the Moors in the 13th century. Although there are several artists who create the masks, the Ayala family artists in Loíza were considered the masters of the form. Prices range from $30-250. *Vejigante* figurines made from a variety of materials, including ceramic, glass, and metal, are also popular collectible items made by local artisans and come in all price ranges.

Puerto Rico's oldest and most traditional craft form is the **santo**, primitive-looking woodcarvings of Catholic saints. Santos originated with low-income families who wanted representations of their favorite saints to display in their homes but couldn't afford the expensive plaster ones available for purchase. Today, santos are highly collectible, and many museums, including Museo de las Americas in Viejo San Juan, exhibit priceless collections of vintage santos. New santos can be found in the island's finer crafts and gift shops and cost $80-500.

Mundillo is a delicate, handmade lace created by tying fine threads using bobbins, which facilitate weaving the threads into an intricate pattern. The lace is used to embellish tablecloths, handkerchiefs, and christening gowns, among other things. The art form has roots in Spain, but the *mundillo* pattern is specific to Puerto Rico. It's primarily produced in and around the tiny town of Moca near Aguadilla on the west coast, where several artisans live. *Mundillo* can be purchased at finer gift shops around the island and at some festivals. Because it is so labor-intensive, *mundillo* is somewhat pricey. A handkerchief rimmed with a small amount of *mundillo* starts around $30, but a handkerchief made entirely of *mundillo* can cost more than $100.

The crafting of woven cotton **hammocks** is an art form that continues a tradition started by the Taíno Indians, who used them not only to sleep on but also for food storage and other utilitarian purposes. The town of San Sebastián in the western fringe of the Cordillera Central is the best-known source of the hammock, but they're available at most crafts and gift shops throughout the island, starting at about $30.

Other popular low-priced craft items include **seed jewelry**, colorful earrings, bracelets, and necklaces made from the seeds of trees and plants on the island; *güiros*, percussion instruments made from gourds; and landscape paintings on pieces of rough-hewn wood.

LITERATURE

Literature in Puerto Rico has historically revolved around national identity and the tension of being U.S. citizens in a Latino culture. Its literary heritage began to emerge in the mid-1800s, and among its earliest notable works was *El Gibaro* (1849) by Manuel Alonso y Pacheco. Part prose, part poetry, *El Gibaro* celebrated the simple life of Puerto Rico's farmers, called *jíbaros*.

But the first writer to receive literary prominence was Alejandro Tapia y Rivera (1826-1882) of San Juan, a playwright and abolitionist who wrote many works, including biographical pieces on important Puerto Ricans such as Spanish admiral Ramón Power y Giralt, artist José Campeche, and the pirate Roberto Cofresí.

One of Puerto Rico's early writers who was revered throughout the Caribbean and South America was Eugenio María de Hostos (1839-1903), a writer and educator who led civic-reform movements throughout Latin America. His seminal work is *Peregrinación de Bayoán* (1863), a work of fiction that illustrated injustices under the Spanish regime and called for independence from Spain.

After Puerto Rico came under control of the United States, a new crop of writers, called the Generation of 1898, began to flourish. Fueled primarily by politics, several writers of this era combined the art of poetry with the craft of journalism. José de Diego (1867-1918) of Aguadilla and Luís Muñoz Rivera (1859-1916) of Barranquitas were significant poets and journalists who fueled the island's independence movement with their words. Diego, considered a precursor of the modernist movement in Puerto Rico, produced several books of poetry, including *Pomarrosas, Jovillos, Cantos de Rebeldia,* and *Cantos del Pitirre*. Rivera's most significant work was a book of poems called *Tropicales*.

One of the most important writers of this era was Antonio S. Pedriera (1899-1939), whose work *Insularismo* examined how U.S. political control had affected Puerto Rican culture in the first 35 years.

In the 1940s, there was a mass migration of Puerto Ricans to the United States—primarily New York City—and the island's literature took a significant shift reflecting that phenomenon. Suddenly there was an output of work by Puerto Rican immigrants who found themselves grappling with issues of dual identity. In 1951 playwright René Marqués (1919-1974) of Arecibo wrote his most critically acclaimed play, *The Oxcart,* which chronicled the mass exodus of Puerto Ricans to New York City. Also noteworthy is *A Puerto Rican in New York* (1961), by Jesús Colón (1918-1974), who was born in Cayey but grew up in the United States. Julia de Burgos (1914-1953) was a celebrated poet, feminist, and nationalist who wrote poems as the land and oppression.

The 1960s and 1970s saw the birth of a literary movement called Nuyorican literature. Nuyorican is the name given to New Yorkers of Puerto Rican heritage. Some of the most notable writers of this movement were Piri Thomas, author of *Down These Mean Streets* (1967), and Nicholasa Mohr, who wrote *Nilda* (1973), both of which dealt with life in the urban barrios of New York City.

By the 1980s, the Nuyorican movement exploded on the spoken-word scene with work that had a strong political message. New York's Nuyorican Poets Café was and still is the epicenter of this movement, providing a forum for such celebrated poets as Ponce-born Pedro Pietri (1944-2004), for whom a street in New York City was recently named, and New York-born Felipe Luciano, founder of the Young Lords activist group. Also once a regular at Nuyorican Poets Café was Gurabo-born Miguel Piñero (1946-1988), who was a playwright and actor. His play *Short Eyes,* about life in prison, won the New York Drama Critics Award for Best American Play in 1974. His life was depicted in a film starring Benjamin Bratt called *Piñero.*

Puerto Rican literature continues to flourish today thanks to many contemporary writers living on the island and in the United States, including poet Victor Hernández Cruz and authors Esmeralda Santiago and Ernesto Quiñonez. Santiago wrote *Conquistador* (2011), a historical novel about a sugar plantation owner in 19th-century Puerto Rico, and *When I Was Puerto Rican* (1993), a memoir about growing up on the island. Quiñonez wrote *Bodega Dreams* (2000) and *Chango's Fire* (2004).

For an excellent survey of Puerto Rican literature, read *Boricuas: The Influential Puerto Rican Writings, an Anthology* (Ballantine, 1995), featuring excerpts of works by some of the writers mentioned here, as well as many others.

DANCE

Dance plays an important role in Puerto Rican culture because it goes hand in hand with the island's rich musical heritage. But for the most part, dance is about moving to the groove of live music or DJs, whether it's at a nightclub, an outdoor concert in the town plaza, or at one of the island's countless festivals. Dance is integral to *bomba, plena,* salsa, and reggaetón music, and the thing all those forms of movement have in common is this: It's all in the hips! The exception is the ballroom style of *danza.*

When it comes to dance performance, the island leader is Guateque, the folkloric ballet of Puerto Rico. For more than 20 years, this 40-member dance company and school based on Corozal has been preserving and performing the island's traditional dances, as well as adapting them into new productions. Past productions include *Los Taínos de Borkén* and *Los Dioses (The Gods),* which depict daily life and spirituality of the island's indigenous people.

Essentials

Transportation

GETTING THERE
Air

Puerto Rico has two international airports, **Luis Muñoz Marín International Airport** (Aeropuerto Internacional Luis Muñoz Marín, SJU) in Isla Verde, San Juan, and **Rafael Hernández International Airport** (Aeropuerto Internacional Rafael Hernández, BQN) in Aguadilla on the west coast. The only other airport to service flights from within the United States is **Mercedita International Airport** (Aeropuerto Internacional Mercedita, PSE) in Ponce on the south coast.

Regional airports serving commercial travel are Isla Grande Airport (SIG) near Viejo San Juan; José Aponte de la Torre Airport (RVR) in Ceiba; Eugenio María de Hostos Airport (MAZ) in Mayagüez; Vieques Airport (VQS) in Isabel Segunda; and Culebra Airport (CPX) in Culebra. Airports in Fajardo and Humacao have been closed to commercial service.

Airfares to Puerto Rico fluctuate in price throughout the year, but the cheapest rates can typically be secured during the off-season, May-October, which is also hurricane season.

FROM NORTH AMERICA
Direct flights to San Juan are available from Atlanta, Boston, Chicago, Dallas/Fort Worth, Fort Lauderdale, Orlando, Miami, New York City, Newark, Philadelphia, and Washington DC.

These airlines offer flights to San Juan, Aguadilla, and Ponce from the United States:

- **American Airlines** (800/433-7300, www. aa.com)
- **Delta Air Lines** (800/221-1212 or 800/325-1999, www.delta.com)
- **JetBlue Airways** (800/538-2583, www. jetblue.com)
- **Southwest** (800-435-9792, www. southwest.com)
- **Spirit Airlines** (800/772-7117, www.spiritairlines.com)
- **United Airlines** (800/864-8331, www. united.com)

In Canada, direct flights to San Juan are operated by **Air Canada** (888/247-2262, www. aircanada.com) from Montréal and Toronto.

FROM EUROPE
British Airways (www.britishairways.com) offers connecting flights from the United Kingdom to San Juan via New York City or Miami. **Iberia** (www.iberia.com) offers connecting flights to San Juan from Spain.

FROM AUSTRALIA
Connecting flights from Australia are operated by **United** (through Los Angeles and Chicago) and **American Airlines** (through New York City).

FROM THE CARIBBEAN
Several small airlines offer flights to San Juan from throughout the Caribbean. They include **Air Sunshine** (888/879-8900, www. airsunshine.com) from St. Croix, St. Thomas, Tortola, Virgin Gorda, and Vieques; **Cape Air** (800/352-0714, www.flycapeair.com) from St. Croix, St. Thomas, and Tortola; and **Liat Airline** (888/844-5428, www.liatairline.com) from 22 destinations in the eastern Caribbean.

Cruise Ship
San Juan is the largest port in the Caribbean, and it is a port of call or point of origin for nearly two dozen cruise lines. The Viejo San Juan Cruise Ship Piers features four piers and two terminals along Calle La Marina. The Pan American Pier on Isla Grande, by the Puerto Rico Convention Center, can accommodate two mega ships. San Juan can dock up to eight cruise ships at one time.

A few of the most popular cruise lines serving San Juan include:

- **Carnival Cruise Lines** (866/299-5698, www.carnival.com)
- **Celebrity Cruises** (800/647-2251, www. celebritycruises.com)
- **Disney Cruise Line** (800/951-3532, www. disneycruise.disney.go.com)
- **Holland America Line** (877/724-5425, www.hollandamerica.com)
- **Norwegian Cruise Line** (800/327-7030, www.ncl.com)

Previous: Rafael Hernández International Airport in Aguadilla.

- **Princess Cruises** (800/774-6237, www. princess.com)
- **Royal Caribbean Cruises** (800/256-6649, www.royalcaribbean.com)
- **Viking Ocean Cruises** (877/668-4546, www.vikingcruises.com)
- **Windstar Cruises** (800/258-7245, www. windstarcruises.com)

GETTING AROUND

Puerto Rico's easy accessibility from the States and the compact lay of the land make it a great place to go for a long weekend. Many visitors simply fly into San Juan and stay there, enjoying the many great restaurants, nightclubs, shopping, beaches, and historical sights within walking or taxi distance. A reliable bus transit system and the modern rapid-transit system, Tren Urbano, provide inexpensive transportation throughout the city. It's understandable why some visitors are hesitant to leave behind the capital city's charms.

But escaping the bustle of the city and experiencing the island's unique natural beauty is highly recommended and easily achieved. Car-rental agencies are plentiful, and the roads are well marked and maintained. Because the island is so small, it's possible to make a day trip to any sight on the island. Just keep in mind that Puerto Rico has a high volume of traffic and the density of development in San Juan and along the north coast can slow your progress. Travel through the central mountain region is also impeded by narrow winding roads. Always figure in extra travel time when planning a road trip. A general rule of thumb is to allow two minutes for every mile.

Car

Visitors who plan to venture outside of San Juan should plan to rent a car. This is by far the best way to explore the island. Most of the major American car-rental agencies have locations throughout the island, and there are several local agencies as well. For the most part, roads are well maintained and marked. Gasoline is sold by the liter, speed limits are measured in miles per hour, and distance is measured in kilometers. And all road signs are in Spanish. International driving licenses are required for drivers from countries other than the United States. GPS apps such as Waze and Google Maps are excellent navigation tools for driving around the island.

Take extra precautions when driving in the mountains. Fortunately, the traffic is light, but the roads are narrow and winding. Drivers who travel these roads every day tend to proceed at a perilously fast clip. If the driver behind you appears impatient or tailgates, pull over and let him or her pass. On roads with a lot of blind curves, it is common practice to blow the car horn to alert oncoming traffic you're approaching. If it's raining, beware of small mudslides and overflowing riverbanks, which sometimes close roads. And whatever you do, don't look down! But really, it's not as bad as it sounds. Driving through Puerto Rico's majestic mountains is well worth a few shattered nerves.

There is an excellent, major, limited-access highway system called *autopista* that dissects and nearly encircles the island, parts of which are toll roads ($0.25-1.25 per toll). The speed limits range 50-65 miles per hour.

The rest of the island's numbered roads are called *carreteras,* typically identified as the abbreviation Carr., followed by a number, such as Carr. 193. But more and more, "PR" is replacing "Carr." in roadway designations. Major *carreteras* often have spur routes that go either into a town's center or along its beachfront. A road number followed by the letter R or the word *ramal* indicates a spur route that goes through a town's commercial district. Beachfront routes are often indicated by the abbreviation *int.* or an addition of the numeral 3 after a road number.

Addresses are typically identified by road and kilometer numbers, for instance: PR 193, km 2. Look for the white numbered kilometer posts alongside the road to identify your location. In towns, streets are called *avenidas* (abbreviated as Ave.) and *calles.*

Highways and Driving Distances

MAJOR HIGHWAYS

- **PR 26:** East-west, San Juan airport to Condado; also known as Baldorioty de Castro Avenue
- **PR 18:** North-south, connecting PR 22 and PR 52, San Juan
- **PR 66:** Northwest-southeast, Canovanas to San Juan
- **PR 22:** East-west, San Juan to Arecibo (toll); also known as Jose de Diego Expressway
- **PR 52:** North-southwest, San Juan to Ponce (partially toll); also known as Luis A. Ferré Expressway
- **PR 30:** Northwest-southeast, Caguas to Humacao
- **PR 53:** North-south, Fajardo to Yabucoa

DRIVING DISTANCES FROM SAN JUAN

- **Aguadilla:** 81 miles (130 kilometers)
- **Arecibo:** 48 miles (77 kilometers)
- **Barranquitas:** 34 miles (55 kilometers)
- **Cabo Rojo:** 111 miles (179 kilometers)
- **Cayey:** 30 miles (48 kilometers)
- **Dorado:** 17 miles (27 kilometers)
- **Fajardo:** 32 miles (52 kilometers)
- **Guánica:** 94 miles (151 kilometers)
- **Humacao:** 34 miles (55 kilometers)
- **Jayuya:** 58 miles (93 kilometers)
- **La Parguera:** 107 miles (172 kilometers)
- **Luquillo:** 28 miles (45 kilometers)
- **Mayagüez:** 98 miles (158 kilometers)
- **Ponce:** 70 miles (113 kilometers)
- **Rincón:** 93 miles (150 kilometers)
- **Salinas:** 46 miles (74 kilometers)
- **Utuado:** 65 miles (105 kilometers)

TRAFFIC

Like any modern metropolitan city, San Juan has a traffic problem. Expect the typical morning commuter rush hour between 7:30am-9am. During the school year, the evening rush hour starts to ramp up around 3pm when schools let out and lasts until 7pm or so. During summer months it starts around 4:30pm.

Driving around San Juan can be nerve-racking for those not accustomed to inner-city driving. The sheer number of cars on

Driving Vocabulary

USEFUL WORDS

al centro: downtown
autopista: limited access toll road
calle: street
carr. or *carretera:* highway
cruce: crossroads
cruzar: to cross
cuadras: blocks
esquina: corner
estacionamiento: parking
derecha: right
derecho: straight ahead
doble: turn
izquierda: left
lejos: far
luces: traffic lights
luz: traffic light
vaya: go

ROAD SIGNS

alto: stop
calle sin salida: dead-end street
cuidado: be careful
despacio: slow
desvio: detour
este: east
hacia: to
int.: approaching intersection, or interior route
norte: north
oeste: west
ramal: business route
salida: exit
sur: south

the island guarantees congested roadways, so be sure to schedule extra time for road trips. Drivers tend to speed and don't leave much space between cars. They also can be creative when it comes to navigating traffic—rolling through stops and driving on the shoulder of the highway is not uncommon. Ponce has, hands-down, the worst drivers. It's practically a free-for-all, and they blow their car horns constantly.

Weekend traffic to popular beaches or towns hosting festivals can be particularly thick. If you're going to Piñones, plan to be there no later than 10am or you could spend hours in traffic trying to get in. Progress on PR 2, the commercial route that runs the length of the north coast from San Juan to Aguadilla, is a grueling drive due to the volume of traffic, the plethora of traffic lights, and the density of development. You're best advised to take PR 22, a divided, controlled-access highway with tolls.

Driving through the Cordillera Central is also slow going, but for a very different reason. There's little development or traffic, but the roads can be very narrow and winding. No matter where you go on the island, a good rule of thumb is to allow two minutes for every mile.

Taxis and Ride-Hailing Services

Most towns in Puerto Rico are served by at least one taxi service. San Juan has several reliable tourist-taxi services that serve the areas where visitors congregate. It's possible to flag one down on the street, but you may have better luck finding a taxi stand on the plaza or at a hotel. You can also call one on the phone.

Operators include **San Juan Taxis** (877/288-8294, www.sanjuantaxis.com), **Metro Taxi** (787/945-5555), and **Rochdale Radio Taxi** (787/721-1900, www.taxiprrochdale.com).

In San Juan, fares from Luis Muñoz Marín International Airport are **fixed rates.** From the airport, the rate is $12 to Isla Verde. The rate is $17 to Condado, Ocean Park, Miramar, Santurce, Isla Grande airport, and the Puerto Rico Convention Center. And the rate is $21 to Viejo San Juan. Metered fares are $3 minimum, $1.75 initial charge, and $0.10 every 19th of a mile. Customers pay all road tolls.

The only ride-hailing service available in Puerto Rico is **Uber** (www.uber.com), and it is only available in San Juan. Drivers are not permitted to pick up passengers at the airport, but they can drop off passengers.

San Juan is the only city with a public bus system, **Autoridad Metropolitana de Autobuses** (AMA, www.fortaleza.pr.gov).

At the main terminal, **Covadonga Bus Terminal,** at the corner of Calle La Marina and Calle J. A. Corretjer in Viejo San Juan near the cruise-ship piers, there are bus schedules and maps, but they are not always current. Bus fare is typically $0.75. Exact change or a fare card, available at Covadonga Bus Terminal and Tren Urbano stations, are required. Bus stops are marked with green signs that say "Parada," except in Viejo San Juan, where you have to catch the bus at Covadonga Bus Terminal. When waiting for a bus at a *parada,* it is necessary to wave to get the driver to stop.

Express routes include **E10** (Mon.-Fri. 5am-8pm), which spans from Sagrado Corazón Tren Urbano station to Covadonga Bus Terminal in Viejo San Juan; and **E40** (Mon.-Fri. 5am-8pm, Sat.-Sun. and holidays 6am-8pm), which goes between Piñero Tren Urbano station in Hato Rey and Luís Muñoz Marín International Airport.

Local routes with multiple stops include **T21** (Mon.-Fri. 5am-9pm, Sat. and holidays 6am-8pm), which spans Sagrado Corazón Tren Urbano station to Covadonga Bus Terminal in Viejo San Juan, via Condado; and **T5** (Mon.-Fri. 5am-9pm, Sat. and holidays 6am-8pm), which goes between Covadonga Bus Terminal in Viejo San Juan and Luís Muñoz Marín International Airport.

Train

Tren Urbano (www.trenurbanoapp.com) is an automated rapid transit system serving San Juan, Guaynabo, Río Piedras, and Bayamón. There are 16 stations on the route, starting in San Juan at Sagrado Corazón near Hato Rey and ending in Bayamón. Many of the train stations sustained damage during Hurricane Maria, and efforts to repair them have been slow, but the trains continue to run. Some elevators, escalators, and automated ticket entries may not be functioning, but riders are assured access. The train does not go to the airport, but it does connect with a bus at Sagrado Corazón station

that provides express service to **Luis Muñoz Marín International Airport.** The train runs daily 5:20am-11:30pm. Fares are $1.50 for two hours, including transfers. Discounts are available for students and senior citizens. A Tren Urbano smartphone app helps riders navigate the system.

Público

Públicos (aka *carros públicos* or *guaguas*) are privately owned, government-regulated transport services that operate passenger vans along local and intercity routes in San Juan and around the island. This is a very slow but inexpensive way to travel. *Públicos* typically wait in the plaza until they fill to capacity with riders before departing for their destinations.

The central terminal is **Terminal de Carros Publicos de Este** (164-166 Calle Arzuaga, San Juan, Mon.-Sat. 4am-6pm). Providers include **Blue Line** (787/765-7733) to Río Piedras, Aguadilla, Aguada, Moca, Isabela, and other areas; **Choferes Unidos de Ponce** (787/764-0540) to Ponce and other areas; **Lina Boricua** (787/765-1908) to Lares, Ponce, Jayuya, Utuado, San Sebastián, and other areas; **Linea Caborrojeña** (787/723-9155) to Cabo Rojo, San Germán, and other areas; **Linea Sultana** (787/765-9377) to Mayagüez and other areas; and **Terminal de Transportación Pública** (787/250-0717) to Fajardo and other areas.

Air

Flights within Puerto Rico, including Vieques and Culebra, are available through **Vieques Air Link** (787/741-8331, www.viequesairlink.com), **Seaborne Airlines** (866/359-8784, www.seaborneairlines.com), Air Sunshine (954/434-8900, www.airsunshine.com), and **Cape Air** (800/227-3247, www.capeair.com).

Ferry

In San Juan, **AcuaExpreso Cataño** (Calle Marina, Pier 2, Viejo San Juan, 787/729-8714 or 787/788-0940) provides ferry service between Viejo San Juan and Cataño, home of Casa Bacardí, for $0.50 each way.

The 10-minute ride operates daily 6am-9:40pm. Frequency is every 30 minutes except Monday-Friday 6am-10am and 3:45pm-7pm, when they run every 15 minutes except on holidays.

For transportation from the main island to Vieques and Culebra, the **Puerto Rico Port Authority** operates a **passenger ferry** (787/497-7740, www.porferry.com, $5.35 one way) daily from Ceiba to Vieques and Culebra, as well as between Vieques and Culebra. But if your travel schedule is not flexible, flying is a better option. The ferry operation has been plagued for years with scheduling irregularities and overcrowding. Weather conditions also affect schedules. In addition, ticket holders are not guaranteed a seat because Puerto Rican residents get priority. Note that ferries are particularly crowded on holiday weekends.

If you do take the ferry, buy your tickets one week in advance online. Only 20 percent of tickets are sold online, so even if the ferry you select appears sold out, you may be able to buy tickets at the gate, beginning one hour prior to departure. On your day of departure, be sure to check the schedule online because it is subject to change.

There is also a **cargo ferry** with a limited amount of passenger space. Car rental companies in Puerto Rico do not permit their cars to be transported to Vieques or Culebra, so plan to park your car on the main island and rent another mode of transportation in Vieques and Culebra.

349

ESSENTIALS
VISAS AND OFFICIALDOM

Visas and Officialdom

No passports or visas are required for U.S. citizens entering Puerto Rico. Those visiting the island from other countries must have the same documentation required to enter the United States. Visitors from the United Kingdom are required to have a British passport but do not need a visa unless their passports are endorsed with British Subject, British Dependent Territories Citizen, British Protected Person, British Overseas Citizen, or British National (Overseas) Citizen. A return ticket or proof of onward travel is necessary. Australian visitors must have a passport and can stay up to 90 days without a visa.

CUSTOMS

Travelers must pass through customs at the airport in Puerto Rico before leaving the island to make sure no prohibited plants or fruits are taken off the island. Permitted items include avocados, coconuts, papayas, and plantains. Mangoes, passion fruits, and plants potted in soil are not permitted. Pre-Columbian items or items from Afghanistan, Cuba, Iran, Iraq, Libya, Serbia, Montenegro, and Sudan may not be brought into the United States. There are no customs duties on items brought into the United States from Puerto Rico.

EMBASSIES

Because Puerto Rico is a commonwealth, there are no U.S. embassies or consulates here. Several countries are represented locally by consulates, though, including the **United Kingdom** (350 Ave. Chardon, Torre Charden, Ste. 1236, San Juan, 787/758-9828, btopr1@coqui.net) and **Canada** (Hato Rey Center, 268 Ponce de Leon, Ste. 1111, Hato Rey, 787/759-6629, sanjuan-honcon@international.gc.ca).

Recreation

WATER SPORTS

Water sports are a huge draw in Puerto Rico. Visitors come from all over the world to surf the western shores, where regional and national competitions are held. Diving and snorkeling are popular on the southwest coast and around the smaller islands off the east coast. Sailing, big game fishing, and stand-up paddleboarding are other popular sports.

Boating
SAN JUAN

Sail the seas on the 83-foot topsail schooner *The Amazing Grace* with **Old San Juan Harbor Tours** (between Piers 3 and 4, Viejo San Juan, 787/860-3434, www.eastislandpr.com). Options include the basic tour, a two-hour sunset tour, dinner cruises, and pirate-themed excursions.

Wow Surfing School & Water Sports (787/955-6059, www.wowsurfingschool.com) offers Jet Ski rentals and tours from San Juan Marina in Miramar and El San Juan Hotel in Isla Verde. Operators must be 21 or older; passengers must be at least 12.

EAST COAST

East Island Excursions (La Guancha, Calle C, Fajardo, 787/860-3434, www.eastislandpr.com) offers day tours to Caja de Muertos on a 65-foot catamaran. Children under 4, pregnant women, and people with back or neck injuries are not permitted.

Sail Getaways (Villa Marina Yacht Harbor, 200 Ave. Marina View, Fajardo, 787/860-7327, http://sailgetaway.com) provides beach snorkeling tours, sailing trips, and private charters to Culebra's Playa Flamenco and Icacos Island. The seven-hour powerboat excursion to Culebra includes snorkel gear, lunch, and drinks.

SOUTH COAST

Island Venture Water Excursions (La Guancha, Ponce, 787/842-8546, www.islandventurepr.com) offers a 6.5-hour, all-inclusive high-speed catamaran tour to Caja de Muertos. It includes lunch, snacks, drinks, beer, kayaks, paddleboards, and snorkel equipment. Children under 4 are not permitted.

WEST COAST

BAMA Boqueron Aqua Marine Adventures (PR 3301, Playa El Combate, Cabo Rojo, 787/472-1321, http://bamapr.com) offers Jet Ski rentals, as well as tours.

Fondo de Cristal III (end of PR 304, La Parguera, 787/899-5891 or 787/344-0593, no reservation required) offers 30-minute nighttime tours of a bioluminescent bay on a 72-foot bi-level glass-bottomed catamaran that is wheelchair-accessible.

Gina at Johnny's Boats (La Parguera, 787/460-8922, cash only) offers guided tours of La Parguera's mangroves and keys, nighttime tours of a bioluminescent bay, and water taxi service to Isla Mata La Gata. No reservations are required.

VIEQUES AND CULEBRA

El Viequesnse Sea Tours (787/644-7112, www.elviequenseseatours.com) offers guided electric boat bio-bay tours of Mosquito Bay in Vieques.

Diving and Snorkeling
SAN JUAN

Aqua Adventure (Caribe Hilton, 1 Calle Geronimo, Puerta de Tierra, 787/636-8811 or 787/860-3483, http://scubapuertorico.net) offers snorkel and scuba tours, plus SNUBA tours, which use floating air tanks to combine snorkeling and scuba diving.

Scuba Dogs (Balneario El Escambrón, Ave. Muñoz Rivera, 787/783-6377 or 787/977-0000, www.scubadogs.net) rents scuba and snorkel equipment and offers tours.

EAST COAST

Caribe Bliss (Puerta del Rey Marina, slip 8102, Fajardo, 787/439-1672 or 772/333-9383, www.caribebliss.com) offers snorkeling tours to Culebra that include lunch, drinks, snorkel gear, and flotation devices.

Pure Adventure (Roosevelt Roads Marina, Ceiba, 787/202-6551, www.pureadventurepr.com) provides snorkel tours to Vieques and dive tours to Culebra.

S. S. Tobias Snorkel and Beach Tours (Villa Marina, Fajardo, 787/567-4495, www.snorkelandbeachtour.com) offers 6.5-hour snorkel tours to Culebra, as well as sailing tours, Laguna Grande bio-bay tours, and more.

Salty Dog (200 Ave. Marina View, Fajardo, 787/717-6378 or 787/717-7259, www.saltydreams.com) offers catamaran snorkeling tours, including all-you-can-eat lunch buffet and unlimited rum drinks. The sunset cruise with cocktails and light snacks lasts about two hours.

Sea Ventures Dive Center (Marina Puerto del Rey, PR 3, km 51.2, Fajardo, 787/739-3483 or 800/863-3483, www.divepuertorico.com) offers dive and snorkel trips to local reefs. Beginners must be at least 10 and a strong swimmer. Tours last about 5.5 hours.

WEST COAST

413 Divers (Ventana del Mar shopping center, PR 115, km 12.9, Rincón, 787/400-2359, http://413divers.com) offers shore dives in Rincón and Aguadilla that are ideally suited for beginning snorkelers and divers.

Aquatica (PR 110, km 10, Gate 5, Ramey, Aguadilla, 787/890-6071, www.aquaticapr.com) offers a two-tank dive and a two-hour guided snorkel tour. Rental equipment is available.

Rincón Diving & Snorkeling (PR 115, km 12.0, Rincón, 787/506-3483, www.rincondiving.com) offers a variety of snorkel and dive lessons and tours for all levels from beginning to experienced. The guided snorkel tour lasts about four hours and is suitable for all ages and experience levels. For children under 8, call to make special arrangements. Novice divers age 10 and up can take a Discover scuba tour and dive down 40 feet underwater. Participants must complete a PADI medical questionnaire upon signing in and can't fly within 18 hours of diving.

Taíno Divers (564 Calle Black Eagle, off PR 413, Barrio Ensenada, Rincón, 787/823-6429, www.tainodivers.com) offers daily snorkeling and dive trips to various dive sites, including Desecheo Island.

VIEQUES AND CULEBRA

Culebra Island Adventures (31 Calle 2, Culebra, 787/529-3536, www.culebraislandadventures.com) leads one-hour snorkeling with turtles tours.

Vieques Sailing Charters (787/435-4858 or 939/332-5778, www.viequessailingcharters.com) offers half-day sailing trips and snorkeling tours for up to eight people ages 12 and up. Private half-day tours for up to four people ages 6 and up are also offered.

Fishing Tours
EAST COAST

Caribbean Outfitters (Cangrejos Yacht Club, Piñones, 787/396-8346, www.fishinginpuertorico.com) offers fishing and fly-fishing charters throughout Puerto Rico, Vieques, Culebra, the Dominican Republic, and St. Thomas with Captain Omar. Options inlcude kayak fishing, light tackle fishing, and deep-sea fishing.

Magic Tarpon (Cangrejos Yacht Club, Piñones, 787/644-1444, www.puertorico-magictarpon.com) offers fly-fishing outings for 1-2 anglers. Reef fishing outings for barracuda, yellow tail, snapper, sharks, and more are available for 1-4 people.

787 Fishing (Marina Puerto Chico, PR 987, km 2.4, Fajardo, 787/347-4464, http://787fishing.com) offers fishing excursions on 22-foot and 26-foot catamarans or 17-foot skiffs.

WEST COAST

Light Tackle Adventure (Boquerón pier, 787/849-1430 or 787/547-7380) specializes in light tackle and fly-fishing excursions. This company also provides kayak trips to the Cabo Rojo salt flats, Boquerón Bay, Joyuda, and La Parguera. Bird-watching tours in Cabo Rojo salt flats are also available.

Makaira Fishing Charters (Rincón, 787/299-7374, http://fishrinconpr.com) offers half-day and full-day charters aboard a 34-foot 2006 Contender. There's a six-passenger maximum.

Parguera Fishing Charters (PR 304, La Parguera, 787/382-4698, www.puertoricofishingcharters.com) offers half-day and full-day trips to fish for dorado, tuna, blue marlin, and wahoo on a 31-foot, twin diesel Bertram Sport Fisherman. Trips include bait, tackle, beverages, snacks, and lunch. They also offer light tackle reef fishing, half-day snorkeling trips, and customized charters.

Taíno Divers (564 Calle Black Eagle, off PR 413, Barrio Ensenada, Rincón, 787/823-6429, www.tainodivers.com) offers half-day offshore fishing charters including tackle, bait, lunch, and soft drinks. It also offers snorkeling, diving, and whale-watching tours.

VIEQUES AND CULEBRA

Go inshore fishing for kingfish, amberjack, barracuda, pompano, and tarpon with **Caribbean Fly Fishing** (787/450-3744, www.facebook.com/cffcinc).

Kayaking

SAN JUAN

E-Bike & Kayak (San Juan Marriott Resort, 1309 Ave. Ashford, Condado, 340/344-4381, www.ebikeandkayak.com) leads one-hour illuminated kayak tours nightly for all ages. There must be at least one participant age 16 or older in each two-person kayak.

Night Kayak (Serafina Beach Hotel, 1045 Ave. Ashford, Condado, 787/248-4569, www.nightkayak.com, $49-59) offers illuminated nighttime tours of the Condado Lagoon. Climb aboard a two-seater kayak tricked out with LED lighting and take a guided tour of the lagoon after dark. If you're lucky, you may see some marine life, including tarpon, sea stars, turtles, lobsters, and stingrays. The tours last one hour and are suitable for all skill levels. One-hour stand-up paddleboard tours are available for experienced boarders only, ages 14 and up.

EAST COAST

Eco Adventures (787/206-0290, www.ecoadventurespr.com) offers bio-bay tours that launch from Las Croabas in Fajardo. Participants must be at least 5 years old.

Kayaking Puerto Rico (PR 987, km 5, Las Croabas, Fajardo, 787/742-0523 or 787/245-4545, www.kayakingpuertorico.com) offers 90-minute bio-bay kayak tours at Laguna Grande. They also offer day-long and half-day Aquafari tours that combine kayaking and snorkeling in Culebra.

Yokahu Kayaks (PR 987, km 6.2, Las Croabas, Fajardo, 787/604-7375, www.yokahukayaks.com) offers two-hour kayak tours to Laguna Grande in Las Cabezas de San Juan with licensed guides and equipment included. Reservations are required.

VIEQUES AND CULEBRA

Jak Water Sports (787/644-7112 or 787/447-8697, www.jakwatersports.com) provides guided bio-bay tours of Mosquito Bay in Vieques in two-person, clear-bottom kayaks for optimum viewing.

Melaya's Tours (787/222-7055, www.melayasours.net) offers 90-minute guided bio-bay tours of Mosquito Bay in Vieques in two-person, clear-bottom kayaks. The weight limit is 250 pounds per person.

Taíno Aqua Adventures (787/349-6964, www.tainoaquaadventures.com) hosts bio-bay tours of Mosquito Bay in Vieques in clear-bottom kayaks for two (450-pound limit). The tour lasts two hours and is appropriate for all skill levels. Call for private tours or groups of 10 or more.

Travesias Isleñas Yaureibo (787/447-4104 or 939/630-1267, www.viequesoutdoors.com) offers nightly two-hour bio-bay tours of Mosquito Bay in Vieques. They also offer extended kayak tours, historical walking tours, and snorkel tours.

Stand-Up Paddleboarding

Aquatica (PR 110, km 10, Gate 5, Ramey, Aguadilla, 787/890-6071, www.aquaticapr.com) offers stand-up paddleboard lessons and tours.

Rincon Paddleboards (Black Eagle beach, south of El Ancla, Rincón, 787/546-9545 or 787/323-6977, http://rinconpaddleboards.com) specializes in paddleboard lessons, guided tours, and equipment rental. They also offer surf lessons and rentals, paddleboard surf lessons, and kayak tours and rentals. If you prefer an adventure after dark, LED nighttime paddleboard tours and nighttime kayak and snorkel tours are also available. Lessons and tours last about two hours.

SUP Action (482 Ave. Manuel Fernández Juncos, San Juan, 787/637-2338, http://supactionpr.com) rents paddleboards and kayaks and leads private tours in Condado Lagoon. The best way to communicate is via text.

Surfing

Caribbean Surf School (2248 Calle Cacique, San Juan, 787/637-8363, www.caribbeansurfpr.com) offers surf lessons, tours, and equipment rental.

Rincón Surf School (787/823-0610, www.rinconsurfschool.com) conducts a surf school for beginners and experienced surfers looking to up their game. You can choose a variety of outings depending on your ability or the surfing experience, such as dawn patrol and sunset sessions. Sessions are three hours long and include board rental. Choose from a group session, private lessons and guided adventures, or the Solo Project, with one-on-one, three-hour sessions.

Surf 787 Summer Camp (PR 115, behind Angelo's Restaurant, Rincón, 787/448-0968, www.surf787.com) offers year-round surfing instruction, including a kids summer camp, private lessons, and group lessons.

Surfing Puerto Rico (La Pared, Luquillo, 787/501-7873, www.surfingpuertorico.com) provides instruction for beginners and intermediate surfers ages 8 and older at La Pared in Luquillo.

Volcom Surf School Puerto Rico (Uma's, PR 4466, km 7.2, Playa Jobos, Isabela, 787/510-3164, www.volcomsurfschoolpr.com) offers surf lessons to beginners and experienced surfers.

Wow Surfing School & Water Sports (787/955-6059, www.wowsurfingschool.com) offers two-hour private surf lessons on land and in the water, including board rentals, at The Ritz Carlton San Juan in Isla Verde. Group rates are also available.

ADVENTURE TOURS AND ACTIVITIES

Cueva Ventana (PR 10, km 75, border of Utuado and Arecibo, 787/322-3554, www.cuevaventanapr.com) is an easily accessible limestone cave that provides a stunning view of the north region's karst country through the cave's gaping back window. Guided tours last 90 minutes and include a 45-minute moderate hike along a dirt path through the woods and up concrete stairs.

Carabalí Rainforest Adventure Forest (PR 3, km 32.4, Luquillo, 787/889-5820, 787/889-4954, or 787/889-2682, www.carabalirainforestpark.com) is a 600-acre ranch offering one- and two-hour guided ATV and UTV off-road adventures and horseback tours along mountainside and beachfront trails. Participants must be at least 16, 60 inches or taller, and have a driver's license to drive an ATV or UTV. Other attractions include go-karts, hayrides, and luxury yacht rental.

Hacienda Campo Rico (end of Ave.

Robert Sánchez, Carolina, 787/523-2001, www.haciendacamporico.com) is a 2,300-acre wonderland for thrill-seekers. Go ziplining, cave rappelling, horseback riding, or take an ATV tour. **Montaña Explora** (PR 191, km. 27.9, Camino Viejo, Charco El Hippie, Barranquitas, 787/516-6194, www.facebook.com/mexplorapr) provides guided extreme adventure tours of San Cristóbal Cañon that include hiking and rappelling. No previous rappelling experience is required. Gear is provided. Other tours include hiking and swimming in a freshwater pond on the less-touristy southern side of El Yunque.

ToroVerde (PR 155, km 32.9, Orocovis, 787/944-1196, 787/944-1195, or 787/867-6606, www.toroverdepr.com) is a popular adventure park that includes ziplines, suspension bridges, and free falls. Closed-toe shoes and reservations are required.

GOLF

Because of its verdant natural beauty, Puerto Rico has become a mecca for golfers and regularly hosts PGA tournaments.

Coco Beach Golf Resort (100 Club House Dr., Río Grande, 787/657-2000, www.cocopuertorico.com) offers 36 holes of oceanside golf on courses designed by Tom Kite and Bruce Besse. The club has hosted the PGA Tour's Puerto Rico Open on multiple occasions.

Costa Caribe Golf and Country Club (Ponce Hilton Golf and Casino Resort, 1150 Ave. Caribe, 787/259-7676, www.costacariberesort.com or www.ponce.hilton.com) is a 27-hole course designed by Bruce Besse on what was once sugarcane fields. It offers spectacular views of the Caribbean and Puerto Rico's central mountain region. The signature hole is number 12, featuring an island green.

Dorado Beach Resort (PR 693, Dorado, 787/626-1010, www.doradobeach.com) is home to two championship Tournament Players Club courses managed by the PGA. Among the tournaments played here are the Senior PGA Tour Championship, the Chi

Chi Rodriguez Pro Am Golf Classic, the Johnnie Walker International Pro Am, and the World Cup golf tournaments. The 72-par East Course was designed and built in 1958 by Robert Trent Jones Sr., modified in 1999, and restored to Jones's original vision by his son, Robert Trent Jones Jr., in 2012. It was named the top golf course in Puerto Rico by *Golf Digest* in 2016. It features panoramic views of the ocean and natural sand bunkers. Even more challenging is the Sugarcane Course, with views of lakes and rivers.

El Legado Golf Resort (PR 52, Guayama, 787/866-8894, www.ellegadopuertorico.com) is an 18-hole course designed by local legend Chi Chi Rodriguez, located in a residential condominium community. It includes several lakes, a waterfall, and a putting green shaped like the island.

The Links at Royal Isabela (396 Ave. Noel Estrada, Isabela, 787/609-5888 or 855/609-5888, www.royalisabela.com) is a spectacular 18-hole course designed to showcase the island's natural beauty on a cliff overlooking the ocean at this luxury resort.

Palmas Athletic Club (Palmas del Mar, Country Club Dr., Humacao, 787/656-3000, www.talgracefeeds.com/palmas) has two 18-hole, 72-par courses. The Golf Club Course was built in 1974 by Gary Player. The Flamboyán Course, considered one of the island's most challenging, was designed by Rees Jones.

Punta Borinquen Golf and Country Club (300 Golf Rd., Ramey Base, Aguadilla, 787/890-2987, www.puntaborinquengolfclub.org) is one of only a handful of courses in Puerto Rico that are not associated with a resort. Designed by Fred Garbin, it opened in 1940 to serve the military base. When the base closed, the course was opened to the public. It features 18 holes with straight and open fairways overlooking the ocean.

Río Bayamón Golf Course (PR 171 at Ave. Laurel, Bayamón, 787/740-1419, www.municipiodebayamon.com) is the only golf course in the metropolitan San Juan area. The public course is 6,870 yards and a par 72.

St. Regis Bahía Beach Resort (PR 187, km 4.2, Río Grande, 787/809-8920, www. marriott.com) is home to the Robert Trent Jones Jr. Golf Course, a par 72, 6,979-yard course that meanders around saltwater lagoons and oceanfront views, with El Yunque National Forest visible in the distance.

Wyndham Grand Río Mar Beach Resort (PR 968, km 1.4, Río Grande, 800/474-6627, teetime-riomar@wyndham.com, www. wyndhamhotels.com) has two courses. The Ocean Course, built in 1975 by George and Tom Fazio, is a 6,716-yard course offering excellent views of the Atlantic Ocean and one of the best-rated holes (16) on the island. The River Course, an 18-hole grass course with water in play, built in 1997 and designed by Greg Norman, runs along the Río Mameyes.

HORSE RACING AND RIDING

The development of the Paso Fino breed of horse is closely intertwined with the history of Puerto Rico, starting with the arrival of Juan Ponce de León in 1508. Among the explorer's cargo were 50 horses from which the birth of the breed can be traced.

Horse races were once held in the streets of Viejo San Juan as far back as 1610. Today, gamblers can bet on winners at the big modern **Hipódromo Camarero** (PR 3, km 15.3, Canóvanas, 787/641-6060, http://hipodromo-camarero.com, Thurs.-Sun., admission free, betting starts at $10), located in the municipality of Canóvanas east of Río Grande.

Horses are still used as a mode of transportation in rural parts of the main island and throughout Vieques and Culebra. There are several stables that offer trail rides.

Esperanza Riding Company (Vieques, 787/435-0073, www.esperanzaridingcompany. com/vieques, cash only, reservations required) offers two-hour guided tours on Paso Fino horses through hills, meadows, riverbeds, and beaches. Children 7 and younger can take a 20-minute, hand-led pony trail ride. Due to the small stature of the breed, there is a weight limit of 225 pounds for riders.

Hacienda Campo Rico (end of Ave. Robert Sánchez, Carolina, San Juan, 787/523-2001, www.haciendacamporico. com) provides guided horseback tours twice a day for two hours. Private tours are also available. Riders must be at least 8 years old and weigh less than 250 pounds. Closed-toe shoes are required.

Hacienda Paraíso (PR 303, km 9.3, El Combate, 787/399-7039, www.facebook.com/ haciendaparaiso303) offers horseback riding on the grounds of a hacienda. Riders must wear long pants and closed-toe shoes, and not exceed 250 pounds. Reservations are required. No experience is necessary.

Jurutungo Farms (PR 997, Vieques, 787/307-1998, www.jurutungo.com) offers 1.5-hour guided horseback riding tours to Playa Negra for groups of four or less. Private tours and combo horseback riding and snorkel tours are available. No previous horseback riding is necessary. Children old enough to sit in a saddle and follow instructions are welcome.

Pintos R Us (PR 413 at Black Eagle, Barrio Ensenada, Rincón, 787/516-7090, www.pintosrus.com, cash only) leads daily rides on Paso Fino horses for beginners and advanced riders. The trail takes you alongside lovely beaches, cliffs, and tropical trails. Pintos R Us also offers riding lessons, trail rides, and full-moon rides.

Tropical Trail Rides (PR 4466, km 1.8, Isabela, 787/872-9256, www.tropicaltrailrides. com) offers two-hour guided tours along tropical trails on Paso Fino horses through an almond forest, along secluded beaches, and to cliffside caves.

BIKING

E-Bike & Kayak (San Juan Marriott Resort, 1309 Ave. Ashford, Condado, San Juan, 340/344-4381, www.ebikeandkayak.com) leads a 2.5-hour bike tour from Condado to Viejo San Juan on electric bicycles available in two styles, a cruiser or a tandem bike built for two. For an added adventure, take the Night E-Bike Tour, illuminated by LED lights.

Puerto Rico Bike Adventures (Playa El Combate, PR 3301, km 2.7, Cabo Rojo, 787/381-4596, www.facebook.com/ puertoricobikeadventures) rents mountain bikes and runs guided tours.

WALKING TOURS

Led by locals from Ponce, **Isla Caribe Tours** (6953 Calle Isabel at Calle Muñoz Rivera, Ponce, 939/265-5691, www.islacaribepr.com) offers daily two-hour walking tours of the city. Other options include coffee-, salsa-, and art-themed tours.

Para la Naturaleza (155 Calle de Tetuan, San Juan, 787/722-5882, www.paralanaturaleza.org) offers educational and historical tours of significant sites around the island, including tours of Canon de San Cristóbal in Barranquitas and the Hacienda Buena Vista coffee plantation in Ponce.

Tour Guide Debbie (Viejo San Juan, 787/605-9060, www.tourguidedebbie.com) offers daytime and nighttime walking tours of Viejo San Juan that revolve around topics from history, pirate legends, and handicrafts.

TENNIS

There is no shortage of tennis courts in San Juan. Many of the large hotels have courts. **Central Park** (Calle Cerra off PR 2, Santurce, 787/722-1646, www.sanjuanciudadpatria.com) has 17 tennis courts. **Isla Verde Tennis Club** (Villamar, Isla Verde, 787/727-6490, www.islaverdetennis.com) has four hard courts lit for night play.

Wyndham Grand Río Mar Beach Resort (6000 Río Mar Blvd., Río Grande, 787/888-7066, www.wyndhamriomar.com) features 11 Har-Tru surface courts and two hard courts, four equipped with lights for nighttime play. There's also a 35,000-square-foot clubhouse and a pro shop. Lessons, clinics, and packages are available.

BASEBALL

With origins dating back to the late 19th century, baseball was the first team sport to emerge in Puerto Rico's modern times.

Currently the island is home to a winter league, **Liga de Béisbol Profesional Roberto Clemente,** featuring five regional teams. Games are played at the 18,000-seat **Hiram Bithorn Stadium** in San Juan, as well as stadiums in Caguas, Carolina, Mayagüez, and Aguadilla. Each year the winning team competes in the Caribbean Series in February.

More than 260 players from Puerto Rico have played on Major League teams. Hall of Famers include Orlando Cepeda, Roberto Alomar, Iván Rodriguez, and the island's most beloved player, Roberto Clemente, who played 18 seasons with the Pittsburgh Pirates.

BASKETBALL

Interest in basketball has waxed and waned in Puerto Rico, but it appears to be on upswing at the moment. The **Baloncesto Superior Nacional** is a first-tier level professional men's basketball league with nine teams. The winningest teams are the Leones de Ponce, Atléticos de San Germán, and Vaqueros de Bayamon. **Baloncesto Superior Nacional Femenino** is the women's national basketball league. It has 11 teams.

The island is also home to the **Puerto Rico National Basketball Team,** which competes in international events. The team made history in 2004 when it defeated the U.S. Dream Team in the Olympics in Greece. It has won more than 24 gold medals in international competitions, including the Pan American Games, FIBA AmeriCup, and Centrobasket. There is also a **Puerto Rico Women's National Basketball Team.**

Athletes from Puerto Rico who have gone on to play for the NBA include Carlos Arroyo and Jose Barea.

BOXING

Puerto Rico has produced many world-class boxers, starting with the island's first National Boxing Association world champion in the bantamweight class, Barceloneta native Sixto Escobar, who first won the title in 1934. In 1948 bantamweight boxer Juan Evangelista Venegas became the first Puerto Rican to win an Olympic medal. To date, Puerto Rico has won six Olympic medals in boxing. Isabela native Juan Ruíz made history by becoming the first Latino World Boxing Association heavyweight champion by beating Evander Holyfield in 2001.

Félix "Tito" Trinidad is considered by many to be Puerto Rico's best all-time boxer. A champion in both welterweight and middleweight divisions, Trinidad announced his retirement in 2002 with a record of 42 wins (35 by knockout) and only two losses. Since then he has come out of retirement twice to compete three more times, losing his last match in 2008 to Roy Jones. Trinidad's most celebrated win was the defeat of welterweight champion Oscar de la Hoya in an event called The Fight of the Millennium held at Mandalay Bay in Las Vegas in 1999. His victorious return to the island was marked by a jubilant turnout of thousands of fans who greeted him at the Luis Muñoz Marín International Airport in San Juan.

COCKFIGHTS

Considered by many people to be cruel and inhumane, cockfighting has been a part of Puerto Rico's culture since the 1700s. Today it is an industry that employs 27,000 people and generates $18 million a year.

Fitted with 1.5-inch long plastic spurs, roosters are pitted against each other in battle while spectators place bets on which bird will win. There are around 60 licensed cockfighting arenas in Puerto Rico.

In 2019 the U.S. Congress passed a law that outlawed cockfighting in Puerto Rico, but the governor of Puerto Rico signed a bill into law that reversed that decision. How the federal government will respond has yet to be determined. For now, cockfights continue on the island.

Accommodations

Accommodations in Puerto Rico run the gamut from world-class luxury resorts to rustic self-serve guesthouses, which offer little more than a bed to crash on and a help-yourself attitude when it comes to getting clean linens, ice, and other items you might need. In between are a variety of American hotel chains in all price ranges and a number of small, independent hotels and inns. There are also some unique hotels of historic significance, such as **Hotel El Convento** in San Juan, a former Carmelite convent built in 1651, and **Hacienda Gripiñas**, a former coffee plantation in Jayuya located high up in the Cordillera Central.

Outside San Juan there are accommodations designated by the Puerto Rico Tourism Co. as *paradores* (www.gotoparadores.com), independently owned and operated country inns. They tend to be economically priced; the quality of the properties can be highly variable.

In recent years, the number of home shares and vacation rentals available through services such as Airbnb and VRBO have exploded, greatly increasing the number of options for overnight accommodations.

RATES

Overnight stays in Puerto Rico can range from $50 a night at a hostel to more than a thousand dollars a night at some of the island's ritziest resorts. Generally, however, room rates fall between $150 and $300. Rates vary depending on the season. They are highest during high season and lowest during low season. High season is typically December through April in San Juan, Dorado, and Río Grande. It's November through April in Vieques, Culebra, and Rincón. Destinations popular with Puerto Rican travelers such as Boquerón, the Cabo Rojo peninsula, and La Parquera experience high season during the summer months when school is out. Rates are usually higher on holiday weekends across the island.

There are few all-inclusive properties in Puerto Rico, but many hotels provide complimentary breakfast. Most accommodations can be booked online.

A tax is applied to all accommodations, ranging from 7 percent on an Airbnb property to 11 percent on a hotel with a casino. Most hotels charge 9 percent tax. Resorts add additional service fees, typically another 9 percent.

Food

CUISINE

Puerto Rican cuisine is a hearty fare called *cocina criolla,* which means creole cooking. A typical *criolla* dish contains fried or stewed meat, chicken, or seafood, combined with or accompanied by rice and beans. Stewed dishes usually begin with a seasoning mix called **sofrito,** which includes salt pork, ham, lard, onions, green peppers, chili peppers, cilantro, and garlic. **Adobo,** a seasoning mix comprising peppercorn, oregano, garlic, salt, olive oil, and vinegar or fresh lime juice, is rubbed into meats and poultry before frying or grilling. Tomato sauce, capers, pimento-stuffed olives, and raisins are also common ingredients in Puerto Rican cuisine. Two items are integral to the preparation of *cocina criolla:* a *caldero* (a cast-iron or cast-aluminum cauldron with a round base, straight sides, and a lid) and a mortar and pestle (used to grind herbs and seeds).

The **plantain** is a major staple of the Puerto Rican diet. Similar to a banana but larger, firmer, and less sweet, it is prepared in a variety of ways. *Tostones* are a popular plantain dish. The fruit is sliced into rounds, fried until soft, mashed flat, and fried again until crisp. They're typically eaten like bread, as a starchy accompaniment to a meal. They're often served with the ubiquitous Puerto Rican condiment, **mayo ketchup.**

But probably the most popular way plantain is served is in mofongo, a mashed mound of fried green plantain, garlic, olive oil, and chicharrón (pork crackling), and you'll find it on the menu of just about every restaurant on the island. *Mofongo relleno* is mofongo stuffed with meat, poultry, or seafood. *Amarillos,* which translates as "yellows," is the same thing as the Cuban *maduras* and is made from ripe plantains that have been sliced lengthwise and fried in oil until soft and sweetly caramelized. Bananas are also popular in *cocina criolla,* especially *guineitos en escabeche,* a green-banana salad marinated with pimento-stuffed olives in vinegar and lime juice.

Rice also figures prominently in Puerto Rican food. Most restaurants serving *comida criolla* will list several *arroz* (rice) dishes, such as *arroz con habichuelas* (beans), *arroz con pollo* (chicken), *arroz con juyeyes* (crab), *arroz con camarones* (shrimp), and *arroz con gandules* (pigeon peas). Typically in this dish the ingredients have been stewed until damp and sticky in a mixture of tomatoes and *sofrito.* A similar dish is paella, a Spanish import featuring an assortment of seafood. *Asopao,* a thick stew, is another popular rice dish, and *arroz con leche* (milk) is a favorite dessert similar to rice pudding.

Pork is very popular in Puerto Rico, and it has a variety of names: *lechón, pernil, cerdo.* But chicken and beef are common, and occasionally you'll come across *cabro* (goat) and guinea hen. Popular meat dishes include *carne guisada* (beef stew), *chuletas fritas* (fried pork chops), *carne empanado* (breaded and fried steak), *carne encebollado* (fried steak smothered in cooked onions), and *churrasco,* an Argentine-style grilled skirt steak. Restaurants along the coast usually specialize in a wide range of seafood, including *camarones* (shrimp), *langosta* (lobster), *pulpo* (octopus), and *carrucho* (conch). Fish—typically fried whole—can be found on nearly every menu, the choices usually being *chillo* (red snapper), *dorado* (mahi-mahi), or occasionally *bacalao* (dried salted cod).

Interestingly, you'll usually find the exact same **dessert** options at most restaurants. They will include flan (a baked caramel custard), *helados* (ice cream), and *dulce de guayaba* (guava in syrup) or *dulce de lechosa* (papaya in syrup) served with *queso del país*, a soft white cheese. Occasionally restaurants will offer *tembleque*, a coconut custard, particularly around the Christmas holidays.

An American-style **breakfast** is commonly found, although Puerto Ricans often eat their eggs and ham in toasted sandwiches called *bocadillos*. American coffee can sometimes be found, but the traditional *café con leche*, a strong brew with steamed milk, is highly recommended. *Bocadillos* are often eaten for lunch, particularly the *cubano*, a toasted sandwich with ham, roasted pork, and cheese. The *medianoche* is similar to the *cubano*, but it's served on a softer, sweeter bread.

Although American fast-food restaurant chains can be found in Puerto Rico, the island has its own traditional style of fast-food fare often sold from roadside kiosks. Offerings usually include fried savory hand pies and fritters made from various combinations of plantain, meat, chicken, cheese, crab, potato, and fish.

DRINKING

The legal drinking age in Puerto Rico is 18. Although all types of alcoholic beverages are available, rum is the number one seller. There are three types of rum: white or silver, which is dry, pale, and light-bodied; gold, which is amber-colored and aged in charred oak casks; and black, a strong, 151-proof variety often used in flambés. Favorite rum drinks are the Cuba libre, a simple mix of rum and Coke with a wedge of lime; the piña colada, a frozen blended combination of rum, cream of coco, and pineapple juice; and the mojito, a Cuban import made from rum, simple syrup, club soda, fresh lime juice, and tons of fresh muddled mint. *Chichaito* is a rum and anise flavored shot often served after a Puerto Rican meal, and a *coquito* is an eggnog-like cocktail made with rum and coconut milk served during the Christmas holidays.

Until the craft beer trend hit Puerto Rico, Medalla, a light pilsner brewed in Mayagüez, was the only local beer produced on the island. But now there are lots of local microbrews available, including Rincón Beer Company, Ocean Lab, and Del Barril.

Conduct and Customs

ETIQUETTE

A certain formality permeates life in Puerto Rico. It's customary to exchange greetings with strangers, including shop owners and hotel desk clerks, before making a request. A simple *buenas días* for good day, *buenas tardes* for good afternoon, and *buenas noches* for good evening will do. If you approach someone to ask the time or for directions, preface your question with *perdóneme* (excuse me) before asking. When a waiter delivers your meal, he or she will say *buen provecho*, and it's customary to say the same to diners already eating when you enter a restaurant.

Traditionally, Puerto Ricans are exceedingly cordial. Even in a big city like San Juan, rudeness is rarely encountered. If you're lost or need help or want a restaurant recommendation, residents generally will cheerfully point you in the right direction.

Things are beginning to change, but many restaurants—especially those that cater primarily to Puerto Rican diners or are located outside cities—do not provide the level of service that stateside Americans may expect. Not

Popular *Cocina Criolla* Dishes

Like the people of Puerto Rico, the cuisine's roots can be found at the intersection of the Taíno, Spanish, and African cultures. Most dishes are either slowly stewed throughout the day or quickly fried just before eating.

Many Puerto Rican dishes start with *sofrito*. Similar to a roux, it is a reduction of tomatoes, green bell pepper, onion, garlic, and cilantro seasoned with salt pork, ham, and/or lard. Plantains, both ripe and green, are eaten at just about every meal.

Here are some dishes commonly served in homes and restaurants throughout Puerto Rico.

- *a la criolla:* a cut of meat or fish served in a sauce made from tomatoes, green bell pepper, onion, garlic, and cilantro

- *amarillos:* a side dish of ripe plantains sliced lengthwise and slowly fried in oil until caramelized; also called maduros or sweet plantains

- *arañitas:* fried balls of shredded plantain; often served as a snack or appetizer with mayo ketchup

- *arroz con gandules:* a thick pigeon peas and rice dish seasoned with *sofrito*

- *arroz con jueyes:* a thick land crab and rice dish seasoned with *sofrito*

- *arroz con pollo:* a thick chicken and rice dish seasoned with *sofrito*

- *asopao:* a thick rice stew made with chicken, pork, beef, or seafood

- *bacalao:* dried salt cod

- *bacalaito:* a fritter made from dried salt cod

- *carne guisado:* beef stew

- *chicharrones:* fried pork skins

- *chicharrones de pollo:* fried chunks of chicken

- *chillo entero frito:* whole fried snapper with the head on

- *chuleta can can:* a thick, deep-fried pork chop specially cut to retain a thick rind of fat and a strip of ribs

- *churrasco:* an Argentine-style grilled skirt steak

- *empanado bifstec:* a slice of steak pounded thin, breaded, and fried

- *encebollado bifstec:* a slice of steak pounded thin, fried, and served with caramelized onions

- *flan:* caramel custard

- *frituras:* fritters, such as *alcapurrias, empanadillas,* and *bacalaito,* typically sold from streetside kiosks, trucks, tents, and vans

only may service be exceptionally slow, but service providers' interactions with customers may be perfunctory at best, and neglectful at worst. But the concept of service is undergoing a shift as young entrepreneurs who take a modern approach to hospitality open more businesses on the island.

Puerto Ricans generally like to dress to impress, especially when dining at upscale restaurants or hitting the nightclubs. Beach attire is never worn anywhere but the pool or beach.

- *guineitos en escabeche:* pickled green banana salad with onions and green olives

- *lechón asado:* whole roasted pig

- *longaniza:* lean, spicy sausage made from pork and chicken seasoned with annatto

- *mallorca:* a slightly sweet knot of bread dough, baked and dusted with powdered sugar—served split, buttered, and toasted or stuffed with hot ham and cheese for breakfast

- *mamposteao:* a thick rice and beans dish seasoned with *sofrito*

- *medianoche:* like a Cuban sandwich but served on egg bread, which is soft and slightly sweet

- *mofongo:* mashed fried green plantain seasoned with olive oil and garlic and fried bits of pork skin, bacon, or ham

- *mofongo relleno:* mofongo stuffed with chicken, meat, or seafood

- *morcilla:* black blood sausage

- *paella:* Spanish dish similar to *arroz con pollo* but with saffron and filled with a variety of seafood instead of chicken

- *panapén:* breadfruit

- *pasteleon:* similar to lasagna but instead of pasta, it's layered with ripe plantains

- *pasteles:* like tamales; mashed plantain or cassava stuffed with pork or chicken and steamed in banana leaves, typically served around the Christmas holidays—don't eat the leaf!

- *pescado en escabeche:* pickled fish served cold; raw fillets are marinated in seasoned vinegar, similar to ceviche

- *pique:* hot sauce made from vinegar, lime juice, and hot peppers

- *quesito:* a sweet, sticky twist of puff pastry with a dab of cream cheese inside

- *salmorejo de jueyes:* stewed land crabmeat served over rice

- *sancocho:* beef stew with potatoes, cassava, and pieces of corn on the cob; a popular hangover remedy

- *tembleque:* coconut custard; often served around Christmas

- *tostones:* slices of green plantain fried twice and smashed; served like bread as an accompaniment to other dishes

- *trifongo:* mofongo made with green plantain, sweet plantain, and yuca

- *tripleta:* sandwich stuffed with chopped steak, ham, and pork

Cover-ups are expected when going from your hotel room to the pool.

Smoking has been banned in all restaurants, lounges, clubs, and bars in Puerto Rico, with the exception of establishments with outdoor seating. Public drinking has also been banned.

MACHISMO

Machismo appears to be becoming somewhat a thing of the past, particularly in San

Juan, where mainland American influence is heaviest. The days of men verbally harassing or flashing young women is no longer a common occurrence, although vestiges of it remain around some wilderness beaches where perpetrators are far from the eyes of the *policía*. Nevertheless, it is interesting that *cabron* is a favored, mock-aggressive greeting among many men in Puerto Rico. Technically it means "goat," but its idiomatic translation is a man who's cuckolded by a cheating wife. There was a time when calling a man a *cabron* was a sure way to get a black eye, and used in the heat of an argument, it still is. But today it's more commonly used as a term of affection between male friends.

Meanwhile, the flip side of machismo—Old World chivalry—is still very much alive and well in Puerto Rico, especially among older men who appear to take pride in their gestures of kindness toward women.

CONCEPTS OF TIME

San Juan operates much like any big American city. The pace of life is fast, service is expedient, and everybody's in a hurry. But the farther you get away from San Juan, and most markedly in Culebra and Vieques, things tend to operate on "island time"—that is, at an extremely leisurely pace. You may be the only person in the restaurant, but it may still take 30 minutes or longer to receive your meal. Posted hours of operation are more suggestion than reality. Visitors are best advised to chill out and accept that this is just the way things are in Puerto Rico. If fawning service is required to have a good time, then stick with the resorts.

Health and Safety

The biggest health danger in Puerto Rico is from mosquito-borne viruses. The most common is **dengue fever.** During non-outbreak years, there are typically between 3,000 and 9,000 suspected dengue cases reported in Puerto Rico. During epidemic years, the numbers can reach the tens of thousands. Symptoms include fever, headache, sore joints, nausea, vomiting, rash, and bleeding. It is typically treatable at home with ibuprofen and liquids, but advanced cases may require hospitalization for treatment of dehydration.

Chikungunya first appeared in 2012. The virus shares many of the same symptoms of dengue; it is also spread by mosquitos. An epidemic occurred in 2014 when 4,000 cases were confirmed. Only two cases were reported in 2019.

Another emergent mosquito-borne virus is **Zika,** which can cause congenital birth defects in pregnant women who contract the virus. Puerto Rico experienced an epidemic in 2016, but no new cases have been reported since then.

To prevent exposure to mosquito-borne illnesses, use bug repellant containing DEET, Picaridin, IR3535, oil of lemon eucalyptus, or para-methane-diol.

Visitors should also take precaution against **sunstroke.** Summer can be brutally hot, especially in urban areas. It's important to drink lots of water, especially if you're doing a lot of walking or other physical activity. A hat and sunscreen are recommended. Or you could do as some of the local women do and use umbrellas to keep the beating rays at bay.

The quality of health care in Puerto Rico is comparable to that in the United States, and all major towns have at least one hospital and pharmacy, including Walgreens. The water is as safe to drink as it is in the United States; the same is true for raw fruits and vegetables.

CRIME

Puerto Rico is a key link in a drug transportation route that begins in Venezuela and passes through the Dominican Republic and into Puerto Rico on the way to the U.S. mainland.

That factor is a major contributor to the island's high murder rate, which spiked in 2011 with 1,135 murders, which translated into 30 deaths for every 100,000 residents. The rate has been on the decline, but it remains high. In early 2019, the rate was 20 murders per 100,000 people.

The good news for visitors is, as long as they stay away from the illegal drug trade, they are unlikely to put themselves in danger. Note that the La Perla neighborhood by Viejo San Juan is a hot spot for illegal drug sales.

The main things the average visitor should be on alert for are the same kinds of petty crimes that plague any U.S. city: thefts from automobiles and snatched purses. Visitors are advised to never leave anything of value visible in their cars and to always keep their cars locked.

If you see a flashing blue light, that doesn't necessarily mean there is any criminal activity going on. Police vehicles often run their lights whenever they're on patrol at night to signal their presence to criminals as a deterrent.

Prostitution is illegal in Puerto Rico, and there is illegal human trafficking. Medical marijuana is legal in Puerto Rico, and clinics can be found in most large cities. Recreational marijuana use is illegal.

For any emergency—crime, fire, car accident, injury—call 911 for help.

Travel Tips

WHAT TO PACK

The activities you plan to pursue in Puerto Rico will dictate what you will need to pack. If you plan to sunbathe by day and hit the club at night, pack your swimsuit, a cover-up, and your trendiest club wear. If a shopping marathon is on the agenda, pack comfortable walking shoes and an empty duffel bag for carrying back your loot. If you want to go hiking in the mountains, long lightweight pants and hiking boots are in order. If you stay in the mountains overnight, bring a light jacket.

No matter what you do, bring **sunscreen, bug spray, a wide-brimmed hat, an umbrella,** and some **bottled water.** You'll need protection from the sun and the occasional sand-flea attack while you're on the beach. And if you're traveling during the rainy season, expect a brief shower every day. You'll be grateful for some **light raingear,** such as a poncho and waterproof shoes or sandals.

U.S. cell phone plans provide coverage in Puerto Rico. Having a smartphone is helpful for using GPS navigation and language translation apps.

Light cotton fabrics are always recommended. Puerto Rico's temperatures fluctuate between 76-88°F on the coastal plains and 73-78°F in the mountain region. The humidity hovers around a steady 80 percent. Note that wearing bathing suits or short shorts is inappropriate anyplace other than the pool or beach, and a few restaurants require a jacket and tie.

Most businesses accept **debit cards** and **credit cards,** although many businesses do not accept American Express or Discover. You may want cash if you want to shop for food and goods from roadside vendors. Some businesses accept payment via **Venmo.**

MONEY

Puerto Rico's form of currency is the U.S. dollar, which is sometimes referred to as *peso.* Full-service banks with ATMs are plentiful, the most common one being Banco Popular. Banking hours are Monday-Friday 9am-3:30pm. Credit cards and debit cards are accepted virtually everywhere, although many businesses do not accept American Express or Discover. The only time cash is required is when buying items from roadside vendors, and occasionally even they will accept plastic.

A sales tax of 10.5 percent has recently

been instituted in Puerto Rico, and hotel taxes can vary depending on the type of property. Hotels with casinos charge 11 percent tax, and hotels without casinos charge 9 percent tax. There may also be resort fees, energy surcharge fees, and other charges. When determining the price of a hotel room, ask whether or not the tax is included in the stated price.

Tipping practices are the same as in the United States—15-20 percent of the bill, unless a gratuity has already been added.

COMMUNICATIONS

Published five days a week, the *San Juan Star* (www.sanjuanweeklypr.com) is San Juan's only English-language newspaper, featuring locally produced content and wire stories from the *New York Times*. *El Nuevo Día* (www.elnuevodia.com) is the islandwide Spanish-language daily newspaper. *La Perla del Sur* (www.periodicolaperla.com) is a daily paper serving Ponce. *El Vocero* (www.elvocero.com) is a free Spanish-language newspaper published five days a week. *The Weekly Journal* is a weekly English-language newspaper with a robust digital presence. The *New York Times* and the *Miami Herald* can be commonly found in hotels and newsstands in San Juan.

The free bimonthly *Qué Pasa!* (www.quepasa.pr) is an English-language travel magazine published by the Puerto Rico Tourism Company. The magazine's current issue is available online, and the publishing company's website is an exhaustive source of information about the entire island.

Television broadcasting is regulated by the U.S. Federal Communications Commission. The major broadcasting companies are **Telemundo** (channel 2) and **Univision** (channel 9), but there are scores of local independent channels, as well as cable and satellite channels. Premium cable channels such as HBO and streaming services such as Netflix are available in Puerto Rico.

Phones

Puerto Rico has two area codes—787 and 939—and they must always be dialed when placing a call. U.S. cell phone service should function fine in Puerto Rico.

Shipping and Postal Service

Mail service is provided by the U.S. Postal Service. Although mailing letters and postcards to and from the island costs the same as in the United States, international rates apply when shipping items to the island. United Parcel Service and overnight shipping companies such as Federal Express also operate on the island.

TIME ZONE

Puerto Rico observes **Atlantic standard time** and does not practice daylight saving time. Therefore, time in Puerto Rico is one hour later than eastern standard time November-March and the same as eastern daylight time from the second Sunday in March until the first Sunday in November.

WEIGHTS AND MEASURES

Puerto Rico uses the metric system. Gasoline is bought in liters (1 gallon = 3.7 liters), and distance is measured in kilometers (1 mile = 1.61 kilometers). The exception is speed, which is measured in miles per hour.

STUDY AND VOLUNTEER OPPORTUNITIES

Spanish Abroad (5112 N. 40th St., Ste. 203, Phoenix, AZ 85018, 888/722-7623 or 602/778-6791, www.spanishabroad.com) offers Spanish-language immersion classes with homestays in Hato Rey, San Juan.

Habitat for Humanity in Puerto Rico (Colegio de Arquitectos, 225 Calle del Parque, Santurce, 787/368-9393, http://habitatpr.org) seeks individuals and organizations who want to help rebuild homes and distribute home repair kits.

Surfrider Foundation (Rincón, http://rincon.surfrider.org) is an environmental organization that protects the health of marine life by keeping beaches clean. Projects include beach cleanups, water testing, tree planting, and debris removal.

Para la Naturaleza (155 Calle de Tetuan, San Juan, 787/722-5882, www.paralanaturaleza.org) is an initiative of the Conservation Trust of Puerto Rico that oversees the management and protection of ecological and natural history sites in Puerto Rico. The organization hosts a wide variety of volunteer events across the island. Activities may include taking a migratory bird census, digging an archaeological site, tending greenhouses, and restoring historic buildings.

ACCESS FOR TRAVELERS WITH DISABILITIES

As a territory of the United States, Puerto Rico must adhere to the Americans with Disabilities Act, which ensures access to public buildings for all. While some historic buildings may be exempt, most have been adapted for access with ramps, elevators, and wheelchair-accessible restrooms. The majority of hotels have at least one accessible hotel room. Most sidewalks have curb cuts at crosswalks to accommodate wheelchairs, scooters, and walkers, and traffic lights have audible signals to assist visitors with sight impairments with street crossings.

TRAVELING WITH CHILDREN

San Juan offers lots to do for families with children of all ages. The historic forts and museums hold plenty of interest for youngsters, and many water sports are suitable as well, including fishing, boating, and swimming. And with a few exceptions, most restaurants welcome young diners. As in any urban center, parents should keep a close watch on their children at the pool and beach, especially if there is no lifeguard on duty, and along busy sidewalks where there is car traffic. It is advisable to keep sunscreen, bug spray, and bottled water on hand at all times.

WOMEN TRAVELING ALONE

Puerto Rico is safe for women traveling alone or in groups. But precautions should be taken. Dressing provocatively will attract attention, and bathing suits should never be worn anywhere but at the beach or pool. Women traveling solo should avoid remote wilderness beaches after dark. Safety in numbers is a good rule to follow when going out at night.

LGBTQ TRAVELERS

Despite Puerto Rico's strong patriarchal society in which a traditional sense of manhood is highly prized, homosexuality is generally accepted, especially in San Juan, which is something of a destination for the LGBTQ traveler. There are a number of nightclubs that cater specifically to gay and lesbian clientele, and certain beaches are known to attract a gay crowd. San Juan is also a popular port of call for gay cruises.

Tourist Information

TOURIST OFFICES

Tourism Company of Puerto Rico (2 Paseo La Princesa, 787/721-2400, www.discoverpuertorico.com, Mon.-Fri. 8am-4:30pm), also known as El Presidio del San Juan and Carcel de San Juan, is located in what was a federal prison built in 1837. The front part of the building contains brochures, maps, and other helpful tourist information. In the center is an art gallery, and in back is what remains of the prison: three cells and the courtyard where executions by hanging were held.

MAPS

There are free maps and travel publications, such as *Places to Go, Bienvenidos,* and *Qué Pasa!* magazines, available at many stores, restaurants, and hotels. But **Waze** and **Google Maps** are your best bet for getting around. These smartphone apps are surprisingly detailed and highly accurate. National Geographic's excellent illustrated map of the Caribbean National Forest is available from its website (www.nationalgeographic.com/maps).

Resources

Glossary

ajillo: garlic

a la criolla: a cut of meat or fish served in a sauce made from tomatoes, green bell pepper, onion, garlic, and cilantro

alcapurria: fritter of mashed yautia, yuca, and green banana stuffed with meat or crab and deep-fried

al centro: downtown

alto: stop

amarillos: fried ripe plantains

appertivos: appetizers

arañitas: fried balls of shredded plantain; often served as a snack or appetizer

arepa: a small, round patty of cornmeal batter fried, split open on one side, and stuffed with meat or seafood

arroz: rice

arroz con gandules: a thick pigeon peas and rice dish seasoned with *sofrito*

arroz con jueyes: a thick land crab and rice dish seasoned with *sofrito*

arroz con pollo: a thick chicken and rice dish seasoned with *sofrito*

asado: roasted

asopao: rice stew

autopista: divided limited-access highway

avenida: avenue

azúcar: sugar

bacalaito: codfish fritter

bahía: bay

balneario: publicly maintained beach

barbacoa: meat grilled over a fire or charcoal; also the name of the grill

barcazas: whole plantains sliced lengthwise, stuffed with ground beef, and topped with cheese

barrio: neighborhood

batata: white yam

batey: ceremonial ball field used by Taíno people

bebida: beverage

bio-bay: shorthand for bioluminescent bay, one of three mangrove lagoons in Puerto Rico that contain microorganisms called dinoflagellates that glow in the dark

bocadillo: sandwich, typically toasted

bohique: Taíno spiritual leader

Borinquen: Taíno name for Puerto Rico

bosque estatal: public forest

botánica: shop that sells herbs, scents, and candles used by practitioners of *espiritismo* or Santería

brazo gitano: translates as "gypsy arm," but it refers to a jelly roll cake filled with fruit traditional to Mayagüez

cabro: goat

cacique: Taíno chief

café: coffee

calle: street

camarones: shrimp

capilla: chapel

carbón: grilled

carne: beef

carne guisado: beef stew

carretera: road

carrucho: conch

cayos: cays, islets

cebollado: onion

cemí: Taíno amulet

cerdo: pork

chicharrones: fried pork skins

chicharrones de pollo: fried chunks of chicken

chillo: red snapper

chillo entero frito: whole fried snapper with the head on

chinchorro: no-frills, open-air restaurant and bar serving *cocina criolla* and drinks for cheap

chorizo: spicy pork sausage

chuleta can can: a thick, deep-fried pork chop specially cut to retain a thick rind of fat and a strip of ribs

chuletas: chops, typically pork

churrasco: grilled, marinated skirt steak

cocina criolla: traditional Puerto Rican cuisine

coco: coconut

coco dulce: an immensely sweet confection of fresh, coarsely grated coconut and caramelized sugar

coco frio: chilled coconut water served in the green husk

conejo: rabbit

coqui: tiny tree frog that emits an eponymous chirp

cordero: lamb

criolla: creole; often refers to a sauce made from tomatoes and green pepper

cruce: crossroad

cruzar: to cross

cuadras: blocks

cubano: toasted sandwich with pork, ham, cheese, and pickles

derecha: right

derecho: straight

doble: turn

dorado: mahi-mahi

empanada or empanadilla: savory turnover stuffed with meat, chicken, seafood, or cheese

empanado: breaded and fried meat

encebollado bifstec: a slice of steak pounded thin and served with caramelized onions

ensalada: salad

espiritismo: Taíno-based religion that believes deities reside in nature

esquina: corner

estacionamiento: parking

este: east

faro: lighthouse

fiestas patronales: festivals that celebrate the patron saints of towns

flan: caramel custard

frito: fried

frituras: fritters

gandules: pigeon peas

guayaba: guava

guineitos en escabeche: pickled green banana salad with onions and green olives

habichuelas: beans

helado: ice cream

hielo: ice

horno: baked

izquierda: left

jámon: ham

jíbaro: rural resident, hillbilly

juevos: eggs

juyeyes: land crab

laguna: lagoon

lancha: ferry

langosta: rock lobster

leche: milk

lechón: pork

lechonera: restaurant serving pit-roasted pork and other local delicacies

lechosa: papaya

lejos: far

luces: traffic lights

luz: traffic light

malécon: seawall promenade

mallorca: a slightly sweet knot of bread dough, baked and dusted with powdered sugar—served split, buttered, and toasted or stuffed with hot ham and cheese for breakfast

mantequilla: butter

mariscos: seafood

máscaras: masks

mavi: a fermented Taíno beverage made from the bark of the *mavi* tree

medianoche: sandwich similar to a *cubano,* but on a softer, sweeter bread

mercado: market

mofongo: cooked unripe plantain mashed with garlic and olive oil

mofongo relleno: mofongo stuffed with chicken, meat, or seafood

mogote: conical, haystack-shaped hill

mondongo: beef tripe stew

mundillo: handmade lace that's created with bobbins

muralla: wall

ñame: yam

norte: north

Nuyorican: a Puerto Rican living in mainland United States

oeste: west

paella: Spanish dish similar to *arroz con pollo* but with saffron and filled with a variety of seafood instead of chicken

pan: bread

panadería: bakery

panapén: breadfruit

papas: potatoes

papas rellenas: a big lump of mashed potatoes stuffed with meat and deep-fried

parador: privately owned inn in a rural area

parque: park

pasteles: like tamales; mashed plantain or cassava stuffed with pork or chicken and steamed in banana leaves, typically served around the Christmas holidays—don't eat the leaf!

pastelillos: savory turnover stuffed with meat, chicken, seafood, or cheese

pechuga de pollo: chicken breast

pernil: pork

pescado: fish

pescado in escabeche: pickled fish served cold; raw fillets are marinated in seasoned vinegar, similar to ceviche

picadillo: seasoned ground beef used to stuff *empanadillas*

pimento: pepper

piña: pineapple

pinchos: chunks of chicken, pork, or fish threaded on a skewer and grilled shish-kebab style

pionono: seasoned ground beef wrapped mummy style in slices of plantain and deep-fried

pique: hot sauce made from vinegar, lime juice, and hot peppers

platano: plantain

playa: beach

postre: dessert

públicos: public transportation in vans that pick up multiple riders along an established route

pueblo: town center

pulpo: octopus

quesito: a sweet, sticky twist of puff pastry with a dab of cream cheese inside

queso: cheese

queso del país: soft white cow cheese

relleno: stuffed food item, as in *mofongo relleno*

reserva forestal: forest reserve

sal: salt

salida: exit

salmorejo de jueyes: stewed land crabmeat served over rice

Santería: Afro-Caribbean-based religion that observes multiple gods

santos: small wood carvings of Catholic saints

setas: mushrooms

sopa: soup

sorullos or sorullitos: fried cheese and cornmeal sticks

sur: south

Taíno: people who were indigenous to Puerto Rico when it became a Spanish colony

taquitos: chicken, ground beef, crab, or fish rolled up in a tortilla and deep-fried

tembleque: coconut custard; often served around Christmas

tocino: bacon

tortilla española: a baked egg and potato dish

tostones: twice-fried, flattened pieces of plantain

vaya: go

vejigante: horned mask worn in festivals

yautia: taro root, similar to a potato

yuca: cassava, a root vegetable

ABBREVIATIONS

Ave.: Avenida

Bo.: Barrio

Carr.: Carretera

Int.: approaching intersection, or interior route

km: kilometer

Spanish Phrasebook

Your Puerto Rico adventure will be more fun if you use a little Spanish. Puerto Ricans, although they may smile at your funny accent, will appreciate your halting efforts to break the ice and transform yourself from a foreigner to a potential friend.

Spanish commonly uses 30 letters—the familiar English 26, plus four straightforward additions: ch, ll, ñ, and rr, which are explained in "Consonants" below.

PRONUNCIATION

Once you learn them, Spanish pronunciation rules—in contrast to English—don't change. Spanish vowels generally sound softer than in English. (Note: The capitalized syllables below receive stronger accents.)

Vowels

a like ah, as in "hah": *agua* AH-gooah (water), *pan* PAHN (bread), and *casa* CAH-sah (house)

e like ay, as in "may": *mesa* MAY-sah (table), *tela* TAY-lah (cloth), and *de* DAY (of, from)

i like ee, as in "need": *diez* dee-AYZ (ten), *comida* ko-MEE-dah (meal), and *fin* FEEN (end)

o like oh, as in "go": *peso* PAY-soh (weight), *ocho* OH-choh (eight), and *poco* POH-koh (a bit)

u like oo, as in "cool": *uno* OO-noh (one), *cuarto* KOOAHR-toh (room), and *usted* oos-TAYD (you); when it follows a "q" the **u** is silent; when it follows an "h" or has an umlaut, it's pronounced like "w"

Consonants

b, d, f, k, l, m, n, p, q, s, t, v, w, x, y, z, ch
pronounced almost as in English

h occurs, but is silent—not pronounced at all

c like k as in "keep": *cuarto* KOOAR-toh (room), Tepic tay-PEEK (capital of Nayarit state); when it precedes "e" or "i," pronounce **c** like s, as in "sit": *cerveza* sayr-VAY-sah (beer), *encima* ayn-SEE-mah (atop)

g like g as in "gift" when it precedes "a," "o," "u," or a consonant: *gato* GAH-toh (cat), *hago* AH-goh (I do, make); otherwise, pronounce **g** like h as in "hat": *giro* HEE-roh (money order), *gente* HAYN-tay (people)

j like h, as in "has": *Jueves* HOOAY-vays (Thursday), *mejor* may-HOR (better)

ll like y, as in "yes": *toalla* toh-AH-yah (towel), *ellos* AY-yohs (they, them)

ñ like ny, as in "canyon": *año* AH-nyo (year), *señor* SAY-nyor (Mr., sir)

r is lightly trilled, with tongue at the roof of your mouth like a very light English d, as in "ready": *pero* PAY-doh (but), *tres* TDAYS (three), *cuatro* KOOAH-tdoh (four)

rr like a Spanish r, but with much more emphasis and trill. Let your tongue flap. Practice with *burro* (donkey), *carretera* (highway), and Carrillo (proper name), then really let go with *ferrocarril* (railroad)

Note: The single small but common exception to all of the above is the pronunciation of Spanish **y** when it's being used as the Spanish word for "and," as in "Ron y Kathy." In such case, pronounce it like the English ee, as in "keep": Ron "ee" Kathy (Ron and Kathy).

Accent

The rule for accent, the relative stress given to syllables within a given word, is straightforward. If a word ends in a vowel, an n, or an s, accent the next-to-last syllable; if not, accent the last syllable.

Pronounce *gracias* GRAH-seeahs (thank you), *orden* OHR-dayn (order), and *carretera* kah-ray-TAY-rah (highway) with stress on the next-to-last syllable.

Otherwise, accent the last syllable: *venir* vay-NEER (to come), *ferrocarril* fay-roh-cah-REEL (railroad), and *edad* ay-DAHD (age).

Exceptions to the accent rule are always marked with an accent sign: (á, é, í, ó, or ú), such as *teléfono* tay-LAY-foh-noh (telephone), *jabón* hah-BON (soap), and *rápido* RAH-pee-doh (rapid).

BASIC AND COURTEOUS EXPRESSIONS

Most Spanish-speaking people consider formalities important. Whenever approaching anyone for information or some other reason, do not forget the appropriate salutation— good morning, good evening, etc. Standing alone, the greeting *hola* (hello) can sound brusque.

Hello. *Hola.*

Good morning. *Buenos días.*

Good afternoon. *Buenas tardes.*

Good evening. *Buenas noches.*

How are you? *¿Cómo está usted?*

Very well, thank you. *Muy bien, gracias.*

Okay; good. *Bien.*

Not okay; bad. *Mal or feo.*

So-so. *Más o menos.*

And you? *¿Y usted?*

Thank you. *Gracias.*

Thank you very much. *Muchas gracias.*

You're very kind. *Muy amable.*

You're welcome. *De nada.*

Goodbye. *Adios.*

See you later. *Hasta luego.*

please *por favor*

yes *sí*

no *no*

I don't know. *No sé.*

Just a moment, please. *Momentito, por favor.*

Excuse me, please (when you're trying to get attention). *Disculpe or Con permiso.*

Excuse me (when you've made a boo-boo). *Lo siento.*

Pleased to meet you. *Mucho gusto.*

What is your name? *¿Cómo se llama usted?*

Do you speak English? *¿Habla usted inglés?*

Is English spoken here? (Does anyone here speak English?) *¿Se habla inglés?*

I don't speak Spanish well. *No hablo bien el español.*

I don't understand. *No entiendo.*

How do you say . . . in Spanish? *¿Cómo se dice . . . en español?*

My name is . . . *Me llamo . . .*

Would you like . . . *¿Quisiera usted . . .*

Let's go to . . . *Vamos a . . .*

TERMS OF ADDRESS

When in doubt, use the formal *usted* (you) as a form of address.

I *yo*

you (formal) *usted*

you (familiar) *tu*

he/him *él*

she/her *ella*

we/us *nosotros*

you (plural) *ustedes*

they/them *ellos* (all males or mixed gender); *ellas* (all females)

Mr., sir *señor*

Mrs., madam *señora*

miss, young lady *señorita*

wife *esposa*

husband *esposo*

friend *amigo* (male); *amiga* (female)

sweetheart *novio* (male); *novia* (female)

son; daughter *hijo; hija*

brother; sister *hermano; hermana*

father; mother *padre; madre*

grandfather; grandmother *abuelo; abuela*

TRANSPORTATION

Where is . . . ? *¿Dónde está . . . ?*

How far is it to . . . ? *¿A cuánto está . . . ?*

from . . . to . . . *de . . . a . . .*

How many blocks? *¿Cuántas cuadras?*

Where (Which) is the way to . . . ? *¿Dónde está el camino a . . . ?*

the bus station *la terminal de autobuses*

the bus stop *la parada de autobuses*

Where is this bus going? *¿Adónde va este autobús?*

the taxi stand *la parada de taxis*

the train station *la estación de ferrocarril*

the boat *el barco*

the launch *lancha; tiburonera*

the dock *el muelle*

the airport *el aeropuerto*
I'd like a ticket to . . . *Quisiera un boleto*
  a . . .
first (second) class *primera (segunda) clase*
roundtrip *ida y vuelta*
reservation *reservación*
baggage *equipaje*
Stop here, please. *Pare aquí, por favor.*
the entrance *la entrada*
the exit *la salida*
the ticket office *la oficina de boletos*
(very) near; far *(muy) cerca; lejos*
to; toward *a*
by; through *por*
from *de*
the right *la derecha*
the left *la izquierda*
straight ahead *derecho; directo*
in front *en frente*
beside *al lado*
behind *atrás*
the corner *la esquina*
the stoplight *la semáforo*
a turn *una vuelta*
right here *aquí*
somewhere around here *por acá*
right there *allí*
somewhere around there *por allá*
road *el camino*
street; boulevard *calle; bulevar*
block *la cuadra*
highway *carretera*
kilometer *kilómetro*
bridge; toll *puente; cuota*
address *dirección*
north; south *norte; sur*
east; west *oriente (este); poniente (oeste)*

ACCOMMODATIONS

hotel *hotel*
Is there a room? *¿Hay cuarto?*
May I (may we) see it? *¿Puedo (podemos)*
  verlo?
What is the rate? *¿Cuál es el precio?*
Is that your best rate? *¿Es su mejor precio?*
Is there something cheaper? *¿Hay algo*
  más económico?

a single room *un cuarto sencillo*
a double room *un cuarto doble*
double bed *cama matrimonial*
twin beds *camas gemelas*
with private bath *con baño*
hot water *agua caliente*
shower *ducha*
towels *toallas*
soap *jabón*
toilet paper *papel higiénico*
blanket *frazada; manta*
sheets *sábanas*
air-conditioned *aire acondicionado*
fan *abanico; ventilador*
key *llave*
manager *gerente*

FOOD

I'm hungry *Tengo hambre.*
I'm thirsty. *Tengo sed.*
menu *carta; menú*
order *orden*
glass *vaso*
fork *tenedor*
knife *cuchillo*
spoon *cuchara*
napkin *servilleta*
soft drink *refresco*
coffee *café*
tea *té*
drinking water *agua pura; agua potable*
bottled carbonated water *agua mineral*
bottled uncarbonated water *agua sin*
  gas
beer *cerveza*
wine *vino*
milk *leche*
juice *jugo*
cream *crema*
sugar *azúcar*
cheese *queso*
snack *antojo; botana*
breakfast *desayuno*
lunch *almuerzo*
daily lunch special *comida corrida (or el*
  menú del día depending on region)

dinner *comida* (often eaten in late
  afternoon); *cena* (a late-night snack)
the check *la cuenta*
eggs *huevos*
bread *pan*
salad *ensalada*
fruit *fruta*
mango *mango*
watermelon *sandía*
papaya *papaya*
banana *plátano*
apple *manzana*
orange *naranja*
lime *limón*
fish *pescado*
shellfish *mariscos*
shrimp *camarones*
meat (without) *(sin) carne*
chicken *pollo*
pork *puerco*
beef; steak *res; bistec*
bacon; ham *tocino; jamón*
fried *frito*
roasted *asada*
barbecue; barbecued *barbacoa; al carbón*

SHOPPING

money *dinero*
money-exchange bureau *casa de cambio*
I would like to exchange traveler's
  checks. *Quisiera cambiar cheques de
  viajero.*
What is the exchange rate? *¿Cuál es el
  tipo de cambio?*
How much is the commission? *¿Cuánto
  cuesta la comisión?*
Do you accept credit cards? *¿Aceptan
  tarjetas de crédito?*
money order *giro*
How much does it cost? *¿Cuánto cuesta?*
What is your final price? *¿Cuál es su último
  precio?*
expensive *caro*
cheap *barato; económico*
more *más*
less *menos*
a little *un poco*
too much *demasiado*

HEALTH

Help me please. *Ayúdeme por favor.*
I am ill. *Estoy enfermo.*
Call a doctor. *Llame un doctor.*
Take me to ... *Lléveme a ...*
hospital *hospital; sanatorio*
drugstore *farmacia*
pain *dolor*
fever *fiebre*
headache *dolor de cabeza*
stomach ache *dolor de estómago*
burn *quemadura*
cramp *calambre*
nausea *náusea*
vomiting *vomitar*
medicine *medicina*
antibiotic *antibiótico*
pill; tablet *pastilla*
aspirin *aspirina*
ointment; cream *pomada; crema*
bandage *venda*
cotton *algodón*
sanitary napkins use brand name, e.g.,
  Kotex
birth control pills *pastillas anticonceptivas*
contraceptive foam *espuma
  anticonceptiva*
condoms *preservativos; condones*
toothbrush *cepilla dental*
dental floss *hilo dental*
toothpaste *crema dental*
dentist *dentista*
toothache *dolor de muelas*

POST OFFICE AND COMMUNICATIONS

long-distance telephone *teléfono larga
  distancia*
I would like to call ... *Quisiera llamar a ...*
collect *por cobrar*
station to station *a quien contesta*
person to person *persona a persona*
credit card *tarjeta de crédito*
post office *correo*
general delivery *lista de correo*
letter *carta*
stamp *estampilla, timbre*
postcard *tarjeta*

aerogram *aerograma*
air mail *correo aereo*
registered *registrado*
money order *giro*
package; box *paquete; caja*
string; tape *cuerda; cinta*

CUSTOMS

border *frontera*
customs *aduana*
immigration *migración*
tourist card *tarjeta de turista*
inspection *inspección; revisión*
passport *pasaporte*
profession *profesión*
marital status *estado civil*
single *soltero*
married; divorced *casado; divorciado*
widowed *viudado*
insurance *seguros*
title *título*
driver's license *licencia de manejar*

AT THE GAS STATION

gas station *gasolinera*
gasoline *gasolina*
unleaded *sin plomo*
full, please *lleno, por favor*
tire *llanta*
tire repair shop *vulcanizadora*
air *aire*
water *agua*
oil (change) *aceite (cambio)*
grease *grasa*
My ... doesn't work. *Mi ... no sirve.*
battery *batería*
radiator *radiador*
alternator *alternador*
generator *generador*
tow truck *grúa*
repair shop *taller mecánico*
tune-up *afinación*
auto parts store *refaccionería*

VERBS

Verbs are the key to getting along in Spanish.
They employ mostly predictable forms and

come in three classes, which end in *ar, er,* and
ir, respectively:

to buy *comprar*
I buy, you (he, she, it) buys *compro, compra*
we buy, you (they) buy *compramos, compran*

to eat *comer*
I eat, you (he, she, it) eats *como, come*
we eat, you (they) eat *comemos, comen*

to climb *subir*
I climb, you (he, she, it) climbs *subo, sube*
we climb, you (they) climb *subimos, suben*

Here are more (with irregularities indicated):

to do or make *hacer* (regular except for *hago,* I do or make)
to go *ir* (very irregular: *voy, va, vamos, van*)
to go (walk) *andar*
to love *amar*
to work *trabajar*
to want *desear, querer*
to need *necesitar*
to read *leer*
to write *escribir*
to repair *reparar*
to stop *parar*
to get off (the bus) *bajar*
to arrive *llegar*
to stay (remain) *quedar*
to stay (lodge) *hospedar*
to leave *salir* (regular except for *salgo,* I leave)
to look at *mirar*
to look for *buscar*
to give *dar* (regular except for *doy,* I give)
to carry *llevar*
to have *tener* (irregular but important: *tengo, tiene, tenemos, tienen*)
to come *venir* (similarly irregular: *vengo, viene, venimos, vienen*)

Spanish has two forms of "to be":

to be *estar* (regular except for *estoy*, I am)
to be *ser* (very irregular: *soy, es, somos, son*)

Use *estar* when speaking of location or a temporary state of being: "I am at home." *"Estoy en casa." "I'm sick." "Estoy enfermo."* Use *ser* for a permanent state of being: "I am a doctor." *"Soy doctora."*

NUMBERS

zero *cero*
one *uno*
two *dos*
three *tres*
four *cuatro*
five *cinco*
six *seis*
seven *siete*
eight *ocho*
nine *nueve*
10 *diez*
11 *once*
12 *doce*
13 *trece*
14 *catorce*
15 *quince*
16 *dieciseis*
17 *diecisiete*
18 *dieciocho*
19 *diecinueve*
20 *veinte*
21 *veinte y uno* or *veintiuno*
30 *treinta*
40 *cuarenta*
50 *cincuenta*
60 *sesenta*
70 *setenta*
80 *ochenta*
90 *noventa*
100 *ciento*
101 *ciento y uno* or *cientiuno*
200 *doscientos*
500 *quinientos*
1,000 *mil*
10,000 *diez mil*
100,000 *cien mil*

1,000,000 *millón*
one half *medio*
one third *un tercio*
one fourth *un cuarto*

TIME

What time is it? *¿Qué hora es?*
It's one o'clock. *Es la una.*
It's three in the afternoon. *Son las tres de la tarde.*
It's 4 a.m. *Son las cuatro de la mañana.*
six-thirty *seis y media*
a quarter till eleven *un cuarto para las once*
a quarter past five *las cinco y cuarto*
an hour *una hora*

DAYS AND MONTHS

Monday *lunes*
Tuesday *martes*
Wednesday *miércoles*
Thursday *jueves*
Friday *viernes*
Saturday *sábado*
Sunday *domingo*
today *hoy*
tomorrow *mañana*
yesterday *ayer*
January *enero*
February *febrero*
March *marzo*
April *abril*
May *mayo*
June *junio*
July *julio*
August *agosto*
September *septiembre*
October *octubre*
November *noviembre*
December *diciembre*
a week *una semana*
a month *un mes*
after *después*
before *antes*

(Courtesy of Bruce Whipperman, author of *Moon Pacific Mexico*.)

Suggested Reading

ARTS AND CULTURE

Delano, Jack. *Puerto Rico Mio: Four Decades of Change.* Washington: Smithsonian Books, 1990. Includes 175 duotones of former Farm Security Administration photographer Jack Delano's visual chronicle of the island and its people. Includes essays in Spanish and English by educator Arturo Morales Carrión, historian Alan Fern, and anthropologist Sidney W. Mintz.

Muckley, Robert L., and Adela Martinez-Santiago. *Stories from Puerto Rico.* New York: McGraw-Hill, 1999. A collection of legends, ghost stories, and beloved true accounts that reflect the island's folklore. In English and Spanish.

Santiago, Roberto, ed. *Boricuas: Influential Puerto Rican Writings—An Anthology.* New York: One World/Ballantine, 1995. A fantastic collection of poems, speeches, stories, and excerpts by Puerto Rico's greatest writers, past and present, including Jesús Colón, Pablo Guzman, Julia de Burgos, and many more.

CHILDREN'S BOOKS

Bernier-Grand, Carmen T. (author), and Ernesto Ramos Nieves (illustrator). *Juan Bobo: Four Folktales from Puerto Rico.* New York: HarperTrophy, 1995. Four humorous folktales about the trials and tribulations of the lovable, misguided little boy Juan Bobo.

Ramirez, Michael Rose (author), and Margaret Sanfilippo (illustrator). *The Legend of the Hummingbird: A Tale from Puerto Rico.* New York: Mondo, 1998. Learn about Puerto Rico's history, climate, and traditions in this beguiling tale of transformation.

HISTORY AND POLITICS

Andrés, José. *We Fed an Island: The True Story of Rebuilding Puerto Rico One Meal at a Time.* New York: Anthony Bourdain/Ecco, 2019. The James Beard Award-winning chef tells the story of his nonprofit organization World Central Kitchen and its efforts to feed the island for months following Hurricane Maria. It also identifies fatal flaws in the U.S. government's emergency relief system.

Carrión, Arturo Morales. *Puerto Rico: A Political and Cultural History.* New York: W. W. Norton & Co., 1984. An examination of Puerto Rico's commonwealth status and how it got there.

Denis, Nelson A. *War Against All Puerto Ricans.* New York: Nation Books, 2015. A deeply researched nonfiction account of Pedro Albizu Campos, president of the National Party, his efforts to gain independence for Puerto Rico, and the U.S. government's efforts to squelch it.

Monge, José Trías. *Puerto Rico: The Trials of the Oldest Colony in the World.* New Haven: Yale University Press, 1999 (paperback). An examination of Puerto Rico's political status through history and an outlook on its future.

Odishelidze, Alexander, and Arthur Laffer. *Pay to the Order of Puerto Rico: The Cost of Dependence.* Dover: Allegiance Press, 2004. A look at Puerto Rico's political status from an outsider—a Russian native. Although Puerto Rico's options for future political status are well documented, the author openly favors statehood.

Rouse, Irving. *The Taínos: Rise and Decline of the People Who Greeted Columbus.* New Haven: Yale University Press, reissue 1993.

A history of the Taíno culture based on intensive study of archaeological sites.

LITERATURE

Ferré, Rosario. *The House on the Lagoon*. New York: Penguin Group, 1995. Historical fiction set during the Spanish-American War about the rebellious wife of a wealthy importer in San Juan who journals about the volatile times on the island.

Santiago, Esmeralda. *Conquistadora*. New York: Knopf, 2012. Historical fiction about a strong-willed Spanish woman who sails to Puerto Rico with her husband and brother-in-law in 1844 to run a sugar plantation.

Santiago, Esmeralda. *When I Was Puerto Rican*. Cambridge: Da Capo Press, 2006. A memoir about growing up in Puerto Rico and immigrating to the United States.

Santiago, Roberto. *Boricua: The Influential Puerto Rican Writings, an Anthology*. New York: Ballantine, 1995. Fifty selections of 19th- and 20th-century works by Puerto Rican writers.

NATURE AND WILDLIFE

Lee, Alfonso Silva. *Natural Puerto Rico/ Puerto Rico Natural*. Saint Paul: Pangaea, 1998. An examination of the fauna of Puerto Rico by Cuban biologist Alfonso Silva Lee. In Spanish and English.

Oberle, Mark W. *Puerto Rico's Birds in Photographs*. Bucharest: Humanitas, 2000. More than 300 color photographs document 181 species of birds found in Puerto Rico. Comes with a CD-ROM including audio clips and more photographs.

Raffaele, Herbert. *A Guide to the Birds of Puerto Rico and the Virgin Islands*. Princeton: Princeton University Press, 1989. Contains information on 284 documented species as well as 273 illustrations.

Simonsen, Steve. *Diving and Snorkeling Guide to Puerto Rico*. Deland: Pisces Books, 1996. A guide to the best diving and snorkeling sites around the island.

Internet Resources

TRAVEL INFORMATION

En Culebra **Magazine**
www.enculebra.com
Well-researched and well-written articles cover various aspects of life in Culebra, with lots of great travel information.

Isla Culebra
www.islaculebra.com
The information on this site is pretty outdated, but the travel forum is active and informative. Post a question and someone will know the answer.

Puerto Rico Day Trips
www.puertoricodaytrips.com
This individually owned and operated site is well researched and updated on a regular basis. Lots of good practical information.

Puerto Rico Tourism Co.
www.discoverpuertorico.com
Produced by the Puerto Rico Tourism Co., this is an excellent source of well-researched information on history, culture, events, and sights with a promotional slant.

Tourism Association of Rincón
www.rincon.org
In addition to a plethora of general tourist information on Rincón, this site provides services of interest to residents, including locations for churches, hair salons, and cleaners. Plus, there's some great photography.

HISTORY, POLITICS, AND CULTURE

Historic Places in Puerto Rico
www.nps.gov/history/nr/travel/prvi
The National Park Service site provides details on all the historic sites that fall under its purview.

Music of Puerto Rico
www.musicofpuertorico.com
An excellent source for information on Puerto Rican music, from folk and *danza* to *bomba* and salsa to reggaetón. It also contains audio clips, biographies of native musicians, lyrics, and musical history.

Public Art
www.artepublicopr.com/english
The official source for Puerto Rico's $25 million public art project, including project proposals, artists' biographies, and maps to the sites.

Puerto Rico and the Dream
www.prdream.com
An intelligent and discriminating site about the history, culture, and politics of Puerto Rico that includes audio files of oral histories, galleries of select art exhibitions, historical timelines, archival photos, and discussion forums. The site really has its finger on the pulse of all matters important to Puerto Ricans.

NATURE AND WILDLIFE

The Conservation Trust of Puerto Rico
www.paralanaturaleza.org
In addition to working to preserve the island's natural beauty, the Conservation Trust of Puerto Rico and Para la Naturaleza offers a variety of educational nature and culture tours.

U.S. Fish and Wildlife Service
www.fws.gov/caribbean
The U.S. Fish and Wildlife Service operates this site featuring information on the island's wildlife refuges, geographic regions, and efforts to restore the population of Puerto Rican parrots.

List of Maps

Photo Credits

Acknowledgments

I want to thank my parents, Ted and Jo Teagle, who instilled in me a passion for travel. Had they not been adventurous enough to move our family to Puerto Rico in the early 1970s, this book would have never happened. I also want to thank my sons, Derrick and Drew, who bring so much joy to my life and inspire me to be my best every day.

Special thanks go to editor Leah Gordon, cartographer Kat Bennett, production coordinator Scott Kimball, and everybody else at Avalon Travel whose expertise and kindness made this fifth edition of *Moon Puerto Rico* such a pleasure to produce.

I owe much gratitude to my dear friends and traveling companions, Sun Rim Brank, Amy Cohen, Anne Mozingo, Scottie Williams, Shelly Williams, and Elizabeth Wylie. Thanks for joining me on my travels. I will always treasure the memories.

I'm also grateful for my friendship with Carlos Davila Rinaldi and Carla Davila Ortiz, who are always so generous with their time and insight into the island's culture.

A final shout-out goes to my oldest, dearest friend, Caryl Altman Howard, who introduced me to this beguiling island and played a major role in some of my fondest memories of life in Puerto Rico.

Trips to Remember

MOON
BALI & LOMBOK
CHANTAE REDEN

MOON
ECUADOR
& THE GALÁPAGOS ISLANDS
BETHANY PITTS

MOON
GREEK ISLANDS & ATHENS
SARAH SOULI

MOON
ICELAND
JENNA GOTTLIEB

MOON
TRIP OF A LIFETIME
MACHU PICCHU
with Lima, Cusco & the Inca Trail
RYAN DUBE

MOON
MOROCCO
LUCAS PETERS

MOON
NEW ZEALAND
JAMIE CHRISTIAN DESPLACES

MOON
OAXACA
SCOTT COPELAND

MOON
TRIP OF A LIFETIME
PATAGONIA
Including the Falkland Islands
WAYNE BERNHARDSON

MOON
PRAGUE, VIENNA & BUDAPEST
JENNIFER WALKER
AUBURN SCALLON

MOON
ROME, FLORENCE & VENICE
ALEXEI J. COHEN

Epic Adventure

MOON
PACIFIC COAST HIGHWAY
Road Trip
CALIFORNIA, OREGON & WASHINGTON
IAN ANDERSON

MOON
ROUTE 66
Road Trip
JESSICA DUNHAM

MOON
YELLOWSTONE TO GLACIER NATIONAL PARK
Road Trip
JACKSON HOLE, CODY, THE GRAND TETONS
& THE ROCKY MOUNTAIN FRONT
CARTER G. WALKER

ROAD TRIPS AND DRIVE & HIKE GUIDES

Beachy Getaways

MOON.COM
@MOONGUIDES

MOON

ARUBA

AMALFI COAST

BAHAMAS

BAJA

BELIZE

BERMUDA

COSTA RICA

DOMINICAN REPUBLIC

FIJI

FLORIDA KEYS

FRENCH RIVIERA: NICE, CANNES, MONACO & ST-TROPEZ

JAMAICA

MAUI

PUERTO RICO

PUERTO VALLARTA

Road Trip USA

Covering more than 35,000 miles of blacktop stretching from east to west and north to south, *Road Trip USA* takes you deep into the heart of America.

This colorful guide covers the top road trips including historic Route 66 and is packed with maps, photos, illustrations, mile-by-mile highlights, and more!

Craft a personalized journey through the top national parks in the U.S. and Canada with Moon Travel Guides.

MOON
USA
NATIONAL
PARKS
THE COMPLETE GUIDE TO ALL
62 PARKS
BECKY LOMAX

MOON
ACADIA
NATIONAL PARK
HILARY NANGLE

MOON
ARCHES &
CANYONLANDS
NATIONAL PARKS

MOON
BANFF
NATIONAL
PARK
HIKE · CAMP · KAYAK
ANDREW HEMPSTEAD

MOON
DEATH VALLEY
NATIONAL PARK

MOON
GLACIER
NATIONAL PARK

MOON
GRAND
CANYON
HIKE · CAMP
RAFT THE
COLORADO RIVER

MOON
GREAT SMOKY
MOUNTAINS
NATIONAL PARK
HIKE · BIKE · CAMP
JASON FRYE

MOUNT RUSHMORE
& THE BLACK HILLS

MOON
ROCKY
MOUNTAIN
NATIONAL PARK
HIKE · CAMP
SEE WILDLIFE

MOON
SEQUOIA &
KINGS CANYON
HIKE · CAMP
SEE REDWOODS

MOON
YELLOWSTONE
& GRAND TETON
HIKE · CAMP
SEE WILDLIFE

MOON
YOSEMITE
SEQUOIA &
KINGS CANYON
ANN MARIE BROWN

MOON
ZION &
BRYCE

For when your friends want your recommendations.
Keep track of your favorite...

Restaurants and Meals

Neighborhoods and Regions

Cultural Experiences

Beaches and Recreation

Day Trips or Scenic Drives

Travel Memories

MAP SYMBOLS

═══	Expressway	○	City/Town	✈	Airport	⚲	Golf Course
───	Primary Road	◉	State Capital	✕	Airfield	🅿	Parking Area
───	Secondary Road	◈	National Capital	▲	Mountain	≜	Archaeological Site
=======	Unpaved Road	✪	Highlight	✛	Unique Natural Feature	⛪	Church
------	Trail	★	Point of Interest			⛽	Gas Station
············	Ferry	•	Accommodation	🜄	Waterfall		
✕─✕─✕	Railroad	▾	Restaurant/Bar	⛰	Park	🎋	Glacier
░░░░	Pedestrian Walkway	■	Other Location	TH	Trailhead	▨	Mangrove
▥▥▥	Stairs	Λ	Campground	⛷	Skiing Area	◩	Reef
						⬚	Swamp

CONVERSION TABLES

°C = (°F − 32) / 1.8
°F = (°C × 1.8) + 32
1 inch = 2.54 centimeters (cm)
1 foot = 0.304 meters (m)
1 yard = 0.914 meters
1 mile = 1.6093 kilometers (km)
1 km = 0.6214 miles
1 fathom = 1.8288 m
1 chain = 20.1168 m
1 furlong = 201.168 m
1 acre = 0.4047 hectares
1 sq km = 100 hectares
1 sq mile = 2.59 square km
1 ounce = 28.35 grams
1 pound = 0.4536 kilograms
1 short ton = 0.90718 metric ton
1 short ton = 2,000 pounds
1 long ton = 1.016 metric tons
1 long ton = 2,240 pounds
1 metric ton = 1,000 kilograms
1 quart = 0.94635 liters
1 US gallon = 3.7854 liters
1 Imperial gallon = 4.5459 liters
1 nautical mile = 1.852 km

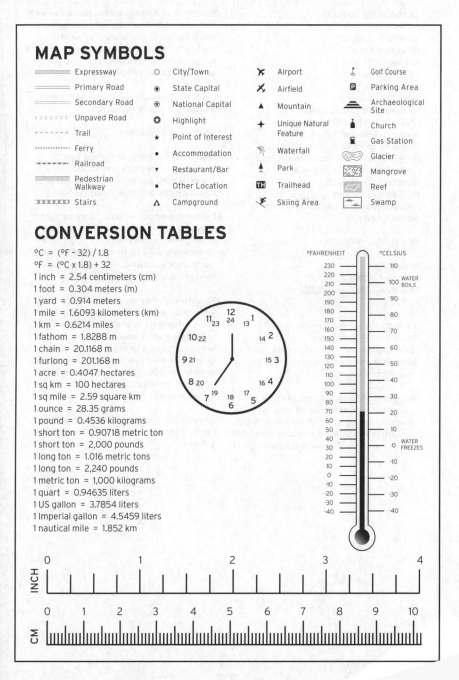

MOON PUERTO RICO

Avalon Travel
Hachette Book Group
1700 Fourth Street
Berkeley, CA 94710, USA
www.moon.com

Editor: Leah Gordon
Series Manager: Kathryn Ettinger
Copy Editor: Callie Stoker-Graham
Graphics Coordinator: Scott Kimball
Production Coordinator: Scott Kimball
Cover Design: Faceout Studios, Charles Brock
Interior Design: Domini Dragoone
Moon Logo: Tim McGrath
Map Editor: Kat Bennett
Cartographers: Kat Bennett, Brian Shotwell
Indexer: Rachel Kuhn

ISBN-13: 978-1-64049-235-6

Printing History
1st Edition — 2006
5th Edition — November 2020
5 4 3 2 1

Front cover photo: Russell Kord, Alamy Stock Photo
Back cover photo: Suzanne Van Atten

Printed in Malaysia for Imago

Avalon Travel is a division of Hachette Book Group, Inc. Moon and the Moon logo are trademarks of Hachette Book Group, Inc. All other marks and logos depicted are the property of the original owners.